Welcome to Europe

There simply is no way to tour Europe and not be awestruck by its scenic beauty, epic history and dazzling arts scene. It also offers delicious culinary diversity and the best nightlife in the world.

Europe's wealth of attractions is its biggest single draw: Florence's Renaissance art, Venice's graceful canals, Paris' Napoleonic splendour, and the multi-layered historical and cultural canvas of London. Less obvious but no less impressive attractions include the ongoing project of Gaudí's La Sagrada Família, in Barcelona, and Iceland's quaint capital Reykjavík with its wonderful cafe and bar scene.

There's a huge diversity of natural scenery: rugged Scottish Highlands with glens and lochs; the flower fields and hilltop villages of Provence; and the Adriatic coastline speckled with thousands of islands. Mountain lovers should head to the Alps: they march across central Europe taking in France, Switzerland, Austria and northern Italy.

London, Berlin and Paris all offer top-class entertainment, especially theatre, live music and clubbing. Those hankering for something cosier can add Dublin's pubs or Vienna's cafes to their itinerary. Continue to party on the continent's streets at a multiplicity of festivals and celebrations.

A European tour is also a chance to indulge in a culinary adventure to beat all others. Go to the source and sample haggis in Scotland and pizza in Rome. But who'd have thought that Amsterdam would be a place to enjoy Indonesian *rijsttafel* (rice table)? That's Europe for you: constantly surprising.

Europe's wealth of attractions is its biggest single draw

Charles Bridge (p535) and the Vltava River, Prague
ROMAN BORODAEV / SHUTTERSTOCK ©

GREENLAND

Greenland Sea

REYKJAVIK (p176) ICELAND

Norwegian Sea

Tron

Shetland **Bergen**

SCOTTISH HIGHLANDS (p96)

Orkney

Inverness

SCOTLAND

Kristiansan

Glasgow Edinburgh *North Sea*

COP

NORTHERN IRELAND

Belfast

Douglas

D

NORTH ATLANTIC OCEAN

Galway

DUBLIN (p114)

IRELAND

Cork

Manchester

WALES

Birmingham

ENGLAND

NETHERLANDS

Ha

AMS (p

Cardiff

LONDON (p50)

English Channel

BELGIUM

BRUSSE

Lille

LUXEMBOUR

Caen Rouen Reims

Rennes

Nantes *Loire*

PARIS (p202)

Dijon

BERN

SWITZERLAND

BASQUE COUNTRY (p308)

Bay of Biscay

Limoges

Bordeaux FRANCE

Geneva

Lyon

M

Vigo

Bilbao

VENICE (p400)

M

Porto

PORTUGAL

PYRENEES

ANDORRA LA VELLA

Montpellier

Marseille

FLOREN (p418)

LISBON (p330)

MADRID

BARCELONA (p268)

TUSC (p44

SPAIN

Valencia

Seville Cordoba

PROVENCE (p252)

Sardin (Italy)

Mediterranean Sea

Gibraltar

MOROCCO ALGERIA

0   1,000 Kilometers
0   500 miles

Tromsø

●Murmansk

KOLA
PENINSULA

FINLAND

White
Sea

Rovaniemi

Luleå

●Petrozavodsk

RUSSIA

●Vaasa

●Sundsvall

●Tampere

dheim●

NORWAY

✪HELSINKI

St Petersburg●

Yaroslavl●

✪TALLINN

Nizhny
Novgorod●

OSLO✪

●STOCKHOLM

ESTONIA

Volga

Pskov●

Tver●

●

SWEDEN

Gotland

LATVIA

MOSCOW✪

RĪGA✪

NHAGEN
(p136)

Öland

Baltic
Sea

LITHUANIA

Smolensk●

NMARK

✪Malmö

Kaliningrad

VILNIUS✪

✪MINSK

Bornholm

●

BELARUS

nburg

Gdansk●

Don

●GERMANY

WARSAW✪

Brest●

Kharkiv●

ERDAM
(54)

✪BERLIN
(p486)

Vistula

POLAND

✪KYIV

Donetsk●

s

Dresden●

Zhytomyr●

Dnipropetrovsk●

Kraków●

SWISS
ALPS
(p586)

✪PRAGUE
(p524)

●Lviv

UKRAINE

CZECH
REPUBLIC

SLOVAKIA

✪VIENNA
(p564)

MOLDOVA

Munich●

✪✪BRATISLAVA

Iaşi●

CHIŞINĂU✪

Zürich
●

AUSTRIA

✪BUDAPEST
(p546)

●Odessa

✪VADUZ

SLOVENIA

HUNGARY

ROMANIA

LJUBLJANA✪

●Sevastapol

an●

✪ZAGREB

SERBIA

Black
Sea

ITALY

CROATIA

BUCHAREST✪

SAN MARINO
●

BOSNIA &
HERCEGOVNIA

●Constanţa

ONACO●

✪SARAJEVO

BULGARIA

E

DUBROVNIK
(p470)

KOSOVO

SOFIA✪

İstanbul●

ANKARA✪

MONTENEGRO

✪PRIŠTINA

ANY
4)

ROME
(p352)

PODGORICA●

MACEDONIA

●Bursa

Bari●

TIRANA✪

SKOPJE✪

●Thessaloniki

TURKEY

Naples●

ALBANIA

●Cagliari

Catanzaro●

GREECE

Corfu

●İzmir

Palermo●

Ionian
Sea

ATHENS✪

NICOSIA✪

Sicily

Aegean
Sea

CYPRUS

TUNISIA

Malta

Sea of
Crete

Karpathos

✪VALLETTA

Crete

EUROPE

TOP SIGHTS, AUTHENTIC EXPERIENCES

Simon Richmond, Alexis Averbuck, Mark Baker, Oliver
Berry, Abigail Blasi, Cristian Bonetto, Kerry Christiani,
Fionn Davenport, Sally Davies, Peter Dragicevich, Steve
Fallon, Emilie Filou, Duncan Garwood, Bridget Gleeson,
Paula Hardy, Damian Harper, Anna Kaminski, Catherine Le
Nevez, Virginia Maxwell, Craig McLachlan, Josephine
Quintero, Kevin Raub, Andrea Schulte-Peevers, Regis St
Louis, Nicola Williams, Neil Wilson

Contents

Contents

Left: Cycling past the Reichstag (p492), Berlin;
Top right: Houses in Lisbon (p330); Bottom right: A Tuscan village (p444)

CANADASTOCK / SHUTTERSTOCK ©

PAVEL ARZAKOV / SHUTTERSTOCK ©

RUDMER ZWERVER / SHUTTERSTOCK ©

Plan Your Trip
Europe's Top 21

JON ARNOLD / SHUTTERSTOCK ©

London, Britain

Truly one of the world's greatest cities

London is mercurial and endlessly fascinating; you could spend a lifetime getting to know it, then realise it's gone and changed again. Stretching back from the mighty River Thames, its lush parks and historic districts are crammed with extraordinary sights: royal palaces, towering cathedrals and remarkable museums and galleries. Add the pick of the world's theatres, restaurants, sports venues and shops, and you'll be very reluctant to leave. Right: Great Court, British Museum (p58)

Venice, Italy

Magical city seemingly floating on water

A sunny winter's day, with far fewer tourists around, is the perfect time to lap up Venice's unique and magical atmosphere. Ditch your map and wander the shadowy backlines of Dorsoduro while imagining secret assignations and whispered conspiracies at every turn. Then visit two of Venice's top galleries, the Gallerie dell'Accademia and the Peggy Guggenheim Collection, which houses works by many of the giants of 20th-century art.

2

BEBOY / 55H-UTTE-STOCK ©

MARCO RUBINO / SHUTTERSTOCK ©

Rome, Italy

Classical ruins mixed with contemporary style

From the crumbling Colosseum to the ancient Forum and the Appian Way, few sights are more evocative than the ruins of ancient Rome. Two thousand years ago this city was the centre of the greatest empire of the ancient world, where gladiators battled and emperors lived in unimaginable luxury. Nowadays it's a haunting spot: as you walk the cobbled paths, you can almost sense the ghosts in the air. Top: Roman Forum (p372); Bottom: Colosseum (p354)

3

ALKPIN / GETTY IMAGES ◈

Paris, France

Up close with an architectural icon

Designed as a temporary exhibit for the 1889 Exposition Universelle (World Fair), Paris' elegant art nouveau Eiffel Tower has become the defining fixture of the skyline. Its recent 1st-floor refit adds two glitzy glass pavilions housing interactive exhibits; outside, peer d-o-w-n through the glass floor to the ground below. Visit at dusk for the best day and night views of the City of Light and make a toast at the sparkling champagne bar.

YONGYUT KUMSRI/ SHUTTERSTOCK ©

Berlin, Germany

Catch the ever-changing zeitgeist

More than 25 years since the fall of the Berlin Wall, it's hard to believe that this most cosmopolitan of cities once marked the frontier
of the Cold War. But reminders of Berlin's divided past still remain:
whether you're passing the Brandenburg Gate, gazing at graffiti
at the East Side Gallery or soaking up the history at Checkpoint
Charlie, it's an essential part of understanding what makes Germany's capital tick. *Drei Mädchen und ein Knabe* (Three Girls and a Boy) by artist
Wilfried Fitzenreiter near the Berliner Dom (p503)

5

6

Dubrovnik, Croatia
Spectacular walled city

Dubrovnik's main claim to fame are its historic ramparts, considered among the finest in the world, which surround luminous marble streets and finely ornamented buildings. Built between the 13th and 16th centuries, the walls are still remarkably intact today, and the vistas over the terracotta rooftops and the Adriatic Sea are sublime, especially at dusk, when the fading light makes the hues dramatic and the panoramas unforgettable.

7

Prague, Czech Republic
An architectural central European jewel

The capital of the Czech Republic is one of Europe's most alluring and dynamic places. For all its modern verve, some parts of the city have hardly changed since medieval times – cobbled cul-de-sacs snake through the Old Town, framed by tee-tering townhouses, baroque buildings and graceful bridges. And if castles are your thing, Prague Castle is an absolute beauty: a 1000-year-old fortress covering around 7 hectares – the world's largest.
Charles Bridge (p535)

Vienna, Austria

Grand heart of a former empire

The monumentally graceful Hofburg whisks you back to the age of empires in Vienna as you marvel at the treasury's imperial crowns, the equine ballet of the Spanish Riding School and the chandelier-lit apartments fit for Empress Elisabeth. The palace, a legacy of the 640-year Habsburg era, is rivalled in grandeur only by the 1441-room Schloss Schön-brunn, a Unesco World Heritage Site, and the baroque Schloss Belvedere, both set in exquisite gardens. Schloss Belvedere (p576)

Amsterdam, The Netherlands

World Heritage–listed canals and gabled buildings

To say Amsterdammers love the water is an understatement. Stroll next to the canals and check out some of the thousands of houseboats. Or better still, go for a ride. From boat level you'll see a whole new set of architectural details such as the ornamentation bedecking the bridges. And when you pass the canalside cafe terraces, you can just look up and wave.

MRPHOTOMANIA / SHUTTERSTOCK ©

Budapest, Hungary

Beautiful Hungarian capital straddling the Danube

Straddling both sides of the romantic Danube River, with the Buda Hills to the west and the start of the Great Plain to the east, Budapest is perhaps the most beautiful city in Eastern Europe. Parks brim with attractions, the architecture is second to none, museums are filled with treasures, pleasure boats sail up and down the scenic Danube Bend, Turkish-era thermal baths belch steam and its nightlife throbs till dawn most nights. Széchenyi Baths (p551)

10

WENDY RAUW PHOTOGRAPHY / GETTY IMAGES ©

Barcelona, Spain

The genius of a visionary architect

Barcelona is famous for its Modernista architecture, much of which was designed by Antoni Gaudí. His masterwork is the mighty cathedral La Sagrada Família, which remains a work in progress close to a century after its creator's death. It's a bizarre combination of crazy and classic: Gothic touches intersect with eccentric experiments and improbable angles. No one is entirely sure when it will be finished; but even half completed, it's a modern-day wonder. La Sagrada Família (p270)

11

Lisbon, Portugal
Soulful city armed with Gothic grit

Alfama, with its labyrinthine alleyways, hidden courtyards and curving, shadow-filled lanes, is a magical place to lose all sense of direction and delve into Lisbon's soul. On the journey, you'll pass breadbox-sized grocers, brilliantly tiled buildings and views of steeply-pitched rooftops leading down to the glittering Tejo. Pause at cosy taverns filled with easygoing chatter, with the scent of chargrilled sardines and the mournful rhythms of fado drifting in the breeze.

12

SWEN STROOP / SHUTTERSTOCK ©

ANDREW SWINBANK / SHUTTERSTOCK ©

The Scottish Highlands

Scenic grandeur and echoes of the past

GEORGECLERK / GETTY IMAGES ©

Breathtaking views abound in the Highlands. From the regal charm of Royal Deeside, via the brooding majesty of Glen Coe, to the mysterious waters of sweeping Loch Ness – these are landscapes that inspire awe. The region is scattered with fairy-tale castles and the hiking is suitably glorious. Add the nooks of warm Highland hospitality found in classic rural pubs and romantic hotels, and you have an unforgettable corner of the country.

13

T.S.ACK / SHUTTERSTOCK ©

Dublin, Ireland

Pints of Guinness and literary connections

Whether you're wandering the leafy Georgian terraces of St Stephen's Green or getting acquainted with the past at Kilmainham Gaol, in Dublin you're never far from a literary or historic sight. And then there are the city's pubs: there are few better places to down a pint than Dublin, and you can even make a pilgrimage to the original Guinness brewery on the city's outskirts. Either way, you'll make a few Irish friends along the way.

14

15

Tuscany, Italy

Italy's most romanticised region

The gently rolling hills of Tuscany, bathed in golden light and dotted with vineyards, sum up Italy's attractions in a nutshell. Battalions of books, postcards and lifestyle TV shows try to do this region justice, but nothing beats a visit. Here picture-perfect hilltop towns vie with magnificent scenery and some of Italy's best food and wine – creating a tourist hotspot. Visit in spring or autumn to see it at its calmest.

16

Pompeii, Italy

Ancient city destroyed and preserved by Vesuvius

Frozen in its death throes, the sprawling, time-warped ruins of Pompeii hurtle you 2000 years into the past. Wander through chariot-grooved Roman streets, lavishly frescoed villas and bathhouses, food stores and markets, theatres and even an ancient brothel. Then, in the eerie stillness, with your eye on ominous Mt Vesuvius, ponder the town's final hours when the skies grew dark and heavy with volcanic ashes.

17

Basque Country, Spain

Home to fabulous food and architecture

This is where mountain peaks reach for the sky and sublime rocky coves are battered by mighty Atlantic swells. Food is an obsession, whether it's the Michelin-starred restaurants of San Sebastián or the fabulous *pintxo* (Basque tapas) bars in the same city or in Bilbao. And the Basque Country has reinvented itself as one of Spain's style and culture capitals, with Bilbao's stunning Museo Guggenheim leading the way.

MARCIN JUCHA ~ SHUTTERSTOCK ©

Reykjavík, Iceland

The world's most northerly capital

Most Icelanders live in Reykjavík and even on the shortest visit you'll be struck by how quirky and creative a population this is. Despite being on the northern margin of Europe, the locals have crafted a town packed with captivating art, rich cuisine and an epic music scene. Learn about a history stretching back to the Vikings and use the city as a base for trips to Iceland's amazing natural wonders.

Far left: Blue Lagoon (p180); Left: Hallgrímskirkja (p184)

Copenhagen, Denmark

Coolest kid on the Nordic block

Scandivania is all about paired-back contemporary style – something that the Danish capital has in spades. Home to a thriving design scene, Copenhagen sports Michelin-starred restaurants, hipster cafes and bars and swoon-worthy boutiques around every corner. Add in top-class museums and galleries and a thousand-year-old harbour town area with handsome historic architecture and you have the perfect Scandi city. Top: Nyhavn (p142); Above Left: Royal Danish Library, designed by Schmidt Hammer Lassen Architects; Above Right: Barista making coffee

19

MASKOT / GETTY IMAGES ©

Matterhorn, Switzerland

Hike, ski and admire this Swiss peak

It graces chocolate-bar wrappers and evokes stereotypical Heidi scenes, but nothing prepares you for the allure of the Matterhorn. This mesmerising peak looms above the timber-chalet-filled Swiss village of Zermatt. Gaze at it from a tranquil cafe, hike in its shadow along the tangle of alpine paths above town, with cowbells clinking in the distance, or pause on a ski slope and admire its craggy, chiselled outline.

Florence, Italy

Tailor-made for fastidious aesthetes

Home to Brunelleschi's Duomo and Masaccio's Cappella Brancacci frescoes, Florence, according to Unesco, contains 'the greatest concentration of universally renowned works of art in the world'. Florence is where the Renaissance kicked off and artists such as Michelangelo, Brunelleschi and Botticelli rewrote the rules of creative expression. The result is a city packed with artistic treasures, blockbuster museums, elegant churches and flawless Renaissance streetscapes. Galleria degli Uffizi (p426)

Plan Your Trip
Need to Know

When to Go?

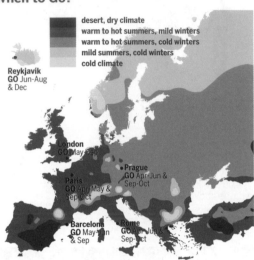

desert, dry climate
warm to hot summers, mild winters
warm to hot summers, cold winters
mild summers, cold winters
cold climate

Reykjavík
GO Jun-Aug & Dec

London
GO May-Sep

Prague
GO Apr-Jun & Sep-Oct

Paris
GO Apr-May & Sep-Oct

Barcelona
GO May-Jun & Sep

Rome
GO Apr-Jun & Sep-Oct

High Season (Jun–Aug)

○ Everybody comes to Europe and all of Europe hits the road.

○ Hotel prices and temperatures are their highest.

Shoulder (Apr–May & Sep–Oct)

○ Crowds and prices drop, except in Italy where it's still busy.

○ Temperatures are comfortable but it can be hot in southern Europe.

○ Overall these are the best months to travel in Europe.

Low Season (Nov–Mar)

○ Outside ski resorts, hotels drop their prices or close down.

○ The weather can be cold and days short, especially in northern Europe.

Currency

Euro (€), Pound (£), Swiss franc (Sfr), Danish krone (Dkr), Hungarian Forint (Ft), Icelandic króna (kr), Czech crown (Koruna česká; Kč), Croatian Kuna (KN)

Language

English, French, German, Italian, Spanish

Visas

EU citizens don't need visas for other EU countries. Australians, Canadians, New Zealanders and Americans don't need visas for visits of less than 90 days.

Money

ATMs are common; credit and debit cards are widely accepted.

Mobile Phones

Europe uses the GSM 900 network. If you're coming from outside Europe it's worth buying a prepaid local SIM.

Time

Britain, Ireland and Portugal (GMT), Central Europe (GMT plus one hour), Greece, Turkey and Eastern Europe (GMT plus two hours).

Daily Costs

Budget: Less than €60

- Dorm beds: €10–20
- Admission to museums: €5–15
- Pizza or pasta: €8–12

Midrange: €60–200

- Double room in a small hotel: €50–100
- Short taxi trip: €10–20
- Meals in good restaurants: around €20 per person

Top end: More than €200

- Stay at iconic hotels, from €150
- Car hire: from around €30 per day
- Theatre tickets: €15–150

Useful Websites

Lonely Planet (www.lonelyplanet.com/europe) Destination information, hotel bookings, traveller forum and more.

The Man in Seat Sixty-One (www.seat61.com) Encyclopedic site dedicated to train travel plus plenty of other tips.

Hidden Europe (www.hiddeneurope.co.uk) Fascinating magazine and online dispatches from all the continent's corners.

VisitEurope (www.visiteurope.com) With information about travel in 33 member countries.

Spotted by Locals (www.spottedbylocals.com) Insider tips for cities across Europe.

Where to Stay

Europe offers the fullest possible range of accommodation for all budgets. Book up to two months in advance for a July visit, or for ski resorts over Christmas and New Year.

Hotels Range from the local pub to restored castles.

B&Bs Small, family-run houses generally provide good value.

Hostels Enormous variety, from backpacker palaces to real dumps.

Homestays and farmstays A great way to really find out how locals live.

Arriving in Europe

Schiphol Airport, Amsterdam (p174) Trains to the centre (20 minutes).

Heathrow Airport, London (p94) Trains (15 minutes) and Tube (one hour) to the centre.

Aéroport de Charles de Gaulle, Paris (p250) Many buses (one hour) and trains (30 minutes) to the centre.

Tegel Airport, Berlin (p517) Buses (40 minutes) and taxis (30 to 45 minutes) to the centre.

Leonardo da Vinci Airport, Rome (p397) Buses (one hour) and trains (30 minutes) to the centre.

El Prat Airport, Barcelona (p306) Buses (35 minutes) to the centre.

Getting Around

In most European countries, the train is the best option for internal transport.

Train Europe's train network is fast and efficient but rarely a bargain unless you book well in advance or use a rail pass wisely.

Bus Usually taken for short trips in remoter areas, though long-distance intercity buses can be cheap.

Car You can hire a car or drive your own through Europe. Roads are excellent but petrol is expensive.

Ferry Boats connect Britain and Ireland with mainland Europe and criss-cross the Mediterranean.

Air Speed things up by flying from one end of the continent to the other.

Bicycle Slow things down on a two-wheeler, a great way to get around just about anywhere.

For more on **getting around**, see p631

Plan Your Trip
Hotspots for...

CRISTIAN PUSCASU / SHUTTERSTOCK ©

History

Europe's epic history is writ large across the continent with headline sights that bring it vividly to life – from Rome's majestic ruins to grand palaces and parliaments.

Rome (p352)
History reverberates all over the Eternal City, from the gladiatorial Colosseum to the Vatican.

Birth of an Empire
Romulus supposedly founded Rome in Palatino (p380).

London (p50)
Indomitable London has seen it all from the Romans and the Great Fire to the Blitz and the Swinging Sixties.

Royal History
Monarchs were crowned in Westminster Abbey (p52).

Berlin (p486)
Reminders of the German capital's glorious and troubled past await you around every corner.

WWII Icon
Brandenburger Tor (p498) is a symbol of the Cold War.

COLIN DEWAR / SHUTTERSTOCK ©

The Great Outdoors

From magnificent mountains and rolling hills covered in flowers and vines to sandy-beach coasts with vistas of charming islands, Europe's landscapes are a visual treat.

Switzerland (p586)
Switzerland's majestic landscapes soaring to the heights of the Alps will make your knees go weak.

Alpine Vistas
Marvel at the iconic Matterhorn (p588) from Zermatt.

Dubrovnik (p470)
An ancient walled town overlooks sapphire waters speckled with countless forested islands.

Coastal Enclaves
Admire the Adriatic from the walls of Dubrovnik (p473).

Scottish Highlands (p96)
Big skies, sweeping landscapes, mysterious lochs (lakes) and spectacular wildlife.

Big Skies
Highland's primary city, Inverness (p104), is on River Ness.

Arts & Architecture

World-class museums and galleries, thriving theatres and concert halls, ancient castles and ornate public buildings: Europe's cultural treasures are guaranteed to excite and delight.

CHAOSS / SHUTTERSTOCK ®

Florence (p418)
Florence is home to a magnificent array of Renaissance art and architecture.

Renaissance Treasures
Swoon over the art at Galleria degli Uffizi (p427).

Vienna (p564)
Grand imperial palaces, revered opera houses and superb art museums can be found in Vienna.

Empire of Art
Kunsthistorisches Museum (p569) brims with works.

Amsterdam (p154)
Ground zero for European art during the Golden Age, fostering the likes of Rembrandt and Vermeer.

Golden Age
Rijksmuseum (p160) is the city's premier art trove.

Food & Drink

Europe's culinary diversity and quality is almost unrivalled; whether you like Michelin-starred restaurants or casual cafes, you'll be treated to delicious local produce.

IRINA MELIUKH / SHUTTERSTOCK ®

Paris (p202)
Food is not fuel here – it's a religion and the reason you get up in the morning.

Artistic Food
Enjoy art-like masterpieces at Restaurant AT (p242).

Barcelona (p268)
This Catalan city has a celebrated food scene fuelled by world-class chefs and imaginative recipes.

Avant Garde
Expect the unexpected at Disfrutar (p300).

Copenhagen (p136)
One of the hottest culinary destinations, with more Michelin stars than any other Scandinavian city.

New Nordic
Geranium (p150) transforms local ingredients into art.

Plan Your Trip
Local Life

Activities

Europe is just one great playground for lovers of the great outdoors. Hiking and biking trails criss-cross mountains, hills, fields, forests and coastlines. Among the huge range of activities you can take part in are fishing, horse riding, skiing, climbing, kayaking and sailing. And if outdoor pursuits are not your thing, then Europe's urban centres are well set up for those interested in learning to cook a local dish, learn a new language or follow a guided specialist tour.

Shopping

You've no doubt heard about the European Union's 'single market'. The reality is infinitely better: a multiplicity of markets and other varied retail options are to found from the highlands of Scotland to the streets of Lisbon. Be it in the grand department stores and fashion houses of Paris, London and Rome, the craft stalls and artists' ateliers of Venice or Prague, or

farmers markets everywhere, there are a million and one ways to find that perfect souvenir to bring home.

Entertainment

When it comes to mass entertainment, Europe practically wrote the book. Rome's Colosseum may no longer be a functioning arena, but there are countless other giant stadiums and storied venues across the continent. The sheer range of performing arts is impressive, spanning classical music to grunge rock, Shakespeare to contemporary dance. Europeans also love their sporting events with soccer being a major preoccupation.

Eating

Europe's delicious cuisine reflects the multitude of different countries and regions spread across the continent. The Mediterranean diet is listed as an 'Intangible Cultural Heritage' by Unesco and has a number of variants, including

FOTOLUPA / SHUTTERSTOCK ©

Italian, Spanish and Greek. French food is practically a religion. Nordic food is the trendy new upstart of the culinary world. The UK excels in cosmopolitan Asian flavours and has invented its own brand of spicy Anglo-Indian cuisine. Wherever you go in Europe, eating is not just a pleasure but a valuable insight into the local history and culture.

Drinking & Nightlife

Whatever your tipple or taste in nightlife, Europe is sure to deliver. Whether you're pounding the streets of Reykjavík, Paris or Barcelona, you're sure to find pumping dance clubs with cutting edge DJs and designer cocktail bars, as well as cosy pubs and third-wave coffee shops. Slip into a local pub in Scotland to sample Highland whiskies, or a bar in Prague to sip on craft beers. And let's not even start on the wonderful wines of France, Spain and Italy – visiting vineyards could keep you occupied the whole trip.

★ Best Restaurants

Dinner by Heston Blumenthal (p89)

Restaurant Guy Savoy (p244)

Cafe Jacques (p461)

Tapas 24 (p300)

Pizzarium (p392)

From left: Market in Prague (p524); Royal Albert Hall (p93), London

Plan Your Trip
Month by Month

February

Carnival, in all its manic glory, sweeps the Catholic regions. Cold temperatures are forgotten amid masquerades, street festivals and general bacchanalia.

❄ Carnevale, Italy

In the period before Ash Wednesday, Venice goes mad for masks (www.venice-carnival-italy.com). Costume balls, many with traditions centuries old, enliven the social calendar in this storied old city.

March

Spring arrives in southern Europe. It's colder further north, though days are often bright.

❄ St Patrick's Day, Ireland

Parades and celebrations with friends and family are held on 17 March across Ireland to honour the country's beloved patron saint.

☆ Budapest Spring Festival, Hungary

This two-week festival in March/April is one of Europe's top classical-music events (www.springfestival.hu). Concerts are held in a number of beautiful venues, including stunning churches, the opera house and the national theatre.

April

Spring arrives with a burst of colour, from the glorious bulb fields of Holland to the blooming orchards of Spain.

❄ Settimana Santa, Italy

Italy celebrates Holy Week with processions and passion plays. By Holy Thursday Rome is thronged with the faithful as hundreds of thousands converge on the Vatican and St Peter's Basilica.

❄ Koninginnedag (Queen's Day), Netherlands

The nationwide celebration on 27 April is especially fervent in Amsterdam, awash

with orange costumes and fake Afros, beer, dope, leather boys, temporary roller coasters, clogs and general craziness.

May

May is usually sunny and warm and full of things to do – an excellent time to visit.

🍺 Beer Festival, Czech Republic

This Prague beer festival (www.ceskypivni festival.cz) offers lots of food, music and – most importantly – around 70 beers from around the country from mid to late May.

June

The sun has broken through the clouds and the weather is generally gorgeous across the continent.

🎊 Karneval der Kulturen, Germany

This joyous street carnival (www.karneval-berlin.de) celebrates Berlin's multicultural tapestry with parties, global nosh and a fun parade of flamboyantly costumed dancers, DJs, artists and musicians.

★ Best Festivals

Carnevale, February

St Patrick's Day, March

Bastille Day, July

Notting Hill Carnival, August

Festes de la Mercè, October

🎊 Festa de Santo António, Portugal

Feasting, drinking and dancing in Lisbon's Alfama in honour of St Anthony (12 to 13 June) top the even grander three-week Festas de Lisboa (http://festasdelisboa. com), which features processions and dozens of street parties.

July

One of the busiest months for travel across the continent with outdoor cafes, beer gardens and beach clubs all hopping.

From left: *Correfoc* during Festes de la Mercè (p34), Barcelona; Dancers at Karneval der Kulturen, Berlin

🐾 Sanfermines (Running of the Bulls), Spain

Fiesta de San Fermín (Sanfermines) is the week-long nonstop Pamplona festival with the daily *encierro* (running of the bulls) as its centrepiece (www.bullrunpamplona. com). The antibullfighting event, the Running of the Nudes (www.runningofthe nudes.com), takes place two days earlier.

🐾 Bastille Day, France

Fireworks, balls, processions and – of course – good food and wine, for France's national day on 14 July, celebrated in every French town and city.

August

Everybody's going someplace as half of Europe shuts down to enjoy the traditional month of holiday with the other half.

🐾 Amsterdam Gay Pride, the Netherlands

Held at the beginning of August, this is one of Europe's best GLBT events (www. amsterdamgaypride.nl). It's more about freedom and diversity than protest.

🐾 Notting Hill Carnival, Great Britain

Europe's largest – and London's most vibrant – outdoor carnival is a two-day event where London's Caribbean community shows the city how to party (www. thelondonnottinghillcarnival.com).

☆ Sziget Music Festival, Hungary

A week-long, great-value world-music festival (www.sziget.hu) held all over Budapest. Sziget features bands from around the world playing at more than 60 venues.

September

Maybe the best time to visit: the weather's still good and the crowds have thinned.

☆ Venice International Film Festival, Italy

Italy's top film fest is a celebration of mainstream and indie moviemaking (www.labiennale.org). The judging here is seen as an early indication of what to look for at the next year's Oscars.

🐾 Festes de la Mercè, Spain

The city's biggest celebration (around 24 September) has four days of concerts, dancing, *castellers* (human-castle builders), fireworks and *correfoc* – a parade of fireworks-spitting dragons and devils.

November

Leaves have fallen, and snow is about to, in much of Europe. Even in the temperate zones around the Med it can get chilly, rainy and blustery.

🐾 Guy Fawkes Night, Great Britain

Bonfires and fireworks erupt across Britain on 5 November, recalling the foiling of a plot to blow up the Houses of Parliament in the 1600s. Go to high ground in London to see glowing explosions erupt everywhere.

☆ Iceland Airwaves, Iceland

Roll on up to Reykjavík for Iceland Airwaves, a great music festival featuring both Icelandic and international acts (www.icelandair waves.is).

December

Despite freezing temperatures this is a magical time to visit, with Christmas markets and decorations brightening Europe's dark streets. Prices remain surprisingly low provided you avoid Christmas and New Year's Eve.

🐾 Natale, Italy

Italian churches set up an intricate crib or a *presepe* (nativity scene) in the lead-up to Christmas. Some are quite famous, most are works of art, and many date back hundreds of years and are venerated for their spiritual ties.

Plan Your Trip
Get Inspired

Read

Neither Here Nor There: Travels in Europe Bill Bryson retraces a youthful European backpacking trip with hilarious observations.

Europe: A History Professor Norman Davies' sweeping overview of European history.

In Europe: Travels through the Twentieth Century Fascinating account of journalist Geert Mak's travels.

Fifty Years of Europe: An Album A lifetime of travel around the continent, distilled by British travel writer Jan Morris.

The Imperfectionists Tom Rachman's novel charts the fortunes of an English-language newspaper based in Rome.

Watch

The Third Man (1949) Classic tale of wartime espionage in old Vienna, starring Orson Welles and that zither theme.

Notting Hill (1999) Superstar Julia Roberts falls for bookshop-owner Hugh Grant in this London-based rom-com.

Amélie (2001) Endearing tale following the quirky adventures of Parisian do-gooder Amélie Poulain.

Vicky Christina Barcelona (2008) Woody Allen–directed drama about the amorous adventures of two young American women in Spain.

Victoria (2016) Thriller set on the streets of Berlin that plays out in one continuous 138-minute camera shot.

Listen

The Original Three Tenors: 20th Anniversary Edition Operatic classics courtesy of Pavarotti, Carreras and Domingo.

The Best of Edith Piaf The sound of France, including a selection of the Little Sparrow's greatest hits.

Chambao Feel-good flamenco fused with electronica from Spain's deep south.

London Calling A post-punk classic from The Clash that incorporates a host of musical influences.

Fado Tradicional A return to basics from Mariza, a top contemporary exponent of Portugal's fado style of music.

Festival performance outside Shakespeare's Globe (p78), London

Plan Your Trip
Five-Day Itineraries

Iberian Excursion

For a short European break, with a bright burst of sunshine whatever the time of year, Portugal and Spain can't be beaten. This quartet of destinations also provides wonderful art, architecture and delicious food.

Bilbao (p316) Devote a day to the monumental contemporary art installations in Bilbao's shimmering Museo Guggenheim. 🚌 1 hr to San Sebastián

San Sebastián (p323) Enjoy a day of grazing on delicious *pintxos* (Basque tapas) in this idyllic seaside town. 🚌 1½ hrs to Barcelona

Barcelona (p268) Ramble along La Rambla; get lost in the medieval streets of the Barri Gòtic; and marvel at La Sagrada Família.

Lisbon (p330) Spend two days exploring this enchanting city from the cobbled lanes of Alfama to seaside Belem. ✈ 2 hrs to Bilbao

Eastern Europe to Berlin

Known as the grim, grey 'Eastern Bloc' until the early 1990s, today this half of Europe is one of the continent's most dynamic and fascinating to visit. The four cities on this itinerary each have a distinct character and charm.

Berlin (p486) Enjoy diversity, alternative culture and the frisson of recent history in Germany's once-divided capital.

Prague (p524) Wander this romantic city for a day, ending up on the iconic Charles Bridge at dusk. 🚆 5 hrs to Berlin

Vienna (p564) Allow two days for Austria's capital; it's packed with palaces, museums and splendid art galleries. 🚆 4 hrs to Prague

Budapest (p546) Spend a day in Hungary's capital with its architectural gems and soothing thermal baths. 🚆 2 ¾ hrs to Vienna

Plan Your Trip
Five-Day Itineraries

Italy & the Adriatic Coast

This whistle-stop itinerary gives a taste of the glories of Italy starting in its ancient capital Rome. Next, the Renaissance crucible of Florence and the floating wonder of Venice, before heading down the Adriatic Coast to historic Dubrovnik in Croatia.

Venice (p400) Hop in a gondola and sail the canals – before the day is out you'll be in love with Venice.
✈ 1½ hrs to Dubrovnik

Florence (p418) You'll need to move at a pace to cram in the art and architecture of this Renaissance beauty in a day. 🚌 2 hrs to Venice

Rome (p352) Allow a couple of days in the Eternal City; home to the Vatican and Colosseum.
🚌 1½ hrs to Florence

Dubrovnik (p470) One of the world's most magnificent walled cities has a pedestrian-only old town and sublime sea views.

Canals & Castles

With only five days, you'll need to fly most of the way between Amsterdam's World Heritage–listed canals and the Schloss Neushwanstein, a classic European castle. Make stops for an injection of Nordic cool in Copenhagen and nightclubbing in Berlin.

Copenhagen (p136) Home to the Tivoli Gardens, palaces, the nonconformist enclave of Christiania and the Little Mermaid.
✈ 1 hr to Berlin

Berlin (p486) With no curfew Berlin parties through the night. Start the evening off in Prater, a historic beer garden. ✈ 1 hr to Munich

Amsterdam (p154) Rent a bike to cycle around this city beside canals, stopping off at art museums and coffeeshops.
✈ 1½ hrs to Copenhagen

Schloss Neuschwanstein (p520) Ludwig II's fantasy castle, two hours southwest of Munich, was a model for the one in Disney's *Sleeping Beauty*.

Plan Your Trip
10-Day Itinerary

Iceland to Ireland

This 1500km journey around northern Europe is one of the continent's most scenic, from the bubbling hot springs outside Reykjavík to the gentle Georgian architecture of Dublin, via the grand Scottish Highlands and the history, culture and fashion of London.

Reykjavík (p176) Allot two days for the city's excellent museums, shops and cafes, as well as its vibrant nightlife.
✈ 4 hrs to London

1

Inverness (p104) This is your three-day base for explorations around the splendid Scottish Highlands.
✈ 1¼ hrs to Dublin

Dublin (p114) Encounter the Dublin of James Joyce as you meander between the literary haunts, museums and pubs of Ireland's capital.

3

4

London (p50) You'll be amazed how much of London you can pack into three days if you try.
✈ 1½ hrs to Inverness

2

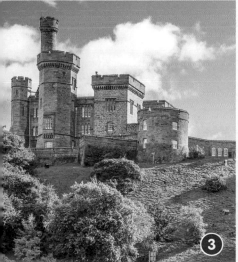

Plan Your Trip
10-Day Itinerary

Southern Mediterranean

Hire a car in Avignon, a great base for touring the hilltop villages and Roman ruins of France's beautiful Provence. Devote a day to travelling the cliffside roads of the Cote d'Azur towards Italy – one of the world's great drives.

1

Avignon (p260) A couple of days is sufficient to see the sights in and around this ancient fortress town.
🚗 7 ¾ hrs to Siena

S.BORISOV / SHUTTERSTOCK ©

2

Florence (p418) Take in the city's Renaissance splendour from the cupola of its landmark Duomo.
🚆 1½ hrs to Rome

3

2

Siena (p452) Spend a day exploring one of Italy's most enchanting medieval settlements.
🚗 1 hr to Florence

Rome (p352) Linger on the Spanish steps, beside the Trevi Fountain and in the Piazza Navona.
🚆 2¾ hrs to Pompeii

4

5

Pompeii (p462) The Unesco-listed ruins provide a remarkable model of a working Roman city, including baths, taverns and a brothel.

4

1

Plan Your Trip
Two-Week Itinerary

Classic Europe

Eight countries in 14 days may
sound like squeezing too much in,
but Europe's extensive network of
budget flights and trains makes this
itinerary easy. It's a great introduction to the continent's infinite variety
of cultures and terrain.

London (p50) Spend a
couple of days in this
endlessly intriguing city, one
of history's great survivors.
🚃 2¼ hrs to Paris

1

3

2

Paris (p202) Swoon for two days over
the beautiful boulevards and romantic
alleys of the City of Light. 🚃 3½ hrs to
Amsterdam

Zermatt (p592) Spend a
day gawping in awe at the
Matterhorn, the Alps'
most famous peak.
🚃 4 hrs to Geneva, then
1 hr to Barcelona

7

Barcelona (p268) Wrap up your tour
on the balmy shores of the
Mediterranean in a city that's both a
visual treat and a foodie heaven.

8

ANASTASIA GALKINA / SHUTTERSTOCK ©

8

Amsterdam (p154) Chill out for a day cruising the canals and art galleries and enjoying the liberal atmosphere. ✈ 1 ½ hrs to Prague

Prague (p524) Devote a day to the town's two big attractions - the castle and the Old Town Square 🚄 4 ½ hrs to Vienna

④

⑤ **Vienna** (p564) Allow two days for the grandeur of the former capital of the Austro-Hungarian empire. ✈ 1 hr to Venice

⑥

Venice (p400) Surrender to the haunting beauty of La Serenissima's watery world of piazza, domes, canals and bridges. 🚄 6 hrs to Zermatt

④

⑤

Plan Your Trip
Family Travel

Getting Around

In general, Europe is an incredibly family-friendly place to travel, but distances can be long, so it's a good idea to break up the trip with things to see and do en route.

Traffic is at its worst during holiday seasons, especially between June and August, and journey times are likely to be much longer during this period.

Trains can be a great option for family travel – kids will have more space to move around, and you can pack books, puzzles and computer games to keep them entertained.

Children and young people qualify for cheap travel on most public transport in Europe (usually around 50% of the adult fare). Look out for railcards and passes that open up extra discounts – many cities offer passes that combine entry to sights and attractions with travel on public transport.

Sights & Attractions

Most attractions offer discounted entry for children (generally for 12 years and under, although this varies). If you can, try to mix up educational activities with fun excursions they're guaranteed to enjoy – balance that visit to the Tate Modern or the Louvre with a trip to the London Aquarium or a day at Disneyland Paris, for example. The number-one rule is to avoid packing too much in – you'll get tired, the kids will get irritable and tantrums are sure to follow. Plan carefully and you'll enjoy your time much more.

Hotels & Restaurants

It's always worth asking in advance whether hotels are happy to accept kids. Many are fully geared for family travel, with children's activities, child-minding services and the like, but others may impose a minimum age limit to deter guests with kids. Family-friendly hotels will usually be

able to offer a large room with two or three beds to accommodate families, or at least neighbouring rooms with an adjoining door. Dining out en famille is generally great fun, but again, it's always worth checking to see whether kids are welcome – generally the posher or more prestigious the establishment, the less kid-friendly they're likely to be. Many restaurants offer cheaper children's menus, usually based around simple staples such as steak, pasta, burgers and chicken. Most will also offer smaller portions of adult meals. If your kids are fussy, buying your own ingredients at a local market can encourage them to experiment – they can choose their own food while simultaneously practising the local lingo.

Need to Know

Changing facilities Found at most supermarkets and major attractions.

Cots and highchairs Available in many restaurants and hotels, but ask ahead.

★ Best Cities for Kids

Paris (p202)

London (p50)

Barcelona (p268)

Copenhagen (p136)

Vienna (p564)

Health Generally good, but pack your own first-aid kit to avoid language difficulties.

Kids' menus Widely available.

Nappies (diapers) Sold everywhere, including pharmacies and supermarkets.

Strollers It's easiest to bring your own.

Transport Children usually qualify for discounts; young kids often travel free.

From left: Carousel in the Tivoli Gardens (p138), Copenhagen; Children in Paris (p202)

GREAT BRITAIN & IRELAND

In This Chapter

London, Great Britain

One of the world's most visited cities, London has something for everyone: from history and culture to fine food and good times. Britain may have voted for Brexit (although the majority of Londoners didn't), but for now London remains one of the world's most cosmopolitan cities, and diversity infuses daily life, food, music and fashion. It even penetrates intrinsically British institutions; the British Museum and Victoria & Albert Museum have collections as varied as they are magnificent, while the flavours at centuries-old Borough Market run the full global gourmet spectrum.

London in Two Days

First stop, **Westminster Abbey** (p52) for an easy intro to the city's (and nation's) history and then to **Buckingham Palace** (p63). Walk up the Mall to **Trafalgar Square** (p75) for its architectural grandeur and photo-op views of **Big Ben** (p74). Art lovers will make a beeline for the **National Gallery** (p74) and and **Tate Britain** (p75).

On day two, visit the **British Museum** (p59) and explore **Soho** (p75), followed by dinner at **Claridge's Foyer & Reading Room** (p90).

London in Four Days

Have a royally good time checking out the Crown Jewels at the **Tower of London** (p67), followed by some retail therapy at **Leadenhall Market** (p70) and a visit to **St Paul's Cathedral** (p78).

Dedicate the fourth day to the **V&A** (p79), **Natural History Museum** (p78) and **Science Museum** (p79). End the day with a show at **Royal Albert Hall** (p93).

After London catch the Eurostar to Paris (p202) or Amsterdam (p154).

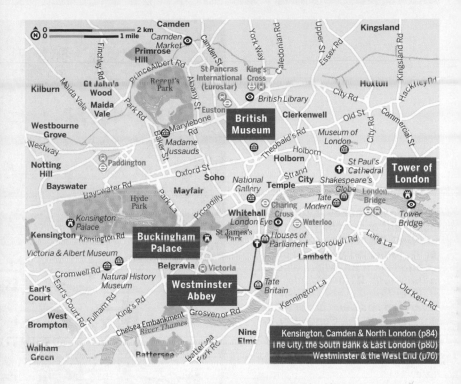

Camden
Camden Market
Primrose Hill
Kingsland
Kilburn
St John's Wood
Maida Vale
Regent's Park
St Pancras International (Eurostar)
King's Cross
British Library
Huxton
Westbourne Grove
Paddington
Euston
Marylebone Rd
British Museum
Clerkenwell
Museum of London
Madame Tussauds
Holborn
Holborn
St Paul's Cathedral
Tower of London
Notting Hill
Bayswater
Oxford St
Soho
National Gallery
Strand
City
Shakespeare's Globe
London Bridge
Mayfair
Temple
Hyde Park
Piccadilly
Charing Cross
Tate Modern
Waterloo
Tower Bridge
Konsington Palace
Whitehall
London Eye
Kensington
Kensington Rd
Buckingham Palace
St James's Park
Houses of Parliament
Borough Rd
Long La
Victoria & Albert Museum
Belgravia
Victoria
Lambeth
Earl's Court
Cromwell Rd
Natural History Museum
Westminster Abbey
Tate Britain
Kennington La
Old Kent Rd
West Brompton
King's Rd
Grosvenor Rd
Chelsea Embankment
River Thames
Nine Elms
Walham Green
Battersea

Kensington, Camden & North London (p84)
The City, the South Bank & East London (p80)
Westminster & the West End (p76)

Arriving in London

Heathrow Airport Trains, the tube and buses head to central London from just after 5am to before midnight (night buses run later and 24-hour tube runs Friday and Saturday) £5.70–21.50; taxi £46–87. From 2018, express trains will run to central London and beyond along the Elizabeth Line (Crossrail).

Gatwick Airport Trains to central London from 4.30am to 1.35am cost £10–20; hourly buses to central London run around the clock, from £5; taxi £100.

St Pancras International Train Station In Central London and connected by many underground lines to other parts of the city.

Where to Stay

Hanging your hat in London can be painfully expensive, and you'll need to book well in advance. Decent hostels are easy to find, but aren't as cheap as you might hope for. Hotels range from no-frills chains through to ultra-ritzy establishments, such as the Ritz itself. B&Bs are often better value and more atmospheric than hotels.

For information on what each London neighbourhood has to offer, see the table on p95.

Westminster Abbey

Westminster Abbey is such an important commemoration site that it's hard to overstate its symbolic value or imagine its equivalent anywhere else in the world. With a couple of exceptions, every English sovereign has been crowned here since William the Conqueror in 1066, and most of the monarchs from Henry III (died 1272) to George II (died 1760) are buried here.

Great For...

❶ Need to Know

Map p76; ☏020-7222 5152; www. westminster-abbey.org; 20 Dean's Yard, SW1; adult/child £20/9, cloister & gardens free; ◷9.30am-4.30pm Mon, Tue, Thu & Fri, to 7pm Wed, to 2.30pm Sat; ⊖Westminster

★ **Top Tip**
The abbey gets incredibly busy, even at opening, so come armed with patience.

There is an extraordinary amount to see at the Abbey. The interior is chock-a-block with ornate chapels, elaborate tombs of monarchs and grandiose monuments to sundry luminaries throughout the ages. First and foremost, however, it is a sacred place of worship.

A Regal History

Though a mixture of architectural styles, the Abbey is considered the finest example of Early English Gothic (1190–1300). The original church was built in the 11th century by King (later St) Edward the Confessor, who is buried in the chapel behind the sanctuary and main altar. Henry III (r 1216–72) began work on the new building, but didn't complete it; the French Gothic nave was finished by Richard II in 1388. Henry VII's huge and magnificent Lady Chapel was added in 1519.

The Abbey was initially a monastery for Benedictine monks, and many of the building's features attest to this collegial past (the octagonal Chapter House, the Quire and four cloisters). In 1536 Henry VIII separated the Church of England from the Roman Catholic Church and dissolved the monastery. The king became head of the Church of England and the Abbey acquired its 'royal peculiar' status, meaning it is administered directly by the Crown and exempt from any ecclesiastical jurisdiction.

North Transept, Sanctuary & Quire

Entrance to the Abbey is via the Great North Door. The North Transept is often referred to as Statesmen's Aisle: politicians

Quire

and eminent public figures are commemorated by large marble statues and imposing marble plaques.

At the heart of the Abbey is the beautifully tiled **sanctuary** (or sacrarium), a stage for coronations, royal weddings and funerals. George Gilbert Scott designed the ornate **high altar** in 1873. In front of the altar is the **Cosmati marble pavement** dating back to 1268. It has intricate designs of small pieces of marble inlaid into plain marble, which predicts the end of the world in AD 19,693! At the entrance to the lovely

> ☑ **Don't Miss**
>
> Poet's Corner, the Coronation Chair, the 14th-century cloisters, the oldest door in the UK, a 900-year-old garden, the royal sarcophagi and much, much more.

Chapel of St John the Baptist is a sublime Virgin and Child bathed in candlelight.

The **Quire**, a magnificent structure of gold, blue and red Victorian Gothic by Edward Blore, dates back to the mid-19th century. It sits where the original choir for the monks' worship would have been, but bears no resemblance to the original. Nowadays, the Quire is still used for singing, but its regular occupants are the Westminster Choir – 22 boys and 12 'lay vicars' (men) who sing the daily services.

Chapels & Chair

The sanctuary is surrounded by chapels. **Henry VII's Lady Chapel**, in the easternmost part of the Abbey, is the most spectacular, with its fan vaulting on the ceiling, colourful banners of the Order of the Bath and dramatic oak stalls. Behind the chapel's altar is the elaborate sarcophagus of Henry VII and his queen, Elizabeth of York.

Beyond the chapel's altar is the **Royal Air Force Chapel**, with a stained-glass window commemorating the force's finest hour, the Battle of Britain (1940), and the 1500 RAF pilots who died. A stone plaque on the floor marks the spot where Oliver Cromwell's body lay for two years (1658) until the Restoration, when it was disinterred, hanged and beheaded. Two bodies, believed to be those of the child princes allegedly murdered in the Tower of London in 1483, were buried here almost two centuries later in 1674.

There are two small chapels either side of Lady Chapel with the tombs of famous monarchs: on the left (north) is where **Elizabeth I** and her half-sister **Mary I** (aka

> ✗ **Take a Break**
>
> Part of the original 14th-century Benedictine monastery, **Cellarium** (Map p76; ✆020-7222 0516; www.benugo.com/restaurants/cellarium-cafe-terrace; Westminster Abbey, 20 Dean's Yard, SW1; mains £9.50-15; ⊗8am-6pm Mon, Tue, Thu & Fri, to 9pm Wed, 9am-5pm Sat, 10am-4pm Sun; ⊜Westminster) has stunning views of the Abbey's architectural details.

Bloody Mary) rest. On the right (south) is the tomb of **Mary Queen of Scots**, beheaded on the orders of her cousin Elizabeth.

The vestibule of the Lady Chapel is the usual place for the rather ordinary-looking **Coronation Chair**, upon which every monarch since the early 14th century has been crowned.

Shrine of St Edward the Confessor

The most sacred spot in the Abbey lies behind the high altar; access is generally restricted to protect the 13th-century flooring. St Edward was the founder of the Abbey and the original building was consecrated a few weeks before his death. His tomb was slightly altered after the original was destroyed during the Reformation, but still contains Edward's remains – the only complete saint's body in Britain. Ninety-minute **verger-led tours** (£5 plus admission) of the Abbey include a visit to the shrine.

South Transept & Nave

The south transept contains **Poets' Corner**, where many of England's finest writers are buried and/or commemorated by monuments or memorials.

In the nave's north aisle is **Scientists' Corner**, where you will find **Sir Isaac Newton's tomb** (note the putto holding a prism to the sky while another feeds material into a smelting oven). Just ahead of it is the north aisle of the Quire, known as **Musicians' Aisle**, where baroque composers Henry Purcell and John Blow are buried, as well as more modern music-makers such as Benjamin Britten and Edward Elgar.

The two towers above the west door are the ones through which you exit. These were designed by Nicholas Hawksmoor and completed in 1745. Just above the door, perched in 15th-century niches, are the additions to the Abbey unveiled in 1998: 10 stone statues of international 20th-century martyrs who died for their Christian faith. These include American pacifist Dr Martin Luther King, the Polish priest St Maximilian Kolbe, who was murdered by the Nazis at Auschwitz, and

Wang Zhiming, publicly executed during the Chinese Cultural Revolution.

Outer Buildings & Gardens

The oldest part of the cloister is the **East Cloister** (or East Walk), dating from the 13th century. Off the cloister is the octagonal **Chapter House**, with one of Europe's best-preserved medieval tile floors and religious murals on the walls. It was used as a meeting place by the House of Commons in the second half of the 14th century. To the right of the entrance to Chapter House is what is claimed to be the **oldest door in Britain** – it's been there for 950 years.

The adjacent **Pyx Chamber** is one of the few remaining relics of the original Abbey, including the 10th-century **Altar of St Dunstan**. The chamber contains the pyx, a chest with standard gold and silver pieces

Statues above the west door

for testing coinage weights in a ceremony called the Trial of the Pyx, which nowadays takes place in Goldsmiths' Hall in the City of London.

To reach the 900-year-old **College Garden** (Map p76; ◷10am-6pm Tue-Thu Apr-Sep, to 4pm Oct-Mar), enter Dean's Yard and the Little Cloisters off Great College St.

New Museum for 2018

Scheduled for completion in 2018 are the **Queen's Diamond Jubilee Galleries**, a new museum and gallery space located in the medieval triforium, the arched gallery above the nave. Its exhibits will include the death masks of generations of royalty, wax effigies representing Charles II and William III (who is on a stool to make him as tall as his wife, Mary II), armour and stained glass. Highlights are the graffiti-inscribed Mary

Chair (used for the coronation of Mary II) and the Westminster Retable, England's oldest altarpiece, from the 13th century.

✕ Take a Break

Not far from the Abbey, the (student-staffed) **Vincent Rooms** (Map p76; ✆020-7802 8391; www.westking.ac.uk/about-us/vincent-rooms-restaurant; Westminster Kingsway College, Vincent Sq, SW1; mains £9-13; ◷noon-3pm Mon-Fri, 6-9pm Tue-Thu; ◉Victoria) is great for top-notch mod European cuisine at rock-bottom prices.

★ Top Tip

By joining a tour of the Abbey (usually two hours) led by an accredited Blue Badge Tourist Guide you can enter via the Dean's Yard and be fast-tracked inside.

KING ROMERO BONHOEFFER ESTHER JOHN

JULES_KITANO/SHUTTERSTOCK ©

Great Court

SONGQUAN DENG/SHUTTERSTOCK ©

British Museum

Britain's most visited attraction – founded in 1753 when royal physician Hans Sloane sold his 'cabinet of curiosities'– is an exhaustive and exhilarating stampede through 7000 years of human civilisation.

The British Museum offers a stupendous selection of tours, many of them free. There are 15 free 30- to 40-minute eyeOpener tours of individual galleries per day. The museum also has free daily gallery talks, a highlights tour (adult/child £12/free, 11.30am and 2pm Friday, Saturday and Sunday) and excellent multimedia iPad tours (adult/child £5/3.50), offering six themed one-hour tours, and a choice of 35-minute children's trails.

Great For...

☑ Don't Miss

The Rosetta Stone, the Mummy of Katebet and the marble Parthenon sculptures.

Great Court

Covered with a spectacular glass-and-steel roof designed by Norman Foster in 2000, the Great Court is the largest covered public square in Europe. In its centre is the world-famous **Reading Room**, formerly the British Library, which has been frequented by all the big brains of history, from Mahatma Gandhi to Karl Marx. It is currently used for temporary exhibits.

Parthenon marble frieze

FLIK47/SHUTTERSTOCK ©

British Museum

Bloomsbury St

Holborn

Tottenham Court Rd

New Oxford St

❶ Need to Know

Map p76; ☎020-7323 8299; www.british museum.org; Great Russell St & Montague Pl, WC1; ⊙10am-5.30pm Sat-Thu, to 8.30pm Fri; ⊖Russell Sq, Tottenham Court Rd FREE

✗ Take a Break

Just around the corner from the museum in a quiet, picturesque square is one of London's most atmospheric pubs, the **Queen's Larder** (Map p84; ☎020-7837 5627; www.queenslarder.co.uk; 1 Queen Sq, WC1; ⊙11.30am-11pm Mon-Fri, noon-11pm Sat, noon-10.30pm Sun; ⊖Russell Sq).

★ Top Tip

The museum is huge, so pick your interests and consider the free tours.

Ancient Egypt, Middle East & Greece

The star of the show here is the Ancient Egypt collection. It comprises sculptures, fine jewellery, papyrus texts, coffins and mummies, including the beautiful and intriguing **Mummy of Katebet** (room 63). The most prized item in the collection (and the most popular postcard in the shop) is the **Rosetta Stone** (room 4), the key to deciphering Egyptian hieroglyphics. In the same gallery is the enormous bust of the pharaoh **Ramesses the Great** (room 4).

Assyrian treasures from ancient Mesopotamia include the 16-tonne **Winged Bulls from Khorsabad** (room 10), the heaviest object in the museum. Behind it are the exquisite **Lion Hunt Reliefs from Ninevah** (room 10) from the 7th century BC, which influenced Greek sculpture. Such antiquities

are all the more significant after the Islamic State's bulldozing of Nimrud in 2015.

A major highlight of the museum is the **Parthenon sculptures** (room 18). The marble frieze is thought to be the Great Panathenaea, a blow-out version of an annual festival in honour of Athena.

Roman & Medieval Britain

Upstairs are finds from Britain and the rest of Europe (rooms 40 to 51). Many items go back to Roman times, when the empire spread across much of the continent, including the **Mildenhall Treasure** (room 49), a collection of pieces of 4th-century Roman silverware from Suffolk with both pagan and early-Christian motifs.

Lindow Man (room 50) is the well-preserved remains of a 1st-century man (comically dubbed Pete Marsh) discovered in a bog near Manchester in northern England in 1984. Equally fascinating are artefacts from the **Sutton Hoo Ship-Burial** (room 41), an elaborate Anglo-Saxon burial site from Suffolk dating back to the 7th century.

Perennial favourites are the lovely **Lewis Chessmen** (room 40), 12th-century game pieces carved from walrus tusk and whale teeth that were found on a remote Scottish island in the early 19th century. They served as models for the game of Wizard Chess in the first Harry Potter film.

Enlightenment Galleries

Formerly known as the King's Library, this stunning neoclassical space (room 1) was built between 1823 and 1827 and was the first part of the new museum building as it is seen today. The collection traces how disciplines such as biology, archaeology, linguistics and geography emerged during the Enlightenment of the 18th century.

What's Nearby?

Sir John Soane's Museum   Museum
(Map p76; ☏020-7405 2107; www.soane. org; 12 Lincoln's Inn Fields, WC2; ⊙10am-5pm Tue-Sat, plus 6-9pm 1st Tue of month; ⊜Holborn) FREE This little museum is one of the most atmospheric and fascinating in London. The building is the beautiful, bewitching home of architect Sir John Soane (1753–1837), which he left brimming with surprising personal effects and curiosities, and the museum represents his exquisite and eccentric taste.

Soane, a country bricklayer's son, is most famous for designing the Bank of England.

The heritage-listed house is largely as it was when Soane died and is itself a main part of the attraction. It has a canopy dome that brings light right down to the crypt, a colonnade filled with statuary and a picture

Buildings along Gordon Square

gallery where paintings are stowed behind each other on folding wooden panes. This is where Soane's choicest artwork is displayed, including *Riva degli Schiavoni, Looking West* by Canaletto, architectural drawings by Christopher Wren and Robert Adam, and the original *Rake's Progress*, William Hogarth's set of satirical cartoons of late-8th-century London lowlife. Among Soane's more unusual acquisitions are an Egyptian hieroglyphic sarcophagus, a mock-up of a monk's cell and slaves' chains.

★ Top Tip

Check out the outstanding *A History of the World in 100 Objects* radio series (www.bbc.co.uk/podcasts/series/ahow), which retraces two million years of history through 100 objects from the museum's collections.

BASPHOTO/SHUTTERSTOCK ©

Charles Dickens Museum Museum

(Map p84; ☎020-7405 2127; www.dickensmuseum.com; 48 Doughty St, WC1; adult/child £9/4; ⏰10am-5pm Tue-Sun; ⊖Chancery Lane, Russell Sq) A £3.5 million renovation has made this museum – located in a handsome four-storey house that was the great Victorian novelist's sole surviving residence in London – bigger and better than ever. The museum showcases the family drawing room (restored to its original condition), a period kitchen and a dozen rooms containing various memorabilia.

The Squares of Bloomsbury

The Bloomsbury Group, they used to say, lived in squares, moved in circles and loved in triangles. **Russell Square** (Map p84; ⊖Russell Square) sits at the very heart of the district. Originally laid out in 1800, a striking facelift at the start of the new millennium spruced it up and gave the square a 10m-high fountain. The centre of literary Bloomsbury was **Gordon Square** (Map p84; ⊖Russell Sq, Euston Sq), where some of the buildings are marked with blue plaques. Lovely **Bedford Square** (Map p76; ⊖Tottenham Court Rd) is the only completely Georgian square still surviving in Bloomsbury.

Tavistock Square (Map p84; ⊖Russell Sq, Euston Sq), the 'square of peace', has a statue of Mahatma Gandhi, a memorial to wartime conscientious objectors and a cherry tree recalling the WWII bombings of Hiroshima and Nagasaki.

Many writers and artists made their home in Gordon Square, including Bertrand Russell (No 57), Lytton Strachey (No 51) and Vanessa and Clive Bell, Maynard Keynes and the Woolf family (No 46). Strachey, Dora Carrington and Lydia Lopokova (the future wife of Maynard Keynes) all took turns living at No 41.

★ Did You Know?

Charles Dickens only spent 2½ years in the house that is now the Charles Dickens Museum, but it was here that he wrote many of his most famous works.

Buckingham Palace

The palace has been the Royal Family's London lodgings since 1837, when Queen Victoria moved in from Kensington Palace as St James's Palace was deemed too old-fashioned.

Great For...

☑ Don't Miss

Peering through the gates, going on a tour of the interior (summer only) or catching the Changing of the Guard at 11.30am.

The State Rooms are only open in August and September, when Her Majesty is holidaying in Scotland. The Queen's Gallery and the Royal Mews are open year-round, however.

State Rooms

The tour starts in the **Grand Hall** at the foot of the monumental **Grand Staircase**, commissioned by George IV in 1828. It takes in John Nash's Italianate **Green Drawing Room**, the **State Dining Room** (all red damask and Regency furnishings), the **Blue Drawing Room** (which has a gorgeous fluted ceiling by Nash) and the **White Drawing Room**, where foreign ambassadors are received.

The **Ballroom**, where official receptions and state banquets are held, was built between 1853 and 1855 and opened with

⏺ Need to Know

Map p76; ☎0303 123 7300; www.royal
collection.org.uk/visit/the-state-rooms-
buckingham-palace; Buckingham Palace Rd,
SW1; adult/child/under 5yr £23/13/free,
evening tour £80; ⏱5.30pm & 6pm late Mar-
Apr, 9.30am-7.30pm late Jul-Aug, to 6.30pm
Sep; ⬒ Green Park or St James's Park

✕ Take a Break

During the summer months, you can
enjoy light refreshments in the **Garden
Café** on the Palace's West Terrace.

★ Top Tip
Come early for front-row views of the
Changing of the Guard.

a ball a year later to celebrate the end of
the Crimean War. The **Throne Room** is
rather anticlimactic, with his-and-hers pink
chairs initialled 'ER' and 'P', sitting under a
curtained theatre arch.

Picture Gallery & Garden

The most interesting part of the tour is
the 47m-long Picture Gallery, featuring
splendid works by such artists as Van Dyck,
Rembrandt, Canaletto, Poussin, Claude
Lorrain, Rubens, Canova and Vermeer.

Wandering the 18 hectares of gardens
is another highlight – as well as admiring
some of the 350 or so species of flowers
and plants and listening to the many birds,
you'll get beautiful views of the palace and
a peek of its famous lake.

Changing of the Guard

At 11.30am daily from April to July (on
alternate days, weather permitting, for
the rest of the year), the old guard (Foot
Guards of the Household Regiment) comes
off duty to be replaced by the new guard on
the forecourt of Buckingham Palace.

Crowds come to watch the carefully
choreographed marching and shouting of
the guards in their bright-red uniforms and
bearskin hats. It lasts about 40 minutes
and is very popular, so arrive early if you
want to get a good **spot** (Map p76; http://
changing-guard.com).

Queen's Gallery

Since the reign of Charles I, the Royal
Family has amassed a priceless collection
of paintings, sculpture, ceramics, furniture and jewellery. The splendid **Queen's
Gallery** (Map p76; www.royalcollection.

org.uk/visit/the-queens-gallery-buckingham-palace; adult/child £10.30/5.30, incl Royal Mews £17.70/9.70; ⊙10am-5.30pm) showcases some of the palace's treasures on a rotating basis.

The gallery was originally designed as a conservatory by John Nash. It was converted into a chapel for Queen Victoria in 1843, destroyed in a 1940 air raid and reopened as a gallery in 1962. A £20-million renovation for Elizabeth II's Golden Jubilee in 2002 added three times as much display space.

Royal Mews

Southwest of the palace, the **Royal Mews** (Map p76; www.royalcollection.org.uk/visit/royalmews; Buckingham Palace Rd, SW1; adult/child £10/5.80, incl Queen's Gallery £17.70/9.70; ⊙10am-5pm Apr-Oct, to 4pm Mon-Sat Feb, Mar & Nov; ⊕Victoria) started life as a falconry, but is now a working stable looking after the royals' three dozen immaculately groomed horses, along with the opulent vehicles – motorised and horse-driven – the monarch uses for transport. The Queen is well known for her passion for horses; she names every horse that resides at the mews.

Nash's 1820 stables are stunning. Highlights of the collection include the enormous and opulent Gold State Coach of 1762, which has been used for every coronation since that of George III; the 1911 Glass Coach used for royal weddings and the Diamond Jubilee in 2012; Queen Alexandra's State Coach (1893), used to transport the Imperial State Crown to the official opening of Parliament; and a Rolls-Royce Phantom VI from the royal fleet.

St James's Park

What's Nearby?

St James's Park   Park

(Map p76; www.royalparks.org.uk/parks/
st-jamess-park; The Mall, SW1; ⊙5am midnight; ⊖St James's Park, Green Park) At just
23 hectares, St James's is one of the
smallest but best-groomed of London's
royal parks.

It has brilliant views of the London Eye,
Westminster, St James's Palace, Carlton
Tce and the Horse Guards Parade; the sight
of Buckingham Palace from the footbridge
spanning the central lake is photo-perfect
and the best you'll find.

> ★ **Did You Know?**
> The State Rooms represent a mere 19
> of the palace's 775 rooms.

WILL RODRIGUES/SHUTTERSTOCK ©

Royal Academy of Arts   Gallery

(Map p76; ☎020-7300 8000; www.royalacad
emy.org.uk; Burlington House, Piccadilly, W1;
adult/child from £13.50/free, exhibition prices
vary; ⊙10am-6pm Sat-Thu, to 10pm Fri; ⊖Green
Park) Britain's oldest society devoted to
fine arts was founded in 1768, moving
to Burlington House exactly a century
later. The collection contains drawings,
paintings, architectural designs, photographs and sculptures by past and present
Academicians such as Joshua Reynolds,
John Constable, Thomas Gainsborough,
JMW Turner, David Hockney and Norman
Foster.

The famous **Summer Exhibition** (adult/
child £14/free; ⊙10am-6pm mid-Jun–mid-Aug),
which has showcased contemporary art
for sale by unknown as well as established
artists for nearly 250 years, is the Academy's biggest annual event.

Horse Guards Parade   Historic Site

(Map p76; http://changing-guard.com/
queens-life-guard.html; Horse Guards Parade,
off Whitehall, SW1; ⊙11am Mon-Sat, 10am Sun;
⊖Westminster, Charing Cross, Embankment) In
a more accessible version of Buckingham
Palace's **Changing of the Guard** (p63),
the mounted troops of the Household
Cavalry change guard here daily, at the
official vehicular entrance to the royal
palaces. A slightly less pompous version
takes place at 4pm when the dismount-
ed guards are changed. On the Queen's
official birthday in June, the Trooping of the
Colour is staged here.

> ★ **Local Knowledge**
> At the centre of Royal Family life is the
> Music Room, where four royal babies
> have been christened – the Prince of
> Wales (Prince Charles), the Princess
> Royal (Princess Anne), the Duke of
> York (Prince Andrew) and the Duke
> of Cambridge (Prince William) – with
> water brought from the River Jordan.

Waterloo Barracks

Tower of London

With a history as bleak as it is fascinating, the Tower of London is now one of the city's top attractions, thanks in part to the Crown Jewels.

Great For...

☑ Don't Miss

The colourful Yeoman Warders (or Beefeaters), the spectacular Crown Jewels, the soothsaying ravens, and armour fit for a king.

Begun during the reign of William the Conqueror (1066–87), the Tower is in fact a castle containing 22 towers.

Tower Green

The buildings to the west and the south of this verdant patch have always accommodated Tower officials. Indeed, the current constable has a flat in Queen's House built in 1540. But what looks at first glance like a peaceful, almost village-like slice of the Tower's inner ward is actually one of its bloodiest.

Scaffold Site & Beauchamp Tower

Those 'lucky' enough to meet their fate here (rather than suffering the embarrassment of execution on Tower Hill, observed by tens of thousands of jeering and cheering onlookers) numbered but a handful

View from the Thames

ⓘ Need to Know

Map p80; ☏0844 482 7777; www.hrp.org.
uk/toweroflondon; Petty Wales, EC3; adult/
child £25/12, audio guide £4/3; ⏱9.30am–
5pm; ⊖Tower Hill

✕ Take a Break

The **Wine Library** (Map p80; ☏020-
7481 0415; www.winelibrary.co.uk; 43 Trinity
Sq, EC3; buffet £18; ⏱buffet noon-3.30pm,
shop 10am-6pm Mon, to 8pm Tue-Fri) is a
great place for a light but boozy lunch
opposite the Tower.

★ Top Tip

Book online for cheaper rates for the
Tower.

and included two of Henry VIII's wives (and
alleged adulterers), Anne Boleyn and Catherine Howard; 16-year-old Lady Jane Grey,
who fell foul of Henry's daughter Mary I by
attempting to have herself crowned queen;
and Robert Devereux, Earl of Essex, once a
favourite of Elizabeth I.

Just west of the scaffold site is
brick-faced Beauchamp Tower, where
high-ranking prisoners left behind unhappy
inscriptions and other graffiti.

Chapel Royal of St Peter ad Vincula

Just north of the scaffold site is the
16th-century Chapel Royal of St Peter ad
Vincula (St Peter in Chains), a rare example
of ecclesiastical Tudor architecture. The
church can be visited on a Yeoman Warder
tour, or during the first and last hour of
normal opening times.

Crown Jewels

To the east of the chapel and north of the
White Tower is **Waterloo Barracks**, the
home of the Crown Jewels, said to be worth
up to £20 billion, but in a very real sense
priceless. Here, you file past film clips of the
jewels and their role through history, and
of Queen Elizabeth II's coronation in 1953,
before you reach the vault itself.

Once inside you'll be greeted by lavishly
bejewelled sceptres, church plate, orbs and,
naturally, crowns. A moving walkway takes
you past the dozen or so crowns and other
coronation regalia, including the platinum
crown of the late Queen Mother, Elizabeth,
which is set with the 106-carat Koh-i-Noor
(Mountain of Light) diamond, and the
State Sceptre with Cross topped with the
530-carat First Star of Africa (or Cullinan I)
diamond. A bit further on, exhibited on its
own, is the centrepiece: the Imperial State
Crown, set with 2868 diamonds (including

the 317-carat Second Star of Africa, or Cullinan II), sapphires, emeralds, rubies and pearls. It's worn by the Queen at the State Opening of Parliament in May/June.

White Tower

Built in stone as a fortress in 1078, this was the original 'Tower' of London – its name arose after Henry III whitewashed it in the 13th century. Standing just 30m high, it's not exactly a skyscraper by modern standards, but in the Middle Ages it would have dwarfed the wooden huts surrounding the castle walls and intimidated the peasantry.

Most of its interior is given over to a **Royal Armouries** collection of cannon, guns, and suits of mail and armour for men and horses. Among the most remarkable exhibits on the entrance floor are Henry VIII's two suits of armour, one made for him when he was a dashing 24-year-old and the other when he was a bloated 50-year-old with a waist measuring 129cm. You won't miss the oversize codpiece. Also here is the fabulous **Line of Kings**, a late-17th-century parade of carved wooden horses and heads of historic kings. On the 1st floor, check out the 2m suit of armour once thought to have been made for the giant like John of Gaunt and, alongside it, a tiny child's suit of armour designed for James I's young son, the future Charles I. Up on the 2nd floor you'll find the block and axe used to execute Simon Fraser at the last public execution on Tower Hill in 1747.

Medieval Palace & the Bloody Tower

The Medieval Palace is composed of three towers: St Thomas's, Wakefield and

Queen's House and Tower Green (p66)

Langthorn. Inside **St Thomas's Tower** (1279) you can look at what the hall and bedchamber of Edward I might once have been like. Here archaeologists have peeled back the layers of newer buildings to find what went before. Opposite St Thomas's Tower is **Wakefield Tower**, built by Edward's father, Henry III, between 1220 and 1240. Its upper floor is entered from St Thomas's Tower and has been even more enticingly furnished with a replica throne and other decor to give an impression of

how an anteroom in a medieval palace might have looked. During the 15th-century Wars of the Roses between the Houses of York and Lancaster, King Henry VI was murdered as (it is said) he knelt in prayer in this tower. A plaque on the chapel floor commemorates this Lancastrian king. The **Langthorn Tower**, residence of medieval queens, is to the east.

Below St Thomas's Tower along Water Lane is the famous **Traitors' Gate**, the portal through which prisoners transported by boat entered the Tower. Opposite Traitors' Gate is the huge portcullis of the Bloody Tower, taking its nickname from the 'princes in the Tower' – Edward V and his younger brother, Richard – who were held here 'for their own safety' and later murdered to annul their claims to the throne. An exhibition inside looks at the life and times of Elizabethan adventurer Sir Walter Raleigh, who was imprisoned here three times by the capricious Elizabeth I and her successor James I.

East Wall Walk

The huge inner wall of the Tower was added to the fortress in 1220 by Henry III to improve the castle's defences. It is 36m wide and is dotted with towers along its length. The East Wall Walk allows you to climb up and tour its eastern edge, beginning in the 13th-century **Salt Tower**, probably used to store saltpetre for gunpowder. The walk also takes in **Broad Arrow Tower** and **Constable Tower**, each containing small exhibits. It ends at the **Martin Tower**, which houses an exhibition about the original coronation regalia. Here you can see some of the older crowns, with their precious stones removed. It was from this tower that Colonel Thomas Blood attempted to steal the Crown Jewels in 1671 disguised as a

KIEV.VICTOR/SHUTTERSTOCK ©

clergyman. He was caught but – surprisingly – Charles II gave him a full pardon.

Yeoman Warders

A true icon of the Tower, the Yeoman Warders have been guarding the fortress since at least the early 16th century. There can be up to 40 – they number 37 at present – and, in order to qualify for the job, they must have served a minimum of 22 years in any branch of the British Armed Forces. They all live within the Tower walls and are known affectionately as 'Beefeaters', a nickname they dislike.

There is currently just one female Yeoman Warder, Moira Cameron, who in 2007 became the first woman to be given the post. While officially they guard the Tower and Crown Jewels at night, their main role is as tour guides. Free tours leave from the bridge near the entrance every 30 minutes; the last tour is an hour before closing.

What's Nearby?

All Hallows by the Tower   Church

(Map p80; ☎020-7481 2928; www.ahbtt. org.uk; Byward St, EC3; ⊗8am-5pm Mon-Fri, 10am-5pm Sat & Sun; ⊖Tower Hill) All Hallows (meaning 'all saints'), which dates from AD 675, survived virtually unscathed by the Great Fire, only to be hit by German bombs in 1940. Come to see the church itself, by all means, but the best bits are in the atmospheric undercroft (crypt), where you'll the discover a pavement of 2nd-century Roman tiles and the walls of the 7th-century Saxon church.

Monument   Tower

(Map p80; ☎020-7403 3761; www.themon ument.org.uk; Fish St Hill, EC3; adult/child £5/2.50, incl Tower Bridge Exhibition £12/5.50; ⊗9.30am-5.30pm; ⊖Monument) Sir Christopher Wren's 1677 column, known simply as the Monument, is a memorial to the Great Fire of London of 1666, whose impact on London's history cannot be overstated. An immense Doric column made of Portland stone, the Monument is 4.5m wide and 60.6m tall – the exact distance it stands

from the bakery in Pudding Lane where the fire is thought to have started.

The Monument is topped with a gilded bronze urn of flames that some think looks like a big gold pincushion. Although Lilliputian by today's standards, the Monument would have been gigantic when built, towering over London.

Climbing up the column's 311 spiral steps rewards you with some of the best 360-degree views over London (due to its central location as much as to its height). And after your descent, you'll also be the proud owner of a certificate that commemorates your achievement.

Leadenhall Market   Market

(Map p80; www.cityoflondon.gov.uk/things-to-do/leadenhall-market; Whittington Ave, EC3; ⊗public areas 24hr; ⊖Bank) A visit to this

'The Gherkin', 30 St Mary Axe

covered mall off Gracechurch St is a step back in time. There's been a market on this site since the Roman era, but the architecture that survives is all cobblestones and late-19th-century Victorian ironwork. Leadenhall Market appears as Diagon Alley in *Harry Potter and the Philosopher's Stone* and an optician's shop was used for the entrance to the Leaky Cauldron wizarding pub in *Harry Potter and the Goblet of Fire*.

30 St Mary Axe Notable Building

(Map p80; www.30stmaryaxe.info; 30 St Mary Axe, EC3; ☻Aldgate) Nicknamed 'the Gherkin' for its unusual shape, 30 St Mary Axe is arguably the City's most distinctive skyscraper, dominating the skyline despite actually being slightly smaller than the neighbouring NatWest Tower. Built in 2003 by award-winning architect Norman Foster, the Gherkin's futuristic exterior has become an emblem of modern London – as recognisable as Big Ben and the London Eye.

The building is closed to the public, though in the past it has opened its doors over the **Open House London** (☎020-7383 2131; www.openhouselondon.org.uk) weekend in September.

★ **Local Knowledge**

Common ravens, which once feasted on the corpses of beheaded traitors, have been here for centuries. Nowadays, they feed on raw beef and biscuits.

★ **Did You Know?**

Yeoman Warders are nicknamed Beefeaters. It's thought to be due to the rations of beef – then a luxury food – given to them in the past.

A Northern Point of View

This walk takes in North London's most interesting locales, including celebrity-infested Primrose Hill and chaotic Camden Town, home to loud guitar bands and the last of London's cartoon punks.
Start ⊖ Chalk Farm
Distance 2.5 miles
Duration Two hours

Classic Photo: of London's skyline from atop Primrose Hill.

2 In **Primrose Hill**, walk to the top of the park where you'll find a classic view of central London's skyline.

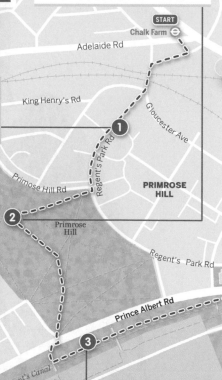

1 Affluent **Regent's Park Rd** is home to many darlings of the celebrity mags, so keep your eyes peeled for famous faces.

3 Walk downhill to Regent's Canal, where you'll pass the large aviary at **London Zoo**, quaint boats, superb mansions and converted industrial buildings.

START
Chalk Farm ⊖

Adelaide Rd

King Henry's Rd

Gloucester Ave

Regent's Park Rd

Primrose Hill Rd

PRIMROSE HILL

Primrose Hill

Regent's Park Rd

Prince Albert Rd

Regent's Canal

ZSL London Zoo

4 At **Camden Lock** turn left into buzzing Lock Market, with its original fashion, ethnic art and food stalls.

5 Exit onto **Camden High St** and turn right onto bar-lined Inverness St, which hosts its own little market.

6 At **Gloucester Cres** turn left and walk past the glorious Georgian townhouses.

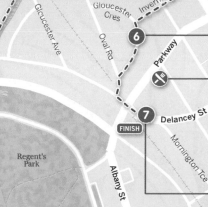

Take a Break... Enjoy excellent fresh fish and seaweed-salted chips at Hook Camden Town (p87).

7 Head towards Delancey St and make a beeline for the **Edinboro Castle** (p92), where this walk ends with a well-deserved drink!

◉ SIGHTS
◎ The West End

Big Ben   Landmark
(Map p76; ⊖Westminster) The most famous feature of the Palace of Westminster (Houses of Parliament) is Elizabeth Tower, more commonly known as Big Ben. To add to the confusion, Big Ben is actually the 13.5-tonne bell hanging inside the 315ft-hight tower and is thought to be named after Benjamin Hall, the commissioner of works when the tower was completed in 1858.

National Gallery   Gallery
(Map p76; ☎020-7747 2885; www.national gallery.org.uk; Trafalgar Sq, WC2; ⊕10am-6pm Sat-Thu, to 9pm Fri; ⊖Charing Cross) FREE
With some 2300 European paintings on display, this is one of the world's great art collections, with seminal works from every important epoch in the history of art – from the mid-13th to the early 20th century, including masterpieces by Leonardo da Vinci, Michelangelo, Titian, Van Gogh and Renoir.

Many visitors flock to the East Wing (1700–1900), where works by 18th-century British artists such as Gainsborough, Constable and Turner, and seminal Impressionist and post-Impressionist masterpieces by Van Gogh, Renoir and Monet await.

National Portrait Gallery   Gallery
(Map p76; ☎020-7321 0055; www.npg.org. uk; St Martin's Pl, WC2; ⊕10am-6pm Sat-Wed, to 9pm Thu & Fri; ⊖Charing Cross, Leicester Sq) FREE What makes the National Portrait Gallery so compelling is its familiarity; in many cases, you'll have heard of the subject (royals, scientists, politicians, celebrities) or the artist (Andy Warhol, Annie Leibovitz, Lucian Freud) but not necessarily recognise the face. Highlights include the famous 'Chandos portrait' of William Shakespeare, the first artwork the gallery acquired (in 1856) and believed to be the only likeness made during the playwright's lifetime, and a touching sketch of novelist Jane Austen by her sister.

Houses of Parliament   Historic Building
(Palace of Westminster; Map p76; www.parlia ment.uk; Parliament Sq, SW1; ⊖Westminster)

Staircase in the Tate Britain

FREE A visit here is a journey to the heart of UK democracy. Officially called the Palace of Westminster, the Houses of Parliament's oldest part is 11th-century **Westminster Hall**, one of only a few sections that survived a catastrophic fire in 1834. Its roof, added between 1394 and 1401, is the earliest known example of a hammerbeam roof. The rest is mostly a neo-Gothic confection built by Charles Barry and Augustus Pugin for 20 years from 1840. The palace's most famous feature is its clock tower, officially the Elizabeth Tower but better known as Big Ben.

Trafalgar Square   Square

(Map p76; ⊖Charing Cross) Trafalgar Square is the true centre of London, where rallies and marches take place, tens of thousands of revellers usher in the New Year and locals congregate for anything from communal open-air cinema and Christmas celebrations to political protests. It is dominated by the 52m-high **Nelson's Column** and ringed by many splendid buildings, including the National Gallery and the church of **St Martin-in-the-Fields**.

Tate Britain   Gallery

(Map p76; ☑020-7887 8888; www.tate.org.uk/visit/tate-britain; Millbank, SW1; ⊗10am-6pm, to 10pm on selected Fri; ⊖Pimlico) **FREE** The older and more venerable of the two Tate siblings celebrates British art from 1500 to the present, with works from Blake, Hogarth, Gainsborough, Hepworth, Whistler, Constable and Turner, as well as vibrant modern and contemporary pieces from Lucian Freud, Francis Bacon and Henry Moore.

Madame Tussauds   Museum

(Map p84; ☑0870 400 3000; www.madame-tussauds.com/london; Marylebone Rd, NW1; adult/child 4-15yr £35/30; ⊗10am-6pm; ⊖Baker St) It may be kitschy and pricey (book online for much cheaper rates), but Madame Tussauds makes for a fun-filled day. There are photo ops with your dream celebrity (be it Daniel Craig, Lady Gaga, Benedict Cumberbatch, Audrey Hepburn or the Beckhams), the Bollywood gathering (sparring studs Hrithik Roshan and Salman

Churchill War Rooms

Winston Churchill helped coordinate the Allied resistance against Nazi Germany on a Bakelite telephone from this **underground complex** (Map p76; www.iwm.org.uk/visits/churchill-war-rooms; Clive Steps, King Charles St, SW1; adult/child £17.25/8.60; ⊗9.30am-6pm; ⊖Westminster) during WWII. The Cabinet War Rooms remain much as they were when the lights were switched off in 1945, capturing the drama and dogged spirit of the time, while the multimedia Churchill Museum affords intriguing insights into the life and times of the resolute, cigar-smoking wartime leader.

BASPHOTO/SHUTTERSTOCK ©

Khan) and the Royal Appointment (the Queen, Harry, William and Kate).

Covent Garden Piazza   Square

(Map p76; ☑020-7836 5221; ⊖Covent Garden) London's fruit-and-vegetable wholesale market until 1974 is now mostly the preserve of visitors, who flock here to shop among the quaint old arcades, eat and drink in any of the myriad of cafes and restaurants, browse through eclectic market stalls, toss coins at street performers pretending to be statues and traipse through the fun **London Transport Museum**. On the square's western side is handsome **St Paul's Church**, built in 1633.

Soho   Area

(Map p76; ⊖Tottenham Court Rd, Leicester Sq) In a district that was once pastureland, the name Soho is thought to have evolved

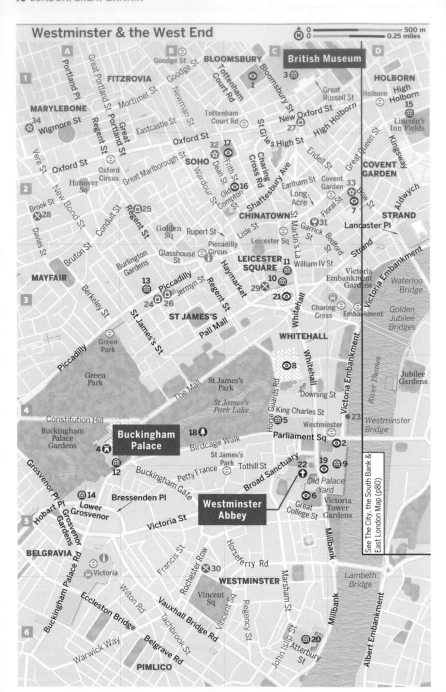

Westminster & the West End

from a hunting cry. While the centre of London nightlife has shifted east, and Soho has recently seen landmark clubs and music venues shut down, the neighbourhood definitely comes into its own in the evenings and remains a proud gay district. During the day you'll be charmed by the area's bohemian side and its sheer vitality.

◎ The City

Tower Bridge
Bridge

(Map p80; ⊖Tower Hill) One of London's most recognisable sights, familiar from dozens of movies, Tower Bridge doesn't disappoint in real life. Its neo-Gothic towers and sky-blue suspension struts add extraordinary elegance to what is a supremely functional structure. London was a thriving port in 1894 when it was built as a much-needed crossing point in the east, equipped with a then-revolutionary steam-driven bascule (counter-balance) mechanism that could raise the roadway to make way for oncoming ships in just three minutes.

Museum of London
Museum

(Map p80; ☏020-7001 9844; www.museumof london.org.uk; 150 London Wall, EC2; ☉10am-6pm; ⊖Barbican) FREE As entertaining as it is educational, the Museum of London meanders through the various incarnations of the city, stopping off in Roman Londinium and Saxon Ludenwic before eventually ending up in the 21st-century metropolis. Interesting objects and interactive displays work together to bring each era to life, without ever getting too whizz-bang, making this one of the capital's best museums. Free themed tours take place throughout the day, check the signs by the entrance for times.

◎ The South Bank

Tate Modern
Museum

(Map p80; www.tate.org.uk; Bankside, SE1; ☉10am-6pm Sun-Thu, to 10pm Fri & Sat; ⊕; ⊖Blackfriars, Southwark or London Bridge) FREE One of London's most amazing attractions, this outstanding modern- and contemporary-art gallery is housed in

St Paul's Cathedral

Towering over diminutive Ludgate Hill in a superb position that's been a place of Christian worship for over 1400 years (and pagan before that), **St Paul's** (Map p80; ☑020-7246 8357; www.stpauls.co.uk; St Paul's Churchyard, EC4; adult/child £18/8; ⊙8.30am-4.30pm Mon-Sat; ⊖St Paul's) is one of London's most magnificent buildings. For Londoners, the vast dome is a symbol of resilience and pride, standing tall for more than 300 years. Viewing Sir Christopher Wren's masterpiece from the inside and climbing to the top for sweeping views of the capital is an exhilarating experience.

CLAUDIO DIVIZIA/SHUTTERSTOCK ©

the creatively revamped Bankside Power Station south of the Millennium Bridge. A spellbinding synthesis of modern art and capacious industrial brick design, Tate Modern has been extraordinarily successful in bringing challenging work to the masses, both through its free permanent collection and fee-paying big-name temporary exhibitions. The stunning Switch House extension opened in 2016, increasing the available exhibition space by 60%.

London Eye   Viewpoint

(Map p80; ☑0871-222 4002; www.londoneye.com; adult/child £23.45/18.95; ⊙11am-6pm Sep-May, 10am-8.30pm Jun-Aug; ⊖Waterloo or Westminster) Standing 135m high in a fairly flat city, the London Eye affords views 25 miles in every direction, weather permitting. Interactive tablets provide great infor-

mation (in six languages) about landmarks as they appear in the skyline. Each rotation – or 'flight' – takes a gracefully slow 30 minutes. At peak times (July, August and school holidays) it can feel like you'll spend more time in the queue than in the capsule; book premium fast-track tickets to jump the queue.

Shakespeare's Globe   Historic Building

(Map p80; www.shakespearesglobe.com; 21 New Globe Walk, SE1; adult/child £16/9; ⊙9am-5pm; ♿; ⊖Blackfriars or London Bridge) Unlike other venues for Shakespearean plays, the new Globe was designed to resemble the original as closely as possible, which means having the arena open to the fickle London skies, leaving the 700 'groundlings' (standing spectators) to weather London's spectacular downpours. Visits to the Globe include tours of the theatre (half-hourly) as well as access to the exhibition space, which has fascinating exhibits on Shakespeare and theatre in the 17th century. Or you can of course take in a **play** (☑020-7401 9919; seats £20-45, standing £5).

Borough Market   Market

(Map p80; www.boroughmarket.org.uk; 8 Southwark St, SE1; ⊙10am-5pm Wed & Thu, 10am-6pm Fri, 8am-5pm Sat; ⊖London Bridge) Located in this spot in some form or another since the 13th century (possibly since 1014), 'London's Larder' has enjoyed an astonishing renaissance in the past 15 years. Always overflowing with food lovers, inveterate gastronomes, wide-eyed visitors and Londoners in search of inspiration for their dinner party, this fantastic market has become firmly established as a sight in its own right. The market specialises in high-end fresh products; there are also plenty of takeaway stalls and an almost unreasonable number of cake stalls.

◎ Kensington & Hyde Park

Natural History Museum   Museum

(Map p84; www.nhm.ac.uk; Cromwell Rd, SW7; ⊙10am-5.50pm; ⊖South Kensington) FREE This colossal and magnificent-looking

GEORGE JOHNSON/500PX ©

London Eye and the Thames

building is infused with the irrepressible Victorian spirit of collecting, cataloguing and interpreting the natural world. The **Dinosaurs Gallery** (Blue Zone) is a must for children, who gawp at the animatronic T-Rex, fossils and excellent displays. Adults for their part will love the intriguing Treasures exhibition in the **Cadogan Gallery** (Green Zone), which houses a host of unrelated objects each telling its own unique story, from a chunk of moon rock to a dodo skeleton.

Victoria & Albert Museum Museum

(V&A; Map p84; ☑020-7942 2000; www.vam.ac.uk; Cromwell Rd, SW7; ☑10am-5.40pm Sat-Thu, to 10pm Fri; ☻South Kensington) FREE The Museum of Manufactures, as the V&A was known when it opened in 1852, was part of Prince Albert's legacy to the nation in the aftermath of the successful Great Exhibition of 1851. It houses the world's largest collection of decorative arts, from Asian ceramics to Middle Eastern rugs, Chinese paintings, Western furniture, fashion from all ages, and modern-day domestic appliances. The (ticketed) temporary

exhibitions are another highlight, covering anything from retrospectives of David Bowie and designer Alexander McQueen to special materials and trends.

Science Museum Museum

(Map p84; www.sciencemuseum.org.uk; Exhibition Rd, SW7; ☑10am-6pm; ☻South Kensington) FREE With seven floors of interactive and educational exhibits, this scientifically spellbinding museum will mesmerise adults and children alike, covering everything from early technology to space travel. A perennial favourite is **Exploring Space**, a gallery featuring genuine rockets and satellites and a full-size replica of the 'Eagle', the lander that took Neil Armstrong and Buzz Aldrin to the moon in 1969. The **Making the Modern World Gallery** next door is a visual feast of locomotives, planes, cars and other revolutionary inventions.

Hyde Park Park

(Map p84; www.royalparks.org.uk/parks/hyde-park; ☑5am-midnight; ☻Marble Arch, Hyde Park Corner or Queensway) At 145 hectares, Hyde Park is central London's

The City, the South Bank & East London

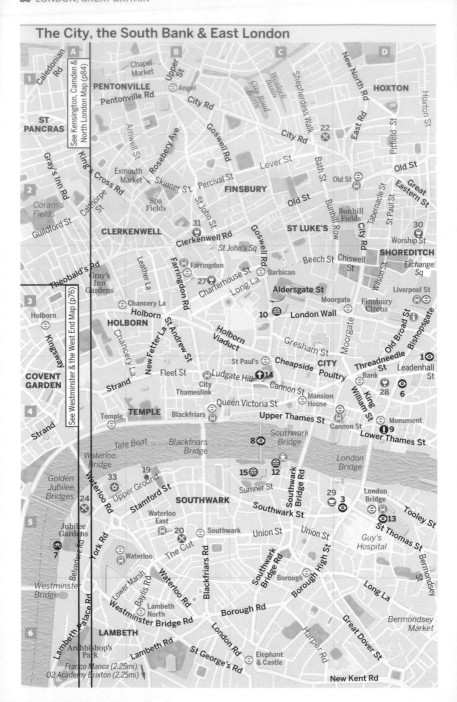

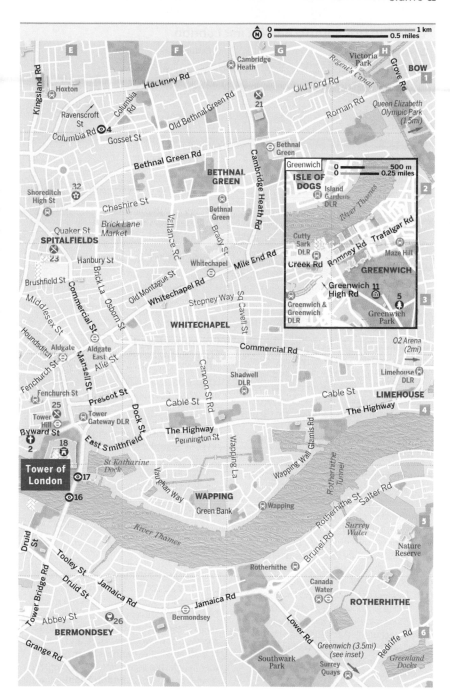

The City, the South Bank & East London

largest open space, expropriated from the Church in 1536 by Henry VIII and turned into a hunting ground and later a venue for duels, executions and horse racing. The 1851 Great Exhibition was held here, and during WWII the park became an enormous potato field. These days, there's boating on the **Serpentine**, summer concerts (Bruce Springsteen, Florence + The Machine, Patti Smith), film nights and other warm-weather events.

Kensington Palace   Palace

(Map p84; www.hrp.org.uk/kensingtonpalace; Kensington Gardens, W8; adult/child £19/free; ⊙10am-6pm Mar-Oct, to 4pm Nov-Feb; ⊖High St Kensington) Built in 1605, the palace became the favourite royal residence under William and Mary of Orange in 1689, and remained so until George III became king and moved out. Today, it is still a royal residence, with the likes of the Duke and Duchess of Cambridge (Prince William and his wife Catherine) and Prince Harry living there. A large part of the palace is open to the public, however, including the King's and Queen's State Apartments.

⊙ East London

Columbia Road Flower Market   Market

(Map p80; www.columbiaroad.info; Columbia Rd, E2; ⊙8am-3pm Sun; ⊖Hoxton) A wonderful explosion of colour and life, this weekly market sells a beautiful array of flowers, pot plants, bulbs, seeds and everything you might need for the garden. It's a lot of fun and the best place to hear proper Cockney barrow-boy banter ('We got flowers cheap enough for ya muvver-in-law's grave' etc). It gets really packed, so go as early as you can, or later on, when the vendors sell off the cut flowers cheaply.

Queen Elizabeth Olympic Park   Park

(www.queenelizabetholympicpark.co.uk; E20; ⊖Stratford) The glittering centrepiece of London's 2012 Olympic Games, this vast 227-hectare expanse includes the main Olympic venues as well as playgrounds, walking and cycling trails, gardens, and a diverse mix of wetland, woodland, meadow and other wildlife habitats as an environmentally fertile legacy for the future. The main focal point is **London Stadium**, with a

Games capacity of 80,000, scaled back to 54,000 seats for its new role as the home ground for West Ham United FC.

◉ Camden & North London

Hampstead Heath   Park

(Map p84; www.cityoflondon.gov.uk; ⊖Hampstead Heath or Gospel Oak) Sprawling Hampstead Heath, with its rolling woodlands and meadows, feels a million miles away – despite being approximately four – from the City of London. Covering 320 hectares, most of it woods, hills and meadows, it's home to about 180 bird species, 23 species of butterflies, grass snakes, bats and a rich array of flora. It's a wonderful place for a ramble, especially to the top of **Parliament Hill**, which offers expansive views across the city.

British Library   Library

(Map p84; www.bl.uk; 96 Euston Rd, NW1; ⊗galleries 9.30am-6pm Mon & Fri, to 8pm Tue-Thu, to 5pm Sat, 11am-5pm Sun; ⊖King's Cross St Pancras) FREE Consisting of low-slung redbrick terraces and fronted by a large plaza featuring an oversized statue of Sir Isaac Newton, Colin St John Wilson's British Library building is a love-it-or-hate-it affair (Prince Charles likened it to a secret-police academy). Completed in 1997, it's home to some of the greatest treasures of the written word, including the *Codex Sinaiticus* (the first complete text of the New Testament), Leonardo da Vinci's notebooks and a copy of the Magna Carta (1215).

Regent's Canal   Canal

(Map p84) To escape the crowded streets and enjoy a picturesque, waterside side stretch of North London, take to the canals that once played such a vital role in the transport of goods across the capital. The towpath of the Regent's Canal also makes an excellent shortcut across North London, either on foot or by bike. In full, the ribbon of water runs 9 miles from Little Venice (where it connects with the Grand Union Canal) to the Thames at Limehouse.

Camden Market

Although – or perhaps because – it stopped being cutting edge several thousand cheap leather jackets ago, **Camden Market** (Map p84; www.camdenmarket.com; Camden High St, NW1; ⊗10am-6pm; ⊖Camden Town or Chalk Farm) attracts millions of visitors each year and is one of London's most popular attractions. What started out as a collection of attractive craft stalls beside Camden Lock on the Regent's Canal now extends most of the way from Camden Town tube station to Chalk Farm tube station.

Abbey Road Studios   Historic Building

(Map p84; www.abbeyroad.com; 3 Abbey Rd, NW8; ⊖St John's Wood) Beatles aficionados can't possibly visit London without making a pilgrimage to this famous recording studio in St John's Wood. The studios themselves are off limits, so you'll have to content yourself with examining the decades of fan graffiti on the fence outside. Stop-start local traffic is long accustomed to groups of tourists lining up on the zebra crossing to re-enact the cover of the fab four's 1969 masterpiece *Abbey Road*. In 2010 the crossing was rewarded with Grade II heritage status.

◉ Greenwich & South London

Greenwich Park   Park

(Map p80; ☑030-0061 2380; www.royalparks.org.uk; King George St, SE10; ⊗6am-around sunset; ⓡDLR Cutty Sark, ⓡGreenwich or Maze Hill) This is one of London's loveliest expanses of green, with a rose garden, picturesque walks, Anglo-Saxon tumuli and astonishing views from the crown of the hill near the Royal Observatory (p85) towards Canary Wharf – the financial district across the Thames. Covering 74 hectares, it's the oldest enclosed royal park and is partly the work of André Le Nôtre, the landscape architect who designed the palace gardens of

Kensington, Camden & North London

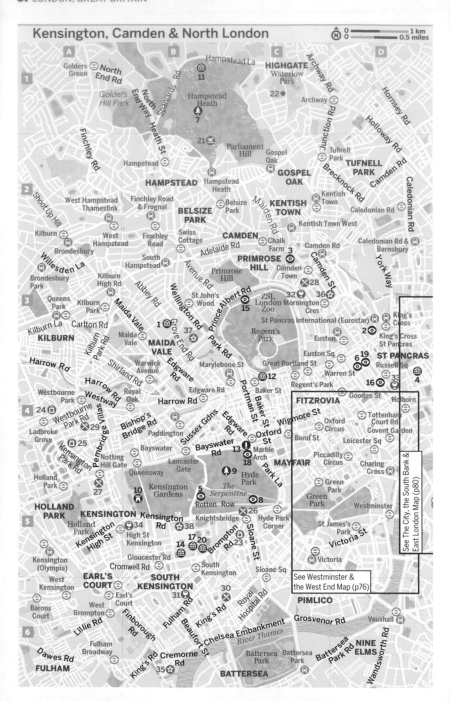

Kensington, Camden & North London

Versailles. Greenwich Park hosted the 2012 Olympic Games equestrian events.

Royal Observatory Historic Building
(Map p80; www.rmg.co.uk; Greenwich Park, Blackheath Ave, SE10; adult/child £9.50/5, incl Cutty Sark £18.50/8.50; ⊙10am-5pm Sep-Jun, to 6pm Jul & Aug; ⊟DLR Cutty Sark, DLR Greenwich or Greenwich) Rising south of Queen's House, idyllic Greenwich Park climbs up the hill, affording stunning views of London from the Royal Observatory, which Charles II had built in 1675 to help solve the riddle of longitude. To the north is lovely **Flamsteed House** and the **Meridian Courtyard**, where you can stand with your feet straddling the western and eastern hemispheres; admission is by ticket. The southern half contains the highly informative and free **Weller Astronomy Galleries** and the **Peter Harrison Planetarium**.

Horniman Museum Museum
(⌨020-8699 1872; www.horniman.ac.uk; 100 London Rd, Forest Hill, SE23; museum & gardens free, exhibitions are ticketed; ⊙museum 10.30am-5.30pm, gardens 7.15am-sunset Mon-Sat, 8am sunset Sun; ⊟Forest Hill) **FREE** This museum is an extraordinary place, comprising the original collection of wealthy tea-merchant Frederick John Horniman. He had this art-nouveau building, with its clock tower and mosaics, specially designed to house his collection. Built in 1901, today it encompasses everything from a dusty walrus and voodoo altars from Haiti and Benin to a mock-up of a Fijian reef and a collection of concertinas. It's wonderful.

⊙ TOURS

City Cruises Boating
(Map p76; ⌨020-7740 0400; www.citycruises. com; adult single/return/day pass from £12.50/16.50/£6.65, child £6.25/8.25/8.35; ⊖Westminster) Ferry service departing every 30 minutes between Westminster, the London Eye, Bankside, Tower and Greenwich

A Shopping Icon

Garish and stylish in equal measures, perennially crowded **Harrods** (Map p84; ☏020-7730 1234; www.harrods.com; 87-135 Brompton Rd, SW1; ⊙10am-9pm Mon-Sat, 11.30am-6pm Sun; ☻Knightsbridge) is an obligatory stop for visitors, from the cash-strapped to the big spenders. The stock is astonishing, as are many of the price tags. High on kitsch, the 'Egyptian Elevator' resembles something out of an *Indiana Jones* epic, while the memorial fountain to Dodi and Di (lower ground floor) merely adds surrealism.

FRANK GAERTNER/SHUTTERSTOCK ©

piers. A 24-hour Rover Ticket is as cheap as adult/child £10/5 online.

London Bicycle Tour — Cycling
(Map p80; ☏020-7928 6838; www.london bicycle.com; 1 Gabriel's Wharf, 56 Upper Ground, SE1; tour incl bike from adult/child £24.95/21.95, bike hire per day £20; ☻Southwark or Waterloo) Three-hour tours begin in the South Bank and take in London's highlights on both sides of the river; the classic tour is available in eight languages. A night ride is available. You can also hire traditional or speciality bikes, such as tandems and folding bikes, by the hour or day.

Highgate Cemetery Tour — Tour
(Map p84; www.highgatecemetery.org; Swain's Lane, N6; adult/child £12/6; ⊙1.45pm Mon-Fri, every 30min 11am-3pm Sat & Sun Nov-Feb, to 4pm Mar-Oct; ☻Archway) The highlight of Highgate Cemetery is the overgrown West Cemetery, where a maze of winding paths leads to the Circle of Lebanon, rings of tombs flanking a circular path and topped with a majestic cedar of Lebanon tree. Admission to the West Cemetery is by guided tour only; weekday tours must be booked in advance but weekend tours are a turn-up-and-pay affair.

🔒 SHOPPING

Fortnum & Mason — Department Store
(Map p76; ☏020-7734 8040; www.fortnum andmason.com; 181 Piccadilly, W1; ⊙10am-8pm Mon-Sat, 11.30am-6pm Sun; ☻Piccadilly Circus) With its classic eau-de-Nil (pale green) colour scheme, 'the Queen's grocery store' established 1707 refuses to yield to modern times. Its staff – men and women – still wear old-fashioned tailcoats and its glamorous food hall is supplied with hampers, cut marmalade, speciality teas, superior fruitcakes and so forth. Fortnum and Mason remains the quintessential London shopping experience.

Hatchards — Books
(Map p76; ☏020-7439 9921; www.hatchards. co.uk; 187 Piccadilly, W1; ⊙9.30am-8pm Mon-Sat, noon-6.30pm Sun; ☻Green Park, Piccadilly Circus) London's oldest bookshop dates drom 1797. Holding three royal warrants, it's a stupendous bookshop now in the Waterstones stable, with a solid supply of signed editions and bursting at its smart seams with very browsable stock. There's a strong selection of first editions on the ground floor and regularly scheduled literary events.

Hamleys — Toys
(Map p76; ☏0371-704 1977; www.hamleys. com; 188-196 Regent St, W1; ⊙10am-9pm Mon-Fri, 9.30am-9pm Sat, noon-6pm Sun; ☻Oxford Circus) Claiming to be the world's oldest (and some say the largest) toy store, Hamleys moved to its address on Regent St in 1881. From the basement's Star Wars Collection and the ground floor where staff blow bubbles and glide foam boomerangs through the air with practised nonchalance

to Lego World and a cafe on the 5th floor, it's a rich layer cake of playthings.

James Smith & Sons
Fashion & Accessories

(Map p70, ☎020-7830 4731, www.james-smith.co.uk; 53 New Oxford St, WC1; ⊘10am-5.45pm Mon, Tue, Thu & Fri, 10.30am-5.45pm Wed, 10am-5.15pm Sat; ⊜Tottenham Court Rd) Nobody makes and stocks such elegant umbrellas (not to mention walking sticks and canes) as this place. It's been fighting the British weather from the same address since 1857 and, thanks to London's ever-present downpours, will hopefully do great business for years to come. Prices start at around £40 for a pocket umbrella.

Portobello Road Market
Clothing, Antiques

(Map p84; www.portobellomarket.org; Portobello Rd, W10; ⊘8am-6.30pm Mon-Wed, Fri & Sat, to 1pm Thu; ⊜Notting Hill Gate or Ladbroke Grove) Lovely on a warm summer's day, Portobello Road Market is an iconic London attraction with an eclectic mix of street food, fruit and veg, antiques, curios,

collectables, vibrant fashion and trinkets. Although the shops along Portobello Rd open daily and the fruit and veg stalls (from Elgin Cres to Talbot Rd) only close on Sunday, the busiest day by far is Saturday, when antique dealers set up shop (from Chepstow Villas to Elgin Cres).

✖ EATING

Franco Manca
Pizza £

(www.francomanca.co.uk; 4 Market Row, SW9; pizzas £4.50-6.95; ⊘noon-5pm Mon, noon-11pm Tue-Fri, 11.30am-11pm Sat, 11.30am-10.30pm Sun; ⊜Brixton) The Brixton branch of Franco Manca remains a perennial local favourite and draws pizza enthusiasts from far and wide. The restaurant only uses its own sourdough, fired up in a wood-burning brick oven. There are no reservations, so beat the queues by arriving early, avoiding lunch hours and Saturday.

Hook Camden Town
Fish & Chips £

(Map p84; www.hookrestaurants.com; 65 Parkway, NW1; mains £8-12; ⊘noon-3pm & 5-10pm Mon-Thu, noon-10.30pm Fri & Sat, to 9pm

Portobello Road Market

WILL JONES/LONELY PLANET ©

Ledbury

Sun; 🐾; ⊖Camden Town) 🍴 In addition to working entirely with sustainable small fisheries and local suppliers, Hook makes all its sauces on site and wraps its fish in recycled materials, supplying diners with extraordinarily fine-tasting morsels. Totally fresh, the fish arrives in panko breadcrumbs or tempura batter, with seaweed salted chips. Craft beers and fine wines are also to hand.

Skylon Modern European ££
(Map p80; 📞020-7654 7800; www.skylon-restaurant.co.uk; 3rd fl, Royal Festival Hall, Southbank Centre, Belvedere Rd, SE1; 3-course menu grill/restaurant £25/30; ⊗grill noon-11pm Mon-Sat, to 10.30pm Sun, restaurant noon-2.30pm & 5.30-10.30pm Mon-Sat & noon-4pm Sun; 🛜; ⊖Waterloo) This excellent restaurant inside the Royal Festival Hall is divided into grill and fine-dining sections by a large bar. The decor is cutting-edge 1950s: muted colours and period chairs (trendy then, trendier now) while floor-to-ceiling windows bathe you in magnificent views of the Thames and the city. The six-course restaurant tasting menu costs £59. Booking is advised.

Anchor & Hope Gastropub ££
(Map p80; www.anchorandhopepub.co.uk; 36 The Cut, SE1; mains £12-20; ⊗noon-2.30pm Tue-Sat, 6-10.30pm Mon-Sat, 12.30-3pm Sun; ⊖Southwark) A stalwart of the South Bank food scene, the Anchor & Hope is a quintessential gastropub: elegant but not formal, and utterly delicious (European fare with a British twist). The menu changes daily but think salt marsh lamb shoulder cooked for seven hours; wild rabbit with anchovies, almonds and rocket; and panna cotta with rhubarb compote.

Corner Room Modern British ££
(Map p80; 📞020-7871 0460; www.townhall hotel.com/cornerroom; Patriot Sq, E2; mains £13-14, 2-/3-course lunch £19/23; ⊗7.30-10am, noon-3pm & 6-9.45pm; ⊖Bethnal Green) Someone put this baby in the corner, but we're certainly not complaining. Tucked away on the 1st floor of the Town Hall Hotel, this relaxed restaurant serves expertly crafted dishes with complex yet delicate flavours, highlighting the best of British seasonal produce.

Rabbit Modern British ££

(Map p84; 020-3750 0172; www.rabbit-restaurant.com; 172 King's Rd, SW3; mains £6-24, set lunch £13.50; noon-midnight Tue-Sat, 6-11pm Mon, noon-6pm Sun; Sloane Sq) Three brothers grew up on a farm. One became a farmer, another a butcher, while the third worked in hospitality. So they pooled their skills and came up with Rabbit, a breath of fresh air in upmarket Chelsea. The restaurant rocks the agri-chic (yes) look and the creative, seasonal modern British cuisine is fabulous.

Geales Seafood ££

(Map p84; 020-7727 7528; www.geales.com; 2 Farmer St, W8; 2-course express lunch £9.95, mains £9-37.50; noon-3pm & 6-10.30pm Tue-Fri, noon 10.30pm Sat, noon-4pm Sun; Notting Hill Gate) Frying since 1939 – a bad year for the European restaurant trade – Geales has endured with its quiet location on the corner of Farmer St. The succulent fish in crispy batter is a fine catch, but the fish pie is also worth angling for. Look out for the good-value (two-course, one coffee) express lunch, available from Tuesday to Friday.

Portrait Modern European £££

(Map p76; 020-7312 2490; www.npg.org.uk/visit/shop-eat-drink.php; 3rd fl, National Portrait Gallery, St Martin's Pl, WC2; mains £19.50-26, 2-/3-course menu £27.50/31.50; 10-11am, 11.45am-3pm & 3.30-4.30pm daily, 6.30-8.30pm Thu, Fri & Sat; Charing Cross) This stunningly located restaurant above the excellent National Portrait Gallery (p74) comes with dramatic views over Trafalgar Sq and Westminster. It's a fine choice for tantalising food and the chance to relax after a morning or afternoon of picture-gazing at the gallery. The breakfast/brunch (10am to 11am) and afternoon tea (3.30pm to 4.30pm) come highly recommended. Booking is advisable.

Ledbury French £££

(Map p84; 020-7792 9090; www.theledbury.com; 127 Ledbury Rd, W11; 4-course set lunch £70, 4-course dinner £115; noon-2pm Wed-Sun

London's Celebrity Chefs

London's food renaissance was partly led by a group of telegenic chefs who built food empires around their names and their TV programs. Gordon Ramsay is the most (in)famous of the lot, but his London venues are still standard-bearers for top-quality cuisine. Other big names include Jamie Oliver, whose restaurant **Fifteen** (Map p80; 020-3375 1515; www.fifteen.net; 15 Westland Pl, N1; mains £22-24, 2-/3-course lunch £19/24, Sun £15-19; noon-3pm & 6-10.30pm; Old St) trains disadvantaged young people, and Heston Blumenthal, whose mad-professor-like experiments with food (molecular gastronomy, as he describes it) have earned him rave reviews at **Dinner by Heston Blumenthal** (Map p84; 020-7201 3833; www.dinnerbyheston.com; Mandarin Oriental Hyde Park, 66 Knightsbridge, SW1; 3 course set lunch £45, mains £28-44; noon-2pm & 6-10.15pm Mon-Fri, noon-2.30pm & 6-10.30pm Sat & Sun; Knightsbridge).

Jamie Oliver's Fifteen

& 6.30-9.45pm daily; Westbourne Park or Notting Hill Gate) Two Michelin stars and swooningly elegant, Brett Graham's artful French restaurant attracts well-heeled diners in jeans with designer jackets. Dishes such as hand-dived scallops, Chinese water deer, smoked bone marrow, quince and red leaves or Herdwick lamb with salt-baked turnips, celery cream and wild garlic are triumphs. London gastronomes have the

Claridge's Foyer & Reading Room

Extend that pinkie finger to partake in afternoon tea within the classic art deco foyer and reading room of this landmark **hotel** (Map p76; ☑020-7107 8886; www.claridges.co.uk; 49-53 Brook St, W1; afternoon tea £68, with champagne £79; ⊙afternoon tea 2.45-5.30pm; 🛜; ⊖Bond St), where the gentle clink of fine porcelain and champagne glasses could be a defining memory of your trip to London. The setting is gorgeous and the dress code is elegant, smart casual (those in ripped jeans and baseball caps won't get served).

Claridge's Hotel
ALEX SEGRE/SHUTTERSTOCK ©

Ledbury on speed-dial, so reservations well in advance are crucial.

Hawksmoor   Steak £££
(Map p80; ☑020-7426 4850; www.thehawksmoor.com; 157 Commercial St, E1; mains £20-50; ⊙noon-2.30pm & 5-10.30pm Mon-Sat, noon-9pm Sun; 🛜; ⊖Liverpool St) You could easily miss discreetly signed Hawksmoor, but confirmed carnivores will find it worth seeking out. The dark wood, bare bricks and velvet curtains make for a handsome setting in which to gorge yourself on the best of British beef. The Sunday roasts (£20) are legendary.

🍷 DRINKING & NIGHTLIFE

Jamaica Wine House   Pub
(Map p80; ☑020-7929 6972; www.jamaicawinehouse.co.uk; 12 St Michael's Alley, EC3; ⊙11am-11pm Mon-Fri; ⊖Bank) Not a wine bar

at all, the 'Jam Pot' is a historic wood-lined pub that stands on the site of what was London's first coffee house (1652). Reached by a narrow alley, it's slightly tricky to find but well worth seeking out for the age-old ambience of its darkened rooms.

Lamb & Flag   Pub
(Map p76; ☑020-7497 9504; www.lambandflagcoventgarden.co.uk; 33 Rose St, WC2; ⊙11am-11pm Mon-Sat, noon-10.30pm Sun; ⊖Covent Garden) Everybody's favourite pub in central London, pint-sized Lamb & Flag is full of charm and history, and stands on the site of a pub that dates back to at least 1772. Rain or shine, you'll have to elbow your way to the bar through the merry crowd drinking outside. Inside are brass fittings and creaky wooden floors.

Oblix   Bar
(Map p80; www.oblixrestaurant.com; 32nd fl, Shard, 31 St Thomas St, SE1; ⊙noon-11pm; ⊖London Bridge) On the 32nd floor of the **Shard** (www.theviewfromtheshard.com; 32 London Bridge St, SE1; adult/child £30.95/24.95; ⊙10am-10pm), Oblix offers mesmerising vistas of London. You can come for anything from a coffee (£3.50) to a cocktail (from £10) and enjoy virtually the same views as the official viewing galleries of the Shard (but at a reduced cost and with the added bonus of a drink). Live music every night from 7pm.

Fabric   Club
(Map p80; www.fabriclondon.com; 77a Charterhouse Street, EC1M; £5-25; ⊙11pm-7am Fri-Sun; ⊖Farringdon or Barbican) London's leading club, Fabric's three separate dance floors in a huge converted cold store opposite Smithfield meat market draws impressive queues (buy tickets online). FabricLive (on selected Fridays) rumbles with drum and bass and dubstep, while Fabric (usually on Saturdays but also on selected Fridays) is the club's signature live DJ night. Sunday's WetYourSelf! delivers house, techno and electronica.

Outside the Lamb & Flag

Roof Gardens Club
(Map p84; www.roofgardens.virgin.com; 99
Kensington High St, W8; club £20, gardens free;
⊙club 10pm-2am Fri & Sat, garden 9am-5pm on
selected dates; 🕾; ⊖High St Kensington) Atop
the former Derry and Toms building is this
enchanting venue – a nightclub with 0.6
hectares of gardens and resident flamin-
gos. The wow-factor requires £20 entry,
you must register on the guest list via the
website before going and drinks are £10 a
pop. Open only to over-21s, the dress code
is 'no effort, no entry' (leave the onesie at
home).

Zetter Townhouse
Cocktail Lounge Cocktail Bar
(Map p80; 🖉020-7324 4545; www.thezetter
townhouse.com; 49-50 St John's Sq, EC1V;
⊙7.30am-12.45am; 🕾; ⊖Farringdon) Tucked
away behind an unassuming door on St
John's Sq, this ground-floor bar is decorated with plush armchairs, stuffed animal
heads and a legion of lamps. The cocktail
list takes its theme from the area's dis-
tilling history – recipes of yesteryear plus
homemade tinctures and cordials are used

*pint-sized Lamb & Flag is full
of charm and history*

to create interesting and unusual tipples.
House cocktails are all £10.50.

Queen of Hoxton Bar
(Map p80; www.queenofhoxton.com; 1 Curtain
Rd, EC2A; ⊙4pm-midnight Mon-Wed, to 2am Thu-
Sat; 🕾; ⊖Liverpool St) This industrial-chic
bar has a games room, basement and varied music nights (including oddballs such
as dance lessons and ukulele jamming
sessions), but the real drawcard is the vast
rooftop bar, decked out with flowers, fairy
lights and even a wigwam. It has fantastic
views across the city.

Netil360 Rooftop Bar
(www.netil360.com; 1 Westgate St, E8; ⊙10am-
10pm Wed-Fri, noon-11pm Sat & Sun Apr-Nov;
🕾; ⊖London Fields) Perched atop Netil
House, this uber-hip rooftop cafe/bar
offers incredible views over London, with
brass telescopes enabling you to get better

acquainted with workers in the Gherkin. In between drinks you can knock out a game of croquet on the AstroTurf, or perhaps book a hot tub for you and your mates to stew in.

Brew By Numbers   Microbrewery

(Map p80; www.brewbynumbers.com; 79 Enid St, SE1; ⊘6-10pm Fri, 11am-8pm Sat; ⊖Bermondsey) This microbrewery's raison d'être is experimentation. Everything from its 'scientific' branding (the numbers refer to the type of beer – porter, pale ale etc – and recipe) to its enthusiasm for exploring new beer styles and refashioning old ones (*saisons* for instance, an old Belgian beer drunk by farm workers) is about broadening the definition of beer.

Glory   Gay & Lesbian

(✆020-7684 0794; www.theglory.co; 281 Kingsland Rd E2; ⊘5pm-midnight Mon-Thu, to 2am Fri & Sat, 1-11pm Sun; ⊠Haggerston) A charming cast has taken over this cosy corner pub, transforming it into one of London's most legendary queer cabaret venues. Order a Twink in Pink or a Schlong

Island Iced Tea from the cocktail list and brace yourself for whatever wackiness is on offer. All genders welcome.

Edinboro Castle   Pub

(Map p84; www.edinborocastlepub.co.uk; 57 Mornington Tce, NW1; ⊘11am-11pm; 🤝; ⊖Camden Town) Large and relaxed Edinboro offers a refined atmosphere, gorgeous furniture perfect for slumping into, a fine bar and a full menu. The highlight, however, is the huge beer garden, complete with warm-weather BBQs and lit up with coloured lights on long summer evenings. Patio heaters come out in winter.

✪ ENTERTAINMENT

Wigmore Hall   Classical Music

(Map p76; www.wigmore-hall.org.uk; 36 Wigmore St, W1; ⊖Bond St) This is one of the best and most active (more than 400 concerts a year) classical-music venues in town, not only because of its fantastic acoustics, beautiful art nouveau hall and great variety of concerts and recitals, but also because of the sheer standard of the performances.

Royal Opera House

Built in 1901, it has remained one of the world's top places for chamber music.

Royal Opera House · Opera

(Map p76; ☑020-7304 4000; www.roh.org.uk; Bow St, WC2, tickets £4-270, ◉Covent Garden) Classic opera in London has a fantastic setting on Covent Garden Piazza and coming here for a night is a sumptuous – if pricey – affair. Although the program has been fluffed up by modern influences, the main attractions are still the opera and classical ballet – all are wonderful productions and feature world-class performers.

National Theatre · Theatre

(Royal National Theatre; Map p80; ☑020-7452 3000; www.nationaltheatre.org.uk; South Bank, SE1; ◉Waterloo) England's flagship theatre showcases a mix of classic and contemporary plays performed by excellent casts in three theatres (Olivier, Lyttelton and Dorfman). Artistic director Rufus Norris, who started in April 2015, made headlines in 2016 for announcing plans to stage a Brexit-based drama.

606 Club · Blues, Jazz

(Map p84; ☑020-7352 5953; www.606club. co.uk; 90 Lots Rd, SW10; ◷7-11.15pm Sun-Thu, 8pm-12.30am Fri & Sat; 🚇Imperial Wharf) Named after its old address on the King's Rd that cast a spell over jazz lovers Londonwide back in the '80s, this fantastic, tuckedaway basement jazz club and restaurant gives centre stage to contemporary British-based jazz musicians nightly. The club can only serve alcohol to nonmembers who are dining, and it is highly advisable to book to get a table.

Royal Albert Hall · Concert Venue

(Map p84; ☑0845 401 5034; www.royalalbert hall.com; Kensington Gore, SW7; ◉South Kensington) This splendid Victorian concert hall hosts classical-music, rock and other performances, but is most famously the venue for the BBC-sponsored Proms. Booking is possible, but from mid-July to mid-September Proms punters queue for £5 standing (or 'promenading') tickets that go on sale one hour before curtain-up. Otherwise, the box

 Anglesea Arms

Seasoned with age and decades of ale-quaffing patrons (including Charles Dickens, who lived on the same road, and DH Lawrence), this old-school **pub** (Map p84; ☑020-7373 7960; www.anglese aarms.com; 15 Selwood Tce, SW7; ◷11am-11pm Mon-Sat, noon-10.30pm Sun; ◉South Kensington) boasts considerable character and a strong showing of brews, while the terrace out front swarms with punters in warmer months. Arch-criminal Bruce Reynolds masterminded the Great Train Robbery over drinks here.

ANA GARCIA BODEGA/GETTY IMAGES ©

office and prepaid-ticket collection counter are through door 12 (south side of the hall).

Electric Cinema · Cinema

(Map p80; ☑020-3350 3490; www.electric cinema.co.uk; 64-66 Redchurch St, E2; tickets £11-19; ◉Shoreditch High St) Run by Shoreditch House, an uber-fashionable private member's club, this is cinema-going that will impress a date, with space for an intimate 48 on the comfy armchairs. There's a full bar and restaurant in the complex, and you can take your purchases in with you. Tickets go like crazy, so book ahead.

Lord's · Spectator Sport

(Map p84; ☑020-7432 1000; www.lords.org; St John's Wood Rd, NW8; 🚻; ◉St John's Wood) For cricket devotees a trip to Lord's is often as much a pilgrimage as anything else. As well as being home to Marylebone Cricket Club, the ground hosts Test matches, oneday internationals and domestic cricket finals. International matches are usually booked months in advance, but tickets for county cricket fixtures are reasonably easy to come by.

Pizza Express Jazz Club   Jazz
(Map p76; ☑020-7439 4962; www.pizzaex presslive.com/venues/soho-jazz-club; 10 Dean St, W1; admission £15-40; ⊖Tottenham Court Rd) Pizza Express has been one of the best jazz venues in London since opening in 1969. It may be a strange arrangement, in a basement beneath a branch of the chain restaurant, but it's highly popular. Lots of big names perform here and promising artists such as Norah Jones, Gregory Porter and the late Amy Winehouse played here in their early days.

O2 Arena   Live Music
(www.theo2.co.uk; Peninsula Sq, SE10; ☎; ⊖North Greenwich) One of the city's major concert venues, hosting all the biggies – the Rolling Stones, Paul Simon and Sting, One Direction, Ed Sheeran and many others – inside the 20,000-capacity arena. It's also a popular venue for sporting events and you can even climb the roof for ranging views with **Up at the O2**.

KOKO   Live Music
(Map p84; www.koko.uk.com; 1a Camden High St, NW1; ⊖Mornington Cres) Once the legendary Camden Palace, where Charlie Chaplin, the Goons and the Sex Pistols performed, and where Prince played surprise gigs, KOKO is maintaining its reputation as one of London's better gig venues. The theatre has a dance floor and decadent balconies, and attracts an indie crowd. There are live bands most nights and hugely popular club nights on Saturdays.

INFORMATION

Visit London (www.visitlondon.com) Visit London can fill you in on everything from tourist attractions and events (such as the Changing of the Guard and Chinese New Year parade) to river trips and tours, accommodation, eating, theatre, shopping, children's London, and gay and lesbian venues. There are helpful kiosks at **Heathrow Airport** (Terminal 1, 2 & 3 Underground station concourse; ⊘7.30am-8.30pm), **King's Cross St Pancras Station** (Western Ticket Hall, Euston Rd N1; ⊘8am-6pm), **Liverpool Street Station** (Map p80; ⊘8am-6pm), **Piccadilly Circus Underground Station** (Map p76; ⊘9.30am-4pm), The City, Greenwich and **Victoria Station** (Map p76; ⊘7.15am-9.15pm Mon-Sat, 8.15am-8.15pm Sun).

ⓘ GETTING THERE & AWAY

AIR

The city has five airports: Heathrow, which is the largest, to the west; Gatwick to the south; Stansted to the northeast; Luton to the northwest; and London City in the Docklands.

RAIL

Main national rail routes are served by a variety of private train-operating companies. Tickets are not cheap, but trains between cities are usually quite punctual. Check National Rail (www.nationalrail.co.uk) for timetables and fares.

EUROSTAR

Eurostar (☑03432 186186; www.eurostar.com) The high-speed passenger rail service links St Pancras International Station with Gare du Nord in Paris (or Bruxelles Midi in Brussels), with between 14 and 16 daily departures. Fares vary wildly, from £69 to £300.

ⓘ GETTING AROUND

Public transport in London is managed by Transport for London (www.tfl.gov.uk). It is extensive, often excellent and always pricey.

The cheapest way to get around is with an Oyster Card or a UK contactless card. Paper tickets still exist, but will work out substantially more expensive than using an Oyster.

The tube, DLR and Overground network are ideal for zooming across more distant parts of the city; buses and the **Santander Cycles** (☑0343 222 6666; www.tfl.gov.uk/modes/cycling/santander-cycles) ('Boris Bikes') are great for shorter journeys.

Where to Stay

Neighbourhood	Atmosphere
The West End	Close to main sights; great transport links; wide accommodation range but expensive; good restaurants; busy tourist areas.
The City	St Paul's and Tower of London; good transport links; handy central location; quality hotels; some cheaper weekend rates; very quiet at weekends; a business district so high prices during week.
The South Bank	Cheaper than West End; excellent pubs and views; many chain hotels; choice and transport limited.
Kensington & Hyde Park	Great accommodation range; stylish area; good transport; quite expensive; drinking and nightlife options limited.
Clerkenwell, Shoreditch & Spitalfields	Trendy area with great bars and nightlife; excellent for boutique hotels; few top sights; transport options somewhat limited.
East London & Docklands	Markets; multicultural feel; great restaurants and traditional pubs; limited sleeping options; some areas less safe at night.
Camden & North London	Leafy; vibrant nightlife; excellent boutique hotels and hostels; quiet during the week; non-central and away from main sights.
Notting Hill & West London	Cool cachet; great shopping, markets and pubs; excellent boutique hotels; good transport; pricey; light on top sights.
Greenwich & South London	Great boutique options; leafy escapes; near top Greenwich sights; sights spread out beyond Greenwich; transport limited.
Richmond, Kew & Hampton Court	Smart riverside hotels; semi-rural pockets; quiet; fantastic riverside pubs; sights spread out; a long way from central London.

Scottish Highlands, Great Britain

The hills and glens and wild coastline of Scotland's Highlands offer the ultimate escape – one of the last corners of Europe where you can discover genuine solitude. Here the landscape is at its grandest, with soaring hills of rock and heather bounded by wooded glens and rushing waterfalls.

Aviemore, Glen Coe and Fort William draw hill walkers and climbers in summer, and skiers, snowboarders and ice climbers in winter. Inverness, the Highland capital, provides urban rest and relaxation, while nearby Loch Ness and its elusive monster add a hint of mystery.

Two Days in the Scottish Highlands

Cruise Royal Deeside on day one, taking in the Queen's estate, **Balmoral** (p108) and nearby **Braemar Castle** (p108). On day two it's time to go Loch Ness Monster-hunting on a **boat trip** (p102). Next up, tour iconic **Urquhart Castle** (p102), before exploring the loch's quieter eastern shore, including a meal at the lovely **Dores Inn** (p103).

Four Days in the Scottish Highlands

Spend day three exploring **Inverness** (p104) or take a dolphin-watching **tour** (p106). Finish up with a drive southwest to **Glen Coe** (p112), stopping en route in Fort William to ride a **steam train** (p111) and tour a **distillery** (p99).

Finished with the Highlands? Take a 13-hour overnight train to London (p50).

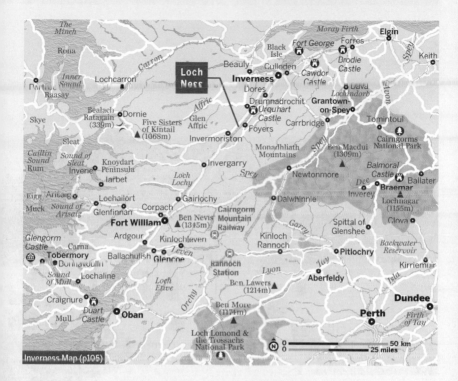

Inverness Map (p105)

Arriving in the Scottish Highlands

Air Inverness Airport at Dalcross has scheduled domestic and some international flights.

Bus There are regular bus services along the Great Glen between Inverness and Fort William.

Train Inverness is connected by train to Glasgow, Edinburgh and London.

Where to Stay

Inverness, Aviemore and Fort William are the main centres for accommodation, but most reasonably sized towns will also have a couple of hotels and a dozen or more B&Bs – many set in superb Victorian villas, farmhouses and manses (former church ministers' houses). Camping is a popular way to enjoy the great outdoors, and there's no shortage of official campsites. Wild camping is also widely practised.

Edradour Distillery

CORNFIELD/SHUTTERSTOCK ©

On the Whisky Trail

Scotland's national drink – in Gaelic uisge bagh, *meaning 'water of life' – has been distilled here for more than 500 years. Over 100 distilleries are still in business, producing hundreds of varieties of single malt, with new operations opening every year.*

Great For...

☑ **Don't Miss**

Fèis Ìle (Islay Festival), which celebrates traditional Scottish music and whisky in May.

Whisky has been distilled in Scotland at least since the 15th century and probably much longer. Learning to distinguish the smoky, peaty whiskies of Islay from, say, the flowery, sherried malts of Speyside has become a hugely popular pastime.

Whisky Central

The Speyside region, around Dufftown and Glenlivet, is the epicentre of the whisky industry. More than 50 distilleries open their doors during the twice yearly **Spirit of Speyside Festival** (www.spiritofspeyside. com), and many are open all year long.

Some pubs in the region have become known as whisky bars, because of their staggering range of single malt whiskies – the famous Quaich bar in the **Craigellachie Hotel** (☎01340-881204; www.craigellachie

JAC_CZ/SHUTTERSTOCK ©

❶ Need to Know

Scotch whisky (always spelt without an 'e' – 'whiskey' is Irish or American) is Scotland's biggest export. The standard measure in pubs is either 25ml or 35ml.

✕ Take a Break

Offering Highland comfort food, Pitlochry's **Moulin Hotel** (☑01796-472196; www.moulinhotel.co.uk; Kirkmichael Rd; mains £9-16; P 🛜 🍴) is within striking distance of both Edradour and Blair Athol Distilleries.

★ Top Tip

Don't ask for 'Scotch' in a bar or pub – what else would you be served in Scotland?

can see the whole process, easily explained, in one building. It's 2.5 miles east of Pitlochry by car, along the Moulin road, or a pleasant 1-mile walk.

Blair Athol Distillery　　Distillery

(☑01796-482003; www.discovering-distilleries. com; Perth Rd; standard tour £7; ⊗10am-5pm Apr-Oct, to 4pm Nov-Mar) Tours here focus on whisky making and the blending of this well-known dram. More detailed private tours give you greater insights and superior tastings.

Ben Nevis Distillery　　Distillery

(☑01397-702476; www.bennevisdistillery.com; Lochy Bridge; guided tour adult/child £5/2.50; ⊗9am-5pm Mon-Fri year-round, 10am-4pm Sat Easter-Sep, noon-4pm Sun Jul & Aug; P) A tour of this distillery makes for a warming rainy-day alternative to exploring the hills.

hotel.co.uk; Craigellachie), established in 1894, offers more than 800 different varieties.

Visiting a Distillery

Many distilleries offer guided tours, rounded off with a tasting session. Trying local varieties is a great way to explore the whisky-making regions, but while visiting a distillery can be a memorable experience, only hardcore malt-hounds will want to go to more than one or two. The following are good options for a day trip from Inverness.

Edradour Distillery　　Distillery

(☑01796-472095; www.edradour.co.uk; Moulin Rd; tour adult/child £7.50/2.50; ⊗10am-5pm Mon-Sat late Apr-late Oct; P 🍴) This is proudly Scotland's smallest and most picturesque distillery and one of the best to visit: you

Urquhart Castle (p102)

Loch Ness

Deep, dark and narrow, the bitterly cold waters of Loch Ness have long drawn waves of people hunting Nessie, the elusive Loch Ness Monster. Despite the crowds, it's still possible to find tranquillity and gorgeous views. Add a highly photogenic castle and some superb hiking and you have a loch with bags of appeal.

Great For...

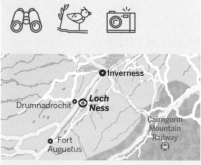

ⓘ Need to Know

A complete circuit of the loch is about 70 miles; travel anticlockwise for the best views.

★ **Top Tip**

Fancy a spot of Nessie hunting?
Check out the latest at www.lochness
sightings.com.

Tales of the Loch Ness Monster truly took off in the 1930s, when reported sightings led to a press furore and a string of high-profile photographs. Reports have tailed off recently, but the bizarre mini-industry that's grown up around Nessie is a spectacle in itself.

Drumnadrochit

Seized by monster madness, its gift shops bulging with Nessie cuddly toys, Drumnadrochit is a hotbed of beastie fever, with Nessie attractions battling it out for the tourist dollar.

The **Loch Ness Centre & Exhibition** (☑01456-450573; www.lochness.com; adult/child £7.95/4.95; ☺9.30am-6pm Jul & Aug, to 5pm Easter-Jun, Sep & Oct, 10am-3.30pm Nov-Easter; P ⛴) adopts a scientific approach that allows you to weigh the evidence for yourself. Exhibits include those on hoaxes and optical illusions and some original equipment – sonar survey vessels, miniature submarines, cameras and sediment coring tools – used in various monster hunts, as well as original photographs and film footage of reported sightings.

To head out yourself, **Nessie Hunter** (☑01456-450395; www.lochness-cruises.com; adult/child £15/10; ☺Easter-Oct) offers one-hour monster-hunting cruises, complete with sonar and underwater cameras. Cruises depart from Drumnadrochit hourly (except 1pm) from 9am to 6pm daily.

Urquhart Castle

Commanding a superb location 1.5 miles east of Drumnadrochit, with outstanding views, **Urquhart Castle** (HS; ☑01456-450551; adult/child £8.50/5.10; ☺9.30am-6pm

Loch Ness

Apr-Sep, to 5pm Oct, to 4.30pm Nov-Mar; P) is a popular Nessie-hunting hotspot. A huge visitor centre (most of which is beneath ground level) includes a video theatre and displays of medieval items discovered in the castle.

The castle has been repeatedly sacked and rebuilt over the centuries; in 1692 it was blown up to prevent the Jacobites from using it. The five-storey tower house at the northern point is the most impressive remaining fragment and offers fine views across the water.

☑ Don't Miss

Climbing to the battlements of the iconic tower of Urquhart Castle, for grandstand views from the rocky headland, up and down Loch Ness.

VISITBRITAIN/JOE CORNISH/GETTY IMAGES ©

Loch Ness' East Side

While tour coaches pour down the west side of Loch Ness to the hotspots of Drumnadrochit and Urquhart Castle, the narrow B862 road along the eastern shore is relatively peaceful. It leads to the village of Foyers, where you can enjoy a pleasant hike to the Falls of Foyers.

It's also worth making the trip just for the **Dores Inn** (☎01463-751203; www.thedoresinn.co.uk; Dores; mains £11-24; ⏰pub 10am-11pm, food served noon-2pm & 6-9pm; P 📶), a beautifully restored country pub adorned with recycled furniture, local landscape paintings and fresh flowers. The menu specialises in quality Scottish produce, from haggis, turnips and *tatties* (potatoes), and haddock and chips, to steaks, scallops and seafood platters. The pub garden has stunning Loch Ness views and a dedicated monster-spotting vantage point.

Hiking at Loch Ness

The South Loch Ness Trail (www.visitinvernesslochness.com) links a series of footpaths and minor roads along the less-frequented southern side of the loch. The 28 miles from Loch Tarff near Fort Augustus to Torbreck on the fringes of Inverness can be done on foot, by bike or on horseback.

The climb to the summit of Meallfuarvonie (699m), on the northwestern shore of Loch Ness, makes an excellent short hill walk: the views along the Great Glen from the top are superb. It's a 6-mile round trip, so allow about three hours. Start from the car park at the end of the minor road leading south from Drumnadrochit to Bunloit.

✕ Take a Break

Drumnadrochit has cafes and restaurants aplenty, but they can get very busy. To avoid the crowds, head for the Dores Inn on the east side.

The Battle of Culloden

The Battle of Culloden in 1746 – the last pitched battle ever fought on British soil – saw the defeat of Bonnie Prince Charlie and the end of the Jacobite dream when 1200 Highlanders were slaughtered by government forces in a 68-minute rout. The Duke of Cumberland, son of the reigning King George II and leader of the Hanoverian army, earned the nickname 'Butcher' for his brutal treatment of the defeated Jacobite forces. The battle sounded the death knell for the old clan system, and the horrors of the Clearances soon followed. The sombre moor where the conflict took place has scarcely changed in the ensuing 260 years.

The impressive **Culloden Visitor Centre** (NTS; www.nts.org.uk/culloden; adult/child £11/8.50; ⏱9am-6pm Jun-Aug, to 5.30pm Apr, May, Sep & Oct, 10am-4pm Nov-Mar; ℗) boasts an innovative film that puts you on the battlefield in the middle of the mayhem, along with a wealth of other audio presentations. The admission fee includes an audio guide for a self-guided tour of the battlefield site.

Thatched cottage on the battlefield site
MATTHI/SHUTTERSTOCK ©

Inverness

Inverness, one of the fastest growing towns in Britain, is the capital of the Highlands. Inverness is a transport hub and jumping-off point for the central, western and northern Highlands, the Moray Firth coast and the Great Glen.

The Great Glen is a geological fault, running in an arrow-straight line across Scotland from Fort William to Inverness. The glaciers of the last ice age eroded a deep trough along the fault line, which is now filled by a series of lochs – Linnhe, Lochy, Oich and Ness.

Inverness was probably founded by King David in the 12th century, but thanks to its often violent history, few buildings of real age or historical significance have survived – much of the older part of the city dates from the period following the completion of the Caledonian Canal in 1822. The broad and shallow River Ness, famed for its salmon fishing, runs through the heart of the city.

◎ SIGHTS

Ness Islands   Park
The main attraction in Inverness is a leisurely stroll along the river to the Ness Islands. Planted with mature Scots pine, fir, beech and sycamore, and linked to the river banks and each other by elegant Victorian footbridges, the islands make an appealing picnic spot. They're a 20-minute walk south of the castle – head upstream on either side of the river (the start of the Great Glen Way), and return on the opposite bank.

Inverness Museum & Art Gallery   Museum
(☏01463-237114; www.inverness.highland.museum; Castle Wynd; ⏱10am-5pm Tue-Sat Apr-Oct, noon-4pm Thu-Sat Nov-Mar) **FREE** Inverness Museum & Art Gallery has wildlife dioramas, geological displays, period rooms with historic weapons, Pictish stones and exhibitions of contemporary Highland arts and crafts.

Cawdor Castle   Castle
(☏01667-404615; www.cawdorcastle.com; Cawdor; adult/child £10.70/6.70; ⏱10am-5.30pm May-Sep; ℗) This castle, 5 miles southwest of Nairn, was once the seat of the Thane of Cawdor, one of the titles bestowed on Shakespeare's *Macbeth*. The real Macbeth – an ancient Scottish king – couldn't have lived here though, since he died in 1057, 300

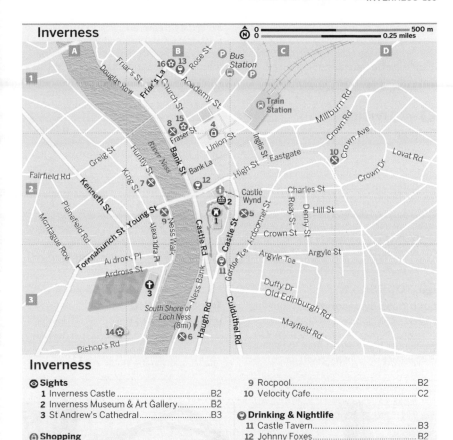

Inverness

Inverness

◉ Sights
1 Inverness Castle B2
2 Inverness Museum & Art Gallery B2
3 St Andrew's Cathedral B3

🅐 Shopping
4 Victorian Market B1

✕ Eating
5 Café 1 .... C2
6 Contrast Brasserie B3
7 Kitchen Brasserie B2
8 Mustard Seed B1

9 Rocpool B2
10 Velocity Cafe C2

🍷 Drinking & Nightlife
11 Castle Tavern B3
12 Johnny Foxes B2
13 Phoenix B1

🎭 Entertainment
14 Eden Court Theatre A3
15 Hootananny B1
16 Ironworks B1

years before the castle was begun. Nevertheless the tour gives a fascinating insight into the lives of the Scottish aristocracy.

Brodie Castle
Castle

(NTS; ☎01309-641371; www.nts.org.uk; Brodie; adult/child £10.50/7.50; ⏰10.30am-5pm daily Jul & Aug, 10.30am-4.30pm Sat-Wed Apr-Jun & Sep-Oct; 🅿) Set in 70 hectares of parkland, Brodie Castle has a library with more than 6000 peeling, dusty volumes, wonderful clocks, a huge Victorian kitchen and

a 17th-century dining room with wildly extravagant moulded plaster ceilings depicting mythological scenes. The Brodies have been living here since 1160, but the present structure dates mostly from 1567, with many additions over the years. The castle is 4 miles west of Forres.

Inverness Castle
Castle

(Castle St) The hill above the city centre is topped by the picturesque Baronial turrets of Inverness Castle, a pink-sandstone confection dating from 1847 that replaced a medieval castle blown up by the Jacobites in 1746; it serves today as the Sheriff's Court. It's not open to the public, but there are good views from the surrounding gardens.

🜚 ACTIVITIES

Dolphin Spirit — Wildlife Watching
(📞07544-800620; www.dolphinspirit.co.uk; Inverness Marina, Longman Dr; adult/child £16/10; 🜚Easter-Oct) Four times a day in season, this outfit runs cruises from Inverness into the Moray Firth to spot the UK's largest pod of bottlenose dolphins – around 130 animals. The dolphins feed on salmon heading for the rivers at the head of the firth, and can often be seen leaping and bow-surfing.

🜚 TOURS

Loch Ness by Jacobite — Boating
(📞01463-233999; www.jacobite.co.uk; Glenurquhart Rd; adult/child £33/26) From June to September, boats depart from Tomnahurich Bridge twice daily for a three-hour cruise along the Caledonian Canal to Loch Ness and back, with a live commentary on local history and wildlife. You can buy tickets at the tourist office and catch a free minibus to the boat. Other cruises and combined cruise/coach tours, from one to 6½ hours, are also available, some year-round.

Happy Tours — Walking
(📞07828-154683; www.happy-tours.biz; £10) Offers 1¼-hour guided walks exploring the town's history and legends, starting at 7pm (must be booked in advance).

Inverness Taxis — Tours
(📞01463-222900; www.inverness-taxis.com) Wide range of day tours to Urquhart Castle, Loch Ness, Culloden and even Skye. Fares per car (up to four people) range from £60 (two hours) to £240 (all day).

🜚 SHOPPING

Victorian Market — Market
(Academy St; 🜚9am-5pm Mon-Sat) If the rain comes down, you could opt for a spot of retail therapy in the Victorian Market, a

Victorian Market

shopping mall that dates from the 1890s and has rather more charm than its modern equivalents.

EATING

Inverness has some of the best – and the best-value – restaurants in the Scottish Highlands.

Velocity Cafe
Cafe £

(☑01463-419956; http://velocitylove.co.uk; 1 Crown Ave; mains £4-7; ◷9am-5pm Mon, Wed, Fri & Sat, 9am-9pm Thu, 11am-5pm Sun; 🛜📶👪) ✿ This cyclists' cafe serves soups, sandwiches and salads prepared with organic, locally sourced produce, as well as yummy cakes and coffee. There's also a workshop where you can repair your bike or book a session with a mechanic.

Café 1
Bistro ££

(☑01463-226200; www.cafe1.net; 75 Castle St; mains £13-25; ◷noon-2.30pm & 5-9.30pm Mon-Fri, noon-2.30pm & 6-9.30pm Sat; 👪) ✿ Café 1 is a friendly, appealing bistro with candlelit tables amid elegant blonde wood and wrought-iron decor. There is an international menu based on quality Scottish produce, from Aberdeen Angus steaks to crisp panfried sea bass and meltingly tender pork belly. The set lunch menu (two courses for £12) is served noon to 2.30pm Monday to Saturday.

Contrast Brasserie
Brasserie ££

(☑01463-223777; www.glenmoristontownhouse. com; 20 Ness Bank; mains £14-21; ◷noon-2.30pm & 5-10pm) Book early for what we think is one of the best-value restaurants in Inverness – a dining room that drips designer style, with smiling professional staff and truly delicious food prepared using fresh Scottish produce. The two-/three-course lunch menu (£11/14) and three-course early-bird menu (£16, 5pm to 6.30pm) are bargains.

Mustard Seed
Bistro ££

(☑01463-220220; www.mustardseedrestaurant. co.uk; 16 Fraser St; mains £13-21; ◷noon-3pm & 5.30-10pm) ✿ The menu at this bright and bustling bistro changes weekly, but focuses

 **Fort George**

One of the finest artillery fortifications in Europe, **Fort George** (HS; ☑01667-462777; adult/child £8.50/5.10; ◷9.30am-5.30pm Apr-Sep, 10am-4pm Oct-Mar; 🅿) was established in 1748 in the aftermath of the Battle of Culloden, as a base for George II's army of occupation in the Highlands. By the time of its completion in 1769 it had cost the equivalent of around £1 billion in today's money. It still functions as a military barracks; public areas have exhibitions on 18th-century soldiery, and the mile-plus walk around the ramparts offers fine views out to sea and back to the Great Glen.

Given its size, you'll need at least two hours to do the place justice. The fort is off the A96 about 11 miles northeast of Inverness; there is no public transport.

JEFF J MITCHELL/GETTY IMAGES ®

on Scottish and French cuisine with a modern twist. Grab a table on the upstairs balcony if you can – it's the best outdoor lunch spot in Inverness, with a great view across the river. And a two-course lunch for £9 – yes, that's right – is hard to beat.

Kitchen Brasserie
Modern Scottish ££

(☑01463-259119; www.kitchenrestaurant. co.uk; 15 Huntly St; mains £9-20; ◷noon-3pm & 5-10pm; 🛜👪) This spectacular glass-fronted restaurant offers a great menu of top Scottish produce with a Mediterranean or Asian touch, and a view over the River Ness – try to get a table upstairs. Great-value

Royal Deeside

The upper valley of the River Dee stretches west from Aboyne and Ballater to Braemar, closely paralleled by the A93 road. Made famous by its long association with the monarchy, the region is often called Royal Deeside.

Built for Queen Victoria in 1855 as a private residence for the royal family, **Balmoral Castle** (☏01339-742534; www. balmoralcastle.com; Crathie; adult/child £11.50/5; ⊗10am-5pm Apr-Jul, last admission 4.30pm; P) kicked off the revival of the Scottish Baronial style of architecture that characterises so many of Scotland's 19th-century country houses. The admission fee includes an interesting and well-thought-out audioguide, but the tour is very much an outdoor one through gardens and grounds.

Just north of Braemar village, turreted **Braemar Castle** (www.braemarcastle. co.uk; adult/child £8/4; ⊗10am-4pm daily Jul & Aug, Wed-Sun Apr-Jun, Sep & Oct; P) dates from 1628 and served as a government garrison after the 1745 Jacobite rebellion. It was taken over by the local community in 2007, and now offers guided tours of the historic castle apartments. There's a short walk from the car park to the castle.

Balmoral Castle

two-course lunch (£9, noon to 3pm) and early-bird menu (£13, 5pm to 7pm).

Rocpool   Mediterranean £££
(☏01463-717274; www.rocpoolrestaurant.com; 1 Ness Walk; mains £13-23; ⊗noon-2.30pm &

5.45-10pm Mon-Sat) ✔ Lots of polished wood, crisp white linen and leather booths and banquettes lend a nautical air to this relaxing bistro, which offers a Mediterranean-influenced menu that makes the most of quality Scottish produce, especially seafood. The two-course lunch is £16.

🍷 DRINKING & NIGHTLIFE

As the 'capital city' of the Highlands, Inverness has the liveliest nightlife in the area. As well as dozens of pubs, clubs and music venues, there's the Eden Court Theatre, the main cultural focus of the region.

Clachnaharry Inn   Pub
(☏01463-239806; www.clachnaharryinn.co.uk; 17-19 High St, Clachnaharry; ⊗11am-11pm Mon-Thu, 11am-1am Fri & Sat, noon-11pm Sun; 🍴) Just over a mile northwest of the city centre, on the bank of the Caledonian Canal just off the A862, this is a delightful old coaching inn (with beer garden out the back) serving an excellent range of real ales and good pub grub.

Phoenix   Pub
(☏01463-233685; 108 Academy St; ⊗11am-1am Mon-Sat, noon-midnight Sun) Beautifully refurbished, this is the most traditional of the pubs in the city centre, with a mahogany horseshoe bar and several real ales on tap, including beers from the Cairngorm, Cromarty and Isle of Skye breweries.

Castle Tavern   Pub
(☏01463-718718; www.castletavern.net; 1-2 View Pl; ⊗11am-11pm) Offering a tempting selection of craft beers, this pub has a wee suntrap of a terrace out the front. It's a great place for a pint on a summer afternoon.

Johnny Foxes   Bar
(☏01463-236577; www.johnnyfoxes.co.uk; 26 Bank St; ⊗11am-3am) Stuck beneath the ugliest building on the riverfront, Johnny Foxes is a big and boisterous Irish bar with a wide range of food served all day and live music nightly. Part of the premises, the **Den** is a smart cocktail bar and late-night club.

☆ ENTERTAINMENT

Hootananny
Live Music

(☎01463-233651; www.hootanannyinverness.
co.uk; 67 Church St) Hootananny is the city's
best live-music venue, with traditional
folk- and/or rock-music sessions nightly,
including big-name bands from all over
Scotland (and, indeed, the world). The bar
is well stocked with a range of beers from
the local Black Isle Brewery.

Ironworks
Live Music, Comedy

(☎0871-789 4173; www.ironworksvenue.com;
122 Academy St) With live bands (rock, pop,
tribute) and comedy shows two or three
times a week, the Ironworks is the town's
main venue for big-name acts.

Eden Court Theatre
Theatre

(☎01463-234234; www.eden-court.co.uk;
Bishop's Rd; 🐾) The Highlands' main cultural
venue – with theatre, art house cinema and
a conference centre – Eden Court stages
a busy program of drama, dance, comedy,
music, film and children's events, and has a
good bar and restaurant. Pick up a program
from the foyer or check the website.

ℹ️ INFORMATION

Inverness Tourist Office (☎01463-252401;
www.visithighlands.com; Castle Wynd; internet
access per 20min £1; ⏰9am-5pm Mon-Sat,
10am-3pm Sun, longer hours Mar-Oct) Bureau de
change and accommodation booking service;
also sells tickets for tours and cruises.

ℹ️ GETTING THERE & AWAY

AIR

Inverness Airport (INV; ☎01667-464000; www.
hial.co.uk/inverness-airport) At Dalcross, 10
miles east of the city, off the A96 towards Aberdeen. There are scheduled flights to Amsterdam,
London, Manchester, Dublin, Orkney, Shetland
and the Outer Hebrides, as well as other places
in the UK.

Stagecoach bus 11/11A runs from the airport
to Inverness bus station (£4, 20 minutes, every
30 minutes).

BUS

Services depart from **Inverness bus station**
(Margaret St). Most intercity routes are served

Highland dancing

LUKASSEK/SHUTTERSTOCK ©

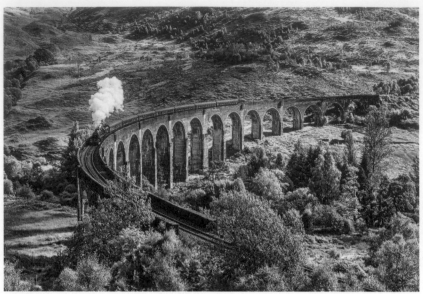

Jacobite Steam Train on the Glenfinnan Viaduct

> *one of the great railway journeys of the world*

by **Scottish Citylink** (✆0871-266 3333; www.citylink.co.uk).

If you book far enough in advance, **Megabus** (✆0141-352 4444; www.megabus.com) offers fares from as little as £1 for buses from Inverness to Glasgow and Edinburgh, and £10 to London.

TRAIN

Inverness is connected by train to Edinburgh (£50, 3½ hours, every two hours) and London (£120, eight to nine hours, one daily direct).

ⓘ GETTING AROUND

BICYCLE

Ticket to Ride (✆01463-419160; www.ticketto ridehighlands.co.uk; Bellfield Park; per day from £25; ☺9am-6pm Apr-Oct) Hires out mountain bikes, hybrids and tandems. Will deliver bikes free to local hotels and B&Bs, and bikes can be dropped off in Fort William.

BUS

City services and buses to places around Inverness, including Nairn, Forres, the Culloden Battlefield, Beauly, Dingwall and Lairg, are operated by **Stagecoach** (✆01463-233371; www.stagecoachbus.com).

An Inverness City Dayrider ticket costs £3.50 and gives unlimited travel for a day on buses throughout the city.

CAR

Focus Vehicle Rental (✆01463-709517; www.focusvehiclerental.co.uk; 6 Harbour Rd) The big boys charge from around £50 to £65 per day, but Focus has cheaper rates starting at £40 per day.

TAXI

Inverness Taxis (✆01463-222222; www.inverness-taxis.com) There's a taxi rank outside the train station.

Fort William

Basking on the shores of Loch Linnhe amid magnificent mountain scenery, Fort William has one of the most enviable settings in the whole of Scotland. It's a good place to base yourself for exploring the surrounding mountains and glens.

⊚ SIGHTS

West Highland Museum · Museum

(☑01397-702169; www.westhighlandmuseum.org.uk; Cameron Sq; ⊙10am-5pm Mon-Sat Apr-Oct, to 4pm Mar & Nov-Dec, closed Jan & Feb) **FREE** This small but fascinating museum is packed with all manner of Highland memorabilia. Look out for the secret portrait of Bonnie Prince Charlie – after the Jacobite rebellions, all things Highland were banned, including pictures of the exiled leader, and this tiny painting looks like nothing more than a smear of paint until viewed in a cylindrical mirror, which reflects a credible likeness of the prince.

⊕ ACTIVITIES

Crannog Cruises · Wildlife

(☑01397-700714; www.crannog.net/cruises; adult/child £15/7.50; ⊙11am, 1pm & 3pm daily Easter-Oct) Operates 1½-hour wildlife cruises on Loch Linnhe, visiting a seal colony and a salmon farm.

⊗ EATING

Lime Tree · Scottish ££

(☑01397-701806; www.limetreefortwilliam.co.uk; Achintore Rd; mains £16-20; ⊙6.30-9.30pm; P ⊛) ✔ Fort William is not over-endowed with great places to eat, but the restaurant at this small hotel and art gallery has put the UK's Outdoor Capital on the gastronomic map. The chef turns out delicious dishes built around fresh Scottish produce, ranging from Loch Fyne oysters to Loch Awe trout and Ardnamurchan venison.

Crannog Seafood Restaurant · Seafood ££

(☑01397-705589; www.crannog.net; Town Pier; mains £15-23; ⊙noon-2.30pm & 6-9pm) ✔ The Crannog wins the prize for the best location in town – perched on the Town Pier, giving

 Jacobite Steam Train

The **Jacobite Steam Train** (☑0844 850 4685; www.westcoastrailways.co.uk; day return adult/child £34/19; ⊙daily Jul & Aug, Mon-Fri mid-May–Jun, Sep & Oct), hauled by a former LNER K1 or LMS Class 5MT locomotive, travels the scenic two-hour run between Fort William and Mallaig. Classed as one of the great railway journeys of the world, the route crosses the historic Glenfinnan Viaduct, made famous in the Harry Potter films – the Jacobite's owners supplied the steam locomotive and rolling stock used in the film.

Trains depart from Fort William train station in the morning and return from Mallaig in the afternoon. There's a brief stop at Glenfinnan station, and you get 1½ hours in Mallaig.

window-table diners an uninterrupted view down Loch Linnhe. Informal and unfussy, it specialises in fresh local fish – there are three or four daily fish specials plus the main menu – though there are lamb, venison and vegetarian dishes, too. Two/three-course lunch £15/19.

Bayleaf · Scottish ££

(Cameron Sq; mains lunch £5-11, dinner £13-20; ⊛) ✔ A great new addition to the town's restaurant scene, this place combines crisp, modern decor, friendly service (the chef often comes out to chat with customers) and the best of Scottish beef, lamb and seafood freshly and simply

🔁 Glen Coe

Scotland's most famous glen is also one of its grandest. It was written into history in 1692 when the resident MacDonalds were murdered by Campbell soldiers in a notorious massacre. Soldiers largely from Campbell clan territory, on government orders, turned on their MacDonald hosts killing 38; another 40 MacDonalds perished having fled into snow-covered hills.

There are several short, pleasant walks around Glencoe Lochan, near the village. To get there, turn left off the minor road to the youth hostel, just beyond the bridge over the River Coe. There are three walks (40 minutes to an hour), all detailed on a signboard at the car park. A more strenuous hike, but well worth the effort on a fine day, is the climb to the Lost Valley, a magical mountain sanctuary still said to be haunted by the ghosts of MacDonalds.

HELEN HOTSON/SHUTTERSTOCK ©

prepared. If Scotland's national dish hasn't appealed, try a haggis fritter with Drambuie mayonnaise!

🍷 DRINKING & NIGHTLIFE

Ben Nevis Bar   Pub
(📞01397-702295; 105 High St; ⏰11am-11pm; 🛜) The lounge here enjoys a good view over the loch, and the bar exudes a relaxed, jovial atmosphere where climbers and tourists can work off leftover energy jigging to live music (Thursday and Friday nights).

Grog & Gruel   Pub
(📞01397-705078; www.grogandgruel.co.uk; 66 High St; ⏰noon-midnight; 🛜) The Grog & Gruel is a traditional-style, wood-panelled pub with an excellent range of cask ales from regional Scottish and English microbreweries.

ℹ️ INFORMATION

Fort William Tourist Office (📞01397-701801; www.visithighlands.com; 15 High St; internet per 20min £1; ⏰9am-5pm Mon-Sat, 10am-3pm Sun, longer hrs Jun-Aug) Has internet access.

ℹ️ GETTING THERE & AWAY

The bus and train stations are next to the huge Morrisons supermarket, reached from the town centre via an underpass next to the Nevisport shop.

BUS

Scottish Citylink (📞0871-266 3333; www.citylink.co.uk) buses link Fort William with other major towns and cities, including Edinburgh (£35, five hours, seven daily with a change at Glasgow; via Glencoe and Crianlarich), Glasgow (£24, three hours, eight daily) and Inverness (£11.60, two hours, six daily).

Shiel Buses (📞01397-700700; www.shielbuses.co.uk) service 500 runs to Mallaig (£6.10, 1½ hours, three daily Monday to Friday, plus one daily weekends April to September) via Glenfinnan (£3.30, 30 minutes) and Arisaig (£5.60, one hour).

CAR

Easydrive Car Hire (📞01397-701616; www.easydrivescotland.co.uk; North Rd) Hires out small cars from £36/165 a day/week, including tax and unlimited mileage, but not Collision Damage Waiver (CDW).

TRAIN

The spectacular West Highland line runs from Glasgow to Mallaig via Fort William. The overnight **Caledonian Sleeper** (www.sleeper.scot) service connects Fort William and London Euston (from £125 sharing a twin-berth cabin, 13 hours).

Lighthouse near Fort William

Edinburgh £35, five hours; change at Glasgow's Queen St station, three daily, two on Sunday

Glasgow £26, 3¾ hours, three daily, two on Sunday

Mallaig £12.20, 1½ hours, four daily, three on Sunday

① GETTING AROUND

BICYCLE

Nevis Cycles (☏01397-705555; www.nevis cycles.com; cnr Montrose Ave & Locheil Rd, Inverlochy; per day from £25; ☺9am-5.30pm) Located a half-mile northeast of the town centre, this place rents everything from hybrid bikes and mountain bikes to full-suspension downhill racers. Bikes can be hired here and dropped off in Inverness.

BUS

A Zone 2 Dayrider ticket (£8.60) gives unlimited travel for one day on Stagecoach bus services in the Fort William area, as far as Glencoe and Fort Augustus. Buy from the bus driver.

In This Chapter

Dublin, Ireland

A small capital with a huge reputation, Dublin's mix of heritage and hedonism will not disappoint. There are fascinating museums, mouth-watering restaurants and the best range of entertainment available anywhere in Ireland – and that's not including the pub, the ubiquitous centre of the city's social life and an absolute must for any visitor. Dubliners at their ease are the greatest hosts of all, a charismatic bunch whose soul and sociability are so compelling and infectious that you mightn't ever want to leave.

Dublin in Two Days

Stroll through the grounds of **Trinity College** (p117), visiting the Long Room and the Book of Kells, before ambling up Grafton St to **St Stephen's Green** (p124). For more beautiful books and artefacts, drop into the **Chester Beatty Library** (p120) on day two. On your way, you can indulge in a spot of retail therapy in **Powerscourt Townhouse Shopping Centre** (p125) or in the many boutiques west of Grafton St.

Dublin in Four Days

After walking the length of **O'Connell St**, and pausing to inspect the bullet holes in the **General Post Office** (p121), explore the collection of the **Dublin City Gallery – Hugh Lane** (p120), including Francis Bacon's reconstructed studio. Begin day four learning some Irish history at **Kilmainham Gaol** (p121). Spend the afternoon at the seven-floor **Guinness Storehouse** (p119), finishing with a pint of the famous black stuff in its Gravity Bar.

Next stop: Lisbon (p330) or the Scottish Highlands (p96).

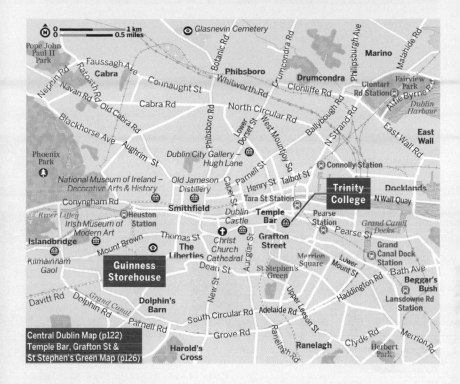

Arriving in Dublin

Dublin Airport Frequent buses to the city centre run from 6am to midnight; taxis (€25) take around 45 minutes.

Dun Laoghaire ferry terminal DART (€3.25) to Pearse Station (for south Dublin) or Connolly Station (for north Dublin); bus 46A to St Stephen's Green, or bus 7, 7A or 8 to Burgh Quay.

Dublin Port terminal Buses (€3) are timed to coincide with arrivals and departures.

Where to Stay

There has only been a handful of hotel openings in Dublin in the last few years, which means that hotel prices in the city are higher than they were during the boom years of the Celtic Tiger.

There are good midrange options north of the Liffey, but the biggest spread of accommodation is south of the river.

For information on what each Dublin neighbourhood has to offer, see the table on p133.

Trinity College

The student body has diversified since those days when a university education was the preserve of a small elite, but Trinity's bucolic charms persist and on a summer's evening it's one of the city's most delightful places to be: a calm retreat from the bustle of contemporary Dublin.

Great For...

☑ **Don't Miss**

The Long Room, which starred as the Jedi Archive in the movie *Star Wars Episode II: Attack of the Clones*.

The college was established by Elizabeth I in 1592 on land confiscated from an Augustinian priory in an effort to stop the brain drain of young Protestant Dubliners, who were skipping across to continental Europe for an education and becoming 'infected with popery'. Trinity went on to become one of Europe's most outstanding universities, producing a host of notable graduates – how about Jonathan Swift, Oscar Wilde and Samuel Beckett at the same alumni dinner?

It remained completely Protestant until 1793, but even when the university relented and began to admit Catholics, the Catholic Church held firm; until 1970, any Catholic who enrolled here could consider themselves excommunicated.

The campus is a masterpiece of architecture and landscaping beautifully preserved in Georgian aspic. Most of the

The Long Room

CLU/GETTY IMAGES ©

❶ Need to Know

Map p126; ☎01-896 1000; www.tcd.ie;
College Green; ⊘8am-10pm; 🚇all city centre)
FREE

✕ Take a Break

Fade Street Social (p129) is an
excellent lunch spot just a few blocks
southwest.

★ Top Tip

Go online and buy a fast-track ticket
(adult/student/family €14/12/28)
to the Old Library, which gives timed
admission to the exhibition and allows
visitors to skip the queue.

buildings and statues date from the 18th
and 19th centuries, each elegantly laid out
on a cobbled or grassy square. The newer
bits include the 1978 Arts & Social Science
Building, which backs on to Nassau St and
forms the alternative entrance to the college. Like the college's Berkeley Library, it
was designed by Paul Koralek; it houses the
Douglas Hyde Gallery of Modern Art.

To the south of Library Sq is the **Old
Library** (Map p126; adult/student/family
€11/9.50/22, fast-track adult/student/family
€14/12/28; ⊘8.30am-5pm Mon-Sat, 9.30am-
5pm Sun May-Sep, 9.30am-5pm Mon-Sat, noon-
4.30pm Sun Oct-Apr), built in a severe style by
Thomas Burgh between 1712 and 1732. It is
one of five copyright libraries across Ireland
and the UK, which means it's entitled to a
copy of every book published in these islands – around five million books, of which

only a fraction are stored here. You can visit
the library as part of a tour, taking in the
Long Room and the famous Book of Kells.

The **Book of Kells** is a breathtaking
illuminated manuscript of the four Gospels
of the New Testament, created around AD
800 by monks on the Scottish island of
Iona. Trinity's other great treasures are kept
in the Old Library's stunning 65m **Long
Room**, which houses about 200,000 of the
library's oldest volumes. Displays include
a rare copy of the Proclamation of the Irish
Republic, which was read out by Pádraig
(Patrick) Pearse at the beginning of the
Easter Rising in 1916.

Also here is the so-called harp of Brian
Ború, which was definitely not in use when
the army of this early Irish hero defeated
the Danes at the Battle of Clontarf in 1014.
It does, however, date from around 1400,
making it one of the oldest harps in Ireland.
Your entry ticket also includes admission
to temporary exhibitions on display in the
East Pavilion.

LITTLENY/SHUTTERSTOCK ©

Guinness Storehouse

More than any beer produced anywhere in the world, Guinness is more than just a brand – for many devotees it's a substance with near spiritual qualities. This beer-lover's Disneyland is a multimedia homage to Ireland's most famous export.

Great For...

☑ Don't Miss

Enjoying the view from the Gravity Bar with your free pint of Guinness (price included with admission).

The mythology of Guinness is remarkably durable: it doesn't travel well; its distinctive flavour comes from Liffey water; and it is good for you – not to mention the generally held belief that you will never understand the Irish until you develop a taste for the black stuff. It's all absolutely true, of course, so it should be no surprise that the Guinness Storehouse, in the heart of the St James's Gate Brewery, is the city's most visited tourist attraction, an all-singing, all-dancing extravaganza that combines sophisticated exhibits, spectacular design and a thick, creamy head of marketing hype.

Grain Storehouse & Brewery

The old grain storehouse, the only part of the massive, 26-hectare St James's Gate Brewery open to the public, is a suitable

Pint of Guinness

ISLAVICEK/SHUTTERSTOCK ©

ℹ Need to Know

Map p122; www.guinness-storehouse.com; St James's Gate, South Market St; adult/child €18/16.50, connoisseur experience €48; ⏱9.30am-5pm Sep-Jun, to 6pm Jul & Aug; 🚌21A, 51B, 78, 78A, 123 from Fleet St, 🚃James's

✕ Take a Break

Gilroy's Bar on the 5th floor of the building serves up a delicious Irish stew.

★ Top Tip

Avoid the queues (and save €2) by buying your ticket online in advance.

cathedral in which to worship the black gold: shaped like a giant pint of Guinness, it rises seven impressive storeys high around a stunning central atrium. At the top is the head, represented by the Gravity Bar, with a panoramic view of Dublin.

Immediately below it is the brewery itself, founded in 1759 by Arthur Guinness and once the employer of over 5000 people; the gradual shift to greater automation has reduced the workforce to around 300.

The Perfect Pour

As you work your way to the top and your prize of arguably the nicest Guinness you could drink anywhere, you'll explore the various elements that made the beer the brand that it is and perhaps understand a little better the efforts made by the company to ensure its quasi-mythical status.

From the (copy of) the original 9000-year lease (in a glass box embedded in the ground floor) to the near scientific lesson in how to pour the perfect pint, everything about this place is designed to make you understand that Guinness isn't just any other beer.

Arthur Guinness

One fun fact you will learn is that genius can be inadvertent: at some point in the 18th century, a London brewer accidentally burnt his hops while brewing ale, and so created the dark beer we know today. It's name of 'porter' came because the dark beer was very popular with London porters. In the 1770s, Arthur Guinness, who had until then only brewed ale, started brewing the dark stuff to get a jump on all other Irish brewers. By 1799 he decided to concentrate all his efforts on this single brew. He died four years later, aged 83, but the foundations for world domination were already in place.

◎ SIGHTS

National Museum of Ireland – Decorative Arts & History   Museum

(Map p122; www.museum.ie; Benburb St; ◎10am-5pm Tue-Sat, 2-5pm Sun; ⊡25, 66, 67, 90 from city centre, ⊡Museum) **FREE** Once the world's largest military barracks, this splendid early neoclassical grey-stone building on the Liffey's northern banks was completed in 1704 according to the design of Thomas Burgh (he of Trinity College's Old Library). It is now home to the Decorative Arts & History collection of the National Museum of Ireland, with a range of superb permanent exhibits ranging from a history of the Easter Rising to the work of iconic Irish designer Eileen Gray (1878-1976).

Chester Beatty Library   Museum

(Map p126; ☎01-407 0750; www.cbl.ie; Dublin Castle; ◎10am-5pm Mon-Fri, 11am-5pm Sat, 1-5pm Sun year-round, closed Mon Nov-Feb, free tours 1pm Wed, 2pm Sat & 3pm Sun; ⊡all city centre) **FREE** This world-famous library, in the grounds of Dublin Castle (p121), houses the collection of mining engineer Sir Alfred Chester Beatty (1875–1968), bequeathed to the Irish State on his death. Spread over two floors, the breathtaking collection includes more than 20,000 manuscripts, rare books, miniature paintings, clay tablets, costumes and other objects of artistic, historical and aesthetic importance.

Dublin City Gallery – Hugh Lane   Gallery

(Map p122; ☎01-222 5550; www.hughlane.ie; 22 N Parnell Sq; ◎9.45am-6pm Tue-Thu, to 5pm Fri & Sat, 11am-5pm Sun; ⊡7, 11, 13, 16, 38, 40, 46A, 123 from city centre) **FREE** Whatever reputation Dublin has as a repository of world-class art has a lot to do with the simply stunning collection at this exquisite gallery, housed in the equally impressive Charlemont House, designed by William Chambers in 1763. Within its walls you'll find the best of contemporary Irish art, a handful of impressionist classics and the relocated Francis Bacon's studio.

> *splendid early neoclassical grey-stone building*

National Museum of Ireland – Decorative Arts & History

CARSO80/SHUTTERSTOCK ©

General Post Office Historic Building

(Map p122; ☑️01-705 7000; www.anpost.ie; Lower O'Connell St; ⏰8am-8pm Mon-Sat; 🚇all city centre, 🚋Abbey) It's not just the country's main post office, or an eye-catching neoclassical building: the General Post Office is at the heart of Ireland's struggle for independence. The GPO served as command HQ for the rebels during the Easter Rising of 1916 and as a result has become the focal point for all kinds of protests, parades and remembrances, and is home to an interactive visitor centre.

Dublin Castle Historic Building

(Map p126; ☑️01-677 7129; www.dublincastle. ie; Dame St; guided tours adult/child €10/4, self-guided tours adult/child €7/3; ⏰9.45am-5.45pm, last admission 5.15pm; 🚇all city centre) If you're looking for a turreted castle straight out of central casting you'll be disappointed: the stronghold of British power in Ireland for 700 years is principally an 18th-century creation that is more hotchpotch palace than medieval castle. Only the Record Tower, completed in 1258, survives from the original Anglo-Norman fortress commissioned by King John from 1204.

Glasnevin Cemetery Museum Museum

(www.glasnevintrust.ie; Finglas Rd; museum €4.50, museum & tour €10; ⏰10am-6pm Mon-Fri; 🚇40, 40A, 40B from Parnell St) The history of Glasnevin Cemetery is told in wonderful, award-winning detail in this museum, which relates the social and political story of Ireland through the lives of the people, known and unknown, buried here. The City of the Dead covers the burial practice and religious beliefs of the roughly 1½ million people whose final resting place this is, while the Milestone Gallery features a 10m-long digitally interactive timeline outlining the lives of the cemetery's most famous residents.

Christ Church Cathedral Church

(Church of the Holy Trinity; Map p126; www. christchurchcathedral.ie; Christ Church Pl; adult/student/child €6.50/4/2.50, with

Gaelic Games

Easily reachable from the city centre, **Experience Gaelic Games** (☑️01-254 4292; www.experiencegaelicgames.com; Saint Mobhi Rd; €25-35; ⏰Mon-Sat Mar-Oct, Fri & Sat Nov- Feb; 🚇4, 9 from O'Connell St) is the only place in Dublin to encounter the unique trio of Gaelic contests: hurling, Gaelic football and handball. The staff have an enormous passion for the sports, and their pride and delight at showing visitors is infectious. You can join one of the open sessions or groups of six or more can book a private session.

Hurleys and helmets
ANNEMARIE MCCARTHY/LONELY PLANET ©

Dublinia €14.50/12/7.50; ⏰9am-5pm Mon-Sat, 12.30-2.30pm Sun year-round, longer hours Mar-Oct; 🚇50, 50A, 56A from Aston Quay, 54, 54A from Burgh Quay) Its hilltop location and eye-catching flying buttresses make this the most photogenic of Dublin's cathedrals. It was founded in 1030 and rebuilt from 1172, mostly under the impetus of Richard de Clare, Earl of Pembroke (better known as Strongbow), the Anglo-Norman noble who invaded Ireland in 1170 and whose monument has pride of place inside.

Guided tours (⏰12.10pm, 2pm & 4pm Mon-Fri, 2pm, 3pm & 4pm Sat) include the belfry, where a campanologist explains the art of bell-ringing and you can even have a go.

Kilmainham Gaol Museum

(Map p122; ☑️01-453 2037; http://kilmainham gaolmuseum.ie; Inchicore Rd; adult/child €8/4; ⏰9.30am-6.45pm Jul & Aug, to 5.30pm rest

Central Dublin

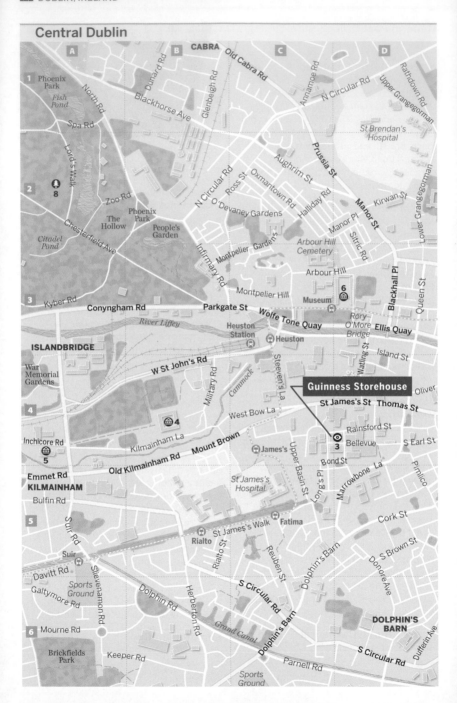

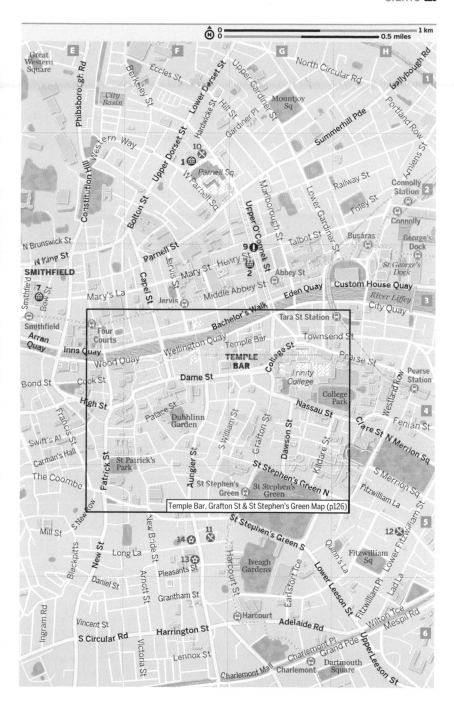

0 ___ 1 km
0 ___ 0.5 miles
N

E

F

G

H

1

Great Western Square

Phibsborough Rd

Eccles St

Berkeley St

Upper Gardiner St

North Circular Rd

Ballybough Rd

City Basin

Lower Dorset St

Hardwicke St

Hill St

Gardiner Pl

Mountjoy Sq

Summerhill Pde

Portland Row

Amiens St

2

Western Way

Upper Dorset St

Bolton St

10
1 🏛

Parnell Sq

W Parnell Sq

Upper O'Connell St

Marlborough St

Railway St

Connolly Station

Connolly

George's Dock

Constitution Hill

N Brunswick St

N King St

SMITHFIELD

Parnell St

Jervis St

Capel St

Mary St

Henry St

9 ℹ️
2 🏛

Abbey St

Lower Gardiner St

Talbot St

Foley St

Busáras

St George's Dock

3

Smithfield

Bow St

Mary's La

Jervis

Middle Abbey St

Eden Quay

Custom House Quay

River Liffey

City Quay

7

Four Courts

Bachelor's Walk

Tara St Station

Townsend St

Smithfield

Arran Quay

Inns Quay

Wood Quay

Wellington Quay

Temple Bar

TEMPLE BAR

College St

Pearse St

Pearse Station

4

Bond St

Cook St

High St

Dame St

Trinity College

College Park

Westland Row

N Merrion Sq

Francis St

Swift's Al

Carman's Hall

Palace St

Dubhlinn Garden

S William St

Grafton St

Dawson St

Nassau St

Clare St

Fenian St

The Coombe

Patrick St

S New Row

St Patrick's Park

Aungier St

St Stephen's Green

Kildare St

St Stephen's Green N

St Stephen's Green

S Merrion Sq

Fitzwilliam La

5

Mill St

New St

Blackpitts

Long La

New Bride St

14 ✪
11 ✗

St Stephen's Green S

Harcourt St

12 ✪

Quinn's La

Lower Fitzwilliam St

Fitzwilliam Sq

Lad La

Temple Bar, Grafton St & St Stephen's Green Map (p126)

13 ✪

Pleasants St

Iveagh Gardens

Earlsfort Tce

Lower Leeson St

Fitzwilliam Pl

Daniel St

Arnott St

Grantham St

Ingram Rd

Vincent St

S Circular Rd

Victoria St

Harrington St

Lennox St

Harcourt

Adelaide Rd

Charlemont Pl

Grand Pde

Charlemont Mall

Charlemont

Dartmouth Square

Mespil Rd

Wilton Tce

Upper Leeson St

6

Central Dublin

of year; 🚍69, 79 from Aston Quay, 13, 40 from
O'Connell St) If you have *any* desire to understand Irish history – especially the juicy
bits about resistance to British rule – then
a visit to this former prison is an absolute
must. This threatening grey building, built
between 1792 and 1795, played a role in
virtually every act of Ireland's painful path
to independence, and even today, despite
closing in 1924, it still has the power to chill.

St Stephen's Green   Park
(Map p126; ⊙dawn-dusk; 🚍all city centre,
🚋St Stephen's Green) As you watch the
assorted groups of friends, lovers and
individuals splaying themselves across
the nine elegantly landscaped hectares
of Dublin's most popular green lung, St
Stephen's Green, consider that those same
hectares once formed a common for public
whippings, burnings and hangings. These
days, the harshest treatment you'll get is
the warden chucking you off the grass for
playing football or Frisbee.

Molly Malone Statue   Statue
(Map p126; Suffolk St; 🚍all city centre) Dublin's most famous statue is that of fictional
fishmonger (and lady of dubious morals)
Molly Malone, she of the song alive, alive-o.
Pending the ongoing expansion of the Luas
tram system, she's been moved from the
bottom of Grafton St to Suffolk St, but that
doesn't halt the never-ending procession of
visitors looking for a selfie with her.

Ha'penny Bridge   Bridge
(Map p126; 🚍all city centre) The Ha'penny
Bridge – officially known as the Liffey

Bridge – was built in 1816 and remains
one of the world's oldest cast-iron bridges.
It was built to replace the seven ferries
that plied a busy route between the two
banks of the river and it gets its name from
the ha'penny toll that was charged until
1919 (for a time the toll was one and a
half pence, and so it was called the Penny
Ha'penny Bridge).

Old Jameson Distillery   Museum
(Map p122; www.jamesonwhiskey.com; Bow
St; adult/student/child €18/15/9, masterclasses
€55; ⊙10am-5pm Mon-Sat, 10.30am-5pm Sun;
🚍25, 66, 67, 90 from city centre, 🚋Smithfield)
Smithfield's biggest draw is devoted to
uisce beatha (ish-kuh ba-ha, 'the water of
life'); that's Irish for whiskey. The museum
(occupying part of the old distillery that
stopped production in 1971) shepherds
visitors through a compulsory tour of the
recreated factory (the tasting at the end
is a lot of fun) and into the inevitable gift
shop.

Phoenix Park   Park
(Map p122; www.phoenixpark.ie; ⊙24hr; 🚍10
from O'Connell St, 25 & 26 from Middle Abbey
St) FREE Measuring 709 glorious hectares,
Phoenix Park is one of the world's largest
city parks; you'll find MP3-rigged joggers,
grannies pushing buggies, ladies walking
poodles, gardens, lakes, a sporting oval,
and 300 deer. There are also cricket and
polo grounds, a motor-racing track and
some fine 18th-century residences, including those of the Irish president and the US
ambassador.

Irish Museum of
Modern Art — Museum
(IMMA; Map p122; www.imma.ie; Military
Rd; ⊗11.30am-5.30pm Tue-Fri, 10am-5.30pm
Sat, noon-5.30pm Sun, tours 1.15pm Wed &
2.30pm Sat & Sun; ⊡51, 51D, 51X, 69, 78, 79
from Aston Quay, ⊡Heuston) **FREE** Ireland's
most important collection of modern and
contemporary Irish and international art is
housed in the elegant, airy expanse of the
Royal Hospital Kilmainham, designed by Sir
William Robinson and built between 1684
and 1687 as a retirement home for soldiers.
It fulfilled this role until 1928, after which it
languished for nearly 50 years until a 1980s
restoration saw it come back to life as this
wonderful repository of art.

Little Museum of Dublin — Museum
(Map p126; ☑01-661 1000; www.littlemuseum.
ie; 15 St Stephen's Green N; adult/student €8/6;
⊗9.30am-5pm Mon-Wed & Fri, to 8pm Thu; ⊡all
city centre, ⊡St Stephen's Green) The idea
is ingeniously simple: a museum, spread
across two rooms of an elegant Georgian
building, devoted to the history of Dublin in
the 20th century, made up of memorabilia
contributed by the general public. Visits are
by guided tour and everyone is presented
with a handsome booklet on the history of
the city.

⊕ TOURS
Dublin Literary Pub Crawl — Walking
(Map p126; ☑01-670 5602; www.dublinpub
crawl.com; 9 Duke St; adult/student €13/11;
⊗7.30pm daily Apr-Oct, 7.30pm Thu-Sun Nov-
Mar; ⊡all city centre) A tour of pubs associated with famous Dublin writers is a sure-fire
recipe for success, and this 2½-hour
tour-performance by two actors is a riotous
laugh. There's plenty of drink taken, which
makes it all the more popular. It leaves from
the Duke on Duke St; get there by 7pm to
reserve a spot for the evening tour.

1916 Rebellion
Walking Tour — Walking
(Map p126; ☑086 858 3847; www.1916rising.
com; 23 Wicklow St; €13; ⊗11.30am Mon-Sat,

1pm Sun Mar-Oct; ⊡all city centre) Superb two-
hour tour starting in the International Bar
on Wicklow St. Lots of information, humour
and irreverence to boot. The guides – all
Trinity graduates – are uniformly excellent
and will not say no to the offer of a pint
back in the International at tour's end. The
also have a tour based around Michael
Collins, hero of the War of Independence.

⊕ SHOPPING
Ulysses Rare Books — Books
(Map p126; ☑01-671 8676; www.rarebooks.
ie, 10 Duke St; ⊗9.30am-5.45pm Mon-Sat; ⊡all
city centre) Our favourite bookshop in the
city stocks a rich and remarkable collection
of Irish-interest books, with a particular
emphasis on 20th-century literature and
a large selection of first editions, including
rare ones by the big guns: Joyce, Yeats,
Beckett and Wilde.

George's Street Arcade — Market
(Map p126; www.georgesstreetarcade.ie; btwn
S Great George's & Drury Sts; ⊗9am-6.30pm
Mon-Wed, to 7pm Thu-Sat, noon-6pm Sun; ⊡all
city centre) Dublin's best nonfood market is
sheltered within an elegant Victorian Gothic
arcade. Apart from shops and stalls selling
new and old clothes, secondhand books,
hats, posters, jewellery and records, there's
a fortune teller, some gourmet nibbles, and
a fish and chipper that does a roaring trade.

Avoca Handweavers — Arts & Crafts
(Map p126; ☑01-677 4215; www.avoca.ie; 11-13
Suffolk St; ⊗9.30am-6pm Mon-Wed & Sat, to 7pm
Thu & Fri, 11am-6pm Sun; ⊡all city centre) Combining clothing, homewares, a basement
food hall and an excellent top-floor cafe,
Avoca promotes a stylish but homey brand
of modern Irish life – and is one of the best
places to find an original present. Many of
the garments are woven, knitted and naturally dyed at its Wicklow factory. There's a
terrific kids' section.

Powerscourt Townhouse
Shopping Centre — Shopping Centre
(Map p126; ☑01-679 4144; 59 S William
St; ⊗10am-6pm Mon-Wed & Fri, to 8pm Thu,

Temple Bar, Grafton St & St Stephen's Green

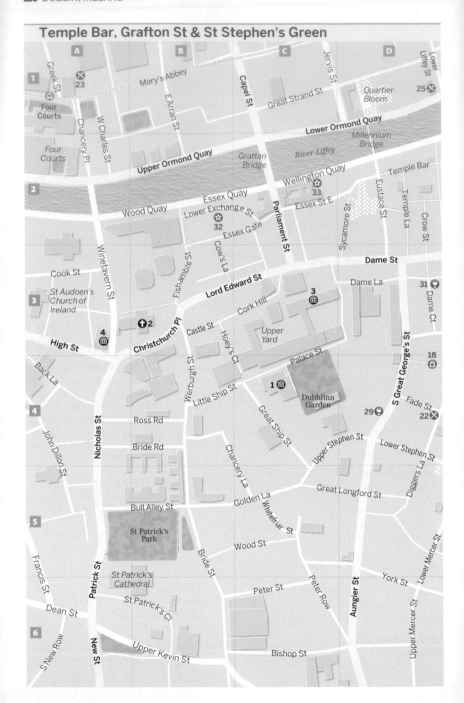

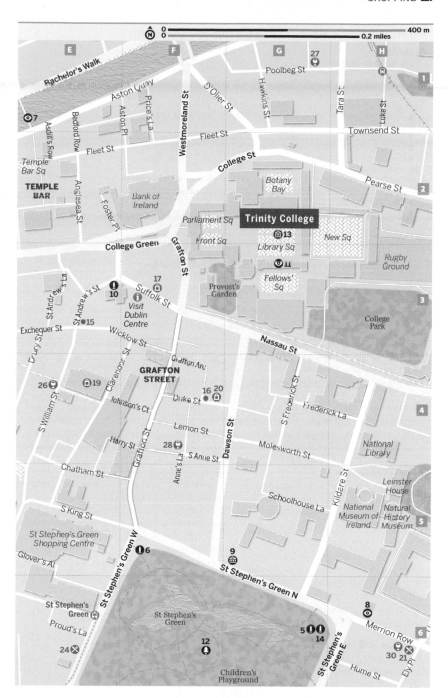

Temple Bar, Grafton St & St Stephen's Green

9am-6pm Sat, noon-6pm Sun; 🚇all city centre)
This absolutely gorgeous and stylish centre
is in a carefully refurbished Georgian
townhouse, built between 1741 and 1744.
These days it's best known for its cafes
and restaurants, but it also does a top-end,
selective trade in high fashion, art, exquisite
handicrafts and other chichi sundries.

❌ EATING

K Chido Mexico   Mexican €
(Map p126; www.kchidomexico.com; 18 Chan-
cery St; tacos €8; ⊙8am-5pm Mon-Fri, 11am-6pm
Sat & Sun; 🚇Four Courts) If you've a craving
for authentic Mexican food, try this food
truck tucked inside a garage. It's a huge
hit with nearby office workers, and seats
can be tough to find weekday lunchtimes,
but for early risers, the breakfast burrito
is great fuel for your sightseeing. The best
Mexican food in the city, no contest.

1837 Bar & Brasserie   Brasserie €
(Map p122; ☎01-471 4602; www.guinness-
storehouse.com; Guinness Storehouse, St

James's Gate; mains €9-14; ⊙noon-3pm; 🚌21A,
51B, 78, 78A, 123 from Fleet St, 🚇James's) This
lunchtime brasserie serves up tasty dishes
from really fresh oysters to an insanely
good Guinness burger, with skin-on fries
and red onion chutney. The drinks menu
features a range of Guinness variants like
West Indian porter and Golden Ale. Highly
recommended for lunch if you're visiting
the museum.

Gerry's   Cafe €
(Map p122; 6 Montague St; Irish fry €6.50;
⊙8am-2pm Mon-Fri, to 2.30pm Sat; 🚌14, 15, 65,
83) A no-nonsense, old-school 'caff' (the
British Isles' equivalent of the greasy-
spoon) is rarer than hen's teeth in the city
centre these days, which makes Gerry's
something of a treasure. You won't find a
more authentic spot to enjoy a traditional
Irish fry-up – and if you want healthy, it
always does porridge, but what's the point?

Etto   Italian €€
(Map p126; ☎01-678 8872; www.etto.ie; 18
Merrion Row; mains €18-23; ⊙noon-10pm
Mon-Fri, 12.30-10pm Sat; 🚇all city centre)

Award-winning restaurant and wine bar that does contemporary versions of classic Italian cuisine. All the ingredients are fresh, the presentation is exquisite and the service is just right. Portions are small, but the food is so rich you won't leave hungry. The only downside is the relatively quick turnover; lingering over the excellent wine would be nice. Book ahead.

Fade Street Social   Modern Irish €€
(Map p126; ☑01 604 0066; www.fadestreetso cial.com; 4–6 Fade St; mains €18-32, tapas €5-12; ☺12.30-10.30pm Mon-Fri, 5-10.30pm Sat & Sun; ☜; ☐all city centre) ✈ Two eateries in one, courtesy of renowned chef Dylan McGrath: at the front, the buzzy tapas bar, which serves up gourmet bites from a beautiful open kitchen. At the back, the more muted restaurant specialises in Irish cuts of meat – from veal to rabbit – served with home-grown, organic vegetables. There's a bar upstairs too. Reservations suggested.

Winding Stair   Modern Irish €€
(Map p126; ☑01-873 7320; www.winding-stair. com; 40 Lower Ormond Quay; 2-course lunch €21.95, mains €22-28; ☺noon-5pm & 5.30–10.30pm; ☐all city centre) In a beautiful Georgian building that once housed the city's most beloved bookshop (the ground floor still is one), the Winding Stair's conversion to elegant restaurant has been faultless. The wonderful Irish menu – creamy fish pie, bacon and organic cabbage, steamed mussels, and Irish farmyard cheeses – coupled with an excellent wine list makes for a memorable meal.

Chapter One   Modern Irish €€€
(Map p122; ☑01-873 2266; www.chapterone restaurant.com; 18 N Parnell Sq; 2-course lunch €32.50, 4-course dinner €75; ☺12.30-2pm Tue-Fri, 7.30-10.30pm Tue-Sat; ☐3, 10, 11, 13, 16, 19, 22 from city centre) Flawless haute cuisine and a relaxed, welcoming atmosphere make this Michelin-starred restaurant in the basement of the Dublin Writers Museum our choice for best dinner experience in town. The food is French-inspired contemporary Irish, the menus change regularly

and the service is top-notch. The three-course pretheatre menu (€39.50) is great.

L'Ecrivain   French €€€
(Map p122; ☑01-661 1919; www.lecrivain.com; 109a Lower Baggot St; 3-course lunch menus €45, 8-course tasting menus €90, mains €45; ☺12.30-2pm Wed-Fri, 6.30-10pm Mon-Sat; ☐38, 39 from city centre) Head chef Derry Clarke is considered a gourmet god for the exquisite simplicity of his creations, which put the emphasis on flavour and the best local ingredients – all given the French once over and turned into something that approaches divine dining. The Michelin people like it too and awarded it one of their stars.

Shanahan's on the Green   Steak €€€
(Map p126; ☑01-407 0939; www.shanahans. ie; 119 St Stephen's Green W; mains €42-49; ☺6-10pm Sat-Thu, noon-10pm Fri; ☐all city centre, ☐St Stephen's Green) You could order seafood or a plate of vegetables, but you'd be missing the point of this supremely elegant steakhouse: the finest cuts of juicy and tender Irish Angus beef you'll find anywhere. The ambience is upmarket Americana – the bar downstairs is called the Oval Office and pride of place goes to a rocking chair once owned by JFK.

🍷 DRINKING & NIGHTLIFE
John Mulligan's   Pub
(Map p126; www.mulligans.ie; 8 Poolbeg St; ☺10.30am-11.30pm Mon-Thu, to 12.30am Fri & Sat, noon-11pm Sun; ☐all city centre) This brilliant old boozer is a cultural institution. Established in 1782 and in this location since 1854, a drink (or more) here is like attending liquid services at a most sacred, secular shrine. John F Kennedy paid his respects in 1945, where he joined a cast of regulars that seems barely to have changed since.

Long Hall   Pub
(Map p126; 51 S Great George's St; ☺10.30am-11.30pm Mon-Thu, to 12.30am Fri & Sat, noon-11pm Sun; ☐all city centre) A Victorian

Live Music

The best place to hear traditional music is in the pub, where the 'session' – improvised or scheduled – is still best attended by foreign visitors who appreciate the form far more than most Dubs and will relish any opportunity to drink and toe-tap to some extraordinary virtuoso performances.

Whelan's (Map p122; ☎01-478 0766; www.whelanslive.com; 25 Wexford St; ☒16, 122 from city centre) Perhaps the city's most beloved live-music venue is this midsized room attached to a tradition-al bar. This is the singer-songwriter's spiritual home: when they're done pouring out the contents of their hearts on stage, you can find them filling up in the bar along with their fans.

O'Donoghue's (Map p126; www. odonoghues.ie; 15 Merrion Row; ☺10.30am-11.30pm Mon-Thu, to 12.30am Fri & Sat, noon-11pm Sun; ☒all city centre) The pub where traditional music stalwarts The Dubliners made their name in the 1960s still hosts live music nightly, but the crowds would gather anyway – for the excellent pints and superb ambience in the old bar or the covered coach yard next to it.

classic that is one of the city's most beau-tiful and best-loved pubs. Check out the ornate carvings in the woodwork behind the bar and the elegant chandeliers. The bartenders are experts at their craft, an

increasingly rare attribute in Dublin these days.

Grogan's Castle Lounge   Pub
(Map p126; www.groganspub.ie; 15 S William St; ☺10.30am-11.30pm Mon-Thu, to 12.30am Fri & Sat, 12.30-11pm Sun; ☒all city centre) This place, known simply as Grogan's (after the original owner), is a city-centre institu-tion. It has long been a favourite haunt of Dublin's writers and painters, as well as others from the alternative bohemian set, who enjoy a fine Guinness while they wait for that inevitable moment when they're discovered.

Kehoe's   Pub
(Map p126; 9 S Anne St; ☺10.30am-11.30pm Mon-Thu, to 12.30am Fri & Sat, noon-11pm Sun; ☒all city centre) This classic bar is the very exemplar of a traditional Dublin pub. The beautiful Victorian bar, wonderful snug, and side room have been popular for Dubliners and visitors for generations, so much so that the publican's living quarters upstairs have since been converted into an exten-sion – simply by taking out the furniture and adding a bar.

John Kavanagh's   Pub
(Gravediggers; ☎01-830 7978; 1 Prospect Sq; ☒13, 19, 19A from O'Connell St) The gravedig-gers from the adjacent **Glasnevin Ceme-tery** (Prospect Cemetery; www.glasnevintrust.ie; Finglas Rd; tours €10; ☺10am-5pm, tours hourly 10.30am-3.30pm; ☒40, 40A, 40B from Parnell St) **FREE** had a secret serving hatch so that they could drink on the job – hence the pub's nickname. Founded in 1833 by one John Kavanagh and still in the family, this pub is one of the best in Ireland, virtually unchanged in 150 years.

Stag's Head   Pub
(Map p126; www.louisfitzgerald.com/stags head; 1 Dame Ct; ☺10.30am-1am Mon-Sat, to midnight Sun; ☒all city centre) The Stag's Head was built in 1770, remodelled in 1895 and has thankfully not changed a bit since then. It's a superb pub: so picturesque that it often appears in films, and also featured

Smock Alley Theatre

in a postage-stamp series on Irish bars. A bloody great pub, no doubt.

⭐ ENTERTAINMENT

Devitt's
Live Music

(Map p122; ☎01-475 3414; www.devittspub.ie; 78 Lower Camden St; ⏰from 9pm Thu–Sat; 🚌14, 15, 65, 83) Devitt's – aka the Cusack Stand – is one of the favourite places for the city's talented musicians to display their wares, with sessions as good as any you'll hear in the city centre. Highly recommended.

Smock Alley Theatre
Theatre

(Map p126; ☎01-677 0014; www.smockalley. com; 6-7 Exchange St) One of the city's most diverse theatres is hidden in this beautifully restored 17th-century building. It boasts a diverse program of events (expect anything from opera to murder mystery nights, puppet shows and Shakespeare) and many events also come with a dinner option.

The theatre was built in 1622 and was the only Theatre Royal to ever be built outside London. It's been reinvented as a warehouse and a Catholic church and

was lovingly restored in 2012 to become a creative hub once again.

Workman's Club
Live Music

(Map p126; ☎01-670 6692; www.theworkmans club.com; 10 Wellington Quay, free-€20; ⏰5pm-3am; 🚌all city centre) A 300-capacity venue and bar in the former workingmen's club of Dublin, the emphasis here is on keeping away from the mainstream, which means everything from singer-songwriters to electronic cabaret. When the live music at the Workman's Club is over, DJs take to the stage, playing rockabilly, hip hop, indie, house and more.

Bord Gáis Energy Theatre
Theatre

(☎01-677 7999; www.grandcanaltheatre.ie; Grand Canal Sq; 🚉Grand Canal Dock) Forget the uninviting sponsored name: Daniel Libeskind's masterful design is a three-tiered, 2100-capacity auditorium where you're as likely to be entertained by the Bolshoi or a touring state opera as you are to see *Disney on Ice* or Barbra Streisand. It's a magnificent venue – designed for classical, paid for by the classics.

Dublinbikes

INFORMATION

Visit Dublin Centre (Map p126; www.
visitdublin.com; 25 Suffolk St; ⊙9am-5.30pm
Mon-Sat, 10.30am-3pm Sun; all city centre) The
main tourist information centre, with free maps,
guides and itinerary planning, plus booking
services for accommodation, attractions and
events.

GETTING THERE & AWAY

Ireland's capital and biggest city is the most
important point of entry and departure for the
country – almost all airlines fly in and out of
Dublin Airport (📞01-814 1111; www.dublinair
port.com). The city has two ferry ports: the **Dun
Laoghaire ferry terminal** (📞01-280 1905; Dun
Laoghaire; 🚌7A or 8 from Burgh Quay, 46A from
Trinity College, 🚉Dun Laoghaire) and the **Dublin**

Port terminal (📞01-855 2222; Alexandra Rd;
🚌53 from Talbot St).

GETTING AROUND

Bus Useful for getting to the west side of the city
and the suburbs.

Bicycle The city's rent-and-ride Dublinbikes
scheme is the ideal way to cover ground quickly.

DART Suburban rail network that runs along the
eastern edge of the city along Dublin Bay.

Luas A two-line light-rail transport system that
links the city centre with southern suburbs.

Taxi Easily recognised by light-green-and-blue
'Taxi' sign on door; can be hailed or picked up at
ranks in the city centre.

Walking Dublin's city centre is compact, flat and
eminently walkable – it's less than 2km from one
end of the city centre to the other.

Where to Stay

Like most cities, the closer to the city centre you want to stay, the more you'll pay – and the room sizes get smaller accordingly. Prices soar during summer and festivals; be sure to book in advance.

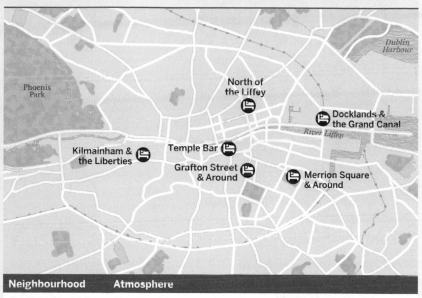

Neighbourhood	Atmosphere
Grafton Street & Around	Close to sights, nightlife and pretty much everything; a good choice of midrange and top-end hotels; generally more expensive than elsewhere; not always good value for money and rooms tend to be smaller
Merrion Square & Around	Lovely neighbourhood, elegant hotels and townhouse accommodation; some of the best restaurants in town are also in the area; not a lot of choice; virtually no budget accommodation; relatively quiet after dark
Temple Bar	In the heart of the action; close to everything, especially the party; noisy and touristy; not especially good value for money; rooms are very small and often less than pristine
Kilmainham & the Liberties	Close to the old city and the sights of west Dublin; no recommended accommodation; only a small selection of restaurants
North of the Liffey	Good range of choices; within walking distance of sights and nightlife; budget accommodation not always good quality; some locations not especially comfortable after dark
Docklands & the Grand Canal	Excellent contemporary hotels with good service, including some top-end choices; isolated in neighbourhood that doesn't have a lot of life after dark; reliant on taxis or public transport to get to city centre

SCANDINAVIA & NORTHERN EUROPE

In This Chapter

Copenhagen, Denmark

Copenhagen is not only the coolest kid on the Nordic block, but it also gets constantly ranked as the happiest city in the world. Ask a dozen locals why and they would probably all zone in on the hygge, which generally means cosiness but encompasses far more. It is this laid-back contentment that helps give the Danish capital the X factor. The backdrop is pretty cool as well: its cobbled, bike-friendly streets are an enticing concoction of sherbet-hued town houses, craft studios and candlelit cafes. Add to this its compact size and it is possibly Europe's most seamless urban experience.

Two Days in Copenhagen

Get your bearings with a canal and harbour tour, wander **Nyhavn** (p142) then seek out a classic smørrebrød (Danish open sandwich), washed down with bracing akvavit (alcoholic spirit, commonly made with potatoes and spiced with caraway). Stroll through the Latin Quarter and the **Nationalmuseet** (p142) and while away the evening at **Tivoli Gardens** (p138).

On day two, walk in royal footsteps at **Rosenborg Slot** (p143) and **Kongens Have** (p143). Lunch at **Designmuseum Danmark** (p140) before exploring its extensive collection. Splurge on New Nordic cuisine at **Geranium** (p150).

Four Days in Copenhagen

If you have a third day, take a trip to **Louisiana** (p148), an easy train ride north of central Copenhagen. Back in the city, dine in Vesterbro's hip Kødbyen (the 'Meatpacking District'), an industrial area turned buzzing hub.

On day four, explore **Statens Museum for Kunst** (p143) and delve into **Torvehallerne KBH** (p148), the city's celebrated food market, and spend the afternoon exploring **Christiania** (p151).

Next up is Berlin (p486), a 7½-hour bus ride away.

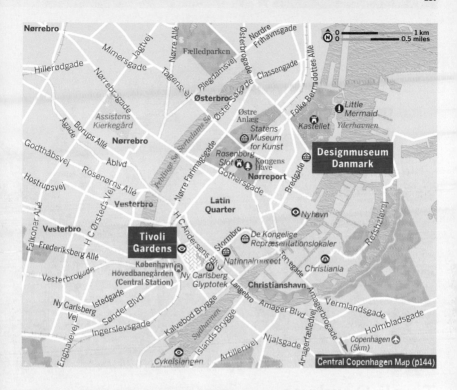

Central Copenhagen Map (p144)

Arriving in Copenhagen

Copenhagen Airport is Scandinavia's busiest hub, with direct flights to cities in Europe, North America and Asia, as well as a handful of Danish cities. Located in Kastrup, 9km southeast of Copenhagen's city centre, it has good eating, retail and information facilities.

All long-distance trains arrive at and depart from **Københavns Hovedbanegård** (Central Station), a 19th-century, wooden-beamed hall with numerous facilities, including currency exchange, a post office, left-luggage facilities and food outlets.

Where to Stay

Copenhagen's accommodation options range from higher-end Danish design establishments to excellent budget hotels and hostels, which are mainly centred on the western side of the Central Station. It's a good idea to reserve rooms in advance, especially hostels, during the busy summer season.

The **Copenhagen Visitors Centre** (p153) can book rooms in private homes. Depending on availability, it also books unfilled hotel rooms at discounted rates.

Tivoli Gardens during Christmas

MARMAGNUM/GETTY IMAGES ©

Tivoli Gardens

The country's top-ranking tourist draw, tasteful Tivoli Gardens has been eliciting gleeful shrills since 1843. Whatever your idea of fun – hair-raising rides, twinkling pavilions, open-air stage shows or al fresco pantomime and beer – this old-timer has you covered.

Great For...

☑ Don't Miss

The city views – taken at 70km/h – from the Star Flyer, one of the world's tallest carousels.

Roller Coasters

The Rutschebanen is the best loved of Tivoli's roller coasters, rollicking its way through and around a faux 'mountain' and reaching speeds of 60km/h. Built in 1914 it claims to be the world's oldest operating wooden roller coaster. If you're after something a little more hardcore, the Dæmonen (Demon) is a 21st-century beast with faster speeds and a trio of hair-raising loops.

The Grounds

Beyond the carousels and side stalls is a Tivoli of landscaped gardens, tranquil nooks and eclectic architecture. Lower the adrenaline under beautiful old chestnut and elm trees, and amble around Tivoli Lake. Formed out of the old city moat, the lake is a top spot to snap pictures of Tivoli's commanding Chinese Tower, built in 1900.

❶ Need to Know

www.tivoli.dk; Vesterbrogade 3, Vesterbro; adult/child under 8yr Mon-Thu Dkr110/free, Fri-Sun Dkr120/free; ☉11am-11pm Sun-Thu, to midnight Fri & Sat Apr-Sep, reduced hours rest of year; 🛉; ₪2A, 5A, 9A, 12, 26, 250S, 350S, 🚆S-train København H

✖ Take a Break

Jolly **Grøften** (📞33 75 06 75; www.groef ten.dk; smørrebrød Dkr69-135, mains Dkr145-385; ☉noon-10pm daily Apr-Sep, reduced hours rest of year; 🛜) is a local institution.

★ Top Tip

Amusement rides cost Dkr25 to Dkr75; consider purchasing a multi-ride ticket for Dkr220.

Illuminations & Fireworks

Throughout the summer season, Tivoli Lake wows the crowds with its nightly laser and water spectacular. The Saturday evening fireworks are a summer season must, repeated again from December 26 to 30 for Tivoli's annual Fireworks Festival.

Live Performances

The indoor **Tivolis Koncertsal** (Concert Hall) hosts mainly classical music, with the odd musical and big-name pop or rock act. All tickets are sold at the **Tivoli Billetcenter** (📞33 15 10 12; ☉10am-8pm Mon-Fri, 11am-5pm Sat & Sun) or online through the Tivoli website.

Pantomime Theatre

Each night during the summer this criminally charming theatre presents silent plays in the tradition of Italy's Commedia dell'Arte. Many of the performers also work at the esteemed Royal Ballet.

When to Go

After dusk Tivoli is at its most enchanting when the park's fairy lights and lanterns are switched on.

Friday evenings From early April to mid-September, the open-air Plænen stage hosts free rock concerts from 10pm – go early if it's a big-name act.

Halloween Tivoli opens for around three weeks. See the website for details.

Christmas From mid-November to early January, Tivoli hosts a large **market**. Entertainment includes costumed staff and theatre shows. Fewer rides are operational but the *gløgg* (mulled wine) and *æbleskiver* (small doughnuts) are ample compensation.

PERNILLE KLEMP/DESIGNMUSEUM DANMARK ©

Designmuseum Danmark

Don't know your Egg from your Swan? What about your PH4 from your PH5? For a crash course in Denmark's incredible design heritage, make an elegant beeline for Designmuseum Danmark.

Housed in a converted 18th-century hospital, the museum is a must for fans of the applied arts and industrial design. Its booty includes Danish silver and porcelain, textiles and the iconic design pieces of modern innovators such as Kaare Klint, Poul Henningsen, Arne Jacobsen and Verner Panton.

20th-Century Crafts & Design

The museum's main permanent exhibition explores 20th-century industrial design and crafts in the context of social, economic, technological and theoretical changes. The collection displays celebrated furniture and applied arts from both Denmark and abroad.

Great For...

☑ **Don't Miss**

The vintage poster collection, including the iconic 1959 'Wonderful Copenhagen' poster.

PERNILLE KLEMP/DESIGNMUSEUM DANMARKS ©

Designmuseum
Danmark

Øster Voldgade
Kongens
Have
Kronprinsessegade
Store Kongensgade
Bredgade
Amaliegade
Yderhavnen
Gothersgade
Holmen
Kongens
Nytorv Ⓜ

❶ Need to Know

www.designmuseum.dk; Bredgade 68,
Østerport; adult/child Dkr100/free; ⏱11am-
5pm Tue & Thu-Sun, to 9pm Wed; 🚌1A, 15,
Ⓜ Kongens Nytorv

✕ Take a Break

The museum's Klint Cafe, located just
off the lobby, serves Danish classics and
has a fine outdoor courtyard.

★ Top Tip

The museum shop is one of the city's
best places to pick up savvy gifts and
easy-to-carry souvenirs.

Fashion & Fabric

This permanent exhibition showcases
around 350 objects from the museum's
rich textile and fashion collections. Spanning four centuries, the collection's treasures include French and Italian silks, ikat
and batik weaving, and two extraordinary
mid-20th-century tapestries based on
cartoons by Henri Matisse. As would you
expect, Danish textiles and fashion feature
prominently, including Danish *hedebo* em-
broidery from the 18th to 20th centuries,
and Erik Mortensen's collection of haute
couture frocks from French fashion houses
Balmain and Jean-Louis Scherrer.

The Danish Chair

An ode to the humble chair and an exploration of what goes into making a 'good'
one, this permanent exhibition displays
more than 100 beautifully designed chairs,
including some international guests. Standing room only.

Porcelain

This detailed exhibition celebrates European porcelain and its journey from initial
attempts through to the current day.

Danish Design Now

Showcasing contemporary fashion,
furniture and products, this captivating
exhibition focuses on 21st-century Danish
design and innovation.

⊙ SIGHTS

One of the great things about Copenhagen is its size. Virtually all of Copenhagen's major sightseeing attractions are in or close to the medieval city centre. Only the perennially disappointing **Little Mermaid** (Den Lille Havfrue; Langelinie, Østerport; 🚌1A, ⚓Nordre Toldbod) lies outside of the city proper, on the harbourfront.

Nyhavn   Canal

There are few nicer places to be on a sunny day than sitting at the outdoor tables of a cafe on the quayside of the Nyhavn canal. The canal was built to connect Kongens Nytorv to the harbour and was long a haunt for sailors and writers, including Hans Christian Andersen, who lived there for most of his life at, variously, numbers 20, 18 and 67.

Nationalmuseet   Museum

(National Museum; www.natmus.dk; Ny Vester-gade 10, Slotsholmen; adult/child Dkr75/60; ⊙10am-5pm Tue-Sun; 🚼; 🚌1A, 2A, 11A, 33, 40, 66, 🚈S-train København H) For a crash course

in Danish history and culture, spend an afternoon at Denmark's National Museum. It has first claims on virtually every antiquity uncovered on Danish soil, including Stone Age tools, Viking weaponry, rune stones and medieval jewellery. Among the many highlights is a finely crafted 3500-year-old Sun Chariot, as well as bronze *lurs* (horns), some of which date back 3000 years and are still capable of blowing a tune.

Ny Carlsberg Glyptotek   Museum

(www.glyptoteket.dk; Dantes Plads 7, Vesterbro, HC Andersens Blvd; adult/child Dkr95/free, Tue free; ⊙11am-6pm Tue-Sun, until 10pm Thu; 🚌1A, 2A, 11A, 33, 40, 66, 🚈S-train København H) Fin de siècle architecture dallies with an eclectic mix of art at Ny Carlsberg Glyptotek. The collection is divided into two parts: Northern Europe's largest trove of antiquities and an elegant collection of 19th-century Danish and French art. The latter includes the largest collection of Rodin sculptures outside of France and no fewer than 47 Gauguin paintings. These are displayed along with works by greats like Cézanne, Van Gogh, Pissarro, Monet and Renoir.

Nyhavn

FRANK FISCHBACH/500PX ©

An added treat for visitors is the August/September Summer Concert Series (admission around Dkr75). Classical music is performed in the museum's concert hall, which is evocatively lined by life-size statues of Roman patricians.

De Kongelige Repræsentationslokaler
Historic Building

(Royal Reception Rooms at Christiansborg Slot; www.christiansborg.dk; Slotsholmen, Christianshavn; adult/child Dkr90/45; ⊙10am-5pm May-Sep, closed Mon Oct-Apr, guided tours in Danish/English 11am/3pm; 🚌1A, 2A, 9A, 11A, 26, 40, 66) The grandest part of Christiansborg Slot is De Kongelige Repræsentationslokaler, an ornate Renaissance hall where the queen holds royal banquets and entertains heads of state. Don't miss the beautifully sewn and colourful wall tapestries depicting Danish history from Viking times to today. Created by tapestry designer Bjørn Nørgaard over a decade, the works were completed in 2000. Look for the Adam and Eve–style representation of the queen and her husband (albeit clothed) in a Danish Garden of Eden.

Rosenborg Slot
Castle

(www.kongernessamling.dk/en/rosenborg; Øster Voldgade 4A, Nørreport; adult/child Dkr105/free, incl Amalienborg Slot Dkr145/free; ⊙10am-5pm Jun-Aug, to 4pm May, Sep & Oct, reduced hours rest of year; 🚌6A, 11A, 42, 150S, 173E, 184, 185, 350S, Ⓜ Nørreport) A 'once-upon-a-time' combo of turrets, gables and moat, the early-17th-century Rosenborg Slot was built in Dutch Renaissance style between 1606 and 1633 by King Christian IV to serve as his summer home. Today, the castle's 24 upper rooms are chronologically arranged, housing the furnishings and portraits of each monarch from Christian IV to Frederik VII. The pièce de résistance is the basement Treasury, home to the dazzling crown jewels.

Statens Museum for Kunst
Museum

(www.smk.dk; Sølvgade 48-50, Østerport; adult/child Dkk110/free; ⊙11am-5pm Tue & Thu-Sun, to 8pm Wed; 🚌6A, 26, 42, 173E, 184, 185) FREE Denmark's National Gallery straddles two contrasting, interconnected buildings: a

 Changing of the Guard

The Royal Life Guard is charged with protecting the Danish royal family and their city residence, Amalienborg Palace. Every day of the year, these soldiers march from their barracks through the streets of Copenhagen to perform the **Changing of the Guard** (www.kongehuset.dk/en/changing-of-the-guard-at-amalienborg; Amalienborg Slotsplads; ⊙noon daily; 🚌1A) FREE. Clad in 19th-century tunics and bearskin helmets, their performance of intricate manoeuvres is an impressive sight. If Queen Margrethe is in residence, the ceremony is even more grandiose, with the addition of a full marching band.

If you miss out on the noon ceremony, a smaller-scale shift change is performed every two hours thereafter.

BIRUTE VIJEIKIENE/SHUTTERSTOCK ©

late-19th-century 'palazzo' and a sharply minimalist extension. The museum houses medieval and Renaissance works and impressive collections of Dutch and Flemish artists including Rubens, Breughel and Rembrandt. It claims the world's finest collection of 19th-century Danish 'Golden Age' artists, among them Eckersberg and Hammershøi, foreign greats like Matisse and Picasso, and modern Danish heavyweights including Per Kirkeby.

Kongens Have
Park

(King's Gardens; http://parkmuseerne.dk/kongens-have/; Øster Voldgade, Nørreport; ⊙8.30am-6pm; 🚌6A, 11A, 42, 150S, 173E, 184, 185, 350S, Ⓜ Nørreport) FREE The oldest park in Copenhagen was laid out in the early

Central Copenhagen (København)

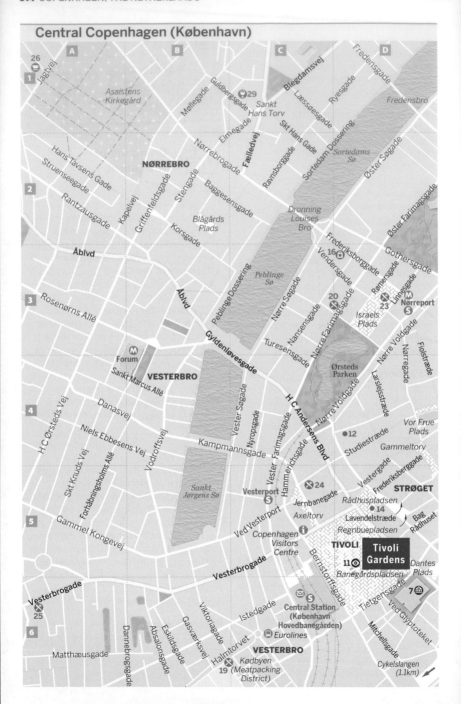

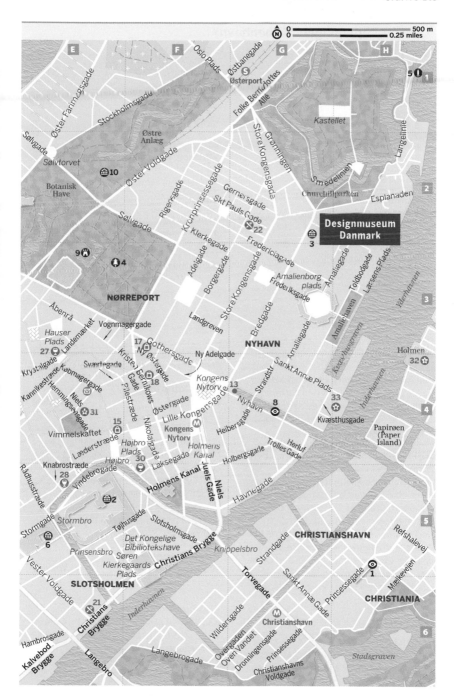

Central Copenhagen (København)

17th century by Christian IV, who used it as his vegetable patch. These days it has a little more to offer, including immaculate flower beds, romantic garden paths and a marionette theatre with free performances during the summer season (2pm and 3pm Tuesday to Sunday).

Superkilen   Park

(Nørrebrogade 210; ☐5A, 66, ⑤Nørrebro) This fascinating one-kilometre-long park showcases objects sourced from around the globe with the aim of celebrating diversity and uniting the community. Items include a tiled fountain from Morocco, bollards from Ghana and swing chairs from Baghdad, as well as neon signs from Russia and China. Even the benches, manhole covers and rubbish bins hail from foreign lands.

TOURS

You can't visit Copenhagen and *not* take a canal boat trip. Not only is it a fantastic way to see the city, but you also see a side of it that landlubbers never see. Be aware that in most boats you are totally exposed to the elements (even during summer).

Bike Copenhagen
with Mike   Cycling

(☑26 39 56 88; www.bikecopenhagenwithmike. dk; Sankt Peders Stræde 47, Strøget; per person Dkr299) If you don't fancy walking, Bike Mike runs three-hour cycling tours of the city, departing Sankt Peders Stræde 47 in the city centre, just east of Ørstedsparken (which is southwest of Nørreport station). Mike is a great character and will really give you the insider's scoop on the city. Book online.

Copenhagen Free
Walking Tours   Walking

(www.copenhagenfreewalkingtours.dk; Rådhus (City Hall), Strøget, H C Andersens Blvd; ⊜noon) FREE Departing daily at noon from outside Rådhus (City Hall), these free, three-hour walking tours take in famous landmarks and include interesting anecdotes. Tours are in English and require a minimum of five people. Free 90-minute tours of Christianshavn depart at 4pm Friday to Monday from the base of the Bishop Absalon statue on Højbro Plads. A tip is expected.

Canal Tours Copenhagen Boating

(📞32 66 00 00; www.stromma.dk; Nyhavn; adult/child Dkr80/40; ⏱9.30am-9pm late Jun-late Aug, reduced hours rest of year; 🚼; Ⓜ Kongens Nytorv) Canal Tours Copenhagen runs one-hour cruises of the city's canals and harbour, taking in numerous major sights, including Christiansborg Slot, Christianshavn, the Royal Library, Opera House, Amalienborg Palace and *The Little Mermaid*. Embark at Nyhavn or Ved Stranden. Boats depart up to six times per hour from late June to late August, with reduced frequency the rest of the year.

🔒 SHOPPING

Most of the big retail names and home-grown heavyweights are centred on the main pedestrian shopping strip, Strøget. The streets running parallel are dotted with interesting jewellery and antique stores while, to the north, the so-called Latin Quarter is worth a wander for books and clothing. Arty Nørrebro is home to Elmegade and Jægersborggade, two streets lined with interesting shops.

Bornholmer Butikken Food & Drinks

(📞30 72 00 07; www.bornholmerbutikken.dk; Frederiksborggade 21; ⏱10am-7pm Mon-Thu, to 8pm Fri, to 6pm Sat, 11am-5pm Sun) The Bornholm Store in Torvehallerne Market offers a range of tasty take-home specialities from the Danish island of Bornholm, which is famed for its incredible local products. Tasty treats to bring home include honeys, relishes and jams, Johan Bulow liquorice, salamis, cheeses, herring, liquors, and beers.

Maduro Homewares

(📞33 93 28 33; www.maduro.dk; Frederiksborggade 39; ⏱11am-6pm Mon-Fri, 10am-4pm Sat) The motto of Maduro owner Jeppe Maduro Hirsch is that 'good style is more than decor and design'. His small shop is an

---

Copenhagen's Cykelslangen

Two of the Danes' greatest passions – design and cycling – meet in spectacular fashion with **Cykelslangen**, or Cycle Snake. Designed by local architects Dissing + Weitling, the 235-metre-long cycling path evokes a slender orange ribbon, its gently curving form contrasting dramatically with the area's block-like architecture. The elevated path winds its way from Bryggebro (Brygge Bridge) west to Fisketorvet Shopping Centre, weaving its way over the harbour and delivering a cycling experience that's nothing short of whimsical. To reach the path on public transport, catch bus 30 to Fisketorvet Shopping Centre. The best way to reach it, however, is on a bike, as Cykelslangen is only accessible to cyclists.

---

eclectic mix of lovely products, including ceramics, posters and jewellery. The style ranges from sleek to traditional to quirky, and the selection of children's items is especially charming.

Posterland Arts

(📞33 11 28 21; www.posterland.dk; Gothersgade 45; ⏱9:30am-6pm Mon-Thu, to 7pm Fri, to 5pm Sat) Posterland is Northern Europe's biggest poster company, and is the perfect place to find something to spruce up your walls. The wide selection of posters includes art, travel and vintage posters, as well Copenhagen posters of every description including Danish icons Hans Christian Andersen, Tivoli Gardens and the Carlsberg Brewery. You can also pick up souvenirs like postcards, maps, calendars and magnets.

Hay House Design

(www.hay.dk; Østergade 61; ⏱10am-6pm Mon-Fri, to 5pm Sat; 🚌11A) Rolf Hay's fabulous interior design store sells its own coveted line of furniture, textiles and design objects, as well as those of other fresh, innovative Danish designers. Easy-to-pack

Louisiana Art Break

Even if you don't have a consuming passion for modern art, Denmark's outstanding **Louisiana** (www.louisiana.dk; Gammel Strandvej 13, Humlebæk; adult/child Dkr115/free; ☺11am-10pm Tue-Fri, to 6pm Sat & Sun) should be high on your 'to do' list. It's a striking modernist gallery, made up of four huge wings, which stretch across a sculpture-filled park, burrowing down into the hillside and nosing out again to wink at the sea (and Sweden). The collection itself is stellar, covering everything from constructivism, CoBrA movement artists and minimalist art to abstract expressionism, pop art and photography.

Louisiana is in the leafy town of **Humlebæk**, 30km north of Copenhagen. From Humlebæk train station, the museum is a 1.5km signposted walk northeast. Trains to Humlebæk run at least twice hourly from Copenhagen (Dkr115, 35 minutes). If day-tripping from Copenhagen, the 24-hour ticket (adult/child Dkr130/65) is much better value.

gifts include anything from notebooks and ceramic cups to building blocks for style-savvy kids. There's a second branch at Pilestræde 29-31.

Wood Wood Fashion & Accessories
(www.woodwood.dk; Grønnegade 1; ☺10.30am-6pm Mon-Thu, to 7pm Fri, to 5pm Sat, noon-4pm Sun; ☐11A, ⓜKongens Nytorv) Unisex Wood Wood's flagship store is a veritable who's who of cognoscenti street-chic labels. Top of the heap are Wood Wood's own hipster-chic creations, made with superlative fabrics and attention to detail. The supporting cast includes solid knits from classic Danish brand SNS Herning, wallets from Comme des Garçons and sunglasses from Kaibosh.

 EATING

Copenhagen remains one of the hottest culinary destinations in Europe, with more Michelin stars than any other Scandinavian city. **Copenhagen Cooking** (www.copenhagencooking.dk), Scandinavia's largest food festival, serves up a gut-rumbling program twice a year.

Lillian's Smørrebrød Danish €
(www.facebook.com/lillianssmorrebrod; Vester Voldgade 108, Slotsholmen; smørrebrød Dkr17-50; ☺6am-1.30pm Mon-Thu, to 1am Fri; ☐1A, 2A, 9A) One of the best, the oldest (dating from 1978) and least costly smørrebrød places in the city, but word is out so you may have to opt for a takeaway as there are just a handful of tables inside and out. The piled-high, open-face sandwiches are classic and include marinated herring, chicken salad and roast beef with remoulade.

Chicky Grill Danish €
(☑33 22 66 96; Halmtorvet 21, Vesterbro; mains from Dkr75; ☺11am-8pm Mon-Sat; ⓘ; ☐10,14, ⓜCentral Station) Blend in with the locals at this perennially popular bar and grill in hip Kødbyen (the 'Meatpacking District'). It has decor that is more diner than 'dining out', but prices are low and portions are huge with a menu of predominantly grilled meats, fried chicken, burgers and that all-time popular Danish speciality, *flæskesteg* (roast pork).

Torvehallerne KBH Market €
(www.torvehallernekbh.dk; Israels Plads, Nørreport; snacks from Dkr80; ☺10am-7pm Mon-Thu, to 8pm Fri, to 6pm Sat, 11am-5pm Sun; ⓜNørreport) Food market Torvehallerne KBH is an essential stop on the Copenhagen foodie trail. A delicious ode to the fresh, the tasty and the artisanal, the market's beautiful stalls peddle everything from seasonal herbs and berries to smoked meats, seafood and cheeses, smørrebrød, fresh pasta and hand-brewed coffee. You could easily spend an hour or more exploring its twin halls.

Smørrebrød, Torvehallerne KBH

WestMarket   Market €

(www.westmarket.dk; Vesterbrogade 97; ⊗bak-
eries & coffee shops 8am-7pm, food stalls 10am-
10pm; ☐6A) Copenhagen's newest foodie
hotspot, WestMarket is both a traditional
market and a hip street food emporium.
The range of cuisines is impressive: visitors
can sample offerings from all over the
world, from Danish smørrebrød at Selma
to Ugandan egg wraps at Ugood. Try bear
sausage at Kød & Bajer for something unusual, or treat yourself to sinfully delicious
desserts at Guilty.

Nyboders Køkken   Danish €€

(☑22 88 64 14; www.nyboderskoekken.dk;
Borgergade 134, Nyhavn; mains Dkr128-185;
⊗5-11.30pm Mon-Fri, noon-3pm Sat & Sun; 🛜;
☐11A, 26, Ⓜ Kongens Nytorv) Located in an
affluent neighbourhood with a fashionably
chic feel, Nyboders Køkken's menu is
purposefully deeply traditional; if you are
Danish, grandma's kitchen may come to
mind. Think apple charlotte, classic wiener
schnitzel, prawn cocktail and Danish junket
with cream. Among the mains, the roasted

slices of pork with parsley sauce has had
local food critics swooning.

Höst   New Nordic €€€

(☑89 93 84 09; www.hostvakst.dk; Nørre
Farimagsgade 41, Nørrebro; mains Dkr205-245,
5-course set menu Dkr395; ⊗5.30pm-midnight,
last order 9.30pm; ☐40, Ⓜ Nørrebro) Höst's
phenomenal popularity is a no-brainer:
warm, award-winning interiors and New
Nordic food that's equally as fabulous and
filling. The set menu is superb, with three
smaller 'surprise dishes' thrown in and
evocative creations like beef tenderloin
from Grambogaard with onion compote,
gherkins, cress and smoked cheese. The
'deluxe' wine menu is significantly better
than the standard option. Book ahead,
especially later in the week.

Uformel   New Nordic €€€

(☑70 99 91 11; www.uformel.dk/en/; Studiestræde 69; dishes Dkr110; ⊗5.30-10pm Sun-Thu,
to 11pm Fri & Sat; ☐5A, 6A, 9A, 10, 12, 14, 31,
Ⓢ Vesterport) The edgier younger brother
of Michelin-starred restaurant Formel B,
Uformel ('Informal') offers a more casual

take on New Nordic cuisine. The restaurant serves up an ever-changing menu featuring local, seasonal ingredients to create its mouth-watering dishes. Diners can choose several small plates to create their own tasting menu, or opt for the set menu of four courses (Dkr775).

Geranium   New Nordic €€€

(☑69 96 00 20; geranium.dk; Per Henrik Lings Allé 4, Østerbro; lunch/dinner tasting menu Dkr1250/1550, lighter lunch tasting menu Dkr950; ⊘lunch noon-1pm Wed-Sat, dinner 6.30-9pm Wed-Sat; 🍴) 🍷 Perched on the 8th floor of Parken football stadium, Geranium is the only restaurant in town sporting three Michelin stars. At the helm is Bocuse d'Or prize-winning chef Rasmus Kofoed, who transforms local ingredients into edible Nordic artworks like venison with smoked lard and beetroot, or king crab with lemon balm and cloudberries.

Kronor-conscious foodies can opt for the slightly cheaper lunch menus, while those not wanting to sample the (swoon-inducing) wines can opt for enlightened juice pairings. Book ahead.

🍷 DRINKING & NIGHTLIFE

Copenhagen is packed with a diverse range of drinking options. Vibrant drinking areas include Kødbyen (the 'Meatpacking District') and Istedgade in Vesterbro; Ravnsborggade, Elmegade and Sankt Hans Torv in Nørrebro; and especially gay-friendly Studiestræde.

Coffee Collective Nørrebro   Cafe

(www.coffeecollective.dk; Jægersborggade 10, Nørrebro; ⊘7am-7pm Mon-Fri, 8am-7pm Sat & Sun; 🚍18, 12, 66) In a city where lacklustre coffee is as common as perfect cheekbones, this microroastery peddles the good stuff – we're talking rich, complex cups of caffeinated magic. The baristas are passionate about their beans and the cafe itself sits on creative Jægersborggade in Nørrebro. There are two other outlets, at food market Torvehallerne KBH (p148) and in **Frederiksberg** (Godthåbsvej 34b; ⊘7.30am-9pm Mon-Fri, from 9am Sat, from 10am Sun).

Ved Stranden 10   Wine Bar

(www.vedstranden10.dk; Ved Stranden 10; ⊘noon-10pm Mon-Sat; 🛜; 🚍1A, 2A, 26, 40, 66)

Politicians and well-versed oenophiles make a beeline for this canalside wine bar, its enviable cellar stocked with classic European vintages, biodynamic wines and more obscure drops. Adorned with modernist Danish design and friendly, clued in staff, its string of rooms lends the place an intimate, civilised air that's perfect for grown-up conversation plus vino-friendly nibbles like cheeses and smoked meats.

Ruby   Cocktail Bar

(www.rby.dk; Nybrogade 10, Strøget; ⊙4pm-2am Mon-Sat, from 6pm Sun; ☎; ☐1A, 2A, 11A, 26, 40, 66) Cocktail connoisseurs raise their glasses to high achieving Ruby. Here, hipster-geek mixologists whip up near-flawless libations such as the Green & White (vodka, dill, white chocolate and liquorice root) and a lively crowd spills into a labyrinth of cosy, decadent rooms. For a gentlemen's club vibe, head downstairs into a world of Chesterfields, oil paintings and wooden cabinets lined with spirits.

Lo-Jo's Social   Bar

(☐53 88 64 65; www.lojossocial.com; Landemærket 7; ⊙bar 11:30am-late Mon-Sat, kitchen to 10pm) It's all in the name: colourful Lo-Jo's is a place to be social, with a range of tasty cocktails available for sharing for up to five people. Wines are largely organic or bio-dynamic, and for something a bit different, there is a bubbly Spritz menu and a refreshing Apple Press menu, using fresh apple juice as a base.

Mikkeller & Friends   Microbrewery

(☐35 83 10 20; www.mikkeller.dk/location/mikkeller-friends; Stefansgade 35; ⊙2pm-midnight Sun-Wed, to 2am Thu & Fri, from noon Sat; ☐5A, 8A) This uniquely designed beer geek hotspot offers 40 kinds of artisan draught beers from local microbreweries and 200 varieties of bottled beers ciders, and soft drinks. Patrons can snack on gourmet sausages and cheese while enjoying their beer.

Rust   Club

(☐35 24 52 00; www.rust.dk; Guldbergsgade 8, Nørrebro; ⊙hours vary, club usually 11pm-5am Fri & Sat; ☎; ☐3A, 5A, 350S) A smashing

 ### Freetown Christiania

Escape the capitalist crunch at Freetown **Christiania** (Prinsessegade, Christianshavn; ☐9A, 2A, 40, 350S, Ⓜ Christianshavn), a free-spirited, eco-oriented commune. Explore beyond the settlement's infamous 'Pusher St' and you'll stumble upon a semibucolic wonderland of whimsical DIY homes, cosy gardens and craft shops, eateries, beer gardens and music venues.

Before its development as an alternative enclave, the site was an abandoned 41-hectare military camp. When squatters took over in 1971, police tried to clear the area. They failed. Bowing to public pressure, the government allowed the community to continue as a social experiment. Self-governing, ecology-oriented and generally tolerant, Christiania residents did, in time, find it necessary to modify their 'anything goes' approach. A new policy was established that outlawed hard drugs and the heroin and cocaine pushers were expelled.

The main entrance into Christiania is on Prinsessegade, 200m northeast of its intersection with Bådsmandsstræde. From late June to the end of August, 60- to 90-minute guided tours (Dkr40) of Christiania run daily at 3pm (weekends only September to late June). Tours commence just inside Christiania's main entrance on Prinsessegade.

History at the Frilandsmuseet

The main sight of interest in the Lyngby area is **Frilandsmuseet** (☏41 20 64 55; www.natmus.dk; Kongevejen 100, Lyngby; ⊙10am-5pm Tue-Sun Jul-Aug, shorter hrs rest of yr) **FREE**, a sprawling open-air museum of old countryside dwellings that have been gathered from sites around Denmark. Its 100-plus historic buildings are arranged in groupings that provide a sense of Danish rural life as it was in various regions and across different social strata.

Frilandsmuseet is a 10-minute sign-posted walk from Sorgenfri station, 25 minutes from Central Station on S-train line B. You can also take bus 184 or 194, both of which stop at the entrance.

Danish farmhouse and windmill
OLIVER FOERSTNER/SHUTTERSTOCK ©

place attracting one of the largest, coolest crowds in Copenhagen. Live acts focus on alternative or upcoming indie rock, hip hop or electronica, while the club churns out hip hop, dancehall and electro on Wednesdays and house, electro and rock on Fridays and Saturdays. From 11pm Friday and Saturday, entrance is only to over 20s.

⭐ ENTERTAINMENT

Copenhagen is home to thriving live-music and club scenes that range from intimate jazz and blues clubs to mega rock venues. Blockbuster cultural venues such as **Operaen** (Copenhagen Opera House; ☏box office 33 69 69 69; www.kglteater.dk; Ekvipagemestervej 10; ☐9A, ⛴Opera) and **Skuespilhuset**

(Royal Danish Playhouse; ☏33 69 69 69; kglteater.dk; Sankt Anne Plads 36; ☐11A, ⓂKongens Nytorv) deliver top-tier opera and theatre. The **Copenhagen Jazz Festival** (www.jazz.dk), the largest jazz festival in northern Europe, hits the city over 10 days in early July.

Jazzhouse   Jazz
(☏33 15 47 00; www.jazzhouse.dk; Niels Hemmingsensgade 10, Strøget; ☎; ☐11A) Copenhagen's leading jazz joint serves up top Danish and visiting talent, with music styles running the gamut from bebop to fusion jazz. Doors usually open at 7pm, with concerts starting at 8pm. On Friday and Saturday, late-night concerts (from 11pm) are also offered. Check the website for details and consider booking big-name acts in advance.

ⓘ INFORMATION

EMERGENCY & IMPORTANT NUMBERS

Dial ☏112 to contact police, ambulance or fire services; the call can be made free from public phones.

DISCOUNT CARDS

The **Copenhagen Card** (www.copenhagencard.com; adult/child 10-15yr 24hr Dkr379/199, 48hr Dkr529/269, 72hr Dkr629/319, 120hr Dkr839/419), available at the Copenhagen Visitors Centre or online, gives you free access to 72 museums and attractions in the city and surrounding area, as well as free travel for all S-train, metro and bus journeys within the seven travel zones.

MONEY

Banks are plentiful, especially in central Copenhagen. Most are open from 10am to 4pm weekdays (to 5.30pm on Thursday). Most banks in Copenhagen have ATMs that are accessible 24 hours per day.

POST

Post Office (Købmagergade 33; ⊙10am-6pm Mon-Fri, to 2pm Sat) A handy post office near Strøget and the Latin Quarter.

København H Post Office (Central Station; ☺9am-7pm Mon-Fri, noon-4pm Sat) Post office in Central Station.

TOURIST INFORMATION

Copenhagen Visitors Centre (70 22 24 42; www.visitcopenhagen.com; Vesterbrogade 4A, Vesterbro; ☺9am-8pm Jul-Sep, to 5pm Mon-Fri, to 2pm Sat Oct-Feb, to 5pm Mon-Fri, to 4pm Sat & Sun Mar-Jun; 🚍; ☐2A, 5A, 9A, 12, 26, 250S, 350S, 🚆S-train København H) Copenhagen's excellent and informative information centre has a superb cafe and lounge with free wi-fi; it also sells the Copenhagen Card.

ⓘ GETTING THERE & AWAY

AIR

If you're waiting for a flight at **Copenhagen Airport** (www.cph.dk; Lufthavnsboulevarden 6, Kastrup), note that this is a 'silent' airport and there are no boarding calls, although there are numerous monitor screens throughout the terminal.

BUS

Eurolines (✆33 88 70 00; www.eurolines.dk; Halmtorvet 5) operates buses to several European cities. The ticket office is behind Central Station. Long-distance buses leave from opposite the DGI-byen sports complex on Ingerslevsgade, just southwest of København H (Central Station). Destinations include Berlin (Dkr329, 7½ hours) and Paris (Dkr699, 19 to 22¼ hours).

TRAIN

DSB Billetsalg (DSB Ticket Office; ✆70 13 14 15; www.dsb.dk; Copenhagen Central Station, Bernstorffsgade 16-22; ☺7am-8pm Mon-Fri, 8am-6pm Sat & Sun) is best for reservations and for purchasing international train tickets.

ⓘ GETTING AROUND

TO/FROM THE AIRPORT

The 24-hour metro (www.m.dk) runs every four to 20 minutes between the airport arrival terminal (the station is called Lufthavnen) and the eastern side of the city centre. It does not stop at København H (Central Station) but is handy for Christianshavn and Nyhavn (get off at Kongens Nytorv for Nyhavn). Journey time to Kongens Nytorv is 14 minutes (Dkr36).

By taxi, it's about 20 minutes between the airport and the city centre, depending on traffic. Expect to pay between Dkr250 and Dkr300.

Trains (www.dsb.dk) connect the airport arrival terminal to Copenhagen Central Station (København Hovedbanegården, commonly known as København H) around every 12 minutes. Journey time is 14 minutes (Dkr36). Check schedules at www.rejseplanen.dk.

BICYCLE

Copenhagen vies with Amsterdam as the world's most bike-friendly city. The superb, city-wide rental system is **Bycyklen** (City Bikes; www.bycyklen.dk). Visit the Bycyklen website for more information.

CAR & MOTORCYCLE

Except for the weekday-morning rush hour, when traffic can bottleneck coming into the city (and vice versa around 5pm), traffic in Copenhagen is generally manageable. Getting around by car is not problematic, except for the usual challenge of finding an empty parking space in the most popular places.

PUBLIC TRANSPORT

Copenhagen has an extensive public transit system consisting of a metro, rail, bus and ferry network. All tickets are valid for travel on the metro, buses and S-tog (S-train or local train) even though they look slightly different, depending on where you buy them. The free Copenhagen city maps that are distributed by the tourist office show bus routes (with numbers) and are very useful for finding your way around the city. Online, click onto the very handy www.rejseplanen.dk for all routes and schedules.

WALKING

The best way to see Copenhagen is on foot. There are few main sights or shopping quarters more than a 20-minute walk from the city centre.

Amsterdam, the Netherlands

Amsterdam works its fairy-tale magic in many ways: via the gabled, Golden Age buildings; glinting, boat-filled canals; and especially the cosy, centuries-old bruin cafés (traditional pubs), where candles burn low and beers froth high. Add in mega art museums and cool street markets, and it's easy to see why this atmospheric city is one of Europe's most popular getaways.

Two Days in Amsterdam

Ogle the masterpieces at the **Van Gogh Museum** (p157) and **Rijksmuseum** (p160) in the Old South and spend the afternoon in the city centre at the Begijnhof or Royal Palace. At night venture into the eye-popping Red Light District, then sip in a brown *café* such as **In 't Aepjen** (p170).

Start the next day at the **Albert Cuypmarkt** (p160) then head to the Southern Canal Ring for a canal boat tour. At night party at hyperactive **Leidseplein** (p164).

Four Days in Amsterdam

On day three head to the haunting **Anne Frank Huis** (p159) and spend the evening in the Jordaan for dinner and canalside drinks.

Begin your fourth day at **Museum het Rembrandthuis** (p161) or cycling around **Vondelpark** (p161), then mosey over to organic brewery **Brouwerij 't IJ** (p172), at the foot of a windmill.

After Amsterdam, hop on a train to Paris (p202), a mere 3¼ hours away, or fly just over an hour to Copenhagen (p136).

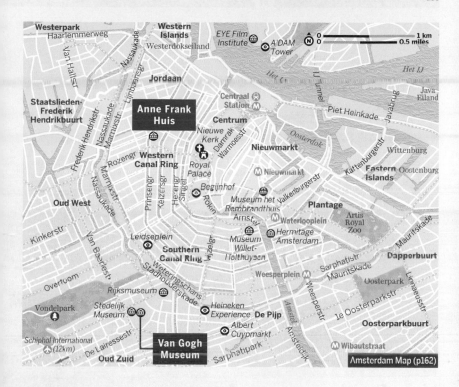

Amsterdam Map (p162)

Arriving in Amsterdam

Schiphol Airport Trains to Centraal Station depart every 10 minutes or so from 6am to 12.30am. The trip takes 17 minutes and costs €5.10; taxis cost €47.

Centraal Station Located in central Amsterdam. Most tram lines connect it to the rest of the city. Taxis queue near the front entrance.

Duivendrecht station Eurolines buses arrive here, south of the centre. Easy links to Centraal Station.

Where to Stay

Amsterdam has loads of accommodation in wild and wonderful spaces: inspired architects have breathed new life into old buildings, from converted schools and industrial lofts to entire rows of canal houses joined at the hip.

Hostels are plentiful, with most geared to youthful party animals. Hotels typically are small and ramble over several floors in charming old buildings.

For information on which neighbourhoods to stay in, see p176.

Van Gogh Museum

The world's largest Van Gogh collection is a superb line-up of masterworks. Opened in 1973 to house the collection of Vincent's younger brother, Theo, the museum comprises some 200 paintings and 500 drawings by Vincent and his contemporaries.

Great For...

☑ Don't Miss

The Potato Eaters, The Yellow House, Wheatfield with Crows and *Sunflowers*.

Entrance & Set-Up

In 2015, a swish new extension and entrance hall added 800 sq metres of space to the museum, which now spreads over four levels, moving chronologically from Floor 0 (aka the ground floor) to Floor 3. It's still a manageable size; allow a couple of hours or so to browse the galleries. Seminal works to look for include the following.

Potato Eaters

Van Gogh's earliest works – shadowy and crude – are from his time in the Dutch countryside and in Antwerp between 1883 and 1885. He was particularly obsessed with peasants. *The Potato Eaters* (1885) is his most famous painting from this period.

Bible & Skeleton

Still Life with Bible (1885) is another early work, and it shows Van Gogh's religious

INGEHOGENBUI - HUTTERSTOCK ©

ℹ️ Need to Know

☑️020-570 52 00; www.vangoghmuseum.
com; Museumplein 6; adult/child €17/free,
audio guide €5; ⊙9am-7pm Sun-Thu, to 9pm
Sat mid-Jul–Aug, to 6pm Sat-Thu Sep–mid-Jul,
to 5pm Jan-Mar, to 10pm Fri; 🚊2/3/5/12 Van
Baerlestraat

✕ Take a Break

Nibble on quiche and sip wine at the
museum cafe. Window tables overlook
the Museumplein.

★ Top Tip

Entrance queues can be long. Try
waiting until after 3pm or buy tickets
online and skip the queue.

inclination. The burnt-out candle is said to
represent the recent death of his father,
who was a Protestant minister. *Skeleton
with Burning Cigarette* (1886) was painted
when Van Gogh was a student at Antwerp's
Royal Academy of Fine Arts.

Self-Portraits

In 1886 Van Gogh moved to Paris, where his
brother, Theo, was working as an art dealer.
Vincent wanted to master the art of portraiture, but was too poor to pay for models.
Several self-portraits resulted. You can see
his palette begin to brighten as he comes
under the influence of the impressionists
in the city.

Sketchbooks & Letters

Intriguing displays enhance what's on
the walls. For instance, you might see Van
Gogh's actual sketchbook alongside an in-

teractive kiosk that lets you page through a
reproduction of it. The museum has catego-
rised all of Van Gogh's letters online at www.
vangoghletters.org. Use the museum's free
Wi-fi to access them with your smartphone.

Other Artists

Thanks to Theo van Gogh's prescient collecting and that of the museum's curators,
you'll also see works by Vincent's contemporaries, including Paul Gauguin, Claude
Monet and Henri de Toulouse-Lautrec.

Extras

The museum has multiple listening stations
for diverse recordings of Van Gogh's letters,
mainly to and from his closest brother
Theo, who championed his work. There
are daily workshops (for adults and kids)
where, suitably inspired, you can create
your own works of art.

KAVALENKAVA/SHUTTERSTOCK ©

Anne Frank Huis

It is one of the 20th century's most compelling stories: a young Jewish girl forced into hiding with her family and their friends to escape deportation by the Nazis. Walking through the bookcase-door is stepping back into a time that seems both distant and tragically real.

Great For...

☑ Don't Miss

Details including Anne's red-plaid diary, WWII news reels and a video of Anne's schoolmate Hanneli Gosler.

Background

It seems impossible now, but it's true: it took the German army just five days to occupy all of the Netherlands, along with Belgium and much of France. And once Hitler's forces had swept across the country, many Jews – like Anne Frank – eventually went into hiding. Anne's diary describes how restrictions were gradually imposed on Dutch Jews: from being forbidden to ride streetcars to being forced to turn in their bicycles and not being allowed to visit Christian friends.

The Franks moved into the upper floors of the specially prepared rear of the building, along with another couple, the Van Pels (called the Van Daans in Anne's diary), and their son Peter. Four months later Fritz Pfeffer (called Mr Dussel in the diary) joined the household. Here they survived until they were discovered by the Gestapo in August 1944.

Anne Frank sculpture by Mari S Andriessen

GIANNIS PAPANIKOS/SHUTTERSTOCK ©

❶ Need to Know

☏020-556 71 05; www.annefrank.org;
Prinsengracht 263-267; adult/child €9/4.50;
🕑9am-10pm Apr-Oct, 9am-7pm Sun-Fri, to
9pm Sat Nov-Mar; 🚊13/14/17 Westermarkt

✕ Take a Break

For pancakes and 18th-century atmosphere aplenty, stroll over to **'t Smalle**
(www.t-smalle.nl; Egelantiersgracht 12;
🕑10am-1am Sun-Thu, to 2am Fri & Sat).

★ Top Tip

Buying timed-entry tickets in advance
allows you to skip the queue entirely
and enter via a separate door (left of
the main entrance).

Ground Floor

After several renovations, the house itself
is now contained within a modern, square
shell that attempts to retain the original
feel of the building (it was used during
WWII as offices and a warehouse).

Offices & Warehouse

The building originally held Otto Frank's
pectin (a substance used in jelly-making)
business. On the lower floors you'll see the
former offices of Victor Kugler, Otto's business partner; and the desks of Miep Gies,
Bep Voskuijl and Jo Kleiman, all of whom
worked in the office and provided food,
clothing and other goods for the household.

Secret Annexe

The upper floors in the *achterhuis* (rear
house) contain the Secret Annexe, where
the living quarters have been preserved in

powerful austerity. As you enter Anne's small
bedroom, you can still sense the remnants
of a young girl's dreams: view the photos of
Hollywood stars and postcards of the Dutch
royal family that she pasted on the wall.

The Diary

More haunting exhibits and videos await after you return to the front house – including
Anne's red-plaid diary itself, sitting alone in
a glass case. Watch the video of Anne's old
schoolmate Hanneli Gosler, who describes
encountering Anne at Bergen-Belsen. Read
heartbreaking letters from Otto, the only
Secret Annexe occupant to survive the
concentration camps.

Renovations

In early 2017 a major renewal project began
at the museum, which will take two years.
The renovations include an expansion to allow more space for school groups and visitor facilities, as well as new displays. Anne
Frank Huis will remain open throughout.

⊙ SIGHTS

Rijksmuseum   Museum
(National Museum; ☎020-674 70 00; www.
rijksmuseum.nl; Museumstraat 1; adult/child
€17.50/free; ☺9am-5pm; 🚋2/5 Rijksmuseum)
The Rijksmuseum is the Netherlands'
premier art trove, splashing Rembrandts,
Vermeers and 7500 other masterpieces
over 1.5km of galleries. To avoid the biggest
crowds, come after 3pm. Or prebook tickets online, which provides fast-track entry.

The Golden Age works are the highlight.
Feast your eyes on still lifes, gentlemen in
ruffled collars and landscapes bathed in
pale yellow light. Rembrandt's *The Night
Watch* (1642) takes pride of place.

Heineken Experience   Brewery
(☎020-523 92 22; https://tickets.heineken
experience.com; Stadhouderskade 78; adult/child
self-guided tour €18/12.50, VIP guided tour €49,
Rock City ticket €25; ☺10.30am-7.30pm Mon-
Thu, to 9pm Fri-Sun; 🚋16/24 Stadhouderskade)
On the site of the company's old brewery,
the crowning glory of this self-guided
'Experience' (samples aside) is a multimedia exhibit where you 'become' a beer by
getting shaken up, sprayed with water and
subjected to heat. True beer connoisseurs
will shudder, but it's a lot of fun. Admission
includes a 15-minute shuttle boat ride to
the Heineken Brand Store near Rembrandtplein. Prebooking tickets online saves you
€2 on the entry fee and allows you to skip
the ticket queues.

Albert Cuypmarkt   Market
(http://albertcuyp-markt.amsterdam; Albert
Cuypstraat, btwn Ferdinand Bolstraat & Van
Woustraat; ☺9.30am-5pm Mon-Sat; 🚋16/24
Albert Cuypstraat) The best place to marvel
at De Pijp's colourful scene is the Albert
Cuypmarkt, Amsterdam's largest and
busiest market. Vendors loudly tout their
odd gadgets and their arrays of fruit, vegetables, herbs and spices. They sell clothes
and other general goods too, often cheaper
than anywhere else. Snack vendors tempt
passers-by with herring sandwiches, egg
rolls, doughnuts and caramel-syrup-filled
stroopwafels. If you have room after all that,
the surrounding area teems with cosy cafes
and eateries.

Cyclists at the Rijksmuseum

MARINADA/SHUTTERSTOCK ©

Vondelpark   Park

(www.hetvondelpark.net; 🚊2/5 Hobbemastraat)
The lush urban idyll of the Vondelpark is
one of Amsterdam's most magical places
– sprawling, English-style gardens, with
ponds, lawns, footbridges and winding footpaths. On a sunny day, an open-air party
atmosphere ensues when tourists, lovers,
cyclists, in-line skaters, pram-pushing
parents, cartwheeling children, football-
kicking teenagers, spliff-sharing friends
and champagne-swilling picnickers all
come out to play.

Museum het
Rembrandthuis   Museum

(Rembrandt House Museum; 🖉020-520 04 00;
www.rembrandthuis.nl; Jodenbreestraat 4; adult/
child €13/4; ☺10am-6pm; 🚊9/14 Waterlooplein)
You almost expect to find the master
himself at the Museum het Rembrandthuis, where Rembrandt van Rijn ran the
Netherlands' largest painting studio, only to
lose the lot when profligacy set in, enemies
swooped and bankruptcy came a-knocking.
The museum has scores of etchings and
sketches. Ask for the free audio guide at
the entrance. You can buy advance tickets
online, though it's not as vital here as at
some of the other big museums.

Royal Palace   Palace

(Koninklijk Paleis; 🖉020-522 61 61; www.
paleisamsterdam.nl; Dam; adult/child €10/free;
☺10am-5pm; 🚊4/9/16/24 Dam) Opened as
a town hall in 1655, this building became
a palace in the 19th century. The interiors
gleam, especially the marble work – at
its best in a floor inlaid with maps of the
world in the great *burgerzaal* (citizens' hall),
which occupies the heart of the building.
Pick up a free audio tour at the desk after
you enter; it will explain everything you see
in vivid detail. King Willem-Alexander uses
the palace only for ceremonies; check the
website for periodic closures.

EYE Film Institute   Museum, Cinema

(🖉589 14 00; www.eyefilm.nl; IJpromenade 1;
☺10am-7pm Sat-Thu, to 9pm Fri; Ⓜ Amsterdam
Central) A modernist architectural triumph,

Exploring
the Jordaan

Though gentrified today, the Jordaan
was once a rough, densely populated
volksbuurt (district for the common
people) until the mid-20th century. That
history still shows amid the cosy pubs,
galleries and markets now squashed
into its grid of tiny lanes.

The area doesn't have many traditional sights, but that's not the point.
It's the little things that are appealing
here – the narrow lanes, the old facades,
the funny little shops. The Jordaan is
about taking your time wandering and
not worrying if you get lost; nothing is
more quintessentially Amsterdam than
losing yourself in the labyrinth of narrow
streets and charming canals before
spending the evening in the neighbourhood's atmospheric brown *cafés*
(traditional pubs).

VERONIKA GALKINA/SHUTTERSTOCK ©

seeming to balance on its edge on the
banks of the river IJ (also pronounced
'eye'), movies from the 40,000-title archive
screen in four theatres, sometimes with
live music. Exhibits (admission €9 to €15)
of costumes, digital art and other cinephile
amusements run in conjunction with what's
playing. A view-tastic bar-restaurant with
a fabulously sunny terrace (when the sun
makes an appearance) is a popular hang-
out on this side of the river.

A'DAM Tower   Notable Building

(www.adamtoren.nl; Overhoeksplein 1; Lookout
adult/child €12.50/6.50, family ticket min 3

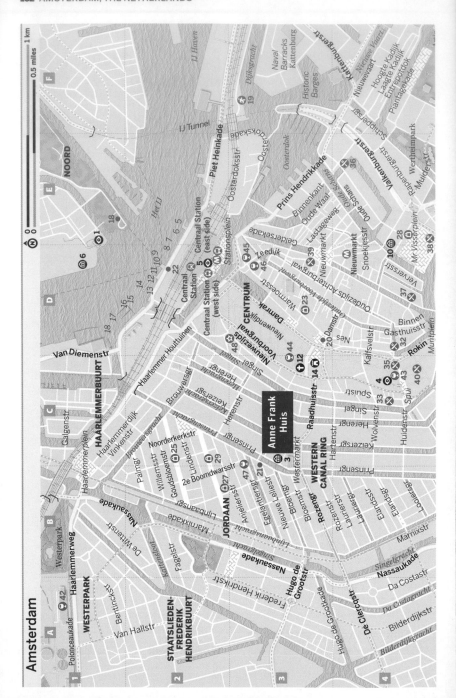

Amsterdam

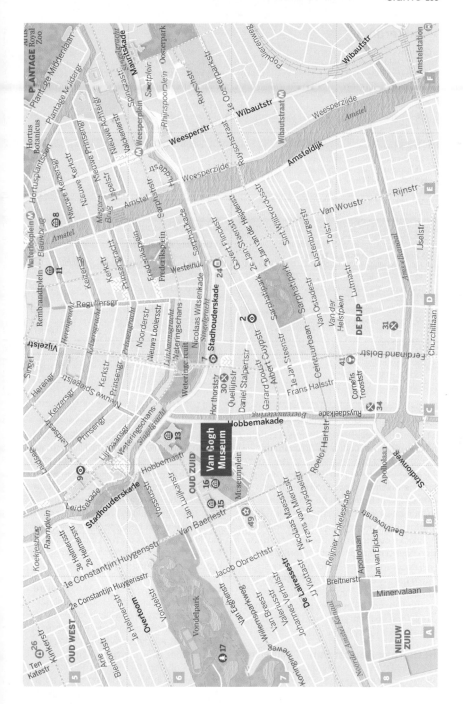

Amsterdam

people from €20; ☺Lookout 10am-10pm; ⛴Badhuiskade) The 22-storey building next to the EYE Film Institute used to be Royal Dutch Shell oil company offices. The oil people would be hard pressed to recognise it now. Take the trippy lift up to the large rooftop for awe-inspiring views in all directions, with large Fat Boy cushions on which to lounge, a red model horse for surreal photoshoots, and a giant four-person swing that kicks out right over the edge for those who have a head for heights (you're very well secured and strapped in). There's a swish bar for drinks and light meals and the Moon revolving restaurant (book ahead) on the 19th floor. There are also two dance clubs (one up high, and one in the basement) and a funky hotel.

Hermitage Amsterdam   Museum
(☑530 74 88; www.hermitage.nl; Amstel 51; adult/child incl audio guide €17.50/free, €25 combined ticket (all exhibitions) €2.50 with Museum Card; ☺10am-5pm; ⓜWaterlooplein, 🚋9/14 Waterlooplein) There have long been links between Russia and the Netherlands – Czar Peter the Great learned shipbuilding here in 1697 – hence this local branch of St Petersburg's State Hermitage Museum. There are no permanent displays: huge temporary exhibitions show work from the Hermitage's vast treasure trove, such as blockbuster shows on the Dutch Golden Age. Come before 11am to avoid the lengthiest queues. Photography isn't permitted.

Leidseplein   Square
(🚋1/2/5/7/10 Leidseplein) Historic architecture, beer, plenty of tourists and an inordinate number of steakhouses – welcome to Leidseplein. Always busy, but coming into its own after dark, this hyperactive square is a major hub both for nightlife and for trams. There are countless pubs and clubs, an aro-

ma of roasted meat, and masses of restaurants. Pavement cafes at the northern end are perfect for watching the human traffic, which gets crazier as the night goes on.

Museum Willet-Holthuysen · Museum

(☎523 18 22; www.willetholthuysen.nl; Herengracht 605; adult/child €9/4.50, audioguide €1; ☺10am-5pm Mon-Fri, from 11am Sat & Sun; Ⓜ Waterlooplein, ☒4/9/14 Rembrandtplein) This exquisite canal house was built in 1685 for Amsterdam mayor Jacob Hop, then remodelled in 1739. It's named after Louisa Willet-Holthuysen who inherited the house from her coal- and glass-merchant father, and lived a bohemian life here with her husband Abraham. She bequeathed the property to the city in 1895. It's a fascinating window into the world of the 18th-century super rich, with displays including part of the family's 275-piece Meissen table service, and the immaculate French-style garden.

Stedelijk Museum · Museum

(☎020-573 29 11; www.stedelijk.nl; Museumplein 10; adult/child €18.75/free; ☺10am-6pm Sat-Thu, to 10pm Fri; ☒2/3/5/12 Van Baerlestraat) This fabulous museum houses the collection amassed by postwar curator Willem Sandberg that makes up the National Museum of Modern Art. Displays rotate but you'll see an amazing selection featuring works by Picasso, Matisse, Mondrian, Van Gogh and more, plus great temporary exhibitions. The building was originally a bank, built in 1895 to a neo-Renaissance design by AM Weissman, and the modern extension is nicknamed 'the bathtub' for reasons obvious when you see it.

Nieuwe Kerk · Church

(New Church; ☎020-638 69 09; www.nieuwekerk.nl; Dam; €8-16; ☺10am-6pm; ☒1/2/5/13/14/17 Dam) This 15th-century, late-Gothic basilica – a historic stage for Dutch coronations – is only 'new' in relation to the Oude Kerk. A few monumental items dominate the otherwise spartan interior – a magnificent carved oak chancel, a bronze choir screen, a massive organ and enormous stained-glass windows. The building is now used for exhibitions and organ concerts. Opening times and admission fees can vary, depending on what's going on.

Begijnhof · Courtyard

(www.nicolaas-parochie.nl; off Gedempte Begijnensloot; ☺9am-5pm; ☒1/2/5 Spui) **FREE** This enclosed former convent dates from the early 14th century. It's a surreal oasis of peace, with tiny houses and postage-stamp gardens around a well-kept courtyard. The Beguines were a Catholic order of unmarried or widowed women who cared for the elderly and lived a religious life without taking monastic vows. The last true Beguine died in 1971.

⚙ ACTIVITIES

Amsterdam has more canals than Venice and getting on the water is one of the best ways to feel the pulse of the city. You could catch the vibe by sitting canalside and watching boats glide by: myriad *cafés* seem purpose-built for this sport. Or you could stroll alongside the canals and check out some of the city's 2500 houseboats. Better yet, hop on a tour boat and cruise the curved passages.

There are more bicycles in Amsterdam than cars. Everyone rides: young, old, club-goers in high heels, cops on duty, bankers in suits with ties flapping in the breeze. Pedal power is what moves the masses to work, to shop and to socialise at the *cafés*. Renting a bike not only puts you shoulder to shoulder with locals but it gives you easy access to the city's outer neighbourhoods and their cool architecture and museums, as well the windmill-dotted countryside and its time-warped villages.

Rederji Lampedusa · Boating

(www.rederjilampedusa.nl; 1-2hr canal tour €17, VIP tours by donation; ☺canal tours weekends, VIP tours Friday fortnightly May-Sept) Take a canal boat tour or a sunset trip around Amsterdam harbour in former refugee boats, brought from Lampedusa by Dutch founder Tuen. The tours are full of heart and offer a

Celebrating King's Day

A celebration of the House of Orange, **King's Day** (Koningsdag) sees more than 400,000 orange-clad people filling Amsterdam's streets for drinking and dancing. The city also becomes one big flea market, as people sell off all their unwanted junk.

For decades it was Queen's Day, but there's a new monarch in the house. So now it's King's Day, celebrated on King Willem-Alexander's birthday of April 27 (unless it falls on a Sunday, in which case it's celebrated the day before). Whatever the name, whatever the date, it's really just an excuse for a gigantic drinking fest and for everyone to wear ridiculous orange outfits, the country's national colour. There's also a free market citywide (where anyone can sell anything) and rollicking free concerts.

fascinating insight, not only into stories of contemporary migration, but also of how immigration shaped Amsterdam's history – especially the canal tour. Both leave from next to Mediamatic.

Wetlands Safari — Boating
(☑06 5355 2669; www.wetlandssafari.nl; adult/child incl transport & picnic €59/33; ☺9.30am Mon-Fri, 10am Sat & Sun early-Apr–late Sep) For a change from Amsterdam's canals, book an exceptional five-hour wetlands boat trip. Participants take a bus to just north of the centre, then canoe through boggy, froggy wetlands and on past windmills and 17th-century villages. Departure is from behind Centraal Station at the 'G' bus stop. Four-hour sunset tours (adult/child €51/29) depart at 5pm from early May to late August.

 TOURS

The following tours provide a good introduction to Amsterdam, particularly if you're short on time:

Sandeman's New Amsterdam Tours
(www.neweuropetours.eu; by donation; ☺up to 8 tours daily; ☑4/9/16/24 Dam) Pay-what-you-can walking tours that cover the Medieval Centre, Red Light District and Jordaan.

Those Dam Boat Guys (☑06 1885 5219; www.thosedamboatguys.com; €25; ☺11am, 1pm, 3pm, 5pm & 7pm Mar-Sep; ☑13/14/17 Westermarkt) Low-key canal tours on small, electric boats where you bring your own picnic.

Orangebike (☑646842083; www.orange-bike.nl; Buiksloterweg 5c; tours €22.50-37.50, hire per hr/day from €5/11; ☺9am-6pm; ⛴Buiksloterweg) Easy cycling jaunts that take in the city's sights, architecture and windmills.

 SHOPPING

During the Golden Age, Amsterdam was the world's warehouse, stuffed with riches from the far corners of the earth. The capital's cupboards are still stocked with all kinds of exotica (just look at that Red Light gear!), but the real pleasure here is finding some odd, tiny shop selling something you wouldn't find anywhere else.

Hutspot — Design
(www.hutspotamsterdam.com; Van Woustraat 4; ☺shop & cafe 10am-7pm Mon-Sat, noon-6pm Sun; ☎; ☑4 Stadhouderskade) Named after the Dutch dish of boiled and mashed vegies, 'Hotchpotch' was founded with a mission to give young entrepreneurs the chance to sell their work. As a result, this concept store is an inspired mishmash of Dutch-designed furniture, furnishings, art, homewares and clothing,` plus a barber and a cool in-store cafe as well as various pop-ups.

Moooi Gallery — Design
(☑020-528 77 60; www.moooi.com; Westerstraat 187; ☺10am-6pm Tue-Sat; ☑3/10 Marnixplein) Founded by Marcel Wanders, this is Dutch design at its most over-the-top, from the life-sized black horse lamp to the 'blow away vase' (a whimsical twist on the classic

Delft vase) and the 'killing of the piggy bank' ceramic pig (with a gold hammer).

Condomerie Het
Gulden Vlies   Adult

(https://condomerie.com; Warmoesstraat 141; ⊙11am-9pm Mon & Wed-Sat, 11am-6pm Tue, 1-6pm Sun; ⊠4/9/14/16/24 Dam) Perfectly positioned for the Red Light District, this boutique sells condoms in every imaginable size, colour, flavour and design (horned devils, marijuana leaves, Delftware tiles...), along with lubricants and saucy gifts. Photos aren't allowed inside the shop.

Local Goods Store   Arts & Crafts

(www.localgoodsstore.nl; Hannie Dankbaar Passage 39, De Hallen; ⊙noon-7pm Tue-Fri & Sun, 11am-7pm Sat; ⊠1/ 1en Katestraat) As the name implies, everything at this concept shop inside De Hallen is created by Dutch designers. Look for Woody skateboards, I Made Gin gin production kits, Carhusa purses and handbags, Timbies wooden bow ties, Lucila Kenny hand-dyed scarves and jewellery, and Neef Louis industrial vintage homewares, as well as racks of

great Dutch-designed casual men's and women's fashion.

EATING

Amsterdam's food scene is woefully underrated. Beyond pancakes and potatoes, Dutch chefs put their spin on all kinds of regional and global dishes using ingredients plucked from local seas and farms. Wherever you go, meals are something to linger over as the candles burn low on the tabletop.

Bakers & Roasters   Cafe €

(www.bakersandroasters.com; 1e Jacob van Campenstraat 54; dishes €7.50-15.50; ⊙8.30am-4pm; ⊠16/24 Stadhouderskade) Sumptuous brunch dishes served up at Brazilian/Kiwi-owned Bakers & Roasters include banana nutbread French toast with homemade banana marmalade and crispy bacon; Navajo eggs with pulled pork, avocado, mango salsa and chipotle cream; and a smoked salmon stack with poached eggs, potato cakes and hollandaise. Wash them

Canalside cafe

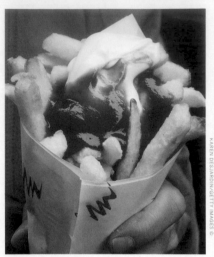

From left: *Frites* (fries); Canalside dining; Shops in an Amsterdam street

down with a fiery Bloody Mary. Fantastic pies, cakes and slices, too.

De Laatste Kruimel   Cafe, Bakery €

(☏020-423 04 99; www.delaatstekruimel.nl; Langebrugsteeg 4; dishes €3.50-7.50; ⊙8am-8pm Mon-Sat, 9am-8pm Sun; ☐4/9/14/16/24 Spui/Rokin) Decorated with vintage objects from the Noordermarkt and wooden pallets upcycled as furniture, and opening to a tiny canalside terrace, the 'Last Crumb' has glass display cases piled high with pies, quiches, breads, cakes and lemon poppy-seed scones. Grandmothers, children, couples on dates and just about everyone else crowds in for the fantastic organic sandwiches and treats.

Gartine   Cafe €

(☏020-320 41 32; www.gartine.nl; Taksteeg 7; dishes €6.50-11.50; high tea €17.50-24.75; ⊙10am-6pm Wed-Sat; ✐; ☐4/9/14/16/24 Spui/Rokin) ✐ Gartine is magical, from its covert location in an alley off busy Kalverstraat to its mismatched antique tableware and its sublime breakfast pastries, sandwiches and salads (made from produce grown in its garden plot and eggs from its

chickens). The sweet-and-savoury high tea, from 2pm to 5pm, is a treat.

Fat Dog   Hot Dogs €

(www.thefatdog.nl; Ruysdaelkade 251; dishes €4.50-12; ⊙noon Wed-Sun; ☐12 Cornelis Troostplein) Überchef Ron Blaauw, of **Ron Gastrobar** (☏020-496 19 43; www.rongas trobar.nl; Sophialaan 55; dishes €15, desserts €9; ⊙noon-2.30pm & 5.30-10.30pm; 📶; ☐2 Amstelveenseweg), elevates the humble hot dog to an art form. Ultra-gourmet options include Naughty Bangkok (pickled vegetables, red curry mayo and dry crispy rice); Vive La France (fried mushrooms, foie gras and truffle mayo); Gangs of New York (sauerkraut, bacon and smoked-onion marmalade) and Vega Gonzalez (vegetarian sausage, corn, guacamole, sour cream and jalapeño mayo).

Vleminckx   Fast Food €

(http://vleminckxdesausmeester.nl; Voet-boogstraat 33; fries €2.30-4.50; sauces €0.70; ⊙noon-7pm Sun & Mon, 11am-7pm Tue, Wed, Fri & Sat, 11am-8pm Thu; ☐1/2/5 Koningsplein) Frying up *frites* (fries) since 1887, Vleminckx has been based at this hole-in-the-wall

takeaway shack near the Spui since 1957.
The standard is smothered in mayonnaise,
though its 28 different sauces also include
apple, green pepper, ketchup, peanut,
sambal and mustard. Queues often stretch
down the block but move fast.

Tokoman   South American €

(Waterlooplein 327; sandwiches €3-4.50, dishes
€6.50-13.50; ⏱11am-8pm Mon-Sat; 🚊9/14
Waterlooplein) Queue with the folks getting
their Surinamese spice on at Tokoman. It
makes a sensational *broodje pom* (a sandwich filled with a tasty mash of chicken and
a starchy Surinamese tuber). You'll want
the *zuur* (pickled-cabbage relish) and *peper*
(chilli) on it, plus a cold can of coconut
water to wash it down.

Sterk Staaltje   Deli €

(www.sterkstaaltje.com; Staalstraat 12; dishes
€4-7.60; ⏱8am-7pm Mon-Fri, 8am-6pm Sat,
11am-5pm Sun; 🚊4/9/14/16/24 Muntplein) With
pristine fruit and veg stacked up outside,
Sterk Staaltje is worth entering just to
breathe in the scent of the foodstuffs,
with a fine range of ready-to-eat treats:
teriyaki meatballs, feta and sundried

tomato quiche, pumpkin-stuffed wraps, a
soup of the day, and particularly fantastic
sandwiches (roast beef, horseradish and
rucola; marinated chicken with guacamole
and sour cream).

Ciel Bleu   Gastronomy €€€

(📞020-450 67 87; www.okura.nl; Hotel Okura
Amsterdam, Ferdinand Bolstraat 333; mains
€45-120, 6-course menu €160, with paired wines
€255; ⏱6.30-10.30pm Mon-Sat; 🚊12 Cornelius
Trootsplein) Mindblowing, two-Michelin-star
creations at this pinnacle of gastronomy
change with the seasons; spring, for instance, might see scallops and oysters with
vanilla sea salt and gin-and-tonic foam,
king crab with salted lemon, beurre blanc
ice cream and caviar, or saddle of lamb
with star anise. Just as incomparable is the
23rd-floor setting with aerial views north
across the city.

D'Vijff Vlieghen   Dutch €€€

(📞020-530 40 60; http://vijffvlieghen.nl;
Spuistraat 294-302; mains €23.50-29.25;
⏱6-10pm; 🚊1/2/5 Spui) Spread across five
17th-century canal houses, the 'Five Flies'
is a classic. Old-wood dining rooms are full

Amsterdam's Best Markets

Albert Cuypmarkt (p160) Europe's largest daily (except Sunday) street market spills over with food, fashion and bargain finds.

Waterlooplein Flea Market (www.waterlooplein.amsterdam; Waterlooplein; ⊘9.30am-6pm Mon-Sat; ⛟9/14 Waterlooplein) Piles of curios, used footwear and cheap bicycle parts for treasure hunters.

Westermarkt (www.jordaanmarkten.nl; Westerstraat; ⊘9am-1pm Mon; ⛟3/10 Marnixplein) Bargain-priced clothing and fabrics at 163 stalls.

Lindengracht Market (www.jordaanmarkten.nl; Lindengracht; ⊘9am-4pm Sat; ⛟3 Nieuwe Willemsstraat) Wonderfully authentic local affair, with bushels of fresh produce.

IJ Hallen (www.ij-hallen.nl; Tt Neveritaweg 15; €5; ⊘9am-4.30pm Sat & Sun monthly; ⛴NDSM-werf) The monthly flea market at NDSM-werf is Europe's largest.

Camera stall at Waterlooplein Flea Market
IVICA DRUSANY/SHUTTERSTOCK ©

---

of character, featuring Delft-blue tiles and original works by Rembrandt; chairs have coppers plates inscribed with the names of its famous guests (Walt Disney, Mick Jagger...). Exquisite dishes span goose breast with apple, sauerkraut and smoked butter to candied haddock with liquorice sauce.

Greetje   Dutch €€€
(☏779 74 50; www.restaurantgreetje.nl; Peperstraat 23-25; mains €23-27; ⊘6-10pm Sun-Fri, to 11pm Sat; ⛟22/34/35/48 Prins Hendrikkade) ✎

Using market-fresh organic produce, Greetje resurrects and re-creates traditional Dutch recipes like pickled beef, braised veal with apricots and leek *stamppot* (traditional mashed potatoes and vegetables), and pork belly with Dutch mustard sauce. A good place to start is the two-person Big Beginning (€15 per person), with a sampling of hot and cold starters.

🍷 DRINKING & NIGHTLIFE

Amsterdam is one of the wildest nightlife cities in Europe and the world, and the testosterone-fuelled stag parties of young chaps roaming the Red Light District know exactly what they're doing here. Yet you can easily avoid the hardcore party scene if you choose to: Amsterdam remains a *café* (pub) society where the pursuit of pleasure centres on cosiness and charm.

For the quintessential Amsterdam experience, pull up a stool in one of the city's famed brown *cafés*. The true specimen has been in business a while and gets its name from the centuries' worth of smoke stains on the walls. Brown *cafés* have candle-topped tables, sandy wooden floors and sometimes a house cat that sidles up for a scratch. Most importantly, they induce a cosy vibe that prompts friends to linger and chat for hours over drinks – the same enchantment the *cafés* have cast for 300 years.

In 't Aepjen   Brown Cafe
(Zeedijk 1; ⊘noon-1am Mon-Thu, to 3am Fri & Sat; ⛟1/2/4/5/9/13/16/17/24 Centraal Station) Candles burn even during the day in this 15th-century building – one of two remaining wooden buildings in the city – which has been a tavern since 1519: in the 16th and 17th centuries it served an inn for sailors from the Far East, who often brought *aapjes* (monkeys) to trade for lodging. Vintage jazz on the stereo enhances the time-warp feel.

Amsterdam Roest   Beer Garden
(www.amsterdamroest.nl; Jacob Bontiusplaats 1; ⊘noon-1am Sun-Thu, to 3pm Fri & Sat; ⛟22 Wittenburgergracht) This is one of those 'only in

Brown *café*

Amsterdam' places, and well worth the trip to what were derelict shipyards and now host an epically cool artist collective/bar/restaurant, Amsterdam Roest (Dutch for 'Rust'), with a canalside terrace, mammoth playground of ropes and tyres, hammocks, street art, a sandy beach in summer and bonfires in winter.

It's slightly tricky to find; the most direct approach is to go along Oostenburgervoorstraat and cross the bridge at the northern end – it's 150m ahead on your left.

Pllek   Bar

(www.pllek.nl; TT Neveritaweg 59; ⊙9.30am-1am Sun-Thu, to 3am Fri & Sat; 🚉NDSM-werf) Ubercool Pllek is one of the key destinations in the Noord, with hip things of all ages streaming over to hang out in its interior made out of old shipping containers, and lie out on its artificial sandy beach. It's a terrific spot for a waterfront beer or glass of wine. Locals flock here for events, too: al fresco film screenings on Tuesday nights in summer, weekend yoga classes and dance parties under the giant disco ball.

Brouwerij Troost   Brewery

(🗲020 760 58 20; http://brouwerijtroost.nl; Cornelis Troostplein 21; ⊙4pm-1am Mon-Thu, 4pm-3am Fri, 2pm-3am Sat, 2pm-midnight Sun; 🚊; 🚋12 Cornelis Troostplein) 🍺 Watch beer being brewed in copper vats behind a glass wall at this outstanding craft brewery. Its dozen beers include a summery blonde, smoked porter, strong tripel, and deep-red Imperial IPA; it also distils cucumber and juniper gin and serves fantastic bar food including crispy prawn tacos and humongous burgers. Book ahead on weekend evenings.

Café de Dokter   Brown Cafe

(www.cafe-de-dokter.nl; Rozenboomsteeg 4; ⊙4pm-1am Wed-Sat; 🚋1/2/5 Spui) Candles flicker on the tables, old jazz records play in the background, and chandeliers and a birdcage hang from the ceiling at atmospheric Café de Dokter, which is said to be Amsterdam's smallest pub. Whiskies and smoked beef sausage are the specialities. A surgeon opened the bar in 1798, hence the name. His descendants still run it.

Vats at the Heineken Experience (p160)

Proeflokaal de Ooievaar Distillery
(www.proeflokaaldeooievaar.nl; St Olofspoort 1;
☺noon-midnight; ☒1/2/4/5/9/13/16/17/24
Centraal Station) Not much bigger than a vat
of *jenever*, this magnificent little tasting
house has been going strong since 1782.
On offer are 14 *jenevers* and liqueurs (such
as Bride's Tears with gold and silver leaf)
from the De Ooievaar distillery, still located
in the Jordaan. Despite appearances, the
house has not subsided but was built
leaning over.

De Drie Fleschjes Distillery
(www.dedriefleschjes.nl; Gravenstraat 18; ☺4-
8.30pm Mon-Wed, 2-8.30pm Thu-Sat, 3-7pm Sun;
☒1/2/5/13/14/17 Dam) A treasure dating
from 1650, with a wall of barrels made by
master shipbuilders, the tasting room of
distiller Bootz specialises in liqueurs including its signature almond-flavoured *bit-
terkoekje* (Dutch-style macaroon) liqueur,
as well as superb *jenever* (Dutch gin). Take
a peek at the collection of *kalkoentjes:*
small bottles with hand-painted portraits of
former mayors.

Brouwerij 't IJ Brewery
(www.brouwerijhetij.nl; Funenkade 7; ☺brewery
2-8pm, English tour 3.30pm Fri-Sun; ☒10 Hoogte
Kadijk) ✏ Beneath the creaking sails of the
1725-built De Gooyer windmill, Amsterdam's leading organic microbrewery
produces delicious (and often very potent)
standard, seasonal and limited-edition
brews. Pop in for a beer in the tiled tasting
room, lined by an amazing bottle collection,
or on the plane tree–shaded terrace. A beer
is included in the 30-minute brewery tour
(€5).

🟊 ENTERTAINMENT

Amsterdam supports a flourishing arts
scene, with loads of big concert halls,
theatres, cinemas and other performance
venues filled on a regular basis. Music fans
will be in their glory, as there's a fervent
subculture for just about every genre, especially jazz, classical and avant-garde beats.

Concertgebouw Classical Music
(☎671 83 45; www.concertgebouw.nl; Concertge-
bouwplein 10; ☺box office 1-7pm Mon-Fri, 10am-

7pm Sat & Sun; 3/5/12/16/24 Museumplein)
Bernard Haitink, former conductor of the
venerable Royal Concertgebouw Orchestra,
once remarked that the world-famous
hall (built in 1888 with near-perfect
acoustics) was the orchestra's best
instrument. Free half-hour concerts take
place every Wednesday at 12.30pm from
mid-September to late June; arrive early.
Try the **Last Minute Ticket Shop** (www.
lastminuteticketshop.nl; online ticket sales
from 10am on day of performance; 1/2/5/7/10
Leidseplein) for half-price seats to all other
performances.

Bitterzoet   Live Music

(020-421 23 18; www.bitterzoet.com; Spuistraat 2; 8pm-late; 1/2/5/13/17 Nieuwezijds
Kolk) Always full, always changing, this
venue with a capacity of just 350 people
is one of the friendliest venues in town,
with a diverse crowd. Music (sometimes
live, sometimes a DJ) can be funk, roots,
drum'n'bass, Latin, Afro-beat, old-school
jazz or hip-hop groove.

INFORMATION

DISCOUNT CARDS

Visitors of various professions, including artists,
journalists, museum conservators and teachers,
may get discounts at some venues if they show
accreditation.

Students regularly get a few euros off museum admission; bring ID.

Seniors over 65, and their partners of 60 or
older, benefit from reductions on public transport, museum admissions, concerts and more.
You may look younger, so bring your passport.

I Amsterdam Card (per 24/48/72 hours
€49/59/69) Provides admission to more than
30 museums (though not the Rijksmuseum), a
canal cruise, and discounts at shops, entertainment venues and restaurants. Also includes
a GVB transit pass. Useful for quick visits to
the city. Available at VVV I Amsterdam Visitor
Centres and some hotels.

Museumkaart (adult/child €55/27.50, plus for
first-time registrants €5) Free and discounted

Gezellig Culture

This particularly Dutch quality, which
is most widely found in old brown *cafés*
(traditional pubs), is one of the best reasons to visit Amsterdam. It's variously
translated as snug, friendly, cosy, informal and convivial, but *gezelligheid* – the
state of being *gezellig* – is something
more easily experienced than defined.
You can get this warm and fuzzy feeling
in many places and situations, often
while nursing a brew with friends. And
nearly any cosy establishment lit by
candles probably qualifies.

entry to some 400 museums all over the country
for one year. Purchase at participating museum
ticket counters or at Uitburo ticket shops.

Holland Pass (2/4/6 attractions €42/62/82)
Similar to the I Amsterdam Card, but without the
rush for usage; you can visit sights over a month.
Prices are based on the number of attractions,
which you pick from tiers (the most popular/
expensive sights are gold tier). Also includes a
train ticket from the airport to the city, and a
canal cruise. Available from GWK Travelex offices
and various hotels.

EMERGENCY NUMBERS
Police, fire, ambulance 112

LEGAL MATTERS
○ Technically, marijuana is illegal. However,
possession of soft drugs (eg cannabis) up to
5g is tolerated. Larger amounts are subject to
prosecution.

Dutch Etiquette

Greetings Do give a firm handshake and a double or triple cheek kiss.

Marijuana and alcohol Don't smoke dope or drink beer on the streets.

Smoking Don't smoke cigarettes in bars or restaurants.

Bluntness Don't take offence if locals give you a frank, unvarnished opinion. It's not considered impolite; rather it comes from the desire to be direct and honest.

Cycling paths Don't walk in bike lanes (which are marked by white lines and bicycle symbols), and do look both ways before crossing a bike lane.

○ Don't light up in an establishment other than a *coffeeshop* (cafe authorised to sell cannabis) without checking that it's OK to do so.

○ Never buy drugs of any kind on the street.

MONEY

ATMs are widely available. Credit cards are accepted in most hotels but not all restaurants; non-European credit cards are sometimes rejected.

TIPPING

Bars Not expected.

Hotels €1 to €2 per bag for porters; not typical for cleaning staff.

Restaurants Leave 5% to 10% for a cafe snack (if your bill comes to €9.50, you might round up to €10) and 10% or so for a restaurant meal.

Taxis Tip 5% to 10%, or round up to the nearest euro.

OPENING HOURS

Hours can vary by season. Our listings depict operating times for peak season (from around May to September). Opening hours often decrease during off-peak months.

GETTING THERE & AWAY

Schiphol International Airport (AMS; www. schiphol.nl) is among Europe's busiest airports and has copious air links worldwide, including many on low-cost European airlines. It's the hub of Dutch passenger carrier KLM.

National and international trains arrive at **Centraal Station** (Stationsplein; 1/2/4/5/9/13/16/17/24 Centraal Station). There are good links with several European cities. The high-speed Thalys (www.thalys.com) runs from Paris (3¼ hours direct, 3¾ hours via Brussels) nearly every hour between 6am and 7pm. Eurostar (www.eurostar.com) runs from London (around five hours); it stops in Brussels, where you transfer onward via Thalys.

Eurolines (www.eurolines.nl; Rokin 38a; ⊙9am-5pm Mon-Sat; 4/9/14/16/24 Dam) buses connect with all major European capitals. Bus travel is typically the cheapest way to get to Amsterdam.

Flights, cars and tours can be booked online at lonelyplanet.com/bookings.

GETTING AROUND

GVB passes in chip-card form are the most convenient option for public transport. Buy them at visitor centres or from tram conductors. Always wave your card at the pink machine when entering and departing.

Walking Central Amsterdam is compact and very easy to cover by foot.

Bicycle This is the locals' main mode of getting around. Rental companies are all over town; bikes cost about €11 per day.

Tram Fast, frequent and ubiquitous, operating between 6am and 12.30am.

Bus and Metro Primarily serve the outer districts; not much use in the city centre.

Ferry Free ferries depart for northern Amsterdam from docks behind Centraal Station.

Taxi Expensive and not very speedy given Amsterdam's maze of streets.

Where to Stay

Book as far in advance as possible, especially in summer and for weekends at any time of the year. Apartment rentals work well for local-life areas such as the Jordaan and De Pijp.

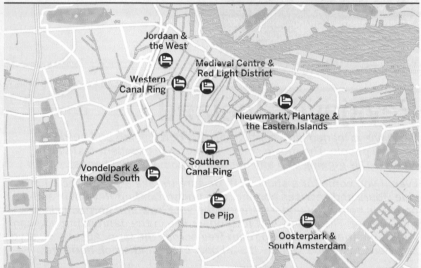

Neighbourhood	Atmosphere
Medieval Centre & Red Light District	In the thick of the action and close to everything. Can be noisy, touristy and seedy; not great value for money.
Nieuwmarkt, Plantage & the Eastern Islands	Nieuwmarkt is near the action, but with a slightly more laid-back vibe than the Centre. Some parts are close enough to the Red Light District to get rowdy spillover.
Western Canal Ring	Tree-lined canals within walking distance of Amsterdam's most popular sights. Rooms book out early and can be pricey.
Southern Canal Ring	Swanky hotels, not far from the restaurants of Utrechtsestraat and the antique shops of Nieuwe Spiegelstraat. Can be loud, crowded, pricey and touristy.
Jordaan & the West	Cosy cafes, quirky shops and charming village character, though sleeping options are few.
Vondelpark & the Old South	Genteel, leafy streets; walking distance to Museumplein; lots of midrange options and cool design hotels.
De Pijp	Ongoing explosion of dining/drinking cool in the area. Easy walking distance to Museumplein, Vondelpark and Leidseplein, but a hike from the Centre.
Oosterpark & South Amsterdam	Lower prices due to location (which is really just a short tram/ metro ride away); a quiet area amid locals.

Reykjavík, Iceland

Reykjavík is loaded with captivating art, rich cuisine and quirky, creative people. The music scene is epic, with excellent festivals, creative DJs gigging and any number of home-grown bands.

Even if you come for a short visit, be sure to take a trip to the countryside. Tours and services abound, and understanding Reykjavík and its people is helped by understanding the vast, raw and gorgeous land they anchor. The majority of Icelanders live in the capital, but you can guarantee their spirits also roam free across the land. Absorb what you see, hear, taste and smell – it's all part of Iceland's rich heritage.

Two Days in Reykjavík

Spend your first morning exploring historic **Old Reykjavík** (p188) and your afternoon wandering up arty **Skólavörðustígur** (p184), shopping and sightseeing. Head to **Laugavegur** (p191) for dinner, drinks and late-night dancing.

On your second day, catch a **whale-watching cruise** (p189) or explore the **Old Harbour** (p185) and its museums in the morning. While away the afternoon at **Laugardalur** (p190) and your evening at a top Icelandic restaurant, such as **Dill** (p191).

Four Days in Reykjavík

On your third day, rent a bike at the Old Harbour and ferry out to historic **Viðey** (p194). Come back in time for last-minute shopping around **Laugavegur** (p190) and **Skólavörðustígur** (p190). Sample the area's seafood before catching a show, an Icelandic movie or some live music.

On your final day take a trip to the **Golden Circle** (p182). If you haven't the time to visit the **Blue Lagoon** (p180) coming or going from the airport, go late this evening, after the crowds have dwindled.

After Reykjavík, catch a three-hour flight to London (p48) or Dublin (p114).

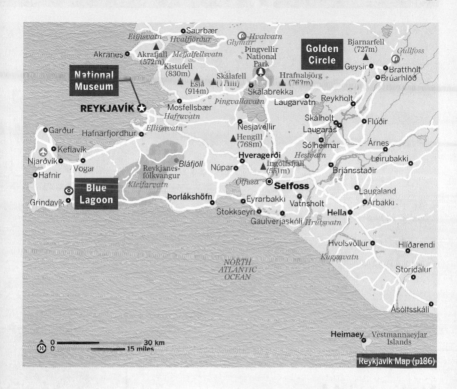

Reykjavik Map (p186)

Arriving in Reykjavík

Keflavík International Airport Iceland's primary international airport is 48km west of Reykjavík.

Reykjavík Domestic Airport Only a 2km walk into town.

Smyril Line (www.smyrilline.com) operates a pricey but well-patronised weekly car ferry from Hirsthals (Denmark) through Tórshavn (Faroe Islands) to Seyðisfjörður in East Iceland. It's possible to make a stopover in the Faroes.

Where to Stay

Reykjavík has loads of accommodation choices, with hostels, midrange guesthouses (often with shared bathrooms, kitchen and lounge) and business-class hotels galore, but top-end boutique hotels and apartments seem to be opening daily. Reservations are essential from June through August and prices are high. Plan for hostels, camping or short-term apartment rentals to save money. Most places open year-round and many offer discounts or variable pricing online.

For information on what each neighbourhood has to offer, see the table on p199.

National Museum

Iceland's premier museum is packed with artefacts and interesting displays. Exhibits give an excellent overview of the country's history and culture, and the audio guide (kr300) adds loads of detail.

The superb National Museum beautifully displays Icelandic artefacts from settlement to the modern age, providing a meaningful overview of Iceland's history and culture. Brilliantly curated exhibits lead you through the struggle to settle and organise the forbidding island, the radical changes wrought by the advent of Christianity, the lean times of domination by foreign powers and Iceland's eventual independence.

Settlement Era Finds

The premier section of the museum describes the Settlement Era – including how the chieftains ruled and the introduction of Christianity – and features swords, meticulously carved **drinking horns**, and **silver hoards**. A powerful **bronze figure of Thor** is thought to date from about 1000. The priceless 13th-century **Valþjófsstaðir**

Great For...

☑ Don't Miss

The gaming pieces made from cod ear bones, and the wooden doll that doubled as a kitchen utensil.

National Museum

University of Iceland

Hljómskálagarður Park

Tjörnin

❶ Need to Know

Þjóðminjasafn Íslands; ☎530 2200; www.
nationalmuseum.is; Suðurgata 41; adult/child
kr1500/free; ⏰10am-5pm May–mid-Sep,
closed Mon mid-Sep–Apr; 🚌1, 3, 6, 12, 14

✕ Take a Break

The ground-floor **Museum Café** (snacks
kr600-1800; ⏰10am-5pm May–mid-Sep,
9am-5pm Tue-Fri, 11am-5pm Sat & Sun mid-
Sep–Apr; 📶) offers wi-fi and a welcome
respite.

★ Top Tip

Free English tours run at 11am on
Wednesdays, Saturdays and Sundays
from May to mid-September.

church door is carved with the story of
a knight, his faithful lion and a passel of
dragons.

Domestic Life

Exhibits explain how the chieftains ruled
and how people survived on little, lighting
their dark homes and fashioning bog iron.
There's everything from the remains of
early *skyr* (yoghurt-like dessert) production
to intricate pendants and brooches. Look
for the Viking-era **hnefatafl game set** (a
bit like chess); this artefact's discovery in a
grave in Baldursheimar led to the founding
of the museum.

Viking Graves

Encased in the floor, you'll find Viking-era
graves, with their precious burial goods:

horse bones, a sword, pins, a ladle and
a comb. One of the tombs containing an
eight-month-old infant is the only one of its
kind ever found.

Ecclesiastical Artefacts

The section of the museum that details
the introduction of Christianity is chock-a-
block with rare art and artefacts, such as
the priceless 13th-century **Valþjófsstaðir
church door**.

The Modern Era

Upstairs, collections span from 1600 to
today and give a clear sense of how Iceland
struggled under foreign rule, finally gained
independence and went on to modernise.
Look for the **papers and belongings of
Jón Sigurðsson**, the architect of Iceland's
independence.

Blue Lagoon

In a magnificent black-lava field, this scenic spa is fed water from the futuristic Svartsengi geothermal plant. With its silver towers, roiling clouds of steam and people daubed in white silica mud, it's an other-worldly place.

Great For...

☑ **Don't Miss**

A bike or quad-bike tour in the lava fields.

A Good Soak

Before your dip, don't forget to practise standard Iceland pool etiquette: naked pre-pool showering.

The super-heated spa water (70% sea water, 30% fresh water) is rich in blue-green algae, mineral salts and fine silica mud, which condition and exfoliate the skin – it sounds like advertising speak, but you really do come out as soft as a baby's bum. The water is hottest near the vents where it emerges, and the surface is several degrees warmer than the bottom.

Towel or bathing-suit hire is €5.

Explore the Complex

The lagoon has been developed for visitors with an enormous, modern complex of changing rooms (with 700 lockers!),

REYKJAVÍK ✪   Mosfellsbær

Garður   Hafnarfjordhur

Keflavík

Njarðvík

Hafnir   Vogar   Reykjanes fólkvangur   Kleifarvatn

Blue Lagoon

Grindavík   Þorlákshöfn

❶ Need to Know

Bláa Lónið; ☑420 8800; www.bluelagoon. com; adult/child Jun-Aug from €50/free, Sep-May from €40/free; ☺8am-midnight Jun–mid-Aug, reduced hours mid-Aug–May

✕ Take a Break

Try the on-site **Blue Café** (snacks kr1000-2100; ☺8am-midnight Jun–mid-Aug, reduced hours mid-Aug–May; ☎) or **LAVA Restaurant** (mains lunch/dinner kr4500/5900; ☺11.30am-9.30pm Jun-Aug, to 8.30pm Sep-May; ☎).

★ Top Tip

Avoid summertime between 10am and 2pm – go early or after 7pm.

restaurants and a gift shop. It is also landscaped with hot-pots, steam rooms, sauna, a silica-mask station, a bar and a piping-hot waterfall that delivers a powerful hydraulic massage. A VIP section has its own interior wading space, lounge and viewing platform.

Massage

For extra relaxation, lie on a floating mattress and have a massage therapist knead your knots (30/60 minutes €75/120). Book spa treatments well in advance; look online for packages and winter rates.

Guided Tours

In addition to the spa opportunities at the Blue Lagoon, you can combine your visit with package tours, or hook up with nearby **ATV Adventures** (☑857 3001; www.atv4x4.is)

for quad bike or cycling tours (kr9900 from the Blue Lagoon through the lava fields) or bicycle rental. The company can pick you up and drop you off at the lagoon.

Planning Your Visit

Many day trips from Reykjavík tie in a visit to the lagoon, which is 47km southwest of the city. It's also seamless to visit on your journey to/from Keflavík International Airport – there's a luggage check in the car park (kr600 per bag, per day).

You should book ahead or risk being turned away. On a tour, always determine whether your ticket for the lagoon is included or if you need to book it separately.

Reykjavík Excursions (Kynnisferðir; ☑580 5400; www.re.is; BSÍ Bus Terminal, Vatnsmýrarvegur 10) and **Bustravel** (☑511 2600; www.bustravel.is) connect the lagoon with Reykjavík and the airport.

Gullfoss waterfall

Golden Circle

The Golden Circle is a beloved tourist circuit that takes in three popular attractions all within 100km of the capital: Þingvellir, Geysir and Gullfoss.

Great For...

☑ Don't Miss

The Sigríður memorial near the foot of the stairs from the Gullfoss visitors centre.

The Golden Circle offers the opportunity to see a meeting-point of the continental plates and the site of the ancient Icelandic parliament (Þingvellir), a spouting hot spring (Geysir) and a roaring waterfall (Gullfoss), all in one doable-in-a-day loop.

Visiting under your own steam allows you to visit at off-hours and explore exciting attractions further afield. Almost every tour company in the Reykjavík area offers a Golden Circle excursion, which can often be confined with virtually any activity from quad-biking to caving and rafting.

If you're planning to spend the night in the relatively small region, Laugarvatn is a good base with excellent dining options.

Þingvellir National Park

Þingvellir National Park (www.thingvellir. is), 40km northeast of central Reykjavík,

Þingvellir National Park

ℹ️ Need to Know

Tours generally go from 8.30am to 6pm or from noon to 7pm. In summer there are evening trips from 7pm to midnight.

✕ Take a Break

Eateries, mini-marts and grocery stores dot the route.

★ Top Tip

To go on to West Iceland afterwards, complete the Circle backwards, finishing with Þingvellir.

is Iceland's most important historical site and a place of vivid beauty. The Vikings established the world's first democratic parliament, the Alþingi, here in AD 930. The meetings were conducted outdoors and, as with many Saga sites, there are only the stone foundations of ancient encampments. The site has a superb natural setting with rivers and waterfalls in an immense, fissured rift valley, caused by the meeting of the North American and Eurasian tectonic plates.

Geysir

One of Iceland's most famous tourist attractions, **Geysir** FREE (*gay*-zeer; literally 'gusher') is the original hot-water spout after which all other geysers are named. Earthquakes can stimulate activity, though eruptions are rare. Luckily for visitors, the

very reliable **Strokkur** geyser sits alongside. You rarely have to wait more than five to 10 minutes for the hot spring to shoot an impressive 15m to 30m plume before vanishing down its enormous hole. Stand downwind only if you want a shower.

The geothermal area containing Geysir and Strokkur was free to enter at the time of writing, though there is discussion of instituting a fee.

Gullfoss

Iceland's most famous waterfall, **Gullfoss** (Golden Falls; www.gullfoss.is) FREE is a spectacular double cascade. It drops 32m, kicking up tiered walls of spray before thundering away down a narrow ravine. On sunny days the mist creates shimmering rainbows, and it's also magical in winter when the falls glitter with ice.

A tarmac path suitable for wheelchairs leads from the tourist information centre to a lookout over the falls, and stairs continue down to the edge. There is also an access road down to the falls.

◎ SIGHTS

◎ Laugavegur & Skólavörðustígur

This district is Reykjavík's liveliest. While it's justifiably well known for its shops and pubs, it's also home to some of the city's top restaurants, local music venues and the city's top art-house cinema.

Hallgrímskirkja   Church

(☎510 1000; www.hallgrimskirkja.is; Skólavörð-ustígur; tower adult/child kr900/100; ☉9am-9pm Jun-Sep, to 5pm Oct-May) Reykjavík's immense white-concrete church (1945–86), star of a thousand postcards, dominates the skyline, and is visible from up to 20km away. Get an unmissable view of the city by taking an elevator trip up the 74.5m-high tower. In contrast to the high drama outside, the Lutheran church's interior is quite plain. The most eye-catching feature is the vast 5275-pipe organ installed in 1992.

> ❝ *sparkling Harpa concert hall and cultural centre is a beauty to behold* ❞

Harpa

Harpa   Arts Centre

(☎box office 528 5050; www.harpa.is; Austurbakki 2; ☉8am-midnight, box office 10am-6pm) With its ever-changing facets glistening on the water's edge, Reykjavík's sparkling Harpa concert hall and cultural centre is a beauty to behold. In addition to a season of top-notch shows (some free), it's worth stopping by to explore the shimmering interior with harbour vistas, or take one of the guided tours and visit areas not open to the general public (see website for daily times and prices).

Culture House   Gallery

(Þjóðmenningarhúsið; ☎530 2210; www.culture house.is; Hverfisgata 15; adult/child kr1200/free; ☉10am-5pm May–mid-Sep, closed Mon mid-Sep–Apr) This superbly curated exhibition covers the artistic and cultural heritage of Iceland from settlement to today. Priceless artefacts are arranged by theme, and highlights include 14th-century manuscripts, contemporary art and items including the skeleton of a great auk (now extinct). The renovated 1908 building is beautiful, with great views of the harbour, and a cafe on the ground floor. Check website for free guided tours.

National Gallery of Iceland
Museum

(Listasafn Íslands; ☑515 9600; www.listasafn. is; Fríkirkjuvegur 7; adult/child kr1500/free; ⊙10am-5pm mid-May mid Sep, 11am-5pm Tue-Sun mid-Sep–mid-May) This pretty stack of marble atriums and spacious galleries overlooking Tjörnin offers ever-changing exhibits drawn from the 10,000-piece collection. The museum can only exhibit a small sample at any time; shows range from 19th- and 20th-century paintings by Iceland's favourite sons and daughters (including Jóhannes Kjarval and Nina Sæmundsson) to sculptures by Sigurjón Ólafsson and others.

◎ Old Harbour

Largely a service harbour until recently, the **Old Harbour** (Geirsgata; ☑1, 3, 6, 11, 12, 13, 14) has blossomed into a hotspot for tourists, with several museums, volcano and Northern Lights films, and excellent restaurants. Whale watching and puffin-viewing trips depart from the pier.

Omnom Chocolate
Factory

(☑519 5959; www.omnomchocolate.com; Hólmaslóð 4, Grandi; adult/child kr3000/1500; ⊙8am-5pm Mon-Fri) Reserve ahead for a tour at this full-service chocolate factory where you'll see how cocoa beans are transformed into high-end scrumptious delights. The shop sells its bonbons and stylish bars, with specially designed labels and myriad sophisticated flavours. You'll find the bars in shops throughout Iceland.

Víkin Maritime Museum
Museum

(Víkin Sjóminjasafnið; ☑517 9400; www. maritimemuseum.is; Grandagarður 8; adult/child kr1500/free; ⊙10am-5pm; ☑14) Based appropriately in a former fish-freezing plant, this museum celebrates the country's seafaring heritage, focusing on the trawlers that transformed Iceland's economy. Guided tours go aboard coastguard ship Óðinn (kr1200, or joint ticket with museum kr2200; check website for times).

The on-site **cafe** (snacks kr800-2200; ⊙10am-5pm) offers relaxing views of the

Reykjavík Art Museum

The excellent **Reykjavík Art Museum** (Listasafn Reykjavíkur; www.artmuseum. is; adult/child kr1600/free) is split over three well-done sites: the large, modern downtown **Hafnarhús** (☑411 6400, Tryggvagata 17; ⊙10am-5pm Fri-Wed, to 10pm Thu) focusing on contemporary art; **Kjarvalsstaðir** (☑411 6420; Flókagata 24, Miklatún Park; ⊙10am-5pm), in a park just east of Snorrabraut, and displaying rotating exhibits of modern art; and **Ásmundarsafn** (Ásmundur Sveinsson Museum; ☑411 6430; ⊙10am-5pm May-Sep, 1-5pm Oct-Apr; ☑2, 5, 15, 17), a peaceful haven near Laugardalur for viewing sculptures by Ásmundur Sveinsson.

One ticket is good at all three sites, and if you buy after 3pm you get a 50% discount should you want a ticket the next day.

Reykjavík Art Museum

boat-filled harbour, and has a great sunny-weather terrace.

Saga Museum
Museum

(☑511 1517; www.sagamuseum.is; Grandagarður 2; adult/child kr2100/800; ⊙10am-6pm; ☑14) The endearingly bloodthirsty Saga Museum is where Icelandic history is brought to life by eerie silicon models and a multilanguage soundtrack with thudding axes and hair-raising screams. Don't be surprised if you see some of the characters wandering around town, as moulds were taken from Reykjavík residents (the owner's daughters

Reykjavík

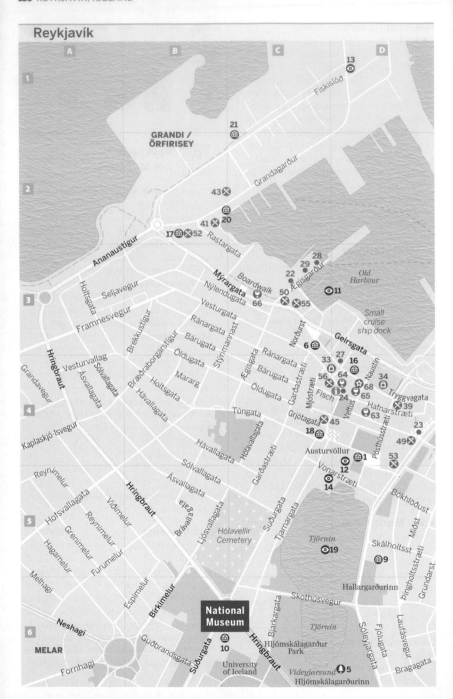

GRANDI /
ÖRFIRISEY

Fiskislóð

Grandagarður

Old
Harbour

Small
cruise
ship dock

Boardwalk

Mýrargata
Nýlendugata
Vesturgata
Rastargata

Ananaustigur

Holtsgata
Seljavegur
Framnesvegur

Vesturvallur
Brekkustigur
Bræðraborgarstigur
Ránargata
Báruqata
Öldugata
Mararg
Styrimannast

Hringbraut
Ásvallagata
Sólvallagata
Holtsgata
Hávallagata

Grandavegur
Túngata
Hólavallagata
Garðastræti
Hávallagata

Kaplaskjó-Isvegur
Sólvallagata
Ásvallagata

Reynimelur
Hringbraut
Bráð...

Hofsvallagata
Viðimelur
Reynimelur
Ljósvallagata

Hagamelur
Grenimelur
Furumelur
Espimelur

Melhagi

Neshagi

MELAR

Fornhagi

Guðbrandsgata
Suðurgata

Norðurstig
Geirsgata

Ránargata
Ránargata
Báruqata
Öldugata
Ægisgata
Garðastræti
Mjöstræti
Fisch
Vellus

Grjótagata
Austurvöllur
Vonarstræti

Naustin
Tryggvagata
Hafnarstræti
Pósthússtræti

Bókhlöðust

Hólavellir
Cemetery

Suðurgata
Tjarnargata

Tjörnin

Skálholtsst
Miðst

Hallargarðurinn

Þingholtsstræti
Grundarst

National
Museum

Bjarkargata
Skothúsvegur

Tjörnin

Laufásvegur
Sóleyjargata
Fjólugata

University
of Iceland

Hljómskálagarður
Park

Viðeyjarsund
Hljómskálagarðurinn

Bragagata

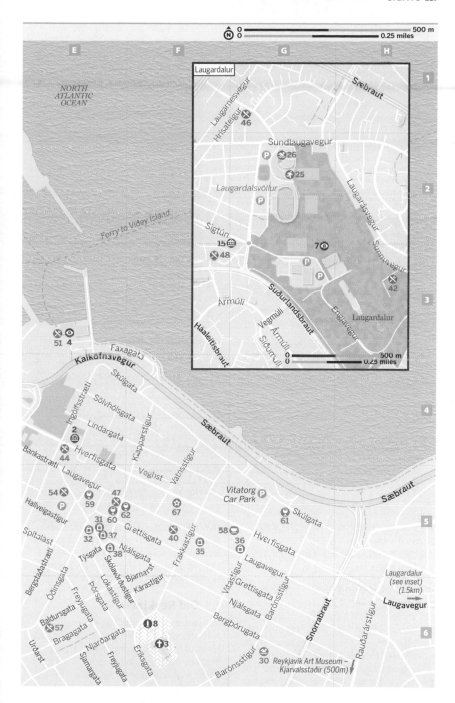

500 m
0.25 miles

E

F

G

H

1

NORTH
ATLANTIC
OCEAN

Sæbraut

Laugardalur

Laugarnesvegur

Hrísateigur

⊗46

Sundlaugavegur

🅿 ⊗26

🛈25

2

Laugarásvegur

Laugardalsvöllur

🅿

Sunnuvegur

Ferry to Viðey Island

Sigtún

15🏛

⊗48

7◉

🅿

🅿

⊗42

Ármúli

Suðurlandsbraut

Englavegur

Laugardalur

3

Vegmúli

Ármúli

Síðumúli

Háaleitisbraut

500 m
0.25 miles

⊗ ◉
51 4

Faxagata

Kalkofnsvegur

Skúlagata

Sölvhólsgata

Ingólfsstræti

Lindargata

Klapparstígur

Sæbraut

4

Bankastræti

Hverfisgata
44

2🏛

Vatnsstígur

Veghst

Sæbraut

Hallveigarstígur

54⊗

🅿

Laugavegur

47
59

Vitatorg 🅿
Car Park

Skúlata

🛈61

5

Spítalast

31 60
🅿 🔒
32 🔒37

62

Grettisgata

⊗
40

⊗
67

58⊗

36
🔒

Hverfisgata

Laugavegur

Bergstaðastræti

Týsgata

38

Njálsgata

Skólavörðustígur

Frakkastígur

35
🔒

Vitastígur

Grettisgata

Barónsstígur

Laugardalur
(see inset)
(1.5km)

Laugavegur

Óðinsgata

Freyjugata

Þórsgata

Lokastígur

Bjarnarst

Kárastígur

Njálsgata

Snorrabraut

Rauðarárstígur

6

Baldursgata

57⊗

Bragagata

Njarðargata

Freyjugata

🛈8

🛈3

Bergþórugata

30

Reykjavík Art Museum –
Kjarvalsstaðir (500m)

Úrðarst

Sjarnagata

Eiríksgata

Barónsstígur

Reykjavík

are the Irish princess and the little slave gnawing a fish!).

There's also a cafe and a room for posing in Viking dress.

Whales of Iceland   Museum

(☏571 0077; www.whalesoficeland.is; Fiskislóð 23-25; adult/child kr2900/1500; ⊙10am-6pm Jun-Aug, to 5pm Sep-May; 🚌14) Ever strolled beneath a blue whale? This museum houses full-sized models of the 23 whales found off Iceland's coast. The largest museum of this type in Europe, it also displays models

of whale skeletons, and has good audio guides and multimedia screens to explain what you're seeing. It has a cafe and gift shop, online ticket discounts and family tickets (kr5800).

⊙ Old Reykjavík

With a series of sights and interesting historic buildings, Old Reykjavík forms the heart of the capital, and the focal point of many historic walking tours. It's a top area for a stroll, from scenic lake Tjörnin to the old-fashioned houses surrounding Austurvöllur and Ingólfstorg squares.

Settlement Exhibition   Museum

(Landnámssýningin; ☑411 6370; www.reykjavik museum.is; Aðalstræti 16; adult/child kr1500/ free; ☺9am-6pm) This fascinating archaeological ruin/museum is based around a 10th-century **Viking longhouse** unearthed here from 2001 to 2002, and other settlement-era finds from central Reykjavík. It imaginatively combines technological wizardry and archaeology to give a glimpse into early Icelandic life.

Tjörnin   Lake

This placid lake at the centre of the city is sometimes locally called the Pond. It echoes with the honks and squawks of over 40 species of visiting birds, including swans, geese and Arctic terns; feeding the ducks is a popular pastime for the under-fives. Pretty sculpture-dotted parks like **Hljómskálagarður** FREE line the southern shores, and their paths are much used by cyclists and joggers. In winter hardy souls strap on ice skates and turn the lake into an outdoor rink.

i8   Gallery

(☑551 3666; www.i8.is; Tryggvagata 16; ☺11am-5pm Tue-Fri, 1-5pm Sat) FREE This gallery represents some of the country's top modern artists, many of whom show overseas as well.

Alþingi   Historic Building

(Parliament; ☑563 0500; www.althingi.is; Kirkjustraeti) FREE Iceland's first parliament, the Alþingi, was created at Þingvellir in AD 930. After losing its independence in the 13th century, the country gradually won back its autonomy, and the modern Alþingi moved into this current basalt building in 1881; a stylish glass-and-stone annexe was completed in 2002. Visitors can attend **sessions** (mid-September to early June; see website for details) when parliament is sitting.

On the northern shore, the postmodern **Ráðhús** (Vonarstræti; ☺8am-4pm Mon-Fri) FREE (city hall) has an interesting topo-map of Iceland inside.

⊕ ACTIVITIES

Creative Iceland   Art

(☑615 3500; www.creativeiceland.is) Get involved with graphic design, cooking, arts, crafts, music...you name it. This service hooks you up with local creative people offering workshops in their art or craft.

Literary Reykjavík   Walking

(www.bokmenntaborgin.is; Tryggvagata 15; ☺3pm Thu Jun-Aug) FREE Part of the Unesco City of Literature initiative, free literary walking tours of the city centre start at the main library and include the Dark Deeds tour focusing on crime fiction. There is also a downloadable *Culture Walks* app with several themes.

Sundhöllin   Geothermal Pool, Hot Pot

(☑411 5350; Barónsstígur 16; adult/child kr900/140; ☺6.30am-10pm Mon-Thu, to 8pm Fri, 8am-4pm Sat, 10am-6pm Sun; ☑) Reykjavík's oldest swimming pool (1937), designed in art deco style by architect Guðjón Samúelsson, is smack in the city centre and offers the only indoor pool within the city, plus Hallgrímskirkja views from the decks. It's been recently renovated.

Elding Adventures at Sea   Wildlife

(☑519 5000; www.whalewatching.is; Ægisgarður 5; adult/child kr9900/4950; ☺harbour kiosk 8am-9pm; ☑14) ✦ The city's most established and ecofriendly outfit, with an included whale exhibition and refreshments sold on board. Elding also offers angling (adult/child kr13,800/6900) and puffin-watching (adult/child from kr6500/3250) trips and combo tours, and runs the ferry to Viðey. Offers pick-up.

Reykjavík Bike Tours   Cycling

(Reykjavík Segway Tours; ☑bike 694 8956, segway 897 2790; www.icelandbike.com; Ægisgarður 7, Old Harbour; bike rental per 4hr from kr3500, tours from kr6500; ☺9am-5pm Jun-Aug, reduced hours Sep-May; ☑14) This outfitter rents out bikes and offers tours of Reykjavík and the countryside: Classic Reykjavík (2½ hours, 7km), Coast of Reykjavík (2½ hours, 18km), and Golden Circle and Bike (eight hours,

Laugardalur: Hot-Springs Valley

Encompassing a verdant stretch of land 4km east of the city centre, **Laugardalur** (🚌2, 5, 14, 15, 17) was once the main source of Reykjavík's hot-water supply: it translates as 'Hot-Springs Valley', and in the park's centre you'll find relics from the old wash house. The park is a favourite with locals for its huge **swimming complex** (📞411 5100; Sundlaugavegur 30a; adult/child kr900/140, suit/towel rental kr850/570; ◎6.30am-10pm Mon-Fri, 8am-10pm Sat & Sun; 🚼), fed by the geothermal spring, alongside a **spa** (📞553 0000; www.laugarspa.com; Sundlaugavegur 30a; day pass kr5490; ◎6am-11.30pm Mon-Fri, 8am-10pm Sat, to 8pm Sun), skating rink, botanical gardens, sporting and concert arenas, and a kids' zoo/entertainment park.

Stop by the sun-dappled tables of **Café Flóra** (Flóran; 📞553 8872; www.floran.is; Botanic Gardens; cakes kr950, mains kr1400-3000; ◎10am-10pm May-Sep; 🍴) 🌿 for lovely food made from wholesome local ingredients – some grown in the gardens themselves! Soups come with fantastic sourdough bread, and snacks range from cheese platters with nuts and honey to pulled-pork sandwiches. Weekend brunch, good coffee and homemade cakes round it all out.

In the surrounding residential streets you'll find **Frú Lauga farmers market** (📞534 7165; www.frulauga.is; Laugalækur 6; ◎11am-6pm Mon-Fri, to 4pm Sat; 🍴) 🌿 and Reykjavík Art Museum – Ásmundarsafn (p185).

25km of cycling in 1½ hours). It also offers Reykjavík Segway (kr12,500) and walking (from kr20,000) tours. Most convenient place to rent a bike before catching the ferry to Viðey island.

Reykjavík By Boat — Boating
(📞841 2030; www.reykjavikbyboat.is; Ægisgarður 11; adult/child kr4500/2200; 🚌14) Offers a 1½-hour boat trip on a small wooden boat from the Old Harbour, around Engey islet (with a puffin colony), to Viðey and back.

Free Walking Tour Reykjavik — Walking
(www.freewalkingtour.is; ◎noon & 2pm Jun-Aug, reduced hours winter) **FREE** One-hour, 1.5km walking tour of the city centre, starting at the little clock tower on Lækjartorg Sq.

Haunted Iceland — Walking
(www.hauntedwalk.is; adult/child kr2500/free; ◎8pm Sat-Thu Jun-early Sep) Ninety-minute tour, including folklore and ghost spotting, departing from the Main Tourist Office.

🛍 SHOPPING

Laugavegur and Skólavörðustígur are the central streets of Reykjavík's shopping scene. You'll find them lined with everything from stereotypical souvenir shops (derisively called 'Puffin Shops' by Reykjavíkers) to design shops and galleries selling beautiful handmade Icelandic arts and crafts, couture clothing lines and cool outdoorwear.

Geysir — Clothing
(📞519 6000; www.geysir.com; Skólavörðustígur 16; ◎9am-10pm) For traditional Icelandic clothing and unique modern designs, Geysir boasts an elegant selection of sweaters, blankets, and men's and women's clothes, shoes and bags.

KronKron — Clothing
(📞562 8388; www.kronkron.com; Laugavegur 63b; ◎10am-6pm Mon-Thu, to 6.30pm Fri, to 5pm Sat) This is where Reykjavík goes high fashion, with the likes of Marc Jacobs and Vivienne Westwood. But we really enjoy its Scandinavian designers (including Kron by KronKron) offering silk dresses, knit capes, scarves and even woollen underwear. Its handmade shoes are off the charts; the shoes are also sold down the street at **Kron** (📞551 8388; www.kron.is; Laugavegur 48; ◎10am-6pm Mon-Thu, to 6.30pm Fri, to 5pm Sat).

Orrifinn — Jewellery
(📞789 7616; www.facebook.com/OrrifinnJewels; Skólavörðustígur 17a; ◎10am-6pm Mon-Fri, to

4pm Sat) Subtle, beautiful jewellery captures the natural wonder of Iceland and its Viking history. Delicate anchors, axes and pen nibs dangle from understated matte chains.

Skúmaskot   Arts & Crafts

(✏663 1013; www.facebook.com/skumaskot. art.design/; Skólavörðustígur 21a; ⊙10am-6pm Mon-Fri, to 5pm Sat, noon-4pm Sun) Ten local designers create these unique handmade porcelain items, women's and kids' clothing, paintings and cards. It's in a recently renovated large gallery beautifully showcasing their creative Icelandic crafts

Kolaportið Flea Market   Market

(www.kolaportid.is; Tryggvagata 19; ⊙11am-5pm Sat & Sun) Held in a huge industrial building by the harbour, this weekend market is a Reykjavík institution. There's a huge tumble of secondhand clothes and old toys, plus cheap imports. There's also a food section that sells traditional eats like *rúgbrauð* (geothermally baked rye bread), *brauðterta* ('sandwich cake'; a layering of bread with mayonnaise-based fillings) and *hákarl* (fermented shark).

Kirsuberjatréð   Arts & Crafts

(Cherry Tree; ✏562 8990; www.kirs.is; Vesturgata 4; ⊙10am-7pm & 8-10pm Mon-Fri, to 5pm Sat, to 4pm Sun) This women's art-and-design collective in an interesting 1882 former bookshop sells weird and wonderful fish-skin handbags, music boxes made from string and, our favourite, beautiful coloured bowls made from radish slices.

EATING

🍴 Laugavegur & Skólavörðustígur

The area around Laugavegur and Skólavörðustígur is packed with eateries, from chilled-out old-school coffeehouses to high-concept Nordic cuisine. Places get crowded in high season, so book ahead if there's somewhere you don't want to miss.

Bakarí Sandholt   Bakery €

(✏551 3524; www.sandholt.is; Laugavegur 36; snacks kr600-1200; ⊙7am-9pm; 🛜) Reykjavík's favourite bakery is usually crammed with folks hoovering up the

KronKron

ICELANDIC PHOTO AGENCY/ALAMY STOCK PHOTO ©

Hallgrímskirkja (p184)
TSUGULIEV/SHUTTERSTOCK ©

generous assortment of fresh baguettes, croissants, pastries and sandwiches. The soup of the day (kr1540) comes with delicious sourdough bread.

Ostabúðin Deli **€€**
(Cheese Shop; 562 2772; www.facebook.com/Ostabudin/; Skólavörðustígur 8; mains kr3600-5000; restaurant 11.30am-9pm Mon-Fri, noon-9pm Sat & Sun, deli 10am-6pm Mon-Thu, to 7pm Fri, 11am-4pm Sat) Head to this gourmet cheese shop and deli, with a large dining room, for the friendly owner's cheese and meat platters (from kr1900 to kr4000), or the catch of the day, accompanied by homemade bread. You can pick up other local goods, like terrines and duck confit, on the way out.

Gló Organic, Vegetarian **€€**
(553 1111; www.glo.is; Laugavegur 20b; mains kr1200-2000; 11am-10pm Mon-Fri, 11.30am-10pm Sat & Sun;) Join the cool cats in this upstairs, airy restaurant serving fresh, large daily specials loaded with Asian-influenced herbs and spices. Though not exclusively vegetarian, it's a wonderland of raw and organic foods with your choice from a broad bar of elaborate salads, from root vegies to Greek. It also has branches in **Laugardalur** (Engjateigur 19; 11am-9pm Mon-Fri;) and **Kópavogur** (Hæðasmári 6; 11am-9pm Mon-Fri, 11.30am-9pm Sat & Sun;).

Dill Icelandic **€€€**
(552 1522; www.dillrestaurant.is; Hverfisgata 12; 5-course meal from kr11,900; 6-10pm Wed-Sat) Top 'New Nordic' cuisine is the major drawcard at this elegant yet simple bistro. The focus is very much on the food – locally sourced produce served as a parade of courses. The owners are friends with Copenhagen's famous Noma clan, and take Icelandic cuisine to similarly heady heights. Reservation is a must.

Þrír Frakkar Icelandic, Seafood **€€€**
(552 3939; www.3frakkar.com; Baldursgata 14; mains kr4000-6000; 11.30am-2.30pm & 6-10pm Mon-Fri, 6-11pm Sat & Sun) Owner-chef Úlfar Eysteinsson has built up a consistently excellent reputation at this snug little restaurant – apparently a favourite of

Jamie Oliver's. Specialities range throughout the aquatic world from salt cod and halibut to *plokkfiskur* (fish stew) with black bread. Non-fish items run towards guillemot, horse, lamb and whale.

Old Harbour

The Old Harbour and nearby Grandi are burgeoning with great spots to eat. Seafood restaurants line the harbour, but it's also a top neighborhood for refined Icelandic cuisine, and some of the best burgers in town.

Sægreifinn — Seafood €
(Seabaron; ☏553 1500; www.saegreifinn.is; Geirsgata 8; mains kr1350-1900; ☉11.30am-11pm mid-May–Aug, to 10pm Sep–mid-May) Sidle into this green harbourside shack for the most famous lobster soup (kr1350) in the capital, or to choose from a fridge full of fresh fish skewers to be grilled on the spot.

Hamborgara Búllan — Burgers €
(Hamborgarabúlla Tómasar; ☏511 1888; www.bullan.is; Geirsgata 1; mains kr1200-1800; ☉11.30am-9pm; ☎🚻) The Old Harbour's outpost of burgerdom and Americana proffers savoury patties that are perennial local favourites.

Coocoo's Nest — Cafe €€
(☏552 5454; www.coocoosnest.is; Grandagarður 23; mains kr1700-4500; ☉11am-10pm Tue-Sat, to 4pm Sun; ☎) Pop into this cool eatery tucked behind the Old Harbour for popular weekend brunches (dishes kr1700 to kr2200, 11am to 4pm Friday to Sunday) paired with decadent cocktails (kr1300). Casual, small and groovy, with mosaic plywood tables; the menu changes and there are nightly themes, but it's always scrumptious.

Matur og Drykkur — Icelandic €€
(☏571 8877; www.maturogdrykkur.is; Grandagarður 2; lunch mains kr1900-3200, dinner menus kr3000-5000; ☉11.30am-3pm Mon-Sat, 6-10.30pm Tue-Sat; 🚌14) One of Reykjavík's top high-concept restaurants, Matur Og Drykkur means 'Food and Drink', and you surely will be plied with the best of

Reykjavík's Best Festivals

Secret Solstice (www.secretsolstice.is; ☉Jun) This excellent music festival with local and international acts coincides with the summer solstice, so there's 24-hour daylight for partying. It's held at Reykjavík's Laugardalur.

Reykjavík Culture Night (www.menningarnott.is; ☉Aug) On Menningarnótt, held mid-month, Reykjavíkers turn out in force for a day and night of art, music, dance and fireworks. Many galleries, ateliers, shops, cafes and churches stay open until late. Your chance to get sporty and sophisticated on the one day, this event is held on the same date as the city's marathon.

Reykjavík International Film Festival (www.riff.is; ☉Sep-Oct) This intimate 11-day event from late September features quirky programming that highlights independent film-making, both home-grown and international.

Iceland Airwaves (www.icelandairwaves.is; ☉Nov) You'd be forgiven for thinking Iceland is just one giant music-producing machine. Since the first edition of Iceland Airwaves was held in 1999, this fab festival has become one of the world's premier annual showcases for new music (Icelandic or otherwise).

Crowd during Secret Solstice
MATTHEW EISMAN/GETTY IMAGES ©

both. The brainchild of brilliant chef Gísli Matthías Auðunsson, who creates inventive versions of traditional Icelandic fare. Book ahead in high season and for dinner.

Day Trip to Viðey

On fine-weather days, the tiny uninhabited island of Viðey (www.reykjavik museum.is) makes a wonderful day trip. Just 1km north of Reykjavík's Sundahöfn Harbour, it feels a world away. Well-preserved historic buildings, surprising modern art, an abandoned village and great birdwatching add to its remote spell.

Iceland's oldest stone house, **Viðeyarstofa**, is just above the harbour. Icelandic Treasurer Skúli Magnússon was given the island in 1751 and he built Viðeyarstofa as his residence. There's also an interesting 18th-century wooden **church**, the second oldest in Iceland, with some original decor and Skúli's tomb (he died here in 1794). Excavations of the old **monastery foundations** unearthed 15th-century wax tablets and a runic love letter, now in the National Museum.

Just northwest along the coast, Yoko Ono's **Imagine Peace Tower** (2007) is a 'wishing well' that blasts a dazzling column of light into the sky every night between 9 October (John Lennon's birthday) and 8 December (the anniversary of his death). Further along, **Viðeyjarnaust day-hut** has a barbecue for use if you bring all your own supplies.

There are usually free **guided walks** in summer. Check online for the current schedule.

Viðey Ferry (🗷533 5055; www.videy. com; return adult/child kr1200/600; ⊙from Skarfabakki hourly 10.15am-5.15pm mid-May–Sep, weekends only Oct–mid-May) takes five minutes from Skarfabakki, 4.5km east of the city centre. During summer, two boats a day start from Elding at the Old Harbour and the Harpa concert hall. Bus 16 stops closest to Skarfabakki, and it's a point on the Reykjavík hop-on-hop-off tour bus.

Bryggjan Brugghús   Pub Food €€
(🗷456 4040; www.bryggjanbrugghus. is; Grandagarður 8; mains kr2300-5000; ⊙11am-midnight Sun-Thu, to 1am Sat & Sun, kitchen 11.30am-11pm; 🛜) This enormous, golden-lit microbrewery and bistro is a welcome pit stop for one of its home-brewed beers (start with IPA, lager and seasonal beers, from 12 taps) or for an extensive menu of seafood and meat dishes, and occasional DJs. You've also got great harbour views out the back windows.

🍴 Old Reykjavík

You'll find some of the city's highest-end restaurants in the Old Reykjavík area, where you should book ahead in high season to guarantee a table. On the other hand, you'll also encounter Reykjavík's famed hot-dog stand, **Bæjarins Beztu** (www.bbp.is; Tryggvagata; hot dogs kr420; ⊙10am-2am Sun-Thu, to 4.30am Fri & Sat; 🚻), and other food trucks set up in Lækjartorg Sq – everything from lobster soup to fish and chips or doughnuts.

Stofan Kaffihús   Cafe €
(🗷546 1842; www.facebook.com/stofan.cafe/; Vesturgata 3; dishes kr1500-1600; ⊙9am-11pm Mon-Wed, to midnight Thu-Sat, 10am-10pm Sun; 🛜) This laid-back cafe in an historic brick building has a warm feel with its worn wooden floors, plump couches and spacious main room. Settle in for coffee, cake or soup, and watch the world go by.

Messinn   Seafood €€
(🗷546 0095; www.messinn.com; Lækjargata 6b; lunch mains kr1900-2100, dinner mains kr2500-3800; ⊙11.30am-3pm & 5-10pm; 🛜) Make a beeline to Messinn for the best seafood that Reykjavík has to offer. The speciality is amazing pan-fries where your pick of fish is served up in a sizzling cast-iron skillet accompanied by buttery potatoes and salad. The mood is upbeat and comfortable, and the staff friendly.

Grillmarkaðurinn   Fusion €€€
(Grill Market; 🗷571 7777; www.grillmarka durinn.is; Lækargata 2a; mains kr4600-7000;

Grillmarkaðurinn

⊗11.30am-2pm Mon-Fri, 6-10.30pm Sun-Thu, to 11.30pm Fri & Sat) From the moment you enter the glass atrium here, high-class dining is the order of the day. Service is impeccable, and locals and visitors alike rave about the food: locally sourced Icelandic ingredients prepared with culinary imagination by master chefs. The tasting menu (kr10,400) is an extravaganza of its best dishes.

Fiskmarkaðurinn   Seafood €€€

(Fishmarket; ☑578 8877; www.fiskmarkadurinn.is; Aðalstræti 12; mains kr5100-5700; ⊗6-11.30pm) This restaurant excels in infusing Icelandic seafood and local produce with unique flavours like lotus root. The tasting menu (kr11,900) is tops, and it is renowned for its excellent sushi bar (kr3600 to kr4600).

🍷 DRINKING & NIGHTLIFE

🍺 Laugavegur & Skólavörðustígur

Laugavegur is the epicentre of Reykjavík's nightlife and you could begin (and end) a night here. Bar hop until the clubs light up for dancing (late), then wander home under the early-morning sun.

Kaffi Vínyl   Cafe

(☑537 1332; www.facebook.com/vinilrvk/; Hverfisgata 76; ⊗9am-11pm Mon-Fri, 10am-11pm Sat, noon-11pm Sun; 🛜) This new entry on the Reykjavík coffee, restaurant and music scene is popular for its chilled vibe, great music, and delicious vegan and vegetarian food.

Mikkeller & Friends   Craft Beer

(www.mikkeller.dk; Hverfisgata 12; ⊗5pm-1am Sun-Thu, 2pm-1am Fri & Sat; 🛜) Climb to the top floor of the building shared by excellent pizzeria Hverfisgata 12 and you'll find this Danish craft-beer pub; its 20 taps rotate through Mikkeller's own offerings and local Icelandic craft beers.

Kaffibarinn   Bar

(www.kaffibarinn.is; Bergstaðastræti 1; ⊗3pm-1am Sun-Thu, to 4.30am Fri & Sat; 🛜) This old house with the London Underground symbol over the door contains one of Reykjavík's coolest bars; it even had a starring role in the cult movie *101 Reykjavík* (2000). At weekends you'll feel like you need a famous face or a battering ram to get in. At other times it's a place for artistic types to chill with their Macs.

Kaldi   Bar

(www.kaldibar.is; Laugavegur 20b; ⊙noon-1am Sun-Thu, to 3am Fri & Sat) Effortlessly cool with mismatched seats and teal banquettes, plus a popular smoking courtyard, Kaldi is awesome for its full range of Kaldi microbrews, not available elsewhere. Happy hour (4pm to 7pm) gets you one for kr700. Anyone can play the in-house piano.

Kiki   Gay

(www.kiki.is; Laugavegur 22; ⊙9pm-1am Thu, to 4.30am Fri & Sat) Ostensibly a queer bar, Kiki is also *the* place to get your dance on (with pop and electronica the mainstays), since much of Reyjavík's nightlife centres on the booze, not the groove.

KEX Bar   Bar

(www.kexhostel.is; Skúlagata 28; ⊙11.30am-11pm; 🛜) Locals like this hostel bar-restaurant (mains kr1800 to kr2600) in an old cookie factory (*kex* means 'cookie') for its broad windows facing the sea, an inner courtyard and kids' play area. Happy hipsters soak up the 1920s Vegas vibe: saloon doors, old-school barber station, scuffed floors and happy chatter.

🟢 Old Reykjavík

Austurstræti is lined with big venues that pull in the drinking crowd. As the night goes on, some of the capital's best dance clubs and late-night hangs can be found around Naustin street.

Micro Bar   Bar

(www.facebook.com/MicroBarIceland/; Vesturgata 2; ⊙2pm-12.30am Sun-Thu, to 2am Fri & Sat) Boutique brews is the name of the game at this low-key spot in the heart of the action. Bottles of beer represent a slew of brands and countries, but more importantly you'll discover 10 local draughts on tap from the island's top microbreweries: one of the best selections in Reykjavík. Happy hour (5pm to 7pm) offers kr850 beers.

A bar in Laugavegur

ICELANDIC PHOTO AGENCY/ALAMY STOCK PHOTO ©

Loftið   Cocktail Bar

(📞551 9400; www.loftidbar.is; 2nd fl, Austurstræti 9; ⏰2pm-1am Sun-Thu, 4pm-3am Fri & Sat)
Loftið is all about high-end cocktails and
good living. Dress up to enter the fray at
this airy upstairs lounge with a zinc bar, retro tailor-shop-inspired decor, vintage tiles
and a swanky, older crowd. The basic booze
here is the top-shelf liquor elsewhere, and
jazzy bands play from time to time.

Paloma   Club

(www.facebook.com/BarPaloma/; Naustin 1-3;
⏰8pm-1am Thu & Sun, to 4.30am Fri & Sat; 👥)
One of Reykjavík's best late-night dance
clubs, with DJs upstairs laying down reggae, electronica and pop, and a dark deep
house dance scene in the basement. Find it
in the same building as the Dubliner.

Old Harbour

Slippbarinn   Cocktail Bar

(📞560 8080; www.slippbarinn.is; Mýrargata 2;
⏰noon-midnight Sun-Thu, to 1am Fri & Sat; 📶)
Jet setters unite at this buzzy restaurant
(mains kr2900 to kr5000) and bar at the
Old Harbour in the Icelandair Hotel Reykjavík Marina. It's bedecked with vintage
record players and chatting locals sipping
some of the best cocktails in town.

✪ ENTERTAINMENT

Bíó Paradís   Cinema

(www.bioparadis.is; Hverfisgata 54; adult kr1600;
📶) This totally cool cinema, decked out
in movie posters and vintage officeware,
screens specially curated Icelandic films
with English subtitles. It has a happy hour
from 5pm to 7.30pm.

Húrra   Live Music

(Tryggvagata 22; ⏰5pm-1am Sun-Thu, to 4.30am
Fri & Sat; 📶) Dark and raw, this large bar
opens up its back room to make a concert
venue, with live music or DJs most nights,
and is one of the best places in town to
close out the night. It's got a range of beers
on tap and happy hour runs till 9pm (beer
or wine kr700).

Icelandic Pop

Iceland's pop music scene is one of its
great gifts to the world. Internationally
famous Icelandic musicians include (of
course) Björk and her former band, the
Sugarcubes. Sigur Rós followed Björk
to stardom; their concert movie *Heima*
(2007) is a must-see. Indie-folk Of Monsters and Men stormed the US charts
in 2011 with *My Head Is an Animal;* their
latest album is *Beneath the Skin (2015)*.
Ásgeir had a breakout hit with *In the
Silence* (2014).

Reykjavík's flourishing music
landscape is constantly changing –
visit www.icelandmusic.is and www.
grapevine.is for news and listings. Just
a few examples of local groups include
Seabear, an indie-folk band, which
spawned top acts like Sin Fang (*Flowers;*
2013) and Sóley (*We Sink;* 2012).
Árstíðir record minimalist indie-folk, and
released Verloren Verleden with Anneke
van Giersbergen in 2016.

Other local bands include GusGus,
a pop-electronica act, FM Belfast
(electronica) and múm (experimental electronica mixed with traditional
instruments). Or check out Singapore
Sling for straight-up rock and roll. If
your visit coincides with one of Iceland's
many music festivals, go!

If you can't get enough, check out **12
Tónar** (www.12tonar.is; Skolavörðustígur 15;
⏰10am-6pm Mon-Sat, from noon Sun). Besides being a very cool place to hang out,
this music store is responsible for launch-
ing some of Iceland's favourite bands.
Drop by to listen to CDs, drink coffee and
sometimes catch a live performance.

ℹ INFORMATION

DISCOUNT CARDS

Reykjavík City Card (www.citycard.is;
24/48/72hr kr3500/4700/5500) offers admission to Reykjavík's municipal swimming/thermal

pools and to most of the main galleries and museums, plus discounts on some tours, shops and entertainment. It also gives free travel on the city's Strætó buses and on the ferry to Viðey.

EMERGENCY NUMBERS
Ambulance, fire brigade & police ☑112

LUGGAGE STORAGE
BSÍ bus terminal, Reykjavík Domestic Airport and several other locations in Reykjavík have luggage lockers (www.luggagelockers.is). Many Reykjavík hotels will keep bags for you if you take off to the countryside for a few days.

MONEY
Credit cards are accepted everywhere (except municipal buses); ATMs are ubiquitous. Currency-exchange fees at hotels or private bureaus can be obscenely high.

It's not customary to tip in restaurants.

TOURIST INFORMATION
The **Main Tourist Office** (Upplýsingamiðstöð Ferðamanna; ☑590 1550; www.visitreykjavik. is; Aðalstræti 2; ☺8am-8pm) has friendly staff and mountains of free brochures, plus maps, Reykjavík City Card and Strætó city bus tickets. It books accommodation, tours and activities.

TRAVEL AGENCIES
Icelandic Travel Market (ITM; ☑522 4979; www. icelandictravelmarket.is; Bankastræti 2; ☺8am-9pm Jun-Aug, 9am-7pm Sep-May) Information and tour bookings.

Trip (☑433 8747; www.trip.is; Laugavegur 54; ☺9am-9pm) Books tours as well lodging, and rents cars.

ℹ GETTING THERE & AWAY
Iceland has become very accessible in recent years, with more flights from more destinations. Ferry transport makes a good alternative for people wishing to bring a car or camper from mainland Europe.

Flights, tours and rail tickets can be booked online at www.lonelyplanet.com/bookings.

ℹ GETTING AROUND
The best way to see compact central Reykjavík is by foot.

TO/FROM THE AIRPORT
The journey from Keflavík International Airport to Reykjavík takes about 50 minutes. Three easy bus services connect Reykjavík and the airport and are the best transport option; kids get discounted fares.

Flybus (☑580 5400; www.re.is; ☎) Meets all international flights. One-way tickets cost kr2200. Pay kr2800 for hotel pickup/drop off, which must be booked a day ahead. A separate service runs to the Blue Lagoon (from where you can continue to the city centre or the airport; kr3900). Flybus will also drop off/pick up in Garðabær and Hafnarfjörður, just south of Reykjavík.

Airport Express (☑540 1313; www.airport express.is; ☎) Operated by Gray Line Tours between Keflavík International Airport and Lækjartorg Sq in central Reykjavík (kr2100) or Mjódd bus terminal, or via hotel pickup/drop off (kr2700; book ahead). Has connections to Borgarnes and points north, including Akureyri.

Airport Direct (☑497 5000; www.reykjaviksight seeing.is/airport-direct; ☎) Minibuses operated by Reykjavík Sightseeing shuttle between hotels and the airport (kr4500, return kr8000).

Strætó (www.bus.is) bus 55 also connects the BSÍ bus terminal and the airport (kr1680, nine daily Monday to Friday in summer).

Taxis cost around kr15,000.

From the Reykjavík Domestic Airport it's a 2km walk into town; there's a taxi rank, or bus 15 stops near the Air Iceland terminal and bus 19 stops near the Eagle Air terminal. Both go to the city centre and the Hlemmur bus stop.

BUS
Strætó (www.bus.is) operates regular, easy buses in the city centre and environs, running 7am until 11pm or midnight daily (from 11am on Sunday). A limited night-bus service runs until 2am on Friday and Saturday.

Where to Stay

Demand always outstrips supply in Reykjavík. Try to book your accommodation three to six months ahead.

Neighbourhood	Atmosphere
Old Reykjavík	Central, easy with higher-end options. Can be crowded, busier and expensive.
Old Harbour	Less busy once back from the harbour. Guesthouses and hostels are more affordable, but it is slightly less central.
Laugavegur & Skólavörðustígur	Perfect for shopping and partying. Good range of options with certain quiet pockets. It's touristy on the main streets.
Hlemmur & Tún	Loads of high-rise hotels are popping up here. The areas are on the bland side and a bit far from the city centre.
Laugardalur	Near a large park and swimming complex. New high-rise hotels. Further from the city centre.

FRANCE, SPAIN & PORTUGAL

In This Chapter

Paris, France

The enchanting French capital is awash with landmarks that need no introduction – the Eiffel Tower and Notre Dame among them – along with a trove of specialist museums and galleries. Creamy-stone, grey-metal-roofed buildings, lamp-lit bridges and geometrically laid-out parks are equally integral elements of the city's fabric. Dining is a quintessential part of the Parisian experience – whether it be in traditional bistros, Michelin-starred restaurants, boulangeries (bakeries) or raucous street markets. Then there's its art repository, one of the world's best. But against this iconic backdrop, Paris' real magic lies in the unexpected: hidden parks, small museums and sun-spangled cafe pavement terraces.

Two Days in Paris

Start early with **Notre Dame** (p217), the **Louvre** (p211) or the **Eiffel Tower** (p204). Afterwards, head to the Champs-Élysées to shop and climb the **Arc de Triomphe** (p229). On day two take a boat cruise along the Seine and visit your pick of **Musée d'Orsay** (p236) or **Musée National du Moyen Âge** (p235). Make soulful St-Germain your dinner date.

Four Days in Paris

Devote day three to **Montmartre** (p229). Begin the fourth day with a top sight you missed on day one. Picnic in a Parisian park and spend the afternoon scouting out treasures at the **St-Ouen flea market** (p238) or checking out famous graves in **Cimetière du Père Lachaise** (p233). By night, take in a performance at **Palais Garnier** (p248) or **Opéra Bastille** (p248), and bar crawl in Le Marais.

Not finished with France? Head south to Provence (p252).

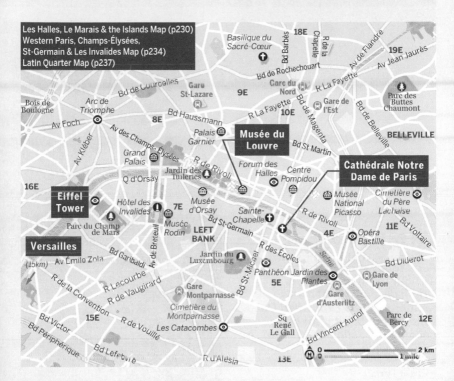

Les Halles, Le Marais & the Islands Map (p230)
Western Paris, Champs-Élysées,
St-Germain & Les Invalides Map (p234)
Latin Quarter Map (p237)

Arriving in Paris

Charles de Gaulle Airport Trains
(RER), buses and night buses to the city
centre €6 to €17; taxi €50 to €55.

Orly Airport Trains (Orlyval then RER),
buses and night buses to the city centre
€8 to €12.05; T7 tram to Villejuif-Louis
Aragon then metro to centre (€3.60);
taxi €30 to €35.

Gare du Nord train station Within central Paris; served by metro (€1.90).

Where to Stay

Paris has a wealth of accommodation
for all budgets, but it's often *complet*
(full) well in advance. Reservations
are recommended year-round and are
essential during the warmer months
(April to October) and on all public and
school holidays.

Parisian hotel rooms tend to be small
by international standards.

Breakfast is rarely included in hotel
rates.

For information on what each Paris
neighbourhood has to offer, see the
table on p251.

Eiffel Tower

Paris today is unimaginable without its signature spire. Originally constructed as a temporary 1889 Exposition Universelle exhibit, it went on to become the defining fixture of the city's skyline.

Great For...

❶ Need to Know

Map p234; ☎08 92 70 12 39; www.toureiffel. paris; Champ de Mars, 5 av Anatole France, 7e; adult/child lift to top €17/8, lift to 2nd fl €11/4, stairs to 2nd fl €7/3; ☉lifts & stairs 9am-12.45am mid-Jun–Aug, lifts 9.30am-11pm, stairs 9.30am-6.30pm Sep–mid-Jun; Ⓜ Bir Hakeim or RER Champ de Mars–Tour Eiffel

★ **Top Tip**

Head here at dusk for the best day-time vistas and glittering night-time city views.

Named after its designer, Gustave Eiffel, the Tour Eiffel was built for the 1889 Exposition Universelle (World Fair). It took 300 workers, 2.5 million rivets and two years of nonstop labour to assemble. Upon completion the tower became the tallest human-made structure in the world (324m or 1063ft) – a record held until the completion of the Chrysler Building in New York (1930). A symbol of the modern age, it faced massive opposition from Paris' artistic and literary elite, and the 'metal asparagus', as some Parisians derided it, was originally slated to be torn down in 1909. It was spared only because it proved an ideal platform for the transmitting antennas needed for the newfangled science of radio-telegraphy.

Tickets & Queues

Buying tickets in advance online usually means you avoid the monumental queues at the ticket offices. Print your ticket or show it on a smartphone screen. If you can't reserve your tickets ahead of time, expect waits of well over an hour in high season.

Stair tickets can't be reserved online. They are sold at the south pillar, where the staircase can also be accessed: the climb to the 2nd floor consists of 704 steps.

Ascend as far as the 2nd floor (either on foot or by lift), from where it is lift-only to the top floor. Prams must be folded in lifts and you are not allowed to take bags or backpacks larger than aeroplane-cabin size.

If you have reservations for either restaurant, you are granted direct access to the lifts.

1st Floor

Of the tower's three floors, the 1st (57m) has the most space, but the least impressive views. The glass-enclosed **Pavillon Ferrié** houses an immersion film along with a small cafe and souvenir shop, while the outer walkway features a discovery circuit to help visitors learn more about

---

☑ Don't Miss

The view of the tower in lights – each night, every hour on the hour, the entire tower sparkles for five minutes with 20,000 6-watt lights. For the best view of the light show, head across the Seine to the Jardins du Trocadéro.

the tower's ingenious design. Check out the sections of glass flooring that proffer a dizzying view of the ant-like people walking on the ground far below.

This level also hosts the **58 Tour Eiffel** (Map p234; ☑01 76 64 14 64; www.restaurants-toureiffel.com; 1st fl; menus lunch €41.50, dinner €85-180; ⊙11.30am-4.30pm & 6.30-11pm; ☑☀) restaurant.

Not all lifts stop at the 1st floor (check before ascending), but it's an easy walk down from the 2nd floor should you accidentally end up one floor too high.

2nd Floor

Views from the 2nd floor (115m) are the best – impressively high, but still close enough to see the details of the city below. Telescopes and panoramic maps placed around the tower pinpoint locations in Paris and beyond. Story windows give an overview of the lifts' mechanics, and the vision well allows you to gaze through glass panels to the ground. Also up here are toilets, a macaron bar and Michelin-starred restaurant **Le Jules Verne** (Map p234; ☑01 45 55 61 44; www.lejulesverne-paris.com; 2nd fl; 5-/6-course menus €190/230, 3-course lunch menu €105; ⊙noon-1.30pm & 7-9.30pm).

Top Floor

Views from the wind-buffeted top floor (276m) stretch up to 60km on a clear day, though at this height the panoramas are more sweeping than detailed. Celebrate your ascent with a glass of bubbly (€12 to €21) from the Champagne bar (open noon to 10pm). Afterwards peep into Gustave Eiffel's restored top-level office where lifelike wax models of Eiffel and his daughter Claire greet Thomas Edison.

To access the top floor, take a separate lift on the 2nd floor (closed during heavy winds).

✕ Take a Break

At the tower's two restaurants, snack bars, macaron bar or top-floor Champagne bar.

What's Nearby?

Parc du Champ de Mars — Park

(Map p234; Champ de Mars, 7e; M École Militaire or RER Champ de Mars–Tour Eiffel) Running southeast from the Eiffel Tower, the grassy Champ de Mars – an ideal summer picnic spot – was originally used as a parade ground for the cadets of the 18th-century **École Militaire**, the vast French-classical building at the southeastern end of the park, which counts Napoléon Bonaparte among its graduates. The steel-and-etched-glass **Wall for Peace Memorial** (Map p234; http://wallforpeace.org), erected in 2000, is by Clara Halter.

Musée du Quai Branly — Museum

(Map p234; ☎01 56 61 70 00; www.quaibranly.fr; 37 quai Branly, 7e; adult/child €10/free; ⊙11am-7pm Tue, Wed & Sun, 11am-9pm Thu-Sat; M Alma Marceau or RER Pont de l'Alma) A tribute to the diversity of human culture, Musée du Quai Branly inspires travellers, armchair anthropologists, and anyone who appreciates the beauty of traditional craftsmanship, through an overview of indigenous and folk art. Spanning four main sections – Oceania, Asia, Africa and the Americas – an impressive array of masks, carvings, weapons, jewellery and more makes up the body of the rich collection, displayed in a refreshingly unique interior without rooms or high walls. Look out for excellent temporary exhibitions and performances.

Musée Guimet des Arts Asiatiques — Gallery

(Map p234; ☎01 56 52 53 00; www.guimet.fr; 6 place d'Iéna, 16e; adult/child €7.50/free; ⊙10am-6pm Wed-Mon; M Iéna) France's foremost Asian art museum has a superb collection of sculptures, paintings and religious articles that originated in the vast stretch of land between Afghanistan and Japan. Observe the gradual transmission of both Buddhism and artistic styles along the Silk Road in pieces ranging from 1st-century Gandhara Buddhas from Afghanistan and Pakistan to later Central Asian, Chinese and Japanese Buddhist sculptures and art. Part of the collection is housed in the nearby

Galeries du Panthéon Bouddhique (Map p234; 19 av d'Iéna, 16e; ⊙10am-5.45pm Wed-Mon, garden to 5pm; M Iéna) with a **Japanese garden**.

Palais de Tokyo — Gallery

(Map p234; www.palaisdetokyo.com; 13 av du Président Wilson, 16e; adult/child €12/free; ⊙noon-midnight Wed-Mon; M Iéna) The Tokyo Palace, created for the 1937 Exposition Internationale des Arts et Techniques dans la Vie Moderne (International Exposition of Art and Technology in Modern Life), has no permanent collection. Instead, its shell-like interior of concrete and steel is a stark backdrop to interactive contemporary-art exhibitions and installations. Its bookshop is fabulous for art and design magazines, and its eating and drinking options are magic.

View of Parc du Champ de Mars from the Eiffel Tower

Musée Marmottan Monet Gallery

(🖉01 44 96 50 33; www.marmottan.fr; 2 rue Louis Boilly, 16e; adult/child €11/7.50; ⏰10am-6pm Tue, Wed & Fri-Sun, to 9pm Thu; Ⓜ La Muette) This museum showcases the world's largest collection of works by impressionist painter Claude Monet (1840–1926) – about 100. Some of the masterpieces to look out for include *La Barque* (1887), *Cathédrale de Rouen* (1892), *Londres, le Parlement* (1901) and the various *Nymphéas*.

Temporary exhibitions, included in the admission price and always excellent, are generally shown either in the basement or on the 1st floor. Also on display are paintings by Gauguin, Sisley, Pissarro, Renoir, Degas, Manet and Berthe Morisot, and an important collection of French, English, Italian and Flemish illuminations from the 13th to 16th centuries.

❶ Did You Know?

Slapping a fresh coat of paint on the tower is no easy feat. It takes a 25-person team 18 months to complete the 60-tonnes of paint task, redone every seven years.

★ Man on a Wire

In 1989 tightrope artist Philippe Petit walked up an inclined 700m cable across the Seine, from Palais Chaillot to the Eiffel Tower's 2nd floor. The act, performed before an audience of 250,000 people, was held to commemorate the French Republic's bicentennial.

NEALE CLARK/ROBERTHARDING/GETTY IMAGES ©

The Louvre

The Mona Lisa *and the* Venus de Milo *are just two of the priceless treasures resplendently housed inside the fortress turned royal palace turned France's first national museum.*

Few art galleries are as prized or as daunting as the Musée du Louvre – one of the world's largest and most diverse museums. Showcasing 35,000 works of art, it would take nine months to glance at every piece, rendering advance planning essential.

Works of art from Europe form the permanent exhibition, alongside priceless collections of Mesopotamian, Egyptian, Greek, Roman and Islamic art and antiquities – a fascinating presentation of the evolution of Western art up through the mid-19th century.

Great For...

☑ Don't Miss

The museum's thematic trails – from the 'Art of Eating' to 'Love in the Louvre'. Download trail brochures in advance from the website.

Visiting

You need to queue twice to get in: once for security and then again to buy tickets. The longest queues are outside the Grande Pyramide; use the Carrousel du Louvre

Canova's Psyche Revived by Cupid's Kiss

❶ Need to Know

Map p234; ☑01 40 20 53 17; www.louvre.fr;
rue de Rivoli & quai des Tuileries, 1er; adult/
child €15/free; ☺9am-6pm Mon, Thu, Sat &
Sun, to 9.45pm Wed & Fri; Ⓜ Palais Royal–
Musée du Louvre

✕ Take a Break

The Hall Napoléon sells sandwiches,
ideal for a picnic in the Jardin des
Tuileries (p233).

★ Top Tip

Tickets are valid for the whole day,
meaning you can come and go.

---

entrance (99 rue de Rivoli or direct from
the metro).

A Paris Museum Pass or Paris City
Passport gives you priority; buying tickets
in advance (on the Louvre website) will also
help expedite the process.

You can rent a Nintendo 3DS multimedia
guide (adult/child €5/3; ID required).
More formal, English-language **guided
tours** (Map p234; ☑01 40 20 52 63; adult/
child €12/7; ☺11.30am & 2pm except 1st Sun
of month) depart from the Hall Napoléon.
Reserve a spot up to 14 days in advance or
sign up on arrival at the museum.

In late 2014, the Louvre embarked on a
30-year renovation plan, with the aim of
modernising the museum to make it more
accessible. Phase 1 increased the number
of main entrances in order to reduce wait
times to get through security. It also revamped the central Hall Napoléon to vastly
improve what was previously bewildering
chaos.

Palais du Louvre

The Louvre today rambles over four floors
and through three wings: the **Sully Wing**
creates the four sides of the Cour Carrée
(literally 'Square Courtyard') at the eastern
end of the complex; the **Denon Wing**
stretches 800m along the Seine to the
south; and the northern **Richelieu Wing**
skirts rue de Rivoli. The building started life
as a fortress built by Philippe-Auguste in
the 12th century – medieval remnants are
still visible on the Lower Ground Floor (Sully). In the 16th century it became a royal
residence, and after the Revolution, in 1793,
it was turned into a national museum. At
the time, its booty was no more than 2500
paintings and objets d'art.

Over the centuries French governments
amassed the paintings, sculptures and
artefacts displayed today. The 'Grand
Louvre' project, inaugurated by the late

President Mitterrand in 1989, doubled the museum's exhibition space, and both new and renovated galleries have since opened, including the state-of-the-art **Islamic art galleries** (Lower Ground Floor, Denon) in the stunningly restored Cour Visconti.

Priceless Antiquities

Whatever your plans are, don't rush by the Louvre's astonishing cache of treasures from antiquity: both Mesopotamia (ground floor, Richelieu) and Egypt (ground and 1st floors, Sully) are well represented, as seen in the *Code of Hammurabi* (Room 3, ground floor, Richelieu) and the *Seated Scribe* (Room 22, 1st floor, Sully). Room 12 (ground floor, Sackler Wing) holds impressive friezes and an enormous two-headed-bull column from the Darius Palace in ancient Iran, while an enormous seated statue of Pharaoh Ramesses II highlights the temple room (Room 12, Sully).

Also worth a look are the mosaics and figurines from the Byzantine empire (lower ground floor, Denon), and the Greek statuary collection, culminating with the world's most famous armless duo, the *Venus de Milo* (Room 16, ground floor, Sully) and the *Winged Victory of Samothrace* (top of Daru staircase, 1st floor, Denon).

French & Italian Masterpieces

The 1st floor of the Denon Wing, where the *Mona Lisa* is found, is easily the most popular part of the Louvre – and with good reason. Rooms 75 through 77 are hung with monumental French paintings, many iconic: look for the *Consecration of the Emperor Napoleon I* (David), *The Raft of the Medusa* (Géricault) and *Grande Odalisque* (Ingres).

Paintings in the Denon Wing

Rooms 1, 3, 5 and 8 are also must-visits. Filled with classic works by Renaissance masters – Raphael, Titian, Uccello, Botticini – this area culminates with the crowds around the *Mona Lisa*. But you'll find plenty else to contemplate, from Botticelli's graceful frescoes (Room 1) to the superbly detailed *Wedding Feast at Cana* (Room 6).

Mona Lisa

Easily the Louvre's most admired work (and the world's most famous painting) is Leonardo da Vinci's *La Joconde* (in French;

La Gioconda in Italian), the lady with that enigmatic smile known as *Mona Lisa* (Room 6, 1st floor, Denon).

Mona (*monna* in Italian) is a contraction of *madonna*, and Gioconda is the feminine form of the surname Giocondo. Canadian scientists used infrared technology to peer through paint layers and confirm *Mona Lisa*'s identity as Lisa Gherardini (1479–1542?), wife of Florentine merchant Francesco de Giocondo. Scientists also discovered that her dress was covered in a transparent gauze veil typically worn in early 16th-century Italy by pregnant women or new mothers; it's surmised that the work was painted to commemorate the birth of her second son around 1503, when she was aged about 24.

The Pyramid Inside & Out

Almost as stunning as the masterpieces inside is the 21m-high glass pyramid designed by Chinese-born American architect IM Pei that bedecks the main entrance to the Louvre. Beneath Pei's Grande Pyramide is the **Hall Napoléon**, the main entrance area, comprising an information booth, temporary exhibition hall, bookshop, souvenir store, cafe and auditoriums. To revel in another Pei pyramid of equally dramatic dimensions, head towards the **Carrousel du Louvre** (Map p234; http://carrouseldulouvre. com; 99 rue de Rivoli, 1er; ◎8.30am-11pm, shops 10am-8pm; 🛜), a busy shopping mall – its centrepiece is Pei's **Pyramide Inversée** (inverted glass pyramid).

★ Italian Sculptures

On the ground floor of the Denon Wing, take time for the Italian sculptures, including Michelangelo's *The Dying Slave* and Canova's *Psyche and Cupid* (Room 4).

TAKASHI IMAGES/SHUTTERSTOCK ©

★ Behind the Smile

Recent tests done with 'emotion recognition' computer software suggest that the smile on 'Madam Lisa' is at least 83% happy. And one other point remains unequivocally certain: she was not the lover of Leonardo, who preferred his *Vitruvian Man* to his Mona.

The Louvre

A HALF-DAY TOUR

Successfully visiting the Louvre is a fine art. Its complex labyrinth of galleries and staircases spiralling three wings and four floors renders discovery a snakes-and-ladders experience. Initiate yourself with this three-hour itinerary – a playful mix of *Mona Lisa*–obvious and up-to-the-minute unexpected.

Arriving in the newly renovated **① Hall Napoléon** beneath IM Pei's glass pyramid, pick up colour-coded floor plans at an information stand, then ride the escalator up to the Sully Wing and swap passport or credit card for a multimedia guide (there are limited descriptions in the galleries) at the wing entrance.

The Louvre is as much about spectacular architecture as masterful art. To appreciate this, zip up and down Sully's Escalier Henri II to admire **② Venus de Milo**, then up parallel Escalier Henri IV to the palatial displays in **③ Cour Khorsabad**. Cross Room 1 to find the escalator up to the 1st floor and the opulent **④ Napoleon III apartments**. Next traverse 25 consecutive galleries (thank you, floor plan!) to flip conventional contemplation on its head with Cy Twombly's **⑤ The Ceiling**, and the hypnotic **⑥ Winged Victory of Samothrace sculpture**, which brazenly insists on being admired from all angles. End with the impossibly famous **⑦ The Raft of the Medusa**, **⑧ Mona Lisa** and **⑨ Virgin & Child**.

TOP TIPS

➡ Don't even consider entering the Louvre's maze of galleries without a floor plan, free from the information desk in the Hall Napoléon.

➡ The Denon Wing is always packed; visit on late nights (Wednesday or Friday) or trade Denon in for the notably quieter Richelieu Wing.

➡ The 2nd floor isn't for first-timers: save its more specialist works for subsequent visits.

Napoleon III Apartments
1st Floor, Richelieu
Napoleon III's gorgeous gilt apartments were built from 1854 to 1861, featuring an over-the-top decor of gold leaf, stucco and crystal chandeliers that reaches a dizzying climax in the Grand Salon and State Dining Room.

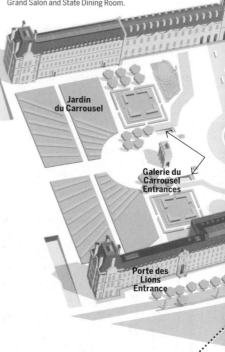

Jardin du Carrousel

Galerie du Carrousel Entrances

Porte des Lions Entrance

LOUVRE AUDITORIUM

Classical-music concerts are staged several times a week at the Louvre Auditorium (off the main entrance hall). Don't miss the Thursday lunchtime concerts featuring emerging composers and musicians. The season runs from September to April or May, depending on the concert series.

Mona Lisa
Room 6, 1st Floor, Denon
No smile is as enigmatic or bewitching as hers. Da Vinci's diminutive *La Joconde* hangs opposite the largest painting in the Louvre – sumptuous, fellow Italian Renaissance artwork *The Wedding at Cana*.

The Raft of the Medusa
Room 77, 1st Floor, Denon
Decipher the politics behind French romanticism in Théodore Géricault's *Raft of the Medusa*.

Cour Khorsabad
Ground Floor, Richelieu
Time travel with a pair of winged human-headed bulls to view some of the world's oldest Mesopotamian art. **DETOUR»** Night-lit statues in Cour Puget.

PRYZMAT/SHUTTERSTOCK ©

The Ceiling
Room 32, 1st Floor, Sully
Admire the blue shock of Cy Twombly's 400-sq-metre contemporary ceiling fresco – the Louvre's latest, daring commission. **DETOUR»** *The Braque Ceiling*, Room 33.

Rue de Rivoli Entrance

3

Cour Khorsabad

Cour Puget

Cour Marly

4

RICHELIEU WING

Cour Napoléon

1

Pyramid Main Entrance

Inverted Pyramid

Cour Carrée

5

SULLY WING

2

6

Cour Visconti

7 **8**

9

DENON WING

Pont des Arts

Pont du Carrousel

Venus de Milo
Room 16, Ground Floor, Sully
No one knows who sculpted this seductively realistic goddess from Greek antiquity. Naked to the hips, she is a Hellenistic masterpiece.

PRYZMAT/SHUTTERSTOCK ©

Winged Victory of Samothrace
Escalier Daru, 1st Floor, Sully
Draw breath at the aggressive dynamism of this headless, handless Hellenistic goddess. **DETOUR»** The razzle-dazzle of the Apollo Gallery's crown jewels.

Virgin & Child
Grande Galerie, 1st Floor, Denon
In the spirit of artistic devotion save the Louvre's most famous gallery for last: a feast of Virgin-and-child paintings by Da Vinci, Raphael, Domenico Ghirlandaio, Giovanni Bellini and Francesco Botticini.

TUTTI FRUTTI/SHUTTERSTOCK ©

ALDORADO/SHUTTERSTOCK ©

Notre Dame

A vision of stained-glass rose windows, flying buttresses and frightening gargoyles, Paris' glorious cathedral, on the larger of the two inner-city islands, is the city's geographic and spiritual heart.

Great For...

☑ **Don't Miss**

Climbing the bell towers, which brings you face to face with the cathedral's ghoulish gargoyles.

When you enter the cathedral its grand dimensions are immediately evident: the interior alone is 127m long, 48m wide and 35m high, and can accommodate some 6000 worshippers.

Architecture

Built on a site occupied by earlier churches and, a millennium prior, a Gallo-Roman temple, Notre Dame was begun in 1163 and largely completed by the early 14th century. The cathedral was badly damaged during the Revolution, prompting architect Eugène Emmanuel Viollet-le-Duc to oversee extensive renovations between 1845 and 1864. Enter the magnificent forest of ornate flying buttresses that encircle the cathedral chancel and support its walls and roof.

Notre Dame is known for its sublime balance, though if you look closely you'll see

Interior of Notre Dame

❶ Need to Know

Map p230; ☎01 42 34 56 10; www.
notredamedeparis.fr; 6 place du Parvis
Notre Dame, 4e; cathedral free, adult/child
towers €10/free, treasury €4/2; ⊙cathedral
7.45am-6.45pm Mon-Fri, to 7.15pm Sat & Sun,
towers 10am-6.30pm Sun-Thu, to 11pm Fri &
Sat Jul & Aug, 10am-6.30pm Apr-Jun & Sep,
10am-5.30pm Oct-Mar, treasury 9.30am-6pm
Apr-Sep, 10am-5.30pm Oct-Mar; Ⓜ Cité

✕ Take a Break

On hidden place Dauphine, **Le Caveau
du Palais** (Map p230; ☎01 43 26 04 28;
www.caveaudupalais.fr; 19 place Dauphine,
1er; mains €21-28; ⊙noon-2.30pm & 7-10pm;
Ⓜ Pont Neuf) serves contemporary
French fare.

> ### ★ Top Tip
> Invariably huge queues get longer
> throughout the day – arrive as early
> as possible.

all sorts of minor asymmetrical elements introduced to avoid monotony, in accordance with standard Gothic practice. These include the slightly different shapes of each of the three main portals, the statues of which were once brightly coloured to make them more effective as a *Biblia pauperum* (a 'Bible of the poor' to help the illiterate faithful understand Old Testament stories, the Passion of the Christ and the lives of the saints).

Rose Windows & Pipe Organ

The most spectacular interior features are three rose windows, particularly the 10m-wide window over the western facade above the organ – one of the largest in the world, with 7800 pipes (900 of which have historical classification), 111 stops, five 56-key manuals and a 32-key pedalboard – and the window on the northern side of

the transept (virtually unchanged since the 13th century).

Towers

A constant queue marks the entrance to the **Tours de Notre Dame**, the cathedral's bell towers. Climb the 400-odd spiralling steps to the top of the western facade of the North Tower, where you'll find yourself on the rooftop **Galerie des Chimères** (Gargoyles Gallery), face to face with frightening and fantastic gargoyles. These grotesque statues divert rainwater from the roof to prevent masonry damage, with the water exiting through the elongated, open mouth; they also, purportedly, ward off evil spirits. Although they appear medieval, they were installed by Eugène Viollet-le-Duc in the 19th century. From the rooftop there's a spectacular view over Paris.

In the South Tower hangs Emmanuel, the cathedral's original 13-tonne bourdon bell (all of the cathedral's bells are named). During the night of 24 August 1944, when the Île de la Cité was retaken by French, Allied and Resistance troops, the tolling of the Emmanuel announced Paris' approaching liberation.

As part of 2013's celebrations for Notre Dame's 850th anniversary since construction began, nine new bells were installed, replicating the original medieval chimes.

Treasury

In the southeastern transept, the *trésor* (treasury) contains artwork, liturgical objects and first-class relics; pay a small fee to enter. Among its religious jewels and gems is the **Ste-Couronne** (Holy Crown), purportedly the wreath of thorns placed on Jesus' head before he was crucified. It is exhibited between 3pm and 4pm on the first Friday of each month, 3pm to 4pm every Friday during Lent, and 10am to 5pm on Good Friday.

Easier to admire is the treasury's wonderful collection, **Les Camées des Papes** (Papal cameos). Sculpted with incredible finesse in shell and framed in silver, the 268-piece collection depicts every pope in miniature from St Pierre to Pope Benoit XVI. Note the different posture, hand gestures and clothes of each pope.

The Mays

Walk past the choir, with its carved wooden stalls and statues representing the Passion of the Christ, to admire the cathedral's wonderful collection of paintings in its

nave side chapels. From 1449 onwards, city goldsmiths offered to the cathedral each year on 1 May a tree strung with devotional ribbons and banners to honour the Virgin Mary – to whom Notre Dame (Our Lady) is dedicated. Fifty years later the goldsmiths' annual gift, known as a May, had become a tabernacle decorated with scenes from the Old Testament, and, from 1630, a large canvas – 3m tall – commemorating one of the Acts of the Apostles, accompanied by a poem or literary explanation. By the early 18th century, when the brotherhood of goldsmiths was dissolved, the cathedral had received 76 such monumental paintings – just 13 can be admired today.

Crypt

Under the square in front of Notre Dame lies the **Crypte Archéologique** (Archaeo-logical Crypt; Map p230; www.crypte.paris.fr; adult/child €8/free; ◷10am-6pm Tue-Sun), a 117m-long and 28m-wide area displaying *in situ* the remains of structures built on this site during the Gallo-Roman period, a 4th-century enclosure wall, the foundations of the medieval foundlings hospice and a few of the original sewers sunk by Haussmann.

Audioguides & Tours

Pick up an audioguide (€5) from Notre Dame's information desk, just inside the entrance. Audio guide rental includes admission to the treasury.

Free one-hour English-language tours take place at 2pm Wednesday and Thursday and 2.30pm Saturday.

Landmark Occasions

Historic events that have taken place at Notre Dame include Henry VI of England's 1431 coronation as King of France, the 1558 marriage of Mary, Queen of Scots, to the Dauphin Francis (later Francis II of France), the 1804 coronation of Napoléon I by Pope Pius VII and the 1909 beatification and 1920 canonisation of Joan of Arc.

Music at Notre Dame

Music has been a sacred part of Notre Dame's soul since birth. The best day to appreciate its musical heritage is on Sunday at a Gregorian or polyphonic Mass (10am and 6.30pm, respectively) or a free organ recital (4.30pm).

From October to June the cathedral stages evening concerts; find the program online at www.musique-sacree-notredame deparis.fr.

MATTEO COLOMBO/GETTY IMAGES ©

★ Square Jean XXIII

One of the best views of the cathedral's forest of flying buttresses is from square Jean XXIII, the little park behind the cathedral.

Notre Dame

TIMELINE

1160 Maurice de Sully becomes bishop of Paris. Mission: to grace growing Paris with a lofty new cathedral.

1182–90 The ❶ **choir with double ambulatory** is finished and work starts on the nave and side chapels.

1200–50 The ❷ **west façade**, with rose window, three portals and two soaring towers, goes up. Everyone is stunned.

1345 Some 180 years after the foundation stone was laid, the Cathédrale de Notre Dame is complete. It is dedicated to notre dame (our lady), the Virgin Mary.

1789 Revolutionaries smash the original ❸ **Gallery of Kings**, pillage the cathedral and melt all its bells except the great bell Emmanuel. The cathedral becomes a Temple of Reason then a warehouse.

1831 Victor Hugo's novel *The Hunchback of Notre Dame* inspires new interest in the half-ruined Gothic cathedral.

1845–64 Architect Viollet-le-Duc undertakes its restoration. Twenty-eight new kings are sculpted for the west façade. The heavily decorated ❹ **portals** and ❺ **spire** are reconstructed. The neo-Gothic ❻ **treasury** is built.

1860 The area in front of Notre Dame is cleared to create the parvis, an al fresco classroom where Parisians can learn a catechism illustrated on sculpted stone portals.

1935 A rooster bearing part of the relics of the Crown of Thorns, St Denis and Ste Geneviève is put on top of the cathedral spire to protect those who pray inside.

1991 The architectural masterpiece of Notre Dame and its Seine-side riverbanks become a Unesco World Heritage Site.

2013 Notre Dame celebrates 850 years since construction began with a bevy of new bells and restoration works.

PAL TERAV/DIMOV PHOTOGRAPHY/GETTY IMAGES ©

Virgin & Child
Spot all 37 artworks representing the Virgin Mary. Pilgrims have revered the pearly-cream sculpture of her in the sanctuary since the 14th century. Light a devotional candle and write some words to the *Livre de Vie* (Book of Life).

North Rose Window
See prophets, judges, kings and priests venerate Mary in vivid blue and violet glass, one of three beautiful rose blooms (1225–70), each almost 10m in diameter.

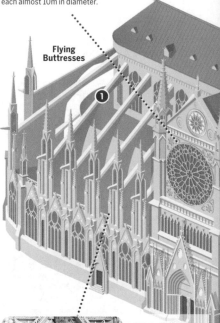

Flying Buttresses

DIGITALIMAGINATION/GETTY IMAGES ©

Choir Screen
No part of the cathedral weaves biblical tales more evocatively than these ornate wooden panels, carved in the 14th century after the Black Death killed half the country's population. The faintly gaudy colours were restored in the 1960s.

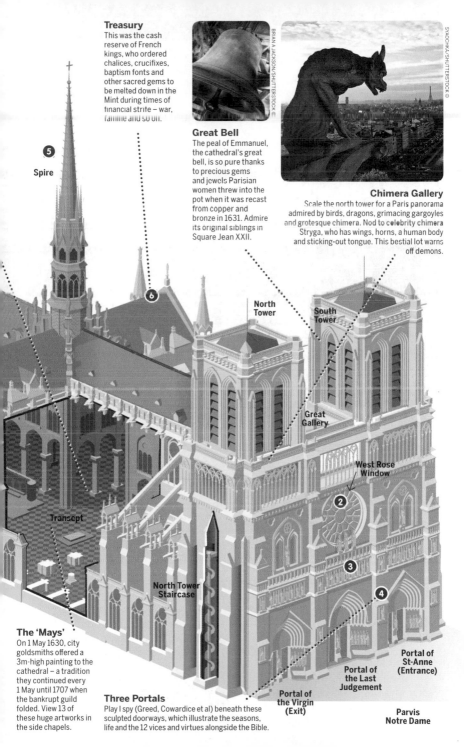

Treasury
This was the cash reserve of French kings, who ordered chalices, crucifixes, baptism fonts and other sacred gems to be melted down in the Mint during times of financial strife – war, famine and so on.

Great Bell
The peal of Emmanuel, the cathedral's great bell, is so pure thanks to precious gems and jewels Parisian women threw into the pot when it was recast from copper and bronze in 1631. Admire its original siblings in Square Jean XXII.

Chimera Gallery
Scale the north tower for a Paris panorama admired by birds, dragons, grimacing gargoyles and grotesque chimera. Nod to celebrity chimera Stryga, who has wings, horns, a human body and sticking-out tongue. This bestial lot warns off demons.

5
Spire

6

North Tower

South Tower

Great Gallery

West Rose Window

2

Transept

3

North Tower Staircase

4

The 'Mays'
On 1 May 1630, city goldsmiths offered a 3m-high painting to the cathedral – a tradition they continued every 1 May until 1707 when the bankrupt guild folded. View 13 of these huge artworks in the side chapels.

Three Portals
Play I spy (Greed, Cowardice et al) beneath these sculpted doorways, which illustrate the seasons, life and the 12 vices and virtues alongside the Bible.

Portal of the Virgin (Exit)

Portal of the Last Judgement

Portal of St-Anne (Entrance)

Parvis Notre Dame

Day Trip: Château de Versailles

This monumental, 700-room palace and sprawling estate – with its gardens, fountains, ponds and canals – is a Unesco World Heritage–listed wonder situated an easy 40-minute train ride from central Paris.

Great For...

☑ Don't Miss

Summertime 'dancing water' displays set to music by baroque- and classical-era composers.

Amid magnificently landscaped formal gardens, this splendid and enormous palace was built in the mid-17th century during the reign of Louis XIV – the Roi Soleil (Sun King) – to project the absolute power of the French monarchy, which was then at the height of its glory. The château has undergone relatively few alterations since its construction, though almost all the interior furnishings disappeared during the Revolution and many of the rooms were rebuilt by Louis-Philippe (r 1830–48).

Some 30,000 workers and soldiers toiled on the structure, the bills for which all but emptied the kingdom's coffers.

Work began in 1661 under the guidance of architect Louis Le Vau (Jules Hardouin-Mansart took over from Le Vau in the mid-1670s), painter and interior designer Charles Le Brun, and landscape artist

ℹ Need to Know

☎01 30 83 78 00; www.chateauversailles.fr; place d'Armes; adult/child passport ticket incl estate-wide access €20/free, with musical events €27/free, palace €15/free; ⏰9am-6.30pm Tue-Sun Apr Oct. to 5.30pm Tue-Sun Nov-Mar; Ⓜ RER Versailles Château–Rive Gauche

✕ Take a Break

Nearby rue de Satory is lined with restaurants and cafes.

★ Top Tip

Prepurchase tickets on the château's website or at Fnac branches (p248) and head straight to the entrance.

André Le Nôtre, whose workers flattened hills, drained marshes and relocated forests as they laid out the seemingly endless **gardens** (free except during musical events; ⏰gardens 8am-8.30pm Apr-Oct, to 6pm Nov-Mar, park 7am-8.30pm Apr-Oct, 8am 6pm Nov Mar), ponds and fountains.

Le Brun and his hundreds of artisans decorated every moulding, cornice, ceiling and door of the interior with the most luxurious and ostentatious of appointments: frescos, marble, gilt and woodcarvings, many with themes and symbols drawn from Greek and Roman mythology. The King's Suite of the Grands Appartements du Roi et de la Reine (King's and Queen's State Apartments), for example, includes rooms dedicated to Hercules, Venus, Diana, Mars and Mercury. The opulence reaches its peak in the Galerie des Glaces (Hall of Mirrors), a 75m-long ballroom with 17 huge mirrors on one side and, on the other, an equal number of windows looking out over the gardens and the setting sun.

Guided Tours

To access areas that are otherwise off-limits and to learn more about Versailles' history, prebook a 90-minute **guided tour** (☎01 30 83 77 88; tours €7, plus palace entry; ⏰English-language tours 9.30am Tue-Sun) of the Private Apartments of Louis XV and Louis XVI and the Opera House or Royal Chapel. Tours also cover the most famous parts of the palace.

Planning Your Visit

The château is situated in the leafy, bourgeois suburb of Versailles, about 22km southwest of central Paris. Take the frequent RER C5 (€4.20) from Paris' Left Bank RER stations to Versailles-Château–Rive Gauche station.

Versailles

A DAY IN COURT

Visiting Versailles – even just the State Apartments – may seem overwhelming at first, but think of it as a house where people ate, drank, worked, slept and conspired and you'll be on the right path.

Some two decades into his long reign, Louis XIV began turning his father's hunting lodge into a palace large enough to house his entire court (to keep closer tabs on the 6000-strong army of courtiers). Sparing no expense, the Sun King employed the greatest artists and craftspeople of the day and by 1682 he'd created the most extravagant dormitory in history.

The royal schedule was as accurate and predictable as a Swiss watch. By following this itinerary of rooms you can recreate the king's day, starting with the ❶ **King's Bedchamber** and the ❷ **Queen's Bedchamber**, where the royal couple was roused at about the same time. The royal procession then leads through the ❸ **Hall of Mirrors** to the ❹ **Royal Chapel** for morning Mass and returns to the ❺ **Council Chamber** for late-morning meetings with ministers. After lunch the king might ride or hunt or visit the ❻ **King's Library**. Later he could join courtesans for an 'apartment evening' starting from the ❼ **Hercules Drawing Room** or play billiards in the **Diana** ❽ **Drawing Room** before supping at 10pm.

VERSAILLES BY NUMBERS

Rooms 700 (11 hectares of roof)

Windows 2153

Staircases 67

Gardens and parks 800 hectares

Trees 200,000

Fountains 50 (with 620 nozzles)

Paintings 6300 (measuring 11km laid end to end)

Statues and sculptures 2100

Objets d'art and furnishings 5000

Visitors 5.3 million per year

Queen's Bedchamber
Chambre de la Reine
The queen's life was on constant public display and even the births of her children were watched by crowds of spectators in her own bedchamber. DETOUR » The Guardroom, with a dozen armed men at the ready.

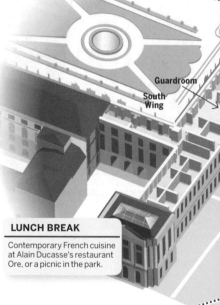

Guardroom

South Wing

LUNCH BREAK

Contemporary French cuisine at Alain Ducasse's restaurant Ore, or a picnic in the park.

Hercules Drawing Room
Salon d'Hercule
This salon, with its stunning ceiling fresco of the strong man, gave way to the State Apartments, which were open to courtiers three nights a week. DETOUR» Apollo Drawing Room, used for formal audiences and as a throne room.

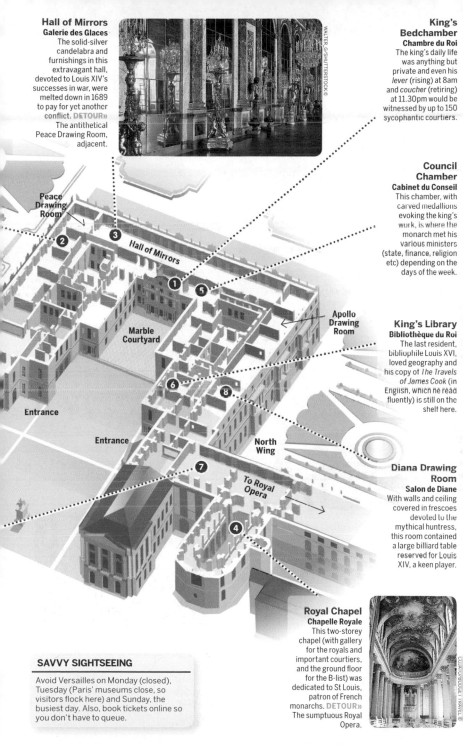

Hall of Mirrors
Galerie des Glaces
The solid-silver candelabra and furnishings in this extravagant hall, devoted to Louis XIV's successes in war, were melted down in 1689 to pay for yet another conflict. DETOUR»
The antithetical Peace Drawing Room, adjacent.

WALTER.G/SHUTTERSTOCK ©

King's Bedchamber
Chambre du Roi
The king's daily life was anything but private and even his *lever* (rising) at 8am and *coucher* (retiring) at 11.30pm would be witnessed by up to 150 sycophantic courtiers.

Council Chamber
Cabinet du Conseil
This chamber, with carved medallions evoking the king's work, is where the monarch met his various ministers (state, finance, religion etc) depending on the days of the week.

King's Library
Bibliothèque du Roi
The last resident, bibliophile Louis XVI, loved geography and his copy of *The Travels of James Cook* (in English, which he read fluently) is still on the shelf here.

Diana Drawing Room
Salon de Diane
With walls and ceiling covered in frescoes devoted to the mythical huntress, this room contained a large billiard table reserved for Louis XIV, a keen player.

Royal Chapel
Chapelle Royale
This two-storey chapel (with gallery for the royals and important courtiers, and the ground floor for the B-list) was dedicated to St Louis, patron of French monarchs. DETOUR» The sumptuous Royal Opera.

GODA/BUDGET TRAVEL ©

Peace Drawing Room

Hall of Mirrors

Marble Courtyard

Apollo Drawing Room

Entrance

Entrance

North Wing

To Royal Opera

SAVVY SIGHTSEEING

Avoid Versailles on Monday (closed), Tuesday (Paris' museums close, so visitors flock here) and Sunday, the busiest day. Also, book tickets online so you don't have to queue.

Seine-Side Meander

The world's most romantic city has no shortage of beguiling spots, but the Seine and its surrounds are Paris at its most seductive. Descend the steps along the quays wherever possible to stroll along the water's edge.
Start Place de la Concorde
Distance 7km
Duration 3 hours

3 Take the steps to **Square du Vert Galant**, before ascending to place du Pont Neuf and place Dauphine.

2 Walk through the Jardin de l'Oratoire to the **Cour Carrée** and exit at the Jardin de l'Infante.

Classic Photo: Enjoy fountain views in this elegant 28-hectare garden.

1 After taking in the panorama at place de la Concorde, stroll through the **Jardin des Tuileries** (p233).

7 End your romantic meander at the tranquil **Jardin des Plantes** (⊙7.30am–8pm early Apr–mid-Sep, shorter hours rest of year). Cruise back along the Seine by Batobus.

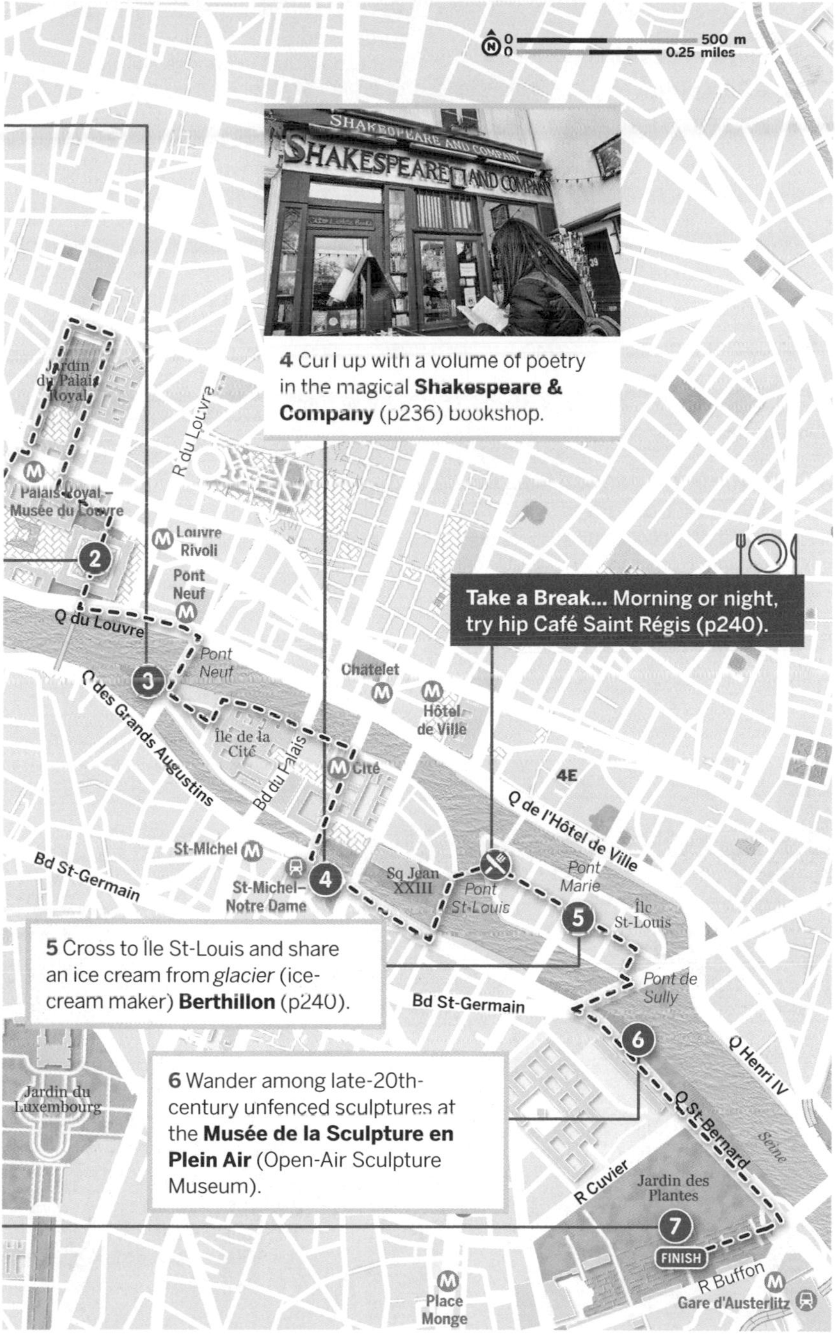

N | 0 — 500 m
0 — 0.25 miles

4 Curl up with a volume of poetry in the magical **Shakespeare & Company** (p236) bookshop.

Jardin du Palais Royal

R du Louvre

M Palais-Royal– Musée du Louvre

2

M Louvre Rivoli

Pont Neuf M

Q du Louvre

Q des Grands Augustins

Pont Neuf

3

Île de la Cité

Bd du Palais

M Cité

Châtelet M

M Hôtel de Ville

4E

Q de l'Hôtel de Ville

Take a Break... Morning or night, try hip Café Saint Régis (p240).

Bd St-Germain

St-Michel M

St-Michel– Notre Dame

4

Sq Jean XXIII

Pont St-Louis

Pont Marie

5

Île St-Louis

Pont de Sully

5 Cross to Île St-Louis and share an ice cream from *glacier* (ice-cream maker) **Berthillon** (p240).

Bd St-Germain

6

Q Henri IV

Q St-Bernard

Jardin du Luxembourg

6 Wander among late-20th-century unfenced sculptures at the **Musée de la Sculpture en Plein Air** (Open-Air Sculpture Museum).

R Cuvier

Jardin des Plantes

Seine

7 FINISH

R Buffon

M Place Monge

M Gare d'Austerlitz

◉ SIGHTS

◉ Louvre & Les Halles

Centre Pompidou   Museum

(Map p230; ☎01 44 78 12 33; www.centrepom
pidou.fr; place Georges Pompidou, 4e; museum,
exhibitions & panorama adult/child €14/free,
panorama ticket only €5; ⊙11am-10pm Wed &
Fri-Mon, to 11pm Thu; Ⓜ Rambuteau) Renowned
for its radical architectural statement, the
1977-opened Centre Pompidou brings
together galleries and cutting-edge exhibitions, hands-on workshops, dance performances, cinemas and other entertainment
venues, with street performers and fanciful
fountains outside. The **Musée National
d'Art Moderne**, France's national collection
of art dating from 1905 onward, is the main
draw; a fraction of its 100,000-plus pieces
– including fauvist, cubist and surrealist
works, pop art and contemporary works
– is on display. Don't miss the spectacular
Parisian panorama from the rooftop.

Église St-Eustache   Church

(Map p230; www.st-eustache.org; 2 impasse
St-Eustache, 1er; ⊙9.30am-7pm Mon-Fri, 9am-
7pm Sat & Sun; Ⓜ Les Halles) Just north of the
gardens adjoining the city's old marketplace, now the **Forum des Halles** (Map
p230; http://forumdeshalles.com; 1 rue Pierre
Lescot, 1er; ⊙shops 10am-8pm Mon-Sat, 11am-
7pm Sun; Ⓜ Châtelet, Les Halles), is one of the
most beautiful churches in Paris. Majestic,
architecturally magnificent and musically
outstanding, St-Eustache was constructed
between 1532 and 1632. It's primarily Gothic, though a neoclassical facade was added
on the western side in the mid-18th century. Highlights include a work by Rubens,
Raymond Mason's colourful bas-relief of
market vendors (1969) and Keith Haring's
bronze triptych (1990) in the side chapels.

◉ The Islands

Sainte-Chapelle   Chapel

(Map p230; ☎01 53 40 60 80, concerts 01 42 77
65 65; www.sainte-chapelle.fr; 8 bd du Palais, 1er;
adult/child €10/free, joint ticket with Conciergerie
€15; ⊙9am-7pm Apr-Sep, to 5pm Oct-Mar; Ⓜ Cité)
Try to save Sainte-Chapelle for a sunny day,
when Paris' oldest, finest stained glass is
at its dazzling best. Enshrined within the

Champs-Élysées and the Arc de Triomphe

KIEV.VICTOR/SHUTTERSTOCK ©

Palais de Justice (Law Courts), this gemlike Holy Chapel is Paris' most exquisite Gothic monument. Sainte-Chapelle was built in just six years (compared with nearly 200 years for Notre Dame) and consecrated in 1248. The chapel was conceived by Louis IX to house his personal collection of holy relics, including the famous Holy Crown (now in Notre Dame).

◎ Champs-Élysées & Grands Boulevards

Arc de Triomphe   Landmark

(Map p234; www.paris-arc-de-triomphe.fr; place Charles de Gaulle, 8e; viewing platform adult/child €12/free, ⏰10am-11pm Apr-Sep, to 10.30pm Oct-Mar; MCharles de Gaulle–Étoile) If anything rivals the Eiffel Tower (p204) as the symbol of Paris, it's this magnificent 1836 monument to Napoléon's victory at Austerlitz (1805), which he commissioned the following year. The intricately sculpted triumphal arch stands sentinel in the centre of the Étoile ('Star') roundabout. From the viewing platform on top of the arch (50m up via 284 steps and well worth the climb) you can see the dozen avenues.

Grand Palais   Gallery

(Map p234; ☎01 44 13 17 17; www.grandpalais.fr; 3 av du Général Eisenhower, 8e; adult/child €11/8; ⏰10am-10pm Wed & Fri-Mon, to 8pm Thu; MChamps-Élysées–Clemenceau) Erected for the 1900 Exposition Universelle (World's Fair), the Grand Palais today houses several exhibition spaces beneath its huge 8.5-tonne art nouveau glass roof. Some of Paris' biggest shows (Renoir, Chagall, Turner) are held in the **Galeries Nationales**, lasting three to four months. Hours, prices and exhibition dates vary significantly for all galleries. Those listed here generally apply to the Galeries Nationales, but always check the website for exact details. Reserving a ticket online for any show is strongly advised.

Le Grand Musée du Parfum   Museum

(Map p234; www.grandmuseeduparfum.fr; 73 rue du Faubourg St-Honoré, 8e; adult/child

👀 Canal St-Martin

The tranquil, 4.5km-long **Canal St-Martin** (Map p230; MRépublique, Jaurès, Jacques Bonsergent) was inaugurated in 1825 to provide a shipping link between the Seine and Paris' northeastern suburbs. Emerging from below ground near de la République, its towpaths take you past locks, bridges and local neighbourhoods. Come for a romantic stroll, cycle, picnic lunch or dusk-time drink. From the iron footbridge by the intersection of rue de la Grange aux Belles and quai de Jemmapes, watch the vintage road bridge swing open to let canal boats pass.

KIEV.VICTOR/T ©

€14.50/9.50; ⏰10.30am-7pm Tue-Thu, Sat & Sun, to 10pm Fri; MMiromesnil) History exhibits (ancient perfume bottles, interpretive French/English panels and dioramas) fill the basement of Paris' 2016-opened perfume museum, but the most engaging sections are upstairs. The 1st floor is a heady sensory guide, revealing the chemical processes while you identify scents. The 2nd floor showcases the art of fragrance creation and the 'instruments' with which professional perfumers work. Afterwards, you'll exit through the ground-floor gift shop where you can see perfume being distilled and bottles hand-painted (and stock up, too).

◎ Montmartre & Northern Paris

Basilique du Sacré-Cœur   Basilica

(Map p230; ☎01 53 41 89 00; www.sacre-coeur-montmartre.com; Parvis du Sacré-Cœur; basilica free, dome adult/child €6/4, cash only; ⏰basilica

Les Halles, Le Marais & the Islands

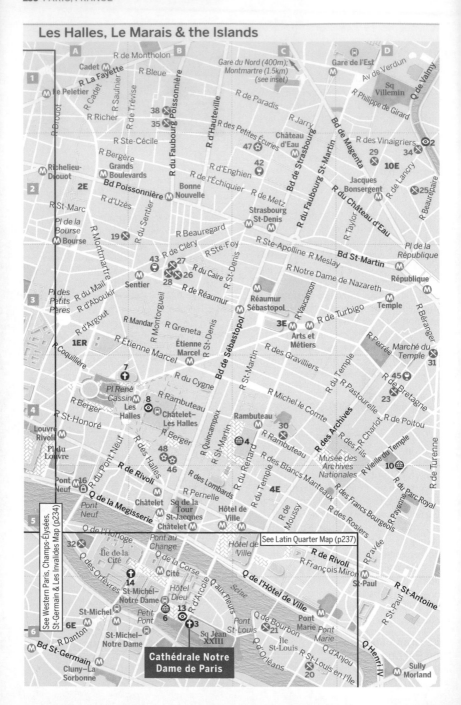

Cadet

R de Montholon

R La Fayette

le Peletier

R Bleue

R Cadet

R Saulnier

R de Trévise

R Richer

R Ste-Cécile

Gare du Nord (400m);
Montmartre (1.5km)
(see inset)

Gare de l'Est

Av de Verdun

Sq
Villemin

R de Valmy

R Philippe de Girard

R de Paradis

38

35

R du Faubourg Poissonnière

R d'Hauteville

R des Petites Écuries

Château
d'Eau

R Jarry

47

R des Vinaigriers

34

2

Bd de Magenta

29

10E

R de Lancry

Richelieu-
Drouot

2E

Grands
Boulevards

Bd Poissonnière

42

R d'Enghien

R de l'Échiquier

R de Metz

Bonne
Nouvelle

Bd de Strasbourg

R du Faubourg St-Martin

Jacques
Bonsergent

R du Château d'Eau

25

R Taylor

R Beaurepaire

R St-Marc

R d'Uzès

Pl de la
Bourse

Bourse

R Montmartre

19

R du Sentier

Strasbourg
St-Denis

Pl de la
République

R Beauregard

R de Cléry

R Ste-Foy

R Ste-Apolline

R Meslay

Bd St-Martin

République

43

27

R du Caire

R St-Denis

R Notre Dame de Nazareth

Sentier

28

26

R de Réaumur

Pl des
Petits
Pères

R du Mail

R d'Aboukir

R d'Argout

R Mandar

R Montorgueil

R Greneta

R de Sébastopol

Réaumur
Sébastopol

3E

R Vaucanson

R de Turbigo

Temple

R Béranger

1ER

R Coquillière

R Étienne Marcel

Étienne
Marcel

R St-Denis

Bd de Sébastopol

Arts et
Métiers

R des Gravilliers

R Perrée

Marché du
Temple

31

7

R du Cygne

R St-Martin

R du Temple

R Pastourelle

45

23

R de Bretagne

Pl René
Cassin

8

Les
Halles

R Rambuteau

Châtelet–
Les Halles

R Michel le Comte

R du Temple

R Charlot

R de Poitou

R Berger

R Berger

Rambuteau

R Quincampoix

R St-Martin

30

R Rambuteau

R des Fils

R des Archives

R de Poitou

R Vieille du Temple

10

R du Parc Royal

Louvre
Rivoli

Pl du
Louvre

R St-Honoré

R du Pont Neuf

R des Halles

48

46

R de Rivoli

R des Lombards

R du Renard

R des Blancs Manteaux

Musée des
Archives
Nationales

R des Francs Bourgeois

R du Parc Royal

R de Turenne

Pont
Neuf

16

Q de la Megisserie

Châtelet

R Berger

R Pernelle

4

4E

R du Temple

R de
Moussy

R des Rosiers

R Payenne

Pont
Neuf

Q de l'Horloge

Sq de la
Tour
St-Jacques

Châtelet

Hôtel de
Ville

Châtelet

Hôtel de
Ville

See Latin Quarter Map (p237)

32

Île de la
Cité

Pont au
Change

Q de la Corse

Cité

R de Rivoli

R François Miron

St-Paul

R St-Antoine

R St-Paul

14

St-Michel–
Notre Dame

Hôtel
Dieu

Q d'Arcole

Q aux Fleurs

Seine

Q de l'Hôtel de Ville

St-Michel

Petit
Pont

6

13

3

Q de Bourbon

21

Île
St-Louis

Pont
Marie

Pont
Marie

Q d'Anjou

Q Henri IV

6E

R Danton

St-Michel–
Notre Dame

Sq Jean
XXIII

Pont
St-Louis

Q d'Orléans

R St-Louis en l'Île

20

Bd St-Germain

Cluny–La
Sorbonne

**Cathédrale Notre
Dame de Paris**

Sully
Morland

See Western Paris, Champs-Élysées,
St-Germain & Les Invalides Map (p234)

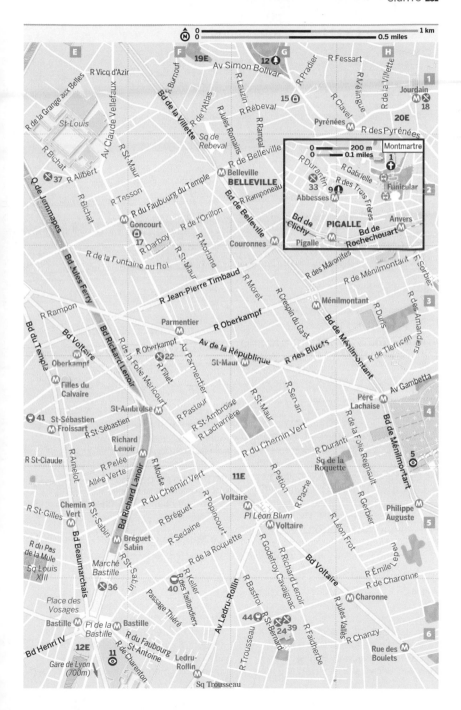

0 | 1 km
0 | 0.5 miles

E

F

19E

12

G

H

R Vicq d'Azir

Av Simon Bolivar

R Fessart

R Burnouf

R Pradier

R Mélingue

R de la Villette

Jourdain

1

R Lauzin

R Jules Romains

R de l'Atlas

R Rébeval

15

R Clavel

Pyrénées

20E

R des Pyrénées

Bd de la Villette

St-Louis

Av Claude Vellefaux

R St-Maur

Sq de Rebeval

R Rampal

R de Belleville

R Bichat

R Albert

37

R Tasson

Belleville

BELLEVILLE

200 m
0.1 miles

Montmartre

R Durantin

R Gabrielle

R des Trois Frères

1

R du Faubourg du Temple

R de l'Orillon

R Ramponeau

Bd de Belleville

33

9

Funicular

2

Q de Jemmapes

R Bichat

Goncourt

17

R Darboy

Couronnes

Abbesses

PIGALLE

Anvers

R Moriana

Bd de Clichy

Bd de Rochechouart

R de la Fontaine au Roi

R St-Maur

Pigalle

R des Maronites

Bd Jules Ferry

R Jean-Pierre Timbaud

R Moret

R des Ménilmontant

R de Ménilmontant

R Sorbier

R Crespin du Gast

Ménilmontant

3

R Rampon

Parmentier

R Oberkampf

Bd de Ménilmontant

R Duris

R des Amandiers

Bd du Temple

Bd Voltaire

Bd Richard Lenoir

R Oberkampf

Av de la République

R des Bluets

R de Tlemcen

Oberkampf

22

R Filet

R de la Folie Méricourt

R Parmentier

St-Maur

Filles du Calvaire

R Pastour

R Serran

Av Gambetta

41

St-Sébastien

St-Ambroise

R St-Ambroise

R Lacharrière

R St-Maur

Père Lachaise

Froissart

R St-Sébastien

R du Chemin Vert

R Duranti

Bd de la Folie Regnault

Bd de Ménilmontant

4

R St-Claude

Richard Lenoir

R Pelée

R Amelot

Allée Verte

R Mouffe

R du Chemin Vert

R Pétion

Sq de la Roquette

5

Chemin Vert

R St-Gilles

R St-Sabin

Bd Beaumarchais

Bd Richard Lenoir

11E

Voltaire

R Bréguet

R Popincourt

Pl Léon Blum

Voltaire

R Pache

R Gerbier

Philippe Auguste

5

R du Pas de la Mule

Bréguet Sabin

R Sédaine

R de la Roquette

R Léon Frot

Sq Louis XIII

Marché Bastille

R St-Sabin

36

40

R Keller

R des Taillandiers

R Godefroy Cavaignac

R Richard Lenoir

Bd Voltaire

R Émile

R de Charonne

Place des Vosages

Passage Thiéré

Av Ledru-Rollin

R Bastroi

Charonne

Bastille

Pl de la Bastille

Bastille

R du Faubourg St-Antoine

44

R St-Bernard

24 39

R Faidherbe

R Jules Vallès

R Chanzy

6

Bd Henri IV

12E

11

Ledru-Rollin

R de Charenton

R Trousseau

Rue des Boulets

Gare de Lyon (700m)

Sq Trousseau

Les Halles, Le Marais & the Islands

6am-10.30pm, dome 8.30am-8pm May-Sep, to 5pm Oct-Apr; Ⓜ Anvers, Abbesses) Begun in 1875 in the wake of the Franco-Prussian War and the chaos of the Paris Commune, Sacré-Cœur is a symbol of the former struggle between the conservative Catholic old guard and the secular, republican radicals. It was finally consecrated in 1919, standing in utter contrast to the bohemian lifestyle that surrounded it. The view over Paris from its parvis is breathtaking. If you don't want to walk the hill, you can use a regular metro ticket aboard the **funicular** (place St-Pierre, 18e; ⏱6am-12.45am).

Art 42   Gallery

(http://art42.fr; 96 bd Bessières, 17e; ⏱tours 7-9pm Tue, 11am-3pm Sat; Ⓜ Porte de Clichy) 🆓 Street art and post-graffiti now have their own dedicated space at this 'anti-museum', with works by Banksy, Bom.K, Miss Van, Ericailcane and Invader (who's

behind the Space Invader motifs on buildings all over Paris), among other boundary-pushing urban artists. Compulsory guided tours (English generally available; confirm ahead) lead you through 4000 sq metres of subterranean rooms sheltering some 150 works. Entry's free but you need to reserve tours online (ideally several weeks in advance, although last-minute cancellations can arise).

Le Mur des je t'aime   Public Art

(Map p230; www.lesjetaime.com; Sq Jehan Rictus, place des Abbesses ,18e; ⏱8am-9.30pm Mon-Fri, 9am-9.30pm Sat & Sun mid-May–Aug, shorter hours Sep–mid-May; Ⓜ Abbesses) Few visitors can resist a selfie in front of Montmartre's 'I Love You' wall, a public artwork created in a small park by artists Frédéric Baron and Claire Kito in the year 2000. Made from dark-blue enamel tiles, the striking mural features the immortal phrase 'I love you' 311 times in 250 different languages (the red fragments, if joined together, would form a heart). Find a bench beneath a maple tree and brush up your language skills romantic Paris-style.

⊙ Le Marais, Ménilmontant & Belleville

Cimetière du
Père Lachaise   Cemetery
(Map p230; ☎01 55 25 82 10; www.pere-lachaise.com; 16 rue du Repos & 8 bd de Ménil-montant, 20e; ☺8am-6pm Mon-Fri, 8.30am-6pm Sat, 9am-6pm Sun mid Mar–Oct, shorter hours Nov–mid-Mar; ⓜPère Lachaise, Gambetta) The world's most-visited cemetery, Père Lachaise opened in 1804. Its 70,000 ornate and ostentatious tombs of the rich and famous form a verdant, 44-hectare sculpture garden. The most visited are those of 1960s rock star Jim Morrison (division 6) and Oscar Wilde (division 89). Pick up cemetery maps at the **conservation office** (Bureaux de la Conservation; ☺8.30am-12.30pm & 2-5pm Mon-Fri; ⓜPhilippe Auguste, Père Lachaise) near the main bd de Ménilmontant entrance. Other notables buried here include composer Chopin; playwright Molière; poet Apollinaire; and writers Balzac, Proust, Gertrude Stein and Colette.

Musée National Picasso   Gallery
(Map p230; ☎01 85 56 00 36; www.musee picassoparis.fr; 5 rue de Thorigny, 3e; adult/child €12.50/free; ☺10.30am-6pm Tue-Fri, 9.30am-6pm Sat & Sun; ⓜSt-Paul, Chemin Vert) One of Paris' most beloved art collections is showcased inside the mid-17th-century Hôtel Salé, an exquisite private mansion owned by the city since 1964. The Musée National Picasso is a staggering art museum devoted to Spanish artist Pablo Picasso (1881–1973), who spent much of his life living and working in Paris. The collection includes more than 5000 drawings, engravings, paintings, ceramic works and sculptures by the *grand maître* (great master), although they're not all displayed at the same time.

 Parisian Parks

Explore the city's lush green parks where Parisians stroll in style, admire art, lounge around fountains on sunchairs, bust out cheese and wine...

Jardin du Luxembourg (Map p237; www.senat.fr/visite/jardin; numerous entrances; ☺hours vary; ⓜMabillon, St-Sulpice, Rennes, Notre Dame des Champs, RER Luxembourg) Paris' most iconic swath of green, where you can stroll among the statues, play tennis, jog in style and entertain the kids.

Jardin du Palais Royal (Map p234; www.domaine-palais royal.fr; 2 place Colette, 1er; ☺8am-10.30pm Apr-Sep, to 8.30pm Oct-Mar; ⓜPalais Royal–Musée du Louvre) The perfect spot to sit, contemplate and picnic between box hedges, or shop in the trio of beautiful arcades that frame the garden.

Jardin des Tuileries (Map p234; rue de Rivoli, 1er; ☺7am-9pm late Mar–late Sep, 7.30am-7.30pm late Sep–late Mar; ♿; ⓜTuileries, Concorde) Leafy Seine-side oasis, perfect for picnics, summer carnival rides, jogging and impossibly magnificent vistas.

Parc des Buttes-Chaumont (Map p230; rue Manin & rue Botzaris, 19e; ☺7am-10pm May-Sep, to 8pm Oct-Apr; ⓜButtes Chaumont, Botzaris) Baron Haussmann's creation, this quirky local spot has a faux Greek temple, abandoned railway line, dance hall and t'ai chi vibes.

Jardin du Luxembourg
XMO/SHUTTERSTOCK ©

Western Paris, Champs-Élysées, St-Germain & Les Invalides

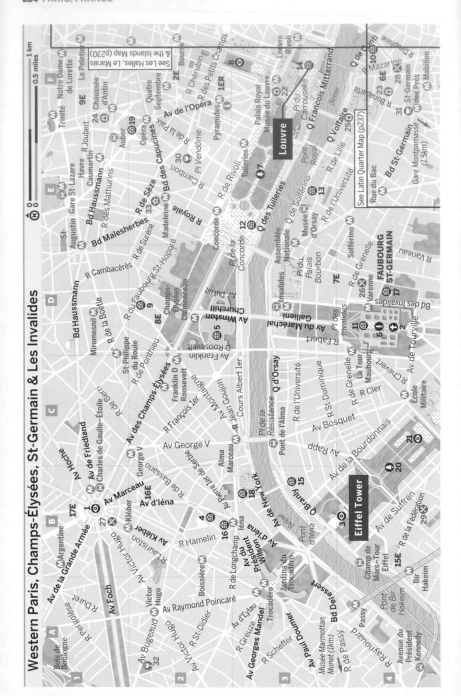

See Les Halles, Le Marais & the Islands Map (p230)

See Latin Quarter Map (p237)

Louvre

Eiffel Tower

1 km
0.5 miles

Western Paris, Champs-Élysées, St-Germain & Les Invalides

⊙ Latin Quarter

Panthéon   Mausoleum

(Map p237; www.paris-pantheon.fr; place du
Panthéon, 5e; adult/child €9/free; ⊙10am-
6.30pm Apr-Sep, to 6pm Oct-Mar; Ⓜ Maubert
Mutualité or RER Luxembourg) Overlooking
the city from its Left Bank perch, the
Panthéon's stately neoclassical dome is an
icon of the Parisian skyline. The vast interior
is an architectural masterpiece: originally a
church and now a mausoleum, it has served
since 1791 as the resting place of some
of France's greatest thinkers, including
Voltaire, Rousseau, Braille and Hugo. A copy
of Foucault's pendulum, first hung from the
dome in 1851 to demonstrate the rotation of
the earth, takes pride of place.

Musée National
du Moyen Âge   Museum

(Map p237; www.musee-moyenage.fr; 6 place
Paul Painlevé, 5e; adult/child incl audioguide
€8/free, during temporary exhibitions €9/
free; ⊙9.15am-5.45pm Wed-Mon; Ⓜ Cluny–La
Sorbonne) The National Museum of the
Middle Ages holds a series of sublime

treasures, from medieval statuary, stained
glass and objets d'art to its celebrated series of tapestries, *The Lady with the Unicorn*
(1500). Throw in the extant architecture –
an ornate 15th-century mansion (the Hôtel
de Cluny) and the *frigidarium* (cold room)
of an enormous Roman-era bathhouse –
and you have one of Paris' top small museums. Outside, four medieval gardens grace
the northeastern corner; more bathhouse
remains are to the west.

⊙ Montparnasse &
Southern Paris

Les Catacombes   Cemetery

(www.catacombes.paris.fr; 1 av Colonel Henri
Roi-Tanguy, 14e; adult/child €12/free, online
booking incl audioguide €27/5; ⊙10am-8pm
Tue-Sun; Ⓜ Denfert Rochereau) Paris' most
macabre sight is its underground tunnels
lined with skulls and bones. In 1785 it was
decided to rectify the hygiene problems of
Paris' overflowing cemeteries by exhuming
the bones and storing them in disused
quarry tunnels and the Catacombes were
created in 1810. After descending 20m (via

Le Jue de Boules

Don't be surprised to see groups of earnest Parisians playing *boules* (France's most popular traditional game, similar to lawn bowls) in the **Jardin du Luxembourg** (p233) and other parks and squares with suitably flat, shady patches of gravel. The **Arènes de Lutèce** (Map p237; 49 rue Monge, 5e; ⊘8am-8.30pm Apr-Oct, to 5.30pm Nov-Mar; M Place Monge) FREE *boulodrome* in a 2nd-century Roman amphitheatre in the Latin Quarter is a fabulous spot to absorb the scene. There are usually places to play at Paris Plages.

ROBERT PAUL VAN BEETS/SHUTTERSTOCK ©

130 narrow, dizzying spiral steps) below street level, you follow the dark, subterranean passages to reach the ossuary (2km in all). Exit back up 83 steps onto rue Remy Dumoncel, 14e.

St-Germain & Les Invalides

Hôtel des Invalides   Monument, Museum

(Map p234; www.musee-armee.fr; 129 rue de Grenelle, 7e; adult/child €11/free; ⊘10am-6pm Apr-Oct, to 5pm Nov-Mar, hours can vary; M Varenne, La Tour Maubourg) Flanked by the 500m-long Esplanade des Invalides lawns, the Hôtel des Invalides was built in the 1670s by Louis XIV to house 4000 *invalides* (disabled war veterans). On 14 July 1789, a mob broke into the building and seized 32,000 rifles before heading on to the prison at Bastille and the start of the French Revolution.

Admission includes entry to all Hôtel des Invalides sights (temporary exhibitions cost extra). Hours for individual sites often vary – check the website for updates.

Musée d'Orsay   Museum

(Map p234; www.musee-orsay.fr; 1 rue de la Légion d'Honneur, 7e; adult/child €12/free; ⊘9.30am-6pm Tue, Wed & Fri-Sun, to 9.45pm Thu; M Assemblée Nationale, RER Musée d'Orsay) The home of France's national collection from the impressionist, post-impressionist and art-nouveau movements spanning from 1848 to 1914 is the glorious former Gare d'Orsay railway station – itself an art-nouveau showpiece – where a roll-call of masters and their world-famous works are on display.

Top of every visitor's must-see list is the museum's painting collections, centred on the world's largest collection of impressionist and post-impressionist art.

Musée Rodin   Museum, Garden

(Map p234; www.musee-rodin.fr; 79 rue de Varenne, 7e; adult/child museum incl garden €10/free, garden only €4/free; ⊘10am-5.45pm Tue-Sun; M Varenne) Sculptor, painter, sketcher, engraver and collector Auguste Rodin donated his entire collection to the French state in 1908 on the proviso that they dedicate his former workshop and showroom, the beautiful 1730 Hôtel Biron, to displaying his works. They're now installed not only in the magnificently restored mansion itself, but also in its rose-filled garden – one of the most peaceful places in central Paris and a wonderful spot to contemplate his famous work *The Thinker*.

Prepurchase tickets online to avoid queuing.

🛍 SHOPPING

Shakespeare & Company   Books

(Map p237; ☎01 43 25 40 93; www.shakespeareandcompany.com; 37 rue de la Bûcherie, 5e; ⊘10am-11pm; M St-Michel) Shakespeare's enchanting nooks and crannies overflow with new and secondhand English-language books. The original shop (12 rue l'Odéon,

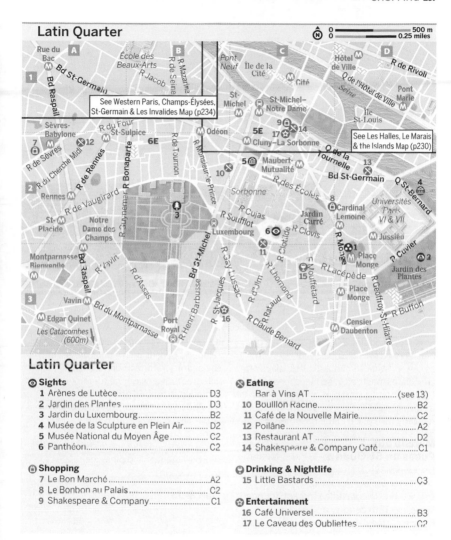

Latin Quarter

Latin Quarter

◉ Sights
1 Arènes de Lutèce..............................D3
2 Jardin des Plantes...........................D3
3 Jardin du Luxembourg.....................B2
4 Musée de la Sculpture en Plein Air.........D2
5 Musée National du Moyen Âge...........C2
6 Panthéon..C2

🏛 Shopping
7 Le Bon Marché..................................A2
8 Le Bonbon au Palais.........................C2
9 Shakespeare & Company...................C1

✗ Eating
Bar à Vins AT.............................(see 13)
10 Bouillon Racine..............................B2
11 Café de la Nouvelle Mairie.............C2
12 Poilâne...A2
13 Restaurant AT.................................D2
14 Shakespeare & Company Café.........C1

◉ Drinking & Nightlife
15 Little Bastards................................C3

✪ Entertainment
16 Café Universel................................B3
17 Le Caveau des Oubliettes...............C2

6e; closed by the Nazis in 1941) was run by Sylvia Beach and became the meeting point for Hemingway's 'Lost Generation'. Readings by emerging and illustrious authors take place at 7pm most Mondays. There's a wonderful **cafe** (Map p237; www.shakespeareandcompany.com; 2 rue St-Julien le Pauvre, 5e; dishes €3.50-10.50; ◷9.30am-7pm Mon-Fri, to 8pm Sat & Sun; 🛜📶♿; Ⓜ St-Michel) 🍴 and various workshops and festivals.

La Grande Épicerie de Paris   Food & Drinks
(www.lagrandeepicerie.com; 36 rue de Sèvres, 7e; ◷8.30am-9pm Mon-Sat, 10am-8pm Sun; Ⓜ Sèvres-Babylone) The magnificent food hall of department store **Le Bon Marché** (Map p237; www.bonmarche.com; 24 rue de Sèvres, 7e; ◷10am-8pm Mon-Wed & Sat, to 8.45pm Thu & Fri, 11am-8pm Sun; Ⓜ Sèvres-Babylone) sells 30,000 rare and/or luxury gourmet

Cycling past *bouquinistes*

products, including 60 different types of bread baked on site and delicacies such as caviar ravioli. Its fantastical displays of chocolates, pastries, biscuits, cheeses, fresh fruit and vegetables and deli goods are a Parisian sight in themselves. Wine tastings regularly take place in the basement.

Marché aux Puces de St-Ouen
Market

(www.marcheauxpuces-saintouen.com; rue des Rosiers, St-Ouen; ⊘Sat-Mon; Ⓜ Porte de Clignancourt) This vast flea market, founded in the late 19th century and said to be Europe's largest, has more than 2500 stalls grouped into 15 *marchés* (markets), each with its own speciality (eg Marché Paul Bert Serpette for 17th-century furniture, Marché Malik for casual clothing, Marché Biron for Asian art). Each market has different opening hours – check the website for details.

Le Bonbon au Palais
Food

(Map p237; www.bonbonsaupalais.fr; 19 rue Monge, 5e; ⊘10.30am-7.30pm Tue-Sat; Ⓜ Cardinal Lemoine) Kids and kids-at-heart will adore this sugar-fuelled *tour de France*. The

school-geography-themed boutique stocks rainbows of artisan sweets from around the country. Old-fashioned glass jars brim with treats like *calissons* (diamond-shaped, icing-sugar-topped ground fruit and almonds from Aix-en-Provence), *rigolettes* (fruit-filled pillows from Nantes), *berlingots* (striped, triangular boiled sweets from Carpentras and elsewhere) and *papalines* (herbal liqueur-filled pink-chocolate balls from Avignon).

Gab & Jo
Fashion & Accessories

(Map p234; www.gabjo.fr; 28 rue Jacob, 6e; ⊘11am-7pm Mon-Sat; Ⓜ St-Germain des Prés) 🖉 Forget mass-produced, imported souvenirs: for quality local gifts, browse the shelves of the country's first-ever concept store stocking only made-in-France items. Designers include La Note Parisienne (scented candles for each Parisian *arrondissement*, such as the 6e, with notes of lipstick, cognac, orange blossom, tuberose, jasmine, rose and fig), Marius Fabre (Marseille soaps), Germaine-des-Prés (lingerie), MILF (sunglasses) and Monsieur Marcel (T-shirts).

Galeries Lafayette Department Store
(Map p234; http://haussmann.galerieslafayette.
com; 40 bd Haussmann, 9e; ⊙9.30am-8.30pm
Mon-Sat, 11am-7pm Sun; 🚇; MChaussée d'Antin or
RER Auber) Grande-dame department store
Galeries Lafayette is spread across the main
store (whose magnificent stained-glass
dome is over a century old), men's store,
and homewares store with a gourmet emporium. Catch modern art in the first-floor
gallery, take in a fashion show, ascend to a
free, windswept rooftop panorama, or take a
break at one of its 24 restaurants and cafes.

Fromagerie Goncourt   Cheese
(Map p230; 📝01 43 57 91 28; 1 rue Abel Rabaud,
11e; ⊙9am-1pm & 4-8.30pm Tue-Fri, 9am-8pm
Sat; MGoncourt) Styled like a boutique,
this contemporary *fromagerie* is a must-
discover. Clément Brossault ditched a
career in banking to become a *fromager*
and his cheese selection – 70-plus types
– is superb. Cheeses flagged with a bicycle
symbol are varieties he discovered in situ
during a two-month French cheese tour he
embarked on as part of his training.

Magasin Sennelier   Arts & Crafts
(Map p234; www.magasinsennelier.com; 3 quai
Voltaire, 7e; ⊙2-6.30pm Mon, 10am-12.45pm
& 2-6.30pm Tue-Sat; MSt-Germain des Prés)
Cézanne and Picasso were among the
artists who helped develop products for
this venerable 1887-founded art supplier
on the banks of the Seine, and it remains
an exceptional place to pick up canvases,
brushes, watercolours, oils, pastels, char-
coals and more. The shop's forest-green
facade with gold lettering, exquisite original
timber cabinetry and glass display cases
also fuel artistic inspiration.

EATING

Louvre & Les Halles

Bambou   Southeast Asian €€
(Map p230; 📝01 40 28 98 30; www.bambou
paris.com; 23 rue des Jeûneurs, 2e; mains €19-28;
⊙noon-2.30pm & 7-11pm, bar to midnight; 📝;
MSentier) One of Paris' most sizzling recent
openings, this spectacular Southeast

Bouquinistes along the Seine

With some 3km of forest-green boxes
lining the Seine – containing over
300,000 secondhand (and often out-of-
print) books, rare magazines, postcards
and old advertising posters – Paris'
bouquinistes (Map p230; quai Voltaire,
7e to quai de la Tournelle, 5e & Pont Marie, 4e
to quai du Louvre, 1er; ⊙11.30am-dusk), or
used-book sellers, are as integral to the
cityscape as Notre Dame. Many open
only from spring to autumn (and many
shut in August), but year-round you'll
still find some to browse.

The *bouquinistes* have been in
business since the 16th century, when
they were itinerant peddlers selling
their wares on Parisian bridges; back
then their sometimes subversive (eg
Protestant) materials could get them in
trouble with the authorities. By 1859 the
city had finally wised up: official licences
were issued, space was rented (10m of
railing) and eventually the permanent
green boxes were installed.

Today, *bouquinistes* (the official count
ranges from 200 to 240) are allowed
to have four boxes, only one of which
can be used to sell souvenirs. Look
hard enough and you just might find
some real treasures: old comic books,
forgotten first editions, maps, stamps,
erotica and pre-war newspapers – as in
centuries past, it's all there, waiting to
be rediscovered.

Asian restaurant occupies a 500-sq-metre
former fabric warehouse, with vintage bird-
cages and a giant metal dragon adorning
the main dining room, a downstairs billiards
room/bar, vast terrace and Zen-like garden.
Chef Antonin Bonnet's specialities include
squid with black pepper and basil, and
aromatic shrimp pad thai.

Frenchie   Bistro €€€
(Map p230; 📝01 40 39 96 19; www.frenchie-
restaurant.com; 5 rue du Nil, 2e; 4-course lunch

Street Markets

Nowhere encapsulates Paris' village atmosphere more than its markets. Not simply places to shop, the city's street markets are social gatherings for the entire neighbourhood, and visiting one will give you a true appreciation for Parisian life. Nearly every little quarter holds its own street market at least once a week (never Monday) where tarpaulin-topped trestle tables bow beneath fresh, cooked and preserved delicacies. *Marchés biologiques* (organic markets) are increasingly sprouting up across the city. Markets in Paris' more multicultural neighbourhoods are filled with the flavours and aromas of continents beyond Europe.

The website www.paris.fr (in French) lists every market by *arrondissement* (city district), including speciality markets such as flower markets.

Marché Bastille (p244) Arguably the best open-air market in the city.

Marché d'Aligre (p244) Wonderfully chaotic market with all the staples of French cuisine.

Marché des Enfants Rouges (p241) Glorious maze of food stalls with ready-to-eat dishes from around the globe.

Marché aux Puces de St-Ouen (p238) Europe's largest flea market, with over 2500 stalls.

MATT MUNRO/LONELY PLANET ©

menu €45, 5-course dinner menu €74, with wine €175; ☷6.30-11pm Mon-Wed, noon-2.30pm & 6.30-11pm Fri; MSentier) Tucked down an

inconspicuous alley, this tiny bistro with wooden tables and old stone walls is always packed and for good reason: excellent-value dishes are modern, market-driven and prepared with unpretentious flair by French chef Gregory Marchand. Reserve well in advance; arrive at 6.30pm and pray for a cancellation (it does happen); or head to neighbouring **Frenchie Bar à Vins** (Map p230; www.frenchie-restaurant.com; 6 rue du Nil, 2e; dishes €9-23; ☷6.30-11pm Mon-Fri; MSentier).

The Islands
Berthillon Ice Cream €
(Map p230; www.berthillon.fr; 31 rue St-Louis en l'Île, 4e; 1/2/3 scoops take away €3/4/6.50, eat in €4.50/7.50/10.50; ☷10am-8pm Wed-Sun, closed Aug; MPont Marie) Founded here in 1954, this esteemed *glacier* (ice-cream maker) is still run by the same family today. Its 70-plus all-natural, chemical-free flavours include fruit sorbets such as blackcurrant or pink grapefruit, and richer ice creams made from fresh milk and eggs, such as salted caramel, *marrons glacés* (candied chestnuts) and Agenaise (Armagnac and prunes), along with seasonal flavours like gingerbread.

Café Saint Régis Cafe €
(Map p230; www.cafesaintregisparis.com; 6 rue Jean du Bellay, 4e; breakfast & snacks €3.50-14.50, mains €18-32; ☷kitchen 8am-midnight, bar to 2am; ☷; MPont Marie) Waiters in long white aprons, a white ceramic-tiled interior and retro vintage decor make hip Le Saint Régis (as regulars call it) a deliciously Parisian hang-out any time of day – from breakfast pastries to mid-morning pancakes, lunchtime salads and burgers and early-evening oyster platters. Come midnight it morphs into a late-night hotspot.

Champs-Élysées & Grands Boulevards
Richer Bistro €
(Map p230; www.lericher.com; 2 rue Richer, 9e; mains €18-20; ☷noon-2.30pm and 7.30-10.30pm; MPoissonnière, Bonne Nouvelle) Run by the same team as across-the-street

neighbour **L'Office** (Map p230; ☑01 47 70 67 31; www.office-resto.com; 3 rue Richer, 9e; 2-/3-course lunch menus €22/27, mains €19-32; ⊘noon-2pm & 7.30-10.30pm Mon-Fri; MPoissonière, Bonne Nouvelle), Richer's pared-back, exposed-brick decor is a smart setting for genius creations like smoked duck breast ravioli in miso broth, and quince and lime cheesecake for dessert. It doesn't take reservations, but it serves up snacks and Chinese tea, and has a full bar (open until midnight). Fantastic value.

❌ Montmartre & Northern Paris

Le Verre Volé   Bistro €€

(Map p230; ☑01 48 03 17 34; http://leverre vole.fr; 67 rue de Lancry, 10e; 2-/3-course lunch menu €19/22, mains €16.50-26; ⊘bistro 12.30-2.30pm & 7.30-11.30pm, wine bar 10am-2am; 🛜; MJacques Bonsergent) The tiny 'Stolen Glass' – a wine shop with a few tables – is one of the most popular wine bar–restaurants in Paris, with outstanding natural and unfiltered wines and expert advice. Unpretentious and hearty *plats du jour* are excellent. Reserve well in advance for meals, or stop by to pick up a gourmet sandwich (€7.90) and a bottle.

Matière à.   Modern French €€

(Map p230; ☑09 83 07 37 85; 15 rue Marie et Louise, 10e; 2-/3-course lunch menu €21/25, 4-course dinner menu €46; ⊘12.30-2pm & 7.30pm-11pm Mon-Fri, 7.30pm-11pm Sat; MGoncourt) The short but stunning seasonal menu changes daily at this unique space. *Table d'hôte*–style dining for up to 14 is around a shared oak table lit by dozens of naked light bulbs. In the kitchen is young chef Anthony Courteille, who prides himself on doing everything *fait maison* (homemade), including bread and butter to die for. Reservations essential.

❌ Le Marais, Ménilmontant & Belleville

Marché des Enfants Rouges   Market €

(Map p230; 39 rue de Bretagne & 33bis rue Charlot, 3e; ⊘8.30am-1pm & 4-7.30pm Tue-Fri, 4-8pm Sat, 8.30am-2pm Sun; MFilles du Calvaire) Built in 1615, Paris' oldest covered

Parisian bistrot

market is secreted behind an inconspicuous green-metal gate. A glorious maze of 20-odd food stalls selling ready-to-eat dishes from around the globe (Moroccan couscous, Japanese bento boxes, and more), as well as produce, cheese and flower stalls, it's a great place to come for a meander and to dine with locals at communal tables. Don't miss out on a sandwich or *galette* (savoury pancake) from **Chez Alain Miam Miam** (Map p230; www.facebook.com/ChezAlainMiamMiam; dishes €3-9.50; ☺9am-3.30pm Wed-Fri, to 5.30pm Sat, to 3pm Sun; ⚲).

Jacques Genin Pastries €

(Map p230; ☎01 45 77 29 01; www.jacques genin.fr; 133 rue de Turenne, 3e; pastries €9; ☺11am-7pm Tue-Sun; Ⓜ Oberkampf, Filles du Calvaire) Wildly creative *chocolatier* Jacques Genin is famed for his flavoured caramels, *pâtes de fruits* (fruit jellies) and exquisitely embossed *bonbons de chocolat* (chocolate sweets). But what completely steals the show at his elegant chocolate showroom is the *salon de dégustation* (aka tearoom), where you can order a pot of outrageously thick hot chocolate and legendary Genin *millefeuille,* assembled to order.

✖ Latin Quarter

Café de la Nouvelle Mairie Cafe €

(Map p237; ☎01 44 07 04 41; 19 rue des Fossés St-Jacques, 5e; mains €9-19; ☺kitchen noon-2.30pm & 8-10.30pm Mon-Thu, 8-10pm Fri; Ⓜ Cardinal Lemoine) Shhhh...just around the corner from the Panthéon (p235) but hidden away on a small, fountained square, this narrow wine bar is a neighbourhood secret, serving blackboard-chalked natural wines by the glass and delicious seasonal bistro fare from oysters and ribs *(à la française)* to grilled lamb sausage over lentils. It takes reservations for dinner but not lunch – arrive early.

Restaurant AT Gastronomy €€€

(Map p237; ☎01 56 81 94 08; www.atsushitana ka.com; 4 rue du Cardinal Lemoine, 5e; 6-course lunch menu €55, 12-course dinner tasting menu €95; ☺12.15-2pm & 8-9.30pm Tue-Sat; Ⓜ Cardinal Lemoine) Trained by some of the biggest names in gastronomy (Pierre Gagnaire

Montmartre

included), chef Atsushi Tanaka showcases abstract art–like masterpieces incorporating rare ingredients (charred bamboo, kohlrabi turnip cabbage, juniper berry powder, wild purple fennel, Nepalese Timut pepper) in a blank-canvas-style dining space on stunning outsized plates. Just off the entrance, steps lead to his cellar wine bar, **Bar à Vins AT** (Map p237; dishes €12-16; ⊘7pm-2am Tue-Sun).

⊗ Montparnasse & Southern Paris

Le Casse Noix   Modern French €€

(Map p234; ☑01 45 66 09 01; www.le-casse noix.fr; 56 rue de la Fédération, 15e; 3-course menus €34; ⊘noon-2.30pm & 7-10.30pm Mon-Fri; Ⓜ Bir Hakeim) Proving that a location footsteps from the Eiffel Tower doesn't mean compromising on quality, quantity or authenticity, 'the nutcracker' is a neighbourhood gem with a cosy retro interior, affordable prices, and exceptional cuisine that changes by season and by the inspiration of owner-chef Pierre Olivier Lenormand, who has honed his skills in some of Paris' most feted kitchens. Book ahead.

Holybelly   International €

(Map p230; http://holybel.ly; 19 rue Lucien Sampaix, 10e; breakfast €5-11.50, lunch mains €15.50-16.50; ⊘kitchen 9am-2.15pm Thu, Fri & Mon, 10am-3.15pm Sat & Sun, cafe to 5pm; Ⓜ Jacques Bonsergent) This outstanding cafe is always rammed with a buoyant crowd, who never tire of its Belleville-roasted coffee, cuisine and exceptional service. Sarah Mouchot's breakfast pancakes (served with egg, bacon, homemade bourbon butter and maple syrup) and black-rice porridge are legendary, while her lunch menu features everything from beetroot gnocchi to almond couscous with tzatziki or beef cottage pie. No reservations.

⊗ St-Germain & Les Invalides

Bouillon Racine   Brasserie €€

(Map p237; ☑01 44 32 15 60; www.bouillon racine.com; 3 rue Racine, 6e; weekday 2-course lunch menu €17, menus €33-46, mains €18.50-

🍽️ Best Boulangeries (Bakeries)

Poilâne (Map p237; www.poilane.com; 8 rue du Cherche Midi, 6e; ⊘7am-8.30pm Mon-Sat; Ⓜ Sèvres Babylone) Turning out distinctive wood-fired, rounded sourdough loaves since 1932.

Besnier (Map p234; 40 rue de Bourgogne, 7e; ⊘7am-8pm Mon-Sat, closed Aug; Ⓜ Varenne) Watch baguettes being made through the viewing window.

Du Pain et des Idées (Map p230; www.dupainetdesidees.com; 34 rue Yves Toudic, 10e; ⊘6.45am-8pm Mon-Fri; Ⓜ Jacques Bonsergent) Traditional bakery near Canal St-Martin with an exquisite 1889 interior.

Au 140 (Map p230; www.au140.com; 140 rue de Belleville, 20e; sandwiches €3-5; ⊘7am-8pm Tue-Fri, 7.30am-8pm Sat, 7am-7pm Sun; Ⓜ Jourdain) Crunchy-to-perfection baguettes and gourmet, wood-fired-oven breads.

Le Grenier à Pain (Map p230; http://legrenierapain.com; 38 rue des Abbesses, 18e; ⊘7.30am-8pm Thu-Mon; Ⓜ Abbesses) Perfect Montmartre picnic stop.

Huré (Map p230; ☑01 42 72 32 18; www.hure-createur.fr; 18 rue Rambuteau, 3e; sandwiches €5-10; ⊘6.30am-8.30pm Tue-Sat; Ⓜ Rambuteau) Contemporary bakery with a graffitied red-brick wall.

Croissants

29; ⊘noon-11pm; 🪑; Ⓜ Cluny-La Sorbonne) Inconspicuously situated in a quiet street, this heritage-listed 1906 art-nouveau 'soup kitchen', with mirrored walls, floral motifs

Gluten-free in Paris

In a city known for its bakeries, it's only right there's **Chambelland** (Map p230; 01 43 55 07 30; http://chambelland.com; 14 rue Ternaux, 11e; lunch menu €10-12; 9am-8pm Tue-Sun; Parmentier) – a 100% gluten-free bakery with serious breads to die for. Using rice and buckwheat flour milled at the bakery's very own mill in southern France, this pioneering bakery creates exquisite cakes and pastries as well as sourdough loaves and brioches (sweet breads) peppered with nuts, seeds, chocolate and fruit.

ROMAN DOMBROWSKI/SHUTTERSTOCK ©

and ceramic tiling, was built in 1906 to feed market workers. Despite the magnificent interior, the food – inspired by age-old recipes – is no afterthought but superbly executed (stuffed, spit-roasted suckling pig, pork shank in Rodenbach red beer, scallops and shrimps with lobster coulis).

Restaurant Guy Savoy
Gastronomy €€€

(Map p234; 01 43 80 40 61; www.guysavoy.com; Monnaie de Paris, 11 quai de Conti, 6e; lunch menu via online booking €110, 12-/18-course tasting menus €420/490; noon-2pm & 7-10.30pm Tue-Fri, 7-10.30pm Sat; Pont Neuf) If you're considering visiting a three-Michelin-star temple of gastronomy, this should certainly be on your list. The world-famous chef needs no introduction (he trained Gordon Ramsay, among others) but now his flagship, entered via a red-carpeted staircase,

is ensconced in the gorgeously refurbished neoclassical **Monnaie de Paris** (Map p234; 01 40 46 56 66; www.monnaiedeparis.fr). Monumental cuisine to match includes Savoy icons like artichoke and black-truffle soup with layered brioche.

Bastille & Eastern Paris

Marché Bastille
Market €

(Map p230; bd Richard Lenoir, 11e; 7am-2.30pm Thu, 7am-3pm Sun; Bastille, Bréguet–Sabin) If you only get to one open-air street market in Paris, this one – stretching between the Bastille and Richard Lenoir metro stations – is among the city's very best.

Marché d'Aligre
Market €

(rue d'Aligre, 12e; 8am-1pm Tue-Sun; Ledru-Rollin) A real favourite with Parisians, this chaotic street market's stalls are piled with fruit, vegetables and seasonal delicacies such as truffles. Behind them, specialist shops stock cheeses, coffee, chocolates, meat, seafood and wine. More stands are located in the adjoining covered market hall, **Marché Beauvau** (place d'Aligre, 12e; 9am-1pm & 4-7.30pm Tue-Fri, 9am-1pm & 3.30-7.30pm Sat, 9am-1.30pm Sun; Ledru-Rollin). The small but bargain-filled flea market **Marché aux Puces d'Aligre** (place d'Aligre, 12e; 8am-1pm Tue-Sun; Ledru-Rollin) takes place on the square.

Septime
Modern French €€€

(Map p230; 01 43 67 38 29; www.septime-charonne.fr; 80 rue de Charonne, 11e; 4-course lunch menu €42, dinner menu €80, with wine €135; 7.30-10pm Mon, 12.15-2pm & 7.30-10pm Tue-Fri; Charonne) The alchemists in Bertrand Grébaut's Michelin-starred kitchen produce truly beautiful creations, while blue-aproned waitstaff ensure culinary surprises are all pleasant. Each dish on the menu is a mere listing of three ingredients, while the mystery *carte blanche* dinner menu puts you in the hands of the innovative chef. Reservations require planning and perseverance – book at least three weeks in advance.

Cheese for sale at a market

⊗ Eiffel Tower & Western Paris

Bustronome Gastronomy €€€

(Map p234; ☑09 54 44 45 55; www.bustro
nome.com; 2 av Kléber, 16e; 4-course lunch
menu €65, with paired wines €85, 6-course
dinner menu €100, with paired wines €130; ⊙by
reservation 12.15pm, 12.45pm, 7.45pm & 8.45pm;
☑☷; ⓂKléber, Charles de Gaulle–Étoile) A true
moveable feast, Bustronome is a voyage
into French gastronomy aboard a glass-
roofed bus, with Paris' famous monuments
– the Arc de Triomphe, Grand Palais, Palais
Garnier, Notre Dame and Eiffel Tower – gliding by as you dine on seasonal creations
prepared in the purpose-built vehicle's
lower-deck galley. Children's menus for
lunch/dinner cost €40/50; vegetarian,
vegan and gluten-free menus are available.

⊙ DRINKING & NIGHTLIFE

Bar Hemingway Cocktail Bar

(Map p234; www.ritzparis.com; Hôtel Ritz Paris,
15 place Vendôme, 1er; ⊙6pm-2am; ☎; ⓂOpéra)
Black-and-white photos and memorabilia
(hunting trophies, old typewriters and

framed handwritten letters by the great
writer) fill this snug bar inside the **Ritz**
(☑01 43 16 30 30; www.ritzparis.com; 15 place
Vendôme, 1er; d from €1000, ste from €1900;
Ⓟ☀@☎≋; ⓂOpéra). Head bartender Colin
Field mixes monumental cocktails, including three different Bloody Marys made
with juice from freshly squeezed seasonal
tomatoes. Legend has it that Hemingway
himself, wielding a machine gun, helped
liberate the bar during WWII.

Lockwood Cocktail Bar

(Map p230; ☑01 77 32 97 21; www.lockwood
paris.com; 73 rue d'Aboukir, 2e; ⊙6pm-2am
Mon-Fri, 10am-4pm & 6pm-2am Sat, 10am-4pm
Sun; ⓂSentier) Cocktails incorporating premium spirits such as Hendrick's rose- and
cucumber-infused gin and Pierre Ferrand
Curaçao are served in Lockwood's stylish
ground-floor lounge and subterranean
candlelit cellar. It's especially buzzing on
weekends, when brunch stretches out
between 10am and 4pm, with Bloody
Marys, coffee brewed with Parisian-roasted
Belleville Brûlerie (Map p230; ☑09 83 75
60 80; http://cafesbelleville.com; 10 rue Pradier,

GLENN BEANLAND/GETTY IMAGES ©

Al fresco diners in Paris

19e; ⊘11.30am-5.30pm Sat; MPyrénées) beans and fare including eggs Benedict and Florentine (dishes €8.50 to €13).

Le Syndicat
Cocktail Bar

(Map p230; http://syndicatcocktailclub.com; 51 rue du Faubourg St-Denis, 10e; ⊘6pm-2am Mon-Sat, 7pm-2am Sun; MChâteau d'Eau) Plastered top to bottom in peeling posters, this otherwise unmarked facade conceals one of Paris' hottest cocktail bars, but it's no fly-by-night. Le Syndicat's subtitle, Organisation de Défense des Spiritueux Français, reflects its impassioned commitment to French spirits. Ingeniously crafted (and named) cocktails include Saix en Provence (Armagnac, chilli syrup, lime and lavender).

Le Mary Céleste
Cocktail Bar

(Map p230; www.quixotic-projects.com/venue/mary-celeste; 1 rue Commines, 3e; ⊘6pm-2am, kitchen 7-11.30pm; MFilles du Calvaire) Snag a stool at the central circular bar at this uber-popular brick-and-timber-floored cocktail bar or reserve one of a handful of tables (in advance online). Creative cocktails such as Ahha Kapehna (grappa, absinthe, beetroot,

fennel and Champagne) are the perfect partner to a dozen oysters (€29 to €38) or tapas-style 'small plates' to share (€7 to €14).

Wild & the Moon
Juice Bar

(Map p230; www.wildandthemoon.com; 55 rue Charlot, 3e; ⊘8am-7pm Mon-Fri, 9am-7pm Sat & Sun; MFilles du Calvaire) A beautiful crowd hobnobs over nut milks, vitality shots, smoothies, cold-pressed juices and raw food in this sleek juice bar in the fashionable Haut Marais. Raw, all-vegan ingredients are fresh, seasonal and organic, and it's one of the few places in town where you can have dishes such as avocado slices on almond and rosemary crackers for breakfast.

Little Bastards
Cocktail Bar

(Map p237; 5 rue Blainville, 5e; ⊘7pm-2am Mon, 6pm-2am Tue-Thu, 6pm-4am Fri & Sat; MPlace Monge) Only house-creation cocktails are listed on the menu at uberhip Little Bastards – among them Fal' in Love (Beefeater gin, cranberry juice, lime, mint, guava puree, and Falernum clove, ginger and almond syrup), Be a Beet Smooth (Jameson, coriander, sherry, egg white and pepper) and Deep Throat (Absolut vodka, watermelon syrup and Pernod) – but they'll also mix up classics if you ask.

Les Deux Magots   Cafe

(Map p234; www.lesdeuxmagots.fr; 170 bd St-Germain, 6e; ⊙7.30am-1am; MSt-Germain des Prés) If ever there was a cafe that summed up St-Germain des Prés' early-20th-century literary scene, it's this former hang-out of anyone who was anyone. You will spend *beaucoup* to sip a coffee in a wicker chair on the terrace shaded by dark-green awnings and geraniums spilling from window boxes, but it's an undeniable piece of Parisian history.

Coutume   Coffee

(www.coutumecafe.com; 47 rue de Babylone, 7e; ⊙8am-6pm Mon-Fri, 9am-6pm Sat & Sun; ☎; MSt-François Xavier) ♪ The dramatic improvement in Parisian coffee in recent years is thanks in no small part to Coutume, artisan roaster of premium beans for scores of establishments around town. Its flagship cafe – a bright, light-filled, postindustrial space – is ground zero for innovative preparation methods including cold extraction and siphon brews. Fabulous organic fare and pastries are also available.

Le Baron Rouge   Wine Bar

(☎01 43 43 14 32; www.lebaronrouge.net; 1 rue Théophile Roussel, 12e; ⊙5-10pm Mon, 10am-2pm & 5-10pm Tue-Fri, 10am-10pm Sat, 10am-4pm Sun; MLedru-Rollin) Just about the ultimate Parisian wine-bar experience, this wonderfully unpretentious local meeting place where everyone is welcome has barrels stacked against the bottle-lined walls and serves cheese, charcuterie and oysters. It's especially busy on Sunday after the Marché d'Aligre (p244) wraps up. For a small deposit, you can fill up 1L bottles straight from the barrel for under €5.

Café des Anges   Cafe

(Map p230; ☎01 47 00 00 63; www.cafedes angesparis.com; 66 rue de la Roquette, 11e; ⊙7.30am-2am; ☎; MBastille) With its pastel-

Jazz Clubs

Café Universel (Map p237; ☎01 43 25 74 20; www.cafeuniversel.com; 267 rue St-Jacques, 5e; ⊙9pm-2am Tue-Sat; ☎; MCensier Daubenton or RER Port Royal) Unpretentious vibe and no cover.

New Morning (Map p230; www.newmorn ing.com; 7 & 9 rue des Petites Écuries, 10e; MChâteau d'Eau) Solid and varied line-up.

Le Baiser Salé (Map p230; ☎01 42 33 37 71; www.lebaisersale.com; 58 rue des Lombards, 1er; ⊙daily; MChâtelet) Focuses on Caribbean and Latin sounds.

Sunset & Sunside (Map p230; ☎01 40 26 46 60; www.sunset-sunside.com; 60 rue des Lombards, 1er; ⊙daily; MChâtelet) Blues, fusion and world sounds.

Le Caveau des Oubliettes (Map p237; ☎01 46 34 23 09; www.caveau-des-oubli ettes.com; 52 rue Galande, 5e; ⊙5pm-2am Sun & Tue, to 4am Wed-Sat; MSt-Michel) Dungeon jam sessions.

shaded paintwork and locals sipping coffee beneath the terracotta-coloured awning on its busy pavement terrace, Angels Cafe lives up to the 'quintessential Paris cafe' dream. In winter wrap up beneath a blanket outside, or squeeze through the crowds at the zinc bar to snag a coveted table inside. Happy hour runs from 5pm to 9pm.

St James Paris   Bar

(Map p234; www.saint-james-paris.com; 43 av Bugeaud, 16e; ⊙7pm-1am Mon-Sat; ☎; MPorte Dauphine) Hidden behind a stone wall, this historic mansion-turned-hotel opens its

Buying Tickets

The most convenient place to purchase concert, theatre and other cultural and sporting-event tickets is from electronics and entertainment megashop **Fnac** (☎08 92 68 36 22; www.fnactickets.com), whether in person at the *billeteries* (ticket offices) or by phone or online. There are branches throughout Paris, including in the Forum des Halles. Tickets generally can't be refunded.

On the day of performance, theatre, opera and ballet tickets are sold for half price (plus €3 commission) at the central **Kiosque Théâtre Madeleine** (Map p234; www.kiosqueculture.com; opposite 15 place de la Madeleine, 8e; ⊗12.30-7.30pm Tue-Sat, to 3.45pm Sun; MMadeleine).

bar each evening to nonguests – and the setting redefines extraordinary. Winter drinks are in the wood-panelled library; in summer they're on the impossibly romantic 300-sq-metre garden terrace with giant balloon-shaped gazebos (the first hot-air balloons took flight here). There are over 70 cocktails and an adjoining Michelin-starred restaurant.

✪ ENTERTAINMENT

Palais Garnier
Opera, Ballet

(Map p234; www.operadeparis.fr; place de l'Opéra, 9e; audio-guided tours €5, guided tours adult/child €15.50/11; ⊗audio-guided tours 10am-5pm, to 1pm on matinee performance days, guided tours by reservation MOpéra) The city's original opera house is smaller than its Bastille counterpart, but has perfect acoustics. Due to its odd shape, some seats have limited or no visibility – book carefully. Ticket prices and conditions (including last-minute discounts) are available from the **box office** (Map p234; ☎international calls 01 71 25 24 23, within France 08 25 05 44 05; ⊗11am-6.30pm Mon-Sat). Online flash sales are held from noon on Wednesdays.

Opéra Bastille
Opera

(Map p230; ☎international calls 01 71 25 24 23, within France 08 92 89 90 90; www.operadeparis.fr; 2-6 place de la Bastille, 12e; ⊗box office 11.30am-6.30pm Mon-Sat, 1hr prior to performances Sun; MBastille) Paris' premier opera hall, Opéra Bastille's 2745-seat main auditorium also stages ballet and classical concerts. Online tickets go on sale up to three weeks before telephone or box office sales (from noon on Wednesdays, online flash sales offer significant discounts). Standing-only tickets (*places débouts*; €5) are available 90 minutes before performances. French-language 90-minute **guided tours** (Map p230; ☎within France 08 92 89 90 90; guided tours adult/child €15/11) take you backstage.

Point Éphémère
Live Music

(☎01 40 34 02 48; www.pointephemere.org; 200 quai de Valmy, 10e; ⊗12.30pm-2am Mon-Sat, to 10pm Sun; 🛜; MLouis Blanc) On the banks of Canal St-Martin in a former fire station and later squat, this arts and music venue attracts an underground crowd for concerts, dance nights and art exhibitions. Its rockin' restaurant, **Animal Kitchen**, fuses gourmet cuisine with music from Animal Records (Sunday brunch from 1pm is a highlight); the rooftop bar, **Le Top**, opens in fine weather.

Le Batofar
Club

(www.batofar.fr; opposite 11 quai François Mauriac, 13e; ⊗club 11.30pm-6am Tue-Sat, bar 6-11pm Tue-Sat May-Sep, 7pm-midnight Tue-Sat Oct-Apr; MQuai de la Gare, Bibliothèque) This much-loved, red-metal tugboat has a rooftop bar that's terrific in summer, and a respected restaurant, while the club underneath provides memorable underwater acoustics between its metal walls and portholes. Le Batofar is known for its edgy, experimental music policy and live performances from 7pm, mostly electro-oriented but also incorporating hip hop, new wave, rock, punk and jazz.

Food is served at the restaurant from 7.30pm to midnight Tuesday and Wednesday, and until 2am Thursday to Saturday.

ℹ️ INFORMATION

DANGERS & ANNOYANCES

In general, Paris is a safe city and random street assaults are rare. The city is generally well lit and there's no reason not to use the metro until it stops running, at some time between 12.30am and just past 1am (2.15am on weekends).

Pickpocketing is typically the biggest concern. Places to be particularly careful include Montmartre (especially around Sacré Cœur); Pigalle; the areas around Forum des Halles and the Centre Pompidou; the Latin Quarter (especially the rectangle bounded by rue St-Jacques, bd St-Germain, bd St-Michel and quai St-Michel); beneath the Eiffel Tower; and on the metro during rush hour (particularly on line 4 and the western part of line 1).

MEDICAL SERVICES

Pharmacies (chemists) are marked by a large illuminated green cross outside. At least one in each neighbourhood is open for extended hours; find a complete night-owl listing at www.parisinfo.com.

American Hospital of Paris (☑01 46 41 25 25; www.american-hospital.org; 63 bd Victor Hugo, Neuilly-sur-Seine; Ⓜ Pont de Levallois) Private hospital; emergency 24-hour medical and dental care.

Hôpital Hôtel Dieu (☑01 42 34 88 19; www.aphp.fr; 1 place du Parvis Notre Dame, 4e; Ⓜ Cité) One of the city's main government-run public hospitals; after 8pm use the emergency entrance on rue de la Cité.

L'Institut Hospitalier Franco-Britannique Hertford British Hospital (IHFB; ☑01 46 39 22 00; www.ihfb.org; 4 rue Kléber, Levallois-Perret, Ⓜ Anatole France) Less expensive, private, English-speaking option.

INTERNET ACCESS

○ Wi-fi (pronounced 'wee-fee' in France) is available in most Paris hotels, usually at no extra cost, and in some museums.

○ Free wi-fi is available in some 300 public places, including parks, libraries and municipal buildings, between 7am and 11pm daily. In parks look for a purple 'Zone Wi-Fi' sign near the entrance. To connect, select the 'PARIS_WI-FI_' network and connect; sessions are limited to

Palais Garnier

GIVAGA/SHUTTERSTOCK ©

two hours. For complete details and a map of hotspots see www.paris.fr/wifi.

TOURIST INFORMATION

Paris Convention & Visitors Bureau (Office du Tourisme et des Congrès de Paris; Map p234; www.parisinfo.com; 25 rue des Pyramides, 1er; ⊙9am-7pm May-Oct, 10am-7pm Nov-Apr; MPyramides) The main branch is 500m northwest of the Louvre. It sells tickets for tours and several attractions, plus museum and transport passes. Also books accommodation.

 GETTING THERE & AWAY

AIR

Paris is a major air-transport hub serviced by virtually all major airlines, with three airports.

Aéroport de Charles de Gaulle (CDG; ☑01 70 36 39 50; www.parisaeroport.fr) Most international airlines fly here; it's 28km northeast of central Paris. In French, the airport is commonly called 'Roissy'.

Aéroport d'Orly (ORY; ☑01 70 36 39 50; www.parisaeroport.fr) Located 19km south of central Paris but not as frequently used by international airlines.

Aéroport de Beauvais (BVA; ☑08 92 68 20 66; www.aeroportbeauvais.com) Not really in Paris at all (75km north of Paris) but served by a few low-cost flights.

CAR

Cars are a hassle in Paris, so it's only worth bringing yours here if you're travelling further afield. To enter the city within the bd Périphérique (ring road) between 8am and 8pm Monday to Friday, cars registered after 1997 (including foreign-registered cars) need a Crit'Air Vignette (compulsory anti-pollution sticker); older vehicles are banned during these hours.

TRAIN

Paris has six major train stations serving both national and international destinations. For mainline train information, check SNCF (www.sncf-voyages.com).

Gare du Nord (rue de Dunkerque, 10e; MGare du Nord) Trains to/from the UK, Belgium, Germany and northern France.

Gare de l'Est (bd de Strasbourg, 10e; MGare de l'Est) Trains to/from Germany, Switzerland and eastern France.

Gare de Lyon (bd Diderot, 12e; MGare de Lyon) Trains to/from Provence, the Riviera, the Alps and Italy. Also serves Geneva.

Gare d'Austerlitz (bd de l'Hôpital, 13e; MGare d'Austerlitz) Trains to/from Spain and Portugal, and non-TGV trains to southwestern France.

Gare Montparnasse (av du Maine & bd de Vaugirard, 15e; MMontparnasse Bienvenüe) Trains to/from western France (Brittany, Atlantic coast) and southwestern France.

Gare St-Lazare (Esplanade de la Gare St-Lazare, 8e; MSt-Lazare) Trains to Normandy.

 GETTING AROUND

Walking is a pleasure in Paris, and the city also has one of the most efficient and inexpensive public-transport systems in the world, making getting around a breeze.

Metro & RER The fastest way to get around. Runs from about 5.30am and finishes around 12.35am or 1.15am (to around 2.15am on Friday and Saturday nights), depending on the line.

Bicycle Virtually free pick-up, drop-off **Vélib** (☑01 30 79 79 30; www.velib.paris.fr; day/week subscription €1.70/8, bike hire up to 30/60/90/120min free/€1/2/4) bikes operate across 1800 stations citywide.

Bus Good for parents with prams/strollers and people with limited mobility.

Boat The **Batobus** (www.batobus.com; adult/child 1-day pass €17/8, 2-day pass €19/10; ⊙10am-9.30pm Apr-Aug, to 7pm Sep-Mar) is a handy hop-on, hop-off service stopping at nine key destinations along the Seine.

Where to Stay

Neighbourhood	Atmosphere
Eiffel Tower & Western Paris	Close to Paris' iconic tower and museums. Upmarket area with quiet residential streets. Limited nightlife.
Champs-Élysées & Grands Boulevards	Luxury hotels, famous boutiques and department stores, gastronomic restaurants, great nightlife. Some areas extremely pricey. Nightlife hotspots can be noisy.
Louvre & Les Halles	Epicentral location, excellent transport links, major museums, shopping galore. Not many bargains. Noise can be an issue.
Montmartre & Northern Paris	Village atmosphere. Further out than some areas. Pigalle's red-light district, although well lit and safe, won't appeal to all.
Le Marais, Ménilmontant & Belleville	Buzzing nightlife, hip shopping, fantastic eating options. Lively gay and lesbian scene. Can be seriously noisy in areas where bars and clubs are concentrated.
Bastille & Eastern Paris	Few tourists, excellent markets, loads of nightlife options. Some areas slightly out of the way.
The Islands	As geographically central as it gets. No metro station on the Île St-Louis. Limited self-catering shops, minimal nightlife.
Latin Quarter	Energetic student area, stacks of eating and drinking options, late-opening bookshops. Rooms hardest to find from March to June and in October.
St-Germain & Les Invalides	Stylish, central location, proximity to the Jardin du Luxembourg. Budget accommodation is seriously short-changed.
Montparnasse & Southern Paris	Good value, few tourists, excellent links to both major airports. Some areas out of the way and/or not well served by metro.

Provence, France

Travelling in this sun-blessed part of southern France translates as touring scenic back roads strewn with stunning landscapes: fields of lavender, ancient olive groves and snow-tipped mountains. Factor in its prehistoric sites, medieval abbeys and elegant churches and Provence begins to feel like a living history book. Attractions can be low key: ambling in pretty villages, wine tasting and enjoying a long afternoon lunch on a panoramic terrace, or more energetic – the area is prime cycling territory, there are dozens of hiking trails and some unique spots to explore, such as the ochre quarries of Roussillon. Take your time.

Two Days in Provence

Spend day one in **Avignon** (p260), exploring the old town and the **Palais des Papes** (p260), and perhaps trying some local wine. On day two, make a day trip to either **Les Baux-de-Provence** (p258) for hilltop-village meandering or to the **Pont du Gard** (p255) for Roman history and memorable canoeing action on the River Gard.

Four Days in Provence

On day three, hop between hilltop villages – don't miss a red-rock hike in **Roussillon** (p259) or wine tasting and truffles in **Ménerbes** (p259). Aim to make it to **Gordes** (p258) for sunset. Devote the fourth day to exploring charming **Moustiers Ste-Marie** (p266).

Finished in Provence? Catch a train to Barcelona (p268) or fly to London (p50).

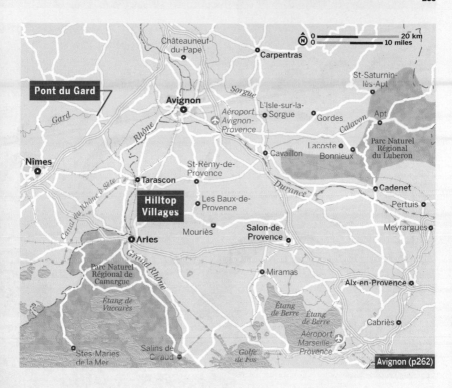

Avignon (p262)

Arriving in Provence

Aéroport Marseille-Provence Buses to Aix-en-Provence every 20 minutes. Direct trains to destinations including Marseille, Arles and Avignon.

Aéroport Avignon-Provence Bus 30 (www.tcra.fr; €1.40; 30 minutes) to the post office and LER bus 22 (www.info-ler.fr; €1.50) to Avignon bus station and TGV station. Taxis about €35.

Where to Stay

Provence has perhaps the most varied range of accommodation anywhere in France, spanning the spectrum from super-luxury hotels to cosy little cottages nestled among vineyards and lavender fields. In summer, prices skyrocket and rooms are scarce. Avignon is an excellent base for Pont du Gard (a 30-minute drive); magical Moustiers Ste-Marie is a key stop for Gorge du Verdon explorers; and Apt and its rural surrounds are perfect for touring the Luberon's hilltop villages.

Pont du Gard

Southern France has some fine Roman sites, but nothing can top the Unesco World Heritage–listed Pont du Gard, a breathtaking three-tiered aqueduct 25km west of Avignon.

The extraordinary three-tiered Pont du Gard, 21km northeast of Nîmes, was once part of a 50km-long system of channels built around 19 BC to transport water from Uzès to Nîmes. The scale is huge: the bridge is 48.8m high, 275m long and graced with 52 precision-built arches. It was sturdy enough to carry up to 20,000 cu metres of water per day.

Great For...

☑ Don't Miss

With kids? Don't miss fun, hands-on learning in the Ludo play area.

Musée de la Romanité

Each block was carved by hand and transported from nearby quarries – no mean feat, considering the largest blocks weighed over 5 tonnes. The height of the bridge descends by 2.5cm across its length, providing just enough gradient to keep the water flowing – an amazing demonstration of the precision of Roman engineering. The Musée de la Romanité

SIQURCAMF/SHUTTERSTOCK ©

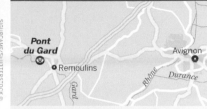

ⓘ Need to Know

📞04 66 37 50 99; www.pontdugard.fr; car
& up to 5 passengers €18, after 8pm €10, by
bicycle or on foot €7, after 8pm €3.50; ⊙site
24hr year-round, visitor centre & museum
9am-8pm Jul & Aug, shorter hours Sep–mid-
Jan & mid-Feb–Jun

✕ Take a Break

Dine at outstanding restaurant **LeTrac-
teur** (www.lucietestud.com/letracteur)
in nearby Argilliers.

★ Top Tip

Evening is a good time to visit: admission is cheaper and the bridge is
illuminated.

provides background on the bridge's construction, and the Ludo play area helps kids
to learn in a fun, hands-on way; both are
closed from mid-January to mid-February.

Mémoires de Garrigue

You can walk across the tiers for panoramic
views over the Gard River, but the best perspective on the bridge is from downstream,
along the 1.4km Mémoires de Garrigue
walking trail.

Canoeing on the Gard

Paddling beneath the Pont du Gard is
unforgettable. The best time to do it is early
spring between April and June, as winter
floods and summer droughts can sometimes make the river impassable. The Gard
flows from the Cévennes mountains all the

way to the aqueduct, passing through the
dramatic Gorges du Gardon en route.

Hire companies are in Collias, 8km from
the bridge, a journey of about two hours by
kayak. Depending on the season and height
of the river, canoe further by being dropped
upstream at Pont St-Nicholas (19km, four
to five hours) or Russan (32km, six to seven
hours); the latter includes a memorable
paddle through the Gorges du Gardon.

There's a minimum age of six. Life jackets are always provided, but you must be a
competent swimmer.

Gordes (p258)

Hilltop Villages

Impossibly perched on a rocky peak, gloriously lost in back country, fortified or château-topped: Provence's impressive portfolio of villages perchés calls for go-slow touring – on foot, by bicycle or by car. Most villages are medieval, built from golden stone and riddled with cobbled lanes, flower-filled alleys and fountain-pierced squares. Combine with a long lazy lunch for a perfect day.

Great For...

❶ Need to Know

Apt Tourist Office (☏04 90 74 03 18; www.luberon-apt.fr; 20 av Philippe de Girard; ⊙9.30am-1pm & 2.30-7pm Mon-Sat, 9.30am-12.30pm Sun Jul & Aug, 9.30am-12.30pm & 2-6pm Mon-Sat Sep-Jun)

★ **Top Tip**
Visit early in the morning or just before sunset for the best light and fewer people.

Les Baux-de-Provence

Clinging precariously to an ancient limestone *baou* (Provençal for 'rocky spur'), this fortified hilltop village is one of the most visited in France. It's easy to understand its popularity: narrow cobbled streets wend car-free past ancient houses, up to a splendid ruined **Château des Baux** (☑04 90 54 55 56; www.chateau-baux-provence.com; adult/child Apr-Sep €10/8, Oct-Mar €8/6; ⊕9am-8pm Jul & Aug, to 7pm Apr-Jun & Sep, reduced hours Oct-Mar), whose dramatic maze-like ruins date from the 10th century. The clifftop castle was largely destroyed in 1633, during the reign of Louis XIII, and is a thrilling place to explore – climb crumbling towers for incredible views, descend into disused dungeons and flex your knightly prowess with giant medieval weapons dotting the open-air site. Medieval-themed entertainment abounds in summer.

Gordes

Like a giant wedding cake rising over the rivers Sorgue and Calavon, the tiered village of Gordes juts spectacularly out of the white-rock face of the Vaucluse plateau. Come sunset, the village glows gold.

From the central square, meander downhill along rue Baptist in Picca to **La Boulangerie de Mamie Jane** (☑04 90 72 09 34; rue Baptistin Picca; lunch menus from €6.50; ⊕6.30am-1pm & 2-6pm Thu-Tue), a pocket-sized family-run bakery with outstanding bread, pastries, cakes and biscuits, including lavender-perfumed *navettes* and delicious peanut-and-almond brittle known as *écureuil* (from the French for squirrel).

Abbaye Notre-Dame de Sénanque

Roussillon

Dazzling Roussillon was once the centre of local ochre mining and is still unmistakably marked by its vivid crimson colour. Artist workshops lace its streets and the **Sentier des Ocres** (Ochre Trail; adult/child €2.50/ free; ☉9.30am-5.30pm; 🚗) plunges intrigued visitors into a mini-desert landscape of chestnut groves, pines and sunset-coloured ochre formations. Information panels along the two circular trails (30 or 50 minutes) highlight flora to spot. Wear walking shoes and avoid white clothing!

☑ Don't Miss

Rows of summertime lavender in bloom at **Abbaye Notre-Dame de Sénanque** (www.abbayedesenanque. com), a supremely peaceful Cistercian abbey 4km northwest of Gordes.

PROCHASSON FREDERIC/SHUTTERSTOCK ©

Ménerbes

Hilltop Ménerbes gained fame as the home of expat British author Peter Mayles, whose book *A Year in Provence* recounts his renovation of a farmhouse just outside the village in the late 1980s. Opposite the village's 12th-century church, the **Maison de la Truffe et du Vin** (House of Truffle & Wine; 📞04 90 72 38 37; www.vin-truffe-luberon. com; place de l'Horloge; ☉10am-noon & 2.30-6pm daily Apr-Oct, Thu-Sat Nov-Mar) represents 60 local *domaines* (wine-growing estates). April to October there is free wine tasting and wine sales at bargain-basement prices. Winter brings truffle workshops.

Lacoste

Lacoste has nothing to do with the designer brand – although it does have couturier connections. In 2001 designer Pierre Cardin purchased the 9th-century **Château de Lacoste** (📞04 90 75 93 12; www.chateau-la-coste.com). The château was looted by revolutionaries in 1789, and the 45-room palace remained an eerie ruin until Cardin arrived. He created a 1000-seat theatre and opera stage adjacent, only open during July's month-long **Festival de Lacoste** (www. festivaldelacoste.com). Daytime visits are possible only by reservation.

Bonnieux

Settled during the Roman era, Bonnieux has preserved its medieval character. It's riddled with alleyways and hidden staircases: from place de la Liberté, 86 steps lead to a 12th-century church. The **Musée de la Boulangerie** (📞04 90 75 88 34; 12 rue de la République; adult/student/child €3.50/1.50/ free; ☉10am-12:30pm & 2.30-6pm Wed-Mon Apr-Oct), in an old 17th-century bakery building, explores the history of bread-making. Time your visit for the lively Friday market.

✗ Take a Break

The villages are the ideal place to try Provençal specialities like aïoli (a fish dish with garlicky mayo) and *daube provençale* (a rich stew).

 ## Rue des Teinturiers

Canalside **rue des Teinturiers** (literally 'street of dyers') is a picturesque pedestrian street known for its alternative vibe in Avignon's old dyers' district. A hive of industrial activity until the 19th century, the street today is renowned for its bohemian bistros, cafes and gallery-workshops. Stone 'benches' in the shade of ancient plane trees make the perfect perch to ponder the irresistible trickle of the River Sorgue.

ANDREA PISTOLESI/GETTY IMAGES ©

Avignon

Attention, quiz fans: name the city where the pope lived during the early 14th century. Answered Rome? Bzzz: sorry, wrong answer. For 70-odd years of the early 1300s, the Provençal town of Avignon served as the centre of the Roman Catholic world, and though its stint as the seat of papal power only lasted a few decades, it's been left with an impressive legacy of ecclesiastical architecture, most notably the soaring, World Heritage–listed fortress-cum-palace known as the Palais des Papes.

Avignon is now best known for its annual arts festival, the largest in France, which draws thousands of visitors for several weeks in July. The rest of the year, it's a lovely city to explore, with boutique-lined streets, leafy squares and some excellent restaurants – as well as an impressive medieval wall that entirely encircles the old city.

◉ SIGHTS

Palais des Papes   Palace

(Papal Palace; www.palais-des-papes.com; place du Palais; adult/child €11/9, with Pont St-Bénezet €13.50/10.50; ⊘9am-8pm Jul, to 8.30pm Aug, shorter hours Sep-Jun) The largest Gothic palace ever built, the Palais des Papes was erected by Pope Clement V, who abandoned Rome in 1309 as a result of violent disorder following his election. It served as the seat of papal power for seven decades, and its immense scale provides ample testament to the medieval might of the Roman Catholic church. Ringed by 3m-thick walls, its cavernous halls, chapels and antechambers are largely bare today, but an audioguide (€2) provides a useful backstory.

Pont St-Bénezet   Bridge

(bd du Rhône; adult/child 24hr ticket €5/4, with Palais des Papes €13.50/10.50; ⊘9am-8pm Jul, to 8.30pm Aug, shorter hours Sep-Jun) Legend says Pastor Bénezet had three saintly visions urging him to build a bridge across the Rhône. Completed in 1185, the 900m-long bridge with 20 arches linked Avignon with Villeneuve-lès-Avignon. It was rebuilt several times before all but four of its spans were washed away in the 1600s.

If you don't want to pay to visit the bridge, admire it for free from Rocher des Doms park or Pont Édouard Daladier, or on Île de la Barthelasse's chemin des Berges.

Don't be surprised if you spot someone dancing: in France, the bridge is known as Pont d'Avignon after the nursery rhyme: 'Sur le pont d'Avignon/L'on y danse, l'on y danse...' (On Avignon Bridge, all are dancing...).

Musée du Petit Palais   Museum

(☏04 90 86 44 58; www.petit-palais.org; place du Palais; adult/child €6/free; ⊘10am-1pm & 2-6pm Wed-Mon) The archbishops' palace during the 14th and 15th centuries now houses outstanding collections of 'primitive', pre-Rennaissance, 13th- to 16th-century Italian religious paintings by artists including Botticelli, Carpaccio and Giovanni di

Paolo – the most famous is Botticelli's *La Vierge et l'Enfant* (1470).

Musée Anglardon   Gallery
(📞04 90 82 29 03; www.angladon.com; 5 rue Laboureur; adult/child €8/6.50; ⏱1-6pm Tue-Sun Apr-Sep, 1-6pm Tue-Sat Oct-Mar) Tiny Musée Angladon harbours an impressive collection of impressionist treasures, including works by Cézanne, Sisley, Manet and Degas – but the star piece is Van Gogh's *Railway Wagons,* the only painting by the artist on display in Provence. Impress your friends by pointing out that the 'earth' isn't actually paint, but bare canvas.

Collection Lambert   Gallery
(📞04 90 16 56 20; www.collectionlambert. com; 5 rue Violette; adult/child €10/8; ⏱11am-6pm Tue-Sun Sep-Jun, to 7pm daily Jul & Aug) Reopened in summer 2015 after significant renovation and expansion, Avignon's contemporary-arts museum focuses on works from the 1960s to the present. Work spans from minimalist and conceptual to video and photography – in stark contrast to the classic 18th-century mansion housing it.

🟢 ACTIVITIES & TOURS

Le Carré du Palais   Wine Tasting
(📞04 90 27 24 00; www.carredupalaisavignon. com; 1 place du Palais) The historic Hôtel Calvet de la Palun building in central Avignon has been renovated into a wine centre promoting and serving Côtes du Rhône and Vallée du Rhône appellations. Stop in to get a taste of the local vintages.

Avignon Wine Tour   Tours
(📞06 28 05 33 84; www.avignon-wine-tour.com; per person €80-110) Visit the region's vineyards with a knowledgeable guide, leaving you free to enjoy the wine.

🍴 EATING

Place de l'Horloge is crammed with touristy restaurants that don't offer the best cuisine or value in town. Delve instead into the pedestrian old city where ample pretty

*the seat of papal power
for seven decades*

Palais des Papes

HANS-GEORG EIBEN/GETTY IMAGES ©

Avignon

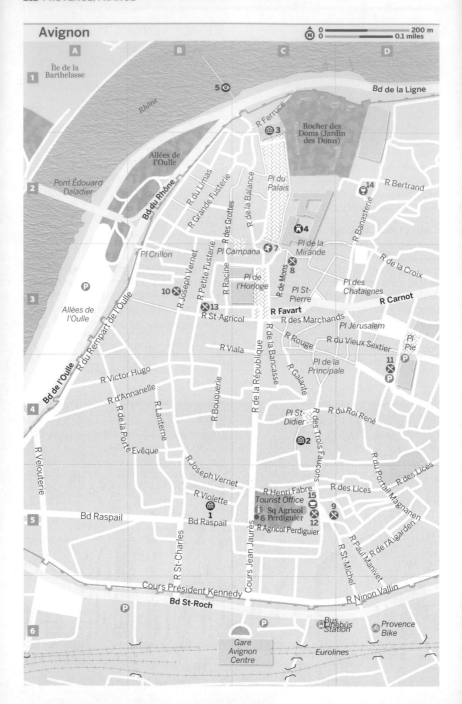

Île de la Barthelasse

Rhône

Bd de la Ligne

5

R Ferruce

Rocher des Doms (Jardin des Doms)

Allées de l'Oulle

Pont Édouard Daladier

Bd du Rhône

3

R du Limas

R Grande Fusterie

R des Grottes

R de la Balance

Pl du Palais

14

R Bertrand

R Banasterie

R de la Croix

4

Pl Crillon

Pl Campana

Pl de la Mirande

R Joseph Vernet

R Petite Fusterie

R Racine

7

R de Mons

8

Pl St-Pierre

Pl des Chataignes

R CARNOT

Allées de l'Oulle

Bd de l'Oulle

R du Rempart de l'Oulle

10

13

R St-Agricol

Pl de l'Horloge

R Favart

R des Marchands

Pl Jérusalem

R du Vieux Sextier

Pl Pie

11

R Viala

R de la République

R de la Bancasse

R Rouge

R Galante

Pl de la Principale

R Victor Hugo

R d'Annanelle

R Lanterne

R de la Porte Evêque

R Bouquerie

Pl St-Didier

R des Trois Faucons

R du Roi René

R du Portail Magnanen

R des Lices

2

R Joseph Vernet

R Violette

Bd Raspail

1

Bd Raspail

R Henri Fabre

Tourist Office

Sq Agricol

6 Perdiguier

R Agricol Perdiguier

15

12

9

R des Lices

R St-Michel

R Paul Manivet

R de l'Aigarden

R Velouterie

R St-Charles

Cours Jean Jaurès

Cours Président Kennedy

Bd St-Roch

R Ninon Vallin

Gare Avignon Centre

Eurolines

Bus Station

Provence Bike

0   200 m
0   0.1 miles

Avignon

squares tempt: place des Châtaignes and place de la Principle are two particularly beautiful restaurant-clad squares.

Restaurants open seven days during the summer festival season, when reservations become essential.

Maison Violette
Bakery €

(📞06 59 44 62 94; place des Corps Saints; ⊙7am-7.30pm Mon-Sat) We simply defy you not to walk into this bakery and not instantly be tempted by the stacks of baguettes, *ficelles* and *pains de campagnes* loaded up on the counter, not to mention the orderly ranks of eclairs, *millefeuilles*, fruit tarts and cookies lined up irresistibly behind the glass. Go on, a little bit of what you fancy does you good, *non*?

Ginette et Marcel
Cafe €

(📞04 90 85 58 70; 27 place des Corps Saints; tartines €4.30-6.90; ⊙11am-11pm Wed-Mon; 🌶) Set on one of Avignon's most happening plane tree shaded squares, this vintage cafe styled like a 1950s grocery is a charming spot to hang out and people-watch over a *tartine* (open-face sandwich), tart, salad or other light dish – equally tasty for lunch or an early-evening *apéro*. Kids adore Ginette's cherry- and violet-flavoured cordials and Marcel's glass jars of old-fashioned sweets.

Restaurant L'Essentiel
French €€

(📞04 90 85 87 12; www.restaurantlessentiel. com; 2 rue Petite Fusterie; menus €32-46; ⊙noon-2pm & 7-9.45pm Tue-Sat) Snug in an elegant, caramel-stone *hôtel particulier*, the Essential is one of the finest places to

eat in town – inside or in the wonderful courtyard garden. Begin with courgette flowers poached in a crayfish and truffle sauce, then continue with rabbit stuffed with candied aubergine, perhaps.

Au Jardin des Carmes
French €€

(📞09 54 25 10 67; 21 place des Carmes; mains €20; ⊙noon-10.30pm Tue-Sat) There's one standout reason to lunch at this lovely little restaurant, and that's the delightful courtyard garden, shaded by sails, tall bamboo and climbing plants. Starters are €10, mains €20 and desserts €9, plus the *plat du jour* at €16. The food is honest rather than *haute cuisine*, but it's prettily presented and packed with flavour.

Christian Etienne
French €€€

(📞04 90 86 16 50; www.christian-etienne.fr; 10 rue de Mons; lunch/dinner menus from €35/75; ⊙noon-2pm & 7.30-10pm Tue-Sat) One of Avignon's top tables, this much-vaunted restaurant occupies a 12th-century palace with a leafy outdoor terrace, adjacent to Palais des Papes. Interiors feel slightly dated, but the refined Provençal cuisine remains exceptional, and the restaurant has earned a Michelin star.

Les 5 Sens
Gastronomy €€€

(📞04 90 85 26 51; www.restaurantles5sens. com; 18 rue Joseph Vernet; menus lunch €16-22, dinner €40-59; ⊙noon-1.30pm & 7.45-11.30pm Tue-Sat) Chef Thierry Baucher, one of France's *meilleurs ouvriers* (top chefs), reveals his southwestern origins in specialities such as *cassoulet* and foie gras, but skews contemporary-Mediterranean

Al fresco dining in Avignon

in gastronomic dishes such as butternut-squash ravioli with *escargots*. Surroundings are sleek; service is impeccable.

🍷 DRINKING & NIGHTLIFE

Chic yet laid-back Avignon is awash with gorgeous, tree-shaded pedestrian squares buzzing with cafe life. Favourite options, loaded with pavement terraces and drinking opportunities, include place Crillon, place Pie, place de l'Horloge and place des Corps Saints.

Students tend to favour the many bars dotted along the aptly named rue de la Verrerie (Glassware St).

La Manutention   Bar
(4 rue des Escaliers Ste-Anne; ⊘noon-midnight)
No address better reflects Avignon's artsy soul than this bistro-bar at cultural centre La Manutention. Its leafy terrace basks in the shade of Palais des Papes' stone walls and, inside, giant conservatory-style windows open onto the funky decor of pocket-size-bar Utopia. There's a cinema too.

Milk Shop   Cafe
(📞09 82 54 16 82; www.milkshop.fr; 26 place des Corps Saints; ⊘7.45am-7pm Mon-Fri, 9.30am-7pm Sat; 📶) Keen to mingle with Avignon students? Make a beeline for this *salon au lait* ('milk bar') where super-thick ice-cream shakes (€4.50) are slurped through extra-wide straws. Bagels (€5 to €7), cupcakes and other American snacks create a deliberate US vibe, while comfy armchairs and wi-fi encourage hanging out.

ℹ️ INFORMATION

Tourist Office (📞04 32 74 32 74; www.avignon-tourisme.com; 41 cours Jean Jaurès; ⊘9am-6pm Mon-Sat, 10am-5pm Sun Apr-Oct, shorter hours Nov-Mar) Offers guided walking tours and information on other tours and activities, including boat trips on the River Rhône and wine-tasting trips to nearby vineyards. Smartphone apps too.

Tourist Office Annexe (Gare Avignon TGV; ⊘Jun-Aug) During summer, Avignon has an information booth at the TGV station.

ℹ️ GETTING THERE & AWAY

AIR

Aéroport Avignon-Provence (AVN; 📞04 90 81 51 51; www.avignon.aeroport.fr; Caumont) In Caumont, 8km southeast of Avignon. Currently has direct flights to London.

BUS

The **bus station** (bd St-Roch; ℹ️information window 8am-7pm Mon-Fri, to 1pm Sat) is next to the central train station. Tickets are sold on board. For schedules, see www.lepilote.com, www.info-ler.fr and www.vaucluse.fr. Long-haul companies **Linebús** (📞04 90 85 30 48; www.linebus.com) and **Eurolines** (📞04 90 85 27 60; www.eurolines.com) have offices at the far end of bus platforms and serve places such as Barcelona.

Aix-en-Provence €17.40; LER Line 23; 1¼ hours; six daily Monday to Saturday, two on Sunday.

Carpentras €2; TransVaucluse Line 5.1; 45 minutes; two or three hourly Monday to Saturday, every two hours Sunday.

TRAIN

If you're arriving in Avignon from elsewhere in France, it's nearly always easier, cheaper (and in many cases faster) to take the train than fly. There are two train stations in Avignon. There is an airport 8km southeast of Avignon in Caumont.

Avignon has two train stations: **Gare Avignon Centre** (42 bd St-Roch), on the southern edge of the walled town, and **Gare Avignon TGV** (Courtine), 4km southwest in Courtine. Local shuttle trains link the two every 20 minutes (€1.60, five minutes, 6am to 11pm). Note that there is no luggage storage at the train station.

Destinations served by TGV include Paris Gare du Lyon (€35 to €80, 3½ hours), Marseille (€17.50, 35 minutes) and Nice (€31 to €40, 3¼ hours). **Eurostar** (www.eurostar.com) services operate one to five times weekly between Avignon TGV and London (from €59.50, 5¾ hours) en route to/from Marseille.

Marseille €17.50, 1¼ to two hours

Marseille airport (Vitrolles station) €14.50, one to 1½ hours

Provençal Produce

Avignon's covered food market, **Les Halles** (www.avignon-leshalles.com; place Pie; ⏰6am-1.30pm Tue-Fri, to 2pm Sat & Sun), has over 40 food stalls showcasing seasonal Provençal ingredients. Even better, free cooking demonstrations are held at 11am Saturday. Outside on place Pie, admire Patrick Blanc's marvellous vegetal wall.

ℹ️ GETTING AROUND

BICYCLE

Vélopop (📞08 10 45 64 56; www.velopop.fr) Shared-bicycle service, with 17 stations around town. The first half-hour is free; each additional half-hour is €1. Membership per day/week is €1/5.

Provence Bike (📞04 90 27 92 61; www.provence-bike.com; 7 av St-Ruf; bicycles per day/week from €12/65, scooters €25/150; ⏰9am-6.30pm Mon-Sat, plus 10am-1pm Sun Jul) Rents city bikes, mountain bikes, scooters and motorcycles.

CAR & MOTORCYCLE

Find car-hire agencies at both train stations (reserve ahead, especially in July). Narrow, one-way streets and impossible parking make driving within the ramparts difficult: park outside the walls. The city has 900 free spaces at **Parking de L'Ile Piot**, and 1150 at **Parking des Italiens**, both under surveillance and served by the free **TCRA shuttle bus** (Transports en Commun de la Région d'Avignon; 📞04 32 74 18 32; www.tcra.

Where to Stay in Avignon

Avignon is an excellent place to base yourself, with a wide range of hotels and B&Bs. **Avignon & Provence** (www.avignon-et-provence.com) is a local tourist site with accommodation listings. Note that parking is pretty much non-existent inside the city walls, so you'll have to drop off your luggage, leave your car at one of the large car parks on the edge of the city and walk.

fr). On directional signs at intersections, 'P' in yellow means pay car parks; 'P' in green, free car parks. Pay **Parking Gare Centre** (☑04 90 80 74 40; bd St-Roch; ☺24hr) is next to the central train station.

Moustiers Ste-Marie

Dubbed 'Étoile de Provence' (Star of Provence), jewel-box Moustiers Ste-Marie crowns towering limestone cliffs, which mark the beginning of the Alps and the end of Haute-Provence's rolling prairies. A 227m-long chain, bearing a shining gold star, is stretched high above the village – a tradition, legend has it, begun by the Knight of Blacas, who was grateful to have returned safely from the Crusades. Twice a century, the weathered chain snaps, and the star gets replaced, as happened in 1996. In summer, it's clear that Moustiers' charms are no secret.

SIGHTS

Chapelle Notre Dame de Beauvoir   Church

(guided tours adult/child €3/free) Lording over the village, beneath Moustiers' star, this 14th-century church clings to a cliff ledge like an eagle's nest. A steep trail climbs beside a waterfall to the chapel, passing 14 stations of the cross en route. On 8 September, Mass at 5am celebrates the na-

tivity of the Virgin Mary, followed by flutes, drums and breakfast on the square.

Musée de la Faïence   Museum

(☑04 92 74 61 64; rue Seigneur de la Clue; adult/student/under 16yr €3/2/free; ☺10am-12.30pm Jul & Aug, to 5pm or 6pm rest of year, closed Tue year-round) Moustiers' decorative *faïence* (glazed earthenware) once graced the dining tables of Europe's most aristocratic houses. Today each of Moustiers' 15 ateliers has its own style, from representational to abstract. Antique masterpieces are housed in this little museum, adjacent to the town hall.

ACTIVITIES

Des Guides pour l'Aventure   Outdoors

(☑06 85 94 46 61; www.guidesaventure.com) Offers activities including canyoning (from €45 per half-day), rock climbing (€40 for three hours), rafting (€45 for 2½ hours) and 'floating' (€50 for three hours) – which is like rafting, except you have a buoyancy aid instead of a boat.

⊗ EATING

La Grignotière   Provencal €

(☑04 92 74 69 12; rte de Ste-Anne; mains €6-15; ☺11.30am-10pm May-Sep, to 6pm Feb–mid-May) Hidden behind the soft pink facade of Moustiers' Musée de la Faïence is this utterly gorgeous, blissfully peaceful garden restaurant. Tables sit between olive trees and the colourful, eye-catching decor – including the handmade glassware – is the handiwork of talented, dynamic owner Sandrine. Cuisine is 'picnic chic', meaning lots of creative salads, tapenades, quiches and so on.

La Treille Muscate   Provencal €€

(☑04 92 74 64 31; www.restaurant-latreillemuscate.fr; place de l'Église; lunch/dinner menus from €24/32; ☺noon-2pm Fri-Wed, 7.30-10.30pm Fri-Tue) The top place to eat in the village proper: classic Provençal cooking served with panache, either in the stone-walled

Moustiers Ste-Marie

dining room or on the terrace with valley views. Expect tasty dishes like oven-roasted lamb served with seasonal veg and rainbow trout with *sauce vierge*. Reservations recommended.

La Ferme Ste-Cécile
Gastronomy €€

(☏04 92 74 64 18; D952; menus €29-38; ⊘noon-2pm Tue-Sun, 7.30-10pm Tue-Sat) Just outside Moustiers, this wonderful *ferme auberge* (country inn) immerses you in the full Provençal dining experience, from the sun-splashed terrace and locally picked wines right through to the chef's meticulous Mediterranean cuisine. It's about 1.2km from Moustiers; look out for the signs as you drive towards Castellane.

La Bastide de Moustiers
Gastronomy €€€

(☏04 92 70 47 47; www.bastide-moustiers.com; chemin de Quinson; lunch menus €40-50, dinner menus €64-82; ⊘noon-2pm & 7.30-9.30pm May-Sep, closed Tue & Wed Oct-Apr; 🖭) Legendary chef Alain Ducasse has created his own Provençal bolthole here, and it's an utter treat from start to finish, from the playful *amuses bouches* to the rich, sauce-heavy mains and indulgent desserts. The views from the terrace are dreamy too. Dress smartly and reserve ahead in high season. It's 500m down a country lane, signposted off the D952 to Ste-Croix de Verdon.

Rooms (double from €280) are spacious and luxurious, and nearly all have valley views.

ⓘ GETTING THERE & AROUND

A car makes exploring the gorges much more fun, though if you're very fit, cycling is an option too. Bus services run to Castellane and Moustiers, but there's scant transport inside the gorges.

Barcelona, Spain

Barcelona is a mix of sunny Mediterranean charm and European urban style. The city bursts with art and architecture (from Gothic to Gaudí), Catalan cooking is among the country's best, summer sun seekers fill the beaches in and beyond the city, and the bars and clubs heave year-round. The city began as a middle-ranking Roman town, of which vestiges can be seen today, and its old centre constitutes one of the greatest concentrations of Gothic architecture in Europe. Beyond this core are some of the world's more bizarre buildings: surreal spectacles capped by Gaudí's church, La Sagrada Família.

Two Days in Barcelona

Start with the Barri Gòtic. After a stroll along **La Rambla** (p278), admire **La Catedral** (p288) and the **Museu d'Història de Barcelona** (p288) on historic **Plaça del Rei** (p289), then visit the **Basílica de Santa Maria del Mar** (p292), and the nearby **Museu Picasso** (p292). Round off with a meal and cocktails in El Born. On day two, experience **Park Güell** (p294) and **La Sagrada Família** (p271). Afterwards, go for dinner at **Suculent** (p299).

Four Days in Barcelona

Start the third day with more Gaudí, visiting **Casa Batlló** (p294) and **La Pedrera** (p294), followed by beachside relaxation and seafood in **Barceloneta** (p300). Day four should be dedicated to **Montjuïc** (p284), with its museums, galleries, fortress, gardens and Olympic stadium.

Looking for more Spain? Drive or catch a train to Basque Country (p308).

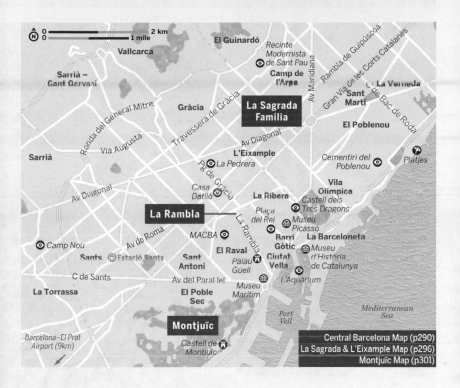

Arriving in Barcelona

Frequent *aerobúses* make the 35-minute run into town (€5.90) from 6am to 1am from **El Prat airport**. Taxis cost around €25. If arriving at the long-distance train station **Estació Sants** near the centre of town, there is a metro connection available to other neighbourhoods. **Estació del Nord** is Barcelona's long-haul bus station in L'Eixample, about 1.5km northeast of Plaça de Catalunya. It's a short walk from several metro stations.

Where to Stay

Barcelona has some fabulous accommodation, but never – and we repeat never – arrive in town without a reservation. Designer digs are something of a Barcelona speciality, with midrange and top-end travellers particularly well served. Apartments are also widespread and a fine alternative to hotels. Prices in Barcelona are generally higher than elsewhere in the country.

For information on what each neighbourhood has to offer, see p307.

La Sagrada Família's interior

JASON WALTMAN/500PX ©

La Sagrada Família

If you have time for only one sightseeing outing, this is it. The Sagrada Família inspires awe by its sheer verticality, inspiring use of light and Gaudí's offbeat design elements.

Great For...

☑ Don't Miss

The apse, the extraordinary pillars and the stained glass.

In the manner of the medieval cathedrals La Sagrada Família emulates, it's still under construction after more than 100 years. When completed, the highest tower will be more than half as high again as those that stand today.

A Holy Mission

The Temple Expiatori de la Sagrada Família (Expiatory Temple of the Holy Family) was Antoni Gaudí's all-consuming obsession. Given the commission by a conservative society that wished to build a temple as atonement for the city's sins of moderni-ty, Gaudí saw its completion as his holy mission. As funds dried up, he contributed his own, and in the last years of his life he was never shy of pleading with anyone he thought a likely donor.

❶ Need to Know

Map p296; ☎93 208 04 14; www.sagrada
familia.cat; Carrer de Mallorca 401; adult/
concession/under 11yr €15/13/free; ☯9am-
8pm Apr-Sep, to 6pm Oct-Mar; Ⓜ Sagrada
Família

✕ Take a Break

Michael Collins (Map p296; ☎93 459 19
04; www.michaelcollinspubs.com; Plaça de la
Sagrada Família 4; ☯1pm-2.30am Sun-Thu,
1pm-3am Fri & Sat; 🛜; Ⓜ Sagrada Família)
across the square is good for a beer.

★ Top Tip

Buying tickets online in advance is a
must to beat the frequently dispiriting
queues.

Gaudí devised a temple 95m long and
60m wide, able to seat 13,000 people,
with a central tower 170m high above the
transept (representing Christ) and another
17 towers of 100m or more. The 12 along
the three facades represent the Apostles,
while the remaining five represent the
Virgin Mary and the four evangelists. With
his characteristic dislike for straight lines
(there were none in nature, he said), Gaudí
gave his towers swelling outlines inspired
by the weird peaks of the holy mountain Montserrat outside Barcelona, and
encrusted them with a tangle of sculpture
that seems an outgrowth of the stone.

At Gaudí's death, only the crypt, the apse
walls, one portal and one tower had been
finished. Three more towers were added by
1930, completing the northeast (Nativity)
facade. In 1936 anarchists burned and
smashed the interior, including workshops,

plans and models. Work began again in
1952, but controversy has always clouded
progress. Opponents of the continuation
of the project claim that the computer
models based on what little of Gaudí's
plans survived the anarchists' ire have led
to the creation of a monster that has little
to do with Gaudí's plans and style. It is a
debate that appears to have little hope of
resolution. Like or hate what is being done,
the fascination it awakens is undeniable.

Guesses on when construction might
be complete range from the 2020s to the
2040s. Even before reaching that point,
some of the oldest parts of the church, especially the apse, have required restoration
work.

The Interior & the Apse

Inside, work on roofing over the church
was completed in 2010. The roof is held up
by a forest of extraordinary angled pillars.

As the pillars soar towards the ceiling, they sprout a web of supporting branches, creating the effect of a forest canopy. The tree image is in no way fortuitous – Gaudí envisaged such an effect. Everything was thought through, including the shape and placement of windows to create the mottled effect one would see with sunlight pouring through the branches of a thick forest. The pillars are of four different types of stone. They vary in colour and load-bearing strength, from the soft Montjuïc stone pillars along the lateral aisles through to granite, dark grey basalt and finally burgundy-tinged Iranian porphyry for the key columns at the intersection of the nave and transept. The stained glass, divided in shades of red, blue, green and ochre, creates a hypnotic, magical atmosphere when the sun hits the windows. Tribunes built high above the aisles can host two choirs: the main tribune up to 1300 people and the children's tribune up to 300.

Nativity Facade

The Nativity Facade is the artistic pinnacle of the building, mostly created under Gaudí's personal supervision. You can climb high up inside some of the four towers by a combination of lifts and narrow spiral staircases – a vertiginous experience. Do not climb the stairs if you have cardiac or respiratory problems. The towers are destined to hold tubular bells capable of playing complex music at great volume. Their upper parts are decorated with mosaics spelling out 'Sanctus, Sanctus, Sanctus, Hosanna in Excelsis, Amen, Alleluia'. Asked why he lavished so much care on the tops of the spires, which

Nativity Facade

no one would see from close up, Gaudí answered: 'The angels will see them'.

Three sections of the portal represent, from left to right, Hope, Charity and Faith. Among the forest of sculpture on the Charity portal you can see, low down, the manger surrounded by an ox, an ass, the shepherds and kings, and angel musicians. Some 30 different species of plant from around Catalonia are reproduced here, and the faces of the many figures are taken from plaster casts done of local people and the occasional one made from corpses in the local morgue.

PECOLD/SHUTTERSTOCK ©

Directly above the blue stained-glass window is the archangel Gabriel's Annunciation to Mary. At the top is a green cypress tree, a refuge in a storm for the white doves of peace dotted over it. The mosaic work at the pinnacle of the towers is made from Murano glass from Venice.

To the right of the facade is the curious Claustre del Roser, a Gothic-style mini-cloister tacked on to the outside of the church (rather than the classic square enclosure of the great Gothic church monasteries). Once inside, look back to the intricately decorated entrance. On the lower right-hand side you'll notice the sculpture of a reptilian devil handing a terrorist a bomb. Barcelona was regularly rocked by political violence, and bombings were frequent in the decades prior to the civil war. The sculpture is one of several on the 'temptations of men and women'.

Passion Facade

The southwest Passion Facade, on the theme of Christ's last days and death, was built between 1954 and 1978 based on surviving drawings by Gaudí, with four towers and a large, sculpture-bedecked portal. The sculptor, Josep Subirachs, worked on its decoration from 1986 to 2006. He did not attempt to imitate Gaudí, rather producing angular, controversial images of his own. The main series of sculptures, on three levels, are in an S-shaped sequence, starting with the Last Supper at the bottom left and ending with Christ's burial at the top right. Decorative work on the Passion Facade continues even today, as construction of the Glory Facade moves ahead.

To the right, in front of the Passion Facade, the Escoles de Gaudí is one of his simpler gems. Gaudí built this as a children's school, creating an original,

ⓘ When to Go

There are always lots of people visiting the Sagrada Família, but if you can get there when it opens, you'll find fewer people.

undulating roof of brick that continues to charm architects to this day. Inside is a recreation of Gaudí's modest office as it was when he died, and explanations of the geometric patterns and plans at the heart of his building techniques.

A Hidden Portrait

Careful observation of the Passion Facade will reveal a special tribute from sculptor Josep Subirachs to Gaudí. The central sculptural group (below Christ crucified) shows, from right to left, Christ bearing his cross, Veronica displaying the cloth with Christ's bloody image, a pair of soldiers and, watching it all, a man called the evangelist. Subirachs used a rare photo of Gaudí, taken a couple of years before his death, as the model for the evangelist's face.

Glory Facade

The Glory Facade is under construction and will, like the others, be crowned by four towers – the total of 12 representing the Twelve Apostles. Gaudí wanted it to be the most magnificent facade of the church. Inside will be the narthex, a kind of foyer made up of 16 'lanterns', a series of hyperboloid forms topped by cones. Further decoration will make the whole building a microcosmic symbol of the Christian church, with Christ represented by a massive 170m central tower above the transept, and the five remaining planned towers symbolising the Virgin Mary and the four evangelists.

Museu Gaudí

Open the same times as the church, the Museu Gaudí, below ground level, includes interesting material on Gaudí's life and other works, as well as models and photos of La Sagrada Família. You can see a good example of his plumb-line models that showed him the stresses and strains he could get away with in construction. A side hall towards the eastern end of the museum leads to a viewing point above the simple crypt in which the genius is buried. The crypt, where Masses are now held, can also be visited from the Carrer de Mallorca side of the church.

What's Nearby?

Església de les Saleses   Church

(Map p296; ☎93 458 76 67; www.parroquia concepciobcn.org; Passeig de Sant Joan 90; ⊙7.30am-1pm & 5-9pm Mon-Fri, 7.30am-2pm & 5-9pm Sun; MTetuan) A singular neo-Gothic effort, this church is interesting because it was designed by Joan Martorell i Montells (1833–1906), Gaudí's architecture professor. It was raised in 1878–85 with an adjacent convent (badly damaged in the civil war and now a school), and the use of brick, mosaics and sober stained glass offers hints of what was to come with Modernisme.

Recinte Modernista de Sant Pau   Architecture

(☎93 553 78 01; www.santpaubarcelona.org; Carrer de Sant Antoni Maria Claret 167; adult/ child €13/free; ⊙10am-6.30pm Mon-Sat, to

Passion facade (p273)

2.30pm Sun Apr-Oct, 10am-4.30pm Mon-Sat Nov-Mar; Ⓜ️Sant Pau/Dos de Maig) Domènech i Montaner outdid himself as architect and philanthropist with the Modernista Hospital de la Santa Creu i de Sant Pau, redubbed in 2014 the 'Recinte Modernista'. It was long considered one of the city's most important hospitals and only recently repurposed, its various spaces becoming cultural centres, offices and something of a monument. The complex, including 16 pavilions, is lavishly decorated and each pavilion is unique. Together with the Palau de la Música Catalana it is a World Heritage site.

Museu del Disseny de Barcelona
Museum

(☑️93 256 68 00, www.museudeldisseny.cat; Plaça de les Glòries Catalanes 37; permanent/temporary exhibition €6/4.40, combination ticket €8; ⊙10am-8pm Tue-Sun; Ⓜ️Glòries) Barcelona's design museum lies inside a new monolithic building with geometric facades and a rather brutalist appearance – which has already earned the nickname *la grapadora* (the stapler) by locals. Architecture aside, the museum houses a dazzling collection of ceramics, decorative arts and textiles, and is a must for anyone interested in the design world.

★ **Did You Know?**

Pope Benedict XVI consecrated the church in a huge ceremony in November 2010.

★ **Top Tip**

Audio guides – including some tailored to children – are available for an additional fee.

La Sagrada Família

A TIMELINE

1882 Construction begins on a neo-Gothic church designed by Francisco de Paula del Villar y Lozano.

1883 Antoni Gaudí takes over as chief architect and plans a far more ambitious church to hold 13,000 faithful.

1926 Gaudí dies; work continues under Domènec Sugrañes i Gras. Much of the **apse ❶** and **Nativity Facade ❷** is complete.

1930 Bell towers ❸ of the Nativity Facade completed.

1936 Construction is interrupted by Spanish Civil War; anarchists destroy Gaudí's plans.

1939–40 Architect Francesc de Paula Quintana i Vidal restores the crypt and meticulously reassembles many of Gaudí's lost models, some of which can be seen in the **museum ❹**.

1976 Passion Facade ❺ completed.

1986–2006 Sculptor Josep Subirachs adds sculptural details to the Passion Facade including the panels telling the story of Christ's last days, amid much criticism for employing a style far removed from what was thought typical of Gaudí.

2000 Central nave vault ❻ completed.

2010 Church completely roofed over; Pope Benedict XVI consecrates the church; work begins on a high-speed rail tunnel that will pass beneath the church's **Glory Facade ❼**.

2020s–40s Projected completion date.

TOP TIPS

➡ The best light through the stained-glass windows of the Passion Facade bursts into the heart of the church in the late afternoon.

➡ Visit at opening time on weekdays to avoid the worst of the crowds.

➡ Head up the Nativity Facade bell towers for the views, as long queues generally await at the Passion Facade towers.

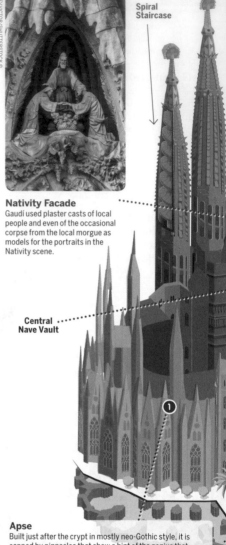

Spiral Staircase

Nativity Facade
Gaudí used plaster casts of local people and even of the occasional corpse from the local morgue as models for the portraits in the Nativity scene.

Central Nave Vault

Apse
Built just after the crypt in mostly neo-Gothic style, it is capped by pinnacles that show a hint of the genius that Gaudí would later deploy in the rest of the church.

Bell Towers

The towers of the three facades will represent the 12 Apostles. Eight are completed. Lifts whisk visitors up one tower of the Nativity and Passion Facades (the latter gets longer queues) for fine views.

NIKADA/GETTY IMAGES ©

Completed Church

Along with the Glory Facade and its four towers, six other towers remain to be completed. They will represent the four Evangelists, the Virgin Mary and, soaring above them all over the transept, a 170m colossus symbolising Christ.

Glory Facade

This will be the most fanciful facade of all, with a narthex boasting 16 hyperboloid lanterns topped by cones that will look something like an organ made of melting ice cream.

Museu Gaudí

Jammed with old photos, drawings and restored plaster models that bring Gaudí's ambitions to life, the museum also houses an extraordinarily complex plumb-line device he used to calculate his constructions.

Escoles de Gaudí

Crypt

The first completed part of the church, the crypt is in largely neo-Gothic style and lies under the transept. Gaudí's burial place here can be seen from the Museu Gaudí.

FOTOKON/SHUTTERSTOCK ©

Passion Facade

See the story of Christ's last days from Last Supper to burial in an S-shaped sequence from bottom to top of the facade. Check out the cryptogram in which the numbers always add up to 33, Christ's age at his death.

YURY DMITRIENKO/SHUTTERSTOCK ©

La Rambla

Barcelona's most famous street is both tourist magnet and window into Catalan culture, with arts centres, theatres and intriguing architecture. The middle is a broad pedestrian boulevard, crowded daily with a wide cross-section of society. A stroll here is pure sensory overload, with souvenir hawkers, buskers, pavement artists and living statues part of the ever-changing street scene.

Great For...

ℹ️ Need to Know

The **Rambla** (Map p290; Ⓜ Catalunya, Liceu, Drassanes) stroll, from Plaça de Catalunya to Plaça del Portal de la Pau, is 1.5km. To get here use the Catalunya, Liceu or Drassanes metro stations.

★ **Top Tip**

Things have improved in recent years, but pickpockets still prey on head-in-air tourists along here.

History

La Rambla takes its name from a seasonal stream (derived from the Arabic word for sand, *raml*) that once ran here. From the early Middle Ages, it was better known as the Cagalell (Stream of Shit) and lay outside the city walls until the 14th century. Monastic buildings were then built and, subsequently, mansions of the well-to-do from the 16th to the early 19th centuries. Unofficially, La Rambla is divided into five sections, which explains why many know it as Las Ramblas.

La Rambla de Canaletes

The section of La Rambla north of Plaça de Catalunya is named after the **Font de Canaletes** (Map p290; M Catalunya), an inconspicuous turn-of-the-20th-century drinking fountain, the water of which supposedly emerges from what were once known as the springs of Canaletes. It used to be said that *barcelonins* 'drank the waters of Les Canaletes'. Nowadays people claim that anyone who drinks from the fountain will return to Barcelona, which is not such a bad prospect. Delirious football fans gather here to celebrate whenever the city's principal team, FC Barcelona, wins a cup or league title.

La Rambla dels Estudis

La Rambla dels Estudis, from Carrer de la Canuda running south to Carrer de la Portaferrissa, was formerly home to a twittering bird market, which closed in 2010 after 150 years in operation.

Església de Betlem

Just north of Carrer del Carme, this **church** (Map p290; ☎ 93 318 38 23; www.mdbetlem. net; Carrer d'en Xuclà 2; ☸ 8.30am-1.30pm &

6-9pm; MLiceu) was constructed in baroque style for the Jesuits in the late 17th and early 18th centuries to replace an earlier church destroyed by fire in 1671. Fire was a bit of a theme for this site: the church was once considered the most splendid of Barcelona's few baroque offerings, but leftist arsonists torched it in 1936.

Palau Moja

Looming over the eastern side of La Rambla, **Palau Moja** (Map p290; 933 16 27 40; https://palaumoja.com; Carrer de Portaferrissa

> ★ **Did You Know**
>
> La Rambla saw plenty of action during the civil war. In *Homage to Catalonia*, George Orwell vividly described the avenue gripped by revolutionary fervour.

KARSOL/SHUTTERSTOCK ©

1; info centre/shop 10am-9pm, cafe 9am-midnight Mon-Fri, 11am-midnight Sat & Sun; MLiceu) FREE is a neoclassical building dating from the second half of the 18th century. Its clean, classical lines are best appreciated from across La Rambla. Unfortunately, interior access is limited, as it houses mostly government offices.

La Rambla de Sant Josep

From Carrer de la Portaferrissa to Plaça de la Boqueria, what is officially called La Rambla de Sant Josep (named after a now nonexistent monastery) is lined with flower stalls, which give it the alternative name La Rambla de les Flors.

Palau de la Virreina

The **Palau de la Virreina** (Map p290; La Rambla 99; MLiceu) is a grand 18th-century rococo mansion (with some neoclassical elements) that houses a municipal arts/entertainment information and ticket office run by the Ajuntament (town hall). Built by Manuel d'Amat i de Junyent, the corrupt captain general of Chile (a Spanish colony that included the silver mines of Potosí), it is a rare example of such a postbaroque building in Barcelona. It's home to the **Centre de la Imatge** (Map p290; 93 316 10 00; www.ajuntament.barcelona.cat; Palau de la Virreina; noon-8pm Tue-Sun; MLiceu) FREE, which has rotating photography exhibits. Admission prices vary.

Mosaïc de Miró

At Plaça de la Boqueria, where four side streets meet just north of Liceu metro station, you can walk all over a Miró – the colourful **mosaic** (Map p290; Plaça de la Boqueria; MLiceu) in the pavement, with one tile signed by the artist. Miró chose this site

> ★ **Local Knowledge**
>
> While there are some decent eateries in the vicinity, the vast majority of cafes and restaurants along La Rambla are expensive, mediocre tourist traps.

as it's near the house where he was born on the Passatge del Crèdit. The mosaic's bold colours and vivid swirling forms are instantly recognisable to Miró fans, though plenty of tourists stroll right over it without realising.

La Rambla dels Caputxins

La Rambla dels Caputxins, named after a former monastery, runs from Plaça de la Boqueria to Carrer dels Escudellers. The latter street is named after the potters' guild, founded in the 13th century, the members of which lived and worked here. On the western side of La Rambla is the **Gran Teatre del Liceu** (Map p290; ☎93 485 99 00; www.liceubarcelona.cat; La Rambla 51-59; tours 45/30min €9/6; ☉45min tours hourly 2-6pm Mon-Fri, from 9.30am Sat, 30min tours 1.30pm daily; MLiceu); to the southeast is the entrance to the palm-shaded Plaça Reial. Below this point La Rambla gets seedier, with the occasional strip club and peep show.

La Rambla de Santa Mònica

The final stretch of La Rambla widens out to approach the Mirador de Colom overlooking Port Vell. La Rambla here is named after the Convent de Santa Mònica, which once stood on the western flank of the street and has since been converted into a cultural centre.

What's Nearby?

Església de Santa Maria del Pi   Church
(Map p290; ☎93 318 47 43; www.basilicadelpi. com; Plaça del Pi; adult/concession/under 6yr €4/3/free; ☉10am-6pm; MLiceu) This striking 14th-century church is a classic of Catalan Gothic, with an imposing facade, a wide interior and a single nave. The simple decor in the main sanctuary contrasts with the gilded chapels and exquisite stained-glass windows that bathe the interior in ethereal light. The beautiful rose window above its entrance is one of the world's largest. Occasional concerts are staged here (clas-

sical guitar, choral groups and chamber orchestras).

Plaça Reial   Sqaure
(Map p290; MLiceu) One of the most photogenic squares in Barcelona, the Plaça Reial is a delightful retreat from the traffic and pedestrian mobs on the nearby Rambla. Numerous eateries, bars and nightspots lie beneath the arcades of 19th-century neoclassical buildings, with a buzz of activity at all hours.

Via Sepulcral
Romana   Archaeological Site
(Map p290; ☎93 256 21 00; www.museuhistor ia.bcn.cat; Plaça de la Vila de Madrid; adult/ concession/child €2/1.50/free; ☉11am-2pm Tue & Thu, to 7pm Sat & Sun; MCatalunya) Along Carrer de la Canuda, a block east

Plaça Reial

of the top end of La Rambla, is a sunken garden where a series of Roman tombs lies exposed. A smallish display in Spanish and Catalan by the tombs explores burial and funerary rites and customs. A few bits of pottery (including a burial amphora with the skeleton of a three-year-old Roman child) accompany the display.

Mirador de Colom   Viewpoint

(☑93 302 52 24; www.barcelonaturisme.com; Plaça del Portal de la Pau; adult/concession €6/4; ◷8.30am-8.30pm; Ⓜ Drassanes) High above the swirl of traffic on the roundabout below, Columbus keeps permanent watch, pointing vaguely out to the Mediterranean. Built for the Universal Exhibition in 1888, the monument allows you to zip up 60m in a lift for bird's-eye views back up La Rambla and across the ports of Barcelona.

Centre d'Art
Santa Mònica   Arts Centre

(☑93 567 11 10; http://artssantamonica.gencat.cat; La Rambla 7; ◷11am-9pm Tue-Sat, 11am-5pm Sun; Ⓜ Drassanes) **FREE** The Convent de Santa Mònica, which once stood on the western flank of the street, has since been converted into the Centre d'Art Santa Mònica, a cultural centre that mostly exhibits modern multimedia installations; admission is free.

Don't Miss

Strolling the whole Rambla from end to end, keeping an eye on the architecture alongside.

★ Top Tip

Take an early morning stroll and another late at night to sample La Rambla's many moods.

Montjuïc

The Montjuïc hillside, crowned by a castle and gardens, overlooks the port with some of the city's finest art collections: the Museu Nacional d'Art de Catalunya, the Fundació Joan Miró and CaixaForum.

Great For...

☑ Don't Miss

The Romanesque frescoes in the Museu Nacional d'Art de Catalunya.

Museu Nacional d'Art de Catalunya

From across the city, the bombastic neobaroque silhouette of the **Museu Nacional d'Art de Catalunya** (MNAC; Map p301; 📞93 622 03 76; www.museunacional.cat; Mirador del Palau Nacional; adult/student/child €12/8.40/free, after 3pm Sat & 1st Sun of month free; ⏱10am-8pm Tue-Sat, to 3pm Sun May-Sep, to 6pm Tue-Sat Oct-Apr; Ⓜ Espanya) can be seen on the slopes of Montjuïc. Built for the 1929 World Exhibition and restored in 2005, it houses a vast collection of mostly Catalan art from the early Middle Ages to the early 20th century. The high point is the collection of extraordinary Romanesque frescoes. Rescued from neglected country churches across northern Catalonia, the collection consists of 21 frescoes, wood-carvings and painted altar frontals.

Museu Nacional d'Art de Catalunya

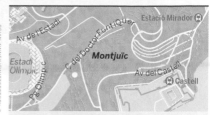

ⓘ Need to Know

The metro stops at the foot of Montjuïc; buses and funiculars go all the way

✕ Take a Break

Montjuïc eateries tend to be overpriced. The gardens surrounding Fundació Joan Miró museum are perfect for a picnic.

★ Top Tip

Ride the Transbordador Aeri from Barceloneta for a bird's-eye approach to Montjuïc.

Fundació Joan Miró

Joan Miró, the city's best-known 20th-century artistic progeny bequeathed the **Fundació Joan Miró** (Map p301; ☏93 443 94 70; www.fmirobcn.org; Parc de Montjuïc; adult/child €12/free; ☉10am-8pm Tue-Wed & Fri, to 9pm Thu, to 3pm Sun Apr-Oct, shorter hours rest of the year; ☒55, 150, ☒Paral·lel) to his home town in 1971. Its light-filled buildings, designed by close friend and architect Josep Lluís Sert (who also built Miró's Mallorca studios), are crammed with seminal works, from Miró's earliest timid sketches to paintings from his last years. Highlights include **Sala Joan Prats**, with works spanning the early years until 1919; **Sala Pilar Juncosa**, which covers his surrealist years 1932–55; and Rooms 18 and 19, which contain masterworks of the years 1956–83.

CaixaForum

The Caixa building society prides itself on its involvement in (and ownership of) art, in particular all that is contemporary. **Caixa-Forum** (Map p301; ☏93 476 86 00; www.fundacio.lacaixa.es; Avinguda de Francesc Ferrer i Guàrdia 6-8; adult/student & child €4/free, 1st Sun of month free; ☉10am-8pm; ℗; ⓂEspanya) hosts part of the bank's extensive collection from around the globe. The setting is a completely renovated former factory, the Fàbrica Casaramona, an outstanding Modernista brick structure designed by Puig i Cadafalch. On occasion portions of La Caixa's own collection goes on display, but more often than not major international exhibitions are the key draw.

Castell de Montjuïc

This forbidding *castell* (castle or fort) dominates the southeastern heights of Montjuïc and enjoys commanding views over the Mediterranean. It dates, in its present form, from the late 17th and 18th centuries. For most of its dark history, it has been used to watch over the city and as a political prison and killing ground.

Treasures in the Barri Gòtic

This scenic walk through the Barri Gòtic will take you back in time, from the early days of Roman-era Barcino through to the medieval era.

Start La Catedral
Distance 1.5km
Duration 1½ hours

Classic Photo: La Catedral

1 Before entering the cathedral, look at three Picasso friezes on the building facing the square. Next, wander through the magnificent **La Catedral** (p288).

2 Pass through the city gates; turn right into **Plaça de Sant Felip Neri**. The shrapnel-scarred church was damaged by pro-Francist bombers in 1939.

3 Head west to the looming 14th-century **Església de Santa Maria del Pi** (p282), famed for its magnificent rose window.

4 Follow the curving road to pretty **Plaça Reial** (p282). Flanking the fountain are Gaudí-designed lamp posts.

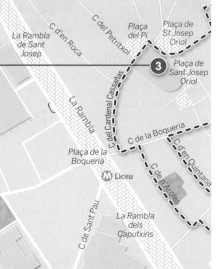

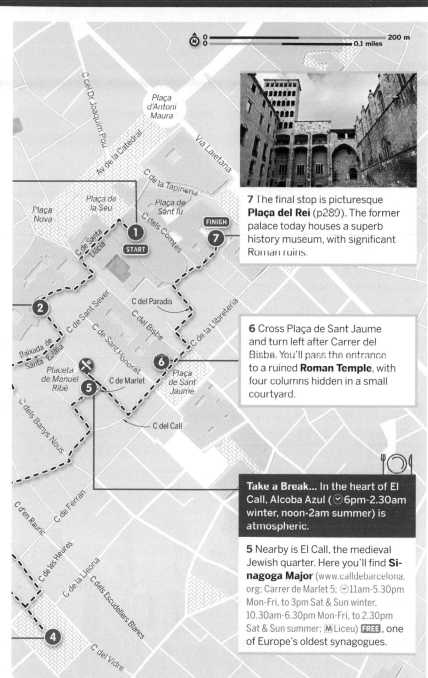

7 The final stop is picturesque **Plaça del Rei** (p289). The former palace today houses a superb history museum, with significant Roman ruins.

6 Cross Plaça de Sant Jaume and turn left after Carrer del Bisbe. You'll pass the entrance to a ruined **Roman Temple**, with four columns hidden in a small courtyard.

Take a Break... In the heart of El Call, Alcoba Azul (⏱6pm-2.30am winter, noon-2am summer) is atmospheric.

5 Nearby is El Call, the medieval Jewish quarter. Here you'll find **Sinagoga Major** (www.calldebarcelona.org; Carrer de Marlet 5; ⏱11am-5.30pm Mon-Fri, to 3pm Sat & Sun winter, 10.30am-6.30pm Mon-Fri, to 2.30pm Sat & Sun summer; Ⓜ Liceu) **FREE**, one of Europe's oldest synagogues.

Map labels:
200 m
0.1 miles

Plaça d'Antoni Maura

C del Dr Joaquim Pou
Av de la Catedral
Via Laietana
C de la Tapineria
Plaça de la Seu
Plaça de Sant Iu
Plaça Nova
C dels Comtes
FINISH
7
C de Santa Llúcia
START
1
2
C del Paradis
C del Bisbe
C de la Llibreteria
C de Sant Sever
C de Sant Honorat
Baixada de Santa Eulàlia
6
Placeta de Manuel Ribé
C de Marlet
5
Plaça de Sant Jaume
C del Call
C dels Banys Nous
C d'en Rauric
C de Ferran
C de les Heures
C de la Lleona
C dels Escudellers Blancs
4
C del Vidre

1 ISMAIL CIYDEM/GETTY IMAGES © 3 JAKOV FILIMONOV/SHUTTERSTOCK © 4 NIKADA/GETTY IMAGES © 7 PERESANZ/GETTY IMAGES ©

◉ SIGHTS
◉ La Rambla & Barri Gòtic
Mercat de la Boqueria   Market

(Map p290; ☎93 412 13 15; www.boqueria.info; La Rambla 91; ⊙8am-8.30pm Mon-Sat; ⓂLiceu) Mercat de la Boqueria is possibly La Rambla's most interesting building, not so much for its Modernista-influenced design (it was actually built over a long period, from 1840 to 1914, on the site of the former St Joseph Monastery), but for the action of the food market within.

La Catedral   Cathedral

(Map p290; ☎93 342 82 62; www.catedralbcn. org; Plaça de la Seu; free, 'donation entrance' €7, choir €3, roof €3; ⊙8am-12.45pm & 5.15-7.30pm Mon-Fri, 8am-8pm Sat & Sun, entry by donation 1-5.30pm Mon, 1-5pm Sat, 2-5pm Sun; ⓂJaume I) Barcelona's central place of worship presents a magnificent image. The richly decorated main facade, laced with gargoyles and the stone intricacies you would expect of northern European Gothic, sets it quite apart from other churches in Barcelona. The facade was actually added in 1870, although the rest of the building was built between 1298 and 1460. The other facades are sparse in decoration, and the octagonal, flat-roofed towers are a clear reminder that, even here, Catalan Gothic architectural principles prevailed.

Museu d'Història de Barcelona   Museum

(MUHBA; Map p290; ☎93 256 21 00; www. museuhistoria.bcn.cat; Plaça del Rei; adult/con-cession/child €7/5/free, 3-8pm Sun & 1st Sun of month free; ⊙10am-7pm Tue-Sat, to 2pm Mon, to 8pm Sun; ⓂJaume I) One of Barcelona's most fascinating museums takes you back through the centuries to the very founda-tions of Roman Barcino. You'll stroll over ru-ins of the old streets, sewers, laundries and wine- and fish-making factories that flour-ished here following the town's founding by Emperor Augustus around 10 BC. Equally impressive is the building itself, which was once part of the Palau Reial Major (Grand Royal Palace) on Plaça del Rei, among the key locations of medieval princely power in Barcelona.

Mosaic chimneys on the roof of Palau Güell

PUMPIZOLDA/GETTY IMAGES ©

Museu Frederic Marès   Museum
(Map p290; ☑93 256 35 00; www.museumares.
bcn.cat; Plaça de Sant Iu 5; adult/concession/
child €4.20/2.40/free, after 3pm Sun & 1st Sun
of month free; ⏰10am-7pm Tue-Sat, 11am-8pm
Sun; Ⓜ Jaume I) One of the wildest collections of historical curios lies inside this vast
medieval complex, once part of the royal
palace of the counts of Barcelona. A rather
worn coat of arms on the wall indicates that
it was also, for a while, the seat of the Spanish Inquisition in Barcelona. Frederic Marès
i Deulovol (1893–1991) was a rich sculptor,
traveller and obsessive collector, and
displays of religious art and vast varieties of
bric-a-brac litter the museum.

Plaça del Rei   Square
(Map p290; Ⓜ Jaume I) Plaça del Rei (King's
Sq) is a picturesque plaza where Fernando
and Isabel received Columbus following his
first New World voyage. It is the courtyard
of the former Palau Reial Major. The palace
today houses a superb history museum
(p288), with significant Roman ruins
underground.

◉ El Raval
MACBA   Arts Centre
(Museu d'Art Contemporani de Barcelona; ☑93
481 33 68; www.macba.cat; Plaça dels Àngels
1; adult/concession/under 12yr €10/8/free;
⏰11am-7.30pm Mon & Wed-Fri, 10am-9pm
Sat, 10am-3pm Sun & holidays; Ⓜ Universitat)
Designed by Richard Meier and opened
in 1995, MACBA has become the city's
foremost contemporary art centre, with
captivating exhibitions for the serious art
lover. The permanent collection is on the
ground floor and dedicates itself to Spanish
and Catalan art from the second half of the
20th century, with works by Antoni Tàpies,
Joan Brossa and Miquel Barceló, among
others, though international artists, such as
Paul Klee, Bruce Nauman and John Cage,
are also represented.

Palau Güell   Palace
(Map p290; ☑93 472 57 75; www.palauguell.cat;
Carrer Nou de la Rambla 3-5; adult/concession/
under 10yr incl audio guide €12/9/free, 1st Sun

Gaudí: a Catholic & a Catalan

Gaudí was a devout Catholic and a
Catalan nationalist. Catalonia's great
medieval churches, in addition to nature, were a source of inspiration to him.
He took pride in utilising the building
materials of the countryside: clay, stone
and timber.

In contrast to his architecture,
Gaudí's life was simple; he was not
averse to knocking on doors, literally
begging for money to help fund construction of the cathedral. As Gaudí became more adventurous he appeared as
a lone wolf. With age he became almost
exclusively motivated by stark religious
conviction, and he devoted much of the
latter part of his life to what remains
Barcelona's call sign – the unfinished La
Sagrada Família. He died in 1926, struck
down by a streetcar while taking his
daily walk to the Sant Felip Neri church.

Wearing ragged clothes with empty
pockets – save for some orange peel
– Gaudí was initially taken for a beggar
and taken to a nearby hospital where
he was left in a pauper's ward; he died
two days later. Thousands attended his
funeral forming a half-mile procession
to La Sagrada Família, where he was
buried in the crypt.

Much like his work in progress, La
Sagrada Família, Gaudí's story is far
from over. In March 2000 the Vatican
decided to proceed with the case for
canonising him, and pilgrims already
stop by the crypt to pay him homage.
One of the key sculptors at work on the
church, the Japanese Etsuro Sotoo,
converted to Catholicism because of his
passion for Gaudí.

of month free; ⏰10am-8pm Tue-Sun Apr-Oct,
to 5.30pm Nov-Mar; Ⓜ Drassanes) Finally reopened in its entirety in 2012 after several
years of refurbishment, this is a magnificent example of the early days of Gaudí's

Central Barcelona

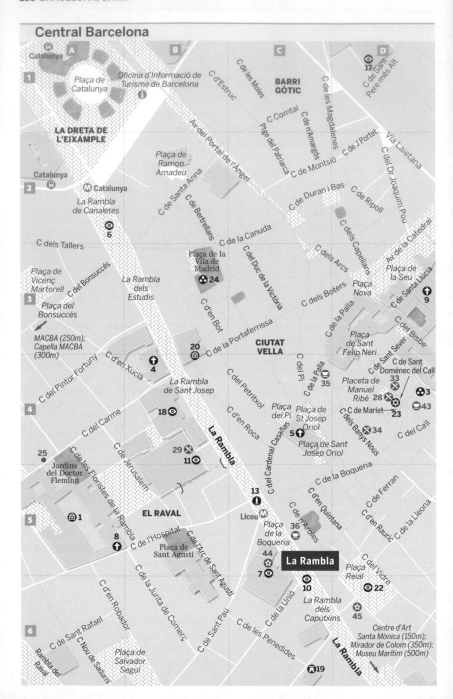

Catalunya

A

B

C

D

1

Plaça de Catalunya

Oficina d'Informació de Turisme de Barcelona

C d'Estruc

C de les Moles

BARRI GÒTIC

C de les Magdalenes

C de Sant Pere més Alt

17

LA DRETA DE L'EIXAMPLE

C d'Amargos

Ptge del Patriarca

C Comtal

C de n'Amargos

C de J Portet

Via Laietana

2

Catalunya

Catalunya

La Rambla de Canaletes

6

Plaça de Ramon Amadeu

C de Santa Anna

C de Bertrellans

C de Montsió

C de Duran i Bas

C del Dr Joaquim Pou

C de Ripoll

C dels Capellans

Av de la Catedral

C dels Tallers

C de la Canuda

C dels Arcs

Plaça de la Seu

C de Santa Llúcia

3

Plaça de Vicenç Martorell

C del Bonsuccés

La Rambla dels Estudis

Plaça de la Vila de Madrid

24

C del Duc de la Victoria

Plaça Nova

9

Plaça del Bonsuccés

MACBA (250m); Capella MACBA (300m)

C del Pintor Fortuny

C d'en Xuclà

C d'en Bot

4

C de la Portaferrissa

CIUTAT VELLA

C dels Boters

C de la Palla

Plaça de Sant Felip Neri

C del Bisbe

C de Sant Sever

4

C del Carme

La Rambla de Sant Josep

18

C del Petritxol

C del Pi

C de la Palla

35

Placeta de Manuel Ribé

28

C de Sant Domènec del Call

33

3

23

43

C de Marlet

C de Jerusalem

C d'en Roca

Plaça del Pi

Plaça de St Josep Oriol

5

34

dels Banys Nous

C del Call

25

Jardins del Doctor Fleming

C de les Floristes de la Rambla

29

11

La Rambla

Plaça de Sant Josep Oriol

C de la Boqueria

C de Ferran

5

1

8

EL RAVAL

C de l'Hospital

C de l'Arc de Sant Agustí

Plaça de Sant Agustí

13

Liceu

Plaça de la Boqueria

36

C d'en Quintana

C d'en Rauric

C de la Lleona

44

7

La Rambla

Plaça Reial

22

45

6

C de Sant Rafael

C Nou de Sadurní

C d'en Robador

C de la Junta de Comerç

C de Sant Pau

C de la Unió

C de les Penedides

10

La Rambla dels Caputxins

C del Vidre

Centre d'Art Santa Mònica (150m); Mirador de Colom (350m); Museu Marítim (500m)

Rambla del Raval

Plaça de Salvador Seguí

19

La Rambla

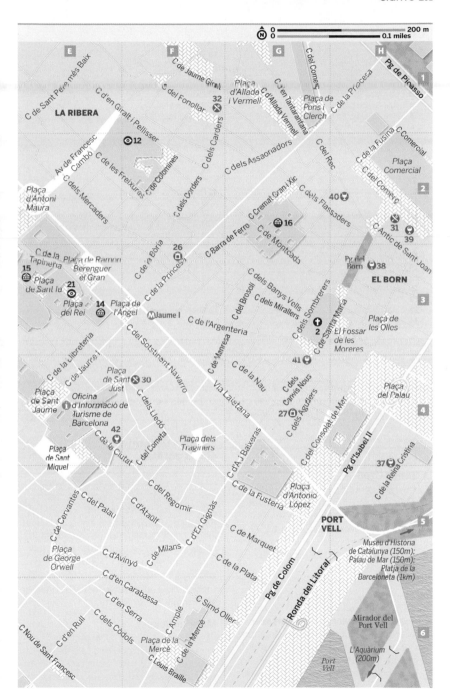

0
0
200 m
0.1 miles

E
F
G
H

C de Jaume Giralt

Pg de Picasso

1

C de Sant Pere més Baix

C del Fonollar

Plaça
d'Allada
i Vermell

C d'en Tantarantana

C d'Allada Vermell

C del Comerç

C de la Princesa

LA RIBERA

32

Plaça de
Pons i
Clerch

Av de Francesc Cambó

C d'en Giralt i Pellisser

12

C de les Freixures

C dels Mercaders

C de les Colomines

C dels Corders

C dels Carders

C dels Assaonadors

C del Rec

C de la Fusina

C Comercial

Plaça
Comercial

2

Plaça
d'Antoni
Maura

C de la
Tapineria

15

21

Plaça
de Sant Iu

C de la Barra de Ferro

C Cremat Gran i Xic

16

C dels Flassaders

C del Comerç

40

C Antic de Sant Joan

31

39

Plaça de Ramon
Berenguer
el Gran

26

C de la Bòria

C Barra de Ferro

C de Montcada

Pg del
Born

38

EL BORN

3

Plaça
del Rei

14

Plaça de
l'Àngel

Jaume I

C de la Princesa

C dels Banys Vells

C del Brosolí

C dels Mirallers

C dels Sombrerers

C de Santa Maria

2

El Fossar
de les
Moreres

Plaça de
les Olles

C de la Llibreteria

C de Jaume I

C del Sotstinent Navarro

C de l'Argenteria

C de Manresa

C de la Nau

41

C dels
Canvis Nous

C dels Agullers

Plaça
del Palau

4

Plaça
de Sant
Jaume

Oficina
d'Informació de
Turisme de
Barcelona

Plaça
de Sant
Just

30

C dels Lledó

42

C de la Ciutat

C del Cometa

Via Laietana

27

C del Consolat de Mar

Pg d'Isabel II

37

C de la Reina Cristina

Plaça
de Sant
Miquel

Plaça dels
Traginers

C d'A J Baixeras

Plaça
d'Antonio
López

5

C de Cervantes

C del Palau

C d'Ataült

C del Regomir

C d'En Gignàs

C de la Fusteria

PORT
VELL

Museu d'Història
de Catalunya (150m);
Palau de Mar (150m);
Platja de la
Barceloneta (1km)

Plaça
de George
Orwell

C d'Avinyó

C de Milans

C de Marquet

C de la Plata

Pg de Colom

Ronda del Litoral

Mirador del
Port Vell

6

C de Cervantes

C d'en Carabassa

C Nou de Sant Francesc

C d'en Rull

C dels Còdols

C d'en Serra

C Ample

C Simó Oller

Plaça de la
Mercè

C de la Mercè

C Louis Braille

Port
Vell

L'Aquàrium
(200m)

Central Barcelona

fevered architectural imagination. The extraordinary neo-Gothic mansion, one of the few major buildings of that era raised in Ciutat Vella, gives an insight into its maker's prodigious genius.

Antic Hospital de la Santa Creu
Historic Building

(Former Hospital of the Holy Cross; Map p290; ☎93 270 16 21; www.bcn.cat; Carrer de l'Hospital 56; ◷9am-8pm Mon-Fri, to 2pm Sat; Ⓜ Liceu) Behind La Boqueria stands the Antic Hospital de la Santa Creu, which was once the city's main hospital. Begun in 1401, it functioned until the 1930s, and was considered one of the best in Europe in its medieval heyday – it is famously the place where Antoni Gaudí died in 1926. Today it houses the **Biblioteca de Catalunya**, and the **Institut d'Estudis Catalans** (Institute for Catalan Studies). The hospital's Gothic chapel, **La Capella** (Map p290; ☎93 256 20 44; www.bcn.cat/lacapella; ◷noon-8pm Tue-Sat, 11am-2pm Sun & holidays; ▯91, 1, 120) **FREE**, shows temporary exhibitions.

◎ La Ribera

Basílica de Santa Maria del Mar
Church

(Map p290; ☎93 310 23 90; www.santamaria delmarbarcelona.org; Plaça de Santa Maria del Mar; €8; ◷guided tours 1.15pm, 2pm, 3pm, 5.15pm; Ⓜ Jaume I) At the southwest end of Passeig del Born stands the apse of Barcelona's finest Catalan Gothic church, Santa Maria del Mar (Our Lady of the Sea). Built in the 14th century with record-breaking alacrity for the time (it took just 54 years), the church is remarkable for its architectural harmony and simplicity.

Museu Picasso
Museum

(Map p290; ☎93 256 30 00; www.museu picasso.bcn.cat; Carrer de Montcada 15-23; adult/ concession/child all collections €14/7.50/free, permanent collection €11/7/free, temporary exhibitions €4.50/3/free, 3-7pm Sun & 1st Sun of month free; ⊙9am-7pm Tue-Sun, to 9.30pm Thu; ⓂJaume I) The setting alone, in five contiguous medieval stone mansions, makes the Museu Picasso unique (and worth the probable queues). The pretty courtyards, galleries and staircases preserved in the first three of these buildings are as delightful as the collection inside.

While the collection concentrates on the artist's formative years – sometimes disappointing for those hoping for a feast of his better-known later works – there is enough material from subsequent periods to give you a thorough impression of the man's versatility and genius. Above all, you come away feeling that Picasso was the true original, always one step ahead of himself (let alone anyone else) in his search for new forms of expression.

Palau de la
Música Catalana   Architecture

(Map p290; ☑93 295 72 00; www.palaumusica. cat; Carrer de Palau de la Música 4-6; adult/ concession/child €18/11/free; ⊙guided tours 10am-3.30pm, to 6pm Easter, Jul & Aug; ⓂUrquinaona) This concert hall is a high point of Barcelona's Modernista architecture, a symphony in tile, brick, sculpted stone and stained glass. Built by Domènech i Montaner between 1905 and 1908 for the Orfeo Català musical society, it was conceived as a temple for the Catalan Renaixença (Renaissance).

Mercat de Santa Caterina   Market

(Map p290; ☑93 319 57 40; www.mercatsanta caterina.com; Avinguda de Francesc Cambó 16; ⊙7.30am-3.30pm Mon, Wed & Sat, to 8.30pm Tue, Thu & Fri, closed afternoons Jul & Aug; ⓂJaume I) Come shopping for your tomatoes at this extraordinary-looking produce market, designed by Enric Miralles and Benedetta Tagliabue to replace its 19th-century predecessor. Finished in 2005, it is distinguished by its kaleidoscopic and undulating roof, held up above the bustling produce stands, restaurants, cafes and bars by twisting slender branches of what look like grey steel trees.

◉ La Barceloneta & the Waterfront

Museu Marítim   Museum

(☑93 342 99 20; www.mmb.cat; Avinguda de les Drassanes; adult/child €5/2.50, 3-8pm Sun free; ⊙10am-8pm; ⓂDrassanes) These mighty Gothic shipyards shelter the Museu Marítim, a remarkable relic from Barcelona's days as the seat of a seafaring empire. Highlights include a full-sized replica (made in the 1970s) of Don Juan of Austria's 16th-century flagship, fishing vessels, antique navigation charts and dioramas of the Barcelona waterfront.

Platjes   Beach

(🚌36, 41, ⓂCiutadella Vila Olímpic, Bogatell, Llacuna, Selva de Mar) A series of pleasant beaches stretches northeast from the Port Olímpic marina. They are largely artificial, but this doesn't stop an estimated seven million bathers from piling in every year!

Museu d'Història
de Catalunya   Museum

(Museum of Catalonian History; ☑93 225 47 00; www.mhcat.net; Plaça de Pau Vila 3; adult/ child €4.50/3.50, last Tue of the month Oct-Jun free; ⊙10am-7pm Tue & Thu-Sat, to 8pm Wed, to 2.30pm Sun; ⓂBarceloneta) Inside the **Palau de Mar**, this worthwhile museum takes you from the Stone Age through the early 1900s. It is a busy hotchpotch of dioramas, artefacts, videos, models, documents and interactive bits: all up, an entertaining exploration of 2000 years of Catalan history. Signage is in Catalan/Spanish.

L'Aquàrium   Aquarium

(☑93 221 74 74; www.aquariumbcn.com; Moll d'Espanya; adult/child €20/15, dive €300; ⊙9.30am-11pm Jul & Aug, to 9pm Sep-Jun; ⓂDrassanes) It is hard not to shudder at the sight of a shark gliding above you, displaying its toothy, wide-mouthed grin. But this, the 80m shark tunnel, is the highlight of one of Europe's largest aquariums. It has the world's best Mediterranean collection and plenty of colourful fish from as far off as the Red Sea, the Caribbean and the Great Barrier Reef. All up, some 11,000 fish

Park Güell

North of Gràcia and about 4km from Plaça de Catalunya, **Park Güell** (📞93 409 18 31; www.parkguell.cat; Carrer d'Olot 7; adult/child €8/6; ☉8am-9.30pm May-Aug, to 8pm Sep-Apr; 🚍24, 🅼Lesseps, Vallcarca) is where Gaudí turned his hand to landscape gardening. It's a strange, enchanting place where his passion for natural forms really took flight – to the point where the artificial almost seems more natural than the natural.

(including a dozen sharks) of 450 species reside here.

Platja de la Barceloneta   Beach

(🅼Barceloneta) This beach, just east of its namesake neighbourhood, has obvious appeal, with Mediterranean delights, plus ample eating and drinking options inland from the beach when you need a bit of refreshment.

◉ L'Eixample

Casa Batlló   Architecture

(Map p296; 📞93 216 03 06; www.casabatllo. es; Passeig de Gràcia 43; adult/concession/under 7yr €23.50/20.50/free; ☉9am-9pm, last admission 8pm; 🅼Passeig de Gràcia) One of the strangest residential buildings in Europe, this is Gaudí at his hallucinatory best. The facade, sprinkled with bits of blue, mauve and green tiles and studded with wave-shaped window frames and balconies, rises to an uneven blue-tiled roof with a solitary tower.

It is one of the three houses on the block between Carrer del Consell de Cent and Carrer d'Aragó that gave it the playful name Manzana de la Discordia, meaning 'Apple (Block) of Discord'. The others are Puig i Cadafalch's **Casa Amatller** (Map p296; 📞93 461 74 60; www.amatller.org; Passeig de Gràcia 41; adult/child 6-12yr/under 6yr 1hr tour €17/8.50/free, 30min tour €14/7/free; ☉11am-6pm) and Domènech i Montaner's

Casa Lleó Morera (Map p296; 📞93 676 27 33; www.casalleomorera.com; Passeig de Gràcia 35; guided tour adult/concession/under 12yr €15/13.50/free, express tour adult/under 12yr €12/free; ☉10am-1.30pm & 3-7pm Tue-Sun). They were all renovated between 1898 and 1906 and show how eclectic a 'style' Modernisme was.

Locals know Casa Batlló variously as the casa dels ossos (house of bones) or casa del drac (house of the dragon). It's easy enough to see why. The balconies look like the bony jaws of some strange beast and the roof represents Sant Jordi (St George) and the dragon. Even the roof was built to look like the shape of an animal's back, with shiny scales – the 'spine' changes colour as you walk around. If you stare long enough at the building, it seems almost to be a living being. Before going inside, take a look at the pavement. Each paving piece carries stylised images of an octopus and a starfish, designs that Gaudí originally cooked up for Casa Batlló.

When Gaudí was commissioned to refashion this building, he went to town inside and out. The internal light wells shimmer with tiles of deep sea blue. Gaudí eschewed the straight line, and so the staircase wafts you up to the 1st (main) floor, where the salon looks on to Passeig de Gràcia. Everything swirls: the ceiling is twisted into a vortex around its sunlike lamp; the doors, window and skylights are dreamy waves of wood and coloured glass. The same themes continue in the other rooms and covered terrace. The attic is characterised by Gaudí trademark hyperboloid arches. Twisting, tiled chimney pots add a surreal touch to the roof.

La Pedrera   Architecture

(Casa Milà; Map p296; 📞902 202138; www. lapedrera.com; Passeig de Gràcia 92; adult/concession/under 13yr/under 7yr €22/16.50/11/free; ☉9am-6.30pm & 7pm-9pm Mon-Sun; 🅼Diagonal) This undulating beast is another madcap Gaudí masterpiece, built in 1905–10 as a combined apartment and office block. Formally called Casa Milà, after the businessman who commissioned it, it

Platja de la Barceloneta

is better known as La Pedrera (the Quarry) because of its uneven grey stone facade, which ripples around the corner of Carrer de Provença.

Pere Milà had married the older and far richer Roser Guardiola, the widow of Josep Guardiola, and clearly knew how to spend his new wife's money. Milà was one of the city's first car owners and Gaudí built parking space into this building, itself a first. When commissioned to design this apartment building, Gaudí wanted to top anything else done in L'Eixample.

The Fundació Caixa Catalunya has opened the top-floor apartment, attic and roof, together called the Espai Gaudí (Gaudí Space), to visitors. The roof is the most extraordinary element, with its giant chimney pots looking like multicoloured medieval knights. Short concerts are often staged up here in summer. Gaudí wanted to put a tall statue of the Virgin up here too: when the Milà family said no, fearing it might make the building a target for anarchists, Gaudí resigned from the project in disgust.

One floor below the roof, where you can appreciate Gaudí's taste for parabolic arches, is a modest museum dedicated to his work.

The next floor down is the apartment (El Pis de la Pedrera). It is fascinating to wander around this elegantly furnished home, done up in the style of a well-to-do family might have enjoyed in the early 20th century. The sensuous curves and unexpected touches in everything from light fittings to bedsteads, from door handles to balconies, might seem admirable to us today, but not everyone thought so at the time. The story goes that one tenant, a certain Mrs Comes i Abril, had complained that there was no obvious place to put her piano in these wavy rooms. Gaudí's response was to suggest that she take up the flute.

For a few extra euros, a 'Premium' ticket means you don't have to queue.

Casa de les Punxes Architecture

(Casa Terrades; Map p296; ☏93 016 01 28; www.casadelespunxes.com; Avinguda Diagonal 420; adult/concession/under 5yr €12.50/€11.25/ free; ⊙9am-8pm; MDiagonal) Puig i Cadafalch's Casa Terrades is better known as the Casa de les Punxes (House of

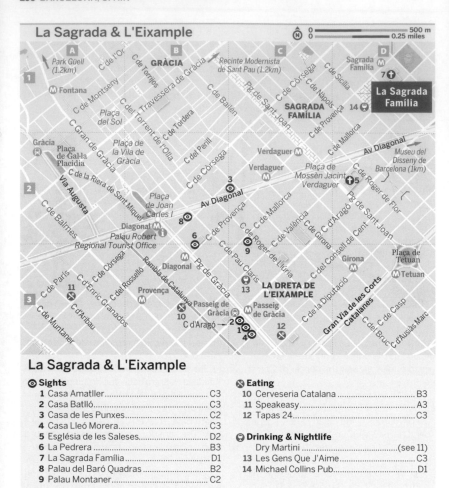

La Sagrada & L'Eixample

La Sagrada & L'Eixample

◎ Sights
1 Casa Amatller	C3
2 Casa Batlló	C3
3 Casa de les Punxes	C2
4 Casa Lleó Morera	C3
5 Església de les Saleses	D2
6 La Pedrera	B3
7 La Sagrada Família	D1
8 Palau del Baró Quadras	B2
9 Palau Montaner	C2

✕ Eating
10 Cerveseria Catalana	B3
11 Speakeasy	A3
12 Tapas 24	C3

◎ Drinking & Nightlife
Dry Martini	(see 11)
13 Les Gens Que J'Aime	C3
14 Michael Collins Pub	D1

Spikes) because of its pointed turrets. This apartment block, completed in 1905, looks like a fairy-tale castle and has the singular attribute of being the only fully detached building in L'Eixample.

Palau Montaner   Architecture
(Map p296; ☑93 317 76 52; www.fundaciotapies. org; Carrer de Mallorca 278; adult/child €7/free; ☺guided tours 11am Sat; ⓂPasseig de Gràcia) Interesting on the outside and made all the more enticing by its gardens, this creation by Domènech i Montaner is spectacular on the inside. Completed in 1896, its central

feature is a grand staircase beneath a broad, ornamental skylight. The interior is laden with sculptures (some by Eusebi Arnau), mosaics and fine woodwork. It is currently only open by guided tour, organised by the Fundació Tàpies and in Catalan only.

Palau del Baró Quadras   Architecture
(Map p296; ☑93 467 80 00; www.llull.cat; Avinguda Diagonal 373; ☺8am-8pm Mon-Fri; ⓂDiagonal) FREE Puig i Cadafalch designed Palau del Baró Quadras (built 1902–06) · in an exuberant Gothic-inspired style. The

main facade is its most intriguing, with a soaring, glassed-in gallery. Take a closer look at the gargoyles and reliefs – the pair of toothy fish and the sword-wielding knight clearly have the same artistic signature as the architect behind Casa Amatller. Decor inside is eclectic, but dominated by Middle Eastern and East Asian themes.

TOURS

Oficina d'Informació de Turisme de Barcelona (Map p290; ☑93 285 38 34; www.barcelonaturisme.com; Plaça de Catalunya 17; ◷9.30am-9.30pm; ⓂCatalunya) Organises a series of guided walking tours. One explores the Barri Gòtic (adult/child €16/free); another follows in Picasso's footsteps and winds up at the Museu Picasso, to which entry is included in the price (adult/child €22/7); and a third takes in the main jewels of Modernisme (adult/child €16/free). There's also a 'gourmet' tour of traditional purveyors of fine foodstuffs across the Ciutat Vella (adult/child €22/7). Stop by the tourist office or go online for the latest schedule. Tours typically last two hours and start at the tourist office.

Barcelona Metro Walks Consists of seven self-guided routes across the city, combining travel on the metro and other public transport as well as stretches on foot. Tourist information points at Plaça de Catalunya and Plaça de Sant Jaume sell the €16 package, which includes a walks guide, two-day transport pass and map.

My Favourite Things (☑637 265405; www.myft.net; tours from €26) Offers tours for no more than 10 participants based on numerous themes: anything from design to food. Other activities include flamenco and salsa classes, and bicycle rides in and out of Barcelona.

Runner Bean Tours (Map p290; ☑636 108776; www.runnerbeantours.com; Carrer del Carme 44; ◷tours 11am year-round & 4.30pm Apr-Sep, 3pm Mar; ⓂLiceu) Has several daily thematic tours. It's a pay-what-you-wish tour, with a collection taken at the end for the guide. The Old City tour explores the Roman and medieval history of Barcelona, visiting highlights in the Ciutat Vella. The Gaudí tour takes in the great works of Modernista Barcelona. It involves two trips on the metro. Runner Bean Tours also has ghostly evening tours and a Kids and Family Walking Tour. Check the website for departure times.

SHOPPING

If your doctor has prescribed an intense round of retail therapy to deal with the blues, then Barcelona is the place. Across Ciutat Vella (Barri Gòtic, El Raval and La Ribera), L'Eixample and Gràcia is spread a thick mantle of boutiques, historic shops, original one-off stores, gourmet corners, wine dens and more designer labels than you can shake your gold card at. You name it, you'll find it here.

El Rei de la Màgia   Magic
(Map p290; ☑93 319 39 20; www.elreydelamagia.com; Carrer de la Princesa 11; ◷10.30am-2pm & 4-7.30pm Mon-Sat; ⓂJaume I) For more than 100 years, the people behind this box of tricks have been keeping locals both astounded and amused. Should you decide to stay in Barcelona and make a living as a magician, this is the place to buy levitation brooms, glasses of disappearing milk and decks of magic cards.

Vila Viniteca   Wine
(Map p290; ☑902 327777; www.vilaviniteca.es; Carrer dels Agullers 7; ◷8.30am-8.30pm Mon-Sat; ⓂJaume I) One of the best wine stores in Barcelona (and there are a few...), this place has been searching out the best local and imported wines since 1932. On a couple of November evenings it organises what has become an almost riotous wine-tasting event in Carrer dels Agullers and surrounding lanes, at which cellars from around Spain present their young new wines.

Els Encants Vells   Market
(Fira de Bellcaire; ☑93 246 30 30; www.encantsbcn.com; Plaça de les Glòries Catalanes; ◷9am-8pm Mon, Wed, Fri & Sat; ⓂGlòries) In a gleaming open-sided complex near Plaça de les Glòries Catalanes, the 'Old Charms' flea

Flea market stalls

market is the biggest of its kind in Barcelona. Over 500 vendors ply their wares beneath massive mirror-like panels. It's all here, from antique furniture through to secondhand clothes. A lot of it is junk, but occasionally you'll stumble across a *ganga* (bargain).

⊗ EATING

Barcelona has a celebrated food scene fuelled by a combination of world-class chefs, imaginative recipes and magnificent ingredients fresh from farms and the sea. Catalan culinary masterminds like Ferran Adrià and Carles Abellan have become international icons, reinventing the world of haute cuisine, while classic old-world Catalan recipes continue to earn accolades in dining rooms and tapas bars across the city.

⊗ La Rambla & Barri Gòtic

Xurreria   Churros €

(Map p290; ☑93 318 76 91; Carrer dels Banys Nous 8; cone €1.20; ⏱7.30am-1.30pm & 3.30-8.15pm; M Jaume I) It doesn't look much from the outside, but this brightly lit street joint is Barcelona's best spot for paper cones of piping-hot churros – long batter sticks fried and sprinkled with sugar and best enjoyed dunked in hot chocolate.

Cafè de l'Acadèmia   Catalan €€

(Map p290; ☑93 319 82 53; Carrer dels Lledó 1; mains €15-20; ⏱1-3.30pm & 8-11.30pm Mon-Fri; 🛜; M Jaume I) Expect a mix of traditional Catalan dishes with the occasional creative twist. At lunchtime, local Ajuntament (town hall) office workers pounce on the *menú del día* (€14.30). In the evening it is rather more romantic, as low lighting emphasises the intimacy of the beamed ceiling and stone walls. On warm days you can also dine on the pretty square at the front.

La Vinateria del Call   Spanish €€

(Map p290; ☑93 302 60 92; www.lavinateria delcall.com; Carrer de Sant Domènec del Call 9; raciones €7-12; ⏱7.30pm-1am; M Jaume I) In a magical setting in the former Jewish quarter, this tiny jewel box of a restaurant (recently extended to add another dining room) serves up tasty Iberian dishes including Galician octopus, cider-cooked chorizo and the Catalan *escalivada* (roasted peppers, aubergine and onions) with anchovies. Portions are small and made for sharing, and there's a good and affordable selection of wines.

El Raval

Mami i Teca   Catalan €€
(93 441 33 35; Carrer de la Lluna 4; mains €10-12; 1-4pm & 8pm-midnight Mon, Wed-Fri & Sun, 8pm-midnight Sat; San Antoni) A tiny place with half a dozen tables, Mam i Teca is as much a lifestyle choice as a restaurant. Locals drop in and hang at the bar, and diners are treated to Catalan dishes made with locally sourced products and that adhere to Slow Food principles (such as cod fried in olive oil with garlic and red pepper, or pork ribs with chickpeas).

Suculent   Catalan €€
(93 443 65 79; www.suculent.com; Rambla del Raval 43; mains €16-22; 1-4pm & 8-11.30pm Wed-Sun; Liceu) Michelin-starred chef Carles Abellan adds to his stable with this old-style bistro, which showcases the best of Catalan cuisine. From the cod brandade to the oxtail stew with truffled sweet potato, only the best ingredients are used. Be warned that the prices can mount up a bit, but this is a great place to sample regional highlights.

Bar Pinotxo   Tapas €€
(Map p290; www.pinotxobar.com; Mercat de la Boqueria; mains €8-17; 7am-4pm Mon-Sat; Liceu) Bar Pinotxo is arguably La Boqueria's, and even Barcelona's, best tapas bar. It sits among the half-dozen or so informal eateries within the market, and the popular owner, Juanito, might serve up chickpeas with pine nuts and raisins, a soft mix of potato and spinach sprinkled with salt, soft baby squid with cannellini beans, or a quivering cube of caramel-sweet pork belly.

La Ribera

El Atril   International €€
(Map p290; 93 310 12 20; www.atrilbarcelona.com; Carrer dels Carders 23; mains €11-15; noon-midnight; ; Jaume I) Aussie owner Brenden is influenced by culinary flavours

Shopping Strips

Avinguda del Portal de l'Àngel This broad pedestrian avenue is lined with high-street chains, shoe shops, bookshops and more. It feeds into Carrer dels Boters and Carrer de la Portaterrissa, characterised by stores offering light-hearted costume jewellery and youth-oriented streetwear.

Avinguda Diagonal This boulevard is loaded with international fashion names and design boutiques, suitably interspersed with cafes to allow weary shoppers to take a load off.

Carrer d'Avinyó Once a fairly squalid old city street, Carrer d'Avinyó has morphed into a dynamic young fashion street.

Carrer de la Riera Baixa The place to look for a gaggle of shops flogging preloved threads.

Carrer del Petritxol Best for chocolate shops and art.

Carrer dels Banys Nous Along with nearby Carrer de la Palla, this is the place to look for antiques.

Passeig de Gràcia This is the premier shopping boulevard, chic with a capital 'C', and mostly given over to big-name international brands.

Shop on Passeig de Gràcia
JZR/SHUTTERSTOCK ©

from all over the globe, so while you'll see plenty of tapas (the *patatas bravas* are recommended for their homemade sauce), you'll also find kangaroo fillet, salmon and date rolls with mascarpone, chargrilled turkey with fried yucca, and plenty more.

Casa Delfín Catalan €€

(Map p290; ☑93 319 50 88; www.tallerdetapas.
com; Passeig del Born 36; mains €10-15;
☺8am-midnight Sun-Thu, to 1am Fri & Sat; ☎;
MBarceloneta) One of Barcelona's culinary
delights, Casa Delfín is everything you
dream of when you think of Catalan (and
Mediterranean) cooking. Start with the
tangy and sweet calçots (a cross between
a leek and an onion; February and March
only) or salt-strewn padron peppers,
moving on to grilled sardines speckled with
parsley, then tackle the meaty monkfish
roasted in white wine and garlic.

❌ La Barceloneta & the Waterfront

La Cova Fumada Tapas €

(☑93 221 40 61; Carrer del Baluard 56; tapas
€4-8; ☺9am-3.20pm Mon-Wed, 9am-3.20pm &
6-8.15pm Thu & Fri, 9am-1pm Sat; MBarceloneta)
There's no sign and the setting is decidedly downmarket, but this tiny, buzzing
family-run tapas spot always packs in a
crowd. The secret? Mouthwatering pulpo
(octopus), calamar, sardinias and 15 or so
other small plates cooked to perfection
in the small open kitchen. The bombas
(potato croquettes served with alioli) and
grilled carxofes (artichokes) are good, and
everything is amazingly fresh.

Can Recasens Catalan €€

(☑93 300 81 23; www.canrecasens.com; Rambla
del Poblenou 102; mains €8-15; ☺9pm-1am Mon-
Fri & 1-4pm & 9pm-1am Sat; MPoblenou) One
of Poblenou's most romantic settings,
Can Recasens hides a warren of warmly lit
rooms full of oil paintings, flickering candles,
fairy lights and baskets of fruit. The food is
outstanding, with a mix of salads, fondues,
smoked meats, cheeses, and open-faced
sandwiches piled high with delicacies like
wild mushrooms and brie, escalivada (grilled
vegetables) and gruyère, and spicy chorizo.

❌ L'Eixample

Tapas 24 Tapas €

(Map p296; ☑93 488 09 77; www.carlesabellan.
com; Carrer de la Diputació 269; tapas €4-9.50;

☺9am-midnight; ☎; MPasseig de Gràcia)
Carles Abellan, master of the now-defunct
Comerç 24 in La Ribera, runs this basement tapas haven known for its gourmet
versions of old faves. Specials include the
bikini (toasted ham and cheese sandwich –
here the ham is cured and the truffle makes
all the difference) and a thick black arròs
negre de sípia (squid-ink black rice).

Cerveseria Catalana Tapas €€

(Map p296; ☑93 216 03 68; Carrer de Mallorca
236; tapas €4-11; ☺8am-1.30am Mon-Fri, 9am-
1.30am Sat & Sun; MPasseig de Gràcia) The 'Catalan Brewery' is good for breakfast, lunch
and dinner. Come for your morning coffee
and croissant, or enjoy the abundance of tapas and montaditos (canapés) at lunch. You
can sit at the bar, on the pavement terrace
or in the restaurant at the back. The variety
of hot tapas, salads and other snacks draws
a well-dressed crowd of locals and outsiders.

Disfrutar Modern European €€€

(☑93 348 68 96; www.en.disfrutarbarcelona.
com; Carrer de Villarroel 163; tasting menus €110-
180; ☺1-2.30pm & 8-9.30pm Tue-Sat; MHospital
Clínic) In its first few months of life, Disfrutar
rose stratospherically to become the city's
finest restaurant – book now while it's still
possible to get a table. Run by alumni of
Ferran Adrià's game-changing El Bulli restaurant, it operates along similar lines.

❌ Montjuïc & Poble Sec

Quimet i Quimet Tapas €€

(Map p301; ☑93 442 31 42; Carrer del Poeta
Cabanyes 25; tapas €4-10, montaditos around €3;
☺noon-4pm & 7-10.30pm Mon-Fri, noon-4pm Sat;
MParal·lel) Quimet i Quimet is a family-run
business that has been passed down
from generation to generation. There's
barely space to swing a calamar in this
bottle-lined, standing-room-only place, but
it is a treat for the palate, with montaditos
(tapas on a slice of bread) made to order.

Palo Cortao Tapas €€

(Map p301; ☑93 188 90 67; www.palocortao.
es; Carrer de Nou de la Rambla 146; mains
€10-15; ☺8pm-1am Tue-Sun, 1-5pm Sat & Sun;

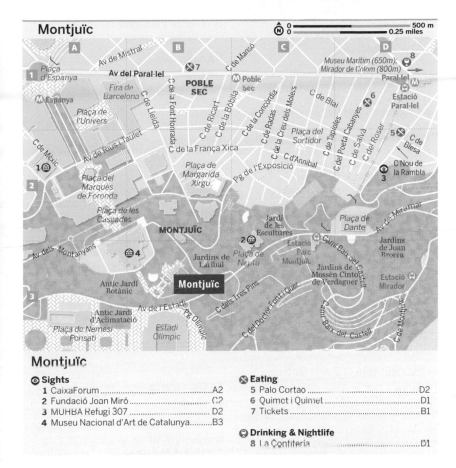

Montjuïc

Montjuïc

ⓂParal·lel) Palo Cortao has a solid reputation for its beautifully executed seafood and meat dishes, served at fair prices. Highlights include octopus with white bean hummus, skirt steak with foie armagnac, and tuna tataki tempura. You can order half sizes of all plates – which will allow you to try more dishes.

Tickets Modern Spanish €€€
(Map p301; ☎606 225545; www.ticketsbar.es; Avinguda del Paral·lel 164; tapas €5-27; ☺6.30-10.30pm Tue-Fri, 1-3pm & 7-10.30pm Sat, closed Aug; ⓂParal·lel) This is, literally, one of the sizzling tickets in the restaurant world, a tapas bar opened by Ferran Adrià, of the leg- endary El Bulli, and his brother Albert. And unlike El Bulli, it's an affordable venture – if you can book a table, that is: you can only book online, and two months in advance (or call for last-minute cancellations).

⊜ DRINKING & NIGHTLIFE

Barcelona is a nightlife lovers' town, with an enticing spread of candlelit wine bars, old-school taverns, stylish lounges and kaleidoscopic nightclubs where the party continues until daybreak. For something a little more sedate, the city's atmospheric cafes and teahouses make a fine retreat when the skies turn grey.

Classic Catalan Cuisine

Traditional Catalan recipes showcase the great produce of the Mediterranean: fish, prawns, cuttlefish, clams, pork, rabbit, game, first-rate olive oil, peppers and loads of garlic. Classic dishes also feature unusual pairings (seafood with meat, fruit with fowl): cuttlefish with chickpeas, cured pork with caviar, rabbit with prawns, goose with pears.

Great Catalan restaurants can be found in nearly every neighbourhood around town. The settings can be a huge part of the appeal – with candle-lit medieval chambers in the Ciutat Vella and Modernista design in L'Eixample setting the stage for a memorable feast. Although there are plenty of high-end places in this city, foodie-minded *barcelonins* aren't averse to eating at humbler, less elegant places – which sometimes cook up the best meals.

🍽 La Rambla & Barri Gòtic

Caelum   Cafe
(Map p290; 🖉93 302 69 93; www.caelumbar celona.com; Carrer de la Palla 8; ⊙10am-8.30pm Mon-Thu, 10.30am-10pm Fri & Sat, to 9pm Sun; ⓂLiceu) Centuries of heavenly gastronomic tradition from across Spain are concentrated in this exquisite medieval space in the heart of the city. The upstairs cafe is a dainty setting for decadent cakes and pastries, while descending into the underground chamber with its stone walls and flickering candles is like stepping into the Middle Ages.

Cafè de l'Òpera   Cafe
(Map p290; 🖉93 317 75 85; www.cafeopera bcn.com; La Rambla 74; ⊙8.30am-2.30am; 🛜; ⓂLiceu) Opposite the Gran Teatre del Liceu is La Rambla's most intriguing cafe. Operating since 1929, it is pleasant enough for an early evening libation or coffee and croissants. Head upstairs for an elevated seat above the busy boulevard. Can you be

tempted by the *cafè de l'Òpera* (coffee with chocolate mousse)?

L'Ascensor   Cocktail Bar
(Map p290; 🖉93 318 53 47; Carrer de la Bellafila 3; ⊙6pm-2.30am Sun-Thu, to 3am Fri & Sat; 🛜; ⓂJaume I) Named after the lift (elevator) doors that serve as the front door, this elegant drinking den with its vaulted brick ceilings, vintage mirrors and marble-topped bar gathers a faithful crowd that comes for old-fashioned cocktails and lively conversation against a soundtrack of up-tempo jazz and funk.

Salterio   Cafe
(Map p290; 🖉933 02 50 28; Carrer de Sant Domènec del Call 4; ⊙12.30pm-1am; 🛜; ⓂJaume I) A wonderfully photogenic candle-lit spot tucked down a tiny lane in El Call, Salterio serves refreshing teas, Turkish coffee, authentic mint teas and snacks amid stone walls, incense and ambient Middle Eastern music. If hunger strikes, try the *sardo* (grilled flat-bread covered with pesto, cheese or other toppings).

🍷 El Raval

La Confitería   Bar
(Map p301; Carrer de Sant Pau 128; ⊙7.30pm-2.30am Mon-Thu, 6pm-3.30am Fri, 5pm-3.30am Sat, 12.45pm-2.45am Sun; ⓂParal·lel) This is a trip into the 19th century. Until the 1980s it was a confectioner's shop, and although the original cabinets are now lined with booze, the look of the place barely changed with its conversion into a laid-back bar. A quiet enough spot for a house *vermut* (€3; add your own soda) in the early evening.

Casa Almirall   Bar
(www.casaalmirall.com; Carrer de Joaquín Costa 33; ⊙6pm-2.30am Mon-Thu, 6.30pm-3am Fri, noon-3am Sat, noon-12.30am Sun; ⓂUniversitat) In business since the 1860s, this unchanged corner bar is dark and intriguing, with Modernista decor and a mixed clientele. There are some great original pieces in here, such as the marble counter, and the cast-iron statue of the muse of the Universal Exposition, held in Barcelona in 1888.

🍸 La Ribera

El Born Bar   Bar

(Map p290; 📞93 319 53 33; www.elbornbar.
neositios.com; Passeig del Born 26; ⏰10am-2am
Mon-Thu, to 3am Fri & Sat, noon-2.30am Sun; 📶;
Ⓜ Jaume I) El Born Bar effortlessly attracts
everyone from cool thirty-somethings from
all over town to locals who pass judgment
on Passeig del Born's passing parade. Its
staying power depends on a good selection
of beers, spirits, and *empanadas*.

Guzzo   Cocktail Bar

(Map p290; 📞93 667 00 36; www.guzzoclub.
es; Plaça Comercial 10; ⏰6pm-3am Mon-Thu, to
3.30am Fri & Sat, noon-3am Sun; 📶; Ⓜ Barceloneta) A swish but relaxed cocktail bar, run by
much-loved Barcelona DJ Fred Guzzo, who
is often to be found at the decks, spinning
his delicious selection of funk, soul and rare
groove. You'll also find frequent live-music
acts of consistently decent quality, and a
funky atmosphere at almost any time of day.

Juanra Falces   Cocktail Bar

(Map p290; 📞93 310 10 27; Carrer del Rec 24;
⏰10am-3pm Sun-Mon, 8pm-3am Tue-Thu, 7pm-

3am Fri & Sat; Ⓜ Jaume I) Transport yourself
to a Humphrey Bogart movie in this narrow
little bar, formerly (and still, at least among
the locals) known as Gimlet. White-jacketed
bar staff with all the appropriate aplomb
will whip you up a gimlet or any other classic cocktail (around €10) that your heart
desires.

La Vinya del Senyor   Wine Bar

(Map p290; 📞93 310 33 79; Plaça de Santa Maria del Mar 5; ⏰noon-1am Mon-Thu, noon-2am Fri
& Sat, noon-midnight Sun; 📶; Ⓜ Jaume I) Relax
on the *terrassa*, which lies in the shadow
of the Basílica de Santa Maria del Mar, or
crowd inside at the tiny bar. The wine list
is as long as *War and Peace* and there's a
table upstairs for those who opt to sample
by the bottle rather than the glass.

🍸 La Barceloneta
& the Waterfront

Absenta   Bar

(📞93 221 36 38; Carrer de Sant Carles 36;
⏰7pm-1am Tue & Wed, from 11am Thu-Mon;
Ⓜ Barceloneta) Decorated with old paintings,

Al fresco dining in the Barri Gòtic

Tickets to FC Barcelona Matches

Tickets to FC Barcelona matches are available at **Camp Nou** (☎902 189900; www.fcbarcelona.com; Carrer d'Arístides Maillol; ⓂPalau Reial), online (through FC Barcelona's official website: www.fcbar celona.com) and through various city locations. Tourist offices sell them – the branch at Plaça de Catalunya is a centrally located option – as do FC Botiga stores. Tickets can cost anything from €39 to upwards of €250, depending on the seat and match. On match day the ticket windows (at gates 9 and 15) open from 9.15am until kick off. Tickets are not usually available for matches with Real Madrid.

vintage lamps and curious sculpture (including a dangling butterfly woman and face-painted TVs), this whimsical and creative drinking den takes its liquor seriously. Stop in for the house-made vermouth or for more bite try one of the many absinthes on hand. Just go easy: with an alcohol content of 50% to 90%, these spirits have kick!

Can Paixano Wine Bar
(Map p290; ☎93 310 08 39; www.canpaixano. com; Carrer de la Reina Cristina 7; Ⓨ9am-10.30pm Mon-Sat; ⓂBarceloneta) This lofty old champagne bar (also called La Xampanyeria) has long been run on a winning formula. The standard poison is bubbly rosé in elegant little glasses, combined with bite-sized *bocadillos* (filled rolls) and tapas (€3 to €7). Note that this place is usually jammed to the rafters, and elbowing your way to the bar can be a titanic struggle.

🍸 L'Eixample

Dry Martini Bar
(Map p296; ☎93 217 50 80; www.drymartini org.com; Carrer d'Aribau 162-166; Ⓨ1pm-2.30am Mon-Thu, 6pm-3am Fri & Sat, 7pm-2.30am Sun; ⓂDiagonal) Waiters with a discreetly knowing smile will attend to your cocktail needs

and make uncannily good suggestions, but the house drink, taken at the bar or in one of the plush green leather banquettes, is a safe bet. The gin and tonic comes in an enormous mug-sized glass – one will take you most of the night.

Monvínic Wine Bar
(☎93 272 61 87; www.monvinic.com; Carrer de la Diputació 249; Ⓨ1-11pm Tue-Fri, 7-11pm Mon & Sat; ⓂPasseig de Gràcia) Apparently considered unmissable by El Bulli's sommelier, Monvínic is an ode, a rhapsody even, to wine loving. The interactive wine list sits on the bar for you to browse, on a digital tablet similar to an iPad, and boasts more than 3000 varieties.

Les Gens Que J'Aime Bar
(Map p296; ☎93 215 68 79; www.lesgensque jaime.com; Carrer de València 286; Ⓨ6pm-2.30am Sun-Thu, 7pm-3am Fri & Sat; ⓂPasseig de Gràcia) This intimate basement relic of the 1960s follows a deceptively simple formula: chilled jazz music in the background, minimal lighting from an assortment of flea-market lamps and a cosy, cramped scattering of red-velvet-backed lounges around tiny dark tables.

🎭 ENTERTAINMENT

Palau de la Música Catalana Classical Music
(Map p290; ☎93 295 72 00; www.palaumusica. cat; Carrer de Palau de la Música 4-6; tickets from €15; Ⓨbox office 9.30am-9pm Mon-Sat, 10am-3pm Sun; ⓂUrquinaona) A feast for the eyes, this Modernista confection is also the city's most traditional venue for classical and choral music, although it has a wide-ranging program, including flamenco, pop and – particularly – jazz. Just being here for a performance is an experience. In the foyer, its tiled pillars all a-glitter, sip a pre-concert tipple.

Gran Teatre del Liceu Theatre, Live Music
(Map p290; ☎93 485 99 00; www.liceu barcelona.cat; La Rambla 51-59; Ⓨbox office 9.30am-8pm Mon-Fri, 9.30am-6pm Sat & Sun;

RODRIGO GARRECO/SHUTTERSTOCK ©

Palau de la Música Catalana

M Liceu) Barcelona's grand old opera house, restored after fire in 1994, is one of the most technologically advanced theatres in the world. To take a seat in the grand auditorium, returned to all its 19th-century glory but with the very latest in acoustics, is to be transported to another age.

Sala Tarantos — Flamenco

(Map p290; ☑ 93 304 12 10; www.masimas. com/tarantos; Plaça Reial 17; tickets €15; ☺ shows 8.30pm, 9.30pm & 10.30pm; M Liceu) Since 1963, this basement locale has been the stage for up-and-coming flamenco groups performing in Barcelona. These days Tarantos has become a mostly tourist-centric affair, with half-hour shows held three times a night. Still, it's a good introduction to flamenco, and not a bad setting for a drink.

ⓘ INFORMATION

SAFE TRAVEL

○ Violent crime is rare in Barcelona, but petty crime (bag-snatching, pickpocketing) is a major problem.

○ You're at your most vulnerable when dragging around luggage to or from your hotel; make sure you know your route before arriving.

○ Be mindful of your belongings, particularly in crowded areas.

○ Avoid walking around El Raval and the southern end of La Rambla late at night.

TOURIST INFORMATION

Several tourist offices operate in Barcelona; the main one is on Plaça de Catalunya (p297). A couple of general information telephone numbers worth bearing in mind are ☑ 010 and ☑ 012. The first is for Barcelona and the other is for all Catalonia (run by the Generalitat). You sometimes strike English speakers, although for the most part operators are Catalan/Spanish bilingual. In addition to tourist offices, information booths operate at Estació del Nord bus station and at Portal de la Pau, at the foot of the Mirador de Colom at the port end of La Rambla. Others set up at various points in the city centre in summer.

Plaça Sant Jaume (Map p290; ☑ 93 285 38 32; www.barcelonaturisme.com; Carrer de la Ciutat

2; ⊗8.30am-8.30pm Mon-Fri, 9am-7pm Sat, 9am-2pm Sun & holidays; MJaume I)

Palau Robert Regional Tourist Office (Map p296; ☑93 238 80 91; www.palaurobert.gencat.cat; Passeig de Gràcia 107; ⊗10am-8pm Mon-Sat, to 2.30pm Sun; MDiagonal) Offers a host of material on Catalonia, audiovisual resources, a bookshop and a branch of Turisme Juvenil de Catalunya (for youth travel).

ℹ GETTING THERE & AWAY

AIR

After Madrid, Barcelona is Spain's busiest international transport hub. A host of airlines fly to **El Prat Airport** (☑902 404704; www.aena.es), including many budget carriers, from around Europe. Ryanair uses Girona and Reus airports (buses link Barcelona to both).

Most intercontinental flights require passengers to change flights in Madrid or another major European hub.

Iberia, Air Europa, Spanair and Vueling all have dense networks across the country, and while flights can be costly, you can save considerable time by flying from Barcelona to distant cities like Seville or Málaga.

BUS

Long-distance buses leave from **Estació del Nord**. A plethora of companies service different parts of Spain; many come under the umbrella of **Alsa** (☑902 422242; www.alsa.es). For other companies, ask at the bus station. There are frequent services to Madrid, Valencia and Zaragoza (20 or more a day) and several daily departures to distant destinations such as Burgos, Santiago de Compostela and Seville.

Eurolines (www.eurolines.com), in conjunction with local carriers all over Europe, is the main international carrier; its website provides links to national operators. It runs services across Europe and to Morocco from Estació del Nord, and from **Estació d'Autobusos de Sants** (☑93 339 73 29; www.adif.es; Carrer de Viriat; MEstació Sants), next to Estació Sants Barcelona.

Much of the Pyrenees and the entire Costa Brava are served only by buses, as train services are limited to important railheads such as Girona, Figueres, Lleida, Ripoll and Puigcerdà.

TRAIN

○ Train is the most convenient overland option for reaching Barcelona from major Spanish centres such as Madrid and Valencia. It can be a long haul from other parts of Europe – budget flights frequently offer a saving in time and money.

○ A network of *rodalies/cercanías* serves towns around Barcelona (and the airport). Contact **Renfe** (☑902 320320; www.renfe.es).

○ Eighteen high-speed Tren de Alta Velocidad Española (AVE) trains between Madrid and Barcelona run daily in each direction, nine of them in under three hours.

○ Most long-distance (*largo recorrido* or *Grandes Línias*) trains have 1st and 2nd classes (known as *preferente* and *turista*). After the AVE, Euromed and several other similarly modern trains, the most common long-distance trains are the slower, all-stops Talgos.

○ The main train station in Barcelona is **Estació Sants** (www.adif.es; Plaça dels Països Catalans; MEstació Sants), located 2.5km west of La Rambla. Direct overnight trains from Paris, Geneva, Milan and Zurich arrive here.

ℹ GETTING AROUND

Barcelona has abundant options for getting around town. The excellent metro can get you most places, with buses and trams filling in the gaps. Taxis are the best option late at night.

Metro The most convenient option. Runs 5am to midnight Sunday to Thursday, till 2am on Friday and 24 hours on Saturday. Targeta T-10 (10-ride passes; €10.30) are the best value; otherwise, it's €2.15 per ride.

Bus A hop-on, hop-off **Bus Turístic** (☑93 298 70 00; www.barcelonabusturistic.cat/en; day ticket adult/child €29/16; ⊗9am-8pm), departing from Plaça de Catalunya, is handy for those wanting to see the city's highlights in one or two days.

Taxi You can hail taxis on the street (try La Rambla, Via Laietana, Plaça de Catalunya and Passeig de Gràcia) or at taxi stands.

On foot To explore the old city, all you need is a good pair of walking shoes.

🛎️ Where to Stay

Barcelona has a wide range of sleeping options, from cheap hostels in the old quarter to luxury hotels overlooking the waterfront. Small-scale apartment rentals around the city are a good-value choice.

Neighbourhood	Atmosphere
La Rambla & Barri Gòtic	Great location, close to major sights, with good nightlife and dining options, this is the perfect area for exploring on foot. It can be very touristy and noisy, while some hotel rooms are small and lack windows.
El Raval	Central option, with good local nightlife and access to sights, it has a bohemian vibe with few tourists. However, it can be noisy, seedy and run-down in parts, with many fleapits best avoided.
La Ribera	Great restaurant scene and neighbourhood exploring, La Ribera is central and close to top sights including the Museu Picasso and the Palau de la Música Catalana. It can be noisy, overcrowded and touristy.
Barceloneta & the Waterfront	Excellent seafood restaurants, with an easygoing local vibe and handy to the promenade and beaches, but it has few sleeping options, and can be far from the action. Better suited to business travellers.
La Sagrada Família & L'Eixample	Offering a wide range of options for all budgets, it is close to Modernista sights, good restaurants and nightlife, and is a prime neighbourhood for the LGBT scene (in the 'Gaixample'). Can be very noisy with lots of traffic though, and is not a great area for walking as it is a little far from the old city.

Basque Country, Spain

No matter where you've just come from – be it the hot, southern plains of Spain or gentle and pristine France – the Basque Country is different. Known to Basques as Euskadi or Euskal Herria ('the land of Basque Speakers') and called El Pais Vasco in Spanish, this is where mountain peaks reach for the sky and sublime rocky coves are battered by mighty Atlantic swells. Food is an obsession in this part of the country, whether it's three-Michelin-starred restaurants or the fabulous pintxos (Basque tapas) bars in San Sebastián or Bilbao. And the Basque Country has reinvented itself as one of Spain's style and culture capitals, with Bilbao's Museo Guggenheim leading the way.

Two Days in Basque Spain

With so little time, you've little choice but to spend a day in **Bilbao** (p316) with the **Museo Guggenheim Bilbao** (p311) as your visit's centrepiece, followed by an afternoon of delicious *pintxos*. On day two, wander around the **Casco Viejo** (p317) and enjoy some shopping – take in the market if you happen to be visiting on a Sunday. Round out the day with some live music.

Four Days in Basque Spain

Spend days three and four in **San Sebastián** (p323), sampling some of the best food Europe has to offer and wandering along the sublime **Playa de la Concha** (p325).

Next stop: Lisbon (p330), only a two-hour flight away from Bilbao.

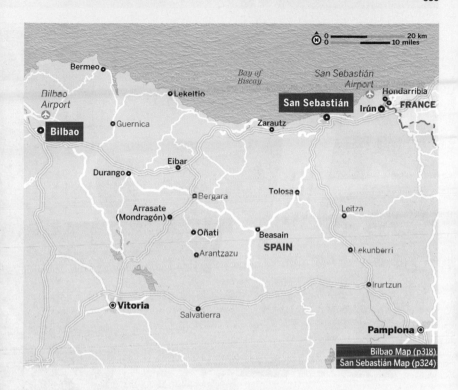

Arriving In Basque Spain

Bilbao is connected by air to numerous European and other Spanish cities; an airport bus connects the airport with the city centre. Otherwise, train and bus services connect Bilbao and San Sebastián with other Basque towns and villages, as well as to Madrid, Barcelona and other northern Spanish cities.

Where to Stay

Bilbao and San Sebastián have the largest selection of places to stay, but you'll need to book ahead at any time of the year. Apart from being fantastic destinations in their own right, these two cities make good bases for exploring the region. The Bilbao tourism authority has a very useful reservations department (p322); if you do turn up in San Sebastián without a booking, head to the tourist office (p329), which keeps a list of available rooms.

Museo Guggenheim Bilbao

Bilbao's titanium Museo Guggenheim Bilbao is one of contemporary architecture's most iconic buildings. It almost single-handedly lifted Bilbao into the international art and tourism spotlight.

Great For...

☑ Don't Miss

The atrium – the interior counterpoint to the facade's flights of fancy.

The Exterior

Some might say, probably quite rightly, that the Guggenheim is more famous for its architecture than its content. But Canadian architect Frank Gehry's inspired use of flowing canopies, cliffs, promontories, ship shapes, towers and flying fins is irresistible.

Gehry designed the Guggenheim with historical and geographical contexts in mind. The site was an industrial wasteland, part of Bilbao's wretched and decaying warehouse district on the banks of the Ría del Nervión. The city's historical industries of shipbuilding and fishing reflected Gehry's own interests, not least his engagement with industrial materials in previous works. The gleaming titanium tiles that sheathe most of the building like giant herring scales are said to have been inspired by the architect's childhood fascination with fish.

ℹ Need to Know

944 35 90 16; www.guggenheim-bilbao.es; Avenida Abandoibarra 2; adult/student/child from €13/7.50/free, depends on exhibits; 10am-8pm, closed Mon Sep-Jun

✕ Take a Break

The museum has a high-class restaurant (p320).

★ Top Tip

The Artean Pass is a joint ticket for the Museo Guggenheim Bilbao and the Museo de Bellas Artes, which, at €16 for adults, offers significant savings. It's available from either museum.

Beyond Gehry

Other artists have added their touch to the Guggenheim as well. Lying between the glass buttresses of the central atrium and the Ría del Nervión is a simple pool of water that emits a mist installation by Fuyiko Nakaya. Near the riverbank is Louise Bourgeois' *Maman,* a skeletal spider-like canopy said to symbolise a protective embrace. In the open area west of the museum, the fountain sculpture randomly fires off jets of water. Jeff Koons' kitsch whimsy *Puppy,* a 12m-tall Highland Terrier made up of thousands of begonias, is on the city side of the museum.

The Interior

The interior of the Guggenheim is purposefully vast. The cathedral-like atrium is more than 45m high, with light pouring in through the glass cliffs. Permanent exhibits fill the ground floor and include such wonders as mazes of metal and phrases of light reaching for the skies.

For most people, though, it is the temporary exhibitions – from the life work of Yoko Ono to the extraordinary sculptures of Brazilian Ernesto Neto – that are the main attraction.

Guggenheim Essentials

Admission prices vary depending on special exhibitions and the time of year. The last ticket sales are half an hour before closing. Free guided tours in Spanish take place at 12.30pm and 5pm. Tours can be conducted in other languages, but you must ask at the information desk beforehand. Excellent self-guided audiotours in various languages are free with admission and there is also a special children's audio guide. Entry queues can be horrendous, with wet summer days and Easter almost guaranteeing you a wait of over an hour. The museum is wheelchair accessible.

Pintxo bar

Pintxo Bars

San Sebastián stands atop a pedestal as one of the planet's culinary capitals. The city overflows with bars, almost all of which have bar tops weighed down under a mountain of Spain's best pintxos.

Great For...

☑ Don't Miss

Bar Border Berri – the essence of *pintxos* San Sebastián style.

The Art of Eating Pintxos

Just rolling the word *pintxo* around your tongue defines the essence of this cheerful, cheeky little slice of Basque cuisine. The perfect *pintxo* should have exquisite taste, texture and appearance and should be savoured in two elegant bites. The Basque version of a tapa, the *pintxo* transcends the commonplace by the sheer panache of its culinary campiness. In San Sebastián especially, Basque chefs have refined the *pintxo* to an art form.

Many *pintxos* are bedded on small pieces of bread or on tiny half-baguettes, upon which towering creations are constructed, often melded with flavoursome mayonnaise and then pinned in place by large tooth-picks. Some bars specialise in seafood, with much use of marinated anchovies, prawns and strips of squid, all topped with anything

CULTURA EXCLUSIVE/RUSS ROHDE/GETTY IMAGES ©

yellow *pintxo* bar really stands out. The house specials are pig's ears served in garlic soup (much better than it sounds!), braised veal cheeks in wine, and a mushroom and *idiazabal* (a local cheese) risotto.

Astelena (☏943 42 58 67; www.restaurante astelena.com; Calle de Iñigo 1; pintxos from €2.50; ⊗1-4.30pm & 8-11pm Tue & Thu-Sat, 1-4.30pm Wed) The *pintxos* draped across the counter in this bar, tucked into the corner of Plaza de la Constitución, stand out. Many are a fusion of Basque and Asian inspirations. The great positioning means that prices are slightly elevated.

Bodega Donostiarra (☏943 42 58 67; www.bodegadonostiarra.com; Calle de Peña y Goñi 13; pintxos from €2.50, mains from €11; ⊗9.30am-midnight Mon-Sat) The stone walls, potted plants and window ornaments give Bodega Donostiarra a real old-fashioned French bistro look, but at the same time it feels very up to date and modern. It's best known for humble *jamón,* chorizo and, most of all, tortilla.

Bar Goiz-Argi (Calle de Fermín Calbetón 4; pintxos from €2.50; ⊗9.30am-3.30pm & 6.30-11.30pm Wed-Sun, 9.30-3.30pm Mon) *Gambas a la plancha* (prawns cooked on a hotplate) are the house speciality. Sounds simple, we know, but never have we tasted prawns cooked quite as perfectly as this.

La Mejillonera (Calle del Puerto 15; pintxos from €2.50; ⊗11.30am-3pm & 6-11pm) If you thought mussels only came with garlic sauce, come here to discover mussels by the thousand in all their glorious forms.

from chopped crab to pâté. Others deal in pepper or mushroom delicacies, or simply offer a mix of everything. And the choice isn't normally limited to what's on the bar top in front of you: many of the best *pintxos* are the hot ones you need to order. These are normally chalked up on a blackboard on the wall somewhere.

San Sebastián's Pintxo Bars

La Cuchara de San Telmo (☏043 44 16 55; www.lacucharadesantelmo.com; Calle de 31 de Agosto 28; pintxos from €2.50; ⊗7.30-11pm Tue, noon-3.30pm & 7.30-11pm Wed-Sun) This unfussy, hard-to-find bar offers miniature *nueva cocina vasca* (Basque nouvelle cuisine) from a supremely creative kitchen.

Bar Borda Berri (☏943 43 03 42; www.bordaberri.com; Calle Fermín Calbetón 12; pintxos from €2.50; ⊗noon-midnight) This mustard-

Mussels not for you? Opt for the calamari and *patatas bravas* (fried potatoes with a spicy tomato and mayo sauce).

Bar Martinez (☏943 42 49 65; www.barmartinezdonosti.com; Calle 31 de Agosto 13; pintxos from €2.50; ⊘9.30am-11pm Tue-Sun, Fri & Sat open late) This small bar, with dusty bottles of wine stacked up, has won awards for its *morros de bacalao* (delicate slices of cod balanced atop a piece of bread) and is one of the more character-laden places to dip into some *pintxos*.

Bar Diz (Calle Zabaleta 17; pintxos from €2.50; ⊘8am-late) In beach-blessed Gros, tiny Bar Diz has massively good *pintxos* (and the breakfast isn't bad either), and other foreign tourists are rare, so it's a totally local affair. If you're hungry opt for a *ración* (plate).

Bergara Bar (www.pinchosbergara.es; General Artetxe 8; pintxos from €2.50; ⊘9am-11pm) The Bergara Bar, which sits on the edge of a busy square, is one of the most highly regarded *pintxo* bars in Gros, a growing powerhouse in the *pintxo*-bar stakes, and has a mouth-watering array of delights piled onto the bar counter as well as others chalked up on the board.

Bilbao's Pintxo Bars

Although it lacks San Sebastián's stellar reputation for *pintxos,* prices are generally slightly lower in Bilbao and the quality is about equal. There are literally hundreds of *pintxo* bars throughout Bilbao, but the Plaza Nueva on the edge of the Casco Viejo offers especially rich pickings, as do Calle de Perro and Calle Jardines. Some of

Pintxos on display, Bilbao

the city's standouts, in no particular order include:

Bar Gure Toki (Plaza Nueva 12; pintxos from €2.50) Has a subtle but simple line in creative *pintxos* including some made with ostrich.

Sorginzulo (Plaza Nueva 12; pintxos from €2.50; ⊗9.30am-12.30am) A matchbox-sized bar with an exemplary spread of *pintxos*. The house special is calamari but it's only served on weekends.

Berton Sasibil (Calle Jardines 8; pintxos from €2.50; ⊗8.30am-midnight Mon-Sat, 10am-4pm Sun) Here you can watch informative films on the crafting of the same superb *pintxos* that you're munching on.

Claudio: La Feria del Jamón (Calle Iparragirre 9-18; pintxos from €2.50; ⊗10am-2pm & 5-9pm Mon-Fri, 10am-2pm & 6-9.30pm Sat) A

creaky old place full of ancient furnishings. As you'll guess from the name and the dozens of legs of ham hanging from the ceiling, it's all about pigs.

La Viña del Ensanche (☎944 15 56 15; www.lavinadelensanche.com; Calle de la Diputación 10; pintxos from €1.35, menú €30; ⊗8.30am-11.30pm Mon-Fri, noon-1am Sat) Hundreds of bottles of wine line the walls of this outstanding *pintxo* bar. And when we say outstanding, we mean that it could well be the best place to eat *pintxos* in the city.

Museo del Vino (Calle de Ledesma 10; pintxos from €2.50; ⊗1-5pm & 8-11pm Mon-Fri) Tiled white interior, Gaudiesque windows, delicious octopus *pintxos* and an excellent wine selection (as you'd hope with a name like this). This place makes us smile.

Bitoque de Albia (www.bitoque.net; Alameda Mazarredo 6; pintxos from €2.50; ⊗1.30-4pm Mon-Wed, 1.30-4pm & 8.30-11.15pm Thu-Sat) Award-winning modern *pintxo* bar serving such unclassic dishes as miniature red tuna burgers, salmon sushi and clams with wild mushrooms. It also offers a *pintxos* tasting menu (€12).

Mugi (www.mugiardotxoko.es; Licenciado Poza 55; pintxos from €2.50; ⊗7am-midnight Mon-Sat, noon-midnight Sun) Widely regarded *pintxo* bar. It can get so busy that you might have to stand outside.

❶ The Price of Pintxos

Most of the San Sebastián bars listed here charge between €2.50 and €3.50 for one *pintxo*. Not so bad if you just take one, but is one ever enough?

Bilbao

Bilbao isn't the kind of city that knocks you out with its physical beauty – head on over to San Sebastián for that particular pleasure – but it's a city that slowly wins you over. Bilbao, after all, has had a tough upbringing. Surrounded for years by an environment of heavy industry and industrial wastelands, its riverfront landscapes and quirky architecture were hardly recognised or appreciated by travellers on their way to more pleasant destinations. But Bilbao's graft paid off when a few wise investments left it with a shimmering titanium landmark, the Museo Guggenheim – and a horde of art world types from around the world started coming to see what all the fuss was about.

The *Botxo* (Hole), as it's fondly known to its inhabitants, has now matured into its role of major European art centre. But at heart it remains a hard-working town, and one that has real character. It's this down-to-earth soul, rather than its plethora of art galleries, that is the real attraction of the vital, exciting and cultured city of Bilbao.

SIGHTS

Many first-time visitors associate Bilbao with its world-famous art museum, the Museo Guggenheim. But there's a wide variety of interesting sights around town, from architectural highlights to landmark bridges, and from bustling plazas to the winding streets of the Casco Viejo (historic centre).

Museo de Bellas Artes Gallery

(☑ 944 39 60 60; www.museobilbao.com; Plaza del Museo 2; adult/student/child €9/7/free, Wed free; ☺10am-8pm Wed-Mon) The Museo de Bellas Artes houses a compelling collection that includes everything from Gothic sculptures to 20th-century pop art. There are three main subcollections: classical art, with works by Murillo, Zurbarán, El Greco, Goya and van Dyck; contemporary art, featuring works by Gauguin, Francis Bacon and Anthony Caro; and Basque art, with works of the great sculptors Jorge de Oteiza and Eduardo Chillida, and strong paintings by the likes of Ignacio Zuloago and Juan de Echevarria.

Zubizuri

Casco Viejo
Old Town

The compact Casco Viejo, Bilbao's atmospheric old quarter, is full of charming streets, boisterous bars and plenty of quirky and independent shops. At the heart of the Casco are Bilbao's original seven streets, Las Siete Calles, which date from the 1400s.

The 14th-century Gothic **Catedral de Santiago** (www.bilbaoturismo.net; Plaza de Santiago; ⊘10am-1pm & 5-7.30pm Tue-Sat, 10am-1pm Sun & holidays) has a splendid Renaissance portico and a pretty little cloister. Further north, the 19th-century arcaded **Plaza Nueva** is a rewarding *pintxo* (Basque tapas) haunt. There's a lively Sunday-morning **flea market** here, which is full of secondhand book and record stalls, and pet 'shops' selling chirpy birds (some kept in old-fashioned wooden cages), fluffy mice and tiny baby terrapins. Elsewhere in the market, children and adults alike swap and barter football cards and old stamps; in between weave street performers and waiters with trays piled high. The market is much more subdued in winter. A sweeter-smelling **flower market** takes place on Sunday mornings in the nearby Plaza del Arenal.

Basilica de Begoña
Basilica

(Calle Virgen de Begoña; ⊘8.30am-1.30pm & 5-8.30pm Mon-Sat, 9am-2pm & 5-9pm Sun) This 16th-century basilica towers over the Casco Viejo from atop a nearby hill. It's mainly Gothic in look, although Renaissance touches, such as the arched main entrance, crept in during its century-long construction. The austere vaulted interior is brightened by a gold altarpiece that contains a statue of the Virgin Begoña, the patron saint of Biscay who's venerated locally as Amatxu (Mother).

Euskal Museoa
Museum

(Museo Vasco; ☏944 15 54 23; www.euskal-museoa.org/es/hasiera; Plaza Miguel Unamuno 4; adult/child €3/free, Thu free; ⊘10am-7pm Mon & Wed-Fri, 10am-1.30pm & 4-7pm Sat, 10am-2pm Sun) This is probably the most complete museum of Basque culture and history in all of Spain. The story begins in prehistory;

 Las Siete Calles

Forming the heart of Bilbao's Casco Viejo are seven streets known as Las Siete Calles (Basque: Zazpi Kaleak). These dark, atmospheric lanes – Barrenkale Barrena, Barrenkale, Carnicería Vieja, Belostikale, Tendería, Artekale and Somera – date from the 1400s when the east bank of the Ría del Nervión was first developed. They originally constituted the city's commercial centre and river port; these days they teem with lively cafes, *pintxo* bars and boutiques.

Casco Viejo
AYHAN ALTUN/GETTY IMAGES ©

from this murky period the displays bound rapidly up to the modern age, in the process explaining just how long the Basques have called this corner of the world home.

Alas, unless you read Spanish (or perhaps you studied Euskara at school?), it's all a little meaningless as there are no English translations.

The museum is housed in a fine old building, at the centre of which is a peaceful cloister that was part of an original 17th-century Jesuit college. In the cloister is the Mikeldi Idol, a powerful pre-Christian symbolic figure, possibly from the Iron Age.

Zubizuri
Bridge

The most striking of the modern bridges that span the Ría del Nervión, the Zubizuri (Basque for 'White Bridge') has become an iconic feature of Bilbao's cityscape since its completion in 1997. Designed by Spanish architect Santiago Calatrava, it has a curved walkway suspended under a flowing

Bilbao

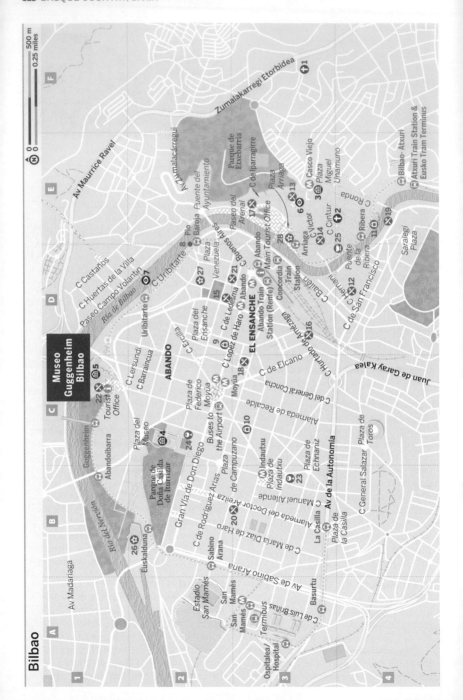

Museo Guggenheim Bilbao

500 m
0.25 miles

Bilbao

white arch to which it's attached by a series of steel spokes.

⊕ TOURS

Bilbao tourist office (p322) organises 1½-hour walking tours covering either the old town or the architecture in the newer parts of town. At busy times tours can run with more frequency.

Bilboats (☑946 42 41 57; www.bilboats.com; Plaza Pío Baroja; adult/child from €12/7) runs boat cruises along the Nervión several times a day.

One of the more original, and interesting, ways to see the city and get to know a local is through the **Bilbao Greeters** (www.bilbaogreeters.com; adult €12) organisation. Essentially a local person gives you a tour of the city showing you their favourite sights, places to hang out and, of course, *pintxos* (Basque tapas) bars. You need to reserve through the website at least a fortnight in advance.

⊙ SHOPPING

For major department stores and big-name fashion labels trawl the streets of El Ensanche. For more one-of-a-kind, independ-

ent boutiques, Casco Viejo is the place to look (although even here the chain shops are increasingly making their presence felt). Bilbao is also a great place for food shopping (of course!).

Mercado de la Ribera   Market
(Calle de la Ribera) Overlooking the river, the Mercado de la Ribera is supposedly one of the largest covered food markets in Spain. It's had a recent makeover, which has sanitised it somewhat, but many of the city's top chefs still come here to select fresh produce each morning.

Arrese   Food
(www.arrese.biz; Calle Lopez de Haro 24; ⊙9am-9pm Mon-Sat, 9am-3pm & 5-9pm Sun) With 160 years of baking experience you'd hope the cakes at this little patissiere would taste divine, but frankly, they're even better than expected.

Chocolates de Mendaro   Food
(www.chocolatesdemendaro.com; Calle de Licenciado Poza 16; ⊙10am-2pm & 4-8pm Mon-Sat) This old-time chocolate shop created its first chocolate treats way back in 1850 and is hands down the best place to ruin a diet in Bilbao.

🗙 EATING

In the world of trade and commerce, the Basques are an outward-looking lot, but when it comes to food they refuse to believe that any other people could possibly match their culinary skills (and they may well have a point). This means that eating out in Bilbao is generally a choice of Basque, Basque or Basque food. Still, life could be worse and there are some terrific places to eat.

The porticoed Plaza Nueva is a good spot for coffee and people-watching, especially in summer.

Agape Restaurante   Basque €€

(📞944 16 05 06; www.restauranteagape.com; Calle de Hernani 13; menú del día €12.90, menús €21-36; ⏰1-4pm Sun-Wed, 1-4pm & 8.30-11.30pm Thu-Sat; 🛜) With a solid reputation among locals for good-value meals that don't sacrifice quality, this is a great place for a slice of real Bilbao culinary life. It's well away from the standard tourist circuit, but is worth the short walk. The lunch menu, at €12.20, is exceptional value, comprising starters such as mushroom risotto and mains like fried anchovies with sweet ratatouille. Book ahead.

Casa Rufo   Basque €€

(📞944 43 21 72; www.casarufo.com; Hurtado de Amézaga 5; mains €10-15; ⏰1.30-4pm & 8.30-11pm Mon-Sat) Despite the emergence of numerous glitzy restaurants that are temples to haute cuisine, this resolutely old-fashioned place, with its shelves full of dusty bottles of top-quality olive oil and wine, still stands out as one of the best places to eat traditional Basque food in Bilbao. The house special is steak – lovingly cooked over hot coals.

Mina Restaurante   Basque €€€

(📞944 79 59 38; www.restaurantemina.es; Muelle Marzana; tasting menu €60-110; ⏰2-3.30pm & 9-10.30pm Wed-Sat, 2-3.30pm Sun & Tue) Offering unexpected sophistication and fine dining in an otherwise fairly grimy neighbourhood, this riverside restaurant has some critics citing it as the current *número uno* in Bilbao. Expect serious culinary creativity: think along the lines of spider crab with passion fruit or frozen 'seawater' with seaweed and lemon sorbet.

Reservations are essential.

Nerua Guggenheim
Bilbao   Basque €€€

(📞944 00 04 30; www.neruaguggenheimbilbao. com; tasting menu from €65, mains €30-35; ⏰1-3pm & 8.30-9.30pm Thu-Sat, 1-3pm Tue, Wed & Sun) The Guggenheim's modernist, chic and very white restaurant is under the direction of Michelin-starred chef Josean Alija (a disciple of Ferran Adria). Needless to say, the *nueva cocina vasca* (Basque nouvelle cuisine) is breathtaking – even the olives are vintage classics: all come from 1000-year-old olive trees!

Reservations are essential.

🍷 DRINKING & NIGHTLIFE

In the Casco Viejo, around Calles Barrenkale, Ronda and de Somera, there are plenty of terrific hole-in-the-wall, no-nonsense bars with a generally youthful crowd.

Across the river, in the web of streets around Muelle Marzana and Bilbao la Vieja, are scores more little bars and clubs. This is gritty Bilbao as it used to be in the days before the arty makeover. It's both a Basque heartland and the centre of the city's ethnic community. The many bars around here are normally welcoming, but one or two can be a bit seedy. It's not a great idea for women to walk here alone at night.

Lamiak   Cafe

(Calle Pelota 8; ⏰4pm-midnight Sun-Thu, 3.30pm-2.30am Fri & Sat) Lamiak, a long-standing Casco Viejo favourite, is a buzzing cafe with a cavernous red and black hall, cast iron columns and upstairs seating on a mezzanine floor. Good for coffees and cocktails, it exudes an arty, laid-back vibe and pulls in a cool weekend crowd.

Lunchtime crowd in a Bilbao restaurant

Geo Cocktail Lounge   Cocktail Bar
(944 66 84 42; Calle Maximo Aguirre 12;
3pm-1.30am Tue-Sun) For a refined
post-dinner cocktail, search out this lounge
bar in the area south of the Guggenheim.
Expect subdued lighting, low-key tunes and
expertly crafted cocktails.

Cotton Club   Club
(944 10 49 51; www.cottonclubbilbao.es; Calle
de Gregorio de la Revilla 25; 8.30pm-3am Tue
& Wed, to 5am Thu, to 6.30am Fri & Sat, 7pm-
1.30am Sun) A historic Bilbao nightspot, the
Cotton Club draws a mixed crowd to its
DJ stoked nights and regular gigs – mainly
blues, jazz and rock. It's a tiny place so
prepare to get up close with your fellow
revellers.

⭐ ENTERTAINMENT

There are plenty of clubs and live venues in
Bilbao, and the vibe is friendly and generally easy-going. Venue websites usually have
details of upcoming gigs.

Kafe Antzokia   Live Music
(944 24 46 25; www.kafeantzokia.com; Calle
San Vicente 2) This is the vibrant heart of
contemporary Basque Bilbao, featuring
international rock, blues and reggae, as well
as the cream of Basque rock-pop. Weekend
concerts run from 10pm to 1am, followed
by DJs until 5am. During the day it's a cafe,
restaurant and cultural centre all rolled into
one and has frequent exciting events on.

Euskalduna Palace   Live Music
(944 03 50 00; www.euskalduna.net; Avenida
Abandoibarra) About 600m downriver from
the Guggenheim is this modernist gem,
built on the riverbank in a style that echoes
the great shipbuilding works of the 19th
century. The Euskalduna is home to the Bilbao Symphony Orchestra and the Basque
Symphony Orchestra, and hosts a wide
array of events.

Teatro Arriaga   Theatre
(944 79 20 36; www.teatroarriaga.com; Plaza
Arriaga) The baroque facade of this venue
commands the open spaces of El Arenal
between the Casco Viejo and the river.

It stages theatrical performances and classical-music concerts.

ℹ INFORMATION

Friendly staff at Bilbao's tourist office are extremely helpful, well informed and, above all, enthusiastic about their city. At all offices ask for the free bimonthly *Bilbao Guía,* which has entertainment listings plus tips on restaurants, bars and nightlife.

At the newly opened, state-of-the-art **main tourist office** (🖉944 79 57 60; www.bilbao turismo.net; Plaza Circular 1; ☉9am-9pm; 🛜), there's free wi-fi access, a bank of touch-screen information computers and, best of all, some humans to help answer questions. There are also branches at the **airport** (🖉944 71 03 01; www. bilbaoturismo.net; Bilbao Airport; ☉9am-9pm Mon-Sat, 9am-3pm Sun) and the **Guggenheim** (www.bilbaoturismo.net; Alameda Mazarredo 66; ☉10am-7pm daily, to 3pm Sun Sep-Jun).

The Bilbao tourism authority has a very useful **reservations service** (🖉902 87 72 98; www. bilbaoreservas.com).

ℹ GETTING THERE & AWAY

AIR

Bilbao's **airport** (BIO; 🖉902 404 704; www.aena. es) is near Sondika, to the northeast of the city. A number of European flag carriers serve the city. Of the budget airlines, EasyJet (www.easyjet. com) and Vueling (www.vueling.com) cover the widest range of destinations.

BUS

Bilbao's main bus station, **Termibus** (🖉944 39 50 77; www.termibus.es; Gurtubay 1, San Mamés), is west of the centre.

Bizkaibus travels to destinations throughout the rural Basque Country, including coastal communities such as Mundaka and Guernica (€2.50). Euskotren buses serve Lekeitio (€6.65).

TRAIN

The Abando train station is just across the river from Plaza Arriaga and the Casco Viejo. There are frequent trains to Barcelona (from €19.60, 6¾ hours), Burgos (from €7, three hours), Madrid (from €20, five hours) and Valladolid (from €12.55, four hours).

Casco Viejo (p317)

Nearby is the **Concordia train station**, with its art-nouveau facade of wrought iron and tiles. It is used by the **FEVE** (www.renfe.com/viajeros/feve), a formerly private rail company that was recently purchased by RENFE. It has trains running west into Cantabria. There are three daily trains to Santander (from €12.55, three hours) where you can change for stations in Asturias.

The **Atxuri train station** is just upriver from Casco Viejo. From here, **Eusko Tren/Ferrocarril Vasco** (www.euskotren.es) operates services every half-hour to Bermeo (€3.70, 1½ hours), Guernica (€3.70, one hour) and Mundaka (€3.70, 1½ hours).

GETTING AROUND

TO/FROM THE AIRPORT

The **airport bus** (Bizkaibus A3247; €1.45) departs from a stand on the extreme right as you leave arrivals. It runs through the northwestern section of the city, passing the Museo Guggenheim, stopping at Plaza de Federico Moyúa and terminating at the Termibus (bus station). It runs from the airport every 20 minutes in summer and every 30 minutes in winter from 6.20am to midnight. There is also a direct hourly bus from the airport to San Sebastián (€16.85, 1¼ hours). It runs from 7.45am to 11.45pm.

Taxis from the airport to the Casco Viejo cost about €23 to €30, depending on traffic.

METRO

There are metro stations at all the main focal points of El Ensanche and at Casco Viejo. Tickets start at €1.65. The metro runs to the north coast from a number of stations on both sides of the river and makes it easy to get to the beaches closest to Bilbao.

TRAM

Bilbao's Eusko Tren tramline is a boon to locals and visitors alike. It runs to and fro between Basurtu, in the southwest of the city, and the Atxuri train station. Stops include the Termibus station, the Guggenheim and Teatro Arriaga by the Casco Viejo. Tickets cost €1.50 and need to be validated in the machine next to the ticket dispenser before boarding.

 Basque Language

Victor Hugo described the Basque language as a 'country', and it would be a rare Basque who'd disagree with him. The language, known as *Euskara*, is the oldest in Europe and has no known connection to any Indo-European languages. Suppressed by Franco, Basque was subsequently recognised as one of Spain's official languages, and it has become the language of choice among a growing number of young Basques.

MONKEY BUSINESS IMAGES/GETTY IMAGES ©

San Sebastián

It's impossible to lay eyes on stunning San Sebastián (Basque: Donostia) and not fall madly in love. This city is cool and happening by night, charming and well mannered by day. It's a city filled with people that love to indulge – and with Michelin stars apparently falling from the heavens onto its restaurants, not to mention *pintxo* (tapas) culture almost unmatched anywhere else in Spain, San Sebastián frequently tops lists of the world's best places to eat.

San Sebastián has four main centres of action. The lively Parte Vieja (old town) lies across the neck of Monte Urgull, the bay's eastern headland, and is where the most popular *pintxo* bars and many of the cheap lodgings are to be found. South of the Parte Vieja is the commercial and shopping district, the Área Romántica, its handsome grid of late-19th-century buildings extending from behind Playa de la Concha to the banks of Río Urumea. On the eastern side

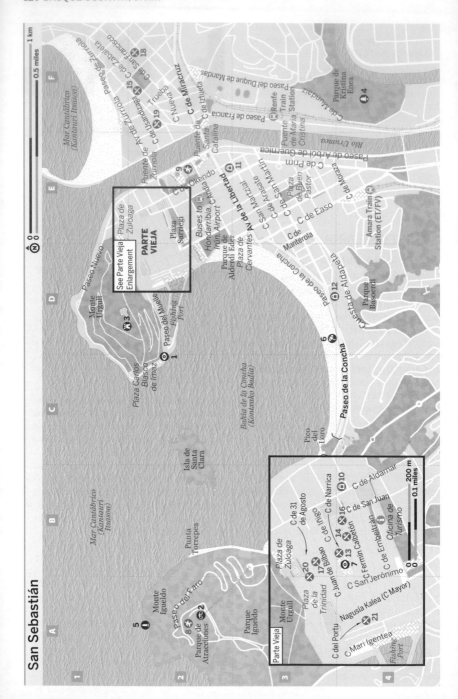

San Sebastián

Mar Cantábrico
(Kantauri Itsasoa)

Monte Igueldo

Parque de
Igueldo

Parque de
Atracciones

5

Paseo del Faro

8 🛈
2

Punta
Torrepea

Isla de Santa
Clara

Bahía de la Concha
(Kontxako Badia)

Monte
Urgull

3

Paseo Nuevo

Plaza Carlos
Blasco
de Imaz

Paseo del Muelle · Fishing Port

1

Pico
del
Loro

Paseo de la Concha

6

Paseo de la Concha

12

Cuesta de Aldapeta

Parque
Basoerdi

See Parte Vieja
Enlargement

**PARTE
VIEJA**

Plaza de
Zuloaga

Plaza
Sarriegi

Buses to
Hondarribia,
Irún, Airport

Plaza de
Alderdi Eder

Plaza de
Cervantes

Parque de
Okendo

9

C de Okendo

AV de la Libertad

11

C San Martín

C de Arasate

C de San Martín

C de
Manterola

C de Easo

C de Easo

Plaza de
Buen Pastor

C de
Prim

Paseo de Árbol de Guernica

Río Urumea

Puente de
Santa
Catalina

Puente de
María
Cristina

Paseo de Francia

Renfe
Train
Station

Paseo del Duque de Mandas

C de Miracruz

C Nueva

C de Iztueta

C de Usandizaga

15

19

Trueba

Puente de
AV de Zurriola

Paseo de Zurriola

Paseo de
Zurriola

Mar Cantábrico
(Kantauri Itsasoa)

C de San Francisco

C de Zabaleta

18

C de Moraza

Amara Train
Station (ET/FV)

Amara Train
Station (ET/FV)

Parque de
Kristina
Enea

4

C de Mundaiz

Parque de
Maria
Cristina

0   0.5 miles   1 km

N

Parte Vieja enlargement

Monte
Urgull

Plaza de
Zuloaga

Plaza
de la
Trinidad

C del Portu

C San Jerónimo

C Mari Igentea

Fishing
Port

Nagusia Kalea (C Mayor)

21

C de Embeltrán

C Fermín Calbetón

C San Juan

C de Aldamar

Oficina de
Turismo

C de 31
de Agosto

C de Iñigo

C de Narrica

C de Bilbao

C Juan de Bilbao

20

17

7

13

14

16

10

0   0.1 miles   200 m

San Sebastián

of the river is the district of Gros, a pleasant enclave that, with its relaxed ambience and the surfing beach of Playa de Gros, makes a cheerful alternative to the honeypots on the western side of the river. Right at the opposite, western end of the city is Playa de Ondarreta (essentially a continuation of Playa de la Concha), a very upmarket district known as a millionaires' belt on account of its lavish holiday homes.

◉ SIGHTS

San Sebastián is more about the beautiful beach – and the world-famous *pintxo* bars, and the quaint streets of the historic quarter – than it is about specific sights and attractions. Still, there's plenty to keep visitors busy here when you tire of sun and sand.

Aquarium   Aquarium
(www.aquariumss.com; Plaza Carlos Blasco de Imaz 1; adult/child €13/6.50; ⊙10am-9pm Jul & Aug, 10am-8pm Mon-Fri, 10am-9pm Sat & Sun Easter-Jun & Sep, shorter hours rest of year) Fear for your life as huge sharks bear down behind glass panes, or gaze in disbelief at tripped-out fluoro jellyfish. The highlights of a visit to the city's excellent aquarium are the cinema-screen-sized deep-ocean and coral-reef exhibits and the long tunnel, around which swim monsters of the deep. The aquarium also contains a maritime

museum section. Allow at least 1½ hours for a visit.

Parque de Cristina Enea   Park
(Paseo Duque de Manda) Created by the Duke of Mandas in honour of his wife, the Parque de Cristina Enea is a favourite escape for locals. This formal park, the most attractive in the city, contains ornamental plants, ducks and peacocks, and open lawns.

Playa de la Concha   Beach
(Paseo de la Concha) Fulfilling almost every idea of how a perfect city beach should be formed, Playa de la Concha (and its westerly extension, Playa de Ondarreta) is easily among the best city beaches in Europe. Throughout the long summer months a fiesta atmosphere prevails, with thousands of tanned and toned bodies spread across the sands. The swimming is almost always safe.

Plaza de la Constitución   Plaza
(Plaza de la Constitución) One of the most attractive city squares in the Basque country, the Plaza de la Constitución sits at the heart of the old town. The square dates from 1813 but sits on the site of an older square. It was once used as a bullring; the balconies of the fringing houses were rented to spectators.

Peine del Viento   Sculpture
A symbol of the city, the *Peine del Viento* (Wind Comb) sculpture, which sits at the

far western end of the Bahía de la Concha, below Monte Igueldo, is the work of the famous Basque sculptor Eduardo Chillida and architect Luis Peña Ganchegui.

Monte Igueldo   Viewpoint

(www.monteigueldo.es; ⊘10am-10pm Jun-Sep, shorter hours rest of year) The views from the summit of Monte Igueldo, just west of town, will make you feel like a circling hawk staring down over the vast panorama of the Bahía de la Concha and the surrounding coastline and mountains. The best way to get there is via the old-world **funicular railway** (www.monteigueldo.es; Plaza del Funicular; return adult/child €3.15/2.35; ⊘10am-9pm Jun-Aug, shorter hours rest of year) to the **Parque de Atracciones** (☑943 21 35 25; www.monteigueldo.es; Paseo de Igeldo; adult/child €3.15/2.35; ⊘11am-2pm & 4-8.30pm Mon-Fri, to 9pm Sat & Sun Jul-Sep, shorter hours rest of year), a slightly tacky theme park at the top of the hill.

Monte Urgull   Castle

You can walk to the summit of Monte Urgull, topped by the low castle walls of the Castillo de la Mota and a grand statue of Christ, by taking a path from Plaza de Zuloaga or from behind the aquarium. The views are breathtaking and the shady parkland on the way up is a peaceful retreat from the city.

⊙ TOURS

The tourist office (p329) runs several different city tours (including a cinema tour) starting at €10.

Sabores de San Sebastián   Tours

(Flavours of San Sebastián; ☑902 44 34 42; www.sansebastianreservas.com; tour €18; ⊘11.30am Tue & Thu Jul & Aug) The tourist office runs the Sabores de San Sebastián, a two-hour tour (in Spanish and English; French tours are available on request) of some of the city's *pintxo* haunts. Tours are also held with less frequency outside high season – contact the tourist office for dates.

San Sebastián Food   Food

(☑943 42 11 43; www.sansebastianfood.com; Hotel Maria Cristina, Paseo de la República Argentina 4) The highly recommended San

From left: Playa de Ondarreta (p325) and Monte Igueldo; San Sebastián's Parte Vieja (Old Town); Bahía de la Concha

Sebastián Food runs an array of *pintxo* tasting tours (from €95) and cookery courses (from €145) in and around the city, as well as wine tastings (from €45). The shop/booking office also sells an array of high-quality local food and drink products.

🔒 SHOPPING

The Parte Vieja is awash with small independent boutiques, while the Área Romántica has all your brand-name and chain-store favourites.

Aitor Lasa   Food
(www.aitorlasa.com; Calle de Aldamar 12) This high-quality deli is the place to stock up on ingredients for a gourmet picnic you'll never forget. It specialises in cheeses, mushrooms and seasonal products.

Follow Me
San Sebastián   Food & Drinks
(www.justfollowme.com; Calle de Zubieta 7; ⊙10am-2pm & 4-8pm Mon-Sat) A small selection of top-quality regional wine and foodstuffs. You can also learn all about their products on one of the gastronomic tours.

Chocolates de Mendaro   Food
(www.chocolatesdemendaro.com; Calle de Echaide 6; ⊙10am 2pm & 4-8pm) We dare you to walk past this fabulous old chocolate shop and resist the temptation to walk inside.

🍴 EATING

With 16 Michelin stars (including three restaurants with the coveted three stars), San Sebastián stands atop a pedestal as one of the culinary capitals of the planet. As if that alone weren't enough, the city is overflowing with bars – almost all of which have bar tops weighed down under a mountain of *pintxos* (p312) that almost every Spaniard will (sometimes grudgingly) tell you are the best in country. These statistics alone make San Sebastián look pretty impressive. But it's not just us who thinks this: a raft of the world's best chefs, including such luminaries as Catalan super-chef Ferran Adriá, have said that San Sebastián is quite

ASIFE/SHUTTERSTOCK ©

Seafood *paella*

> *San Sebastián stands atop a pedestal as one of the culinary capitals of the planet*

possibly the best place on the entire planet to eat.

La Fábrica
Basque €€

(☎943 98 05 81; www.restaurantelafabrica.es; Calle del Puerto 17; mains €15-20, menús from €28; ◷12.30-4pm & 7.30-11.30pm Mon-Fri, 1-4pm & 8-11pm Sat-Sun) The red-brick interior walls and white tablecloths lend an air of class to this restaurant, whose modern takes on Basque classics have been making waves with San Sebastián locals over the last couple of years. At just €25, the multi-dish tasting *menú* is about the best-value deal in the city. Advance reservations are essential.

Arzak
Basque €€€

(☎943 27 84 65; www.arzak.info; Avenida Alcalde Jose Elosegui 273; meals around €195; ◷Tue-Sat, closed Nov & late Jun) With three shining Michelin stars, acclaimed chef Juan Mari

Arzak is king when it comes to *nueva cocina vasca* and his restaurant is considered one of the best in the world. Arzak is now assisted by his daughter Elena, and they never cease to innovate. Reservations, well in advance, are obligatory.

The restaurant is located just east of San Sebastián.

Martín Berasategui Restaurant
Basque €€€

(☎943 36 64 71; www.martinberasategui. com; Calle Loidi 4, Lasarte-Oria; tasting menu €195; ◷Wed-Sun lunch) This superlative restaurant, about 9km southwest of San Sebastián, is considered by foodies to be one of the best restaurants in the world. The chef, Martín Berasategui, approaches cuisine as a science and the results are tastes you never knew existed. Reserve well ahead.

Akelaŕe
Basque €€€

(☎943 31 12 09; www.akelarre.net; Paseo Padre Orcolaga 56; tasting menu €170; ◷1-3.30pm & 8.30-11pm Tue-Sat Jul-Dec, Wed-Sat Jan-Jun) This is where chef Pedro Subijana creates cuisine that is a feast for all five senses. As with most of the region's top *nueva cocina vasca* restaurants, the emphasis here is on using fresh, local produce and turning it into something totally unexpected. It's in the suburb of Igeldo just west of the city.

DRINKING & NIGHTLIFE

It would be hard to imagine a town with more bars than San Sebastián. Most of the city's bars mutate through the day from calm morning-coffee hang-outs to *pintxo*-laden delights, before finally finishing up as noisy bars full of writhing, sweaty bodies. Nights in San Sebastián start late and go on until well into the wee hours.

INFORMATION

Oficina de Turismo (943 48 11 66; www. sansebastianturismo.com; Alameda del Boulevard 8; 9am-8pm Mon-Sat, 10am-7pm Sun Jul-Sep, shorter hours rest of year) This friendly office offers comprehensive information on the city and the Basque Country in general.

GETTING THERE & AWAY

AIR

The city's **airport** (free call 902 404704; www. aena.es) is 22km out of town, near Hondarribia. There are regular flights to Madrid and Barcelona and occasional charters to other major European cities. Biarritz, just over the border in France, is served by Ryanair and EasyJet, among various other budget airlines, and is generally much cheaper to fly into.

BUS

The main bus stop is a 20-minute walk south of the Parte Vieja, between Plaza de Pío XII and the river. Local buses 28 and 26 connect the bus station with Alameda del Boulevard (€1.65, 10 minutes), but it's also a pleasant stroll into the historic center from here, especially if you walk along the river. There's no real station here, but all the bus companies have offices and ticket booths near the bus stop.

TRAIN

The main **Renfe train station** (Paseo de Francia) is just across Río Urumea, on a line linking Paris to Madrid. There are several services daily to Madrid (from €27, 5½ hours) and two to Barcelona (from €19.25, six hours).

GETTING AROUND

Buses to Hondarribia (€2.35, 45 minutes) and the airport (€2.35, 45 minutes) depart from Plaza de Gupúzkoa.

In This Chapter

Lisbon, Portugal

Spread across steep hillsides that overlook the Rio Tejo, Lisbon has captivated visitors for centuries. Windswept vistas reveal the city in all its beauty: Roman and Moorish ruins, white-domed cathedrals, grand plazas. However, the real delight of discovery is delving into the narrow cobblestone lanes.

As yellow trams clatter through tree-lined streets, lisboêtas stroll through lamp-lit old quarters. Gossip is exchanged over wine at tiny restaurants as fado singers perform in the background. In other neighbourhoods, Lisbon reveals her youthful alter ego at bohemian bars and late-night street parties.

Lisbon in Two Days

Explore Lisbon's old town – the **Alfama** (p336) – on day one, perhaps taking a ride on **tram 28** (p335) part of the way. Round off with a **fado performance** (p347) in the evening. On day two explore **Belém** (p341) and the **Mosteiro dos Jerónimos** (p332). In the evening sample some of Lisbon's famous **nightlife** (p346).

Lisbon in Four Days

On day three hit the museums – Lisbon has plenty dedicated to a range of subjects, but one highlight is the **Museu Nacional do Azulejo** (p337) packed with traditional tiles. On day four seek out a a picnic lunch at the **Mercado da Ribeira** (p344) and laze the day away at the **Jardim da Cerca da Graça** (p337).

Finished in Lisbon? Fly to Copenhagen (p136) or Prague (p524).

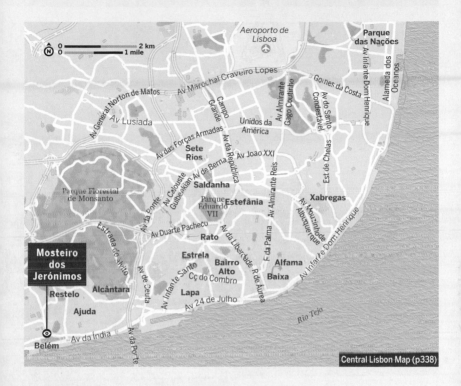

Central Lisbon Map (p338)

Arriving in Lisbon

Aeroporto de Lisboa Direct flights to major international hubs including London, New York, Paris and Frankfurt.

Sete Rios bus station The main long-distance bus terminal.

Gare do Oriente bus station Bus services to the north and Spain.

Gare do Oriente train station Lisbon's largest train station.

Where to Stay

Lisbon has an array of boutique hotels, upmarket hostels and both modern and old-fashioned guesthouses. Be sure to book ahead for high season (July to September). A word to those with weak knees and/or heavy bags: many guesthouses lack lifts, meaning you'll have to haul your luggage up three flights or more. If this disconcerts, be sure to book a place with a lift.

For information on what each Lisbon neighbourhood has to offer, see the table on p349.

KIEV.VICTOR/SHUTTERSTOCK ©

Mosteiro dos Jerónimos

One of Lisbon's top attractions is this Unesco-listed monastery, an outstanding example of the elaborate Manueline style.

Great For...

☑ Don't Miss

The rows of seats in the church are Portugal's first Renaissance woodcarvings.

The Monastery's Story

Belém's undisputed heart-stealer is the stuff of pure fantasy: a fusion of Diogo de Boitaca's creative vision and the spice-and-pepper dosh of Manuel I, who commissioned it to trumpet Vasco da Gama's discovery of a sea route to India in 1498. The building embodies the golden age of Portuguese discoveries and was funded using the profits from the spices da Gama brought back from the subcontinent. Building began in 1502 but was not completed for almost a century. Wrought for the glory of God, Jerónimos was once populated by monks of the Order of St Jerome, whose spiritual job for four centuries was to comfort sailors and pray for the king's soul. The monastery withstood the 1755 earthquake but fell into disrepair when the order was dissolved in 1833. It was later used as a

The cloisters

TAKASHI IMAGES/SHUTTERSTOCK ©

ℹ Need to Know

www.mosteirojeronimos.pt; Praça do Império; adult/child €10/5, 1st Sun of month free, ☺10am-6.30pm Tue-Sun, to 5.30pm Oct-May

✕ Take a Break

Pão Pão Queijo Queijo (☎213 626 369; Rua de Belém 124; mains €4-8; ☺10am-midnight Mon-Sat, to 8pm Sun; 🛜🖉) is a popular fast-food stop selling sandwiches and snacks.

★ Top Tip

A €12 admission pass is valid for both the monastery and the nearby Torre de Belém.

soft golden light over the church. Superstar Vasco da Gama is interred in the lower chancel, just left of the entrance, opposite venerated 16th-century poet Luís Vaz de Camões. From the upper choir, there's a superb view of the church.

The Cloisters

There's nothing like the moment you walk into the honey-stone Manueline cloisters, dripping with organic detail in their delicately scalloped arches, twisting auger-shell turrets and columns intertwined with leaves, vines and knots. It will simply wow. Keep an eye out for symbols of the age such as the armillary sphere and the cross of the Military Order, plus gargoyles and fantastical beasties on the upper balustrade.

school and orphanage until about 1940. In 2007 the now much-discussed Treaty of Lisbon was signed here.

Vasco da Gama

Born in Alentejo in the 1460s, Vasco da Gama was the first European explorer to reach India by ship. This was a key moment in Portuguese history as it opened up trading links to Asia and established Portugal's maritime empire, the wealth from which made the country into a world superpower. Da Gama died from malaria on his third voyage to India in 1524.

The Church

Entering the church through the western portal, you'll notice tree-trunk-like columns that seem to grow into the ceiling, which is itself a spiderweb of stone. Windows cast a

JORGE CASAS/SHUTTERSTOCK ©

Lisbon's Trams

Quintessentially Lisbon, a ride on one of the city's typical yellow trams should be on your to-do list. Tram 28 climbs through the Alfama and is a must for every visitor.

Great For...

☑ Don't Miss

In addition to tram 28, other city-centre tram routes are 12, 15, 18 and 25.

Lisbon's Old Trams

Lisbon's old yellow streetcars are a nostalgic throwback to the early days of urban public transport and would have long since been pensioned off to a transport museum in most other European countries. They have survived largely because they were specially designed for a specific task – to trundle up and down central Lisbon's steep gradients (just like their San Francisco cousins) and would be much too expensive to replace. These roller-coaster vintage trams date from the 1930s and are called *remodelados* (remodelled). The name comes from the fact the cars were slightly upgraded in the 1990s to include such luxuries as late 20th-century brakes. There were once 27 lines in the city, but the construction of the metro put the system

PETER ADAMS/GETTY IMAGES ©

ⓘ Need to Know

Companhia Carris de Ferro de Lisboa
(Carris; ☎213 500 115; http://carris.trans
porteslisboa pt) operates all transport in
Lisbon proper except the metro.

✕ Take a Break

Many cafes and restaurants line the
route of tram 28 – take your pick.

★ Top Tip

Ride tram 28 early in the morning or
at night to avoid the tourist mobs.

Tram 28

The famous tram 28, Lisbon's longest tram
route, is extremely popular with tourists as
it heads through Baixa, Graça, Alfama and
Estrela, climbing the steep hill from Baixa
to the castle and Alfama as well as three of
the city's seven other hills en route. There
are 34 stops between Campo Ourique
in the west of the city centre to Martim
Monique, though the most interesting section is between Estrela and Graça. Trams
depart every 11 minutes, though the last
leaves fairly early (before 10pm, depending on the day). The experience on the
museum-piece tram can be an uncomfort-
able one for some, with varnished wooden
benches, steps and crowds of tourists
getting in each other's way. But it's worth it
for the ride – there's no cheaper way to see
the city and it's a great option to take when
the weather is not playing ball.

into decline. Today there are only five lines
left – *remodelados* run on all of them.

Tram Stops & Fares

Lisbon's tram stops are marked by a small
yellow *paragem* (stop) sign hanging from a
lamp post or from the overhead wires. You'll
pay more for a tram ride if you buy your
ticket on board rather than purchasing a
prepaid card. On-board one-way prices are
€2.90, but a day pass costs just €6.15 and
is valid on all of the city's public transport
for 24 hours.

Pickpockets

With groups of tourists crammed into a
small space, sadly tram 28 is a happy hunting ground for pickpockets. Take the usual
precautions to avoid being parted from
your possessions.

◎ SIGHTS

At the riverfront is the grand Praça do Comércio. Behind it march the pedestrian-filled streets of Baixa (lower) district, up to Praça da Figueira and Praça Dom Pedro IV (aka Rossio). From Baixa it's a steep climb west, through swanky shopping district Chiado, into the narrow streets of night-life-haven Bairro Alto. Eastwards from the Baixa it's another climb to Castelo de São Jorge and the Moorish, labyrinthine Alfama district around it. The World Heritage Sites of Belém lie further west along the river – an easy tram ride from Praça do Comércio.

◎ Alfama, Castelo & Graça

Castelo de São Jorge   Castle
(www.castelodesaojorge.pt; adult/student/child €8.50/5/free; ⊙9am-9pm Mar-Oct, to 6pm Nov-Feb) Towering dramatically above Lisbon, the mid-11th-century hilltop fortifications of Castelo de São Jorge sneak into almost

> *the anachronous feeling of stepping back in time*

every snapshot. Roam its snaking ramparts and pine-shaded courtyards for superlative views over the city's red rooftops to the river. Three guided tours daily (Portuguese, English and Spanish) at 1pm and 5pm are included in the admission price.

These smooth cobbles have seen it all – Visigoths in the 5th century, Moors in the 9th century, Christians in the 12th century, royals from the 14th to 16th centuries, and convicts in every century.

Inside the **Ulysses Tower**, a camera obscura offers a unique 360-degree angle on Lisbon, with demos every 20 minutes. There are also a few galleries displaying relics from past centuries, including traces of the Moorish neighbourhood dating from the 11th century at the **Archaeological Site**. But the standout attraction is the view – as well as the anachronous feeling of stepping back in time amid fortified courtyards and towering walls. There are a few cafes and restaurants to while away time in as well.

Bus 737 from Sé or Praça da Figueira goes right to the gate. Tram 28 also passes nearby.

Castelo de São Jorge

Miradouro do Castelo de São Jorge   Viewpoint

One of Lisbon's privileged views is on offer from this outstanding lookout point on the grounds of the Castelo.

Jardim da Cerca da Graça   Park

(Calçada Do Monte 46;) Closed for centuries, this 1.7-hectare green space debuted in 2015 and clocks in as Lisbon's second-biggest park, offering a lush transition between the neighbourhoods of Graça and Mouraria. There are superb city and castle views from several points and a shady picnic park along with a playground, an orchard and a peaceful kiosk with a terrace.

Load up on wine and cheese and call it an afternoon!

Museu do Fado   Museum

(www.museudofado.pt; Largo do Chafariz de Dentro; adult/child €5/3; ◷10am-6pm Tue-Sun) Fado (traditional Portuguese melancholic song) was born in the Alfama. Immerse yourself in its bittersweet symphonies at the Museu do Fado. This engaging museum traces fado's history from its working class roots to international stardom.

Museu de Artes Decorativas   Museum

(Museum of Decorative Arts; www.fress.pt; Largo das Portas do Sol 2; adult/child €4/free; ◷10am-5pm Wed-Mon) Set in a petite 17th-century palace, the Museu de Artes Decorativas creaks under the weight of treasures including blingy French silverware, priceless Qing vases and Indo-Chinese furniture, a collection amassed by a wealthy Portuguese banker from the age of 16. It's worth a visit alone to admire the lavish apartments, embellished with baroque *azulejos,* frescoes and chandeliers.

It's a particularly atmospheric spot for live **fado** on Wednesday at 6pm.

Mosteiro de São Vicente de Fora   Church

(Largo de São Vicente; adult/child €5/free; ◷10am-6pm Tue-Sun) Graça's Mosteiro de São Vicente de Fora was founded in 1147

☀ **When to Go to Lisbon**

The peak summer season (June to August) serves up hot weather and is the best time for open-air festivals, beach days and al fresco dining. However, the perfect season for exploring may be spring (March to May) – it has milder but often sunny days, and accommodation is still reasonably priced.

and revamped by Italian architect Felipe Terzi in the late 16th century. Since the adjacent church took the brunt of the 1755 earthquake (the church's dome crashed through the ceiling of the **sacristy,** but emerged otherwise unscathed), elaborate blue-and-white *azulejos* dance across almost every wall, echoing the building's architectural curves.

Museu Nacional do Azulejo   Museum

(www.museudoazulejo.pt; Rua Madre de Deus 4; adult/child €5/2.50, free 1st Sun of the month; ◷10am-6pm Tue-Sun) Housed in a sublime 16th-century convent, Lisbon's Museu Nacional do Azulejo covers the entire *azulejo* (hand-painted tile) spectrum. Star exhibits feature a 36m-long panel depicting pre-earthquake Lisbon, a Manueline cloister with web-like vaulting and exquisite blue-and-white *azulejos,* and a gold-smothered baroque chapel.

Here you'll find every kind of *azulejo* imaginable, from early Ottoman geometry to zinging altars, scenes of lords a-hunting and Goan intricacies. Bedecked with food-inspired *azulejos* – ducks, pigs and the like – the **restaurant** opens onto a vine-clad courtyard.

Sé de Lisboa   Cathedral

(Largo de Sé; ◷9am-7pm Tue-Sat, to 5pm Mon & Sun) FREE One of Lisbon's icons is the fortress-like Sé de Lisboa, built in 1150 on the site of a mosque soon after Christians recaptured the city from the Moors.

Central Lisbon

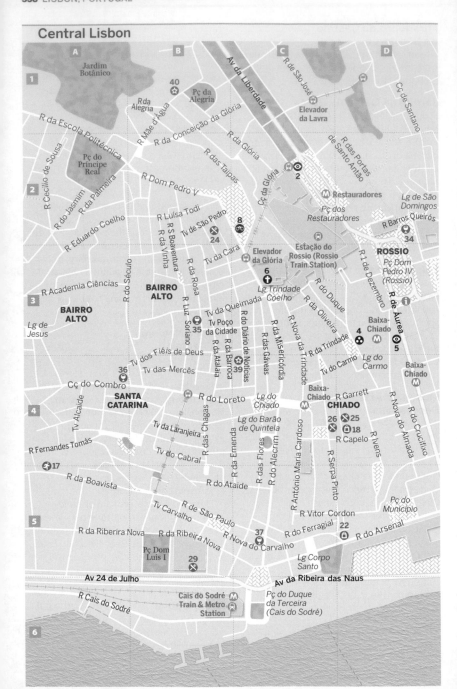

Jardim Botânico

Av da Liberdade

R de São José

Cç de Santião

40

Pç da Alegria

R da Alegria

R Mae d'Água

R da Conceição da Glória

R da Glória

Elevador da Lavra

R das Portas de Santo Antão

R da Escola Politécnica

Pç do Príncipe Real

R das Taipas

R Dom Pedro V

Cç da Glória

2

Restauradores

Lg de São Domingos

R Cecílio de Sousa

R do Jasmim

R da Palmeira

R Eduardo Coelho

R Luísa Todi

R S Boaventura

R da Vinha

Tv de São Pedro

8

Pç dos Restauradores

R Barros Queirós

34

ROSSIO

R Academia Ciências

BAIRRO ALTO

R do Século

R da Rosa

24

Tv da Cara

Elevador da Glória

6

Estação do Rossio (Rossio Train Station)

Pç Dom Pedro IV (Rossio)

R de Áurea

BAIRRO ALTO

R Luz Soriano

Tv da Queimada

Lg Trindade Coelho

R do Duque

R da Oliveira

Baixa-Chiado

4

Lg de Jesus

35

Tv Poço da Cidade

R do Diário de Notícias

R da Misericórdia

R Nova da Trindade

R da Trindade

Baixa-Chiado

5

Tv dos Fiéis de Deus

R da Atalaia

R da Barroca

R das Gáveas

39

Tv do Carmo

Lg do Carmo

Baixa-Chiado

36

Tv das Mercês

Cç do Combro

SANTA CATARINA

R do Loreto

Lg do Chiado

Baixa-Chiado

CHIADO

R Garrett

R Nova do Almada

R do Crucifixo

Tv Alcaide

R das Chagas

Lg do Barão de Quintela

R da Emenda

R das Flores

R do Alecrim

R António Maria Cardoso

26

25

18

R Capelo

R Ivens

R Fernandes Tomás

17

Tv da Laranjeira

Tv do Cabral

R do Ataíde

R Serpa Pinto

Pç do Município

R da Boavista

R Vitor Cordon

R do Ferragial

22

R do Arsenal

Tv Carvalho

R de São Paulo

R Nova do Carvalho

37

Lg Corpo Santo

R da Ribeira Nova

R da Ribeira Nova

Pç Dom Luis I

29

Av 24 de Julho

Av da Ribeira das Naus

R Cais do Sodré

Cais do Sodré Train & Metro Station

Pç do Duque da Terceira (Cais do Sodré)

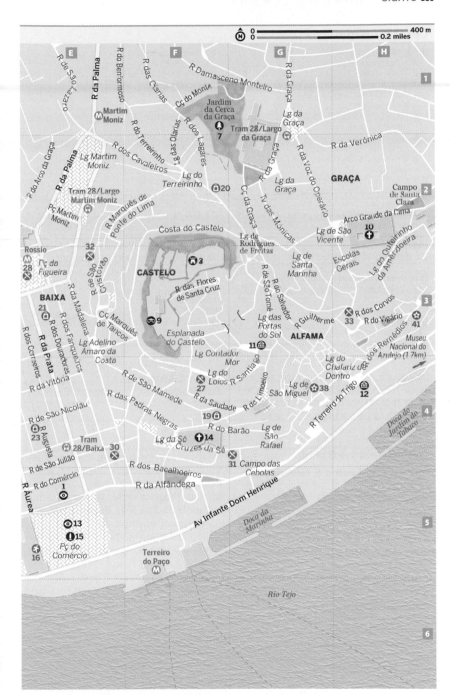

N 0   400 m
   0   0.2 miles

R de São Lázaro
R da Palma
R do Benformoso
R das Clarias
Cç do Monte
R Damasceno Monteiro
R da Graça

Martim Moniz
R do Terreirinho
Tv das Olarias
R dos Lagares
Jardim da Cerca da Graça
7
Tram 28/Largo da Graça
Lg da Graça
R da Verónica

R do Arco da Graça
R da Palma
Lg Martim Moniz
R dos Cavaleiros
Lg do Terreirinho
20
Lg da Graça
R da Voz do Operário
GRAÇA

Tram 28/Largo Martim Moniz
R Marquês de Ponte do Lima
Cç da Graça
Campo de Santa Clara
2

Pç Martim Moniz
Costa do Castelo
Lg de Rodrigues de Freitas
Tv das Mónicas
Arco Grande da Cima
R do Outeirinho da Amendoeira

Rossio
32
R de São Cristóvão
CASTELO
3
Lg de Santa Marinha
Lg de São Vicente
10
Escolas Gerais

Pç da Figueira
28
R da Madalena
R das Flores de Santa Cruz
R de São Tomé
R de Salvador
R Guilherme
33
R dos Corvos
R do Vigário
3
41

BAIXA
21
Cç Marquês de Tancos
9
Lg das Portas do Sol
ALFAMA
R dos Remédios
Museu Nacional do Azulejo (1.7km)

R dos Fanqueiros
R dos Douradores
R dos Cerraeiros
Lg Adelino Amaro da Costa
Esplanada do Castelo
11
Lg Contador Mor
Lg do Chafariz de Dentro

R da Prata
R da Vitória
R de São Mamede
Lg do Loios
27
R Santiago
R do Limoeiro
Lg de São Miguel
38
R Terreiro do Trigo
12

R de São Nicolau
R das Pedras Negras
R da Saudade
19
Lg de São Rafael
Doca do Jardim do Tabaco
4

23
R Augusta
Tram 28/Baixa
30
Lg da Sé
14
R do Barão
Cruzes da Sé

R de São Julião
R dos Bacalhoeiros
31
Campo das Cebolas
Doca da Marinha
5

R do Comércio
R da Alfândega
Av Infante Dom Henrique

R Áurea
1
13
15
16
Pç do Comércio
Terreiro do Paço

Rio Tejo

6

Central Lisbon

It was sensitively restored in the 1930s. Despite the masses outside, the rib-vaulted interior, lit by a rose window, is calm. Stroll around the cathedral to spy leering gargoyles peeking above the orange trees.

⊚ Bairro Alto & Chiado

Convento do Carmo & Museu Arqueológico   Ruins
(Largo do Carmo; adult/child €3.50/free; ⊙10am-7pm Mon-Sat, to 6pm Oct-May) Soaring above Lisbon, the skeletal Convento do Carmo was all but devoured by the 1755 earthquake and that's precisely what makes it so captivating. Its shattered pillars and wishbone-like arches are completely exposed to the elements. The Museu Arqueológico shelters archaeological treasures, such as 4th-century sarcophagi, griffin-covered column fragments, 16th-century azulejo (hand-painted tile) panels and two gruesome 16th-century Peruvian mummies.

Igreja & Museu São Roque   Church, Museum
(www.museu-saoroque.com; Largo Trindade Coelho; church free, museum adult/child €2.50/free, free 10am-2pm Sun; ⊙2-7pm Mon, 10am-7pm Tue-Wed & Fri-Sun, 10am-8pm Thu) The plain facade of 16th-century Jesuit Igreja de São Roque belies its dazzling interior of gold, marble and Florentine azulejos – bankrolled by Brazilian riches. Its star attraction is **Capela de São João Baptista**, a lavish confection of amethyst, alabaster, lapis lazuli and Carrara marble. The **museum** adjoining the church is packed with elaborate sacred art and holy relics.

Free guided tours are offered in four languages. For English, arrive on Thursdays (3pm), Fridays (11.30am and 4.30pm), Saturdays (10am) and Sundays (3pm).

Miradouro de São Pedro de Alcântara   Viewpoint
(Rua São Pedro de Alcântara; ⊙viewpoint 24hr, kiosk 10am-midnight Mon-Wed, to 2am Thu-

Sun) Hitch a ride on vintage **Ascensor da Glória** (www.transporteslisboa.pt; return €3.60; ☉7am-midnight Mon-Thu, 7am-12.30pm Fri, 8.30am-12.30am Sat, 9am-midnight Sun) from Praça dos Restauradores, or huff your way up steep Calçada da Glória to this terrific hilltop viewpoint. Fountains and Greek busts add a regal air to the surroundings, and the open-air kiosk doles out wine, beer and snacks, which you can enjoy while taking in the castle views and live music.

Elevador de Santa Justa   Elevator
(www.transporteslisboa.pt; cnr Rua de Santa Justa & Largo do Carmo; return trip €5; ☉7am-11pm, to 10pm Oct-May) If the lanky, wrought-iron Elevador de Santa Justa seems uncannily familiar, it's probably because the neo Gothic marvel is the handiwork of Raul Mésnier, Gustave Eiffel's apprentice. It's Lisbon's only vertical street lift, built in 1902 and steam-powered until 1907. Get there early to beat the crowds and zoom to the top for sweeping views over the city's skyline.

Bear in mind, however, some call the €5 fee Santa Injusta! You can save €3.50 by entering the platform from the top (behind Convento do Carmo) and paying just €1.50 to access the viewing platform.

◉ Baixa & Rossio
Praça do Comércio   Plaza
(Terreiro do Paço) With its grand 18th-century arcades, lemon meringue facades and mosaic cobbles, the riverfront Praça do Comércio is a square to out-pomp them all. Everyone arriving by boat used to disembark here, and it still feels like the gateway to Lisbon, thronging with activity and rattling trams.

At its centre rises the dashing equestrian **statue of Dom José I**, hinting at the square's royal roots as the pre-earthquake site of Palácio da Ribeira. In 1908, the square witnessed the fall of the monarchy, when anarchists assassinated Dom Carlos I and his son. The biggest crowd-puller is Verissimo da Costa's triumphal **Arco da Rua Augusta** (Rua Augusta 2-10; €2.50; ☉9am-7pm), crowned with bigwigs such

as 15th-century explorer Vasco da Gama; come at dusk to see the arch glow gold.

◉ Belém
Torre de Belém   Tower
(www.torrebelem.pt; adult/child €6/3, 1st Sun of month free; ☉10am-6.30pm Tue-Sun, to 5.30pm Oct-Apr) Jutting out onto the Rio Tejo, this Unesco World Heritage–listed fortress epitomises the Age of Discoveries. You'll need to breathe in to climb the narrow spiral staircase to the tower, which affords sublime views over Belém and the river.

Francisco de Arruda designed the pearly-grey chess piece in 1515 to defend Lisbon's harbour and nowhere else is the lure of the Atlantic more powerful. The Manueline show-off flaunts filigree stonework, meringue-like cupolas and – just below the western tower – a stone rhinoceros.

The ungulate depicts the one Manuel I sent Pope Leo X in 1515, which inspired Dürer's famous woodcut. Crowds can be intense on weekends (especially Sunday) – a warning to claustrophobes.

Museu Colecção Berardo   Museum
(www.museuberardo.pt; Praça do Império; ☉10am-7pm) **FREE** Culture fiends get their contemporary art fix for free at Museu Colecção Berardo, the star of the Centro Cultural de Belém. The ultrawhite, minimalist gallery displays millionaire José Berardo's eye-popping collection of abstract, surrealist and pop art, including Hockney, Lichtenstein, Warhol and Pollack originals.

Temporary exhibitions are among the best in Portugal. Also in the complex is a cafe-restaurant that faces a grassy lawn, a bookshop and a crafty museum store.

⊕ ACTIVITIES
Sipping away summer on numerous hilltop and waterfront *esplanadas* (terraces) and plaza kiosks is a quintessential Lisbon experience. Fancy some football? Two of Portugal's big three clubs, Benfica and Sporting, call Lisbon home. Guided tours are extremely popular and, for certified beach

Torre de Belém (p341)

bums, idyllic sands at Carcavelos, Parede, Estoril and Cascais are easy train rides away.

ViniPortugal
Wine

(www.winesofportugal.info; Praça do Comércio; ⊙11am-7pm Tue-Sat) Under the arcades on Praça do Comércio, this viticultural organisation offers €6 themed wine tastings, if booked in advance. Otherwise, pop in and grab a €3 enocard, which allows you to taste between two and four Portuguese wines, from Alentejo whites to full-bodied Douro reds.

Kiss the Cook
Cooking

(☑968 119 652; www.kissthecook.pt; Rua Rodrigues Faria 103, LX Factory; classes €65; ⊙noon-3pm) If you're into Portuguese food in a big way and fancy picking up a few tips and tricks from the experts, why not pass by Kiss the Cook? Here you can prepare (and devour) traditional dishes. The cookery classes are totally hands-on and the price includes lunch and wine.

Teleférico
Cable Car

(Telecabine Lisboa; www.telecabinelisboa.pt; Passeio do Tejo; 1-way adult/child €3.95/2;

⊙10.30am-8pm, 11am-7pm low season) Hitch a ride on this 20m-high cable car, linking Torre Vasco da Gama to the Oceanário. The ride affords bird's-eye views across Parque das Nações' skyline and the glittering Tejo that will have you burning up the pixels on your camera.

Zeev
Cycling

(☑915 100 242; www.rent.zeev.pt; Rua da Boavista 166; bike hire per 3/8/24hr €16/22/30; ⊙9am-7pm Mon-Sat) ⚡ Rents electric bikes (you'll appreciate the pedal-assist on Lisbon's hills), Renault Twizy electric two-person buggies, and full-size electric cars. Charging is free as is parking for electric vehicles within Lisbon city limits.

⊕ TOURS

Culinary Backstreets
Food & Drink

(☑963 472 188; www.culinarybackstreets.com/culinary-walks/lisbon; 3/6hr tours €85/118) *Eat Portugal* co-author Célia Pedroso leads epic culinary walks through Lisbon, a fantastic way to take in some of the best treats in town. Try *ginjinha* (cherry liqueur) followed by *pastel de nata* (custard tarts) and *porco preto* (Iberian black pork), paired with killer local wines. Tours are available Monday to Saturday. Expect tantalising multiple food-gasms followed by a debilitating food coma.

Lisbon Explorer   Walking
(☎213 629 263; www.lisbonexplorer.com; tour per person/group from €60/150) Top-notch English-speaking guides peel back the many layers of Lisbon's history during the three-hour walking tours offered by this highly rated outfit. Fees do not include admissions but often include public-transport costs during the tour. Tours typically depart from Praça do Comércio or other central locations. You'll receive the meeting point upon booking.

🔒 SHOPPING

Bairro Alto attracts vinyl lovers and vintage devotees to its cluster of late-opening boutiques. Alfama, Baixa and Rossio have frozen-in-time stores dealing exclusively in buttons and kid gloves, tawny port and tinned fish. Elegant Chiado is the go-to place for high-street and couture shopping to the backbeat of buskers.

Arte da Terra   Gifts & Souvenirs
(www.aartedaterra.pt; Rua Augusto Rosa 40; ⊘11am-8pm) In the stables of a centuries-old bishop's palace, Arte da Terra brims with authentic Portuguese crafts including Castello Branco embroideries, nativity figurines, hand-painted *azulejos,* fado CDs and quality goods (umbrellas, aprons, writing journals) made from cork. Some items are beautifully lit in former troughs.

Cortiço & Netos   Homewares
(www.corticoenetos.com; Calçada de Santo André 66; ⊘10am-1pm & 2-7pm Mon-Sat) A wonder wall of fabulous *azulejos* greets you as you enter this very special space. It's the vision of brothers Pedro, João, Ricardo and Tiago Cortiço, whose grandfather dedicated more than 30 years to gathering, storing and selling discontinued Portuguese industrial tiles. Reviving the family trade, they are

experts on the *azulejo* and how it can be interpreted today.

Garrafeira Nacional   Wine
(www.garrafeiranacional.com; Rua de Santa Justa 18; ⊘9.30am-7.30pm Mon Fri, to 7.30pm Sat) This Lisbon landmark has been slinging Portuguese juice since 1927 and is easily the best spot to pick up a bevy of local wines and spirits. It is especially helpful and will steer you towards lesser-known boutique wines and vintage ports in addition to the usual suspects. The small museum features vintages dating to the 18th century.

There is a second, smaller outlet in the Mercado da Ribeira.

Typographia   Clothing
(www.typographia.com; Rua Augusta 93; T-shirts €16-24; ⊘10am-9pm) With shops in Porto and Madrid as well, this high-design T-shirt shop is one of Europe's best. It features a select, monthly-changing array of clever and artsy, locally designed T-shirts, which everyone else won't be wearing once you get back home.

A Vida Portuguesa Gifts & Souvenirs
(www.avidaportuguesa.com; Rua Anchieta 11; ⊘10am-8pm Mon-Sat, from 11am Sun) A flashback to the late 19th century with its high ceilings and polished cabinets, this former warehouse and perfume factory lures nostalgics with all-Portuguese products from retro-wrapped Tricona sardines to Claus Porto soaps, heart-embellished Viana do Castelo embroideries and Bordallo Pinheiro porcelain swallows. Also in Intendente.

Loja das Conservas   Food
(www.facebook.com/lojadasconservas; Rua do Arsenal 130; ⊘10am-9pm Mon-Sat, noon-8pm Sun) What appears to be a gallery is on closer inspection a fascinating temple to tinned fish (or *conservas* as the Portuguese say), the result of an industry on its deathbed revived by a savvy marketing about-face and new generations of hipsters. The retro-wrapped tins, displayed along with the history of each canning factory, are the artworks.

Craft Beer

Lisboêtas have finally been released from the decades-long suds purgatory imposed on them by commoner lagers Super Bock and Sagres. IPAs, stouts, porters, *saisons* and sours are booming – keep an eye out for an ever-expanding list of local standouts that includes Dois Corvos, Oitava Colina, Passarola, Mean Sardine, Amnesia and Musa. Drink in the local scene at several new craft-beer bars and brewpubs. The hops revolution has begun!

AFRICA STUDIO/SHUTTERSTOCK ©

✖ EATING

Mercado da Baixa   Market €
(www.adbaixapombalina.pt; Praça da Figueira; ⊙10am-10pm Fri-Sun) This tented market/glorious food court on Praça da Figueira has been slinging cheese, wine, smoked sausages and other gourmet goodies since 1855. It takes place on the last weekend of each month and it is fantastic fun to stroll the stalls eating and drinking yourself into a gluttonous mess.

Nova Pombalina   Portuguese €
(www.facebook.com/anovapombalina; Rua do Comércio 2; sandwiches €2.20-4; ⊙7am-7.30pm, closed Sun) The reason this bustling traditional restaurant is always packed around midday is its delicious *leitão* (suckling pig) sandwich, served on freshly baked bread in 60 seconds or less by the lightning-fast crew behind the counter.

Ti-Natércia   Portuguese €
(🖁218 862 133; Rua Escola Gerais 54; mains €5-12; ⊙7pm-midnight Mon-Fri, noon-3pm & 7pm-midnight Sat) A decade in and a legend in the making, 'Aunt' Natércia and her downright delicious Portuguese home cooking is a tough ticket: there are but a mere six tables and they fill up fast. She'll talk your ear off (and doesn't mince words!) while you devour her excellent take on the classics. Reservations essential (and cash only).

If you do manage to get a seat, you're in for a treat, especially with the *bacalhau com natas* (shredded codfish with bechamal, served au gratin) or *à Brás* (shredded codfish with eggs and potatoes) or, well, anything you else you might order. President Marcelo Rebelo de Sousa approved – his photo is on the wall.

Pois Café   Cafe €
(www.poiscafe.com; Rua de São João da Praça 93; mains €7-10; ⊙noon-11pm Mon, 10am-11pm Tue-Sun; 🛜) Boasting a laid-back vibe under dominant stone arches, atmospheric Pois Café has creative salads, sandwiches and fresh juices, plus a handful of heartier daily specials (salmon quiche, sirloin steak). Its sofas invite lazy afternoons spent reading novels and sipping coffee, but you'll fight for space with the laptop brigade.

Mercado da Ribeira   Market €
(www.timeoutmarket.com; Av 24 de Julho; ⊙10am-midnight Sun-Wed, to 2am Thu-Sat; 🛜) Doing trade in fresh fruit and veg, fish and flowers since 1892, this oriental-dome-topped market hall is the word on everyone's lips since *Time Out* transformed half of it into a gourmet food court in 2014. Now it's like Lisbon in microcosm, with everything from Garrafeira Nacional wines to Conserveira de Lisboa fish, Arcádia chocolate and Santini gelato.

Follow the lead of locals and come for a browse in the morning followed by lunch at one of 35 kiosks – there's everything from Café de São Bento's famous steak and fries to a stand by top chef Henrique Sá Pessoa. Do not miss it.

Dona Quitéria Portuguese €
(☎213 951 521; Travessa de São José 1; small plates €5-12; ⏰7pm-midnight Tue-Sun) Locals do their best to keep this quaint corner *petiscaria* (small plates restaurant), a former grocery store from 1870, all to themselves – no such luck. Pleasant palette surprises such as tuna *pica-pau* instead of steak, or a pumpkin-laced cream-cheese mousse for dessert, put tasty creative spins on tradition. It's warm, welcoming and oh so tiny – so reserve ahead.

Chapitô à Mesa Portuguese €€
(☎218 875 077; www.facebook.com/chapitoamesa; Rua Costa do Castelo 7; mains €18-21; ⏰noon-11pm Mon-Fri, 7.30-11pm Sat-Sun; 📶) Up a spiral iron staircase from this circus school's casual cafe, the decidedly creative menu of Chef Bertílio Gomes is served alongside views worth writing home about. His modern takes include classic dishes (*bacalhau à Brás,* stewed veal cheeks, suckling pig), plus daring ones (rooster testicles – goes swimmingly with a drop of Quinta da Silveira Reserva).

Tasca Zé dos Cornos Portuguese €€
(☎218 869 641; www.facebook.com/ZeCornos; Beco Surradores 5; mains €10-15; ⏰8am-11pm Mon-Sat) This family owned tavern welcomes regulars and first-timers with the same undivided attention. Lunchtime is particularly busy but the service is whirlwind quick and effective. Space is tight so sharing tables is the norm. The menu is typical Portuguese cuisine with emphasis on pork and *bacalhau* (salted cod) grilled on the spot, served in very generous portions.

Alma Contemporary, Portuguese €€€
(☎213 470 650; www.almalisboa.pt; Rua Anchieta 15; mains €25-29, tasting menus €60-80; ⏰noon-3pm & 7-11pm Tue-Sun; 📶) Henrique Sá Pessoa, one of Portugal's most talented chefs, moved his flagship Alma from Santos to more fitting digs in Chiado in 2015. The casual space exudes understated style amid its original stone flooring and gorgeous hardwood tables, but it's Pessoa's outrageously good nouveau Portuguese cuisine that draws the foodie flock from far and wide.

Mercado da Ribeira

100 Maneiras   Fusion €€€

(☏910 307 575; www.restaurante100maneiras.
com; Rua do Teixeira 35; tasting menu €58,
with classic/premium wine pairing €93/118;
⊙7.30pm-2am; 📶) How do we love 100
Maneiras? Let us count the 100 ways... The
nine-course tasting menu changes twice
yearly and features imaginative, delicately
prepared dishes. The courses are all a
surprise – part of the charm – though
somewhat disappointingly, the chef will
only budge so far to accommodate special
diets and food allergies. Reservations are
essential for the elegant and small space.

Belcanto   Portuguese €€€

(☏213 420 607; www.belcanto.pt; Largo de São
Carlos 10; mains €45, tasting menu €125-145,
with 5/7 wines €50/60; ⊙12.30-3pm & 7.30-
11pm Tue-Sat; 📶) Fresh off a 2016 intimacy
upgrade, José Avillez' two-Michelin-starred
cathedral of cookery wows diners with
painstaking creativity, polished service and
first-rate sommelier. Standouts among
Lisbon's culinary adventure of a lifetime
include suckling pig with orange purée,
sea bass with seaweed and bivalves and

a stunning roasted butternut squash with
miso; paired wines sometimes date to the
'70s! Reservations essential.

🍷 DRINKING & NIGHTLIFE

Park   Bar

(www.facebook.com/00park; Calçada do Combro
58; cocktails €6.50-8; ⊙1pm-2am Tue-Sat, 1-8pm
Sun; 📶) If only all multistorey car parks
were like this... Take the elevator to the 5th
floor, and head up and around to the top,
which has been transformed into one of
Lisbon's hippest rooftop bars, with sweeping views reaching right down to the Tejo
and over the bell towers of Santa Catarina
Church.

Pensão Amor   Bar

(www.pensaoamor.pt; Rua do Alecrim 19;
cocktails €5.50-13; ⊙noon-3am Mon-Wed, to
4am Thu-Sat, to 3am Sun) Set inside a former
brothel, this cheeky bar pays homage to
its passion-filled past with colourful wall
murals, a library of erotic-tinged works, and
a small stage where you can sometimes
catch burlesque shows. The Museu Erótico

Fado performer

de Lisboa (MEL) was on the way at time of research.

BA Wine Bar
do Bairro Alto · Wine Bar

(☑213 461 182; bawinebar@gmail.com; Rua da Rosa 107; wines from €3, tapas from €12; ⊘6-11pm Tue-Sun; ☏) Reserve ahead unless you want to get shut out of Bairro Alto's best wine bar, where the genuinely welcoming staff will offer you three fantastic choices to taste based on your wine proclivities. The cheeses (from small artisanal producers) and charcuterie (melt-in-your-mouth black-pork *presuntos*) are not to be missed, either. You could spend the night here.

A Ginjinha · Bar

(Largo de Saõ Domingos 8; ⊘9am 10pm) Hipsters, old men in flat caps, office workers and tourists all meet at this microscopic *ginjinha* (cherry liqueur) bar for that moment of cherry-licking, pip-spitting pleasure (€1.40 a shot).

Watch the owner line 'em up at the bar under the beady watch of the drink's 19th-century inventor, Espinheira. It's less about the grog, more about the event.

Lux-Frágil · Club

(www.luxfragil.com; Av Infante Dom Henrique, Armazém A - Cais de Pedra, Santo Apolónia; ⊘11pm-6am Thu-Sat) Lisbon's ice-cool, must-see club, Lux hosts big-name DJs spinning electro and house. It's run by ex-Frágil maestro Marcel Reis and part-owned by John Malkovich. Grab a spot on the terrace to see the sun rise over the Tejo; or chill like a king on the throne-like giant interior chairs.

Style policing is heartwarmingly lax but arrive after 4am at weekends and you might have trouble getting in because of the crowds.

⭐ ENTERTAINMENT

Infused by Moorish song and the ditties of homesick sailors, bluesy, bittersweet fado encapsulates the Lisbon psyche like nothing else. There's usually a minimum cover

Lisbon Online

Lonely Planet (www.lonelyplanet.com/lisbon) Destination information, hotel bookings, traveller forum and more.

Visit Lisboa (www.visitlisboa.com) Comprehensive tourist office website.

Lisbon Lux (www.lisbonlux.com) Trendy city guide.

Spotted by Locals (www.spottedbylocals.com/lisbon) Insider tips.

Go Lisbon (www.golisbon.com) Dining, drinking and nightlife insight.

of €15 to €25. Book ahead at weekends. If you prefer a spontaneous approach, seek out *fado vadio* where anyone can – and does – have a warble.

Hot Clube de Portugal · Jazz

(☑213 460 305; www.hcp.pt; Praça da Alegria 48; ⊘10pm-2am Tue-Sat) As hot as its name suggests, this small, poster-plastered cellar (and newly added garden) has staged top-drawer jazz acts since the 1940s. It's considered one of Europe's best.

A Baîuca · Fado

(☑218 867 284; Rua de São Miguel 20; ⊘8pm-midnight Thu-Mon) On a good night, walking into A Baîuca is like gatecrashing a family party. It's a special place with *fado vadio,* where locals take a turn and spectators hiss if anyone dares to chat during the singing. There's a €25 minimum spend, which is as tough to swallow as the food, though the fado is spectacular. Reserve ahead.

A Tasco do Chico · Fado

(☑961 339 696; www.facebook.com/atasca.dochico; Rua Diário de Notícias 39; ⊘noon-2am, to 3am Fri-Sat) This crowded dive (reserve ahead), full of soccer banners and spilling over with people of all ilk is a fado free-for-all. It's not uncommon for taxi drivers to roll up, hum a few bars, and hop right back into their cabs, speeding off into the night.

Portugal's most famous fado singer, Mariza, brought us here in 2005. It's legit.

Senhor Fado   Fado
(218 874 298; www.sr-fado.com; Rua dos Remédios 176; ⊗8pm-2am Wed-Sat) Small and lantern-lit, this is a cosy spot for *fado vadio* (street fado). *Fadista* Ana Marina and guitarist Duarte Santos make a great double act.

ⓘ INFORMATION

The largest and most helpful tourist office in the city, **Ask Me Lisboa** (⊘213 463 314; www.askme lisboa.com; Praça dos Restauradores, Palácio Foz; ⊗9am-8pm) faces Praça dos Restauradaures inside the Palácio Foz. Staff dole out maps and information, book accommodation and reserve rental cars.

Ask Me Lisboa runs several information kiosks, which are handy places for maps and quick information:

Airport (⊘218 450 660; Aeroporto de Lisboa, Arrivals Hall; ⊗7.30am-9.30am Tue-Sat)

Belém (⊘213 658 435; Largo dos Jernónimos; ⊗10am-1pm & 2-6pm Tue-Sat)

Santa Apolónia (⊘910 517 982; Door 48, Santa Apolónia train station; ⊗7.30am-9.30pm Tue-Sat)

Rossio Square (⊘910 517 914; Praça Dom Pedro IV; ⊗10am-1pm & 2-6pm)

Parque das Nações (⊘910 518 028; Alameda dos Oceanos; ⊗10am-1pm & 2-7pm Apr-Sep, to 6pm Oct-Mar)

ⓘ GETTING THERE & AWAY

AIR
Situated around 6km north of the centre, the ultramodern **Aeroporto de Lisboa** (Lisbon Airport; 218 413 700; www.ana.pt; Alameda das Comunidades Portuguesas) operates direct flights to major international hubs including London, New York, Paris and Frankfurt. Several low-cost carriers (easyJet, Ryanair, Transavia, Norwegian etc) leave from the less-efficient terminal 2 – you'll need to factor in extra time for the shuttle ride if arriving at the airport on the metro.

BUS
Lisbon's main long-distance bus terminal is **Rodoviário de Sete Rios** (Praça General Humberto Delgado, Rua das Laranjeiras), adjacent to both Jardim Zoológico metro station and Sete Rios train station. The big carriers, **Rede Expressos** (⊘707 223 344; www.rede-expressos.pt) and **Eva** (⊘707 223 344; www.eva-bus.com), run frequent services to almost every major town. You can buy your ticket up to seven days in advance.

TRAIN
Lisbon is linked by train to other major cities. Check the **Comboios de Portugal** (⊘707 210 220; www.cp.pt) website for schedules.

ⓘ GETTING AROUND

BUS, TRAM & FUNICULAR
Companhia Carris de Ferro de Lisboa (Carris; 213 500 115; http://carris.transporteslisboa. pt) operates all transport in Lisbon proper except the metro. Its buses and trams run from about 5am or 6am to about 10pm or 11pm; there are some night bus and tram services.

Pick up a transport map, *Rede de Transportes de Lisboa,* from tourist offices. The Carris website has timetables and route details.

METRO
The **metro** (www.metro.transporteslisboa.pt; single/day ticket €1.40/6; ⊗6.30am-1am) is useful for short hops, and to reach the stations.

Buy tickets from metro ticket machines, which have English-language menus. The Lisboa Card is also valid.

Entrances are marked by a big red 'M'. Useful signs include *correspondência* (transfer between lines) and *saída* (exit to the street).

TICKETS & PASSES
On-board one-way prices are €1.80 for buses, €2.85 for trams and €3.60 (return) for funicular rides (one-way tickets not available). A day pass for all public transport is €6.

Where to Stay

You're spoilt for choice in the Portuguese capital when it comes to places to unpack your duffle bag. Room rates tend to be lower than in most of Western Europe.

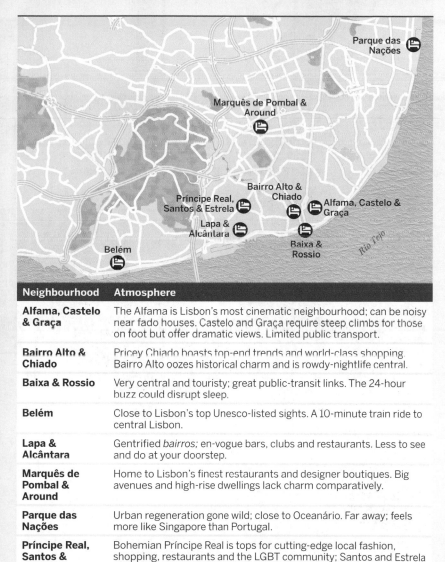

Neighbourhood	Atmosphere
Alfama, Castelo & Graça	The Alfama is Lisbon's most cinematic neighbourhood; can be noisy near fado houses. Castelo and Graça require steep climbs for those on foot but offer dramatic views. Limited public transport.
Bairro Alto & Chiado	Pricey Chiado boasts top-end trends and world-class shopping. Bairro Alto oozes historical charm and is rowdy-nightlife central.
Baixa & Rossio	Very central and touristy; great public-transit links. The 24-hour buzz could disrupt sleep.
Belém	Close to Lisbon's top Unesco-listed sights. A 10-minute train ride to central Lisbon.
Lapa & Alcântara	Gentrified *bairros*; en-vogue bars, clubs and restaurants. Less to see and do at your doorstep.
Marquês de Pombal & Around	Home to Lisbon's finest restaurants and designer boutiques. Big avenues and high-rise dwellings lack charm comparatively.
Parque das Nações	Urban regeneration gone wild; close to Oceanário. Far away; feels more like Singapore than Portugal.
Príncipe Real, Santos & Estrela	Bohemian Príncipe Real is tops for cutting-edge local fashion, shopping, restaurants and the LGBT community; Santos and Estrela are ideal for escapists who prefer pin-drop peace to central bustle.

ITALY & CROATIA

Rome, Italy

A heady mix of haunting ruins, breathtaking art, vibrant street life and incredible food, Italy's hot-blooded capital is one of the world's most romantic and inspiring cities. Ancient icons such as the Colosseum, Roman Forum and Pantheon recall the city's golden age as caput mundi (capital of the world), while monumental basilicas testify to the role that great popes have played in its history. And Rome's astonishing artistic heritage is almost unrivalled. A walk around the centre will have you encountering masterpieces by the giants of Western art: sculptures by Michelangelo, canvases by Caravaggio, frescoes by Raphael and fountains by Bernini.

Rome in Two Days

Start early at the **Colosseum** (p354), then visit the **Palatino** (p380) and **Roman Forum** (p372). Spend the afternoon in the *centro storico* (historic centre) exploring **Piazza Navona** (p381) and the **Pantheon** (p358). On day two, hit the **Vatican Museums** (p367) and **St Peter's Basilica** (p363). Afterwards, check out the **Spanish Steps** (p387) and **Trevi Fountain** (p387). Round the day off in the **Campo de' Fiori** (p383).

Rome in Four Days

Spend day three investigating **Villa Borghese** (p389) – make sure to book for the **Museo e Galleria Borghese** (p389) – and **Piazza del Popolo** (p387). End the day with dinner in Trastevere. Next day, admire classical art at the **Capitoline Museums** (p380) before checking out the basilicas on the Esquiline.

Next up? Catch the train to Florence (p418) or step back in time at Pompeii (p462).

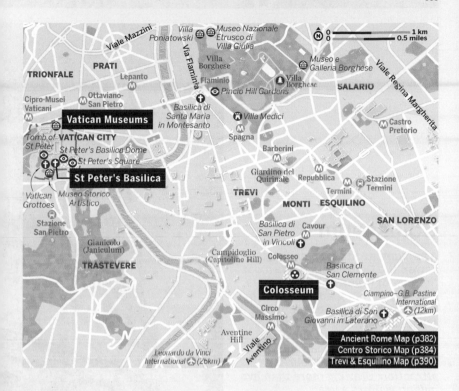

Arriving in Rome

Leonardo da Vinci (Fiumicino) Airport Half-hourly Leonardo Express trains run to Stazione Termini (€14, 30 minutes). A taxi to the centre is €48.

Ciampino Airport Arrival point for Ryanair flights to Rome. SIT Bus and Terravision run regular services to Via Marsala outside Termini (from €5, 45 minutes). Taxi fare is €30.

Stazione Termini Rome's principal train station.

Where to Stay

Rome has many boutique-style guesthouses offering chic accommodation at midrange to top-end prices. Alternatively, try a *pensione* (a small family-run hotel with simple rooms, most with private bathroom). Some religious institutions also offer good-value rooms, though many have strict curfews and the rooms are no-frills.

For information on what each Roman neighbourhood has to offer, see the table on p399.

Colosseum

A monument to raw, merciless power, the Colosseum is the most thrilling of Rome's ancient sights. It was here that gladiators met in mortal combat and condemned prisoners fought off wild beasts in front of baying, bloodthirsty crowds. Two thousand years on and it's Italy's top tourist attraction, drawing more than five million visitors a year.

Great For...

Parco del Colle Oppio

Ⓜ Colosseo

Colosseum ◉

Piazza del Colosseo

Via Celio Vibenna

❶ Need to Know

Colosseo; ☎06 3996 7700; www.coopculture.it; Piazza del Colosseo; adult/reduced incl Roman Forum & Palatino €12/7.50; ⊗8.30am-1hr before sunset; ⓂColosseo

★ Top Tip

Beat the queues by buying your ticket at the Palatino (Via di San Gregorio 30).

Built by Vespasian (r AD 69–79) in the grounds of Nero's vast Domus Aurea complex, the arena was inaugurated in AD 80, eight years after it had been commissioned. To mark the occasion, Vespasian's son and successor Titus (r 79–81) staged games that lasted 100 days and nights, during which 5000 animals were slaughtered. Trajan (r 98–117) later topped this, holding a marathon 117-day killing spree involving 9000 gladiators and 10,000 animals.

The 50,000-seat arena was originally known as the Flavian Amphitheatre, and although it was Rome's most fearsome arena it wasn't the biggest – the Circo Massimo could hold up to 250,000 people. The name Colosseum, when introduced in medieval times, was a reference not to its size but to the Colosso di Nerone, a giant statue of Nero that stood nearby.

With the fall of the Roman Empire in the 5th century, the Colosseum was abandoned and gradually became overgrown. In the Middle Ages it served as a fortress for two of the city's warrior families, the Frangipani and the Annibaldi. Later, during the Renaissance and baroque periods, it was plundered of its precious travertine, and the marble stripped from it was used to make huge palaces such as Palazzo Venezia, Palazzo Barberini and Palazzo Cancelleria.

More recently, pollution and vibrations caused by traffic and the metro have taken their toll, but the first stage of a €25 million clean-up, the first in its 2000-year history, has once again revealed the creamy hues of the Colosseum walls.

Exterior

The outer walls have three levels of arches, framed by Ionic, Doric and Corinthian columns. These were originally covered in travertine, and marble statues filled the niches on the 2nd and 3rd storeys. The upper level, punctuated with windows and slender Corinthian pilasters, had supports for 240 masts that held up a huge canvas awning over the arena, shielding spectators from sun and rain. The 80 entrance arches, known as *vomitoria,* allowed the spectators to enter and be seated in a matter of minutes.

> ☑ **Don't Miss**
>
> The hypogeum's network of dank tunnels beneath the main arena. Visits require advance booking and cost an extra €9.

GEORGY KURYATOV/SHUTTERSTOCK ©

Arena

The arena originally had a wooden floor covered in sand to prevent the combatants from slipping and to soak up the blood. It could also be flooded for mock sea battles. Trapdoors led down to the hypogeum, a subterranean complex of corridors, cages and lifts beneath the arena floor.

Stands

The *cavea,* for spectator seating, was divided into three tiers: magistrates and senior officials sat in the lowest tier, wealthy citizens in the middle, and the plebeians in the highest tier. Women (except for vestal virgins) were relegated to the cheapest sections at the top. As in modern stadiums, tickets were numbered and spectators assigned a seat in a specific sector – in 2015, restorers uncovered traces of red numerals on the arches, indicating how the sectors were numbered. The podium, a broad terrace in front of the tiers of seats, was reserved for the emperor, senators and VIPs.

Hypogeum

The hypogeum served as the stadium's backstage area. Sets for the various battle scenes were prepared here and hoisted up to the arena by a complicated system of pulleys. Caged animals were kept here and gladiators would gather here before showtime, having come in through an underground corridor from the nearby Ludus Magnus (gladiator school).

✕ Take a Break

Cafè Cafè (☏06 700 87 43; www.cafe cafebistrot.it; Via dei Santi Quattro 44; meals €15-20; ⊙9.30am-8.50pm; ☐Via di San Giovanni in Laterano) is the perfect venue for a post-arena break, for tea and cake or a light meal.

Pantheon

A striking 2000-year-old temple that's now a church, the Pantheon is Rome's best-preserved ancient monument and one of the most influential buildings in the Western world. Its greying, pockmarked exterior may look its age, but inside it's a different story. It's a unique and exhilarating experience to pass through the vast bronze doors and gaze up at the largest unreinforced concrete dome ever built.

Great For...

❶ Need to Know

Map p384; www.pantheonroma.com; Piazza della Rotonda; ⊘8.30am-7.15pm Mon-Sat, 9am-5.45pm Sun; 🚊Largo di Torre Argentina
`FREE`

★ **Top Tip**

Mass is celebrated at the Pantheon at 5pm on Saturday and 10.30am on Sunday.

In its current form the Pantheon dates from around AD 125. The original temple, built by Marcus Agrippa in 27 BC, burnt down in AD 80, and although it was rebuilt by Domitian, it was struck by lightning and destroyed for a second time in 110. The emperor Hadrian had it reconstructed between 118 and 125, and it's this version that you see today.

Hadrian's temple was dedicated to the classical gods – hence the name Pantheon, a derivation of the Greek words *pan* (all) and *theos* (god) – but in 608 it was consecrated as a Christian church. It's now officially known as the Basilica di Santa Maria ad Martyres.

Thanks to this consecration, it was spared the worst of the medieval plundering that reduced many of Rome's ancient buildings to near dereliction. But it didn't escape entirely unscathed – its gilded-bronze roof tiles were removed and bronze from the portico was used by Bernini for the *baldachino* at St Peter's Basilica.

Exterior

The dark-grey pitted exterior faces onto busy, cafe-lined Piazza della Rotonda. And while its facade is somewhat the worse for wear, it's still an imposing sight. The monumental entrance **portico** consists of 16 Corinthian columns, each 13m high and made of Egyptian granite, supporting a triangular **pediment**. Behind the columns, two 20-tonne **bronze doors** – 16th-century restorations of the original portal – give onto the central rotunda. Rivets and holes in the building's brickwork indicate where marble-veneer panels were originally placed.

The oculus

Inscription

For centuries the inscription under the pediment – M:AGRIPPA.L.F.COS.TERTIUM. FECIT or 'Marcus Agrippa, son of Lucius, consul for the third time built this' – led scholars to think that the current building was Agrippa's original temple. However, 19th-century excavations revealed traces of an earlier temple and historians realised that Hadrian had simply kept Agrippa's original inscription.

Interior

Although impressive from outside, it's only when you get inside that you can really

> ☑ **Don't Miss**
>
> The 7m-high bronze doors, which provide a suitably grand entrance to your visit.

appreciate the Pantheon's full size. With light streaming in through the **oculus** (the 8.7m-diameter hole in the centre of the dome), the cylindrical marble-clad interior seems vast.

Opposite the entrance is the church's main **altar**, over which hangs a 7th-century icon of the *Madonna col Bambino* (Madonna and Child). To the left are the tombs of the artist Raphael, King Umberto I and Margherita of Savoy. Over on the opposite side of the rotunda is the tomb of King Vittorio Emanuele II

Dome

The Pantheon's dome, considered to be the Romans' most important architectural achievement, was the largest dome in the world until Brunelleschi beat it with his Florentine cupola. Its harmonious appearance is due to a precisely calibrated symmetry – its diameter is exactly equal to the building's interior height of 43.3m. At its centre, the oculus, which symbolically connected the temple with the gods, plays a vital structural role by absorbing and redistributing the dome's huge tensile forces.

What's Nearby?
Basilica di Santa Maria
Sopra Minerva   Basilica

(Map p384, www.santamariasopraminerva.it; Piazza della Minerva 42; ⊘6.40am-7pm Mon-Fri, 6.40am-12.30pm & 3.30-7pm Sat, 8am-12.30pm & 3.30-7pm Sun; ☐Largo di Torre Argentina) Built on the site of three pagan temples, including one to the goddess Minerva, the Dominican Basilica di Santa Maria Sopra Minerva is Rome's only Gothic church. However, little remains of the original 13th-century structure and these days the main drawcard is a minor Michelangelo sculpture and the colourful, art-rich interior.

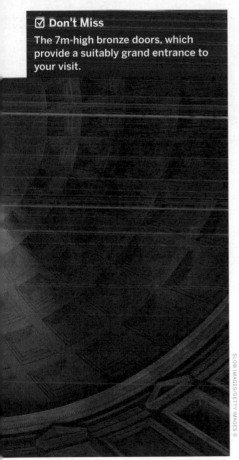

> ✕ **Take a Break**
>
> Get caffeinated at Caffè Sant'Eustachio (p394), known to serve some of the best coffee in town.

St Peter's Basilica

In this city of outstanding churches, none can hold a candle to St Peter's, Italy's largest, richest and most spectacular basilica.

Great For...

☑ Don't Miss

Climbing the (numerous, steep and tiring, but worth it) steps of the dome for views over Rome.

The original church was commissioned by the emperor Constantine and built around 349 on the site where St Peter is said to have been buried between AD 64 and 67. But like many medieval churches, it eventually fell into disrepair. It wasn't until the mid-15th century that efforts were made to restore it, first by Pope Nicholas V and then, rather more successfully, by Julius II.

In 1506 construction began on a design by Bramante, but ground to a halt when the architect died in 1514. In 1547 Michelangelo stepped in to take on the project. He simplified Bramante's plans and drew up designs for what was to become his greatest architectural achievement: the dome. He didn't live to see it built, though, and it was left to Giacomo della Porta, Domenico Fontana and Carlo Maderno to complete the basilica, which was finally consecrated in 1626.

St Peter's Basilica and the Tiber River

MAPICS/SHUTTERSTOCK ©

❶ Need to Know

Basilica di San Pietro; 📞06 6988 5518; www.
vatican.va; St Peter's Square; ⏰7am-7pm
summer, to 6.30pm winter; 🚇Piazza del
Risorgimento, Ⓜ️Ottaviano-San Pietro FREE

✗ Take a Break

With more than 200 teas to choose
from, you'll find the perfect cuppa at
Makasar Bistrot (📞06 687 46 02; www.
makasar.it; Via Plauto 33; ⏰noon-midnight
Mon-Thu, to 2am Fri & Sat, 5pm-midnight Sun;
🚇Piazza del Risorgimento).

★ Top Tip

Strict dress codes are enforced, which
means no shorts, miniskirts or bare
shoulders.

Facade

Built between 1608 and 1612, Maderno's
immense facade is 48m high and 118.6m
wide. Eight 27m-high columns support
the upper attic on which 13 statues stand
representing Christ the Redeemer, St John
the Baptist and the 11 apostles. The central
balcony, the **Loggia della Benedizione**, is
where the pope stands to deliver his *Urbi et
Orbi* blessing at Christmas and Easter.

Interior

At the beginning of the right aisle is Michelangelo's hauntingly beautiful **Pietà**. Sculpted when the artist was 25 (in 1499), it's the
only work he ever signed; his signature is
etched into the sash across the Madonna's
breast.

On a pillar just beyond the *Pietà,* Carlo
Fontana's gilt and bronze **monument to
Queen Christina of Sweden** commemorates the far-from-holy Swedish monarch
who converted to Catholicism in 1655.

Moving on, you'll come to the **Cappella di San Sebastiano**, home of Pope
John Paul II's tomb, and the **Cappella del
Santissimo Sacramento**, a sumptuously
decorated baroque chapel.

Dominating the centre of the basilica is
Bernini's 29m-high **baldachin**. Supported
by four spiral columns and made with
bronze taken from the Pantheon, it stands
over the **high altar**, which itself sits on the
site of St Peter's grave.

Above the baldachin, Michelangelo's
dome soars to a height of 119m. Based on
Brunelleschi's cupola in Florence, it's supported by four massive stone piers named
after the saints whose statues adorn the
Bernini-designed niches – Longinus, Hele-
na, Veronica and Andrew.

At the base of the **Pier of St Longinus** is Arnolfo di Cambio's much-loved 13th-century bronze **statue of St Peter**, whose right foot has been worn down by centuries of caresses.

Dominating the tribune behind the altar is Bernini's extraordinary **Cattedra di San Pietro**, centred on a wooden seat that was once thought to have been St Peter's, but in fact dates from the 9th century.

To the right of the throne, Bernini's **monument to Urban VIII** depicts the pope flanked by the figures of Charity and Justice.

Near the head of the left aisle are the so-called **Stuart monuments**. On the right is the monument to Clementina Sobieska, wife of James Stuart, by Filippo Barigioni, and on the left is Canova's vaguely erotic monument to the last three members of the Stuart clan, the pretenders to the English throne who died in exile in Rome.

Dome

From the **dome** (with/without lift €8/6; ☺8am-6pm summer, to 5pm winter) entrance on the right of the basilica's main portico, you can walk the 551 steps to the top or take a small lift halfway and then follow on foot for the last 320 steps. Either way, it's a long, steep climb and not recommended for anyone who suffers from claustrophobia or vertigo. Make it to the top, though, and you're rewarded with stunning views.

Museo Storico Artistico

Accessed from the left nave, the **Museo Storico Artistico** (Tesoro, Treasury; adult/reduced €7/5; ☺8am-6.50pm summer, to 5.50pm winter) sparkles with sacred relics.

Top of St Peter's Square and the basilica

Highlights include a tabernacle by Donatello and the 6th-century *Crux Vaticana* (Vatican Cross).

Vatican Grottoes

Extending beneath the basilica, the **Vatican Grottoes** (⊗8am-6pm summer, to 5.30pm winter) `FREE` contain the tombs and sarcophagi of numerous popes, as well as several columns from the original 4th-century basilica. The entrance is in the Pier of St Andrew.

★ Free Tours

Between October and late May, free English-language tours of the basilica are run by seminarians from the Pontifical North American College, usually departing 2.15pm Monday to Friday from Centro Servizi Pellegrini e Turisti.

MARHA GOLOVIANKO/SHUTTERSTOCK ©

St Peter's Tomb

Excavations beneath the basilica have uncovered part of the original church and what archaeologists believe is the **Tomb of St Peter** (☑06 6988 5318; www.scavi.va; €13, over 15s only).

The excavations can only be visited by guided tour. To book a spot, email the Ufficio Scavi (scavi@fsp.va) as far in advance as possible.

What's Nearby?

St Peter's Square   Piazza

(Piazza San Pietro; MOttaviano-San Pietro) Overlooked by St Peter's Basilica, the Vatican's central square was laid out between 1656 and 1667 to a design by Gian Lorenzo Bernini. Seen from above, it resembles a giant keyhole with two semicircular colonnades, each consisting of four rows of Doric columns, encircling a giant ellipse that straightens out to funnel believers into the basilica. The effect was deliberate – Bernini described the colonnades as representing 'the motherly arms of the church'.

Castel Sant'Angelo   Museum, Castle

(Map p384; ☑06 681 91 11; www.castelsant angelo.beniculturali.it; Lungotevere Castello 50; adult/reduced €10/5; ⊗9am-7.30pm, ticket office to 6.30pm; ☐Piazza Pia) With its chunky round keep, this castle is an instantly recognisable landmark. Built as a mausoleum for the emperor Hadrian, it was converted into a papal fortress in the 6th century and named after an angelic vision that Pope Gregory the Great had in 590. Nowadays it houses the **Museo Nazionale di Castel Sant'Angelo** and its eclectic collection of paintings, sculpture, military memorabilia and medieval firearms.

★ Local Knowledge

Near the main entrance, a red floor disc marks the spot where Charlemagne and later Holy Roman Emperors were crowned by the pope.

Spiral staircase

GIORGIO ART/SHUTTERSTOCK ©

Vatican Museums

Founded in the 16th century, the Vatican Museums boast one of the world's greatest art collections. Highlights include spectacular classical statuary, rooms frescoed by Raphael, and the Michelangelo-decorated Sistine Chapel.

Great For...

☑ Don't Miss

The Museo Gregoriano Egizio's fascinating 3rd-century linen 'Shroud of the Lady of the Vatican'.

Housing the museums are the lavishly decorated halls and galleries of the Palazzo Apostolico Vaticano. This vast 5.5-hectare complex consists of two palaces – the Vatican palace (nearer to St Peter's) and the Belvedere Palace – joined by two long galleries. Inside are three courtyards: the Cortile della Pigna, the Cortile della Biblioteca and, to the south, the Cortile del Belvedere. You'll never cover it all in one day, so it pays to be selective.

Pinacoteca

Often overlooked by visitors, the papal picture gallery contains Raphael's last work, *La Trasfigurazione* (Transfiguration; 1517–20), and paintings by Giotto, Fra Angelico, Filippo Lippi, Perugino, Titian, Guido Reni, Guercino, Pietro da Cortona, Caravaggio and Leonardo da Vinci, whose

Gallery in the Vatican Museums

❶ Need to Know

Musei Vaticani; ☑06 6988 4676; www.musei
vaticani.va; Viale Vaticano; adult/reduced
€16/8, last Sun of month free; ⊙9am-6pm
Mon-Sat, 9am-2pm last Sun of month, last
entry 2hr before close; ☐Piazza del Risorgimento, ⓂOttaviano-San Pietro

✗ Take a Break

Snack on a scissor-cut square of pizza
or a rice croquette from Pizzarium
(p392).

★ Top Tip

Avoid queues by booking tickets online (http://biglietteriamusei.vatican.
va/musei/tickets/do); the booking
fee is €4.

haunting *San Gerolamo* (St Jerome; c
1400) was never finished.

Museo Chiaramonti & Braccio Nuovo

The Museo Chiaramonti is effectively the
long corridor that runs down the eastern
side of the Belvedere Palace. Its walls are
lined with thousands of statues and busts
representing everything from immortal
gods to playful cherubs and unattractive
Roman patricians. Near the end of the hall,
off to the right, is the Braccio Nuovo (New
Wing), which contains a famous statue of
the Nile as a reclining god covered by 16
babies.

Museo Pio-Clementino

This stunning museum contains some of
the Vatican Museums' finest classical statu-

ary, including the peerless *Apollo Belvedere*
and the 1st-century *Laocoön*, both in the
Cortile Ottagono (Octagonal Courtyard).
Before you go into the courtyard, take a
moment to admire the 1st-century *Apoxy-
omenos*, one of the earliest known sculptures to depict a figure with a raised arm.

To the left as you enter the courtyard, the
Apollo Belvedere is a 2nd-century Roman
copy of a 4th-century-BC Greek bronze.
A beautifully proportioned representation
of the sun god Apollo, it's considered one
of the great masterpieces of classical
sculpture. Nearby, the *Laocoon* depicts a
muscular Trojan priest and his two sons in
mortal struggle with two sea serpents.

Back inside, the **Sala degli Animali** is
filled with sculpted creatures and some
magnificent 4th-century mosaics. Continuing on, you come to the **Sala delle Muse**,
centred on the *Torso Belvedere,* another of
the museum's must-sees. A fragment of a

muscular 1st-century-BC Greek sculpture, it was found in Campo de' Fiori and used by Michelangelo as a model for his *ignudi* (male nudes) in the Sistine Chapel. It's currently undergoing restoration.

The next room, the **Sala Rotonda**, contains a number of colossal statues, including a gilded-bronze *Ercole* (Hercules) and an exquisite floor mosaic. The enormous basin in the centre of the room was found at Nero's Domus Aurea and is made out of a single piece of red porphyry stone.

Museo Gregoriano Egizio

Founded by Gregory XVI in 1839, this museum contains pieces taken from Egypt in Roman times. The collection is small, but there are fascinating exhibits including the *Trono di Ramses II* (part of a statue of the seated king), vividly painted sarcophagi dating from around 1000 BC, and some macabre mummies.

Museo Gregoriano Etrusco

At the top of the 18th-century Simonetti staircase, the Museo Gregoriano Etrusco contains artefacts unearthed in the Etruscan tombs of northern Lazio, as well as a superb collection of vases and Roman antiquities. Of particular interest is the *Marte di Todi* (Mars of Todi), a black bronze of a warrior dating from the late 5th century BC.

Galleria delle Carte Geografiche & Sala Sobieski

The last of three galleries – the other two are the **Galleria dei Candelabri** (Gallery of the Candelabra) and the **Galleria degli**

Cortile della Pigna

Arazzi (Tapestry Gallery) – this 120m-long corridor is hung with 40 huge topographical maps. These were created between 1580 and 1583 for Pope Gregory XIII based on drafts by Ignazio Danti, one of the leading cartographers of his day.

Beyond the gallery, the **Sala Sobieski** is named after an enormous 19th-century painting depicting the victory of the Polish king John III Sobieski over the Turks in 1683.

Stanze di Raffaello

These four frescoed chambers, currently undergoing partial restoration, were part of Pope Julius II's private apartments. Raphael himself painted the Stanza della Segnatura (1508–11) and the Stanza d'Eliodoro (1512–14), while the Stanza dell'Incendio (1514–17) and Sala di Costantino (1517–24) were decorated by students following his designs.

The first room you come to is the **Sala di Costantino**, which features a huge fresco depicting Constantine's defeat of Maxentius at the battle of Milvian Bridge.

The **Stanza d'Eliodoro**, which was used for private audiences, takes its name from the *Cacciata d'Eliodoro* (Expulsion of Heliodorus from the Temple), an allegorical work reflecting Pope Julius II's policy of forcing foreign powers off Church lands. To its right, the *Messa di Bolsena* (Mass of Bolsena) shows Julius paying homage to the relic of a 13th-century miracle at the lakeside town of Bolsena. Next is the *Incontro di Leone Magno con Attila* (Encounter of Leo the Great with Attila) by Raphael and his school, and, on the fourth wall, the *Liberazione di San Pietro* (Liberation of St Peter), a brilliant work illustrating Raphael's masterful ability to depict light.

The **Stanza della Segnatura**, Julius' study and library, was the first room that Raphael painted, and it's here that you'll find his great masterpiece, *La Scuola di Atene* (The School of Athens), featuring philosophers and scholars gathered around Plato and Aristotle. The seated figure in front of the steps is believed to be Michelangelo, while the figure of Plato is said to be a portrait of Leonardo da Vinci, and Euclide (the bald man bending over) is Bramante. Raphael also included a self-portrait in the

★ **Top Tip**

Most exhibits are not well labelled. Consider hiring an audio guide (€7) or buying the excellent *Guide to the Vatican Museums and City* (€14).

GUZEL STUDIO/SHUTTERSTOCK ©

lower right corner – he's the second figure from the right.

The most famous work in the **Stanza dell'Incendio di Borgo** is the *Incendio di Borgo* (Fire in the Borgo), which depicts Pope Leo IV extinguishing a fire by making the sign of the cross. The ceiling was painted by Raphael's master, Perugino.

Sistine Chapel

The jewel in the Vatican's crown, the Sistine Chapel (Cappella Sistina) is home to two of the world's most famous works of art: Michelangelo's ceiling frescoes and his *Giudizio Universale* (Last Judgment).

The chapel was originally built for Pope Sixtus IV, after whom it's named, and was consecrated on 15 August 1483. However, apart from the wall frescoes and floor, little remains of the original decor, which was sacrificed to make way for Michelangelo's two masterpieces. The first, the ceiling, was commissioned by Pope Julius II and painted between 1508 and 1512; the second, the spectacular *Giudizio Universale,* was painted between 1535 and 1541.

Michelangelo's ceiling design, which is best viewed from the chapel's main entrance in the far east wall, covers the entire 800-sq-m surface. With painted architectural features and a cast of colourful biblical characters, it's centred on nine panels depicting scenes from the Creation, the story of Adam and Eve, the Fall, and the plight of Noah.

As you look up from the east wall, the first panel is the *Drunkenness of Noah,* followed by *The Flood* and the *Sacrifice of Noah.* Next, *Original Sin and Banishment from the Garden of Eden* famously depicts Adam and Eve being sent packing after accepting the forbidden fruit from Satan, represented by a snake with the body of a woman coiled around a tree. The *Creation of Eve* is then followed by the *Creation of Adam.* This, one of the most famous images in Western art, shows a bearded God pointing his finger at Adam, thus bringing him to life. Completing the sequence are the *Separation of Land from Sea;* the *Creation*

of the Sun, Moon and Plants; and the *Separation of Light from Darkness,* featuring a fearsome God reaching out to touch the sun. Set around the central panels are 20 athletic male nudes, known as *ignudi.*

Opposite, on the west wall, is Michelangelo's mesmeric *Giudizio Universale,* showing Christ – in the centre near the top – passing sentence over the souls of the dead as they are torn from their graves to face him. The saved get to stay in heaven (in the upper right); the damned are sent down to face the demons in hell (in the bottom right).

Near the bottom, on the right, you'll see a man with donkey ears and a snake wrapped around him. This is Biagio de Cesena, the papal master of ceremonies, who was a fierce critic of Michelangelo's composition. Another famous figure is St

Raphael's Stanza della Segnatura

Bartholomew, just beneath Christ, holding his own flayed skin. The face in the skin is said to be a self-portrait of Michelangelo, its anguished look reflecting the artist's tormented faith.

The chapel's walls also boast superb frescoes. Painted between 1481 and 1482 by a crack team of Renaissance artists, including Botticelli, Ghirlandaio, Pinturicchio, Perugino and Luca Signorelli, they represent events in the lives of Moses (to the left looking at the *Giudizio Universale*) and Christ (to the right). Highlights include Botticelli's *Temptations of Christ* and Perugino's *Handing over of the Keys*.

As well as providing a showcase for priceless art, the Sistine Chapel serves an important religious function as the place where the conclave meets to elect a new pope.

✕ Take a Break

For something quick and delicious, stop by **Fa-Bìo** (☑06 6452 5810; www. fa-bio.com; Via Germanico 43; sandwiches €5; ☉10.30am-5.30pm Mon-Fri, to 4pm Sat; ☐Piazza del Risorgimento, ⓂOttaviano-San Pietro) 🍴 for a healthy salad or a tasty sandwich.

★ Did You Know

A popular Sistine Chapel myth is that Michelangelo painted the ceilings lying down. In fact, he designed a curved scaffolding that allowed him to work standing up.

Tempio di Saturno (Temple of Saturn; p374)

Roman Forum

The Roman Forum was ancient Rome's showpiece centre, a grandiose district of temples, basilicas and vibrant public spaces. Nowadays, it's a collection of impressive, if badly labelled, ruins that can leave you drained and confused. But if you can get your imagination going, there's something wonderfully compelling about walking in the footsteps of Julius Caesar and other legendary figures of Roman history.

Great For...

Map

Largo della Salara Vecchia

Via dei Fori Imperiali

Roman Forum

Colosseo

❶ Need to Know

Foro Romano; Map p382; ☎06 3996 7700; www.coopculture.it; Largo della Salara Vecchia, Piazza di Santa Maria Nova; adult/reduced incl Colosseum & Palatino €12/7.50; ☉8.30am-1hr before sunset; ☐Via dei Fori Imperiali

MARTIN M303/SHUTTERSTOCK ©

Originally an Etruscan burial ground, the Forum was first developed in the 7th century BC, growing over time to become the social, political and commercial hub of the Roman Empire. In the Middle Ages it was reduced to pasture land and extensively plundered for its marble. The area was systematically excavated in the 18th and 19th centuries and work continues to this day.

Via Sacra Towards Campidoglio

Entering the Forum from Largo della Salara Vecchia, you'll see the **Tempio di Antonino e Faustina** ahead to your left. Erected in AD 141, this was transformed into a church in the 8th century, the **Chiesa di San Lorenzo in Miranda**. To your right, is the 179 BC **Basilica Fulvia Aemilia**.

At the end of the path, you'll come to **Via Sacra**, the Forum's main thoroughfare,

and the **Tempio di Giulio Cesare**, which stands on the spot where Julius Caesar was cremated.

Heading right brings you to the **Curia**, the original seat of the Roman Senate, though what you see today is a reconstruction of how it looked in the reign of Diocletian (r 284–305).

At the end of Via Sacra, the **Arco di Settimio Severo** (Arch of Septimius Severus) is dedicated to the eponymous emperor and his sons, Caracalla and Geta. Close by the **Colonna di Foca** (Column of Phocus) rises above what was once the Forum's main square, Piazza del Foro.

The eight granite columns that rise behind the Colonna are all that survive of the **Tempio di Saturno** (Temple of Saturn), an important temple that doubled as the state treasury.

Basilica di Massenzio

Tempio di Castore e Polluce & Casa delle Vestali

From the path that runs parallel to Via Sacra, you'll pass the stubby ruins of the **Basilica Giulia**, which was begun by Caesar and finished by Augustus. At the end of the basilica, three columns remain from the 5th-century BC **Tempio di Castore e Polluce** (Temple of Castor and Pollux). Nearby, the 6th-century **Chiesa di Santa Maria Antiqua** (currently closed) is the oldest Christian church in the Forum.

Back towards Via Sacra is the **Casa delle Vestali** (House of the Vestal Virgins), home

of the virgins who tended the flame in the adjoining **Tempio di Vesta**.

Via Sacra Towards the Colosseum

Heading up Via Sacra past the **Tempio di Romolo** (Temple of Romulus), you'll come to the **Basilica di Massenzio** (Basilica di Costantino; Piazza di Santa Maria Nova), the largest building on the forum.

Beyond the basilica, the **Arco di Tito** (Arch of Titus; Piazza di Santa Maria Nova) was built in AD 81 to celebrate Vespasian and Titus' victories against rebels in Jerusalem.

What's Nearby?

Imperial Forums Archaeological Site
(Fori Imperiali; Via dei Fori Imperiali; Map p382; Via dei Fori Imperiali) The forums of Trajan, Augustus, Nerva and Caesar are known collectively as the Imperial Forums. These were largely buried when Mussolini bulldozed Via dei Fori Imperiali through the area in 1933, but excavations have since unearthed much of them. The standout sights are the **Mercati di Traiano** (Trajan's Markets), accessible through the Museo dei Fori Imperiali, and the landmark **Colonna di Traiano**.

Mercati di Traiano Museo dei Fori Imperiali Museum
(Map p382; 06 06 08; www.mercatiditraiano.it; Via IV Novembre 94; adult/reduced €11.50/9.50; 9.30am 7.30pm, last admission 6.30pm; Via IV Novembre) This striking museum brings to life the **Mercati di Traiano**, emperor Trajan's great 2nd-century complex, while also providing a fascinating introduction to the Imperial Forums with multimedia displays, explanatory panels and a smattering of archaeological artefacts.

✕ **Take a Break**

Continue up to the Capitoline Museums (p380) to enjoy inspiring views and coffee at the Caffè Capitolino.

Roman Forum

A HISTORICAL TOUR

In ancient times, a forum was a market place, civic centre and religious complex all rolled into one, and the greatest of all was the Roman Forum (Foro Romano). Situated between the Palatino (Palatine Hill), ancient Rome's most exclusive neighbourhood, and the Campidoglio (Capitoline Hill), it was the city's busy, bustling centre. On any given day it teemed with activity. Senators debated affairs of state in the ❶ Curia, shoppers thronged the squares and traffic-free streets and crowds gathered under the ❷ Colonna di Foca to listen to politicians holding forth from the ❷ Rostrum. Elsewhere, lawyers worked the courts in basilicas including the ❸ Basilica di Massenzio, while the Vestal Virgins quietly went about their business in the ❹ Casa delle Vestali.

Special occasions were also celebrated in the Forum: religious holidays were marked with ceremonies at temples such as ❺ Tempio di Saturno and ❻ Tempio di Castore e Polluce, and military victories were honoured with dramatic processions up Via Sacra and the building of monumental arches like ❼ Arco di Settimio Severo and ❽ Arco di Tito.

The ruins you see today are impressive but they can be confusing without a clear picture of what the Forum once looked like. This spread shows the Forum in its heyday, complete with temples, civic buildings and towering monuments to heroes of the Roman Empire.

TOP TIPS

➡ Get grandstand views of the Forum from the Palatino and Campidoglio.

➡ Visit first thing in the morning or late afternoon; crowds are worst between 11am and 2pm.

➡ In summer it gets hot in the Forum and there's little shade, so take a hat and plenty of water.

Colonna di Foca & Rostrum

The free-standing, 13.5m-high Column of Phocus is the Forum's youngest monument, dating to AD 608. Behind it, the Rostrum provided a suitably grandiose platform for pontificating public speakers.

Campidoglio (Capitoline Hill)

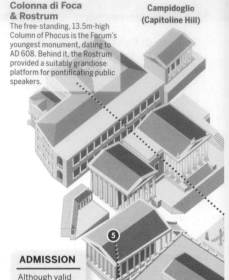

ADMISSION

Although valid for two days, admission tickets only allow for one entry into the Forum, Colosseum and Palatino.

Tempio di Saturno

Ancient Rome's Fort Knox, the Temple of Saturn was the city treasury. In Caesar's day it housed 13 tonnes of gold, 114 tonnes of silver and 30 million sestertii worth of silver coins.

IASCIC/SHUTTERSTOCK©

VIACHESLAV LOPATIN/SHUTTERSTOCK ©

Tempio di Castore e Polluce

Only three columns of the Temple of Castor and Pollux remain. The temple was dedicated to the Heavenly Twins after they supposedly led the Romans to victory over the Latin League in 496 BC.

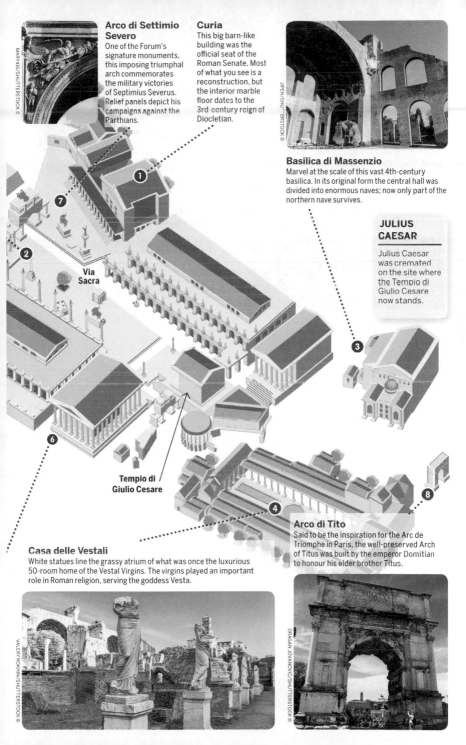

Arco di Settimio Severo
One of the Forum's signature monuments, this imposing triumphal arch commemorates the military victories of Septimius Severus. Relief panels depict his campaigns against the Parthians.

Curia
This big barn-like building was the official seat of the Roman Senate. Most of what you see is a reconstruction, but the interior marble floor dates to the 3rd-century reign of Diocletian.

Basilica di Massenzio
Marvel at the scale of this vast 4th-century basilica. In its original form the central hall was divided into enormous naves; now only part of the northern nave survives.

JULIUS CAESAR

Julius Caesar was cremated on the site where the Tempio di Giulio Cesare now stands.

Via Sacra

Templo di Giulio Cesare

Casa delle Vestali
White statues line the grassy atrium of what was once the luxurious 50-room home of the Vestal Virgins. The virgins played an important role in Roman religion, serving the goddess Vesta.

Arco di Tito
Said to be the inspiration for the Arc de Triomphe in Paris, the well-preserved Arch of Titus was built by the emperor Domitian to honour his elder brother Titus.

Centro Storico Piazzas

Rome's *centro storico* boasts some of the city's most celebrated piazzas, and several lovely but lesser-known squares. Each has its own character, but together they encapsulate much of the city's beauty, history and drama.

Start Piazza Colonna
Distance 1.5km
Duration 3½ hours

Classic Photo: Piazza della Rotonda with the Pantheon in the background.

4 It's a short walk along Via del Seminario to Piazza della Rotonda, where the **Pantheon** (p358) needs no introduction.

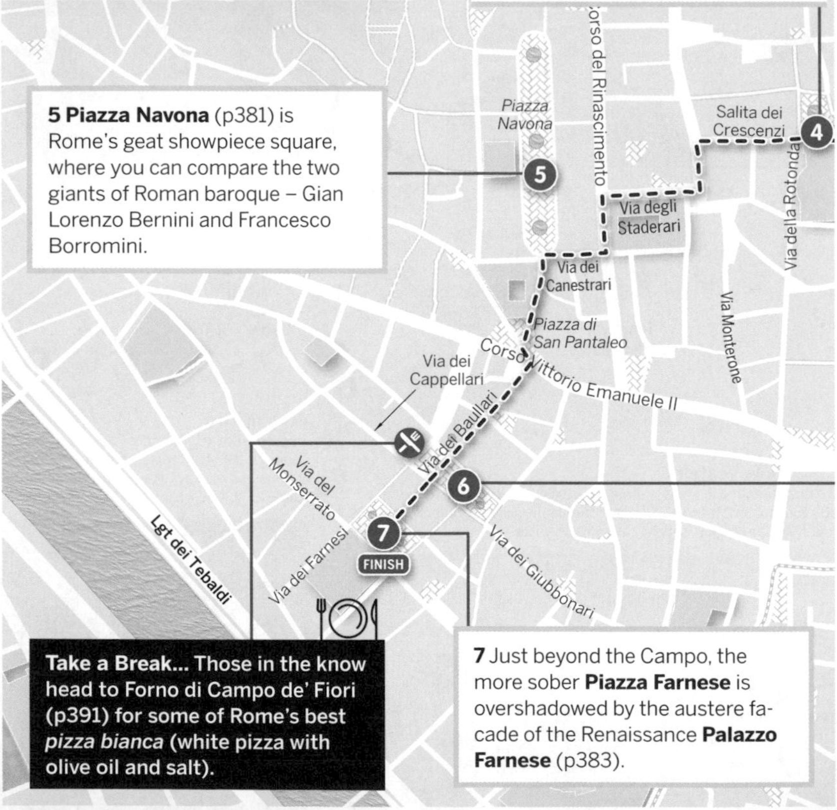

5 Piazza Navona (p381) is Rome's geat showpiece square, where you can compare the two giants of Roman baroque – Gian Lorenzo Bernini and Francesco Borromini.

Take a Break... Those in the know head to Forno di Campo de' Fiori (p391) for some of Rome's best *pizza bianca* (white pizza with olive oil and salt).

7 Just beyond the Campo, the more sober **Piazza Farnese** is overshadowed by the austere facade of the Renaissance **Palazzo Farnese** (p383).

1 Piazza Colonna is dominated by the 30m-high Colonna di Marco Aurelio and flanked by Palazzo Chigi, the official residence of the Italian PM.

2 Follow Via dei Bergamaschi to **Piazza di Pietra**, a refined space overlooked by the 2nd-century Tempio di Adriano.

3 Continue down Via de' Burro to **Piazza di Sant'Ignazio Loyola**, a small piazza with a church boasting celebrated *trompe l'œil* frescoes.

6 On the other side of Corso Vittorio Emanuele II, **Campo de' Fiori** (p383) hosts a noisy market and boisterous drinking scene.

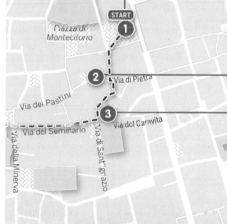

START

Piazza di Montecitorio

Via di Pietra

Via dei Pastini

Via del Seminario

Via del Caravita

Via di Sant'Ignazio

Via della Minerva

200 m
0.1 miles

◎ SIGHTS

◎ Ancient Rome

Palatino   Archaeological Site
(Palatine Hill; Map p382; ☑06 3996 7700; www.
coopculture.it; Via di San Gregorio 30, Piazza di
Santa Maria Nova; adult/reduced incl Colosseum
& Roman Forum €12/7.50; ⊙8.30am-1hr before
sunset; MColosseo) Sandwiched between the
Roman Forum and the Circo Massimo, the
Palatino (Palatine Hill) is an atmospheric
area of towering pine trees, majestic ruins
and memorable views. It was here that
Romulus supposedly founded the city in 753
BC and Rome's emperors lived in unabashed
luxury. Look out for the **stadio** (stadium), the
ruins of the **Domus Flavia** (imperial palace),
and grandstand views over the Roman
Forum from the **Orti Farnesiani**.

Capitoline Museums   Museum
(Musei Capitolini; Map p382; ☑06 06 08; www.
museicapitolini.org; Piazza del Campidoglio 1;

> *atmospheric area of towering
> pine trees, majestic ruins
> and memorable views*

Stadio in the Palatino

adult/reduced €11.50/9.50; ⊙9.30am-7.30pm,
last admission 6.30pm; ☐Piazza Venezia) Dating
from 1471, the Capitoline Museums are the
world's oldest public museums. Their collection of classical sculpture is one of Italy's
finest, including crowd-pleasers such as
the iconic *Lupa capitolina* (Capitoline Wolf),
a sculpture of Romulus and Remus under a
wolf, and the *Galata morente* (Dying Gaul),
a moving depiction of a dying Gaul warrior.
There's also a formidable picture gallery
with masterpieces by the likes of Titian,
Tintoretto, Rubens and Caravaggio.

Ticket prices increase when there's a
temporary exhibition on.

Vittoriano   Monument
(Victor Emmanuel Monument; Map p382;
Piazza Venezia; ⊙9.30am-5.30pm summer, to
4.30pm winter; ☐Piazza Venezia) FREE Love it
or loathe it, as many Romans do, you can't
ignore the Vittoriano (aka the Altare della
Patria, Altar of the Fatherland), the massive
mountain of white marble that towers over
Piazza Venezia. Begun in 1885 to honour
Italy's first king, Victor Emmanuel II – who's
immortalised in its vast equestrian statue

VIACHESLAV LOPATIN/SHUTTERSTOCK ©

– it incorporates the **Museo Centrale del Risorgimento** (📞06 679 35 98; www.risorgimento.it; adult/reduced €5/2.50; ⊙9.30am-6.30pm), a small museum documenting Italian unification, and the **Tomb of the Unknown Soldier**.

For Rome's best 360-degree views, take the **Roma dal Cielo** (adult/reduced €7/3.50; ⊙9.30am-7.30pm, last admission 7pm) lift to the top.

Bocca della Verità   Monument

(Mouth of Truth; Map p382; Piazza Bocca della Verità 18; ⊙9.30am-5.50pm; 🚇Piazza Bocca della Verità) A bearded face carved into a giant marble disc, the *Bocca della Verità* is one of Rome's most popular curiosities. Legend has it that if you put your hand in the mouth and tell a lie, the Bocca will slam shut and bite your hand off.

The mouth, which was originally part of a fountain, or possibly an ancient manhole cover, now lives in the portico of the **Chiesa di Santa Maria in Cosmedin**, a handsome medieval church.

◎ Centro Storico

Piazza Navona   Piazza

(Map p384; 🚇Corso del Rinascimento) With its showy fountains, baroque *palazzi* (mansions) and colourful cast of street artists, hawkers and tourists, Piazza Navona is central Rome's elegant showcase square. Built over the 1st-century **Stadio di Domiziano** (Domitian's Stadium; 📞06 4568 6100; www.stadiodomiziano.com; Via di Tor Sanguigna 3; adult/reduced €8/6; ⊙10am-7pm Sun-Fri, to 8pm Sat; 🚇Corso del Rinascimento), it was paved over in the 15th century and for almost 300 years hosted the city's main market. Its grand centrepiece is Bernini's **Fontana dei Quattro Fiumi** (Fountain of the Four Rivers), a flamboyant fountain featuring an Egyptian obelisk and muscular personifications of the rivers Nile, Ganges, Danube and Plate.

Galleria Doria Pamphilj   Gallery

(Map p384; 📞06 679 73 23; www.doriapamphilj.it; Via del Corso 305; adult/reduced €12/8; ⊙9am-7pm, last admission 6pm; 🚇Via del Corso) Hidden behind the grimy grey exterior of

 Via Appia Antica

Completed in 190 BC, the Appian Way connected Rome with Brindisi on Italy's Adriatic coast. It's now a picturesque area of ancient ruins, grassy fields and towering pine trees. But it has a dark history – this is where Spartacus and 6000 of his slave rebels were crucified in 71 BC, and where the ancients buried their dead. Well-to-do Romans built elaborate mausoleums, while the early Christians went underground, creating a 300km network of subterranean burial chambers – the catacombs.

Highlights include the **Catacombe di San Sebastiano** (📞06 785 03 50; www.catacombe.org; Via Appia Antica 136; adult/reduced €8/5; ⊙10am-5pm Mon-Sat Jan-Nov; 🚇Via Appia Antica) and the nearby **Catacombe di San Callisto** (📞06 513 01 51; www.catacombe.roma.it; Via Appia Antica 110-126; adult/reduced €8/5; ⊙9am-noon & 2-5pm Thu-Tue Mar-Jan; 🚇Via Appia Antica).

To get to the Via, take bus 660 from Colli Albani metro station (line A) or bus 118 from Circo Massimo (line B).

IANNIS TORIAS WERNER/SHUTTERSTOCK ©

Palazzo Doria Pamphilj, this wonderful gallery boasts one of Rome's richest private art collections, with works by Raphael, Tintoretto, Titian, Caravaggio, Bernini and Velázquez, as well as several Flemish masters. Masterpieces abound, but the undisputed star is Velázquez' portrait of an implacable Pope Innocent X, who grumbled that the depiction was 'too real'. For a comparison, check out Gian Lorenzo

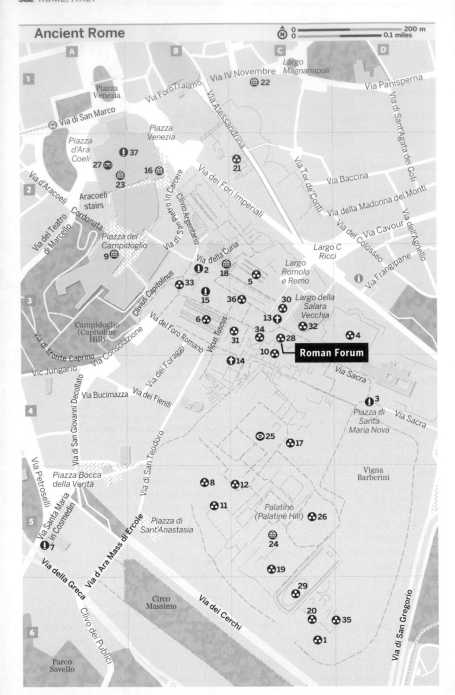

Ancient Rome

N 0 — 200 m
0 — 0.1 miles

Ancient Rome

Bernini's sculptural interpretation of the same subject.

Chiesa del Gesù — Church

(Map p384; ☑06 69 70 01; www.chiesadelgesu. org; Piazza del Gesù; ⊙7am-12.30pm & 4-7.45pm, St Ignatius rooms 4-6pm Mon-Sat, 10am-noon Sun; 🚇Largo di Torre Argentina) An imposing example of Counter Reformation architecture, Rome's most important Jesuit church is a fabulous treasure trove of baroque art. Headline works include a swirling vault fresco by Giovanni Battista Gaulli (aka Il Baciccia), and Andrea del Pozzo's opulent tomb for Ignatius Loyola, the Spanish soldier and saint who founded the Jesuits in 1540. St Ignatius lived in the church from 1544 until his death in 1556 and you can visit his private rooms to the right of the main building in the Cappella di Sant'Ignazio.

Palazzo Farnese — Historic Building

(Map p384; www.inventerrome.com; Piazza Farnese; €9; ⊙guided tours 3pm, 4pm & 5pm Mon, Wed & Fri; 🚇Corso Vittorio Emanuele II) Home of the French Embassy, this formidable Renaissance *palazzo,* one of Rome's finest, was started in 1514 by Antonio da Sangallo the Younger, continued by Michelangelo and finished by Giacomo della Porta. Inside it boasts a series of frescoes by Annibale and Agostino Carracci that are said by some to rival Michelangelo's in the Sistine Chapel. The highlight, painted between 1597 and 1608, is the monumental ceiling fresco *Amori degli Dei* (The Loves of the Gods) in the Galleria dei Carracci.

Campo de' Fiori — Piazza

(Map p384; 🚇Corso Vittorio Emanuele II) Noisy, colourful 'Il Campo' is a major focus of Roman life: by day it hosts one of Rome's best-known markets, while at night it morphs into a raucous open-air pub as drinkers spill out from its many bars and eateries. For centuries the square was the site of public executions, and it was here that philosopher Giordano Bruno was burned for heresy in 1600. The spot is marked by a sinister statue of the hooded monk, which was created by Ettore Ferrari in 1889.

Elefantino — Monument

(Map p384; Piazza della Minerva; 🚇Largo di Torre Argentina) Just south of the Pantheon, the Elefantino is a curious and much-loved statue of a puzzled-looking elephant carrying a 6th-century-BC Egyptian obelisk. Commissioned by Pope Alexander VII and completed in 1667, the elephant, symbolising strength and wisdom, was sculpted by Ercole Ferrata to a design by Gian Lorenzo

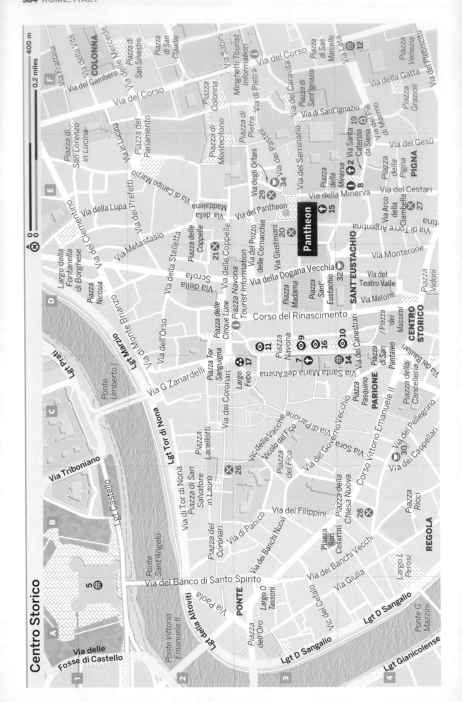

Centro Storico

400 m
0.2 miles

Via delle
Fosse di Castello

Via Triboniano

Lgt Prati

Ponte
Umberto I

Lgt Castello

Lgt Sant'Angelo

Ponte
Sant'Angelo

Ponte Vittorio
Emanuele II

Lgt della Altoviti

Via Paola

Largo O
Tassoni

Piazza
dell'Oro

Lgt D Sangalio

Vic del Cefalo

PONTE

Via del Banco di Santo Spirito

Via dei Banchi Nuovi

Largo L
Perosi

Ponte G
Mazzini

Lgt D Sangalio

Lgt Gianicolense

Via Giulia

Piazza
San
Cesarini

Via dei Banchi Vecchi

Piazza
Ricci

28

Piazza della
Chiesa Nuova

Via dei Filippini

Via di Panico

Piazza del
Coronari

Piazza di San
Salvatore
in Lauro

Via di Tor di Nona

Piazza
Lacellotti

Piazza Tor
Sanguigna

26

Via dei Coronari

Vic del Fico

Piazza
del Fico

Vic delle Vacche

Via Sora

Via del Governo Vecchio

Via di Parione

Corso Vittorio Emanuele II

PARIONE

Piazza
Pasquino

Piazza della
Cancelleria

Via del Pellegrino

Via dei Cappellari

30

REGOLA

Lgt Tor di Nona

Via di Monte Brianzo

Via dell'Orso

Ponte
Umberto I

Via G Zanardelli

Largo
Febo

17

Via Santa Maria dell'Anima

7

Piazza
Navona

11

9

16

10

14

Piazza di San
Pantaleo

Via dei Baullari

Piazza
del
Massimi

CENTRO
STORICO

Largo della
Fontanella
di Borghese

Piazza
Nicosia

Via del Clementino

Via della Stelletta

Via Metastasio

Via della Scrofa

Piazza delle
Coppelle

Piazza delle
Cinque Lune

Piazza Navona
Tourist Information

Corso del Rinascimento

Piazza
Madama

Piazza
Sant'
Eustachio

Via delle Coppelle

21

Via della Dogana Vecchia

Via del Canestrari

SANT'EUSTACHIO

Via del
Teatro Valle

Via Melone

32

Via Monterone

Via dei Prefetti

Via della Lupa

Via di Campo Marzio

Piazza del
Parlamento

Via In Lucina

Piazza di
San Lorenzo
in Lucina

Piazza del
Monticitorio

Piazza di
Montecitorio

Via del Corso

Via della
Maddalena

Via della
Maddalena

Via del Pantheon

29

34

Via degli Orfani

Via del Pozzo
delle Cornacchie

20

Via Giustiniani

Pantheon

15

Minghetti/Tourist
Information

Piazza di
Pietra

Via di Pietra

Via del Seminario

Piazza di
Sant'Ignazio

Via di Sant'Ignazio

Piazza
della
Minerva

Via della Minerva

2

1

8

19

Via Santa
Caterina
da Siena

Pie
di Marmo

Via del Gesù

Piazza
della
Pigna

PIGNA

Via dei Cestari

Via Arco
della
Ciambella

27

Via di Torre Argentina

Via del Corso

Piazza di
Claudio

Piazza
di San
Claudio

Piazza della
Vite

Piazza di
San Silvestro

COLONNA

Via del Gambero

Via Frattina

Via delle Mercede

Piazza di
Colonna

Via Sabini

Via di
San
Marcello

Via Lata

12

Piazza di
San Marcello

Piazza della Gatta

Piazza
Grazioli

Piazza
Venezia

Piazza del Plebiscito

F

E

D

C

B

A

1

2

3

4

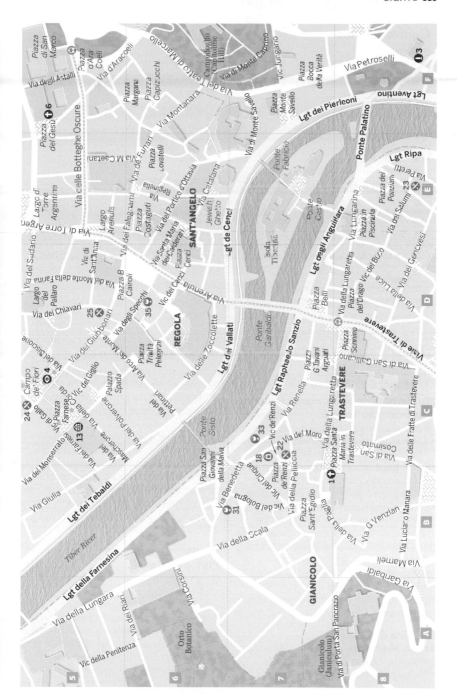

Centro Storico

Bernini. The obelisk was taken from the nearby Basilica di Santa Maria Sopra Minerva (p361).

◎ Monti & Esquilino

Museo Nazionale Romano: Palazzo Massimo alle Terme   Museum
(Map p390; ☏06 3996 7700; www.coopculture.it; Largo di Villa Peretti 1; adult/reduced €7/3.50; ⊗9am-7.45pm Tue-Sun; Ⓜ Termini) One of Rome's great unheralded museums, this is a fabulous treasure trove of classical art. The ground and 1st floors are devoted to sculpture with some breathtaking pieces – check out the *Pugile* (Boxer), a 2nd-century-BC Greek bronze; the graceful 2nd-century-BC *Ermafrodite dormiente* (Sleeping Hermaphrodite); and the idealised *Il discobolo* (Discus Thrower). It's the magnificent and vibrantly coloured frescoes on the 2nd floor, however, that are the undisputed highlight.

Basilica di Santa Maria Maggiore   Basilica
(Map p390; ☏06 6988 6800; Piazza Santa Maria Maggiore; basilica free, museum adult/reduced €3/2, museum & loggia €5/4; ⊗7am-7pm, loggia guided tours 9.30am-5.45pm; 🚇Piazza Santa Maria Maggiore) One of Rome's four patriarchal basilicas, this monumental 5th-century church stands on the summit of the Esquiline Hill, on the spot where snow is said to have miraculously fallen in the summer of AD 358. To commemorate the event, every year on 5 August thousands of white petals are released from the basilica's coffered ceiling. Much altered over the centuries, it's an architectural hybrid with 14th-century Romanesque belfry, 18th-century baroque facade, largely baroque interior and a series of glorious 5th-century mosaics.

Basilica di San Pietro in Vincoli   Basilica
(Piazza di San Pietro in Vincoli 4a; ⊗8am-12.30pm & 3-7pm summer, to 6pm winter; Ⓜ Cavour) Pilgrims and art lovers flock to this 5th-century basilica for two reasons: to marvel at Michelangelo's colossal *Moses* (1505) sculpture and to see the chains that supposedly bound St Peter when he was imprisoned in the Carcere Mamertino (near the Roman Forum). Access to the church is

via a flight of steps through a low arch that leads up from Via Cavour.

⊙ Tridente & Trevi

Trevi Fountain   Fountain

(Fontana di Trevi; Map p390; Piazza di Trevi; MBarberini) The Fontana di Trevi, scene of Anita Ekberg's dip in *La Dolce Vita,* is a flamboyant baroque ensemble of mythical figures and wild horses taking up the entire side of the 17th-century Palazzo Poli. After a Fendi-sponsored restoration finished in 2015, the fountain gleams brighter than it has for years. The tradition is to toss a coin into the water, thus ensuring that you'll return to Rome – on average about €3000 is thrown in every day.

Palazzo Barberini   Gallery

(Galleria Nazionale d'Arte Antica; Map p390; ☑06 481 45 91; www.barberinicorsini.org; Via delle Quattro Fontane 13; adult/reduced €5/2.50, incl Palazzo Corsini €10/5; ⊗8.30am-7pm Tue-Sun; MBarberini) Commissioned to celebrate the Barberini family's rise to papal power, Palazzo Barberini is a sumptuous baroque palace that impresses even before you clap eyes on the breathtaking art. Many high-profile architects worked on it, including rivals Bernini and Borromini; the former contributed a large squared staircase, the latter a helicoidal one. Amid the masterpieces, don't miss Pietro da Cortona's *Il Trionfo della Divina Provvidenza* (Triumph of Divine Providence; 1632–39), the most spectacular of the *palazzo*'s ceiling frescoes in the 1st-floor main salon.

Piazza di Spagna & the Spanish Steps   Piazza

(Map p390; MSpagna) A magnet for visitors since the 18th century, the Spanish Steps (Scalinata della Trinità dei Monti) provide a perfect people-watching perch. The 135 steps, gleaming after a recent clean-up, rise from Piazza di Spagna to the landmark **Chiesa della Trinità dei Monti** (Map p390; ☑06 679 41 79; Piazza Trinità dei Monti 3; ⊗7.30am-8pm Tue-Fri, 10am-5pm Sat & Sun).

Piazza di Spagna was named after the Spanish Embassy to the Holy See, although the staircase, designed by the Italian Francesco de Sanctis, was built in 1725 with money bequeathed by a French diplomat.

Piazza del Popolo   Piazza

(MFlaminio) This dazzling piazza was laid out in 1538 to provide a grandiose entrance to what was then Rome's main northern gateway. It has since been remodelled several times, most recently by Giuseppe Valadier in 1823. Guarding its southern approach are Carlo Rainaldi's twin 17th-century churches, **Chiesa di Santa Maria dei Miracoli** (Via del Corso 528; ⊗6.45am-12.30pm & 4.30-7.30pm Mon-Sat, 8am-1.15pm & 4.30-7.45 Sun) and **Chiesa di Santa Maria in Montesanto** (Chiesa degli Artisti; www.chiesadegliartisti.it; Via del Babuino 198; ⊗5.30-8pm Mon-Fri, 11am-1.30pm Sun). In the centre, the 36m-high **obelisk** (Piazza del Popolo) was brought by Augustus from ancient Egypt; it originally stood in Circo Massimo.

Villa Medici   Palace

(☑06 676 13 11; www.villamedici.it; Viale Trinità dei Monti 1; 1½hr guided tour adult/reduced €12/6; ⊗10am-7pm Tue-Sun; MSpagna) This sumptuous Renaissance palace was built for Cardinal Ricci da Montepulciano in 1540, but Ferdinando dei Medici bought it in 1576. It remained in Medici hands until 1801, when Napoleon acquired it for the French Academy. Guided tours take in the wonderful landscaped gardens, cardinal's painted apartments, and incredible views over Rome – tours in English depart at noon. Note the pieces of ancient Roman sculpture from the Ara Pacis embedded in the villa's walls.

Keats-Shelley House   Museum

(Map p390; ☑06 678 42 35; www.keats-shelley-house.org; Piazza di Spagna 26; adult/reduced €5/4; ⊗10am-1pm & 2-6pm Mon-Sat; MSpagna) The Keats-Shelley House is where Romantic poet John Keats died of TB at the age of 25, in February 1821. Keats came to Rome in 1820 to try to improve his health in the Italian climate, and rented two rooms on the 3rd floor of a townhouse next to the Spanish Steps, with painter companion Joseph Severn (1793–1879). Watch a film

From left: Temple and lake in Villa Borghese ; A pizzeria in Trastevere; Trevi Fountain (p387)

on the 1st floor about the Romantics, then head upstairs to see where Keats and Severn lived and worked.

Trastevere

Trastevere is one of central Rome's most vivacious neighbourhoods, a tightly packed warren of ochre *palazzi,* ivy-clad facades and photogenic lanes. Originally working class, it's now a trendy hang-out full of bars and restaurants.

Basilica di Santa Maria in Trastevere · Basilica

(Map p384; ☎06 581 4802; Piazza Santa Maria in Trastevere; ◷7.30am-9pm Sep-Jul, 8am-noon & 4-9pm Aug; ☒Viale di Trastevere, ☒Viale di Trastevere) Nestled in a quiet corner of Trastevere's focal square, this is said to be the oldest church dedicated to the Virgin Mary in Rome. In its original form, it dates from the early 3rd century, but a major 12th-century makeover saw the addition of a Romanesque bell tower and glittering facade. The portico came later, added by Carlo Fontana in 1702. Inside, the 12th-century mosaics are the headline feature.

San Giovanni & Testaccio

Basilica di San Giovanni in Laterano · Basilica

(Piazza di San Giovanni in Laterano 4; basilica/cloister free/€5 with audio guide; ◷7am-6.30pm, cloister 9am-6pm; ☒San Giovanni) For a thousand years this monumental cathedral was the most important church in Christendom. Commissioned by Constantine and consecrated in AD 324, it was the first Christian basilica built in the city and, until the late 14th century, was the pope's main place of worship. It's still Rome's official cathedral and the pope's seat as the bishop of Rome.

The basilica has been revamped several times, most notably by Borromini in the 17th century, and by Alessandro Galilei, who added the immense white facade in 1735.

Basilica di San Clemente · Basilica

(www.basilicasanclemente.com; Piazza San Clemente; excavations adult/reduced €10/5; ◷9am-12.30pm & 3-6pm Mon-Sat, 12.15-6pm Sun; ☒Via Labicana) Nowhere better illustrates the various stages of Rome's turbulent past than this fascinating multilayered church. The ground-level 12th-century basilica sits

NIKI.E.I/GETTY SHUTTERSTOCK ©

atop a 4th-century church, which, in turn, stands over a 2nd-century pagan temple and a 1st-century Roman house. Beneath everything are foundations dating from the Roman Republic.

◉ Villa Borghese

Accessible from Piazzale Flaminio, Pincio Hill and the top of Via Vittorio Veneto, **Villa Borghese** (www.sovraintendenzaroma.it; entrances at Piazzale San Paolo del Brasile, Piazzale Flaminio, Via Pinciana, Via Raimondo, Largo Pablo Picasso; ☉sunrise-sunset; 🚊Via Pinciana) is Rome's best-known park.

Museo e Galleria Borghese   Museum

(☏06 3 28 10; www.galleriaborghese.it; Piazzale del Museo Borghese 5; adult/reduced €15/8.50; ☉9am-7pm Tue-Sun; 🚊Via Pinciana) If you only have the time (or inclination) for one art gallery in Rome, make it this one. Housing what's often referred to as the 'queen of all private art collections', it boasts paintings by Caravaggio, Raphael and Titian, as well as some sensational sculptures by Bernini. Highlights abound, but look out

for Bernini's *Ratto di Proserpina* (Rape of Proserpina) and Canova's *Venere vincitrice* (Venus Victrix).

To limit numbers, visitors are admitted at two-hourly intervals, so you'll need to pre-book your ticket and get an entry time.

Museo Nazionale Etrusco di Villa Giulia   Museum

(☏06 322 65 71; www.villagiulia.beniculturali. it; Piazzale di Villa Giulia; adult/reduced €8/4; ☉8.30am-7.30pm Tue-Sun; 🚊Via delle Belle Arti) Pope Julius III's 16th-century villa provides the charming setting for Italy's finest collection of Etruscan and pre-Roman treasures. Exhibits, many of which came from tombs in the surrounding Lazio region, range from bronze figurines and black *bucchero* tableware to temple decorations, terracotta vases and a dazzling display of sophisticated jewellery.

Must-sees include a polychrome terracotta statue of Apollo from a temple in Veio and the 6th-century-BC *Sarcofago degli Sposi* (Sarcophagus of the Betrothed), found in 1881 in Cerveteri.

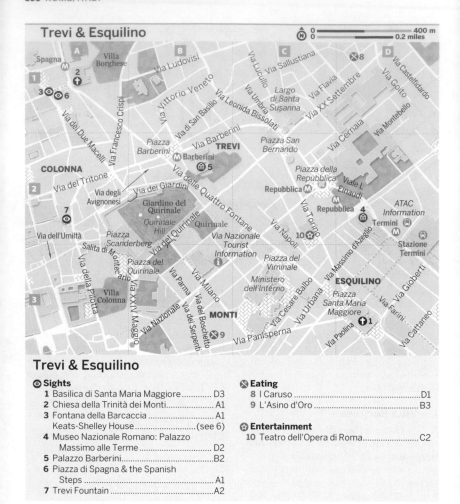

Trevi & Esquilino

🔒 SHOPPING

Rome boasts the usual cast of flagship chain stores and glitzy designer outlets, but what makes shopping here fun is its legion of small, independent shops: family-run delis, small-label fashion boutiques, artisans' studios and neighbourhood markets.

Antica Caciara Trasteverina
Food & Drinks

(📞 06 581 28 15; www.anticacaciara.it; Via San Francesco a Ripa 140; ⊙ 7am-2pm & 4-8pm Mon-Sat; 🚊 Viale di Trastevere, 🚊 Viale di Trastevere) The fresh ricotta is a prized possession at this century-old deli, and it's all usually snapped up by lunchtime. If you're too late, take solace in the to-die-for *ricotta infornata* (oven-baked ricotta), 35kg wheels of famous, black-waxed *pecorino romano* DOP (€16.50 per kilo), and aromatic garlands of *guanciale* (pig's jowl) begging to be chopped up, pan-fried and thrown into the perfect carbonara.

Benheart
Fashion & Accessories

(Map p384; 📞06 5832 0801; www.benheart.it; Via del Moro 47; ⏰11am-11pm; 🚃Piazza Triussa) From the colourful resin floor papered with children's drawings to the vintage typewriter, dial-up telephone and old-fashioned tools decorating the interior, everything about this artisanal leather boutique is achingly cool. Benheart, a young Florentine designer, is one of Italy's savviest talents and his fashionable handmade shoes (from €190) and jackets for men and women are glorious

Confetteria Moriondo & Gariglio
Chocolate

(Map p384; 📞06 699 0856; Via del Piè di Marmo 21-22; ⏰9am-7.30pm Mon-Sat; 🚃Via del Corso) Roman poet Trilussa was so smitten with this historic chocolate shop – established by the Torinese confectioners to the royal house of Savoy – that he was moved to mention it in verse. And we agree: it's a gem. Decorated like an elegant tearoom with crimson walls, tables and glass cabinets, it specialises in delicious handmade chocolates, many prepared according to original 19th-century recipes.

Re(f)use
Design

(📞06 6813 6975; www.carminacampus.com; Via della Fontanelle di Borghese 40; ⏰11am-7pm; 🚃Via del Corso) Fascinating to browse, this clever boutique showcases unique Carmina Campus pieces – primarily bags and jewellery – made from upcycled objects and recycled fabrics. The brand is the love child of Rome-born designer Ilaria Venturini Fendi (of the Fendi family), a passionate advocate of ethical fashion, who crafts contemporary bracelets from beer and soft drink cans, and bold bags from recycled materials.

Porta Portese Market
Market

(Piazza Porta Portese; ⏰6am-2pm Sun; 🚃Viale di Trastevere, 🚃Viale di Trastevere) To see another side of Rome, head to this mammoth flea market. With thousands of stalls selling everything from rare books and fell-off-a-lorry bikes to Peruvian shawls and MP3 players, it's crazily busy and a lot of fun. Keep your valuables safe and wear your haggling hat.

🍴 EATING

The most atmospheric neighbourhoods to dine in are the *centro storico* and Trastevere. There are also excellent choices in boho Monti and Testaccio. Watch out for overpriced tourist traps around Termini and the Vatican.

🍴 Centro Storico

Supplizio
Fast Food €

(Map p384; 📞06 8987 1920; www.facebook.com/supplizioroma; Via dei Banchi Vecchi 143; suppli €3-7; ⏰noon-8pm Mon-Thu, noon-3.30pm & 6.30-10.30pm Fri & Sat; 🚃Corso Vittorio Emanuele II) Rome's favourite snack, the *supplì* (a fried croquette filled with rice, tomato sauce and mozzarella), gets a gourmet makeover at this elegant street food joint. Sit back on the vintage leather sofa and dig into a crispy classic or push the boat out and try something different, maybe a little fish number stuffed with fresh anchovies, cheese, bread and raisins.

Forno Roscioli
Pizza, Bakery €

(Map p384; 📞06 686 4045; www.anticoforno roscioli.it; Via dei Chiavari 34; pizza slices from €2, snacks €2; ⏰6am-8pm Mon-Sat, 9am-7pm Sun; 🚃Via Arenula) This is one of Rome's top bakeries, much loved by lunching locals who crowd here for luscious sliced pizza, prized pastries and hunger-sating *supplì* (risotto balls). The *pizza margherita* is superb, if messy to eat, and there's also a counter serving hot pastas and vegetable side dishes.

Forno di Campo de' Fiori
Pizza, Bakery €

(Map p384; www.fornocampodefiori.com; Campo de' Fiori 22; pizza slices around €3; ⏰7.30am-2.30pm & 4.45-8pm Mon-Sat, closed Sat dinner Jul & Aug; 🚃Corso Vittorio Emanuele II) This buzzing bakery on Campo de' Fiori, divided into two adjacent shops, does a roaring trade in *panini* and delicious fresh-from-the-oven *pizza al taglio* (pizza by the slice). Aficionados swear by the *pizza bianca* ('white' pizza with olive oil, rosemary and salt), but the *panini* and *pizza rossa* ('red' pizza, with olive oil, tomato and oregano) taste plenty good too.

La Ciambella
Italian €€

(Map p384; ☎06 683 2930; www.la-ciambella. it; Via dell'Arco della Ciambella 20; meals €35-45; ⊘bar 7.30am-midnight, wine bar & restaurant noon-11pm Tue-Sun; ☐Largo di Torre Argentina) Central but largely undiscovered by the tourist hordes, this friendly wine-bar-cum-restaurant beats much of the neighbourhood competition. Its spacious, light-filled interior is set over the ruins of the Terme di Agrippa, visible through transparent floor panels, and its kitchen sends out some excellent food, from tartares and chickpea pancakes to slow-cooked beef and traditional Roman pasta.

Armando al Pantheon
Roman €€

(Map p384; ☎06 6880 3034; www.armandoal-pantheon.it; Salita dei Crescenzi 31; meals €40; ⊘12.30-3pm Mon-Sat & 7-11pm Mon-Fri; ☐Largo di Torre Argentina) With its cosy wooden interior and unwavering dedication to old-school Roman cuisine, Armando al Pantheon is a regular go-to for local foodies. It's

been trading for more than 50 years and has served its fair share of celebs, but it hasn't let fame go to its head and it remains as popular as ever. Reservations essential.

Casa Coppelle
Ristorante €€€

(Map p384; ☎06 6889 1707; www.casacoppelle. it; Piazza delle Coppelle 49; meals €65, tasting menu €85; ⊘noon-3.30pm & 6.30-11.30pm; ☐Corso del Rinascimento) Boasting an enviable setting near the Pantheon and a plush, theatrical look – think velvet drapes, black lacquer tables and bookshelves – Casa Coppelle sets a romantic stage for high end Roman-French cuisine. Gallic trademarks like snails and onion soup feature alongside updated Roman favourites such as pasta *amatriciana* (with tomato sauce and pancetta) and *cacio e pepe* (pecorino and black pepper), here re-invented as a risotto with prawns.

✖ Vatican City, Borgo & Prati

Pizzarium
Pizza €

(☎06 3974 5416; Via della Meloria 43; pizza slices €5; ⊘11am-10pm; Ⓜ Cipro-Musei Vaticani) When a pizza joint is packed on a wet

Market on Campo de' Fiori (p383)

KEN WELSH/GETTY IMAGES ©

winter lunchtime, you know it's something special. Pizzarium, the takeaway of Gabriele Bonci, Rome's acclaimed pizza king, serves Rome's best sliced pizza, bar none. Scissor-cut squares of soft, springy base are topped with original combinations of seasonal ingredients and served on paper trays for immediate consumption. Also worth trying are the freshly fried *supplì* (crunchy rice croquettes).

✪ Monti & Esquilino

L'Asino d'Oro Italian €€

(Map p390; ✆06 4891 3832; www.facebook. com/asinodoro; Via del Boschetto 73; weekday lunch menu €16, meals €45; ☺12.30-2.30pm & 7.30-11pm Tue-Sat; Ⓜ Cavour) This fabulous restaurant was transplanted from Orvieto, and its Umbrian origins resonate in Lucio Sforza's exceptional cooking. Unfussy yet innovative dishes feature bags of flavourful contrasts, like lamb meatballs with pear and blue cheese. Save room for the equally amazing desserts. Intimate, informal and classy, this is one of Rome's best deals – its lunch menu is a steal.

✪ Trastevere

Da Augusto Trattoria €

(Map p384; ✆06 580 37 98; Piazza de' Renzi 15; meals €25; ☺12.30-3pm & 8-11pm; 🚃 Viale di Trastevere, 🚃 Viale di Trastevere) Bag one of Augusto's rickety tables outside and tuck into some truly fabulous mamma-style cooking on one of Trastevere's prettiest piazza terraces. Hearty portions of all the Roman classics are dished up here as well as lots of rabbit, veal, hare and *pajata* (calf intestines). Winter dining is around vintage formica tables in a bare-bones interior, unchanged for decades. Be prepared to queue. Cash only.

Da Enzo Trattoria €

(Map p384; ✆06 581 22 60; www.daenzoal29. com; Via dei Vascellari 29; meals €30; ☺12.30-3pm & 7-11pm Mon-Sat; 🚃 Viale di Trastevere, 🚃 Viale di Trastevere) Vintage buttermilk walls, red chequered tablecloths and a traditional menu featuring all the Roman classics: what

🍽 Rome's Best Gelato

Fatamorgana (✆06 3265 2238; www. gelateriafatamorgana.com; Via Laurina 10; 2/3/4/5 scoops €2.50/3.50/4.50/5; ☺noon-11pm; Ⓜ Flaminio) Superb artisanal flavours at multiple central locations.

Gelateria del Teatro (Map p384; ✆06 4547 4880; www.gelateriadelteatro.it; Via dei Coronari 65; gelato €2.50-5; ☺10.30am-8pm winter, 10am-10.30pm summer; 🚃 Via Zanardelli) Seasonal fruit and spicy chocolate flavours, all made on site.

I Caruso (Map p390; ✆06 4201 6420; Via Collina 13-15; cones & tubs from €2.50; ☺noon-midnight; Ⓜ Repubblica) A small but perfect selection of creamy flavours.

Venchi (Map p384; ✆06 6992 5423; www. venchi.com; Via degli Orfani 87; gelato €2.50-5; ☺10.30am-11pm Sun-Thu, to midnight Fri & Sat summer, 10am-10pm Sun-Thu, to 11pm Fri & Sat winter; 🚃 Via del Corso) Nirvana for chocoholics.

makes this staunchly traditional trattoria exceptional is its careful sourcing of local, quality products, many from nearby farms in Lazio. The seasonal, deep-fried Jewish artichokes and the *pasta cacio e pepe* (cheese and black pepper pasta) in particular are among the best in Rome.

✪ San Giovanni & Testaccio

Sbanco Pizza €€

(✆06 78 93 18; Via Siria 1; pizzas €7.50-12.50; ☺7.30pm-midnight; 🚃 Piazza Zama) With its informal warehouse vibe and buzzing

Rome for Free

Some of Rome's most famous sights are free, including all state museums and monuments on the first Sunday of the month, and all of Rome's churches.

Vatican Museums (p367) Free on the last Sunday of the month.

Trevi Fountain (p387)

Spanish Steps (p387)

Pantheon (p358)

St Peter's Basilica (p363)

atmosphere, Sbanco is one of the capital's hottest pizzerias. Since opening in 2016, it has quickly made a name for itself with its creative, wood-fired pizzas and sumptuous fried starters – try the carbonara *supplì* (risotto balls). To top things off, it serves some deliciously drinkable craft beer.

🍷 DRINKING & NIGHTLIFE

Much of the drinking action is in the *centro storico*: Campo de' Fiori is popular with students, while the area around Piazza Navona hosts a more upmarket scene. Over the river, Trastevere is another favoured spot with dozens of bars and pubs.

Rome's clubbing scene is centred on Testaccio and the Ostiense area, although you'll also find places in Trastevere and the *centro storico*. Admission to clubs is often free, but drinks are expensive.

Il Tiaso   Bar

(☎06 4547 4625; www.iltiaso.com; Via Ascoli Piceno 25; ☺6pm-2am; ⛛; ⛽Circonvallazione Casilina) Think living room with zebra-print chairs, walls of indie art, Lou Reed biographies wedged between wine bottles, and 30-something owner Gabriele playing a New York Dolls album to neo-beatnik chicks, corduroy-clad professors and the odd neighbourhood dog. Expect well-priced wine, an intimate chilled vibe, regular live music and lovely pavement terrace.

Barnum Cafe   Cafe

(Map p384; ☎06 6476 0483; www.barnumcafe. com; Via del Pellegrino 87; ☺9am-10pm Mon, to 2am Tue-Sat; ⛛; ⛽Corso Vittorio Emanuele II) A laid-back *Friends*-style cafe, evergreen Barnum is the sort of place you could quickly get used to. With its shabby-chic vintage furniture and white bare-brick walls, it's a relaxed spot for a breakfast cappuccino, a light lunch or a late afternoon drink. Come evening, a coolly dressed-down crowd sips seriously good cocktails.

Caffè Sant'Eustachio   Coffee

(Map p384; www.santeustachioilcaffe.it; Piazza Sant'Eustachio 82; ☺8.30am-1am Sun-Thu, to 1.30am Fri, to 2am Sat; ⛽Corso del Rinascimento) This small, unassuming cafe, generally three deep at the bar, is reckoned by many to serve the best coffee in town. To make it, the bartenders sneakily beat the first drops of an espresso with several teaspoons of sugar to create a frothy paste to which they add the rest of the coffee. It's superbly smooth and guaranteed to put some zing into your sightseeing.

Open Baladin   Bar

(Map p384; ☎06 683 8989; www.openbaladinroma.it; Via degli Specchi 6; ☺noon-2am; ⛛; ⛽Via Arenula) For some years, this cool, modern pub near Campo de' Fiori has been a leading light in Rome's craft beer scene, and it's still a top place for a pint with more than 40 beers on tap and up to 100 bottled brews, many from Italian artisanal microbreweries. There's also a decent food menu with *panini*, gourmet burgers and daily specials.

La Casa del Caffè
Tazza d'Oro   Coffee

(Map p384; ☎06 678 9792; www.tazzadorocoffeeshop.com; Via degli Orfani 84-86; ☺7am-8pm Mon-Sat, 10.30am-7.30pm Sun; ⛽Via del Corso) A busy, stand-up affair with burnished 1940s fittings, this is one of Rome's best coffee houses. Its espresso hits the mark nicely and there's a range of delicious coffee concoctions, including a cooling *granita di caffè*, a crushed-ice coffee drink served with whipped cream. There's also a small shop and, outside, a coffee *bancomat* for those out-of-hours caffeine emergencies.

Bir & Fud   Craft Beer

(Map p384; ☑06 589 40 16; www.birandfud.it; Via Benedetta 23; ⊘noon-2am; ☐Piazza Trilussa) On a narrow street lined with raucous drinking holes, this brick-vaulted bar-pizzeria wins plaudits for its outstanding collection of craft *bir* (beer), many on tap, and equally tasty *fud* (food) for when late-night munchies strike. Its Neapolitan-style wood-fired pizzas are particularly excellent.

Freni e Frizioni   Bar

(Map p384; ☑06 4549 7499; www.freniefrizioni. com; Via del Politeama 4-6; ⊘7pm-2am; ☐Piazza Trilussa) This perennially cool Trastevere bar is housed in an old mechanic's workshop – hence its name ('brakes and clutches') and tatty facade. It draws a young *spritz*-loving crowd that swells onto the small piazza outside to sip superbly mixed cocktails (€10) and seasonal punches, and fill up on its lavish early-evening *aperitivo* buffet (7pm to 10pm). Table reservations are essential on Friday and Saturday evenings.

⊕ ENTERTAINMENT

Rome has a thriving cultural scene, with a year-round calendar of concerts, performances and festivals. Upcoming events are also listed on www.turismoroma.it and www.inromenow.com.

Auditorium Parco
della Musica   Concert Venue

(☑06 8024 1281; www.auditorium.com; Viale Pietro de Coubertin; ☐Viale Tiziano) The hub of Rome's thriving cultural scene, the Auditorium is the capital's premier concert venue. Its three concert halls offer superb acoustics, and together with a 3000-seat open-air arena, stage everything from classical music concerts to jazz gigs, public lectures and film screenings.

The Auditorium is also home to Rome's world-class **Orchestra dell'Accademia Nazionale di Santa Cecilia** (www.santa cecilia.it).

Alexanderplatz   Jazz

(☑06 8377 5604; www.facebook.com/alex ander.platz.37; Via Ostia 9; ⊘8.30pm-1.30am;

Restaurants in Trastevere

Teatro dell'Opera di Roma

Ⓜ Ottaviano-San Pietro) Intimate, underground, and hard to find – look for the discreet black door – Rome's most celebrated jazz club draws top Italian and international performers and a respectful cosmopolitan crowd. Book a table for the best stage views or to dine here, although note that it's the music that's the star act not the food.

Teatro dell'Opera di Roma
Opera, Ballet

(Map p390; 📞 06 48 16 01; www.operaroma.it; Piazza Beniamino Gigli 1; ⊙ box office 10am-6pm Mon-Sat, 9am-1.30pm Sun; Ⓜ Repubblica) Rome's premier opera house boasts a plush gilt interior, a Fascist 1920s exterior and an impressive history: it premiered Puccini's *Tosca,* and Maria Callas once sang here. Opera and ballet performances are staged between September and June.

❶ INFORMATION

DANGERS & ANNOYANCES

Rome is not a dangerous city, but petty theft can be a problem. Watch out for pickpockets around the big tourist sites, at Stazione Termini and on crowded public transport – the 64 Vatican bus is notorious.

MEDICAL SERVICES

Policlinico Umberto I (📞 06 4 99 71; www.policlinicoumberto1.it; Viale del Policlinico 155; Ⓜ Policlinico, Castro Pretorio) Rome's largest hospital is located near Stazione Termini.

TOURIST INFORMATION

For phone enquiries, there's a **tourist information line** (📞 06 06 08; www.060608.it; ⊙ 9am-9pm), and for information about the Vatican, contact the **Centro Servizi Pellegrini e Turisti** (📞 06 6988 1662; St Peter's Square; ⊙ 8.30am-6.30pm Mon-Sat; 🚇 Piazza del Risorgimento, Ⓜ Ottaviano-San Pietro).

There are tourist information points at **Fiumicino** (Fiumicino Airport; International Arrivals, Terminal 3; ⊙ 8am-8.45pm) and **Ciampino** (Arrivals Hall; ⊙ 8.30am-6pm) airports, and at locations across town.

Fori Imperiali Tourist Information (Via dei Fori Imperiali; ⊙ 9.30am-7pm; 🚇 Via dei Fori Imperiali)

Has a useful panel illustrating the Roman and Imperial Forums.

Minghetti Tourist Information (06 06 08; www.turismoroma.it; Via Marco Minghetti; 9.30am-7pm; Via del Corso) Info kiosk between Via del Corso and the Trevi Fountain.

Piazza Navona Tourist Information (Piazza delle Cinque Lune; 9.30am-7pm; Corso del Rinascimento) Located just off Piazza Navona.

Stazione Termini Tourist Information (06 06 08; www.turismoroma.it; Via Giovanni Giolitti 34; 9am-5pm; Termini) Located inside the station next to the Mercato Centrale, not far from the car rental and left luggage desk. Pick up city maps and reserve city tours.

Via Nazionale Tourist Information (06 06 08; www.turismoroma.it; Via Nazionale 184; 9.30am-7pm; Via Nazionale) In front of Palazzo delle Esposizioni.

 GETTING THERE & AWAY

AIR

Rome's main international airport, **Leonardo da Vinci** (Fiumicino; 06 6 59 51; www.adr.it/fiumicino), better known as Fiumicino, is on the coast 30km west of the city.

The much smaller **Ciampino Airport** (www.ciampino-airport.info), 15km southeast of the city centre, is the hub for European low-cost carrier Ryanair.

BOAT

The nearest port to Rome is at Civitavecchia, about 80km north. Ferries sail here from Spain, Tunisia, Sicily and Sardinia. Book tickets at travel agents or online at www.traghettiweb.it. You can also buy directly at the port.

Half-hourly trains connect Civitavecchia and Termini (€5 to €15.50, 40 minutes to 1¼ hours).

BUS

Long-distance national and international buses use the **Autostazione Tiburtina** (Tibus; Largo Guido Mazzoni; Tiburtina). Get tickets at the bus station or at travel agencies.

 Roma Pass

A cumulative sightseeing and transport card, available online or from tourist information points and participating museums, the Roma Pass (www.romapass.it) comes in two forms:

72 hours (€38.50) Provides free admission to two museums or sites, as well as reduced entry to extra sites, unlimited city transport, and discounted entry to other exhibitions and events.

48 hours (€28) Gives free admission to one museum or site, and then as per the 72-hour pass.

CAR & MOTORCYCLE

Rome is circled by the Grande Raccordo Anulare (GRA), to which all autostrade (motorways) connect, including the main A1 north–south artery, and the A12, which runs to Civitavecchia and Fiumicino airport.

Car hire is available at the airport and Stazione Termini.

TRAIN

Rome's main station is **Stazione Termini** (www.romatermini.com; Piazza dei Cinquecento; Termini). It has regular connections to other European countries, all major Italian cities and many smaller towns. **Left luggage** (Stazione Termini; 1st 5hr €6, 6-12hr per hour €0.90, 13hr & over per hour €0.40; 6am-11pm; Termini) is in the wing on the Via Giolitti side of the station, near the tourist office.

Rome's other principal train stations are Stazione Tiburtina and Stazione Roma-Ostiense.

 GETTING AROUND

TO/FROM THE AIRPORTS

FIUMICINO

The easiest way to get to/from Fiumicino is by train, but there are also bus services. The set taxi fare to the city centre is €48 (valid for up to four people with luggage).

Leonardo Express Train (one way €14) Runs to/from Stazione Termini. Departures from Fiumicino airport every 30 minutes between 6.23am and 11.23pm; from Termini between 5.35am and 10.35pm. Journey time is 30 minutes.

FL1 Train (one way €8) Connects to Trastevere, Ostiense and Tiburtina stations, but not Termini. Departures from Fiumicino airport every 15 minutes (half-hourly on Sundays and public holidays) between 5.57am and 10.42pm; from Tiburtina every 15 minutes between 5.01am and 7.31pm, then half-hourly to 10.01pm.

CIAMPINO

The best option from Ciampino is to take one of the regular bus services into the city centre. The set taxi fare to the centre is €30.

SIT Bus – Ciampino (☑06 591 68 26; www.sitbusshuttle.com; from/to airport €5/6, return €9) Regular departures from the airport to Via Marsala outside Stazione Termini between 7.45am and 11.15pm; from Termini between 4.30am and 9.30pm. Get tickets on the bus. Journey time is 45 minutes.

Schiaffini Rome Airport Bus – Ciampino (☑06 713 05 31; www.romeairportbus.com; Via Giolitti; one way/return €4.90/7.90) Regular departures to/from Via Giolitti outside Stazione Termini. From the airport, services are between 4am and 10.50pm; from Via Giolitti, buses run from 4.50am to midnight. Buy tickets onboard, online, at the airport, or at the bus stop. Journey time is approximately 40 minutes.

PUBLIC TRANSPORT

Rome's public transport system includes buses, trams, a metro and a suburban train network.

Tickets are valid on all forms of public transport, except for routes to Fiumicino airport. Buy tickets at *tabacchi*, newsstands or from vending machines. They come in various forms:

BIT (€1.50) Valid for 100 minutes and one metro ride.

Roma 24h (€7) Valid for 24 hours.

Roma 48h (€12.50) Valid for 48 hours.

Roma 72h (€18) Valid for 72 hours.

BUS

○ Rome's buses and trams are run by **ATAC** (☑06 5 70 03; www.atac.roma.it).

○ The main bus station is in front of Stazione Termini on Piazza dei Cinquecento, where there's an **information booth** (Piazza dei Cinquecento; ⊙8am-8pm; Ⓜ Termini).

○ Other important hubs are at Largo di Torre Argentina and Piazza Venezia.

○ Buses run from about 5.30am to midnight, with limited services throughout the night.

METRO

○ Rome has two main metro lines, A (orange) and B (blue), which cross at Termini.

○ Trains run from 5.30am to 11.30pm (to 1.30am on Fridays and Saturdays).

TAXI

○ Official licensed taxis are white with an ID number and *Roma Capitale* on the sides.

○ Always go with the metered fare, never an arranged price (the set fares to and from the airports are exceptions).

Where to Stay

Accommodation in Rome is expensive, and with the city busy year-round, you'll want to book as far ahead as you can to secure the best deal.

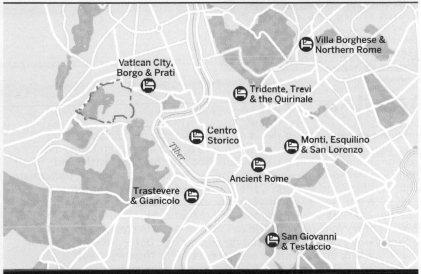

Neighbourhood	Atmosphere
Ancient Rome	Close to major sights such as the Colosseum and Roman Forum; quiet at night; not cheap; restaurants are touristy.
Centro Storico	Atmospheric area with everything on your doorstep – Pantheon, Piazza Navona, restaurants, bars, shops, most expensive part of town; can be noisy.
Tridente, Trevi & the Quirinale	Good for Spanish Steps, Trevi Fountain and designer shopping; excellent midrange to top end options; good transport links.
Vatican City, Borgo & Prati	Near St Peter's Basilica; decent range of accommodation; some excellent shops and restaurants; on the metro; not much nightlife; sells out quickly for religious holidays.
Monti, Esquilino & San Lorenzo	Lots of budget accommodation around Stazione Termini; top eating in Monti and good nightlife in San Lorenzo; good transport links; some dodgy streets near Termini.
Trastevere & Gianicolo	Gorgeous, atmospheric area; party vibe with hundreds of bars, cafes and restaurants; expensive; noisy, particularly in summer.
San Giovanni & Testaccio	Authentic atmosphere with good eating and drinking options; Testaccio is a top food and nightlife district; not many big sights.
Villa Borghese & Northern Rome	Largely residential area good for the Auditorium and Stadio Olimpico; some top museums; generally quiet after dark.

In This Chapter

Venice, Italy

Imagine the audacity of deciding to build a city of marble palaces on a lagoon. Instead of surrendering to acque alte (high tides) like reasonable folk might do, Venetians flooded the world with vivid painting, baroque music, modern opera, spice-route cuisine, bohemian-chic fashions and a Grand Canal's worth of spritz: the signature prosecco and Aperol cocktail. Today, cutting-edge architects and billion-aire benefactors are spicing up the art scene, musicians are rocking out 18th-century instruments and backstreet osterie (taverns) are winning a Slow Food following. Your timing couldn't be better: the people who made walking on water look easy are well into their next act.

Venice in Two Days

Spend your first day in Venice cruising the **Grand Canal** (p402), hopping on and off *vaporetti* as the mood takes you.

On the second day rise early to get to **Basilica di San Marco** (p405) and **Palazzo Ducale** (p407), then revive your spirits (but not your wallet!) at **Caffè Florian** (p416). Glimpse gorgeous **La Fenice** (p416), and make sure you don't leave Venice without indulging in an evening **gondola trip**.

Venice in Four Days

Explore **Ca' Rezzonico** (p410), then choose between the **Gallerie dell'Accademia** (p410) and the **Peggy Guggenheim** (p410) before finishing at the **Basilica di Santa Maria della Salute** (p411). On day four begin at the **Rialto Market** (p411), then wander to Gothic **I Frari** (p411). Once admired, slip into **Scuola Grande di San Rocco** (p410) for prime-time-drama Tintorettos.

After Venice hop on the train to Rome (p352) or glam out in the Swiss Alps (p586).

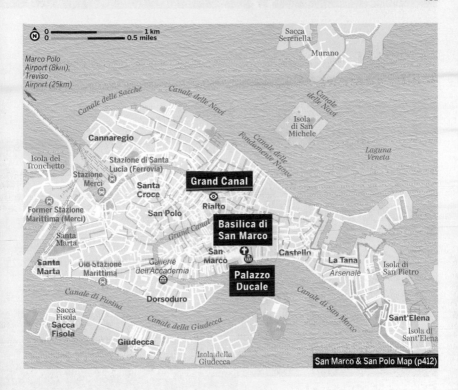

Marco Polo
Airport (8km);
Treviso
Airport (25km)

Sacca
Serenella

Murano

Canale delle Sacche

Canale delle Navi

Canale
della Navi

Cannaregio

Isola
di San
Michele

Laguna
Veneta

Isola del
Tronchetto

Stazione di Santa
Lucia (Ferrovia)

Canale delle
Fondamente Nuove

Stazione
Merci

Santa
Croce

Grand Canal

Former Stazione
Marittima (Merci)

San Polo

Rialto

Santa
Marta

Grand Canal

**Basilica di
San Marco**

Santa
Marta

Old Stazione
Marittima

Gallerie
dell'Accademia

San
Marco

Castello

La Tana

Isola di
San Pietro

Arsenale

**Palazzo
Ducale**

Canale di San Marco

Canale di Fusina

Dorsoduro

Sacca
Fisola

**Sacca
Fisola**

Canale della Giudecca

Sant'Elena

Isola di
Sant'Elena

Giudecca

Isola della
Giudecca

San Marco & San Polo Map (p412)

Arriving in Venice

Marco Polo airport Located on the mainland 12km from Venice. Alilaguna operates a ferry service (€15) to Venice from the airport ferry dock. Water taxis cost from €110. Half-hourly buses (€6) connect with Piazzale Roma.

Stazione Santa Lucia Venice's train station. *Vaporetti* (small passenger boats) depart from Ferrovia (Station) docks.

Stazione Venezia Mestre The mainland train station; transfer here to Stazione Santa Lucia.

Where to Stay

With many Venetians opening their homes to visitors, you can become a local overnight. Venice was once known for charmingly decrepit hotels where English poets quietly expired, but new design-literate boutique hotels are glamming up historic palaces. In peak seasons quality hotels fill up fast. In summer, many people decamp to the Lido where prices are more reasonable.

Grand Canal

Never was a thoroughfare so aptly named as the Grand Canal. Snaking through the heart of the city, Venice's signature waterway is flanked by a magnificent array of Gothic, Moorish, Renaissance and Rococo palaces.

Great For...

☑ **Don't Miss**

The Ponte di Rialto, the Palazzo Grassi and the iconic Basilica di Santa Maria della Salute.

For most people, a trip down the Canal starts near the train station, near the Ponte di Calatrava. Officially known as the Ponte della Costituzione (Constitution Bridge), this contemporary bridge, designed by avant-garde Spanish architect Santiago Calatrava in 2008, is one of the few modern structures you'll see in central Venice.

To the Rialto

Leaving the bridge in your wake, one of the first landmarks you'll pass is the arcaded Gothic facade of the **Ca' d'Oro** (☏041 520 03 45; www.cadoro.org; Calle di Ca' d'Oro 3932; adult/reduced €8.50/4.25; ⏱8.15am-2pm Mon, to 7.15pm Tue-Sun; ⛴Ca' d'Oro), a 15th-century palazzo that now houses an art museum.

Ponte di Rialto & Around

A short way on, the Ponte di Rialto (p411) is the oldest of the four bridges that cross

Stazione di Santa
Lucia (Ferrovia)

Stazione
Merci

Grand Canal ⊙

*Canale di
San Marco*

---

❶ Need to Know

Take *vaporetti* 1 or 2 from the Ferrovia;
it takes 35 to 40 minutes to Piazza San
Marco.

✕ Take a Break

Jump off at Rialto and search out **Cantina Do Spade** (⊘041 521 05 83; www.
cantinadospade.com; Calle delle Do Spade
860, San Polo; ⊙10am-3pm & 6-10pm; 🕿;
🚣Rialto-Mercato) for a cosy drink.

★ Top Tip

Avoid the crowds and tour the canal in
the early evening or at night.

---

the canal. Nearby, local shoppers crowd to
the Rialto Market (p411) and Pescaria
fish market (p411).

Palazzo Grassi

The clean, geometric form of **Palazzo
Grassi** (⊘041 200 10 57; www.palazzograssi.
it; Campo San Samuele 3231; adult/reduced
incl Punta della Dogana €18/15; ⊙10am-7pm
Wed-Mon mid-Apr–Nov; 🚣San Samuele) comes
into view on the first bend after the Rialto. A
noble 18th-century palace, it now provides
the neo-classical setting for show-stopping
contemporary art. Over the water, spy out
the sumptuous Ca' Rezzonico (p410).

Ponte dell'Accademia & Around

A couple of ferry stops further down and
you arrive at the wooden Ponte dell'Accademia, a bridge whose simple design
seems strangely out of place amid Venice's

fairy-tale architecture. For an art gallery
interlude, head to the nearby Gallerie
dell'Accademia (p410) or the Peggy
Guggenheim (p410).

Basilica di Santa Maria della Salute

The imperious dome of the Basilica di
Santa Maria della Salute (p411) has been
overlooking the canal's entrance since
the 17th century. Beyond the basilica, the
Punta della Dogana (⊘041 271 90 39; www.
palazzograssi.it; Fondamente della Dogana alla
Salute 2, Dorsoduro; adult/reduced €15/10, incl
Palazzo Grassi €18/15; ⊙10am-7pm Wed-Mon
Apr-Nov; 🚣Salute) is a former customs
warehouse that now stages contemporary
art exhibitions.

St Marks & Palazzo Ducale

You're now at the mouth of the canal, where
you can disembark for Piazza San Marco.
Dominating the waterside here is Palazzo
Ducale (p407), the historic residence of
the Venetian Doges.

Claudio Stocco/Shutterstock ©

Basilica di San Marco

With its profusion of spires and domes, lavish marble-work and 8500 sq metres of luminous mosaics, the Basilica di San Marco, Venice's signature basilica, is an unforgettable sight.

Great For...

☑ Don't Miss

Loggia dei Cavalli, where reproductions of the four bronze horses gallop off the balcony over Piazza San Marco.

The basilica was founded in the 9th century to house the corpse of St Mark after wily Venetian merchants smuggled it out of Egypt in a barrel of pork fat. When the original burnt down in 932 Venice rebuilt the basilica in its own cosmopolitan image, with Byzantine domes, a Greek cross layout and walls clad in marble from Syria, Egypt and Palestine.

Exterior & Portals

The front of St Mark's ripples and crests like a wave, its five niched portals capped with shimmering mosaics and frothy stonework arches. The oldest mosaic on the facade (1270) is in the lunette above the far-left portal, depicting St Mark's stolen body arriving at the basilica. The theme is echoed in three of the other lunettes,

Gold-leaf mosaics inside Basilica di San Marco

❶ Need to Know

St Mark's Basilica; ☑041 270 83 11; www.
basilicasanmarco.it; Piazza San Marco;
☉9.45am-5pm Mon-Sat, 2 5pm Sun summer,
to 4pm Sun winter; ⛴San Marco FREE

✕ Take a Break

Treat yourself to a *bellini* at world-
famous **Harry's Bar** (☑041 528 57 77;
www.harrysbarvenezia.com; Calle Vallaresso
1323; ☉10.30am-11pm).

★ Top Tip

There's no charge to enter the church
and wander around the roped-off
central circuit, although you'll need
to dress modestly, with knees and
shoulders covered.

including one showing turbaned officials
recoiling from the hamper of pork fat containing the sainted corpse.

Mosaics

Blinking is natural upon your first glimpse
of the basilica's glittering ceiling mosaics,
many made with 24-carat gold leaf. Just
inside the vestibule are the basilica's oldest
mosaics: Apostles with the Madonna,
standing sentry by the main door for more
than 950 years. Inside the church proper,
three golden domes vie for your attention.
The Pentecost Cupola shows the Holy Spirit, represented by a dove, shooting tongues
of flame onto the heads of the surrounding
saints. In the central 13th-century Ascen-
sion Cupola, angels swirl around the central
figure of Christ hovering among the stars.

Pala d'Oro

Tucked behind the main altar (€2), this
stupendous golden screen is studded with
2000 emeralds, amethysts, sapphires,
rubies, pearls and other gemstones. But
the most priceless treasures here are
biblical figures in vibrant cloisonné, begun
in Constantinople in AD 976 and elaborated
by Venetian goldsmiths in 1209.

Tesoro & Museum

Holy bones and booty from the Crusades
fill the Tesoro (Treasury; €3); while ducal
treasures on show in the **museum** (adult/
reduced €5/2.50; ☉9.45am-4.45pm) would
put a king's ransom to shame. A highlight is
the Quadriga of St Mark's, a group of four
bronze horses originally plundered from
Constantinople and later carted off to Paris
by Napoleon before being returned to the
basilica and installed in the 1st-floor gallery.

Palazzo Ducale

Gothic Palazzo Ducale was the doge's official residence and the seat of the Venetian Republic's government (and location of its prisons) for over seven centuries.

Although the ducal palace probably moved to this site in the 10th century, the current complex only started to take shape in around 1340. In 1424 the wing facing Piazzetta San Marco was added and the palace assumed its final form, give or take a few major fires and refurbishments.

First Floor

The doge's suite of private 1st-floor rooms is now used to house temporary art exhibitions, which are ticketed separately (around €10 extra). The doge lived like a caged lion in his gilded suite in the palace, which he could not leave without permission. The most intriguing room is the Sala dello Scudo (Shield Room), covered with world maps that reveal the extent of Venetian power (and the limits of its cartographers).

Great For...

☑ Don't Miss

The face of a grimacing man with his mouth agape at the top of the Scala d'Oro; this was a post box for secret accusations.

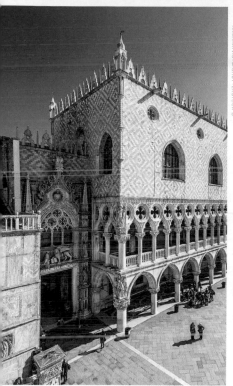

Piazza
San Marco

**Palazzo
Ducale**

Piazzetta
San Marco

Canale di
San Marco

❶ Need to Know

Ducal Palace; ☎041 271 59 11; www.palazzo
ducale.visitmuve.it; Piazzetta San Marco 1;
adult/reduced incl Museo Correr €19/12, or
with Museum Pass; ⏰8.30am-7pm Apr-Oct, to
5.30pm Nov-Mar; ⛴San Zaccaria

✖ Take a Break

Continue the rarefied vibe within the
jewellery-box interior of Caffè Florian
(p416).

★ Top Tip

Check www.palazzoducale.visitmuve.
it for details of Secret Itineraries tours
and special openings.

Second Floor

Ascend Sansovino's 24-carat gilt stucco-
work Scala d'Oro (Golden Staircase) and
emerge into 2nd-floor rooms covered with
gorgeous propaganda. In the Palladio-
designed Sala delle Quattro Porte (Hall
of the Four Doors), ambassadors awaited
ducal audiences under a lavish display of
Venice's virtues by Giovanni Cambi, Titian
and Tiepolo.

Few were granted an audience in the
Palladio-designed Collegio (Council Room),
where Veronese's 1575–78 *Virtues of the
Republic* ceiling shows Venice as a bewitching blonde waving her sceptre like a wand
over Justice and Peace. Father-son team
Jacopo and Domenico Tintoretto attempt
similar flattery, showing Venice keeping
company with Apollo, Mars and Mercury in

their *Triumph of Venice* ceiling for the Sala
del Senato (Senate Hall).

Government cover-ups were never so
appealing as in the Sala Consiglio dei Dieci
(Trial Chambers of the Council of Ten), where
Venice's star chamber plotted under Ve-
ronese's *Juno Bestowing Her Gifts on Venice*.
Arcing over the Sala della Bussola (Compass
Room) is his *St Mark in Glory* ceiling.

Sala del Maggior Consiglio

The cavernous 1419 Sala del Maggior
Consiglio (Grand Council Hall) provides the
setting for Domenico Tintoretto's swirling
Paradise, a work that's more politically correct than pretty: heaven is crammed with
500 prominent Venetians, including several
Tintoretto patrons. Veronese's political pos-
turing is more elegant in his oval *Apotheosis of Venice* ceiling, where gods marvel at
Venice's coronation by angels, with foreign
dignitaries and Venetian blondes rubber-
necking on the balcony below.

Venice Gourmet Crawl

From market discoveries to delectable gelato, Venice is a gourmand's paradise waiting to be explored.

Start Rialto Market
Distance 2.9km
Duration Two hours

7 Finish with a wine or a cocktail at a bar such as **Al Prosecco** (p416),

6 Savour a sinful scoop of organic gelato at standout **Gelato di Natura** (www.gelatodinatura.com; Calle Larga 1628).

5 Impress your dinner guests with for to-die-for menu cards or invitations printed at **Veneziastampa** (www.veneziastampa.com; Campo Santa Maria Mater Domini 2173; 🕒8.30am-7.30pm Mon-Fri, 9am-12.30pm Sat).

FINISH 7

Campo San Giacomo dell'Orio 6

Campo Santa Maria Mater Domini

5

SAN POLO

0 — 200 m
0 — 0.1 miles

Classic Photo: Colourful produce at the Rialto Market.

2 At **Drogheria Mascari** (www. imascari.com; Ruga degli Spezieri 381; ⊙8am-1pm & 4-7.30pm Mon, Tue & Thu-Sat, 8am-1pm Wed) glimpse the fragrant spices and trade-route treasures that made Venice's fortune.

1 A trip through gourmet history starts at the **Rialto Market** (p411), where fishmongers artfully arrange the day's catch.

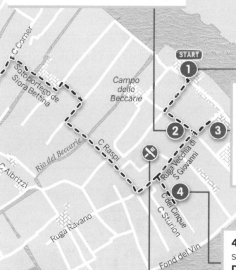

START
1

Rio dei Santi Apostoli

C Corner

Sotoportego de Siora Bettina

Campo dello Beccarie

2 **3**

Rio del Beccarie

C Raspi

C Albrizzi

Ruga Vecchia di S Giovanni

4

C del Cinque

C Sturion

Ponte di Rialto

Ruga Ravano

Fond del Vin

SAN MARCO

Rio di San Salvador

3 Casa del Parmigiano (www. aliani-casadelparmigiano.it; Campo Cesare Battisti 214; ⊙8am-1.30pm Mon-Wed, to 7.30pm Thu-Sat) is a historic deli laden with hard-to-find cheeses and mouth-watering cured meats.

4 Stop for an aromatic espresso at specialist coffee pedlar **Caffè del Doge** (www.caffedeldoge.com; Calle dei Cinque 609; ⊙7am-7pm).

Take a Break... Duck into All'Arco (p414) for some of the city's best *cicheti*.

◉ SIGHTS

Gallerie dell'Accademia   Gallery

(☑041 520 03 45; www.gallerieaccademia.
org; Campo della Carità 1050, Dorsoduro; adult/
reduced €12/6, 1st Sun of month free; ⊙8.15am-
2pm Mon, to 7.15pm Tue-Sun; ⛴Accademia) Venice's historic gallery traces the development
of Venetian art from the 14th to 18th centuries, with works by Bellini, Titian, Tintoretto,
Veronese and Canaletto, among others. The
former Santa Maria della Carità convent
complex housing the collection maintained
its serene composure for centuries until
Napoleon installed his haul of Venetian art
trophies here in 1807. Since then there's
been nonstop visual drama on its walls.

Peggy Guggenheim
Collection   Museum

(☑041 240 54 11; www.guggenheim-venice.it;
Palazzo Venier dei Leoni 704, Dorsoduro; adult/
reduced €15/9; ⊙10am-6pm Wed-Mon; ⛴Acca-
demia) After losing her father on the *Titanic*,
heiress Peggy Guggenheim became one
of the great collectors of the 20th century.
Her palatial canalside home, Palazzo Venier
dei Leoni, showcases her stockpile of surre-

alist, futurist and abstract expressionist art
with works by up to 200 artists, including
her ex-husband Max Ernst, Jackson Pollock
(among her many rumoured lovers), Picasso and Salvador Dalí.

Ca' Rezzonico   Museum

(Museum of the 18th Century; ☑041 241 01
00; www.visitmuve.it; Fondamenta Rezzonico
3136, Dorsoduro; adult/reduced €10/7.50;
⊙10am-6pm Wed-Mon summer, to 5pm winter;
⛴Ca' Rezzonico) Baroque dreams come
true at Baldassare Longhena's Grand
Canal palace, where a marble staircase
leads to gilded ballrooms, frescoed salons
and sumptuous boudoirs. Giambattista
Tiepolo's Throne Room ceiling is a masterpiece of elegant social climbing, showing
gorgeous Merit ascending to the Temple of
Glory clutching the Golden Book of Venetian nobles' names – including Tiepolo's
patrons, the Rezzonico family.

Scuola Grande
di San Rocco   Museum

(☑041 523 48 64; www.scuolagrandesanrocco.it;
Campo San Rocco 3052, San Polo; adult/reduced
€10/8; ⊙9.30am-5.30pm; ⛴San Tomà) Every-

Gondola ride past Basilica di Santa Maria della Salute

one wanted the commission to paint this building dedicated to the patron saint of the plague-stricken, St Roch, so Tintoretto cheated: instead of producing sketches like rival Veronese, he gifted a splendid ceiling panel of St Roch, knowing it couldn't be refused, or matched by other artists. The artist documents Mary's life story in the assembly hall, and both Old and New Testament scenes in the Sala Grande Superiore upstairs.

Ponte di Rialto   Bridge
(🚤Rialto-Mercato) A superb feat of engineering, Antonio da Ponte's 1592 Istrian stone span took three years and 250,000 gold ducats to construct. Adorned with stone reliefs depicting St Mark, St Theodore and the Annunciation, the bridge crosses the Grand Canal at its narrowest point, connecting the neighbourhoods of San Polo and San Marco.

When crowds of shutterbugs clear out around sunset, the bridge's southern side offers a romantic view of black gondolas pulling up to golden Grand Canal *palazzi*.

Basilica di Santa
Maria della Salute   Basilica
(La Salute; www.basilicasalutevenezia.it; Campo della Salute 1b, Dorsoduro; basilica free, sacristy adult/reduced €4/2; ☉basilica 9.30am-noon & 3-5.30pm, sacristy 10am-noon & 3-5pm Mon-Sat, 3-5pm Sun; 🚤Salute) Guarding the entrance to the Grand Canal, this 17th-century domed church was commissioned by Venice's plague survivors as thanks for their salvation. Baldassare Longhena's uplifting design is an engineering feat that defies simple logic; in fact, the church is said to have mystical curative properties. Titian eluded the plague until age 94, leaving 12 key paintings in the basilica's art-slung sacristy.

Rialto Market   Market
(📞041 296 06 58; San Polo; ☉7am-2pm; 🚤Rialto-Mercato) Venice's Rialto Market has been whetting appetites for seven centuries. To see it at its best arrive in the morning with trolley-totting shoppers

Top Tours

and you'll be rewarded by pyramids of colourful seasonal produce like Sant'Erasmo *castraure* (baby artichokes), *radicchio trevisano* (bitter red chicory) and thick, succulent white asparagus. If you're in the market for picnic provisions, vendors may offer you samples. The **Pescaria** (Fish Market; Rialto, San Polo; ☉7am-2pm Tue-Sun; 🚤Rialto-Mercato) is closed Monday.

I Frari   Church
(Basilica di Santa Maria Gloriosa dei Frari; 📞041 272 86 18; www.basilicadeifrari.it; Campo dei Frari 3072, San Polo; adult/reduced €3/1.50; ☉9am-6pm Mon-Sat, 1-6pm Sun; 🚤San Tomà) A soaring Gothic church, I Frari's assets include marquetry choir stalls, Canova's pyramid mausoleum, Bellini's achingly sweet *Madonna with Child* triptych in the sacristy, and Longhena's creepy Doge Pesaro funereal monument. Upstaging them all, however, is the small altarpiece. This is Titian's 1518 *Assunta* (Assumption), in which a radiant red-cloaked Madonna reaches heavenward, steps onto a cloud and escapes this mortal coil. Titian himself – lost to the plague in 1576 at the age 94 – is buried near his celebrated masterpiece.

🟢 ACTIVITIES
Row Venice   Boating
(📞347 7250637; www.rowvenice.org; Fondamenta Gasparo Contarini; 90min lessons 1-2 people €85, 3/4 people €120/140; 🚤Orto) The next best thing to walking on water: rowing

San Marco & San Polo

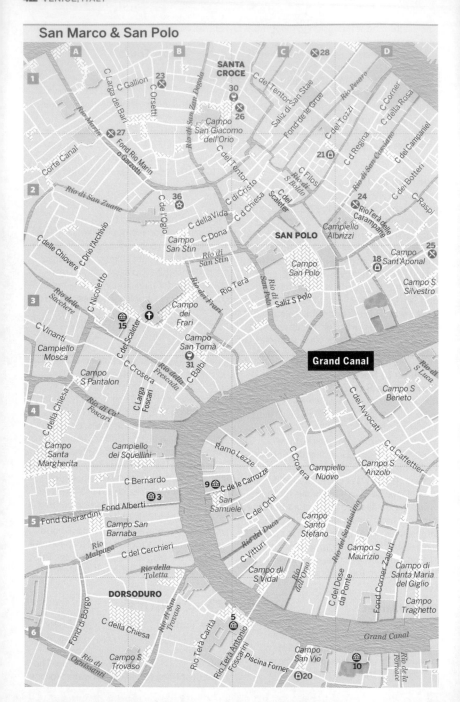

SANTA CROCE

SAN POLO

Grand Canal

DORSODURO

Grand Canal

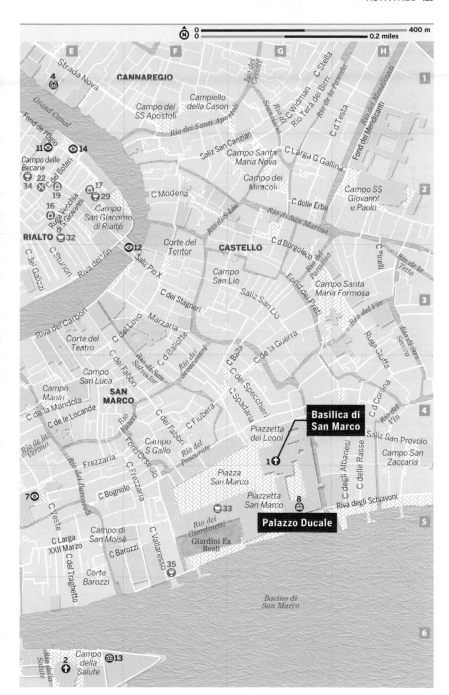

N

0   400 m
0   0.2 miles

4

Strada Nova

CANNAREGIO

Grand Canal

Fond de l'Ogio

Campiello
della Cason

Campo dei
SS Apostoli

Rio dei Santi Apostoli

Rio dei Gesuiti

C Stella

C Widman

Rio di Scoacigra

C Rio Tera del Birri

Rio de la Panada

C d'Testa

Fond dei Mendicanti

Rio dei Mendicanti

1

Saliz San Canzian

11   **14**

Campo delle
Becarie

22
34   C   **17**
19   **29**

16

Ruga Vecchia
S Giovanni

C del Boteri

Campo
San Giacomo
di Rialto

Campo Santa
Maria Nova

C Larga G Gallina

Campo dei
Miracoli

C Modena

C delle Erbe

Campo SS
Giovanni
e Paolo

2

RIALTO   **32**

C 3e Gai'zi

C Sturion

Riva del Vin

12

Saliz Pio X

Corte del
Tentor

Rio di S Lio

Rio de San Marina

CASTELLO

C d Burgoloco

Fond dei Paradiso

C Pinelli

Rio de la Tetta

3

Campo
San Lio

Saliz San Lio

Campo Santa
Maria Formosa

Rio del Vin

Riva del Carbon

Corte del
Teatro

C del Lovo

Marzaria

C d Ballotte

Rio di San Salvador

C dei Stagneri

Rio de Scoacigra

C de la Guerra

Ruge Giuffa

Rio dei Ferri Sarca

Campo
San Luca

C dei Fabbri

**SAN
MARCO**

Campo
Manlin

C de la Mandola

C de le Locande

Rio Fuseri

C dei Fabbri

C Fiubera

C Babbi

C C dei Specchieri

C Spadaria

Piazzetta
dei Leoni

**Basilica di
San Marco**

C d Corona

Rio del Vin

4

Saliz San Provolo

Campo San
Zaccaria

Rio de la
Verona

Rio dei Barcaroli

Frezzaria

C Frezzaria

Fond Orseolo

Campo
S Gallo

Rio del
Procurate

1

C degli Albanesi

C delle Rasse

7

C Bognolo

Piazza
San Marco

Piazzetta
San Marco

8

Riva degli Schiavoni

5

C Veste

C Larga
XXII Marzo

Campo di
San Moisè

C del Traghetto

C Barozzi

C Vallaresso

Rio dei
Giordinetti

Giardini Ex
Reali

35

33

Palazzo Ducale

Corte
Barozzi

Bacino di
San Marco

6

Rio de la
Salute

Campo
della
Salute

2

13

E   F   G   H

San Marco & San Polo

a traditional *batellina coda di gambero* (shrimp-tailed boat) standing up like gondoliers do. Tours must be pre-booked and commence at the wooden gate of the Sacca Misericordia boat marina.

🔒 SHOPPING

Marina e Susanna Sent   Glass
(📞041 520 81 36; www.marinaesusannasent. com; Campo San Vio 669, Dorsoduro; ⊙10am-1pm & 1.30-6.30pm; 🚤Accademia) Wearable waterfalls and soap-bubble necklaces are Venice style signatures, thanks to the Murano-born Sent sisters. Defying centuries-old beliefs that women can't handle molten glass, their minimalist art-glass statement jewellery is featured in museum stores worldwide, from Palazzo Grassi to MoMA.

Alberto Sarria   Arts & Crafts
(📞041 520 72 78; www.masksvenice.com; San Polo 777, San Polo; ⊙10am-7pm; 🚤San Stae) Go Gaga or channel Casanova at this atelier, dedicated to the art of masquerade for over 30 years. Sarria's *commedia dell'arte*

masks are worn by theatre companies from Argentina to Osaka – ominous burnished black leather for dramatic leads, harlequin-chequered *cartapesta* (papier-mâché) for comic foils, starting from around €20. Beyond the masks is a cast of one-of-a-kind marionettes.

Damocle Edizioni   Books
(📞346 8345720; www.edizionidamocle.com; Calle Perdon 1311, San Polo; ⊙10am-1pm & 3-7pm Mon-Fri, 10am-1pm Sat; 🚤San Silvestro) Pocket-sized Damocle is both a bookshop and publisher, translating literary greats and showcasing emerging writing talent. Most of Damocle's creations feature beautiful artwork created through collaborations with local and foreign artists.

✖ EATING

All'Arco   Venetian €
(📞041 520 56 66; Calle dell'Ochialer 436, San Polo; cicheti from €2; ⊙8am-2.30pm Mon, Tue & Sat, to 7pm Wed-Fri summer, 8am-2.30pm Mon-Sat winter; 🚤Rialto-Mercato) Search out this authentic neighbourhood *osteria* (casual

tavern) for the best *cicheti* (bar snacks) in town. Armed with ingredients from the nearby Rialto Market, father-son team Francesco and Matteo serve miniature masterpieces such as *cannocchia* (mantis shrimp) with pumpkin and roe, and *otrega crudo* (raw butterfish) with mint-and-olive-oil marinade. Even with copious *prosecco,* hardly any meal here tops €20.

Dai Zemei   Venetian, Cicheti €

(☑041 520 85 96; www.ostariadaizemei.it; Ruga Vecchia San Giovanni 1045, San Polo; cicheti from €1.50; ⏲8.30am-8.30pm Mon-Sat, 9am-7pm Sun; ⛴San Silvestro) Running this closet-sized *cicheti* counter are *zemei* (twins) Franco and Giovanni, who serve loyal regulars small meals with plenty of imagination. A gourmet bargain for inspired bites and impeccable wines – try a crisp *nosiola* or invigorating *prosecco* brut.

Osteria Trefanti   Venetian €€

(☑041 520 17 89; www.osteriatrefanti.it; Fondamenta Garzotti 888, Santa Croce; meals €40; ⏲noon-2.30pm & 7-10.30pm Tue-Sun; 📶; ⛴Riva de Biasio) 🍃 La Serenissima's spice trade lives on at simple, elegant Trefanti, where a dish of marinated prawns, hazelnuts, berries and caramel might get an intriguing kick from garam masala. Sip a small, beautifully curated selection of local and organic wines served among old pews and recycled copper lamps.

Antica Besseta   Venetian €€

(☑041 72 16 87; www.anticabesseta.it; Salizada de Cà Zusto 1395, Santa Croce; meals €35; ⏲6.30-10pm Mon, Wed & Thu, noon-2pm & 6.30-10.30pm Fri-Sun; 📶; ⛴Riva de Biasio) Wood panelling and fresh flowers set the scene at this veteran trattoria, known for giving contemporary verve to regional classics. The *delizie di pesce dell'Adriatico* – a tasting plate which might see seared scallops served with a brandy and asparagus salsa – makes for a stimulating prologue to dishes like almond-crusted turbot with artichokes and cherry tomatoes.

Gondola Rides

Cheesy or the ultimate romance? You choose. Daytime rates run to €80 for 30 minutes (six passengers maximum) or €100 for 35 minutes from 7pm to 8am, not including songs (negotiated separately) or tips.

Antiche Carampane Venetian €€€

(☑041 524 01 65; www.antichecarampane.com; Rio Terà delle Carampane 1911, San Polo; meals €50; ⏲12.45-2.30pm & 7.30-10.30pm Tue-Sat; ⛴San Stae) Hidden in the once-shady lanes behind Ponte delle Tette, this culinary indulgence is a trick to find. Once you do, say goodbye to soggy lasagne and hello to a market-driven menu of silky *crudi* (raw fish/seafood), surprisingly light *fritto misto* (fried seafood) and *caramote* prawn salad with seasonal vegetables. Never short of a smart, convivial crowd, it's a good idea to book ahead.

Riviera   Venetian €€€

(☑041 522 76 21; www.ristoranteriviera.it; Fondamenta Zattere al Ponte Lungo 1473, Dorsoduro; meals €70-85; ⏲12.30-3pm & 7-10.30pm Fri-Tue; ⛴Zattere) Seafood connoisseurs concur that dining at GP Cremonini's restaurant is a Venetian highlight. A former rock musician, GP now focuses his considerable talents on delivering perfectly balanced octopus stew, feather-light gnocchi with lagoon crab, and risotto with langoustine and hop shoots. The setting, overlooking the Giudecca Canal, is similarly spectacular,

Opera at La Fenice

From January to July and September to October, opera season is in full swing at **La Fenice** (📞041 78 66 75; www. teatrolafenice.it; Campo San Fantin 1977; audioguide adult/reduced €10/7; ⏰9.30am-6pm; 🚏Giglio), Venice's gorgeous gilt opera house. If you can't attend a performance, it's possible to explore the theatre with an audio guide.

PISAPHOTOGRAPHY/SHUTTERSTOCK ©

encompassing views of Venetian domes backed by hot pink sunsets.

Ristorante Glam   Venetian €€€

(Palazzo Venart; 📞041 523 56 76; www.enrico bartolini.net/i-ristoranti/glam; Calle Tron 1961, Santa Croce; tasting menu €90-110; ⏰12.30-2.30pm & 7.30-10.30pm; 🚏San Stae) Step out of your water taxi into the canalside garden of Enrico Bartolini's new Venetian restaurant in the Venart Hotel. The tasting menus focus on local ingredients, pepping up Veneto favourites with unusual spices that would once have graced the tables of this trade route city.

🍸 DRINKING & NIGHTLIFE

Al Mercà   Wine Bar

(📞346 8340660; Campo Cesare Battisti 213, San Polo; ⏰10am-2.30pm & 6-8pm Mon-Thu, to 9.30pm Fri & Sat; 🚏Rialto-Mercato) Discerning drinkers throng to this cupboard-sized counter on a Rialto Market square to sip on top-notch *prosecco* and DOC wines by the glass (from €3). Edibles usually include

meatballs and mini *panini* (€1.50), proudly made using super-fresh ingredients.

Al Prosecco   Wine Bar

(📞041 524 02 22; www.alprosecco.com; Campo San Giacomo dell'Orio 1503, Santa Croce; ⏰10am-8pm Mon-Fri, to 5pm Sat Nov-Mar, to 10.30pm Apr-Oct; 🚏San Stae) 🍷 The urge to toast sunsets in Venice's loveliest *campo* is only natural – and so is the wine at Al Prosecco. This forward-thinking bar specialises in *vini naturi* (natural-process wines) – organic, biodynamic, wild-yeast fermented – from enlightened Italian winemakers like Cinque Campi and Azienda Agricola Barichel. So order a glass of unfiltered 'cloudy' *prosecco* and toast the good things in life.

Caffè Florian   Cafe

(📞041 520 56 41; www.caffeflorian.com; Piazza San Marco 57; ⏰9am-11pm; 🚏San Marco) The oldest still-operating cafe in Europe and one of the first to welcome women, Florian maintains rituals (if not prices) established in 1720: be-suited waiters serve cappuccino on silver trays, lovers canoodle in plush banquettes and the orchestra strikes up as the sunset illuminates San Marco's mosaics. Piazza seating during concerts costs €6 extra, but dreamy-eyed romantics hardly notice.

Basegò   Bar

(📞041 850 02 99; www.basego.it; Campo San Tomá, San Polo; ⏰9am-11pm; 🚏San Tomà) Focusing on three essential ingredients – good food, good wine and good music – newly opened Basegò has rapidly formed a dedicated group of drinkers. Indulge in a *cicheti* feast of lagoon seafood, Norcia prosciutto, smoked tuna and Lombard cheeses.

🎭 ENTERTAINMENT

Palazzetto Bru Zane   Classical Music

(Centre du Musique Romantique Française; 📞041 521 10 05; www.bru-zane.com; Palazzetto Bru Zane 2368, San Polo; adult/reduced €15/5; ⏰box office 2.30-5.30pm Mon-Fri, closed late Jul–mid-Aug; 🚏San Tomà) Pleasure palaces don't get more romantic than Palazetto Bru Zane on concert nights, when exquisite harmonies tickle Sebastiano Ricci angels tumbling across stucco-frosted ceilings. Multi-year restorations returned the 1695–97 Casino Zane's 100-seat music room to its original function, attracting world-class musicians to enjoy its acoustics from late September to mid-May.

INFORMATION

Vènezia Unica (☏041 24 24; www.veneziaunica. it) runs all tourist information services and offices in Venice. It provides information on sights, itineraries, day trips, transport, special events, shows and temporary exhibitions. Discount passes can be pre-booked on its website.

GETTING THERE & AWAY

AIR

Most flights to Venice fly into **Marco Polo Airport** (☏flight information 041 260 92 60; www.veniceairport.it, Via Galileo Galilei 30/1, Tessera), 12km outside Venice, east of Mestre. Ryanair and some other budget airlines also use **Treviso Airport** (☏042 231 51 11; www.trevisoairport.it; Via Noalese 63), about 4km southwest of Treviso and a 26km, one-hour drive from Venice.

BOAT

Venice has regular ferry connections with Greece, Croatia and Slovenia. However, remember that long-haul ferries and cruise ships have an outsized environmental impact on tiny Venice and its fragile lagoon aquaculture. Consider the lower-impact train instead – Venice will be grateful.

CAR

If you drive to Venice, you have to park at the western end of the city and then walk or take a *vaporetto*.

You'll find car parks in Piazzale Roma or on Isola del Tronchetto. Prices in Venice start at €3.50 per hour and rise to €32 for five to 24 hours. At peak times, many car parks become completely full. However, you can book a parking place ahead of time at www.veneziaunica.it. To make the most of the cheaper car parks, consider parking in Mestre, and take the bus or train into Venice instead.

For a range of parking options in Venice and Mestre, including prices and directions, head to www.avmspa.it.

TRAIN

Direct intercity services operate out of Venice to most major Italian cities, as well as to points in France, Germany, Austria, Switzerland, Slovenia and Croatia.

GETTING AROUND

Vaporetto (small passenger ferry) Venice's main public transport. Single rides cost €7.50; for frequent use, get a timed pass for unlimited travel within a set period (1-/2-/3-/7-day passes cost €20/30/40/60). Tickets and passes are available dockside from ACTV ticket booths and ticket vending machines, or from tobacconists.

Traghetto Locals use this daytime public gondola service (€2) to cross the Grand Canal between bridges.

Water taxi Sleek teak boats offer taxi services for €15 plus €2 per minute, plus €5 for pre-booked services and extra for night-time, luggage and large groups.

In This Chapter

Florence, Italy

Cradle of the Renaissance – romantic, enchanting and utterly irresistible – Florence (Firenze) is a place to feast on world-class art and gourmet Tuscan cuisine. Few cities are so compact in size or so packed with extraordinary art and architecture at every turn. The urban fabric of this small city, on the banks of the Arno river in northeastern Tuscany, has hardly changed since the Renaissance and its narrow cobbled streets are a cinematic feast of elegant 15th- and 16th-century palazzi (mansions), medieval chapels, fresco-decorated churches, marble basilicas and world-class art museums. Unsurprisingly, the entire city centre is a Unesco World Heritage Site.

Florence in Two Days

Start with a coffee on **Piazza della Repubblica** (p433) before hitting the **Uffizi** (p427). After lunch visit the **Duomo** (p420), **Baptistry** (p433) and **Grande Museo del Duomo** (p432). Set aside day two to explore the **Galleria dell'Accademia** (p425) and **Museo di San Marco** (p433). In the evening, venture across to the Oltrarno, stopping en route to admire sunset views from **Ponte Vecchio** (p436) and **Piazzale Michelangelo** (p437).

Florence in Four Days

On day three, explore **Palazzo Pitti** (p436) and the **Giardino di Boboli** (p437) or visit the city's major basilicas – **San Lorenzo** (p437), **Santa Croce** (p437) and **Santa Maria Novella** (p437). Stop by **Il Teatro del Sale** (p440) for dinner and a show. On day four, take a guided tour of **Palazzo Vecchio** (p432) and explore the city's artisanal shops.

Where next? The Tuscan countryside (p444) and Rome (p352) are both waiting.

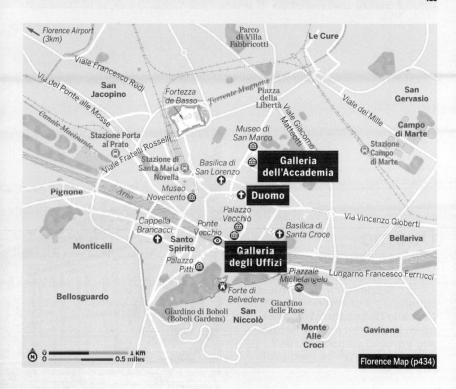

Florence Map (p434)

Arriving in Florence

Pisa International Airport Tuscany's main international airport. There are regular buses to Stazione di Santa Maria Novella (€5). Buy tickets online, on board or at the information desk in the arrivals hall.

Florence Airport ATAF operates a half-hourly Volainbus shuttle (€6) to Florence bus station. A taxi costs €20.

Stazione di Santa Maria Novella A 10-minute walk from the historic centre, Florence's main train station is on the Rome–Milan line.

Where to Stay

Advance reservations are essential between Easter and September, while winter ushers in some great deals for visitors – room rates are practically halved. Many top-end boutique options hide in courtyards or behind the inconspicuous door of a *residenza d'epoca* (historical residence) – not listed as hotel or graced with any stars, making such addresses all the more atmospheric and oh-so-Florentine.

Duomo

Florence's Duomo is the city's most iconic landmark. Capped by Filippo Brunelleschi's red-tiled cupola, it's a staggering construction, and its breathtaking pink, white and green marble facade and graceful campanile (bell tower) dominate the medieval cityscape.

Great For...

Stazione di Santa Maria Novella

Via dei Panzani

Via de' Cerretani

Duomo

❶ Need to Know

Cattedrale di Santa Maria del Fiore; ☎055 230 28 85; www.ilgrandemuseodelduomo. it; Piazza del Duomo; ⏰10am-5pm Mon-Wed & Fri, to 4.30pm Thu, to 4.45pm Sat, 1.30-4.45pm Sun FREE

★ **Top Tip**

Reservations are required to climb the dome. Book online or at the ticket office at Piazza San Giovanni 7, opposite the Baptistry's northern entrance.

Sienese architect Arnolfo di Cambio began work on the Duomo in 1296, but construction took almost 150 years and it wasn't consecrated until 1436.

Facade

The neo-Gothic facade was designed in the 19th century by architect Emilio de Fabris to replace the uncompleted original, torn down in the 16th century. The oldest and most clearly Gothic part of the cathedral is its south flank, pierced by the Porta dei Canonici (Canons' Door), a mid-14th-century High Gothic creation (you enter here to climb up inside the dome).

Dome

One of the finest masterpieces of the Renaissance, the **cupola** (Brunelleschi's Dome; adult/reduced incl cupola, baptistry, campanile, crypt & museum €15/3; ⊘8.30am-7pm Mon-Fri, to 5pm Sat, 1-4pm Sun) is a feat of engineering that cannot be fully appreciated without climbing its 463 interior stone steps. It was built between 1420 and 1436 to a design by Filippo Brunelleschi, and is a staggering 91m high and 45.5m wide.

Taking his inspiration from Rome's Pantheon, Brunelleschi arrived at an innovative engineering solution of a distinctive octagonal shape of inner and outer concentric domes resting on the drum of the cathedral rather than the roof itself, allowing artisans to build from the ground up without needing a wooden support frame. Over four million bricks were used in the construction, all of them laid in consecutive rings in horizontal courses using a vertical herringbone pattern.

The climb up the spiral staircase is relatively steep. Make sure to pause when

The Duomo is the city's most iconic landmark

you reach the balustrade at the base of the dome, which gives an aerial view of the octagonal *coro* (choir) in the cathedral below and the seven round stained-glass windows (by Donatello, Andrea del Castagno, Paolo Uccello and Lorenzo Ghiberti) that pierce the octagonal drum.

Interior

After the visual wham-bam of the facade, the sparse decoration of the cathedral's vast interior, 155m long and 90m wide, comes as a surprise – most of its artistic treasures have been removed over the centuries according to the vagaries of ecclesiastical fashion, and many are on show

> ☑ **Don't Miss**
>
> The flamboyant dome frescoes by Giorgio Vasari and Federico Zuccari.

ROSSHELEN/SHUTTERSTOCK ©

in the Grande Museo del Duomo (p432). The interior is also unexpectedly secular in places (a reflection of the sizeable chunk of the cathedral not paid for by the church): down the left aisle two immense frescoes of equestrian statues portray two *condottieri* (mercenaries) – on the left Niccolò da Tolentino by Andrea del Castagno (1456), and on the right Sir John Hawkwood (who fought in the service of Florence in the 14th century) by Uccello (1436).

Between the left (north) arm of the transept and the apse is the Sagrestia delle Messe (Mass Sacristy), its panelling a marvel of inlaid wood carved by Benedetto and Giuliano da Maiano. The fine bronze doors were executed by Luca della Robbia – his only known work in the material. Above the doorway is his glazed terracotta *Resurrezione* (Resurrection).

A stairway near the main entrance of the cathedral leads down to the Cripta Santa Reparata (crypt), where excavations between 1965 and 1974 unearthed parts of the 5th-century Chiesa di Santa Reparata that originally stood on the site.

Campanile

The 414-step climb up the cathedral's 85m-tall **campanile** (Bell Tower; 🎫 adult/reduced incl campanile, baptistry, cupola, crypt & museum €15/3; ⏱ 8.15am 8pm), bogun by Giotto in 1334, rewards with a staggering city panorama. The first tier of bas-reliefs around the base of its elaborate Gothic facade are copies of those carved by Pisano depicting the Creation of Man and the *attività umane* (arts and industries). Those on the second tier depict the planets, the cardinal virtues, the arts and the seven sacraments. The sculpted Prophets and Sibyls in the upper-storey niches are copies of works by Donatello and others.

✕ Take a Break

Take time out over a taste of Tuscan wine at stylish **Coquinarius** (www.coquin arius.com; Via delle Oche 11r; ⏱ 12.30-3pm & 6.30-10.30pm Wed-Mon).

SYLVAIN SONNET/GETTY IMAGES ©

Galleria dell'Accademia

A lengthy queue marks the door to the Galleria dell'Accademia, the late 18th-century gallery that's home to one of the Renaissance's most iconic masterpieces, Michelangelo's David.

Great For...

☑ Don't Miss

David – look for the two pale lines visible on his lower left arm where it was broken in 1527.

David

Fortunately, the world's most famous statue is worth the wait. Standing at over 5m tall and weighing in at 19 tonnes, *David* is a formidable sight. But it's not just its scale that impresses, it's also the subtle detail – the veins in his sinewy arms, the muscles in his legs, the change in expression as you move around him. Carved from a single block of marble, Michelangelo's most famous work was also his most challenging – he didn't choose the marble himself, it was veined, and its larger-than-life dimensions were already decided.

When the statue of the boy-warrior, depicted for the first time as a man in the prime of life rather than a young boy, assumed its pedestal in front of Palazzo Vecchio on Piazza della Signoria in 1504,

Michelangelo's *David*

MARVIN E. BEWMAN/GETTY IMAGES ©

❶ Need to Know

www.firenzemusei.it; Via Ricasoli 60; adult/
reduced €8/4, incl temporary exhibition
€12.50/6.25; ⊙8.15am-6.50pm Tue-Sun

✗ Take a Break

Grab a pizza slice at the much-loved
Pugi (☑055 28 09 81; www.focacceria-
pugi.it; Piazza San Marco 9b; per kg €15-24;
⊙7.45am-8pm Mon-Sat, closed 2 weeks mid-
Aug), a stone's throw from the Galleria.

★ Top Tip

Cut queuing time by booking tickets
in advance at www.firenzemusei.it; the
reservation fee is €4.

Florentines immediately adopted it as a
powerful emblem of Florentine power, liberty and civic pride. It stayed in the piazza
until 1873 when it was moved to its current
purpose-built tribune in the Galleria.

Other Works

Michelangelo was also the master behind
the unfinished *San Matteo* (St Matthew;
1504–08) and four *Prigioni* ('Prisoners' or
'Slaves'; 1521–30), also displayed in the
gallery. The prisoners seem to be writhing
and struggling to free themselves from the
marble; they were meant for the tomb of
Pope Julius II, itself never completed.

Adjacent rooms contain paintings by
Andrea Orcagna, Taddeo Gaddi, Domenico
Ghirlandaio, Filippino Lippi and Sandro
Botticelli.

What's Nearby?

To the east of the Galleria, Giambologna's
equestrian statue of Grand Duke Ferdinando I de' Medici lords it over **Piazza della
Santissima Annunziata**, a majestic square
dominated by the facades of the **Chiesa
della Santissima Annunziata**, built in
1250, then rebuilt by Michelozzo et al in the
mid-15th century, and the **Ospedale degli
Innocenti** (Hospital of the Innocents),
Europe's first orphanage founded in 1421.
Look up to admire Brunelleschi's classically
influenced portico, decorated by Andrea
della Robbia (1435–1525) with terracotta
medallions of babies in swaddling clothes.

About 200m southeast of the piazza is
the **Museo Archeologico** (☑055 23 57; www.
archeotoscana.beniculturali.it; Piazza della SS Annunziata 9b; adult/reduced €4/2; ⊙8.30am-7pm
Tue-Fri, to 2pm Sat-Mon). Its rich collection of
finds, including most of the Medici hoard of
antiquities, plunges you deep into the past
and offers an alternative to Renaissance
splendour.

Galleria degli Uffizi

An art lover's paradise, the Galleria degli Uffizi houses the world's finest collection of Renaissance paintings, including masterpieces by Giotto, Botticelli, Michelangelo, da Vinci, Raphael, Titian and Caravaggio, in a magnificent 16th-century palazzo.

The gallery is undergoing a €65 million refurbishment (the Nuovi Uffizi project) that will eventually see the doubling of exhibition space. Work is pretty much complete on the permanent collection, which has grown over the years from 45 to 101 revamped rooms split across two floors; but there is much to be done still on areas earmarked for temporary exhibitions. Until the project is completed (date unknown) expect some halls to be closed and the contents of others changed.

Tuscan Masters: 13th to 14th Centuries

Starting in the Primo Corridoio (First Corridor) on the 2nd floor, Rooms 2 to 7 are dedicated to pre- and early Renaissance Tuscan art. Among the 13th-century Sienese works displayed in Room 2 are

Great For...

☑ Don't Miss

The reverse side of *The Duke and Duchess of Urbino*, depicting the duke and duchess accompanied by the Virtues.

JULIAN ELLIOTT PHOTOGRAPHY/GETTY IMAGES ©

❶ Need to Know

Uffizi Gallery; ☎055 29 48 83; www.uffizi.
beniculturali.it; Piazzale degli Uffizi 6; adult/
reduced €8/4, incl temporary exhibition
€12.50/6.25; ⊙8.15am-6.50pm Tue-Sun

✕ Take a Break

To clear your head of art overload, stop
by the gallery's rooftop cafe, for fresh air
and fabulous views.

★ Top Tip
Save money and visit on the first Sunday of the month – admission is free.

three large altarpieces by Duccio di Buoninsegna, Cimabue and Giotto. These clearly
reflect the transition from the Gothic to the
nascent Renaissance style.

The highlight in Room 3 is Simone Martini's shimmering *Annunciazione* (1333),
painted with Lippo Memmi and setting the
Madonna in a sea of gold.

In Room 4 savour the realism of the *Lam-
entation over the Dead Christ* (1360–65) by
gifted Giotto pupil, Giottino.

Renaissance Pioneers

Florence's victory over the Sienese at the
Battle of San Romano, near Pisa, in 1432,
is brought to life with outstanding realism
and increased use of perspective in Paolo
Uccello's magnificent *Battaglia di San
Romano* (1435–40) in Room 8. In the same
room, don't miss the exquisite *Madonna*

con bambino e due angeli (Madonna and
Child with Two Angels; 1460–65) by Fra'
Filippo Lippi.

In Room 9, Piero della Francesca's
famous profile portraits (1465) of the
crooked-nosed, red-robed duke and
duchess of Urbino are wholly humanist
in spirit: the former painted from the left
side as he'd lost his right eye in a jousting
accident, and the latter painted a deathly
stone-white, reflecting the fact the portrait
was painted posthumously.

In the same room, the seven cardinal and
theological values of 15th-century Florence
by brothers Antonio and Piero del Pollaiolo
– commissioned for the merchant's
tribunal in Piazza della Signoria – radiate
energy. The only canvas in the theological
and cardinal virtues series not to be painted by the Pollaiolos is *Fortitude* (1470), the
first documented work by Botticelli.

Botticelli Room

The spectacular Sala del Botticelli,
numbered as Rooms 10 to 14, is one of the

Uffizi's hot spots and is always packed. Of the 18 Botticelli works displayed in the Uffizi in all, the iconic *La nascita di Venere* (The Birth of Venus; c 1485), *Primavera* (Spring; c 1482) and *Madonna del Magnificat* (Madonna of the Magnificat; 1483) are the best known by the Renaissance master known for his ethereal figures. Take time to study the lesser-known *Annunciazione* (Annunciation), a 6m-wide fresco painted by Botticelli in 1481 for the San Martino hospital in Florence.

True aficionados rate his twin set of miniatures depicting a sword-bearing Judith returning from the camp of Holofernes and the discovery of the decapitated Holofernes in his tent (1495–1500) as being among his finest works.

La Tribuna

The Medici clan stashed away their most precious masterpieces in this octagonal-shaped treasure trove (Room 18). Perfectly restored to its original exquisite state, a small collection of classical statues and paintings adorn its crimson silk walls and 6000 mother-of-pearl shells painted with crimson varnish encrust the domed ceiling.

Elsewhere in Italy: 15th Century

In Rooms 19 to 23, the ornate vaulted ceilings – frescoed in the 16th and 17th centuries with military objects, allegories, battles and festivals held on piazzas in Florence – are as compelling as the art strung on the walls.

Sculptures in the Primo Corridoio (First Corridor; p426)

High Renaissance to Mannerism

Passing through the loggia or Secondo Corridoio (Second Corridor), visitors enjoy wonderful views of Florence before entering the Terzo Corridoio (Third Corridor).

Michelangelo dazzles with the *Doni Tondo*, a depiction of the Holy Family that steals the High Renaissance show in Room 35. The composition is unusual – Joseph holding an exuberant Jesus on his muscled mother's shoulder as she twists round to gaze at him, the colours as vibrant as when they were first applied in 1506–08.

First-Floor Galleries

Head downstairs to the 1st-floor galleries where Rooms 46 to 55 display 16th- to 18th-century works by foreign artists, including Rembrandt (Room 49), and Rubens and Van Dyck (who share Room 55). In Room 66, Raphael's *Madonna del cardellino* (Madonna of the Goldfinch; 1505–06) steals the show.

Room 65 is dedicated to Medici portrait artist, Agnolo Bronzino (1503–72), who worked at the court of Cosimo I from 1539 until 1555. His 1545 portraits of the Grand Duchess Eleonora of Toleto and her son Giovanni together, and the 18-month-old Giovanni alone holding a goldfinch – symbolising his calling into the church – are considered masterpieces of 16th-century European portraiture.

As part of the seemingly endless New Uffizi expansion project, four early Florentine works by Leonardo da Vinci are currently displayed in Room 79. His *Annunciazione* (Annunciation; 1472) was deliberately painted to be admired, not face on (from where Mary's arm appears too long, her face too light, the angle of buildings not quite right), but rather from the lower right-hand side of the painting.

Room 90, with its canary-yellow walls, features works by Caravaggio, deemed vulgar at the time for his direct interpretation of reality. *The Head of Medusa* (1598–99) is supposedly a self-portrait of the young artist who died at the age of 39. The biblical drama of an angel steadying the hand of Abraham as he holds a knife to his son Isaac's throat in Caravaggio's *Sacrifice of Isaac* (1601–02) is glorious in its intensity.

★ **Local Knowledge**

In 1966 flood waters threatened to destroy the Uffizi Gallery. Locals and tourists rushed to the gallery to help rescue the artworks, and these saviours became known as 'mud angels'.

Heart of the City

Every visitor to Florence spends time navigating the cobbled medieval lanes that run between Via de' Tornabuoni and Via del Proconsolo, but few explore them thoroughly.
Start Piazza della Repubblica
Distance 2km
Duration Two hours

4 Head past the market and along Via Porta Rossa to **Palazzo Davanzati** with its magnificent studded doors and fascinating museum.

6 Wander down the narrow **Via del Parione** to spy out old mansions and artisans workshops.

5 Hidden behind the unassuming facade of the **Chiesa di Santa Trinita** are some of the city's finest 15th-century frescoes.

Classic Photo: The Arno river and Ponte Vecchio.

7 Finish with a sundowner and spectacular Ponte Vecchio views at **La Terrazza Lounge Bar** (p442).

0   100 m
0   0.05 miles

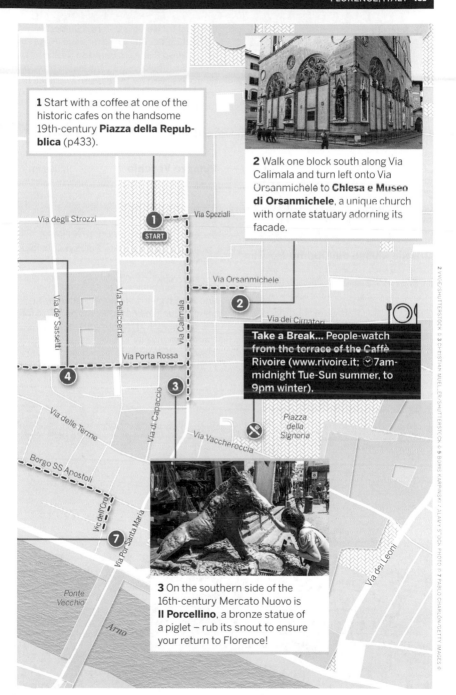

1 Start with a coffee at one of the historic cafes on the handsome 19th-century **Piazza della Repubblica** (p433).

2 Walk one block south along Via Calimala and turn left onto Via Orsanmichele to **Chiesa e Museo di Orsanmichele**, a unique church with ornate statuary adorning its facade.

Via degli Strozzi

Via Speziali

Via Orsanmichele

Via de' Sassetti

Via Pellicceria

Via Calimala

Via Porta Rossa

Via dei Cimatori

Take a Break... People-watch from the terrace of the Caffè Rivoire (www.rivoire.it; ⊙7am–midnight Tue-Sun summer, to 9pm winter).

Via delle Terme

Via di Capaccio

Via Vaccherreccia

Piazza della Signoria

Borgo SS Apostoli

Vic dell'Oro

Via Por Santa Maria

Ponte Vecchio

Arno

Via dei Leoni

3 On the southern side of the 16th-century Mercato Nuovo is **Il Porcellino**, a bronze statue of a piglet – rub its snout to ensure your return to Florence!

◉ SIGHTS

Florence's wealth of museums and galleries house many of the world's most exquisite examples of Renaissance art, and its architecture is unrivalled. Yet don't feel pressured to see everything: combine your personal pick of sights with ample meandering through the city's warren of narrow streets broken by cafe and *enoteca* (wine bar) stops.

Churches enforce a strict dress code for visitors: no shorts, sleeveless shirts or plunging necklines. Photography with no flash is allowed in museums, but leave the selfie stick at home – they are officially forbidden.

Grande Museo del Duomo Museum

(Cathedral Museum; ☑055 230 28 85; www.ilgrandemuseodelduomo.it; Piazza del Duomo 9; adult/reduced incl cathedral bell tower, cupola, baptistry & crypt €15/3; ⊘9am-7.30pm) This awe-inspiring museum tells the magnificent story of how the Duomo and its cupola was built through art and short films. Among its many sacred and liturgical treasures is Lorenzo Ghiberti's original 15th-century masterpiece, *Porta del paradiso* (Gates of Paradise; 1425–52) – gloriously golden, 16m-tall gilded bronze doors designed for the eastern entrance to the Baptistry – as well as those he sculpted for the northern entrance (1403–24). Michelangelo's achingly beautiful *La pietà*, sculpted when he was almost 80 and intended for his own tomb, is also here.

Palazzo Vecchio Museum

(☑055 276 85 58, 055 27 68 22; www.musefirenze.it; Piazza della Signoria; adult/reduced museum €10/8, tower €10/8, museum & tower €14/12, archaeological tour €4, combination ticket €18/16; ⊘museum 9am-11pm Fri-Wed, to 2pm Thu Apr-Sep, 9am-7pm Fri-Wed, to 2pm Thu Oct-Mar, tower 9am-9pm Fri-Wed, to 2pm Thu Apr-Sep, 10am-5pm Fri-Wed, to 2pm Thu Oct-Mar) This fortress palace, with its crenellations and 94m-high tower, was designed by Arnolfo di Cambio between 1298 and 1314 for the *signoria* (city government). It remains the seat of the city's power, home to the mayor's office and the municipal council. From the top of the **Torre d'Arnolfo** (tow-

Palazzo Vecchio

er), you can revel in unforgettable rooftop views. Inside, Michelangelo's *Genio della vittoria* (Genius of Victory) sculpture graces the Salone dei Cinquecento, a magnificent painted hall created for the city's 15th-century ruling Consiglio dei Cinquecento (Council of 500).

Battistero di San Giovanni   Landmark

(Baptistry; ☎055 230 28 85; www.ilgrandemuseodelduomo.it; Piazza di San Giovanni; adult/reduced incl baptistry, campanile, cupola, crypt & museum €15/3; ⊗8.15am-10.15am & 11.15am-7.30pm Mon-Fri, 8.15am-6.30pm Sat, 8.15am-1.30pm Sun) This 11th-century baptistry is a Romanesque, octagonal-striped structure of white-and-green marble with three sets of doors conceived as panels illustrating the story of humanity and the Redemption. Most celebrated are Lorenzo Ghiberti's gilded bronze doors at the eastern entrance, the *Porta del paradiso* (Gates of Paradise). What you see today are copies – the originals are in the Grande Museo del Duomo. Buy tickets online or at the ticket office at Piazza di San Giovanni 7, opposite the main baptistry entrance.

Piazza della Signoria   Piazza

Florentines flock to this square, the hub of local life since the 13th century, to meet friends and chat over early-evening *aperitivi* at historic cafes. Presiding over everything is Palazzo Vecchio (p432), Florence's city hall, and the 14th-century **Loggia dei Lanzi** FREE, an open-air gallery showcasing Renaissance sculptures, including Giambologna's *Rape of the Sabine Women* (c 1583), Benvenuto Cellini's bronze *Perseus* (1554) and Agnolo Gaddi's *Seven Virtues* (1384–89).

Piazza della Repubblica   Piazza

The site of a Roman forum and heart of medieval Florence, this busy civic space was created in the 1880s as part of a controversial plan of 'civic improvements' involving the demolition of the old market, Jewish ghetto and slums, and the relocation of nearly 6000 residents. Vasari's lovely *Log-*

Florence by Fiat

Hook up with Florence's **500 Touring Club** (☎346 8262324; www.500touringclub.com; Via Gherardo Silvani 149a) for a guided tour in a vintage motor – with you behind the wheel! Every car has a name in this outfit's fleet of gorgeous vintage Fiat 500s from the 1960s. Motoring tours are guided – hop in your car and follow the leader – and themed – families love the picnic trip, couples the wine tasting.

ALEXSTEPANOV/GETTY IMAGES ©

gia del Pesce (Fish Market) was saved and re-erected on Via Pietrapiana.

Museo delle Cappelle Medicee   Mausoleum

(Medici Chapels; www.firenzemusei.it; Piazza Madonna degli Aldobrandini 6; adult/reduced €8/4; ⊗8.15am-1.50pm, closed 1st, 3rd & 5th Mon, 2nd & 4th Sun of month) Nowhere is Medici conceit expressed so explicitly as in the Medici Chapels. Adorned with granite, marble, semi-precious stones and some of Michelangelo's most beautiful sculptures, it is the burial place of 49 dynasty members. Francesco I lies in the dark, imposing **Cappella dei Principi** (Princes' Chapel) alongside Ferdinando I and II and Cosimo I, II and III. Lorenzo il Magnifico is buried in the graceful **Sagrestia Nuova** (New Sacristy), which was Michelangelo's first architectural work.

Museo di San Marco   Museum

(☎055 238 86 08; Piazza San Marco 3; adult/reduced €4/2; ⊗8.15am-1.50pm Mon-Fri,

Florence

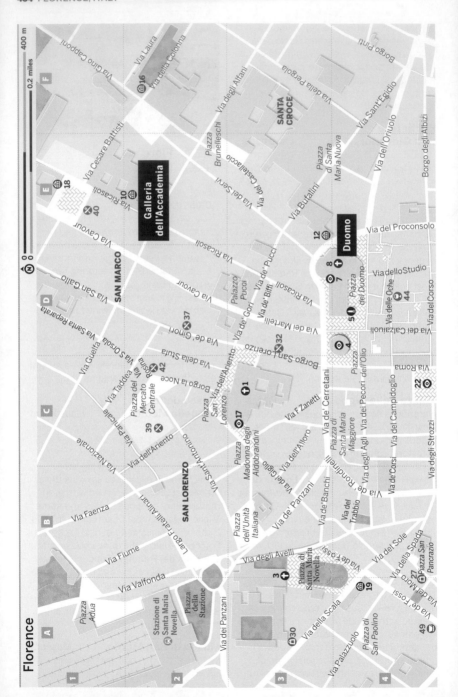

Galleria dell'Accademia

Duomo

400 m
0.2 miles

SANTA CROCE

SAN MARCO

SAN LORENZO

Piazza del Duomo

Piazza di Santa Maria Nuova

Piazza Brunelleschi

Piazza della Stazione

Piazza Adua

Piazza dell'Unità Italiana

Piazza Madonna degli Aldobrandini

Piazza del Mercato Centrale

Piazza di Santa Maria Novella

Piazza di San Paolino

Piazza San Pancrazio

Piazza di Santa Maria Maggiore

Stazione di Santa Maria Novella

Via Gino Capponi
Via Laura
Via della Colonna
Borgo Pinti
Via degli Alfani
Via della Pergola
Via Cesare Battisti
Via dei Servi
Via del Castellaccio
Via Sant'Egidio
Via dell'Oriuolo
Borgo degli Albizi
Via Ricasoli
Via Cavour
Via San Gallo
Via Santa Reparata
Via Guelfa
Via S Orsola
Via Taddea
Via Panicale
Via Nazionale
Via Faenza
Via Fiume
Via Valfonda
Via dei Panzani
Via del Proconsolo
Via dello Studio
Via delle Oche
Via del Corso
Via dei Calzaiuoli
Via Roma
Via del Campidoglio
Via de' Pecori
Via del Tebrio
Via de' Martelli
Via dei Biffi
Via de' Gori
Via de' Pucci
Via Ricasoli
Via Bufalini
Via de' Cerretani
Via degli Agli
Via de' Rondinelli
Via de' Banchi
Via del Giglio
Via dell'Alloro
Via de' Panzani
Via F Zanetti
Borgo San Lorenzo
Via Sant'Antonino
Via dell'Ariento
Via della Stufa
Via de' Ginori
Largo Fratelli Alinari
Via degli Avelli
Via della Scala
Via del Sole
Via del Moro
Via della Spada
Via de' Fossi
Via de' Fossi
Via Palazzuolo
Via dei Pecori dell'Olio

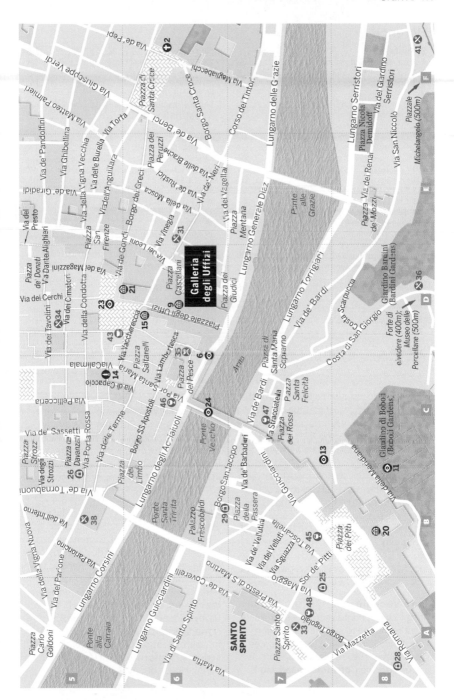

Galleria
degli Uffizi

Florence

8.15am-4.50pm Sat & Sun, closed 1st, 3rd & 5th Sun, 2nd & 4th Mon of month) At the heart of Florence's university area sits **Chiesa di San Marco** and adjoining 15th-century Dominican monastery where both gifted painter Fra' Angelico (c 1395–1455) and the sharp-tongued Savonarola piously served God. Today the monastery, aka one of Florence's most spiritually uplifting museums, showcases the work of Fra' Angelico. After centuries of being known as 'Il Beato Angelico' (literally 'The Blessed Angelic One') or simply 'Il Beato' (The Blessed), the Renaissance's most blessed religious painter was made a saint by Pope John Paul II in 1984.

Ponte Vecchio   Bridge
Dating to 1345, Ponte Vecchio was the only Florentine bridge to survive destruction at the hands of retreating German forces in 1944. Above the jewellers' shops on the eastern side, the **Corridoio Vasariano**

(Vasarian Corridor; ⊘by guided tour; ▣B) is a 16th-century passageway between the Uffizi and Palazzo Pitti that runs around, rather than through, the medieval **Torre dei Mannelli** at the bridge's southern end. The first documentation of a stone bridge here, at the narrowest crossing point along the entire length of the Arno, dates from 972.

Palazzo Pitti   Museum
(www.uffizi.beniculturali.it; Piazza dei Pitti; ⊘8.15am-6.50pm Tue-Sun) Commissioned by banker Luca Pitti and designed by Brunelleschi in 1457, this vast Renaissance palace was later bought by the Medici family. Over the centuries, it served as the residence of the city's rulers until the Savoys donated it to the state in 1919. Nowadays it houses an impressive silver museum, a couple of art museums and a series of rooms recreating life in the palace during House of Savoy times.

Giardino di Boboli Gardens

(☑055 29 48 83; www.polomuseale.firenze.it; Palazzo Pitti, Piazza dei Pitti; adult/reduced incl Tesoro del Granduchi, Museo delle Porcellane & Museo della Moda e del Costume €7/3.50, during temporary exhibition €10/5; ⊗8.15am-7.30pm summer, reduced hours winter, closed 1st & last Mon of month) Behind Palazzo Pitti, the Boboli Gardens were laid out in the mid-16th century to a design by architect Niccolò Pericoli. At the upper, southern limit, beyond the box-hedged rose garden and **Museo delle Porcellane** (Porcelain Museum), beautiful views over the Florentine countryside unfold. Within the lower reaches of the gardens, don't miss the fantastical shell- and gem-encrusted **Grotta del Buontalenti**, a decorative grotto built by Bernardo Buontalenti between 1583 and 1593 for Francesco I de' Medici.

Basilica di San Lorenzo Basilica

(www.operamedicealaurenziana.org; Piazza San Lorenzo; €6, with Biblioteca Medicea Laurenziana €8.50; ⊗10am-5pm Mon-Sat, plus 1.30-5pm Sun Mar-Oct) Considered one of Florence's most harmonious examples of Renaissance architecture, this unfinished basilica was the Medici parish church and mausoleum. It was designed by Brunelleschi in 1425 for Cosimo the Elder and built over an earlier 4th-century church. In the solemn interior, look for Brunelleschi's austerely beautiful **Sagrestia Vecchia** (Old Sacristy) with its sculptural decoration by Donatello. Michelangelo was commissioned to design the facade in 1518, but his design in white Carrara marble was never executed, hence the building's rough unfinished appearance.

Basilica di Santa Maria Novella Church

(☑055 21 92 57; www.smn.it; Piazza di Santa Maria Novella 18; adult/reduced €5/3.50; ⊗9am-7pm Mon-Thu, 11am-7pm Fri, 9am-6.30pm Sat, noon-6.30pm Sun summer, shorter hours winter) The striking green-and-white marble facade of 13th- to 15th-century Basilica di Santa Maria Novella fronts an entire monastical complex, comprising romantic church cloisters and a frescoed chapel. The basilica itself is a treasure chest of artistic masterpieces, climaxing with frescoes by Domenico Ghirlandaio. The lower section of the basilica's striped marbled facade is transitional from Romanesque to Gothic; the upper section and the main doorway (1456–70) were designed by Leon Battista Alberti. Book tickets in advance online to cut queuing time.

Museo Novecento Museum

(Museum of the 20th Century; ☑055 28 61 32, www.museonovecento.it; Piazza di Santa Maria Novella 10; adult/reduced €8.50/4; ⊗9am-7pm Mon-Wed, Sat & Sun, to 2pm Thu, to 11pm Fri summer, 9am-6pm Fri-Wed, to 2pm Thu winter) Don't allow the Renaissance to distract from Florence's fantastic modern art museum, in a 13th-century *palazzo* previously used as a pilgrim shelter, hospital and school. A well-articulated itinerary guides visitors through modern Italian painting and sculpture from the early 20th century to the late 1980s. Installation art makes effective use of the outside space on the 1st-floor loggia. Fashion and theatre get a nod on the 2nd floor, and the itinerary ends with a 20-minute cinematic montage of the best film set in Florence.

Basilica di Santa Croce Church, Museum

(☑055 246 61 05; www.santacroceopera.it; Piazza di Santa Croce; adult/reduced €8/4; ⊗9.30am-5.30pm Mon-Sat, 2-5.30pm Sun) The austere interior of this Franciscan basilica is a shock after the magnificent neo-Gothic facade enlivened by varying shades of coloured marble. Most visitors come to see the tombs of Michelangelo, Galileo and Ghiberti inside this church, but frescoes by Giotto in the chapels right of the altar are the real highlights. The basilica was designed by Arnolfo di Cambio between 1294 and 1385 and owes its name to a splinter of the Holy Cross donated by King Louis of France in 1258.

Piazzale Michelangelo Viewpoint

(◻13) Turn your back on the bevy of ticky-tacky souvenir stalls flogging *David* statues and boxer shorts and take in the

🍽 Florence's Best Panini

Semel (Piazza Ghiberti 44r; panini €3.50-5; ⊗11.30am-3pm Mon-Sat) Irresistibly creative sandwiches to go in Sant'Ambrogio.

'Ino (📞055 21 45 14; www.inofirenze.com; Via dei Georgofili 3r-7r; bruschette/panini €6/8; ⊗noon-4.30pm) 🥪 Made-to-measure, gourmet *panini* by the Galleria degli Uffizi.

Mariano (📞055 21 40 67; Via del Parione 19r; panini €3.50; ⊗8am-3pm & 5-7.30pm Mon-Fri, 8am-3pm Sat) Local neighbourhood cafe serving super-fresh *panini* to boot.

Gustapanino (www.facebook.com/pages/Gustapanino; Piazza Santa Spirito; focacce from €3.50; ⊗11am-8pm Mon-Sat, noon-5pm Sun) Hole-in-the-wall *enopaninoteca* (wine and sandwich stop) in Santa Croce.

Dal Barone (📞366 1479432; https://dalbarone.jimdo.com; Borgo San Lorenzo 30; sandwiches €5-10; ⊗11am-8pm) Hot and gooey *panini* to go by San Lorenzo market.

I Due Fratellini (📞055 239 60 96; www.iduefratellini.com; Via dei Cimatori 38r; panini €4; ⊗10am-7pm) Memorable vintage kid on the block, around since 1875.

spectacular city panorama from this vast square, pierced by one of Florence's two *David* copies. Sunset here is particularly dramatic. It's a 10-minute uphill walk along the serpentine road, paths and steps that scale the hillside from the Arno and Piazza Giuseppe Poggi; from Piazza San Niccolò walk uphill and bear left up the long flight of steps signposted Viale Michelangelo. Or take bus 13 from Stazione di Santa Maria Novella.

🛍 SHOPPING

Officina Profumo-Farmaceutica di Santa Maria Novella   Beauty, Gifts

(📞055 21 62 76; www.smnovella.it; Via della Scala 16; ⊗9.30am-8pm) In business since 1612, this exquisite perfumery-pharmacy began life when Santa Maria Novella's Dominican friars began to concoct cures and sweet-smelling unguents using medicinal herbs cultivated in the monastery garden. The shop, with interior from 1848, sells fragrances, skincare products, ancient herbal remedies and preparations for everything from relief of heavy legs to improving skin elasticity, memory and mental energy

It also sells teas, herbal infusions, liqueurs and scented candles. A real treasure, the shop has touchscreen catalogues and a state-of-the-art payment system, yet still manages to ooze vintage charm. After a day battling crowds at the Uffizi or Accademia, you might just want to come here for a cup of carefully prepared tea in its **Tisaneria** (Tearoom) or to buy a bottle of Aqua di Santa Maria Novella, one of the pharmacy's oldest herbal concoctions, taken to cure hysterics since 1614.

La Bottega Della Frutta   Food & Drinks

(📞055 239 85 90; Via dei Federighi 31r; ⊗8.30am-7.30pm Mon-Sat, closed Aug) Follow the trail of knowing Florentines, past the flower- and veg-laden bicycle parked outside, into this enticing food shop bursting with boutique cheeses, organic fruit and veg, biscuits, chocolates, conserved produce, excellent-value wine et al. Mozzarella oozing raw milk arrives fresh from Eboli in Sicily every Tuesday, and if you're looking to buy olive oil, this is the place to taste. Simply ask Elisabeta or husband Francesco.

Piazza Santa Trinita

&Co · Arts & Crafts

(And Company; 055 21 99 73; www.andcom-panyshop.com; Via Maggio 51r; 10.30am-1pm & 3-7pm Mon-Sat) Souvenir shopping at its best! This Pandora's box of beautiful objects is the love child of Florence-born, British-raised callligrapher and graphic designer Betty Soldi and her vintage-loving husband, Matteo Perduca. Their extraordinary boutique showcases Betty's customised cards, decorative paper products, upcycled homewares and custom fragrances alongside work by other designers (including super-chic leather-printed accessories by Danish design company Edition Poshette).

Obsequium · Wine

(055 21 68 49; www.obsequium.it; Borgo San Jacopo 17/39; 10am-10pm Mon, to 9pm Tue & Wed, to midnight Thu-Sat, noon-midnight Sun) Tuscan wines, wine accessories and gourmet foods, including truffles, in one of the city's finest wine shops – on the ground floor of one of Florence's best-preserved medieval towers to boot. Not sure which

wine to buy? Linger over a glass or indulge in a three-wine tasting with (€20 to €40) or without (€15 to €30) an accompanying *taglieri* (board) of mixed cheese and salami.

Lorenzo Perrone · Art

(340 274402; www.libribianchi.info; Borgo Tegolaio 59r; hours vary) Every book tells a different story in this absolutely fascinating artist's workshop, home to Milan-born Lorenzo Perrone who creates snow-white *Libri bianchi* (White Books) – aka sublime book sculptures – out of plaster, glue, acrylic and various upcycled objects. His working hours are somewhat predictably erratic; call ahead.

Il Papiro · Gifts & Souvenirs

(055 21 65 93; http://ilpapirofirenze.eu/en/; Via Porta Rosso 76; 10am-7pm) One of several branches around town, this elegant boutique specialises in books, journals, writing paper, cards and other stationery made from Florence's signature, hand-decorated marbled paper.

A terrace cafe

🍽 EATING

Mercato Centrale   Food Hall €

(📞055 239 97 98; www.mercatocentrale.it;
Piazza del Mercato Centrale 4; dishes €7-15;
🕙10am-midnight; 📶) Meander the maze
of stalls rammed with fresh produce at
Florence's oldest and largest food market,
on the ground floor of a fantastic iron-
and-glass structure designed by architect
Giuseppe Mengoni in 1874. Head to the 1st
floor's buzzing, thoroughly contemporary
food hall with dedicated bookshop, cookery
school and artisan stalls cooking steaks,
burgers, tripe *panini,* vegetarian dishes,
pizza, gelato, pastries and pasta.

Load up and find a free table.

Trattoria Mario   Tuscan €

(📞055 21 85 50; www.trattoria-mario.com; Via
Rosina 2; meals €25; 🕙noon-3.30pm Mon-Sat,
closed 3 weeks Aug; ❄) Arrive by noon to
ensure a stool around a shared table at this
noisy, busy, brilliant trattoria – a legend
that retains its soul (and allure with locals)
despite being in every guidebook. Charming Fabio, whose grandfather opened the

place in 1953, is front of house while big
brother Romeo and nephew Francesco
cook with speed in the kitchen. No advance
reservations; no credit cards.

All'Antico Vinaio   Osteria €

(📞055 238 27 23; www.allanticovinaio.com; Via
de' Neri 65r; tasting platters €10-30; 🕙10am-
4pm & 6-11pm Tue-Sat, noon-3.30pm Sun) The
crowd spills out the door of this noisy
Florentine thoroughbred. Push your way to
the tables at the back to taste cheese and
salami in situ (advance reservations recommended). Or join the queue at the deli
counter for a well-stuffed foccacia wrapped
in waxed paper to take away – quality is
outstanding. Pour yourself a glass of wine
while you wait.

Il Teatro del Sale   Tuscan €€

(📞055 200 14 92; www.teatrodelsale.com; Via
dei Macci 111r; lunch/dinner/weekend brunch
€15/35/20; 🕙11am-3pm & 7.30-11pm Tue-Sat,
11am-3pm Sun, closed Aug) Florentine chef
Fabio Picchi is one of Florence's living
treasures who steals the Sant' Ambrogio show with this eccentric, good-value

members-only club (everyone welcome; membership €7) inside an old theatre. He cooks up weekend brunch, lunch and dinner, culminating at 9.30pm in a live performance of drama, music or comedy arranged by his wife, artistic director and comic actress Maria Cassi.

Dinners are hectic: grab a chair, serve yourself water, wine and antipasti and wait for the chef to yell out what's about to be served before queuing at the glass hatch for your *primo* (first course) and *secondo* (second course).

San Niccolò 39   Seafood €€

(055 200 13 97; www.sanniccolo39.com; Via di San Niccolò 39; meals €40; ⊗7-10.30pm Tue, 12.30-2.30pm & 7-10.30pm Wed-Sat;) With street terrace in front and hidden summer garden out the back, this contemporary address in quaint San Niccolò is a gem. Fish – both raw and cooked – is the house speciality, with chef Vanni cooking up a storm with his creative salted-cod burgers, swordfish steak with radicchio, and famous linguine with squid ink and Cetara anchovy oil.

Essenziale   Tuscan €€

(055.247 69 56; http://essenziale.me; Piazza di Cestello 3r; 3-/5-/7-course tasting menu €35/55/75, brunch €28; ⊗7-10pm Tue-Sat, 11am-4pm Sun;) There's no finer showcase for modern Tuscan cuisine than this loft-style restaurant in a 19th-century warehouse. Preparing dishes at the kitchen bar, in rolled-up shirt sleeves and navy butcher's apron, is dazzling young chef Simone Cipriani. Order one of his tasting menus to sample the full range of his inventive, thoroughly modern cuisine inspired by classic Tuscan dishes.

La Ménagère   International €€

(055 075 06 00; www.lamenagere.it; Via de' Ginori 8r; meals €15-70; ⊗7am-2am;) Be it breakfast, lunch, dinner, good coffee or cocktails after dark, this bright industrial-styled space lures Florence's hip brigade. A concept store, the Housewife is a fashionable one-stop shop for chic china and tableware, designer kitchen gear and fresh flowers. For daytime dining and drinking,

Aperitivo Time

No ritual is more sacrosanct than *aperitivo* or 'Happy Hour' as many bars call it in English when friends gather for pre-dinner drinks accompanied by gourmet tapas or a banquet of savoury snacks. Be it a perfectly mixed cocktail at **Mad Souls & Spirits** (055 627 16 21; www.facebook.com/madsoulsandspirits; Borgo San Frediano 38r; ⊗6pm-2am Thu-Sun, to midnight Mon & Wed;), or a glass of Tuscan wine paired with cured meats at **Enoteca Pitti Gola e Cantina** (p442) or **Le Volpi e l'Uva** (p442), *aperitivo* is a cherished Florentine tradition that should be embraced with gusto when in town.

Aperol spritz

pick from retro sofas in the boutique area, or banquet seating and bar stools in the jam-packed bistro.

La Leggenda dei Frati   Tuscan €€€

(055 068 05 45; www.laleggendadeifrati.it; Villa Bardini, Costa di San Giorgio 6a; menus €60 & €75, meals €70; ⊗12.30-2pm & 7.30-10pm Tue-Sun;) Summertime's hottest address. At home in the grounds of historic Villa Bardini, Michelin-starred Legend of Friars enjoys the most romantic terrace with view in Florence. Veggies are plucked fresh from the vegetable patch, tucked between waterfalls and ornamental beds in Giardino Bardini, and contemporary art jazzes up the classically chic interior. Cuisine is Tuscan, gastronomic and well worth the vital advance reservation.

Florence Online

The Florentine (www.theflorentine.net) English-language newspaper.

Girl in Florence (www.girlinflorence.com) Inside musings, practical tips and smart drinking and dining recommendations from an American gal called Georgette, at home in Florence.

Lost in Florence (www.lostinflorence.it) Great for 'hipster chic' boutique openings in the city.

Art Trav (www.arttrav.com) Florence-based art historian's museum and sightseeing recommendations.

Emiko Davies (www.emikodavies.com) Exceptional, Florence-based food blogger, cookbook writer and photographer; author of *Florentine: Food and Stories from the Renaissance City* (2016).

🍷 DRINKING & NIGHTLIFE

Le Volpi e l'Uva   Wine Bar

(📞055 239 81 32; www.levolpieluva.com; Piazza dei Rossi 1; ⊙11am-9pm Mon-Sat) This unassuming wine bar hidden away by Chiesa di Santa Felicità remains as appealing as the day it opened over a decade ago. Its food and wine pairings are first class – taste and buy boutique wines by small producers from all over Italy, matched perfectly with cheeses, cold meats and the best crostini in town. Wine-tasting classes too.

Rasputin   Cocktail Bar

(📞055 28 03 99; www.facebook.com/rasputin firenze; Borgo Tegolaio 21r; ⊙8pm-2am) The 'secret' speakeasy everyone knows about. It has no sign outside and is disguised as a chapel of sorts; look for the tiny entrance with two-seat wooden pew, crucifix on the wall, vintage pics and tea lights flickering in the doorway. Inside, it's back to the 1930s with period furnishings, an exclusive vibe and barmen mixing prohibition-era cocktails. Reservations (phone or Facebook page) recommended.

Todo Modo   Cafe

(📞055 239 91 10; www.todomodo.org; Via dei Fossi 15r; ⊙10am-8pm Tue-Sun) This contemporary bookshop with hip cafe and pocket theatre at the back makes a refreshing change from the usual offerings. A salvaged mix of vintage tables and chairs sits between book- and bottle-lined shelves in the relaxed cafe, actually called 'UqBar' after the fictional place of the same name in a short story by Argentinian writer Jorges Luis Borges.

Its weekend lunches are particularly popular: think healthy salads, a couple of homemade mains chalked on the board, and delicious muffins and cakes.

La Terrazza Lounge Bar   Bar

(📞055 272 659 87; www.lungarnocollection.com; Vicolo dell' Oro 6r; ⊙2.30-11.30pm Apr-Sep) This rooftop bar with wooden-decking terrace accessible from the 5th floor of the 1950s-styled, design Hotel Continentale is as chic as one would expect of a fashion-house hotel. Its *aperitivo* buffet is a modest affair, but who cares with that fabulous, drop-dead-gorgeous panorama of one of Europe's most beautiful cities. Dress the part or feel out of place. Count on €19 for a cocktail.

Santarosa Bistrot   Bar

(📞055 230 90 57; www.facebook.com/santa rosa.bistrot; Lungarno di Santarosa; ⊙8am-midnight; 🛜) The living is easy at this hipster garden bistro-bar, snug against a chunk of ancient city wall in the flowery Santarosa gardens. Comfy cushioned sofas built from recycled wooden crates sit beneath trees al fresco; the food is superb (meals €30); and mixologists behind the bar complement an excellent wine list curated by **Enoteca Pitti Gola e Cantina** (📞055 21 27 04; www.pittigo-laecantina.com; Piazza dei Pitti 16; ⊙1pm-midnight Wed-Mon) with serious craft cocktails.

ℹ️ INFORMATION

There are several places in the city to get information, including the following:

Airport tourist office (📞055 31 58 74; www.firenzeturismo.it; Florence Airport, Via del Termine 11; ⊙9am-7pm Mon-Sat, to 2pm Sun)

Wine bar

Central tourist office (055 29 08 32; www. firenzeturismo.it; Via Cavour 1r; ⊙9am-1pm Mon-Fri)

Infopoint Bigallo (☑055 28 84 96; www.firen-zeturismo.it; Piazza San Giovanni 1; ⊙9am-7pm Mon-Sat, to 2pm Sun)

Infopoint Stazione (☑055 21 22 45; www. firenzeturismo.it; Piazza della Stazione 4; ⊙9am-6.30pm Mon-Sat, to 1.30pm Sun)

GETTING THERE & AWAY

Most people arrive one of two ways: by air from international airports in Florence and Pisa, or by train to Stazione Campo di Marte or **Stazione di Santa Maria Novella** (Piazza della Stazione), both in central Florence. Florence is on the Rome–Milan train line.

GETTING AROUND

Florence itself is small and best navigated on foot; most major sights are within easy walking distance.

Bicycle Rent city bikes from in front of Stazione di Santa Maria Novella and elsewhere in the city.

Car & Motorcycle Nonresident traffic is banned from the historic centre; parking is an absolute headache and best avoided

Public Transport There's an efficient network of buses and trams, most handy for visiting Fiesole and getting up the hill to Piazzale Michelangelo.

Taxi Cabs can't be hailed on the street; find ranks at the train and bus stations or call ☑055 42 42 or ☑055 43 90.

Tuscany, Italy

With its lyrical landscapes, superlative art and superb cucina contadina (food from the farmer's kitchen), Tuscany offers a splendid array of treats for travellers. No land is more caught up with the fruits of its fertile earth than Tuscany, a gourmet destination where locality, seasonality and sustainability are revered. And oh, the art! During the medieval and Renaissance periods, Tuscany's painters, sculptors and architects created world-class masterpieces. Squirrelled away and safeguarded today in churches, museums and galleries all over the region, Tuscan art is truly unmatched.

Tuscany in Two Days

Base yourself in **Siena** (p452), and spend your first day exploring this charming town, including a visit to the Duomo and the Museo Civico. On day two, head northwest to San Gimignano's famed **towers** (p446), or east to **Arezzo** (p455) for churches, museums and, if the timing is right, antiques.

Tuscany in Four Days

With an additional two days, head southwest to **Montepulciano** and **Montalcino** on day three, and over to Pisa and its famous **tower** (p448) on day four. Or, for a little luxury, spend some time in a local **spa** (p457).

After leaving Tuscany, Rome (p352) and Venice (p400) are ideal next stops.

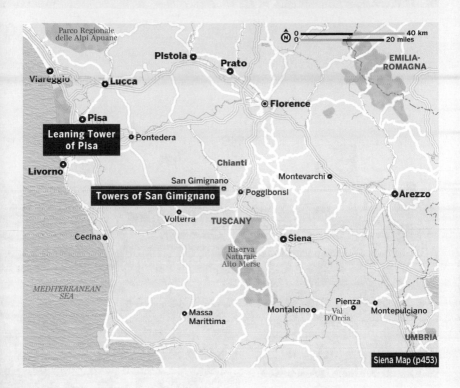

Arriving in Tuscany

Pisa International Airport Tuscany's principal international gateway; from here, buses run to Pisa, Florence and Siena.

Florence Airport This smaller airport serves flights from Italian and European destinations.

Stazione di Santa Maria Novella Florence's station is the region's biggest and busiest; it's served by regular fast trains on the main Rome–Milan line.

Where to Stay

An *agriturismo* (rural accommodation on a working farm, winery or agricultural domain) is an idyllic five-star way of experiencing country life in Tuscany. It's perfect for those with a car, and usually highly practical for those travelling with children. Tuscany also abounds in *palazzo* hotels: these historic 'palace' hotels, designer in vibe, are the boutique option for those in towns and cities with a midrange to top-end budget.

CANADASTOCK/SHUTTERSTOCK ©

Towers of San Gimignano

A mecca for day trippers, San Gimignano lies deep in the Tuscan countryside northwest of Siena. Known as the 'medieval Manhattan', it features 15 11th-century towers that soar above its hilltop centro storico (historic centre).

Great For...

☑ Don't Miss

The town's **Galleria Continua** (☏0577 94 31 34; www.galleriacontinua.com; Via del Castello 11; ☉10am-1pm & 2-7pm) FREE.

Originally an Etruscan village, the town was named after the bishop of Modena, San Gimignano, who is said to have saved it from Attila the Hun. It became a *comune* in 1199 and quickly flourished, thanks in no small part to its position on the Via Francigena. Up to 72 towers were built as the town's prosperous burghers sought to outdo their neighbours and flaunt their wealth.

Collegiata

San Gimignano's Romanesque cathedral, the **Collegiata** (Duomo; Basilica di Santa Maria Assunta; ☏0577 94 01 52; www.duomosangimignano.it; Piazza del Duomo; adult/reduced €4/2; ☉10am-7pm Mon-Sat, to 4.30pm winter), is named after the college of priests who originally managed it. Parts of the building

CAN/ADASTOCK/SHUTTERSTOCK ©

Palazzo Comunale

The 12th-century **Palazzo Comunale** (☎0577 99 03 12; www.sangimignanomusei.it; Piazza del Duomo 2; combined Civic Museums ticket adult/reduced €9/7; ⊗10am-7.30pm summer, 11am-5.30pm winter) has always been the centre of local government – its Sala di Dante is where the great poet addressed the town's council in 1299, urging it to support the Guelph cause. The room (also known as the Sala del Consiglio) is home to Lippo Memmi's early 14th-century *Maestà*, which portrays the enthroned Virgin and Child surrounded by angels, saints and local dignitaries.

Upstairs, the pinacoteca has a charming collection of paintings from the Sienese and Florentine schools of the 12th to 15th centuries.

In the Camera del Podestà is a meticulously restored cycle of frescoes by Memmo di Filippuccio, illustrating a moral history – the rewards of marriage are shown in the scenes of a husband and wife naked in a bath and in bed.

After you've enjoyed the art, be sure to climb the 218 steps of the palazzo's 54m-tall Torre Grossa for spectacular views of the town and surrounding countryside.

were built in the second half of the 11th century, but its remarkably vivid frescoes date from the 14th century.

Entry is via the side stairs and through a loggia that originally functioned as the baptistry. Once in the main space, face the altar and look to your left (north). On the wall are scenes from Genesis and the Old Testament by Bartolo di Fredi, dating from around 1367. On the right (south) wall are scenes from the New Testament by the workshop of Simone Martini, which were completed in 1336. On the inside of the front facade is Taddeo di Bartolo's striking depiction of the *Last Judgment* – on the upper-left side is a fresco depicting *Paradiso* (Heaven) and on the upper-right *Inferno* (Hell).

Leaning Tower of Pisa

One of Italy's signature sights, Pisa's stunning Torre Pendente (Leaning Tower) truly lives up to its name, leaning a startling 3.9 degrees off the vertical. Visit Pisa as a day trip from Florence or one of the charming Tuscan towns further south.

Great For...

☑ Don't Miss

Planning an enchanting after-dark visit: if you're in Pisa from mid-June to late August, doors don't close till 10pm.

The 56m-high tower, officially the Duomo's *campanile* (bell tower), took almost 200 years to build, but was already listing when it was unveiled in 1372. Over time, the tilt, caused by a layer of weak subsoil, steadily worsened until it was finally halted by a major stabilisation project in the 1990s.

Planning Your Visit

Access to the Leaning Tower is limited to 40 people at a time – children under eight are not allowed in and those aged eight to 10 years must hold an adult's hand.

Visits last 35 minutes and involve a steep climb up 251 occasionally slippery steps. All bags, handbags included, must be deposited at the free left-luggage desk next to the central ticket office – cameras are about the only thing you can take up.

The Duomo and the Leaning Tower

JAVEN/SHUTTERSTOCK ©

❶ Need to Know

Torre Pendente; ☑050 83 50 11; www.opa-pisa.it; Piazza dei Miracoli; €18; ⊗8am-8pm Apr-Sep, 9am-7pm Oct, to 6pm Mar, 10am-5pm Nov-Feb

✕ Take a Break

Grab a huge gourmet *panino* from **L'Ostellino** (Piazza Cavallotti 1; panini €3.50-7; ⊗noon-4.30pm Mon-Fri, to 6pm Sat & Sun) for a picnic beside the tower.

★ Top Tip

With two million visitors every year, crowds are the norm. Visit between November and March for shorter queues.

Tower & Combo Tickets

To guarantee your visit and cut the long high-season queue, buy tickets in advance online (maximum 20 days before visiting), or go straight to a ticket office when you arrive in Pisa to book a slot for later in the day.

Buy tickets from the main **ticket office** (⊗8.30am-7.30pm summer, to 5.30pm winter) behind the tower or the smaller office inside Museo delle Sinopie (on Piazza dei Miracoli). Ticket offices in Pisa also sell combination tickets for other city sights.

What's Nearby?

Pisa's medieval heart lies north of the water; from **Piazza Cairoli**, with its evening bevy of bars and gelato shops, meander along **Via Cavour**. A daily fresh-produce market fills **Piazza delle Vettovaglie**.

Duomo   Cathedral

(Duomo di Santa Maria Assunta; ☑050 83 50 11; www.opapisa.it; Piazza dei Miracoli; ⊗10am-8pm Apr-Sep, to 7pm Oct, to 6pm Nov-Mar) **FREE** The Romanesque Duomo was begun in 1064 and consecrated in 1118. Admission is free, but you'll need an entrance coupon from the ticket office or a ticket from one of the other Piazza dei Miracoli sights.

Battistero   Christian Site

(Battistero di San Giovanni; ☑050 83 50 11; www.opapisa.it; Piazza dei Miracoli; €5, combination ticket with Camposanto or Museo delle Sinopie €7, Camposanto & Museo €8; ⊗8am-8pm Apr-Sep, 9am-7pm Oct, to 6pm Mar, 10am-5pm Nov-Feb) This unusual round baptistry (1395) has one dome piled on top of another, each roofed half in lead, half in tiles, and topped by a gilt bronze John the Baptist.

Tuscan Road Trip

Taking in Tuscany's two great medieval rivals, Florence and Siena, Chianti's wine-rich hills, and the Unesco-listed Val d'Orcia, this drive offers artistic masterpieces, soul-stirring scenery and captivating Renaissance towns.

Start Florence
Distance 185km
Duration Four days

1 Start your journey in the cradle of the Renaissance, **Florence**. Admire Brunelleschi's Duomo dome, wander around the Galleria degli Uffizi, and greet Michelangelo's *David* at the Galleria dell'Accademia.

START 1

SR222

RA3

Badia a Passignano 2

Take a Break... Enjoy a meal at Osteria di Passignano (www.osteriadipassignano.com; Via di Passignano 33; ⏰12.15-2.15pm & 7.30-10pm Mon-Sat) in Badia a Passignano, about 20 minutes from Greve.

3

Riserva Naturale Alto Merse

SR2

SS223

4

3 The medieval cityscape of **Siena** is one of Italy's most captivating. Be inspired by the Duomo's intricate facade, bustling Piazza del Campo, and fine art in the Museo Civico.

4 Take the SR2 (Via Cassia) to **Montalcino**, known to wine buffs around the world for its celebrated local drop, Brunello.

San
Godenzo

Parco Nazionale
delle Foreste
Casentinesi, Monte
Falterona e Campigna

Monte
Falterona

40 km

20 miles

2 Pick up the SR222 (Via Chianti-giana) and head south to Chianti wine country. Stop off in the centuries-old wine centre of **Greve**, then continue south to Siena.

Classic Photo: The stunning Val d'Orcia offers open views of undulating fields, stone farmhouses and rows of elegant cypresses.

5 Head east to the Val d'Orcia and pretty **Pienza**. Check out the magnificent Renaissance buildings in and around Piazza Pio II, which went up in just four years in the 15th century and haven't been remodelled since.

5

6
FINISH

SR2

6 Steeply stacked **Montepulciano** harbours a wealth of *palazzi* and fine buildings, plus grandstand views over the Val di Chiana and Val d'Orcia. Round off your trip with a glass or two of the local Vino Nobile.

Siena

Siena is one of Italy's most enchanting medieval towns. Its walled centre is a beautifully preserved warren of dark lanes punctuated with Gothic *palazzi*, and at its heart, Piazza del Campo, the sloping square that is the venue for the city's famous annual horse race, Il Palio.

◉ SIGHTS

Piazza del Campo   Square

This sloping piazza, popularly known as Il Campo, has been Siena's civic and social centre since being staked out by the ruling Consiglio dei Nove in the mid-12th century. It was built on the site of a Roman marketplace, and its pie-piece paving design is divided into nine sectors to represent the number of members of that ruling council.

Palazzo Pubblico   Historic Building

(Palazzo Comunale; Piazza del Campo) The restrained, 14th-century Palazzo Comunale serves as the grand centrepiece of the square in which it sits – notice how its concave facade mirrors the opposing convex curve. From the *palazzo* soars a graceful bell tower, the **Torre del Mangia** (☑0577 29 23 43; www.enjoysiena.it; €10; ☺10am-6.15pm summer, to 3.15pm winter), 102m high and with 500-odd steps. The views from the top are magnificent.

Museo Civico   Museum

(Civic Museum; ☑0577 29 22 32; Palazzo Pubblico, Piazza del Campo 1; adult/reduced €9/8; ☺10am-6.15pm summer, to 5.15pm winter) Siena's most famous museum occupies rooms richly frescoed by artists of the Sienese school. Commissioned by the governing body of the city, rather than by the Church, many – unusually – depict secular subjects. The highlight is Simone Martini's celebrated *Maestà* (Virgin Mary in Majesty; 1315) in the **Sala del Mappamondo** (Hall of the World Map). It features the Madonna beneath a canopy surrounded by saints and angels, and is Martini's first known work.

Duomo   Cathedral

(Cattedrale di Santa Maria Assunta; ☑0577 28 63 00; www.operaduomo.siena.it; Piazza Duomo; summer/winter €4/free, when floor displayed €7; ☺10.30am-7pm Mon-Sat, 1.30-6pm Sun summer, to 5.30pm winter) Siena's cathedral is one of Italy's most awe-inspiring churches. Construction started in 1215 and over the centuries many of Italy's top artists have contributed: Giovanni Pisano designed the intricate white, green and red marble facade; Nicola Pisano carved the elaborate pulpit; Pinturicchio painted some of the frescoes; Michelangelo, Donatello and Gian Lorenzo Bernini all produced sculptures. Buy tickets from the **duomo ticket office** (Santa Maria della Scala, Piazza del Duomo; ☺10am-6.30pm summer, to 5pm winter).

Museale Santa
Maria della Scala   Museum

(☑0577 53 45 71, 0577 53 45 11; www.santamariadellascala.com; Piazza Duomo 1; adult/reduced €9/7; ☺10am-5pm Mon, Wed & Thu, to 8pm Fri, to 7pm Sat & Sun, extended hours in summer) This former hospital, parts of which date from the 13th century, was built as a hospice for pilgrims travelling the Via Francigena pilgrimage trail. Its highlight is the upstairs Pellegrinaio (Pilgrim's Hall), with vivid 15th-century frescoes by Lorenzo Vecchietta, Priamo della Quercia and Domenico di Bartolo lauding the good works of the hospital and its patrons.

Pinacoteca Nazionale   Gallery

(☑0577 28 11 61; http://pinacotecanazionale.siena.it; Via San Pietro 29; adult/reduced €4/2; ☺8.15am-7.15pm Tue-Sat, 9am-1pm Sun & Mon) An extraordinary collection of Gothic masterpieces from the Sienese school sits inside the once grand but now sadly dishevelled 14th-century Palazzo Buonsignori. The pick of the collection is on the 2nd floor, including magnificent works by Duccio di Buoninsegna, Simone Martini, Niccolò di Segna, Lippo Memmi, Ambrogio and Pietro Lorenzetti, Bartolo di Fredi and Taddeo di Bartolo.

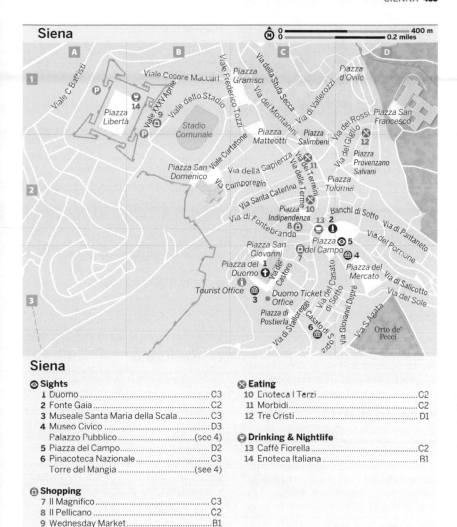

Siena

⊕ SHOPPING

Il Magnifico   Food

(☏0577 28 11 06; www.ilmagnifico.siena.it; Via
dei Pellegrini 27; ⊙7.30am-7.30pm Mon-Sat)
Lorenzo Rossi is Siena's best baker, and his
panforte, *ricciarelli* (sugar-dusted chewy
almond biscuits) and *cavallucci* (almond
biscuits made with Tuscan millefiori honey)
are a weekly purchase for most local

households. Try them at his bakery and
shop behind the *duomo*, and you'll understand why.

Il Pellicano   Ceramics

(☏0577 24 79 14; www.siena-ilpellicano.it; Via
Diaccето 17a; ⊙10.30am-7pm summer, hours
vary in winter) Elisabetta Ricci has been
making traditional hand-painted Sienese
ceramics for over 30 years. She shapes,

Celebrating Il Palio

Dating from the Middle Ages, Il Palio is a spectacular annual event in July and August that includes a series of colourful pageants and a wild horse race in Piazza del Campo. Ten of Siena's 17 *contrade* (town districts) compete for the coveted *palio* (silk banner). Each *contrada* has its own traditions, symbol and colours, plus its own church and *palio* museum.

LONGJON/SHUTTERSTOCK ©

fires and paints her creations, often using Renaissance-era styles or typical *contrade* designs. Elisabetta also conducts lessons in traditional ceramic techniques.

Wednesday Market   Market
(⊘7.30am-2pm) Spreading around Fortezza Medicea and towards the Stadio Comunale, this is one of Tuscany's largest markets and is great for cheap clothing; some food is also sold. An antiques market is held here on the third Sunday of each month.

✷ EATING & DRINKING

Morbidi   Deli €
(⌨0577 28 02 68; www.morbidi.com; Via Banchi di Sopra 75; lunch €12, aperitivo buffet from €7; ⊘8am-8pm Mon-Thu, to 10pm Fri & Sat) Possibly the classiest cheap feed in Siena: set in the stylish basement of Morbidi's deli, the lunch buffet on offer here is excellent. For a mere €12, you can join the well-dressed locals sampling antipasti, salads, risottos, pastas and a dessert of the day. Bottled water is supplied; wine and coffee cost extra.

Buy your ticket upstairs before heading down.

Enoteca I Terzi   Tuscan €€
(⌨0577 4 43 29; www.enotecaiterzi.it; Via dei Termini 7; meals €35; ⊘11am-3pm & 6.30pm-1am Mon-Sat, shorter hrs in winter) A favourite for many locals who head to this historic *enoteca* (wine bar) to linger over lunches, *aperitivi* and casual dinners featuring top-notch Tuscan *salumi* (cured meats), delicate handmade pasta and wonderful wines.

Tre Cristi   Seafood €€€
(⌨0577 28 06 08; www.trecristi.com; Vicolo di Provenzano 1-7; meals €45, tasting menus €40-65; ⊘12.30-2.30pm & 7.30-10pm Mon-Sat) Seafood restaurants are thin on the ground in this meat-obsessed region, so the long existence of Tre Cristi (it's been around since 1830) should be heartily celebrated. The menu here is as elegant as the decor, and touches such as a complimentary glass of *prosecco* (dry sparkling wine) at the start of the meal add to the experience.

Enoteca Italiana   Wine Bar
(⌨0577 22 88 43; www.enoteca-italiana.it; Fortezza Medicea, Piazza Libertà 1; ⊘noon-7.30pm Mon & Tue, to midnight Wed-Sat) The former munitions cellar and dungeon of this Medici fortress has been artfully transformed into a classy *enoteca* that carries more than 1500 Italian labels. You can take a bottle with you, ship a case home or just enjoy a glass in the attractive courtyard or vaulted interior. There's usually food available, too.

Caffè Fiorella   Cafe
(Torrefazione Fiorella; www.torrefazionefiorella.it; Via di Città 13; ⊘7am-6pm Mon-Sat) Squeeze into this tiny, heart-of-the-action space to enjoy some of Siena's best coffee. In summer, the coffee granita with a dollop of cream is a wonderful indulgence.

ℹ INFORMATION

Tourist Office (⌨0577 28 05 51; www.enjoysiena.it; Piazza Duomo 1, Santa Maria della Scala; ⊘9am-6pm summer, to 5pm winter)

Siena's Duomo (p452)

ℹ️ GETTING THERE & AWAY

Bus service **Siena Mobilità** (📞800 922984; www.sienamobilita.it) links Siena with Florence (€7.80, 1¼ hours, at least hourly) and San Gimignano (€6, 1¼ hours, 10 daily Monday to Saturday).

Arezzo

Arezzo may not be a Tuscan centrefold, but those parts of its historic centre that survived merciless WWII bombings are as compelling as any destination in the region – the city's central square is as beautiful as it appears in Roberto Benigni's classic film *La vita è bella* (Life is Beautiful).

Today, the city is known for its churches, museums and fabulously sloping Piazza Grande, across which a huge antiques fair spills during the first weekend of each month. Come dusk, Arentini (locals of Arezzo) spill along the length of shop-clad Corso Italia for the ritual *passeggiata* (evening stroll).

> *Siena's cathedral is one of Italy's most awe-inspiring churches*

◎ SIGHTS

Cappella Bacci   Church
(📞0575 35 27 27; www.pierodellafrancesca.it; Piazza San Francesco; adult/reduced €8/5; ⏰9am-6pm Mon-Fri, to 5.30pm Sat, 1-5.30pm Sun) This chapel, in the apse of 14th-century **Basilica di San Francesco**, safeguards one of Italian art's greatest works: Piero della Francesca's fresco cycle of the *Legend of the True Cross*. Painted between 1452 and 1466, it relates the story of the cross on which Christ was crucified. Only 25 people are allowed in every half-hour, making advance booking (by telephone or email) essential in high season. The ticket office is down the stairs by the basilica's entrance.

Chiesa di Santa Maria della Pieve   Church
(Corso Italia 7; ⏰8am-12.30pm & 3-6.30pm) **FREE** This 12th-century church – Arezzo's

oldest – has an exotic Romanesque arcaded facade adorned with carved columns, each uniquely decorated. Above the central doorway are 13th-century carved reliefs called *Cyclo dei mesi* representing each month of the year. The plain interior's highlight – removed for restoration work at the time of writing – is Pietro Lorenzetti's polyptych *Madonna and Saints* (1320–24), beneath the semidome of the apse. Below the altar is a 14th-century silver bust reliquary of the city's patron saint, San Donato.

Duomo di Arezzo Cathedral

(Cattedrale di SS Donato e Pietro; Piazza del Duomo; ⊙7am-12.30pm & 3.30-6.30pm) **FREE** Construction started in the 13th century but Arezzo's cathedral wasn't completed until the 15th century. In the northeast corner, left of the intricately carved main altar, is an exquisite fresco of *Mary Magdalene* (c 1459) by Piero della Francesca. Also notable are five glazed terracottas by Andrea della Robbia and his studio. Behind the cathedral is the pentagonal **Fortezza Medicea** (1502) atop the crest of one of Arezzo's two hills – the *duomo* was built on the crest of the other.

Museo Archeologico Nazionale 'Gaio Cilnio Mecenate' Museum

(Gaius Cilnius Maecenas Archeological Museum; ☑0575 2 08 82; www.facebook.com/archeologicoarezzo; Via Margaritone 10; adult/reduced €6/3; ⊙8.30am-7.30pm, to 1.30pm Nov) Overlooking the remains of a Roman amphitheatre that once seated up to 10,000 spectators, this museum in a 14th-century convent building exhibits Etruscan and Roman artefacts. The highlight is the *Cratere di Euphronios*, a 6th-century BC Etruscan vase decorated with vivid scenes showing Hercules in battle. Also of note is an exquisite tiny portrait of a bearded man from the second half of the 3rd century AD, executed in chrysography whereby a fine sheet of gold is engraved then encased between two glass panes.

⊗ EATING & DRINKING

Antica Osteria Agania Tuscan €

(☑0575 29 53 81; www.agania.com; Via G Mazzini 10; meals €20; ⊙noon-3pm & 6-10.30pm Tue-Sun) Agania has been around for years and her fare is die-hard traditional – the tripe

Cobblestone alley

and *grifi con polenta* (lambs' cheeks with polenta) are sensational. But it is timeless, welcoming addresses like this, potted fresh herbs on the doorstep, that remain the cornerstone of Tuscan dining. Begin with *antipasto misto* (mixed appetisers) followed by your choice combo of six pastas and eight sauces.

Arrive by 1pm to beat the crowd of regulars.

Osteria dell'Acquolina   Tuscan €€

(055 97 74 97; www.acquolina.it; Via Setteponti Levante 26, Terranuova Bracciolini; meals €30; noon-4pm & 7-11pm Tue-Sun) Heading east from Florence to Arezzo, this vivid pink villa in an olive grove is the perfect lunch stop, especially in summer when the dining action spills out onto the terracotta-brick terrace with 360-degree view of olive trees, vines and hills beyond. Cuisine is Tuscan and there's no written menu – the chef cooks different dishes every day.

Take the Valdarno exit off the A1 and follow signs for 'Terranuova Bracciolini' and 'Arezzo' until you pick up 'Osteria dell'Acquolina' signs.

Trattoria del Leone   Tuscan €€

(0575 35 79 27; www.trattoriadelleone.it; Piazza del Popolo 11; meals €30; noon-2.30pm Tue-Sun, 7.30-10pm Tue-Sat, closed Aug) A perfect example of the trattoria model that is trending in Tuscany today, del Leone is found in a slightly obscure location on some stairs leading down into Piazza del Popolo. The food is delicious – smallish portions of beautifully prepared modern riffs on Tuscan classics, with homemade pasta, bruschetta and salads.

Caffè dei Costanti   Cafe

(0575 182 40 75; www.caffedeicostanti.it; Piazza San Francesco 19-20; 7.30am-2am summer, to 9.30pm Wed-Sun winter) Arezzo's oldest and most atmospheric cafe is located directly opposite the Basilica di San Francesco, so it's a perfect coffee stop before or after a visit to the Cappella Bacci. The coffee is excellent, as are the home-baked pastries. The outdoor tables are popular with the *aperitivo* set.

Thermal Spas

Tuscany is one of Italy's thermal activity hotspots, with the province of Siena particularly rich in mineral-packed waters. Ranging from swish indoor spas to natural woodland pools, tracking them down – and trying them out – is a delight.

Terme di Saturnia (0564 60 01 11; www.termedisaturnia.it; day pass €25, after 2pm €20; 9.30am-7pm summer, to 5pm winter) A stunning, cascading cluster of open-air pools near Pitigliano.

Bagni di Lucca Terme (0583 8 72 21; www.termebagnidilucca.it; Piazza San Martino 11) Thermal swims and massage treatments in a northwestern spa town.

Bagni San Filippo (24hr) **FREE** Free, alfresco backwoods bathing at its best in the Val d'Orcia, about 15km south of Bagno Vignoni along the SR2.

Calidario Terme Etrusche (0565 85 15 04; www.calidario.it; Via del Bottaccio 40, Venturina; pool entry per day adult/child €20/10, spa package per person €29-55; 1-4pm & 4.30-7.30pm Mon-Fri, 9.30am-12.30pm, 1-4pm & 4.30-7.30pm Sat & Sun, closed early Jan–early Mar & weekends Jul & Aug) Spa treatments and atmospheric outdoor swims on the Etruscan coast.

Bagni San Filippo

ℹ INFORMATION

Tourist Office (0575 40 19 45; Piazza della Libertà; 2-4pm) Find another **branch** (0575 2 68 50; Piazza della Repubblica 22-23;

Talking to Locals

Many locals in towns and cities speak at least one language other than Italian – usually English or French. But in the Tuscan countryside you'll need that Italian phrasebook. Region-wide, many traditional places to eat have no written menu or only a menu penned in Italian in spidery handwriting.

⊘10.30am-12.30pm) to the right as you exit the train station.

Una Vetrina per Arezzo e Le Sue Vallate (☑0575 182 27 70; www.arezzoturismo.it; Emiciclo Giovanni Paolo II, Scale Mobili di Arezzo; ⊘9am-6pm Mon-Fri, to 7pm Sat & Sun) Private tourist office on the *scala mobile* (escalator) leading up to Piazza del Duomo; it has toilet facilities (€0.50).

❶ GETTING THERE & AWAY

To drive here from Florence, take the A1. Parking at the train station costs €2 per hour. By train, Arezzo is on the Florence–Rome line.

Montepulciano

Exploring this reclaimed narrow ridge of volcanic rock will push your quadriceps to failure point. When this happens, self-medicate with a generous pour of the highly reputed Vino Nobile while drinking in the spectacular views over the Val di Chiana and Val d'Orcia.

◉ SIGHTS

Il Corso   Street
Montepulciano's main street – called in stages Via di Gracciano, Via di Voltaia, Via dell'Opio and Via d'Poliziano – climbs up the eastern ridge of the town from **Porta al Prato** and loops to meet Via di Collazzi on the western ridge. To reach the centre of town (Piazza Grande) take a dog-leg turn into Via del Teatro.

In Piazza Savonarola, up from the Porta al Prato, is the **Colonna del Marzocca**, erected in 1511 to confirm Montepulciano's allegiance to Florence. The splendid stone lion, squat as a pussycat atop this column is, in fact, a copy; the original is in the town's Museo Civico.

Notable buildings further along the street include the late-Renaissance **Palazzo Avignonesi** (Via di Gracciano nel Corso 91); **Palazzo di Bucelli** (Via di Gracciano nel Corso 73) – look for the recycled Etruscan and Latin inscriptions and reliefs on the lower facade; and **Palazzo Cocconi** (Via di Gracciano nel Corso 70).

Continuing uphill, you'll find Michelozzo's **Chiesa di Sant'Agostino** (www.montepul cianochiusipienza.it; Piazza Michelozzo; ⊘9am-noon & 3-6pm), with its lunette above the entrance holding a terracotta Madonna and Child, John the Baptist and St Augustine. Opposite, the **Torre di Pulcinella**, a medieval tower house, is topped by the town clock and the hunched figure of Pulcinella (Punch of Punch and Judy fame), which strikes the hours. After passing historic **Caffè Poliziano** (☑0578 75 86 15; www.caffepoliziano.it; Via di Voltaia 27; ⊘7am-8pm Mon-Fri, to 11pm Sat, to 9pm Sun; 🛜), the Corso continues straight ahead and Via del Teatro veers off to the right.

Museo Civico & Pinocoteca Crociani   Gallery, Museum
(☑0578 71 73 00; www.museocivicomonte pulciano.it; Via Ricci 10; adult/reduced €5/3; ⊘10.30am-6.30pm Wed-Mon summer, reduced hours winter) Montepulciano's modest museum and pinacoteca have recently had a curatorial dream come true: a painting in

their collections has been attributed to Caravaggio. The masterpiece is a characteristic *Portrait of a Gentleman*. Worth the entrance fee alone, it's accompanied by high-tech, touchscreen interpretation, which allows you to explore details of the painting, its restoration and diagnostic attribution.

Palazzo Comunale   Palace
(Piazza Grande; terrace & tower adult/reduced €5/2.50, terrace only €2.50; ☉10am-6pm) Built in the 14th-century in Gothic style and remodelled in the 15th century by Michelozzo, the Palazzo Comunale still functions as the town hall. The main reason to head inside is to drink in the extraordinary views from the panoramic terrace and the tower – from the latter you can see as far as Pienza, Montalcino and even, on a clear day, Siena.

✪ EATING & DRINKING

Osteria Acquacheta   Tuscan €€
(☎0578 71 70 86; www.acquacheta.eu; Via del Teatro 22; meals €25-30; ☉12.30-3pm & 7.30-10.30pm Wed-Mon mid-Apr–Dec) Hugely

popular with locals and tourists alike, this bustling *osteria* (tavern) specialises in *bistecca alla fiorentina* (chargrilled T-bone steak), which comes to the table in huge, lightly seared and exceptionally flavoursome slabs (don't even *think* of asking for it to be served otherwise). Book ahead; no email reservations.

La Grotta   Ristorante €€€
(☎0578 75 74 79; www.lagrottamontepulciano. it; Via di San Biagio 15, meals €40; ☉12.30 2pm & 7.30-10pm Thu-Tue, closed mid-Jan–mid-Mar) The ingredients, and sometimes dishes, may be traditional, but the presentation is full of refined flourishes – artfully arranged Parmesan shavings and sprigs of herbs crown delicate towers of pasta, vegetables and meat. The service is exemplary and the courtyard garden divine. It's just outside town on the road to Chiusi. Booking recommended.

E Lucevan Le Stelle   Wine Bar
(☎0578 75 87 25; www.lucevanlestelle.it; Piazza San Francesco 5; ☉11.30am-11.30pm mid-Mar–Dec; 🌐) The decked terrace here is

Al fresco diners in Montalcino (p460)

ATLANTIDE PHOTOTRAVEL/GETTY IMAGES ©

A wine bar in Montalcino

the top spot in Montepulciano to watch the sun go down. Inside squishy sofas, modern art and jazz on the sound system give the place a chilled-out vibe. Dishes (antipasto plates €4.50 to €8; *piadinas* €6; pastas €6.50 to €9) are simple but tasty, and there's Montepulciano Nobile by the glass (€5 to €7).

Or opt for a tasting flight featuring three wines (€15); choose from Tuscany (Chianti, Montepulciano Nobile and Brunello) or Montepulciano (Rosso, Nobile and Nobile Riserva).

ℹ️ INFORMATION

Tourist Office (📠0578 75 73 41; www. prolocomontepulciano.it; Piazza Don Minzoni 1; 🕑9am-1pm)

ℹ️ GETTING THERE & AWAY

If driving from Florence, take the Valdichiana exit off the A1 (direction Bettolle-Sinalunga) and then follow the signs. From Siena, take the Siena–Bettolle–Perugia Super Strada.

Siena Mobilità runs four buses daily between Siena and Montepulciano (€6.60, one hour) stopping at Pienza (€2.50) en route. There are three services per day to/from Florence (€11.20, 1½ hours).

Montalcino

Known globally as the home of one of the world's great wines, Brunello di Montalcino, the attractive hilltop town of Montalcino has number of *enoteche* lining its medieval streets, and is surrounded by hugely picturesque vineyards. There's history to explore, too; the town's efforts to hold out against Florence even after Siena had fallen earned it the title 'the Republic of Siena in Montalcino'.

✖️ EATING & DRINKING

Poggio Antico   Wine €€

(📠0577 84 80 44, restaurant 0577 84 92 00; www.poggioantico.com; Località Poggio Antico, off SP14; 🕑cantina 10am-6pm, restaurant noon-2.30pm & 7-9.30pm Tue-Sun, closed Sun evening winter) Located 5km outside Montalcino on the road to Grosseto, Poggio Antico is a superb foodie one-stop-shop. It makes award-winning wines (try its Brunello Altero or Riserva), conducts free cellar tours in Italian, English and German, offers tastings (approximately €25 depending on wines) and has an on-site restaurant (meals €40). Book tours in advance.

Il Leccio   Tuscan €€

(☑0577 84 41 75; www.illeccio.net; Via Costa Castellare 1/3, Sant'Angelo in Colle; meals €30, 4-course set menu €36; ⏰noon-2.30pm & 7-9pm Thu-Tue; ✐) Watching the chef make his way between his stove and kitchen garden to gather produce for each order puts a whole new spin on the word 'fresh', and both the results and the house Brunello are spectacular.

Sant'Angelo in Colle is 10km southwest of Montalcino along Via del Sole (and 10km west of the Abbazia di Sant'Antimo) along an unsealed but signed road through vineyards.

Enoteca Osteria Osticcio   Wine Bar

(☑0577 84 82 71; www.osticcio.it; Via Giacomo Matteotti 23; antipasto & cheese plates €7-17, meals €40; ⏰noon-4pm & 7-11pm Fri-Wed, plus noon-7pm Thu summer) In a town overflowing with *enoteche,* this is definitely one of the best. A huge selection of Brunello and its more modest sibling Rosso di Montalcino accompanies tempting dishes such as

marinated anchovies, *cinta senese* (Tuscan pork) crostini, and pasta with pumpkin and *pecorino* (sheep's milk cheese). The panoramic view, meanwhile, almost upstages it all.

Caffè Fiaschetteria
Italiana 1888   Cafe

(☑0577 84 90 43; Piazza del Popolo 6; ⏰7.30am-11pm, closed Thu winter) You could take a seat in the slender square outside this atmosphere-laden *enoteca*-cafe, but then you'd miss its remarkable 19th-century decor – all brass, mirrors and ornate lights. It's been serving coffee and glasses of Brunello to locals since 1888 (hence the name) and is still chock-full of charm.

ℹ INFORMATION

The **Tourist Office** (☑0577 84 93 31; www.prolocomontalcino.com; Costa del Municipio 1; ⏰10am-1pm & 2-5.50pm, closed Mon winter) is just off the main square. It can book cellar-door visits and accommodation.

ℹ GETTING THERE & AWAY

If driving from Siena, take the SS2 (Via Cassia), after Buonconvento, turn off onto the SP45. There's plenty of parking around the *fortezza* (€1.50 per hour 8am to 8pm).

By bus, Siena Mobilità buses (€5, 1½ hours, six daily Monday to Saturday) run to/from Siena

Teatro Grande (p465)

Ruins of Pompeii

Around 30 minutes by train from Naples, you'll find Europe's most compelling archaeological site: the ruins of Pompeii. Sprawling and haunting, the site is a remarkably well-preserved slice of ancient life. Here you can walk down Roman streets and snoop around millennia-old houses, temples, shops, cafes, amphitheatres and even a brothel.

Great For...

ℹ Need to Know

✆081 857 53 47; www.pompeiisites.org; entrances at Porta Marina, Piazza Esedra & Piazza Anfiteatro; adult/reduced €13/7.50, incl Herculaneum €22/12; ☉9am-7.30pm, last entry 6pm Apr-Oct, to 5pm, last entry 3.30pm Nov-Mar

★ **Top Tip**
The ruins are not well labelled, so pick up a free booklet or an audio guide (€6.50) to enhance your visit.

Visiting the Site

Much of the site's value lies in the fact that the city wasn't blown away by Vesuvius in AD 79, but buried beneath a layer of lapilli (burning fragments of pumice stone). The remains first came to light in 1594, but systematic exploration didn't begin until 1748. Since then 44 of Pompeii's original 66 hectares have been excavated.

Remember that you'll need sustenance for your explorations. You'll find an on-site cafeteria at the ruins, and no shortage of touristy, mediocre eateries directly outside the site. The modern town is home to a few better-quality options, or bring your own snacks and beverages.

Before entering the site through **Porta Marina**, the gate that originally connected the town with the nearby harbour,

duck into the **Terme Suburbane**. This 1st-century-BC bathhouse is famous for several erotic frescoes that scandalised the Vatican when they were revealed in 2001. The panels decorate what was once the *apodyterium* (changing room). The room leading to the colourfully frescoed *frigidarium* (cold-water bath) features fragments of stucco-work, as well as one of the few original roofs to survive at Pompeii.

Done in the Terme, continue through the city walls to the main part of the site. Highlights to look out for here include:

Foro

A huge grassy rectangle flanked by limestone columns, the **foro** (forum) was ancient Pompeii's main piazza, as well as the site of gladiatorial battles before the

Impluvium (rain tank) in a Pompeii house

Anfiteatro was constructed. The buildings surrounding the forum are testament to its role as the city's hub of civic, commercial, political and religious activity.

Lupanare

Ancient Pompeii's only dedicated brothel, **Lupanare** is a tiny two-storey building with five rooms on each floor. Its collection of raunchy frescoes was a menu of sorts for clients. The walls in the rooms are carved with graffiti – including declarations of love and hope written by the brothel workers – in various languages.

★ **Top Tip**

On the first Sunday of the month, all tickets are free; see www.pompeii sites.org.

DE AGOSTINI / L ROMANO/GETTY IMAGES ©

Teatro Grande

The 2nd-century-BC **Teatro Grande** was a huge 5000-seat theatre carved into the lava mass on which Pompeii was originally built.

Anfiteatro

Gladiatorial battles thrilled up to 20,000 spectators at the grassy **anfiteatro** (Amphitheatre). Built in 70 BC, it's the oldest known Roman amphitheatre in existence.

Casa del Fauno

Covering an entire *insula* (city block) and boasting two atria at its front end (humbler homes had one), Pompeii's largest **private house** (House of the Faun) is named after the delicate bronze statue in the *impluvium* (rain tank). It was here that early excavators found Pompeii's greatest mosaics, most of which are now in Naples' **Museo Archeologico Nazionale** (848 80 02 88, from mobile 06 399 67050; www.museoarcheologiconapoli.it; Piazza Museo Nazionale 19; adult/reduced €12/6; 9am-7.30pm Wed-Mon; Museo, Piazza Cavour). Valuable on-site survivors include a beautiful, geometrically patterned marble floor.

Villa dei Misteri

This recently restored, 90-room **villa** is one of the most complete structures left standing in Pompeii. The dionysiac frieze, the most important fresco still on site, spans the walls of the large dining room. One of the biggest and most arresting paintings from the ancient world, it depicts the initiation of a bride-to-be into the cult of Dionysus, the Greek god of wine.

✗ **Take a Break**

For a memorable bite in Pompeii town, head to Michelin-starred **President** (081 850 72 45; www.ristorantepresident.it; Piazza Schettini 12; meals from €40, tasting menus €65-90; noon-3.30pm & 7pm-late Tue-Sun; FS to Pompei, Circumvesuviana to Pompei Scavi-Villa dei Misteri), where you can try bread made to ancient Roman recipes and sweet slow-cooked snapper.

A farm for much of its life, the villa has a vino-making area that is still visible at the northern end.

Follow Via Consolare out of the town through **Porta Ercolano**. Continue past **Villa di Diomede**, turn right, and you'll come to Villa dei Misteri.

Body Casts

One of the most haunting sights at Pompeii are the body casts in the **Granai del Foro** (Forum Granary). These were made in the late 19th century by pouring plaster into the hollows left by disintegrated bodies. Among the casts is a pregnant slave; the belt around her waist would have displayed the name of her owner.

Tours

You'll almost certainly be approached by a guide outside the *scavi* (excavations) ticket office: note that authorised guides wear identification tags. If considering a guided tour of the ruins, reputable tour operators include **Yellow Sudmarine** (☑329 1010328; www.yellowsudmarine.com; 2½hr Pompeii guided tour €135, plus entrance fee) and **Walks of Italy** (www.walksofitaly.com; 3hr Pompeii guided tour per person €59), both of which also offer excursions to other areas of Campania.

Getting to Pompeii

Circumvesuviana trains run to Pompei-Scavi-Villa dei Misteri station from Naples (€3.20, 36 minutes) and Sorrento (€2.80, 30 minutes). By car, take the A3 from Naples, then use the Pompeii exit and follow signs to Pompeii Scavi. Car parks (approximately €5 per hour) are clearly marked and vigorously touted.

What's Nearby?

If you have time for further exploration in the area, check out these ancient sites.

Ruins of Herculaneum   Archaeological Site

(☑081 857 53 47; www.pompeiisites.org; Corso Resina 187, Ercolano; adult/reduced €11/5.50, incl Pompeii €22/12; ☾8.30am-7.30pm Apr-Oct, to 5pm Nov-Mar; ☒Circumvesuviana to Ercolano-Scavi) Upstaged by its larger rival, Pompeii, Herculaneum harbours a wealth of archaeological finds, from ancient advertisements and stylish mosaics to carbonised furniture and terror-struck skeletons. This superbly conserved Roman fishing town is easier to navigate than Pompeii, and can be explored in a half-day with a map and audio guide (€6.50).

From the site's main gateway on Corso Resina, head down the walkway to the ticket office (at the bottom on your left). Ticket purchased, follow the walkway to the actual entrance to the ruins.

MAV   Museum

(Museo Archeologico Virtuale; ☑081 1777 6843; www.museomav.com; Via IV Novembre 44; adult/reduced €7.50/6, with 3D documentary

€11.50/10; ⊙9am-5.30pm daily Mar-May, 10am-6.30pm daily Jun-Sep, 10am-4pm Tue-Sun Oct-Feb; 🛜🚻; 🚊Circumvesuviana to Ercolano-Scavi) Using high-tech holograms and computer-generated recreations, this 'virtual archaeological museum' brings ancient ruins alive; it's especially fun for kids. The museum is on the main street linking Ercolano-Scavi train station to the ruins of Herculaneum.

Mt Vesuvius

Towering darkly over Naples and its environs, 1281m Mt Vesuvius (Vesuvio) is the only active volcano on the European mainland. From the summit car park, an 860m path leads up to the volcano's **crater** (Vesuvius National Park; www.epnv.it).

From Ercolano, **Vesuvio Express** (☏081 739 36 66; www.vesuvioexpress.it; Piazzale Stazi-one Circumvesuviana, Ercolano; return incl admission to summit €20; ⊙every 40min, 9.30am to 4pm) runs shuttle buses from outside the train station up to the summit car park. The journey time is 20 minutes each way.

From Pompeii, **Busvia del Vesuvio** (☏081 878 21 03; www.busviadelvesuvio.com; Via Villa dei Misteri, Pompeii; return incl entry to summit adult/reduced €22/7; ⊙hourly from 9am-5pm) runs hourly shuttle services between Pompei-Scavi-Villa dei Misteri train station (steps away from the ruins of Pompeii) and Boscoreale Terminal Interchange, from where a bus continues the journey up the slope to the summit car park.

★ Top Tip

For the Mt Vesuvius climb, take water, sunscreen and a hat. You'll also need sturdy shoes, as the path can have loose stones.

Tragedy in Pompeii

24 AUGUST AD 79

8am Buildings including the **❶ Terme Suburbane** and the **❷ Foro** are still undergoing repair after an earthquake in AD 63 caused significant damage to the city. Despite violent earth tremors overnight, residents have little idea of the catastrophe that lies ahead.

Midday Peckish locals pour into the **❸ Thermopolium di Vetutius Placidus**. The lustful slip into the **❹ Lupanare**, and gladiators practise for the evening's planned games at the **❺ Anfiteatro**. A massive boom heralds the eruption. Shocked onlookers witness a dark cloud of volcanic matter shoot some 14km above the crater.

3pm–5pm Lapilli (burning pumice stone) rains down on Pompeii. Terrified locals begin to flee; others take shelter. Within two hours, the plume is 25km high and the sky has darkened. Roofs collapse under the weight of the debris, burying those inside.

25 AUGUST AD 79

Midnight Mudflows bury the town of Herculaneum. Lapilli and ash continue to rain down on Pompeii, bursting through buildings and suffocating those taking refuge within.

4am–8am Ash and gas avalanches hit Herculaneum. Subsequent surges smother Pompeii, killing all remaining residents, including those in the **❻ Orto dei Fuggiaschi**. The volcanic 'blanket' will safeguard frescoed treasures like the **❼ Casa del Menandro** and **❽ Villa dei Misteri** for almost two millennia.

Terme Suburbane
The *laconicum* (sauna), *caldarium* (hot bath) and large, heated swimming pool weren't the only sources of heat here; scan the walls of this suburban bathhouse for some of the city's raunchiest frescoes.

Villa di Diomede

Casa del Poeta Tragico

Porta Ercolano

Casa del Fauno

Basilica

Tempio di Apollo

Porta Marina

Terme del Foro

Macellum

Teatro Grande

Quadriportico dei Teatri

Porta di Stabia

Teatro Piccolo

Foro
An ancient Times Square of sorts, the forum sits at the intersection of Pompeii's main streets and was closed to traffic in the 1st century AD. The plinths on the southern edge featured statues of the imperial family.

TOP TIPS

➜ Visit in the afternoon.
➜ Allow three hours.
➜ Wear comfortable shoes and a hat.
➜ Bring drinking water.
➜ Don't use flash photography.

Villa dei Misteri
Home to the world-famous *Dionysiac Frieze* fresco. Other highlights at this villa include *trompe l'oeil* wall decorations in the *cubiculum* (bedroom) and Egyptian-themed artwork in the *tablinum* (reception).

Lupanare
The prostitutes at this brothel were often slaves of Greek or Asian origin. Mattresses once covered the stone beds and the names engraved in the walls are possibly those of the workers and their clients.

Thermopolium di Vetutius Placidus
The counter at this ancient snack bar once held urns filled with hot food. The *lararium* (household shrine) on the back wall depicts Dionysus (the god of wine) and Mercury (the god of profit and commerce).

Casa dei Vettii

Porta del Vesuvio

EYEWITNESS ACCOUNT

Pliny the Younger (AD 61–c 112) gives a gripping, first-hand account of the catastrophe in his letters to Tacitus (AD 56–117).

Porta di Nola

Casa della Venere in Conchiglia

Porta di Sarno

3

7

6

Grande Palestra

5

Templo di Iside

Orto dei Fuggiaschi
The Garden of the Fugitives showcases the plaster moulds of 13 locals seeking refuge during Vesuvius' eruption – the largest number of victims found in any one area. The huddled bodies make for a moving scene.

Anfiteatro
Magistrates, local senators and the games' sponsors and organisers enjoyed front-row seating at this veteran amphitheatre, home to gladiatorial battles and the odd riot. The parapet circling the stadium featured paintings of combat, victory celebrations and hunting scenes.

Casa del Menandro
This dwelling most likely belonged to the family of Poppaea Sabina, Nero's second wife. A room to the left of the atrium features Trojan War paintings and a polychrome mosaic of pygmies rowing down the Nile.

Dubrovnik, Croatia

Regardless of whether you are visiting Croatia's Dubrovnik for the first time or the hundredth, the sense of awe never fails to descend when you set eyes on the beauty of the old town. Indeed it's hard to imagine anyone becoming jaded by the city's marble streets, baroque buildings and the endless shimmer of the Adriatic, or failing to be inspired by a walk along the ancient city walls that protected a civilised, sophisticated republic for centuries.

Although the shelling of Dubrovnik in 1991 horrified the world, the city has bounced back with vigour to enchant visitors again.

Two Days in Dubrovnik

Start early with a walk along the **city walls** (p473), before it's too hot, then wander the marbled streets and call into whichever church, palace or museum takes your fancy.

On day two, take the **cable car** (p479) up Mt Srđ and visit the exhibition **Dubrovnik During the Homeland War** (p477). Afterwards, continue exploring the old town. When it starts to bake, wander along to **Banje Beach** (p479).

Four Days in Dubrovnik

With another couple of days you'll have the luxury of confining your old-town explorations to the evenings, when it's quieter. On day three, visit the island of **Lokrum** (p477). On your final day, jump on a boat to **Cavtat** (p480), allowing a couple of hours to stroll around the historic town.

Moving on from Dubrovnik? It's a short flight to Rome (p352) or Venice (p400).

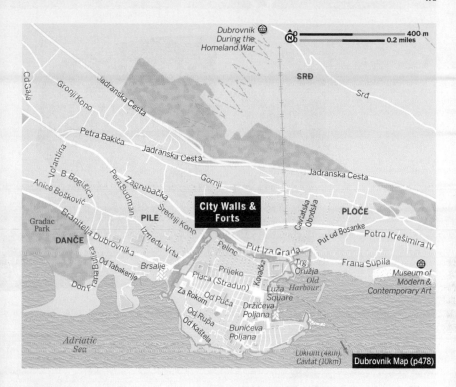

Dubrovnik
During the
Homeland War

400 m
0.2 miles

SRĐ

Srd

City Walls &
Forts

PLOČE

Museum of
Modern &
Contemporary Art

Old
Harbour

Luža
Square

Trg.
Oružja

Frana Supila

Put od Bosanke

Potra Krešimira IV

Jadranska Cesta

Gornji

Jadranska Cesta

Petra Bakića

Gronji Kono

Cd Gaja

Volantina

B. Bogišća

Anice Bošković

Pera Budman

Zagrebačka

Srednji Kono

PILE

Izmedu Vrta

Branitelja Dubrovnika

Gradac
Park

DANČE

Od Tabakerije

Brsalje

Don F

Feline

Prijeko

Put Iza Grada

Kovačka

Placa (Stradun)

Za Rokom

Od Puča

Od Rupa

Od Kaštela

Držićeva
Poljana

Bunićeva
Poljana

Adriatic
Sea

Lokrum (4km),
Cavtat (10km)

Caviatska
Obodska

Dubrovnik Map (p478)

Arriving in Dubrovnik

Dubrovnik Airport In Čilipi, 19km southeast of Dubrovnik. Allow up to 280KN for a taxi, or Atlas runs the airport bus service (40KN, 30 minutes), which stops at the Pile Gate and the bus station.

Dubrovnik Bus Station Times are detailed at www.libertasdubrovnik.hr.

Where to Stay

There's limited accommodation in the compact old town itself. You should book well in advance, especially in summer.

Private accommodation can be a good, well-priced alternative; contact local travel agencies or the tourist office for options.

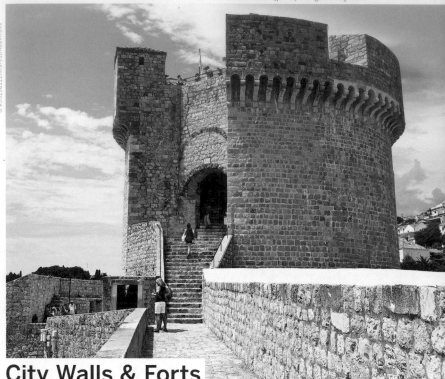

Minčeta Tower (p475) along the city walls

ANSHARPHOTO/SHUTTERSTOCK ©

City Walls & Forts

No visit to Dubrovnik would be complete without a walk around the spectacular city walls – the finest in the world and the city's main claim to fame.

Great For...

☑ Don't Miss

The sublime view over the old town and the shimmering Adriatic from the top of the walls.

Walking the Walls

There are entrances to the walls from near the Pile Gate (p476), the **Ploče Gate** (Vrata od Ploča) and the **Maritime Museum** (Pomorski muzej; www.dumus.hr). The Pile Gate entrance tends to be the busiest, and entering from the Ploče side has the added advantage of getting the steepest climbs out of the way first (you're required to walk in an anticlockwise direction).

The round Minčeta Tower protects the landward edge of the city from attack, while Fort Revelin and Fort St John guard the eastern approach and the Old Harbour.

The Bokar Tower and Fort Lawrence look west and out to sea. St Blaise gazes down from the walls of **Fort Lawrence** (Tvrđava Lovrjenac; admission 30KN; ☺8am-7.30pm), a large free-standing fortress. There's

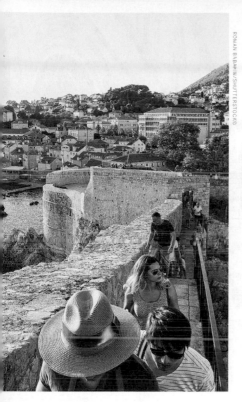

ROMAN BABAKIN/SHUTTERSTOCK©

❶ Need to Know

Gradske zidine; adult/child 150/50KN; ☺8am-7.30pm Apr-Oct, 9am-3pm Nov-Mar

✕ Take a Break

Bring your own snacks, and especially your own drinks: the few vendors selling water on the route tend to be overpriced.

★ Top Tip

Don't underestimate how strenuous the wall walk can be, particularly on a hot day.

Recent History

Caught in the cross-hairs of the war that ravaged the former Yugoslavia, Dubrovnik was pummelled with some 2000 shells in 1991 and 1992, suffering considerable damage. There were 111 strikes on the walls.

The walls themselves and all of the damaged buildings have since been restored, but you can get a good handle on the extent of the shelling damage by gazing over the rooftops as you walk the walls: those sporting bright new terracotta suffered damage and had to be replaced.

Guided Tours

Dubrovnik Walks (☏095 80 64 526; www. dubrovnikwalks.com; Brsalje bb; ☺Apr-Nov) runs excellent English-language guided walks departing from near the Pile Gate. The two-hour 'Walls & Wars' tour is 190KN. No reservations necessary.

not a lot inside, but the battlements offer wonderful views over the old town and its large courtyard is often used as a venue for summer theatre and concerts.

History of the Walls

The first set of walls to enclose the city was built in the 9th century. In the middle of the 14th century the 1.5m-thick defences were fortified with 15 square forts. The threat of attacks from the Turks in the 15th century prompted the city to strengthen the existing forts and add new ones, so that the entire old town was contained within a stone barrier 2km long and up to 25m high. The walls are thicker on the land side – up to 6m – and range from 1.5m to 3m on the sea side.

Rector's Palace

Game of Thrones Locations

Dubrovnik is like a fantasy world for many, but fans of Game of Thrones *have more reason to indulge in flights of fancy than most, as much of the immensely popular TV series was filmed here.*

Great For...

☑ Don't Miss

The city walls, which have often featured in the TV series, particularly during the siege of King's Landing.

City Walls & Fort Lawrence

Tyrion Lannister commanded the defence of King's Landing from the seaward-facing walls (p473) during the Battle of the Blackwater. Fort Lawrence (p472) is King's Landing's famous Red Keep and both the interior and the exterior will be familiar. Cersei farewelled her daughter Myrcella from the little harbour beneath the fort.

Rector's Palace

The grand atrium of the **Rector's Palace** (Knežev dvor; ☎020-321 422; www.dumus.hr; Pred Dvorom 3; adult/child multimuseum pass 100/25KN; ⊙9am-6pm Apr-Oct, to 4pm Nov-Mar) featured as the palace of the Spice King of Qarth – they didn't even bother moving the statue! Built in the late 15th century for the elected rector who governed Dubrovnik,

ROMAN BABAKIN/SHUTTERSTOCK ©

Fort Lawrence

SABINE LUBENOW/GETTY IMAGES ©

this Gothic-Renaissance palace contains the rector's office, his private chambers, public halls, administrative offices and a dungeon. Today the palace has been turned into the Cultural History Museum, with artfully restored rooms, portraits, coats of arms and coins, evoking the glorious history of Dubrovnik.

Trsteno Arboretum

The Red Keep gardens, where the Tyrells chatted and plotted endlessly during seasons three and four, are at the **Trsteno Arboretum** (☑020-751 019; adult/child 45/25KN; ⊙8am-7pm Jun-Sep, to 4pm Oct-May). These leafy gardens, 14km northwest of Dubrovnik, are the oldest of their kind in Croatia and well worth a visit. There is a Renaissance layout, with a set of geometric shapes made with plants and bushes, cit-

rus orchards, a maze, a fine palm collection and a gorgeous pond. To get to Trsteno, catch local bus 12, 15, 22 or 35 from Dubrovnik's bus station.

Other Notable Spots

Minčeta Tower (Tvrđava Minčeta; City Walls) The exterior of Qarth's House of Undying.

Uz Jezuite The stairs connecting the St Ignatius of Loyola Church to Gundulić Sq were the starting point for Cersei Lannister's memorable naked penitential walk. The walk continued down Stradun.

Gradac Park The site of the Purple Wedding feast, where King Joffrey finally got his comeuppance.

Sv Dominika street The street and staircase outside the Dominican Monastery (p479) were used for various King's Landing market scenes.

Ethnographic Museum (Etnografski muzej; www.dumus.hr; Od Rupa 3; adult/child multimuseum pass 100/25KN; ⊙9am-4pm Wed-Mon) Littlefinger's brothel.

Lokrum (p477) The reception for Daenerys in Qarth was held in the monastery cloister.

◎ SIGHTS

Today Dubrovnik is the most prosperous, elegant and expensive city in Croatia. In many ways it still feels like a city state, isolated from the rest of the nation by geography and history. It's become such a tourism magnet that there's even talk of having to limit visitor numbers in the car-free old town – the main thoroughfares can get impossibly crowded, especially when multiple cruise ships disgorge passengers at the same time.

Pile Gate   Gate

(Gradska vrata Pile) The natural starting point to any visit to Dubrovnik, this fabulous city gate was built in 1537. While crossing the drawbridge, imagine that this was once lifted every evening, the gate closed and the key handed to the rector. Notice the statue of St Blaise, the city's patron saint, set in a niche over the Renaissance arch.

After passing through the outer gate you'll come to an inner gate dating from 1460, and soon after you'll be struck by the gorgeous view of the main street, Placa, or as it's commonly known, Stradun, Dubrovnik's pedestrian promenade.

Onofrio Fountain   Fountain

(Velika Onofrijeva fontana; Placa bb) One of Dubrovnik's most famous landmarks, this large fountain was built in 1438 as part of a water-supply system that involved bringing water from a well 12km away. Originally the fountain was adorned with sculpture, but it was heavily damaged in the 1667 earthquake and only 16 carved masks remain, with water dribbling from their mouths into a drainage pool.

War Photo Limited   Gallery

(☑020-322 166; www.warphotoltd.com; Antuninska 6; adult/child 50/40KN; ☺10am-10pm daily May-Sep, 10am-4pm Wed-Mon Apr & Oct) An immensely powerful experience, this gallery features intensely compelling exhibitions curated by New Zealand photojournalist Wade Goddard, who worked in the Balkans in the 1990s. Its declared intention is to 'expose the myth of war...to let people see war as it is, raw, venal, frightening, by focusing on how war inflicts injustices on innocents

Onofrio Fountain

IRINA SEN/SHUTTERSTOCK ©

and combatants alike'. There's a permanent exhibition on the upper floor devoted to the wars in Yugoslavia, but the changing exhibitions cover a multitude of conflicts.

Lokrum   Island

(www.lokrum.hr; adult/child incl boat 100/20KN; ☺Apr-Nov) Lush Lokrum is a beautiful, forested island full of holm oaks, black ash, pines and olive trees, and an ideal escape from urban Dubrovnik. It's a popular swimming spot, although the beaches are rocky. To reach the nudist beach, head left from the ferry and follow the signs marked FKK; the rocks at the far end are Dubrovnik's de facto gay beach. Also popular is the small saltwater lake known as the **Dead Sea**.

The island's main hub is its large medieval **Benedictine monastery**, which houses a restaurant and a display on the island's history and the TV show *Game of Thrones,* which was partly filmed in Dubrovnik. This is your chance to pose imperiously in a reproduction of the Iron Throne. The monastery has a pretty cloister garden and a significant botanical garden, featuring giant agaves and palms from South Africa and Brazil.

Lokrum is only a 10-minute ferry ride from Dubrovnik's Old Harbour. Boats leave roughly hourly in summer (half-hourly in July and August). Make sure you check what time the last boat to the mainland departs. Note that no one can stay overnight and smoking is not permitted anywhere on the island.

Dubrovnik During the Homeland War   Museum

(Dubrovnik u domovinskom ratu; Fort Imperial, Srđ; adult/child 30/15KN; ☺8am-10pm) Set inside a Napoleonic fort near the cable-car terminus, this permanent exhibition is dedicated to the siege of Dubrovnik during the 'Homeland War', as the 1990s war is dubbed in Croatia. The local defenders stationed inside this fort ensured the city wasn't captured. If the displays are understandably one-sided, they still provide in-depth coverage of the events, including plenty of video footage.

Deconstruction & Reconstruction

From late 1991 to May 1992, images of the shelling of Dubrovnik dominated the news worldwide. While memories may have faded for those who watched it from afar, those who suffered through it will never forget – and the city of Dubrovnik is determined that visitors don't either. You'll see reminders of it on several plaques throughout the old town, especially at the main gates.

Shells struck 68% of the 824 buildings in the old town, leaving holes in two out of three tiled roofs. Building facades and the paving stones of streets and squares suffered 314 direct hits and there were 111 strikes on the great wall. Nine historic palaces were completely gutted by fire, while the Sponza Palace, Rector's Palace, St Blaise's Church, Franciscan Monastery and the carved fountains Amerling and Onofrio all sustained serious damage. It was quickly decided that the repairs and rebuilding would be done with traditional techniques, using original materials whenever feasible.

Dubrovnik has since regained most of its original grandeur. The town walls are once again intact, the gleaming marble streets are smoothly paved and famous monuments have been lovingly restored, with the help of an international brigade of specially trained stonemasons.

Museum of Modern & Contemporary Art   Museum

(Umjetnička galerija; ☎020-426 590; www.ug dubrovnik.hr; Frana Supila 23; adult/child multimuseum pass 100/25KN; ☺9am-8pm Tue-Sun) Spread over three floors of a significant modernist building east of the old town, this excellent gallery showcases Croatian artists, particularly painter Vlaho Bukovac from nearby Cavtat. Head up to the sculpture terrace for excellent views.

Dubrovnik

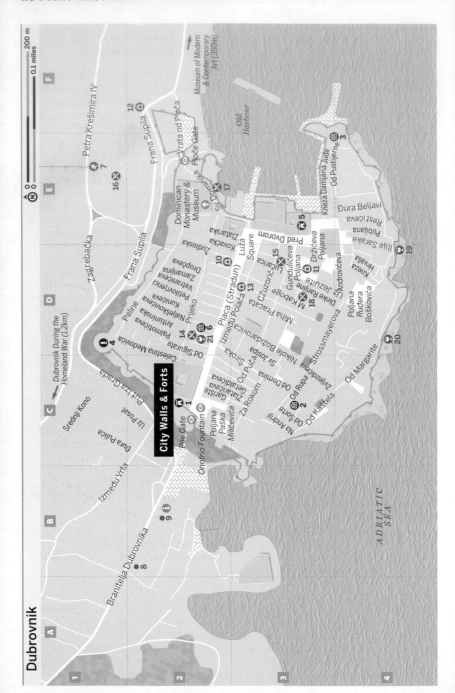

City Walls & Forts

ADRIATIC
SEA

Museum of Modern
& Contemporary
Art (350m)

Old
Harbour

Dubrovnik During the
Homeland War (1.2km)

200 m
0.1 miles

Dubrovnik

Dominican Monastery & Museum
Christian Monastery

(Muzej Dominikanskog samostana; Sv Dominika 4; 30KN; ◉9am-5pm) This imposing structure is an architectural highlight, built in a transitional Gothic-Renaissance style, and containing an impressive art collection. Constructed around the same time as the city walls in the 14th century, the stark exterior resembles a fortress more than a religious complex. The interior contains a graceful 15th-century **cloister** constructed by local artisans after the designs of the Florentine architect Maso di Bartolomeo.

◉ ACTIVITIES

Cable Car
Cable Car

(Žičara; ☎020-414 355; www.dubrovnikcable car.com; Petra Krešimira IV bb; return adult/child 120/50KN; ◉9am-5pm Nov-Mar, to 9pm Apr, May, Sep & Oct, to midnight Jun-Aug) Dubrovnik's cable car whisks you from just north of the city walls to Mt Srđ in under four minutes. At the end of the line there's a stupendous perspective of the city from a lofty 405m, taking in the terracotta-tiled rooftops of the old town and the island of Lokrum, with the Adriatic and distant Elafiti Islands filling the horizon.

Banje Beach
Swimming

(www.banjebeach.eu; Frana Supila 10) Banje Beach is the closest beach to the old town, just beyond the 17th-century Lazareti (a former quarantine station) outside Ploče Gate. Although many people rent lounge chairs and parasols from the beach club, there's no problem with just flinging a towel on the beach if you can find a space.

Bellevue Beach
Swimming

The nicest beach within an easy walk of the old town is below the Hotel Bellevue. This pebbly cove is sheltered by high cliffs, which provide a platform for daredevil cliff divers but also cast a shadow over the beach by late afternoon – a boon on a scorching day. Public access is via a steep staircase off Kotorska street.

Way of the Cross Walking Trail
Hiking

(Križni Put; Jadranska) Filled with jaw-dropping views of the entire town and art reliefs illustrating the Stations of the Cross, the hike up the 418m Mt Srđ takes roughly an hour. This free alternative to the cable-car ride starts nearby the eastern entrance to the Adriatic Motorway and runs up to the Fort Imperial on top. It's best done early in the morning or at sunset.

Keep in mind there is no shade along the way, so pack ample water, a hat and sunscreen, and skip the hike altogether in peak summer heat. On the top, consider descending straight to the old town with a one-way cable-car ticket.

Detour: Cavtat

Without Cavtat, there'd be no Dubrovnik, as it was refugees from the original Cavtat town who established the city of Dubrovnik in 614. But Cavtat is interesting in itself. A lot more 'local' than Dubrovnik – read, not flooded by tourists on a daily basis – it has its own charm. Wrapped around a very pretty harbour that's bordered by beaches and backed by a curtain of imposing hills, the setting is lovely.

Cavtat's most famous personality is the painter Vlaho Bukovac (1855–1922), one of the foremost exponents of Croatian modernism. His paintings are liberally distributed around the town's main sights.

From June to September there are 11 sailings a day between Dubrovnik's Old Harbour and Cavtat (one-way/return 50/80KN, 45 minutes). For the rest of the year this reduces to three to five a day, weather dependent.

LUKASZIMILENA/SHUTTERSTOCK ©

⊕ TOURS

Dubrovnik Shore Tours　　Tours
(☑095 80 33 587; www.dubrovnikshoretours.net; Branitelja Dubrovnika 15) Offers tailored small-group tours; popular options include a trip to Mt Srđ and Cavtat followed by a guided walk in the old town (four hours), or to the Pelješac Peninsula for wine and oysters (four hours).

Dubrovnik Day Tours　　Tours
(☑091 44 55 846; www.dubrovnikdaytours.net) Private day trips led by licensed guides to as far away as Korčula, Split, Kotor, Mostar and Sarajevo, as well as sightseeing and *Game of Thrones* tours around Dubrovnik.

ⓐ SHOPPING

Gundulić Square Market　　Market
(Gundulićeva poljana; ⊙6am-1pm Mon-Sat) Stallholders sell mainly produce, local artisanal products and craft at this open-air market.

Algoritam　　Books
(www.algoritam.hr; Placa 8; ⊙9am-9pm Mon-Sat, 10am-1pm Sun) A good bookshop with a wide range of English-language books and a variety of guides on Dubrovnik and Croatia.

Uje　　Food & Drinks
(www.uje.hr; Placa 5; ⊙9am-11pm) Uje specialises in olive oils – among the best is Brachia, from the island of Brač – along with a wide range of other locally produced epicurean delights, including some excellent jams (the lemon spread is divine), pickled capers, local herbs and spices, honey, figs in honey, chocolate, wine and *rakija* (grappa).

KAWA　　Gifts & Souvenirs
(☑091 89 67 509; www.kawa.life; Hvarska 2; ⊙10am-midnight) Selling 'wonderful items made by Croatians', KAWA combines an inviting, smart interior with a heartfelt appreciation of Croatian artisans and culture. From wines and craft beers to jewellery, clothing, homewares and even its own line of products under the Happy Čevapi label, KAWA's selection reflects a refined taste and great passion. Superb service rounds off the experience.

⊗ EATING

Pizzeria Tabasco　　Pizza €
(☑020-429 595; www.pizzeriatabasco.hr; Hvarska 48; pizzas 55-120KN; ⊙9.30am-midnight; ☑) Positioned right above the old town

and just underneath the cable-car station, Tabasco is a tasty stopover between the two attractions and a local's fave. Wood-fired pizzas with an ample variety of toppings, plus shaded terraces and a maze-like interior definitely compensate for a seemingly unsexy location at the end of a parking lot.

Oliva Pizzeria   Pizza €

(📞020-324 594; www.pizza-oliva.com; Lučarica 5; mains 41-86KN; ⊙10am-midnight) There are a few token pasta dishes on the menu, but this attractive little place is really all about pizza. And the pizza is worthy of the attention. Grab a seat on the street and tuck in.

Pantarul   Modern European €€

(📞020 333 486; www.pantarul.com; Kralja Tomislava 1; mains 70-128KN; ⊙noon-4pm & 6pm-midnight) This breezy bistro serves exceptional homemade bread, pasta and risotto, alongside the likes of pork belly, steaks, ox cheeks, burgers and a variety of fish dishes. There's a fresh modern touch to most dishes but chef Ana-Marija Bujić knows her way around traditional

Dalmatian cuisine too – she's got her own cookbook to prove it.

Nishta   Vegetarian €€

(📞020-322 088; www.nishtarestaurant.com; Prijeko 29; mains 77-85KN; ⊙11.30am-11.30pm; 🛜🍽️) The popularity of this tiny old-town eatery (expect to queue) is testament not just to the paucity of options for vegetarians and vegans in Croatia but to the excellent, imaginative food produced within. Alongside the expected curries, pastas and vegie burgers, the menu delivers more unusual delicious options such as eggplant tartare, 'tempehritos' and pasta free zucchini 'spaghetti'.

Shizuku   Japanese €€

(📞020 311 493; www.facebook.com/Shizuku Dubrovnik; Kneza Domagoja 1f; mains 65-99KN; ⊙noon-midnight Tue-Sun; 🛜) Tucked away in a residential area between the harbour and Lapad Bay, this charming little restaurant has an appealing front terrace and an interior decorated with silky draperies, paper lampshades and colourful umbrellas. The Japanese owners will be in the kitchen,

Al fresco dining

preparing authentic sushi, sashimi, udon and gyoza. Wash it all down with Japanese beer or sake.

Restaurant
360°   Modern European €€€
(☑020-322 222; www.360dubrovnik.com; Sv Dominika bb; mains 240-290KN, 5-course degustation 780KN; ☺6.30-11pm) Dubrovnik's glitziest restaurant offers fine dining at its finest, with flavoursome, beautifully presented, creative cuisine, and slick, professional service. The setting is unrivalled, on top of the city walls with tables positioned so you can peer through the battlements over the harbour.

Amfora   International €€€
(☑020-419 419; www.amforadubrovnik.com; Obala Stjepana Radića 26; mains 145-185KN; ☺noon-4pm & 7-11pm) From the street, Amfora looks like just another local cafe-bar, but the real magic happens at the six-table restaurant at the rear. Dalmatian favourites such as *pašticada* (stew with gnocchi) and black risotto sit alongside fusion dishes such as swordfish sashimi, veal kofte, and miso fish soup.

Restaurant
Dubrovnik   European €€€
(☑020-324 810; www.restorandubrovnik.com; Marojice Kaboge 5; mains 105-210KN; ☺noon-midnight) One of Dubrovnik's most upmarket restaurants has a wonderfully unstuffy setting, occupying a covered rooftop terrace hidden among the venerable stone buildings of the old town. A strong French influence pervades a menu full of decadent and rich dishes, such as confit duck and plump Adriatic lobster tail served on homemade pasta.

🍷 DRINKING & NIGHTLIFE
Bard   Bar
(off Ilije Sarake; ☺9am-3am) The more upmarket and slick of two cliff bars pressed up against the seaward side of the city walls, this one is lower on the rocks and has a shaded terrace where you can lose a day

quite happily, mesmerised by the Adriatic vistas. At night the surrounding stone is lit in ever-changing colours.

Cave Bar More   Bar
(www.hotel-more.hr; Hotel More, Šetalište Nika i Meda Pucića; ☺10am-midnight) This little beach bar serves coffee, snacks and cocktails to bathers reclining by the dazzlingly clear waters of Lapad Bay, but that's not the half of it – the main bar is set in an actual cave. Cool off beneath the stalactites in the side chamber, where a glass floor exposes a water-filled cavern.

D'vino   Wine Bar
(☑020-321 130; www.dvino.net; Palmotićeva 4a; ☺10am-late; 🛜) If you're interested in sampling top-notch Croatian wine, this upmarket little bar is the place to go. As well as a large and varied wine list, it offers themed tasting flights (multiple wine tastings; three wines for 50KN) accompanied by a thorough description by the knowledgable staff.

Buža   Bar
(off Od Margarite; ☺8am-2am) Finding this ramshackle bar-on-a-cliff feels like a real discovery as you duck and dive around the city walls and finally see the entrance tunnel. However, Buža's no secret – it gets insanely busy, especially around sunset. Wait for a space on one of the concrete platforms, grab a cool drink in a plastic cup and enjoy the vibe and views.

ℹ️ INFORMATION
Dubrovnik Tourist Board Has offices in **Pile** (☑020-312 011; www.tzdubrovnik.hr; Brsalje 5; ☺8am-9pm Jun-Sep, 8am-7pm Mon-Sat, 9am-3pm Sun Oct-May), **Gruž** (☑020-417 983; Obala Pape Ivana Pavla II 1; ☺8am-9pm Jun-Sep, to 3pm Mon-Sat Oct-May) and **Lapad** (☑020-437 460; Kralja Tomislava 7; ☺8am-8pm Mon-Fri, 9am-noon & 5-8pm Sat & Sun Jun-Sep).

Dubrovnik General Hospital (Opća bolnica Dubrovnik; ☑020-431 777; www.bolnica-du.hr; Dr Roka Mišetića 2; ☺emergency department 24hr) On the southern edge of the Lapad peninsula.

Travel Corner (020-492 313; Obala Stjepana Radića 40; internet per hr 25KN, left luggage 2hr 10KN then per hr 4KN, per day 40KN; ⊘9am-8pm Mon-Sat, 9am-4.30pm Sun) This handy one-stop shop has a left-luggage service and internet terminals, dispenses tourist information, books excursions and sells Kapetan Luka ferry tickets.

🛈 GETTING THERE & AWAY

Dubrovnik Airport (DBV, Zračna luka Dubrovnik; ☏020-773 100; www.airport dubrovnik.hr) is in Čilipi, 19km southeast of Dubrovnik. Both Croatia Airlines and British Airways fly to Dubrovnik year-round. In summer they're joined by dozens of other airlines flying seasonal routes and charter flights.

Croatia Airlines has domestic flights from Zagreb (year-round), Split and Osijek (both May to October only).

A taxi to the old town costs up to 280KN.

🛈 GETTING AROUND

BUS

Dubrovnik has a superb bus service; buses run frequently and generally on time. The key tourist routes run until after 2am in summer. The fare is 15KN if you buy from the driver, and 12KN if you buy a ticket at a *tisak* (news stand). Timetables are available at www.libertasdubrovnik.hr.

To get to the old town from the bus station, take buses 1a, 1b, 3 or 8.

CAR

The entire old town is a pedestrian area, public transport is good and parking is expensive, so you're better off not hiring a car until you're

 Where to Stay

Croatia is traditionally seen as a summer destination and good places book out well in advance in July and August. It's also very busy in June and September.

Accommodation in Dubrovnik's old town is limited. Private accommodation is a good alternative but beware the scramble of private owners at the bus station and ferry terminal. Some provide what they say they offer, others are scamming – try to pin down the location in advance if you want to be able to walk to the old town. Note that if you stay in unlicensed accommodation you are unprotected in case of a problem; all registered places should have a blue *'sobe'* (rooms available) sign.

Dubrovnik's Old Town
IHOR PASTERNAK/SHUTTERSTOCK ©

ready to leave the city. All of the street parking surrounding the old town is metered from May to October (40KN per hour). Further out it drops to 20KN or 10KN per hour.

All of the usual car-hire companies are represented at the airport and most also have city branches.

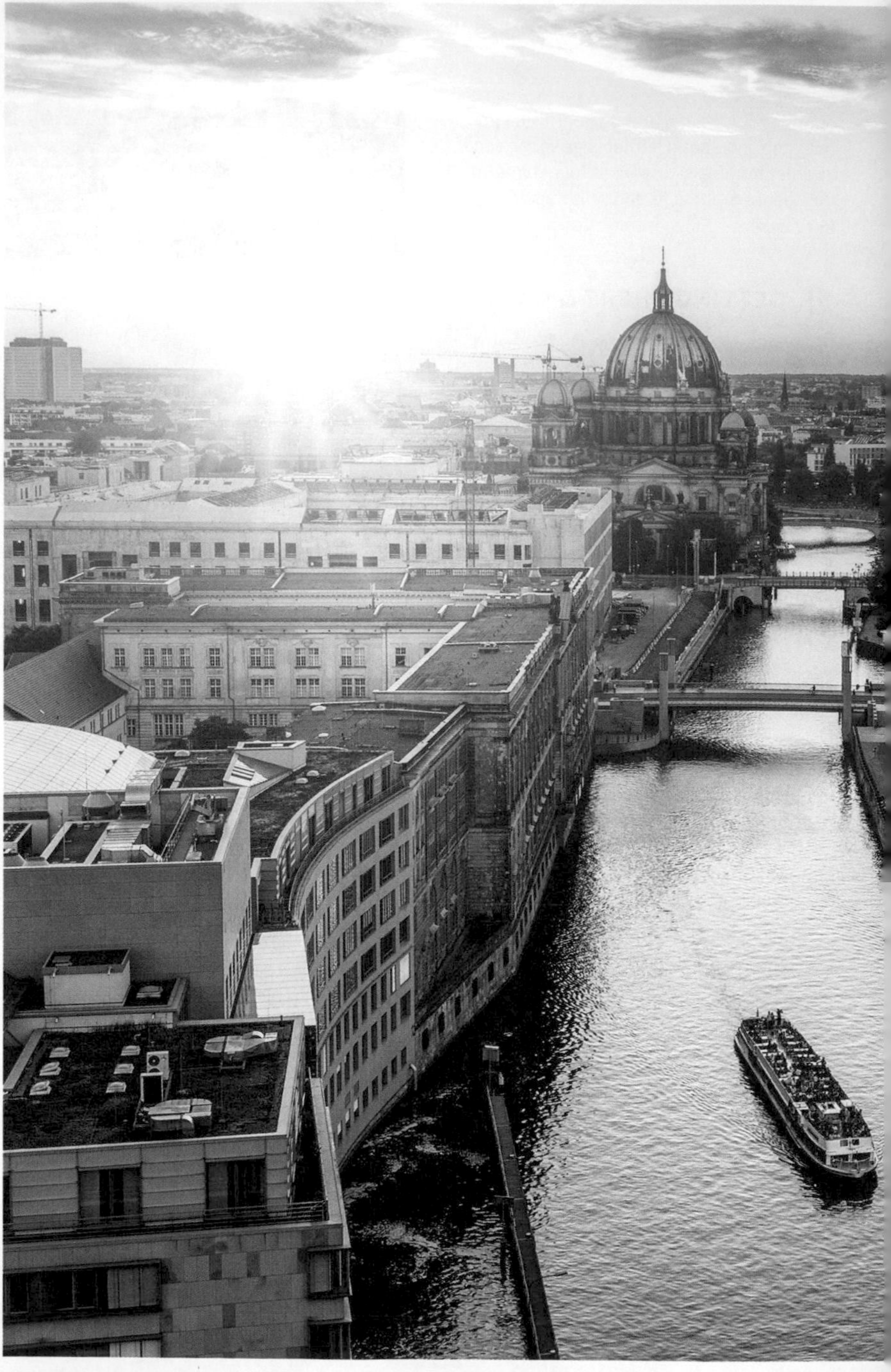

PATINO/SHUTTERSTOCK ©

GERMANY & EASTERN EUROPE

In This Chapter

Berlin, Germany

Berlin's combo of glamour and grit is bound to mesmerise anyone keen to explore its vibrant culture, cutting-edge architecture, fabulous food, intense parties and tangible history.

It's a city that staged a revolution, was headquartered by Nazis, bombed to bits, divided in two and finally reunited – and that was just in the 20th century! Berlin is a big multicultural metropolis, but deep down it maintains the unpretentious charm of an international village.

Two Days in Berlin

Start your first day at the **Reichstag** (p493), then stroll over to the iconic **Brandenburger Tor** (p498). Next, head west along Strasse des 17 Juli, passing the Soviet War memorial before you reach the **Siegessäule** (p505). Take the steps to the top to view the beautiful **Tiergarten** (p504), before getting lost in the park itself. Dedicate your second day to exploring the museums and galleries at **Museumsinsel** (p503).

Four Days in Berlin

Start your third day at the vast **Holocaust Memorial** (p498). Stroll through nearby **Potsdamer Platz** (p504) and then on to the **Topographie des Terrors** (p504) documentation centre and **Checkpoint Charlie** (p499). Use day four to visit the **Gedenkstätte Berliner Mauer** (p489) before heading to the **East Side Gallery** (p489), the longest surviving piece of the Berlin Wall.

Next stop: **Schloss Neuschwanstein** (p520) or beautiful Prague (p524).

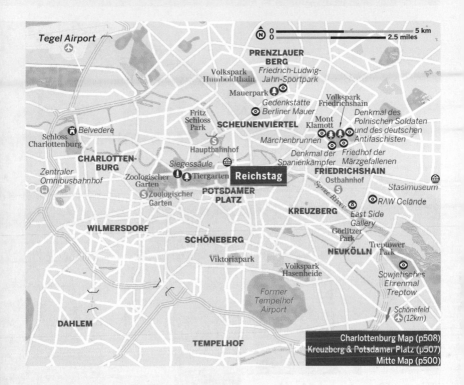

Arriving in Berlin

Tegel & Schönefeld Airports Handle domestic and international flights. Tegel is served directly only by bus and taxi. From Schönefeld, take the S-Bahn or a regional train to the city centre.

Hauptbahnhof Main train station in the city centre; served by S-Bahn, U-Bahn, tram, bus and taxi.

Zentraler Omnibusbahnhof (ZOB) Point of arrival for most long-haul buses.

Where to Stay

Berlin has over 137,000 hotel rooms, but the most desirable properties book up quickly, especially in summer and around major holidays; prices soar and reservations are essential. Otherwise, rates are low by Western capital standards. Options range from chain hotels and Old Berlin–style B&Bs to happening hostels, handy self-catering apartments and trendy boutique hotels.

For information on what each Berlin neighbourhood has to offer, see the table on p519.

The Berlin Wall

For 28 years the Berlin Wall was the most potent symbol of the Cold War. Surprisingly very few of its reinforced concrete slabs remain in today's reunited Berlin.

Great For...

☑ **Don't Miss**

The open-air mural collection of the East Side Gallery.

Construction

Shortly after midnight on 13 August 1961 East German soldiers and police began rolling out miles of barbed wire that would soon be replaced with prefab concrete slabs. The wall was a desperate measure taken by the German Democratic Republic (GDR) government to stop the sustained brain and brawn drain it had experienced since its 1949 founding. Around 3.6 million people had already left for the West, putting the GDR on the verge of economic and political collapse.

Demise

The Wall's demise in 1989 came as unexpectedly as its construction. Once again the GDR was losing its people in droves, this time via Hungary, which had opened its borders with Austria. Something had to give. It did on 9 November 1989 when a GDR

Mural by Thierry Noir on the Wall

Gedenkstätte Berliner Mauer

Ⓢ Nordbahnhof

❶ Need to Know

A double row of cobblestones guides you along 5.7km of the Wall's course. Track down remaining fragments of the Wall using Memorial Landscape Berlin Wall (www.berlin-wall-map.com).

✕ Take a Break

Not far from the Berlin Wall Memorial is the famous Konnopke's Imbiss (p510).

★ Top Tip

There's a great view from the Documentation Centre's viewing platform.

Eberswalder Strasse) **FREE** extends for 1.4km along Bernauer Strasse and integrates an original section of Wall, vestiges of the border installations and escape tunnels, a chapel and a monument. Multimedia stations, panels, excavations and a Documentation Centre provide context and explain what the border fortifications looked like and how they shaped the everyday lives of people on both sides of it.

spokesperson (mistakenly, it later turned out) announced during a press conference that all travel restrictions to the West would be lifted. When asked when, he said simply 'Immediately'. Amid scenes of wild partying, the two Berlins came together again.

In the course of 1990 the Wall almost disappeared from Berlin, some bits smashed up and flogged to tourists, other sections carted off to museums, parks, embassies, exhibitions and even private gardens across the globe. The longest section to survive intact is the East Side Gallery.

Gedenkstätte Berliner Mauer

The outdoor **Berlin Wall Memorial** (☎030-467 986 666; www.berliner-mauer-gedenkstaette. de; Bernauer Strasse, btwn Schwedter Strasse & Gartenstrasse; ⊘visitor & documentation centre 10am-6pm Tue-Sun, open-air exhibit 8am-10pm daily; Ⓢ Nordbahnhof, Bernauer Strasse,

East Side Gallery

The year was 1989. After 28 years, the Berlin Wall, that grim and grey divider of humanity, finally met its maker. Most of it was quickly dismantled, but along Mühlenstrasse, paralleling the Spree, a 1.3km stretch became the **East Side Gallery** (www.eastsidegallery-berlin. de; Mühlenstrasse btwn, Oberbaumbrücke & Ostbahnhof; ⊘24hr; Ⓤ Warschauer Strasse, Ⓢ Ostbahnhof, Warschauer Strasse) **FREE**, the world's largest open-air mural collection. In more than 100 paintings, dozens of international artists translated the era's global euphoria and optimism into a mix of political statements, drug-induced musings and truly artistic visions.

The Berlin Wall

The construction of the Berlin Wall was a unique event in human history, not only for physically bisecting a city but by becoming a dividing line between competing ideologies and political systems. It's this global impact and universal legacy that continue to fascinate people more than a quarter century after its triumphant tear-down. Fortunately, plenty of original Wall segments and other vestiges remain, along with museums and memorials, to help fathom the realities and challenges of daily life in Berlin during the Cold War.

Our illustration points out the top highlights you can visit to learn about different aspects of these often tense decades. The best place to start is the ❶ **Gedenkstätte Berliner Mauer**, for an excellent introduction to what the inner-city border really looked liked and what it meant to live in its shadow. Reflect upon what you've learned while relaxing along the former death strip, now the ❷ **Mauerpark**, before heading to the emotionally charged exhibit at the ❸ **Tränenpalast**, an actual border-crossing pavilion. Relive the euphoria of the

Tränenpalast
This modernist 1962 glass-and-steel border pavilion was dubbed 'Palace of Tears' because of the many tearful farewells that took place outside the building as East Germans and their western visitors had to say goodbye.

Brandenburg Tor
People around the world cheered as East and West Berliners partied together atop the Berlin Wall in front of the iconic city gate, which today is a photogenic symbol of united Germany.

Potsdamer Platz
Nowhere was the death strip as wide as on the former no-man's-land around Potsdamer Platz from which sprouted a new postmodern city quarter in the 1990s. A tiny section of the Berlin Wall serves as a reminder.

Checkpoint Charlie
Only diplomats and foreigners were allowed to use this border crossing. Weeks after the Wall was built, US and Soviet tanks faced off here in one of the hottest moments of the Cold War.

Bernauer Strasse

Chausseestr

Unter den Linden

Leipziger Str

Wall's demise at the **❹ Brandenburg Tor**, then marvel at the revival of **❺ Potsdamer Platz**, which was nothing but death-strip wasteland until the 1990s. The Wall's geopolitical significance is the focus at **❻ Checkpoint Charlie**, which saw some of the tensest moments of the Cold War. Wrap up with finding your favourite mural motif at the **❼ East Side Gallery**.

It's possible to explore these sights by using a combination of walking and public transport, but a bike ride is the best method for gaining a sense of the former Wall's erratic flow through the central city.

FAST FACTS

Beginning of construction 13 August 1961
Total length 155km
Height 3.6m
Weight of each segment 2.6 tonnes
Number of watchtowers 300

❷ .... Remnants of the Wall ──⟩

Mauerpark
Famous for its flea market and karaoke, this popular park actually occupies a converted section of death strip. A 30m segment of surviving Wall is now an official practice ground for budding graffiti artists.

Gedenkstätte Berliner Mauer
Germany's central memorial to the Berlin Wall and its victims exposes the complexity and barbaric nature of the border installation along a 1.4km stretch of the barrier's course.

Alexanderplatz

Alexanderstr

East Side Gallery
Paralleling the Spree for 1.3km, this is the longest Wall vestige. After its collapse, more than a hundred international artists expressed their feelings about this historic moment in a series of colourful murals.

❼

The Reichstag

Reinstated as the home of the German parliament in 1999, the late 19th-century Reichstag is one of Berlin's most iconic buildings.

The Reichstag's Beginnings

It's been burned, bombed, rebuilt, buttressed by the Wall, wrapped in plastic and finally brought back from the dead by Norman Foster: 'turbulent history' just doesn't do it when describing the life this most famous of Berlin's landmarks has endured. This neo-baroque edifice was finished in 1894 to house the German Imperial Diet and served its purpose until 1933 when it was badly damaged by fire in an arson attack carried out by Marinus van der Lubbe, a young Dutch communist. This shocking event conveniently gave Hitler a pretext to tighten his grip on the German state. In 1945 the building was a major target for the Red Army who raised the red flag from the Reichstag, an act that became a symbol of the Soviet defeat of the Nazis.

Great For...

☑ Don't Miss

Free auto-activated audioguides provide info on the building, landmarks and the workings of parliament.

❶ Need to Know

Map p500; www.bundestag.de; Platz der Republik 1, Visitors' Service, Scheidemann-strasse; ⊙lift ride 8am–midnight, last entry 10pm, Visitors' Service 8am–8pm Apr–Oct, to 6pm Nov–Mar; ⓠ100, Ⓢ Brandenburger Tor, Hauptbahnhof, Ⓤ Brandenburger Tor, Bundestag FREE

✗ Take a Break

For quick feeds, the tourist-geared, self-service **Berlin Pavillon** (Map p500; ☐030-2065 4737; www.berlin-pavillon. de; Scheidemannstrasse 1; mains €3.50–9; ⊙8am–9pm) comes in handy.

★ Top Tip

For guaranteed access, make free ticket reservations online before you leave home. Note that all visitors must show ID to enter the building.

The Cold War Years

Although in West Berlin, the Reichstag found itself very near the dividing line between East and West Berlin and from the early 1960s, the Berlin Wall. With the German government sitting safely in faraway Bonn, this grand facade lost its purpose and in the 1950s some in West Berlin thought it should be demolished. However, the wrecking balls never got their day and the Reichstag was restored, albeit without a lot of the decoration which had adorned the old building.

Reunification & Norman Foster

Almost a year after the Wall came down, the official reunification ceremony was symbolically held at the Reichstag which, it was later decided, would become the seat of the German Bundestag (parliament)

once again. Before Norman Foster began his reconstruction work, the entire Reichstag was spectacularly wrapped in plastic sheeting by the Bulgarian-American artist Christo in the summer of 1995. The following four years saw the erection of Norman Foster's now famous glittering glass copula, the centrepiece of the visitor experience today. It is the Reichstag's most distinctive feature, serviced by lift and providing fabulous 360-degree city views and the opportunity to peer down into the parliament chamber. To reach the top, follow the ramp spiralling up around the dome's mirror-clad central cone. The cupola was a spanking new feature, but Foster's brief also stipulated that some parts of the building were to be preserved. One example is the Cyrillic graffiti left by Soviet soldiers in 1945.

MARFMAGNUM/GETTY IMAGES ©

Berlin Nightlife

With its well-deserved reputation as one of Europe's primo party capitals, Berlin offers a thousand-and-one scenarios for getting your cocktails and kicks (or wine or beer, for that matter).

Great For...

☑ **Don't Miss**

Café am Neuen See (p514), generally regarded as Berlin's best beer garden.

Bars & Cafes

Berlin is a notoriously late city: bars stay packed from dusk to dawn and beyond, and some clubs don't hit their stride until 4am. The lack of a curfew never created a tradition of binge drinking.

Edgier, more underground venues cluster in Kreuzberg, Friedrichshain, Neukölln and up-and-coming outer boroughs like Wedding (north of Mitte) and Lichtenberg (past Friedrichshain). Places in Charlottenburg, Mitte and Prenzlauer Berg tend to be quieter and close earlier. Some proprietors have gone to extraordinary lengths to come up with special design concepts.

The line between cafe and bar is often blurred, with many changing stripes as the hands move around the clock. Alcohol, however, is served pretty much all day. Cocktail bars are booming in Berlin and

Beach bars along the Spree River

several new arrivals have measurably elevated the 'liquid art' scene. Dedicated drinking dens tend to be elegant cocoons with mellow lighting and low sound levels. A good cocktail will set you back between €10 and €15.

Beaches & Outdoor Drinking

Berliners are sun cravers and as soon as the first rays spray their way into spring, outdoor tables show up faster than you can pour a pint of beer. The most traditional places for outdoor chilling are, of course, the beer gardens with long wooden benches set up beneath leafy old chestnuts and with cold beer and bratwurst on the menu. In 2002, Berlin also jumped on the 'sandwagon' with the opening of its first beach bar, Strandbar Mitte (p513), in a prime location on the Spree River. Many

that followed have since been displaced by development, which has partly fuelled the latest trend: rooftop bars.

Clubbing

Over the past 25 years, Berlin's club culture has put the city firmly on the map of hedonists. With more than 200 venues, finding one to match your mood isn't difficult. Electronic music in its infinite varieties continues to define Berlin's after-dark action but other sounds like hip-hop, dancehall, rock, swing and funk have also made inroads. The edgiest clubs have taken up residence in power plants, transformer stations, abandoned apartment buildings and other repurposed locations. The scene is in constant flux as experienced club owners look for new challenges and a younger generation of promoters enters the scene with new ideas and impetus.

Historical Highlights

This walk checks off Berlin's blockbuster landmarks as it cuts right through the historic city centre, Mitte (literally 'Middle'). This is the birthplace and glamorous heart of Berlin, a high-octane cocktail of culture, architecture and commerce.

Start Reichstag
Distance 3.5km
Duration Three hours

Classic Photo: The iconic Brandenburger Tor is now a symbol of German reunification.

2 The **Brandenburger Tor** (p498) became an involuntary neighbour of the Berlin Wall during the Cold War.

3 Unter den Linden has been Berlin's showpiece road since the 18th century.

Take a Break... Stop in at Augustiner am Gendarmenmarkt (p509) for some German fare.

1 The sparkling glass dome of the **Reichstag** (p493) has become a shining beacon of unified Berlin.

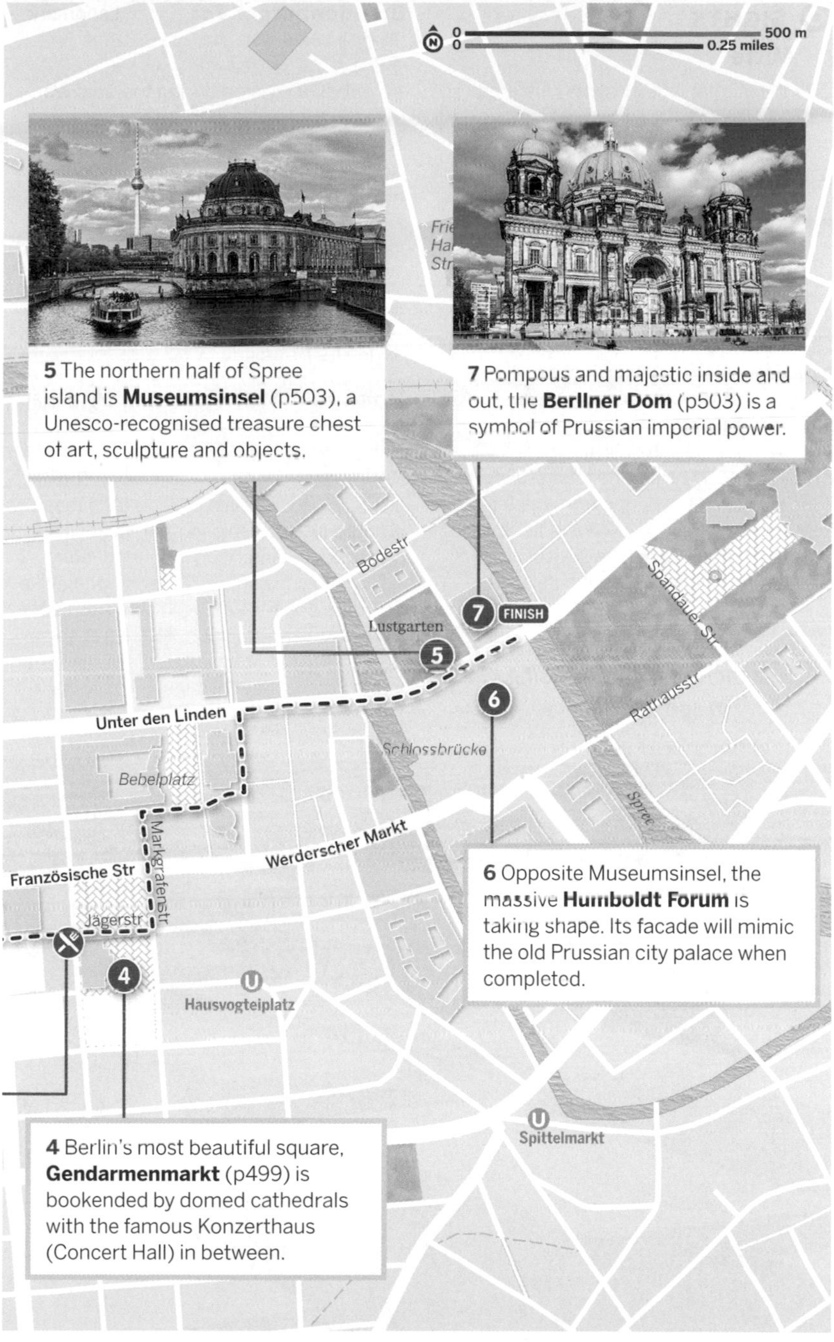

0 ____ 500 m
0 ____ 0.25 miles

5 The northern half of Spree island is **Museumsinsel** (p503), a Unesco-recognised treasure chest of art, sculpture and objects.

7 Pompous and majestic inside and out, the **Berliner Dom** (p503) is a symbol of Prussian imperial power.

Bodestr

Lustgarten

7 FINISH

5

Unter den Linden

6

Schlossbrücke

Bebelplatz

Spandauer Str

Rathausstr

Spree

Werderscher Markt

Französische Str

Jägerstr

4

Hausvogteiplatz

Spittelmarkt

6 Opposite Museumsinsel, the massive **Humboldt Forum** is taking shape. Its facade will mimic the old Prussian city palace when completed.

4 Berlin's most beautiful square, **Gendarmenmarkt** (p499) is bookended by domed cathedrals with the famous Konzerthaus (Concert Hall) in between.

◎ SIGHTS

◎ Mitte

With the mother lode of sights clustered within a walkable area, the most historic part of Berlin is a prime port of call for visitors.

Deutsches Historisches Museum   Museum

(Map p500; German Historical Museum; ☎030-203 040; www.dhm.de; Unter den Linden 2; adult/concession/under 18 €8/4/free; ☺10am-6pm; ☒100, 200, Ⓤ Hausvogteiplatz, Ⓢ Hackescher Markt) If you're wondering what the Germans have been up to for the past two millennia, take a spin around this engaging museum in the baroque Zeughaus, formerly the Prussian arsenal and now home of the German Historical Museum. Upstairs, displays concentrate on the period from the 1st century AD to the end of WWI in 1918, while the ground floor tracks the 20th century all the way through to German reunification.

> *sarcophagi-like concrete columns rising in sombre silence*

Brandenburger Tor   Landmark

(Brandenburger Gate; Map p500; Pariser Platz; Ⓢ Brandenburger Tor, Ⓤ Brandenburger Tor) A symbol of division during the Cold War, the landmark Brandenburg Gate now epitomises German reunification. Carl Gotthard Langhans found inspiration in Athens' Acropolis for the elegant triumphal arch, completed in 1791 as the royal city gate. It stands sentinel over Pariser Platz, a harmoniously proportioned square once again framed by banks, a hotel and the US, British and French embassies, just as it was during its 19th-century heyday.

Holocaust Memorial   Memorial

(Memorial to the Murdered Jews of Europe; Map p500; ☎030-2639 4336; www.stiftung-denkmal.de; Cora-Berliner-Strasse 1; ☺24hr; Ⓢ Brandenburger Tor, Ⓤ Brandenburger Tor) **FREE** Inaugurated in 2005, this football-field-sized memorial by American architect Peter Eisenman consists of 2711 sarcophagi-like concrete columns rising in sombre silence from undulating ground. You're free to access this maze at any point and make your individual journey through it. For context

Holocaust Memorial

ANTON HAVELAAR/SHUTTERSTOCK ©

visit the subterranean **Ort der Information** (Information Centre; Map p500; ☎030-7407 2929; www.holocaust-mahnmal.de; audio guide adult/concession €4/2; ⊙10am-8pm Tue-Sun Apr-Sep, to 7pm Oct-Mar, last admission 45min before closing) FREE whose exhibits will leave no one untouched. Audioguides and audio translations of exhibit panels are available.

Gendarmenmarkt · Square

(Map p500; U Französische Strasse, Stadtmitte) The Gendarmenmarkt area is Berlin at its ritziest, dappled with luxury hotels, fancy restaurants and bars. The graceful square is bookended by the domed 18th century German and French cathedrals and punctuated by a grandly porticoed concert hall, the **Konzerthaus** (Map p500; ☎030-203 092 333; www.konzerthaus.de; tours €3). It was named for the Gens d'Armes, an 18th-century Prussian regiment consisting of French Huguenot refugees whose story is chronicled in a museum inside the **Französischer Dome** (French Cathedral; Map p500; www.franzoesischer-dom.de; church free, museum adult/concession €3.50/2, tower adult/child €3/1; ⊙church & museum noon-5pm Tue-Sun, tower 10am-7pm Apr-Oct, noon-5pm Jan-Mar, last entry 1hr before closing). Climb the tower here for grand views of historic Berlin.

Checkpoint Charlie · Historic Site

(Map p507; cnr Zimmerstrasse & Friedrichstrasse; ⊙24hr; U Kochstrasse) FREE Checkpoint Charlie was the principal gateway for foreigners and diplomats between the two Berlins from 1961 to 1990. Unfortunately, this potent symbol of the Cold War has degenerated into a tacky tourist trap, though a free open-air exhibit that illustrates milestones in Cold War history is one redeeming aspect.

◉ Scheunenviertel

Hackesche Höfe · Historic Site

(Map p500; ☎030-2809 8010; www.hackesche-hoefe.com; enter from Rosenthaler Strasse 40/41 or Sophienstrasse 6; ☐M1, S Hackescher Markt, U Weinmeisterstrasse) FREE The Hackesche Höfe is the largest and most famous of the

Treptower Park & the Soviet Memorial

The former East Berlin district of Treptow gets its character from the Spree River and two parks: Treptower Park and Plänterwald. Both are vast sweeps of expansive lawns, shady woods and tranquil riverfront and are popular for strolling, jogging and picnicking.

Treptower Park's main sight is the gargantuan **Sowjetisches Ehrenmal Treptow** (Soviet War Memorial; ⊙24hr; ☐Treptower Park) FREE, which stands above the graves of 5000 Soviet soldiers killed in the 1945 Battle of Berlin. Inaugurated in 1949, it's a bombastic and sobering testament to the immensity of Russia's wartime losses. Coming from the S-Bahn station, you'll first be greeted by a **statue of Mother Russia** grieving for her dead children. Beyond, two mighty walls fronted by soldiers kneeling in sorrow flank the gateway to the memorial itself; the red marble used here was supposedly scavenged from Hitler's ruined chancellery. Views open up to an enormous sunken lawn lined by **sarcophagi** representing the then 16 Soviet republics, each decorated with war scenes and Stalin quotations. The epic dramaturgy reaches a crescendo at the **mausoleum**, topped by a 13m statue of a Russian soldier clutching a child, his sword resting melodramatically on a shattered swastika. The socialist-realism mosaic within the plinth shows grateful Soviets honouring the fallen.

Sowjetisches Ehrenmal Treptow
CAROL.ANNE/SHUTTERSTOCK ©

Mitte

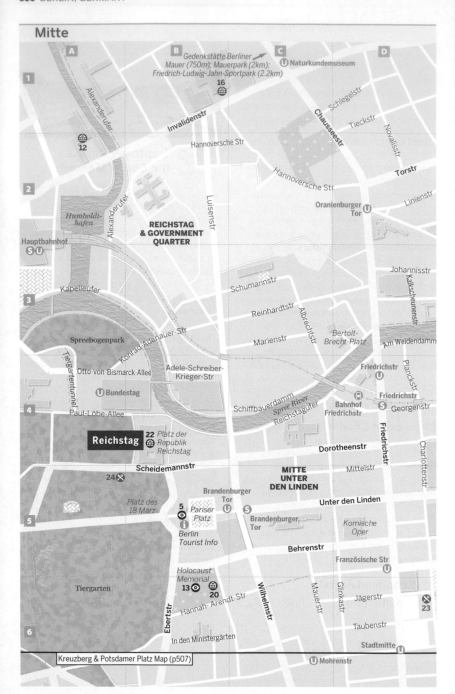

Gedenkstätte Berliner
Mauer (750m); Mauerpark (2km);
Friedrich-Ludwig-Jahn-Sportpark (2.2km)

Naturkundemuseum

16

12

Invalidenstr

Hannoversche Str

Schlegelstr

Tieckstr

Chausseestr

Novalisstr

Hannoversche Str

Torstr

Luisenstr

**REICHSTAG
& GOVERNMENT
QUARTER**

Oranienburger
Tor

Linienstr

7

Humboldt-
hafen

Hauptbahnhof

Johannisstr

Kalkscheunenstr

Kapelleufer

Schumannstr

Reinhardtstr

Albrechtstr

Bertolt-
Brecht-Platz

Am Weidendamm

Spreebogenpark

Konrad-Adenauer-Str

Marienstr

Planckstr

Tiergartentunnel

Otto-von-Bismarck-Allee

Adele-Schreiber-
Krieger-Str

Friedrichstr

Friedrichstr

Bundestag

Schiffbauerdamm

Spree River

Reichstagufer

Bahnhof
Friedrichstr

Georgenstr

Paul-Löbe-Allee

Friedrichstr

Reichstag

22 Platz der
Republik
Reichstag

Dorotheenstr

Charlottenstr

Scheidemannstr

**MITTE
UNTER
DEN LINDEN**

Mittelstr

24

Platz des
18 März

Brandenburger
Tor

5 Pariser
Platz

Unter den Linden

Berlin
Tourist Info

Brandenburger
Tor

Komische
Oper

Behrenstr

Französische Str

Holocaust
Memorial

13

20

Tiergarten

Hannah-Arendt-Str

Wilhelmstr

Mauerstr

Glinkastr

Jägerstr

23

Ebertstr

Taubenstr

In den Ministergärten

Stadtmitte

Kreuzberg & Potsdamer Platz Map (p507)

Mohrenstr

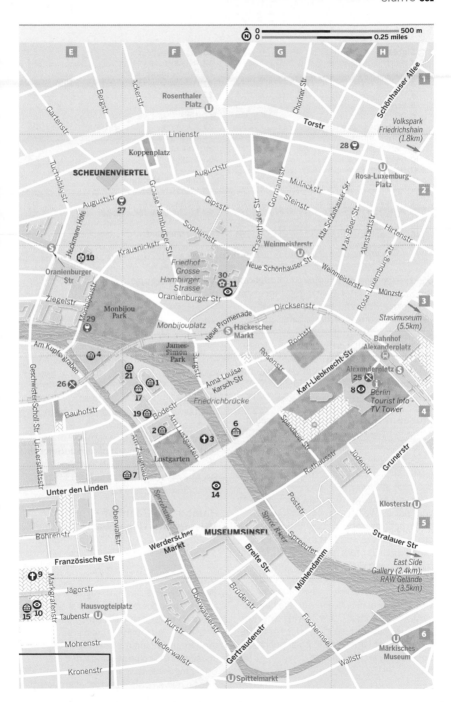

Mitte

courtyard ensembles peppered throughout the Scheunenviertel. Built in 1907, the eight interlinked *Höfe* (courtyards) reopened in 1996 with a congenial mix of cafes, galleries, boutiques and entertainment venues. The main entrance on Rosenthaler Strasse leads to **Court I**, prettily festooned with art nouveau tiles, while Court VII segues to the romantic **Rosenhöfe** with a sunken rose garden and tendril-like balustrades.

Museum für Naturkunde   Museum
(Museum of Natural History; Map p500; ☑030-2093 8591; www.naturkundemuseum.berlin; Invalidenstrasse 43; adult/concession incl audioguide €8/5; ☻9.30am-6pm Tue-Fri, 10am-6pm Sat & Sun; ☷M5, M8, M10, 12, ☝Naturkundemuseum) Fossils and minerals don't quicken your pulse? Well, how about Tristan, one of the best-preserved *Tyrannosaurus rex* skeletons in the world, or the 12m-high *Brachiosaurus branchai,* the world's largest mounted dino skeleton? These Jurassic superstars are joined by a dozen other buddies, some of which are brought to virtual flesh-and-bone life with the help of clever 'Juraskopes'. Other crowd favourites in this excellent museum include Knut, the world's most famous dead polar bear, and an ultrarare archaeopteryx.

Neue Synagoge   Synagogue
(Map p500; ☑030-8802 8300; www.centrumju daicum.de; Oranienburger Strasse 28-30; adult/concession €5/4; ☻10am-6pm Mon-Fri, to 7pm Sun, closes 3pm Fri & 6pm Sun Oct-Mar; ☷M1, ☝Oranienburger Tor, ⎈Oranienburger Strasse) The gleaming gold dome of the Neue Synagoge is the most visible symbol of Berlin's revitalised Jewish community. The 1866 original was Germany's largest synagogue but its modern incarnation is not so much a house of worship (although prayer services do take place), as a museum and place of remembrance called **Centrum Judaicum**. The dome can be climbed from April to September (adult/concession €3/2.50). An audioguide costs €3.

**Hamburger Bahnhof –
Museum für Gegenwart**   Museum
(Contemporary Art Museum; Map p500; ☑030-266 424 242; www.smb.museum; Invalidenstrasse 50-51; adult/concession €14/7; ☻10am-6pm Tue, Wed & Fri, 10am-8pm Thu, 11am-6pm Sat & Sun; ☷M5, M8, M10, ⎈Hauptbahnhof, ☝Hauptbahnhof) Berlin's contemporary art showcase opened in 1996 in an old railway station, whose loft and grandeur are a great backdrop for this Aladdin's cave of paintings, installations, sculptures and video art. Changing exhibits span the arc of post-1950 artistic movements – from conceptual art

and pop art to minimal art and Fluxus – and include seminal works by such major players as Andy Warhol, Cy Twombly, Joseph Beuys and Robert Rauschenberg.

◎ Alexanderplatz

It's practically impossible to visit Berlin without spending time in this area, which packs some of Berlin's must-see sights into a very compact frame.

Museumsinsel — Museum
(Museum Island; Map p500; ☑030-266 424 242, www.smb.museum; day tickets for all 5 museums adult/concession/under 18 €18/9/free; ☼varies by museum; ☐100, 200, TXL, Ⓤ Hackescher Markt, Friedrichstrasse) Walk through ancient Babylon, meet an Egyptian queen, clamber up a Greek altar or be mesmerised by Monet's ethereal landscapes. Welcome to Museumsinsel (Museum Island), Berlin's most important treasure trove, spanning 6000 years' worth of art, artefacts, sculpture and architecture from Europe and beyond. Spread across five grand museums built between 1830 and 1930, the complex takes up the entire northern half of the little Spree Island where Berlin's settlement began in the 13th century.

The first repository to open was the **Altes Museum** (Old Museum; Map p500; Am Lustgarten; adult/concession €10/5; ☼10am-6pm Tue, Wed & Fri-Sun, to 8pm Thu), which presents Greek, Etruscan and Roman antiquities. Behind it, the **Neues Museum** (New Museum; Map p500; Bodestrasse 1-3; adult/concession €12/6; ☼10am-6pm, to 8pm Thu) showcases the Egyptian collection, most famously the bust of Queen Nefertiti, and also houses the Museum of Pre- and Early History. The temple-like **Alte Nationalgalerie** (Old National Gallery; Map p500; Bodestrasse 1-3; adult/concession €12/6; ☼10am-6pm Tue, Wed & Fri-Sun, to 8pm Thu) trains the focus on 19th-century European art. The island's top draw is the **Pergamonmuseum** (Map p500; Bodestrasse 1-3; adult/concession €12/6; ☼10am-6pm Fri-Wed, to 8pm Thu), with its monumental architecture from ancient worlds, including the namesake Pergamonaltar. The **Bode-Museum** (Map

p500; cnr Am Kupfergraben & Monbijoubrücke; adult/concession €12/6; ☼10am-6pm Tue, Wed & Fri-Sun, to 8pm Thu), at the island's northern lip, is famous for its medieval sculptures.

DDR Museum — Museum
(GDR Museum; Map p500; ☑030-847 123 731; www.ddr-museum.de; Karl-Liebknecht-Strasse 1; adult/concession €9.50/6; ☼10am-8pm Sun-Fri, to 10pm Sat; ☐100, 200, TXL, Ⓢ Hackescher Markt) This interactive museum does an entertaining job of pulling back the iron curtain on an extinct society. You'll learn how, under communism, kids were put through collective potty training, engineers earned little more than farmers, and everyone, it seems, went on nudist holidays. A highlight is a simulated ride in a Trabi (an East German car).

Fernsehturm — Landmark
(TV Tower; Map p500; ☑030-247 575 875; www.tv-turm.de; Panoramastrasse 1a; adult/child €13/8.50, premium ticket €19.50/12; ☼9am-midnight Mar-Oct, 10am-midnight Nov-Feb, last ascent 11.30pm; ☐100, 200, TXL, Ⓤ Alexanderplatz, Ⓢ Alexanderplatz) Germany's tallest structure, the TV Tower has been soaring 368m high since 1969 and is as iconic to Berlin as the Eiffel Tower is to Paris. On clear days, views are stunning from the panorama level at 203m or from the upstairs **restaurant** (☑030-247 5750; www.tv-turm.de/en/bar-restaurant; mains lunch €9.50-18.50, dinner €14.50-28.50; ☼10am-midnight), which makes one revolution per hour. To shorten the wait, buy a timed ticket online.

Berliner Dom — Church
(Berlin Cathedral; Map p500; ☑030-2026 9136; www.berlinerdom.de; Am Lustgarten; adult/concession/under 18 €7/5/free; ☼9am-8pm Apr-Oct, to 7pm Nov-Mar; ☐100, 200, TXL, Ⓢ Hackescher Markt) Pompous yet majestic, the Italian Renaissance–style former royal court church (1905) does triple duty as house of worship, museum and concert hall. Inside it's gilt to the hilt and outfitted with a lavish marble-and-onyx altar, a 7269-pipe Sauer organ and elaborate royal sarcophagi. Climb up the 267 steps to the gallery for glorious city views.

Potsdamer Platz & Tiergarten

Potsdamer Platz Area

(Map p507; Alte Potsdamer Strasse; 🚌200, Ⓢ Potsdamer Platz, Ⓤ Potsdamer Platz) The rebirth of the historic Potsdamer Platz was Europe's biggest building project of the 1990s, a showcase of urban renewal masterminded by such top international architects as Renzo Piano and Helmut Jahn. An entire city quarter sprouted on terrain once bifurcated by the Berlin Wall and today houses offices, theatres and cinemas, hotels, apartments and museums. Highlights include the glass-tented **Sony Center** (Map p507; Potsdamer Strasse) and the **Panoramapunkt** (Map p507; 🕾030-2593 7080; www.panoramapunkt.de; Potsdamer Platz 1; adult/concession €6.50/5, without wait €10.50/8; ⊙10am-8pm Apr-Oct, to 6pm Nov-Mar) observation deck.

Topographie des Terrors Museum

(Topography of Terror; Map p507; 🕾030-2548 0950; www.topographie.de; Niederkirchner Strasse 8; ⊙10am-8pm, grounds close at dusk or 8pm at the latest; Ⓢ Potsdamer Platz, Ⓤ Potsdamer Platz) FREE In the same spot where the most feared institutions of Nazi Germany (including the Gestapo headquarters and the SS central command) once stood, this compelling exhibit chronicles the stages of terror and persecution, puts a face on the perpetrators and details the impact these brutal institutions had on all of Europe. A second exhibit outside zeroes in on how life changed for Berlin and its people after the Nazis made it their capital.

Tiergarten Park

(Map p507; Strasse des 17 Juni; 🚌100, 200, Ⓢ Potsdamer Platz, Brandenburger Tor, Ⓤ Brandenburger Tor) FREE Berlin's rulers used to hunt boar and pheasants in the rambling Tiergarten until garden architect Peter Lenné landscaped the grounds in the 18th century. Today it's one of the world's largest urban parks, popular for strolling, jogging, picnicking, Frisbee tossing and, yes, nude sunbathing and gay cruising (especially around the Löwenbrücke). It is bisected by a major artery, the Strasse des 17 Juni. Walking across the entire park takes about an hour, but even a shorter stroll has its rewards.

DE VISU?/SHUTTERSTOCK ©

Gemäldegalerie — Gallery

(Gallery of Old Masters; Map p507; ☎030-266 424 242; www.smb.museum/gg; Matthäikirchplatz; adult/concession €10/5; ⏰10am-6pm Tue, Wed & Fri, 10am-8pm Thu, 11am-6pm Sat & Sun; ♿; ☐M29, M48, M85, 200, ⑤Potsdamer Platz, ⓤPotsdamer Platz) This museum ranks among the world's finest and most comprehensive collections of European art with about 1500 paintings spanning the arc of artistic vision from the 13th to the 18th century. Wear comfy shoes when exploring the 72 galleries: a walk past masterpieces by Titian, Dürer, Hals, Vermeer, Gainsborough and many more Old Masters covers almost 2km. Don't miss the Rembrandt Room (Room X).

Siegessäule — Monument

(Victory Column; Grosser Stern; adult/concession €3/2.50; ⏰9.30am-6.30pm Mon-Fri, to 7pm Sat & Sun Apr-Oct, 10am-5pm Mon-Fri, to 5.30pm Sat & Sun Nov-Mar; ☐100, 200, ⓤHansaplatz, ⑤Bellevue) Like arms of a starfish, five roads merge into the Grosser Stern roundabout at the heart of the huge Tiergarten park. The Victory Column at its centre is crowned by a gilded statue of the goddess Victoria in celebration of 19th-century Prussian military triumphs. Today it is also a symbol of Berlin's gay community. Climb 285 steps for sweeping views of the park.

Bauhaus Archiv — Museum

(Map p507; ☎030-254 0020; www.bauhaus. de; Klingelhöferstrasse 14; adult/concession/ under 18 incl audioguide Wed-Fri €7/4/free, Sat-Mon €8/5/free; ⏰10am-5pm Wed-Mon; ☐100, ⓤNollendorfplatz) Founded in 1919, the Bauhaus was a seminal school of avant-garde architecture, design and art. This avant-garde building, designed by Bauhaus' founder Walter Gropius, presents paintings, drawings, sculptures, models and other objects and documents by such famous artist-teachers as Klee, Feininger and Kandinsky. There's a decent cafe and good gift shop. A building expansion by Berlin architect Volker Staab is planned to open in 2021.

◉ Prenzlauer Berg

Prenzlauer Berg doesn't have any blockbuster sights, and most of what it does have is concentrated in the pretty southern section around Kollwitzplatz.

> ★ **Top Five Historical Sites**
> Gedenkstätte Berliner Mauer (p409)
> Topographie des Terrors (p504)
> Jüdisches Museum (p506)
> Sachsenhausen (p514)
> Deutsches Historisches Museum (p498)

From left: Sony Center, Potsdamer Platz; Bauhaus Archiv; Goddess Victoria on top of the Siegessäule

HINTERHOF/SHUTTERSTOCK ©

CINEBERG/SHUTTERSTOCK ©

The neighbourhood does include the city's most important exhibit on the Berlin Wall, the Gedenkstätte Berliner Mauer (p489), which begins in Wedding and stretches for 1.4km all the way into Prenzlauer Berg.

Mauerpark   Park

(www.mauerpark.info; btwn Bernauer Strasse, Schwedter Strasse & Gleimstrasse; M1, M10, 12, Eberswalder Strasse) With its wimpy trees and anaemic lawn, Mauerpark is hardly your typical leafy oasis, especially given that it was forged from a section of Cold War–era death strip (a short stretch of Berlin Wall survives). It's this mystique combined with an unassuming vibe and a hugely popular Sunday flea market and karaoke show that has endeared the place to locals and visitors alike.

◎ Kreuzberg

Jüdisches Museum   Museum

(Jewish Museum; Map p507; 030-2599 3300; www.jmberlin.de; Lindenstrasse 9-14; adult/concession €8/3, audioguide €3; 10am-8pm Tue-Sun, to 10pm Mon, last entry 1hr before closing; Hallesches Tor, Kochstrasse) In a landmark building by American-Polish architect Daniel Libeskind, Berlin's Jewish Museum offers a chronicle of the trials and triumphs in 2000 years of Jewish life in Germany. The exhibit smoothly navigates all major periods, from the Middle Ages via the Enlightenment to the community's post-1990 renaissance. Find out about Jewish cultural contributions, holiday traditions, the difficult road to emancipation and outstanding individuals (eg Moses Mendelssohn, Levi Strauss) and the fates of ordinary people.

Deutsches Technikmuseum   Museum

(German Museum of Technology; Map p507; 030-902 540; www.sdtb.de; Trebbiner Strasse 9; adult/concession/under 18 €8/4/after 3pm free, audioguide adult/concession €2/1; 9am-5.30pm Tue-Fri, 10am-6pm Sat & Sun; P; Gleisdreieck, Möckernbrücke) A roof-mounted 'candy bomber' (the plane used in the 1948 Berlin airlift) is merely the over-ture to this enormous and hugely engaging shrine to technology. Fantastic for kids, the giant museum counts the world's first computer, an entire hall of vintage locomotives and extensive exhibits on aerospace and navigation among its top attractions. At the adjacent **Science Center Spectrum** (enter Möckernstrasse 26; same ticket) kids can participate in hands-on experiments.

◎ Friedrichshain

This notorious party district also has a serious side, especially when it comes to blockbuster vestiges of the GDR era such as the East Side Gallery (p489), Karl-Marx-Allee and the Stasi HQ. Alas, the key sights are all pretty spread out and best reached by public transport.

Volkspark Friedrichshain   Park

(bounded by Am Friedrichshain, Friedenstrasse, Danziger Strasse & Landsberger Allee; P; 142, 200, M5, M6, M8, M10, Schillingstrasse) Berlin's oldest public park has provided relief from urbanity since 1840, but has been hilly only since the late 1940s when wartime debris was piled up here to create two 'mountains' – the taller one, **Mont Klamott** (24hr) **FREE**, rises 78m high. Diversions include expansive lawns for lazing, tennis courts, a halfpipe for skaters, a couple of handily placed beer gardens and an outdoor cinema.

◎ Charlottenburg

Schloss Charlottenburg   Palace

(Map p508; 030-320 910; www.spsg.de; Spandauer Damm 10-22; day passes to all 4 buildings adult/concession €12/9; hours vary by building; P; M45, 109, 309, Richard-Wagner-Platz, Sophie-Charlotte-Platz) Charlottenburg Palace is one of the few sites in Berlin that still reflects the one-time grandeur of the Hohenzollern clan that ruled the region from 1415 to 1918. Originally a petite summer retreat, it grew into an exquisite baroque pile with opulent private apartments, richly festooned festival halls, collections of precious porcelain and paintings by French 18th-century masters. It's lovely

Kreuzberg & Potsdamer Platz

Kreuzberg & Potsdamer Platz

in fine weather when you can fold a stroll in the palace park into a day of peeking at royal treasures.

Kaiser-Wilhelm-Gedächtniskirche Church

(Kaiser Wilhelm Memorial Church; Map p508; ☏030-218 5023; www.gedaechtniskirche.com; Breitscheidplatz; ⊙church 9am-7pm, memorial hall 10am-6pm Mon-Fri, 10am-5.30pm Sat, noon-5.30pm Sun; 🚌100, 200, ⓤZoologischer Garten, Kurfürstendamm, Ⓢ Zoologischer Garten) FREE

Allied bombing in 1943 left only the husk of the west tower of this once magnificent neo-Romanesque church standing. Now an antiwar memorial, it stands quiet and dignified amid the roaring traffic. Historic photographs displayed in the **Gedenkhalle** (Hall of Remembrance), at the bottom of the tower, help you visualise the former grandeur of this 1895 church. The adjacent octagonal hall of worship, added in 1961, has glowing midnight-blue glass walls and a giant 'floating' Jesus.

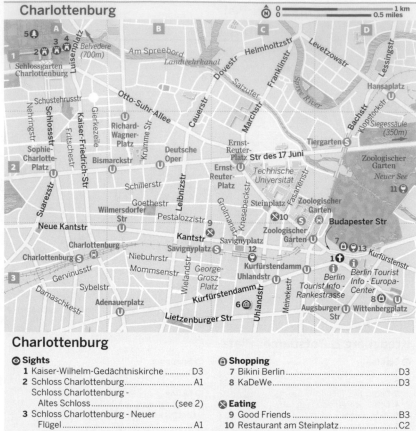

Charlottenburg

Story of Berlin   Museum

(Map p508; ☎030-8872 0100; www.story-of-berlin.de; Kurfürstendamm 207-208, enter via Ku'damm Karree mall; adult/concession €12/9; ☺10am-8pm, last admission 6pm; ☒X9, X10, 109, 110, M19, M29, TXL, ⓊUhlandstrasse) This engaging museum breaks 800 years of Berlin history down into bite-size chunks that are easy to swallow but substantial enough to be satisfying. Each of the 23 rooms uses sound, light, technology and original objects to zero in on a specific theme or epoch in the city's history, from its founding in 1237 to the fall of the Berlin Wall. The creepily fascinating climax is a tour (in English) of a still-functional atomic bunker beneath the building.

🎫 TOURS

Berliner Unterwelten   Tours

(☎030-4991 0517; www.berliner-unterwelten.de; Brunnenstrasse 105; adult/concession €11/9;

⊙Dark Worlds tours in English 1pm Mon & 11am Thu-Mon year-round, 11am Wed Mar-Nov, 3pm Wed-Mon & 1pm Wed-Sun Apr-Oct; Ⓢ Gesundbrunnen, Ⓤ Gesundbrunnen) After you've checked off the Brandenburg Gate and the TV Tower, why not explore Berlin's dark and dank underbelly? Join Berliner Unterwelten on its 'Dark Worlds' tour of a WWII underground bunker (available in English) and pick your way through a warren of claustrophobic rooms, past heavy steel doors, hospital beds, helmets, guns, boots and lots of other wartime artefacts.

Berlin on Bike — Cycling
(☑030-4373 9999; www.berlinonbike.de; Knaackstrasse 97, Kulturbrauerei, Court 4; tours incl bike adult/concession €21/18; ⊙8am-8pm mid Mar–mid Nov, 10am-4pm Mon-Sat mid-Nov–mid-Mar; Ⓜ M1, Ⓤ Eberswalder Strasse) This well-established company has a busy schedule of insightful and fun bike tours led by locals. There are daily English-language city tours (Berlin's Best) and Berlin Wall tours as well as an Alternative Berlin tour three times weekly. Other tours (eg street art, night tours) run in German or in English on request.

Original Berlin Walks — Walking
(☑030-301 9194; www.berlinwalks.de; adult/concession from €14/12) Berlin's longest-running English-language walking tour company has a large roster of general and themed tours (eg Hitler's Germany, Jewish Life, Berlin Wall), as well as trips out to Sachsenhausen concentration camp, Potsdam and Wittenberg. The website has details on timings and meeting points.

🅐 SHOPPING
KaDeWe — Department Store
(Map p508; ☑030-212 10; www.kadewe.de; Tauentzienstrasse 21-24; ⊙10am-8pm Mon-Thu, 10am-9pm Fri, 9.30am-8pm Sat; Ⓤ Wittenbergplatz) Every day some 180,000 shoppers invade continental Europe's largest department store. Going strong since 1907, it boasts an assortment so vast that a pirate-style campaign is the best way to

plunder its bounty. If pushed for time, at least hurry up to the legendary 6th-floor gourmet food hall. The name, by the way, stands for *Kaufhaus des Westens* (department store of the West).

LP12 Mall of Berlin — Mall
(Map p507; www.mallofberlin.de; Leipziger Platz 12; ⊙10am-9pm Mon-Sat; 📶; 🚌200, Ⓤ Potsdamer Platz, Ⓢ Potsdamer Platz) This spanking new retail quarter is tailor-made for black-belt mall rats. More than 270 shops vie for your shopping euros, including flagship stores by Karl Lagerfeld, Hugo Boss, Liebeskind, Marc Cain, Muji and other international high-end brands alongside the usual high-street chains like Mango and H&M. Free mobile-phone recharge station on the 2nd floor.

Bikini Berlin — Mall
(Map p508; www.bikiniberlin.de; Budapester Strasse 38-50; ⊙shops 10am-8pm Mon-Sat, building 9am-9pm Mon-Sat, 1-6pm Sun; 📶; 🚌100, 200, Ⓤ Zoologischer Garten, Ⓢ Zoologischer Garten) Germany's first concept mall opened in 2014 in a spectacularly rehabilitated 1950s architectural icon nicknamed 'Bikini' because of its design: 200m-long upper and lower sections separated by an open floor, now chastely covered by a glass facade. Inside are three floors of urban indie boutiques and short-lease pop-up 'boxes' that offer a platform for up-and-coming designers.

❌ EATING
🍴 Mitte
Augustiner am Gendarmenmarkt — German €€
(Map p500; ☑030-2045 4020; www.augustinerbraeu-berlin.de; Charlottenstrasse 55; mains €6.50-26.50; ⊙10am-2am; Ⓤ Französische Strasse) Tourists, concert-goers and hearty-food lovers rub shoulders at rustic tables in this authentic Bavarian beer hall. Soak up the down-to-earth vibe right along with a mug of full-bodied Augustiner brew. Sausages, roast pork and pretzels provide rib-sticking sustenance, but there's also plenty of lighter (even meat-free) fare as well as good-value lunch specials.

Flea Markets

Berlin's numerous flea markets set up on weekends (usually Sunday) year-round – rain or shine – and are also the purview of fledgling local fashion designers and jewellery makers.

Flohmarkt im Mauerpark (www.flohmarktimmauerpark.de; Bernauer Strasse 63-64; ⊙9am-6pm Sun; 🚃M1, M10, 12, ⓤEberswalder Strasse) Join the throngs of thrifty trinket hunters, bleary-eyed clubbers and excited tourists sifting for treasure at this always busy flea market with cult status, running right where the Berlin Wall once ran. Source new faves among retro threads, local-designer T-shirts, vintage vinyl and offbeat stuff. Street-food stands and beer gardens, including **Mauersegler** (📞030-9788 0904; www.mauersegler-berlin.de; ⊙2pm-2am May-Oct; 🛜), provide sustenance.

Nowkoelln Flowmarkt (www.nowkoelln. de; Maybachufer; ⊙10am-6pm 2nd & 4th Sun of month Mar-Oct or later; ⓤKottbusser Tor, Schönleinstrasse) This hipster-heavy flea market sets up twice-monthly along the scenic Landwehrkanal and delivers secondhand bargains galore along with handmade threads and jewellery.

RAW Flohmarkt (www.raw-flohmarkt-berlin.de; Revaler Strasse 99, RAW Gelände; ⊙9am-7pm Sun; 🚃M10, M13, ⓢWarschauer Strasse, ⓤWarschauer Strasse) Bargains abound at this smallish flea market right on the grounds of **RAW Gelände** (www.raw-tempel.de), a former train repair station turned party village. It's wonderfully free of professional sellers, meaning you'll find everything from the proverbial kitchen sink to 1970s go-go boots. Bargains are plentiful, and food, a beer garden and cafes are nearby.

Zwölf Apostel   Italian €€

(Map p500; www.12-apostel.de; Georgenstrasse 2; pizza €10-15, mains €16.50-22.50; 🚃M1, ⓢFriedrichstrasse, ⓤFriedrichstrasse) A pleasant pit stop between museums, this place beneath the railway arches has over-the-top religious decor and tasty thin-crust pizzas named after the 12 apostles, plus good-value lunch specials.

Restaurant Tim Raue   Asian €€€

(Map p507; 📞030-2593 7930; www.tim-raue. com; Rudi-Dutschke-Strasse 26; 3-/4-course lunch €48/58, 8-course dinner €198, mains €55-66; ⊙noon-3pm & 7pm-midnight Wed-Sat; ⓤKochstrasse) Now here's a two-Michelin-starred restaurant we can get our mind around. Unstuffy ambience and a reduced design with walnut and Vitra chairs perfectly juxtapose with Raue's brilliant Asian-inspired plates that each shine the spotlight on a few choice ingredients. His interpretation of Peking duck is a perennial bestseller. Popular at lunchtime too.

 Prenzlauer Berg

Kanaan   Middle Eastern €

(📞0176 2258 6673; www.facebook.com/kanaan restaurantberlin; Kopenhagener Strasse 17; dishes €4-7; ⊙noon-4pm Mon-Fri, to 10pm Sat & Sun; 🛜🍽; 🚃M1, ⓤSchönhauser Allee, ⓢSchönhauser Allee) In this feel-good venture, an Israeli biz whiz and a Palestinian chef have teamed up to bring a progressive blend of Middle Eastern fare to Berlin. Top menu picks are hummus, *shakshuka* and *sabich*. For now, weekday lunch is served from a rakishly ramshackle hut, while on weekends a bigger menu is dished up across the street at Kohlenquelle, a funky bar in a former coal cellar.

Konnopke's Imbiss   German €

(📞030-442 7765; www.konnopke-imbiss. de; Schönhauser Allee 44a; sausages €1.30-2; ⊙9am-8pm Mon-Fri, 11.30am-8pm Sat; 🚃M1, M10, ⓤEberswalder Strasse) Brave the inevitable queue at this famous sausage kitchen, ensconced in the same spot below the elevated U-Bahn tracks since 1930, but now equipped with a heated pavilion and an English menu. The 'secret' sauce topping its classic *Currywurst* comes in a four-tier heat scale from mild to wild.

Outdoor cafe

Umami   Vietnamese €€

(☑030-2886 0626; www.umami restaurant.de, Knaackstrasse 16-18; mains €7.50-15; ⓧnoon-11.30pm; ☎◢; ⊜M2, ⓤSenefelderplatz) A mellow 1950s lounge-vibe and an inspired menu of Indochine home cooking divided into 'regular' and 'vegetarian' choices are the main draws of this restaurant with large pavement terrace. Leave room for the green-tea apple pie or a Vietnamese cupcake called 'popcake'. The six-course family meal is a steal at €20 (€9 per additional person).

Bird   American €€

(☑030-5105 3283; www.thebirdinberlin.com; Am Falkplatz 5; burgers €9.50-14, steaks from €22.50; ⓧ6pm-midnight Mon-Thu, 4pm-midnight Fri, noon-midnight Sat & Sun; ☎; ⊜M1, ⓤSchön-hauser Allee, Ⓢ Schönhauser Allee) New York meets Berlin at this expat favourite whose dry-aged steaks, burgers and hand-cut fries might just justify the hype. Sink your teeth into a dripping half-pounder made from freshly ground premium German beef trapped between a toasted English muffin (yes, it's messy – that's what the kitchen paper is for!).

✖ Kreuzberg

Curry 36   German €

(Map p507; ☑030-2580 088 336; www.curry36. de; Mehringdamm 36; snacks €2-6; ⓧ9am-5am; ⓤMehringdamm) Day after day, night after night, a motley crowd – cops, cabbies, queens, office jockeys, savvy tourists etc – wait their turn at this top-ranked *Curry-wurst* snack shop that's been frying 'em up since 1981.

Cafe Jacques   International €€

(☑030-694 1048; Maybachufer 14; mains €12-20; ⓧ6pm-late; ⓤSchönleinstrasse) A favourite with off-duty chefs and loyal foodies, Jacques infallibly charms with flattering candlelight, arty-elegant decor and fantastic wine. It's the perfect date spot but, quite frankly, you only have to be in love with good food to appreciate the French- and North African–inspired blackboard menu. Fish and meat are always tops and the pasta is homemade. Reservations essential.

Restaurant Richard   French €€€

(☑030-4920 7242; www.restaurant-richard.de; Köpenicker Strasse 174; 4-course dinner €58,

Berlin nightlife

additional courses €10; ⊙7pm-midnight Tue-Sat; ⓊSchlesisches Tor) A venue where Nazis partied in the 1930s and leftists debated in the '70s has been reborn as a fine-dining shrine solidly rooted in the French tradition and, since 2015, endowed with a Michelin star. With its coffered ceiling, bubble chandeliers and risqué canvases, the decor is as luscious as the fancy food while the vibe remains charmingly relaxed.

✖ Charlottenburg

Good Friends   Chinese €€

(Map p508; ☎030-313 2659; www.goodfriends-berlin.de; Kantstrasse 30; 2-course lunches €7, dinner mains €7-20; ⊙noon-1am; ⓈSavignyplatz) Good Friends is widely considered Berlin's best Cantonese restaurant. The ducks dangling in the window are merely an overture to a menu long enough to confuse Confucius, including plenty of authentic homestyle dishes. If sea cucumber with fish belly proves too challenging, you can always fall back on sweet-and-sour pork or fried rice with shrimp.

Lucky Leek   Vegan €€

(☎030-6640 8710; www.lucky-leek.de; Kollwitzstrasse 54; mains €14-20, 3-/5-course dinners €33/55; ⊙6-10pm Wed-Sun; ✚; ⓊSenefelderplatz) Josita Hartanto has a knack for coaxing maximum flavour out of the vegetable kingdom and for boldly combining ingredients in unexpected ways. Hers is one of the best vegan restaurants in town and is especially lovely in the summer, when seating expands to a leafy pavement terrace. No à la carte on Fridays and Saturdays.

Restaurant am Steinplatz   German €€€

(Map p508; ☎030-5544 447 053; www.hotelsteinplatz.com; Steinplatz 4; mains €18-38, 4-/5-course dinners €56/65; ⊙noon-2.30pm & 6.30-10.30pm; Ⓟ; ⎇M45, ⓊErnst-Reuter-Platz, Zoologischer Garten, ⓈZoologischer Garten) The 1920s get a 21st-century makeover at this stylish outpost with an open kitchen where Marcus Zimmer feeds regional products into classic German and Berlin recipes. Even rustic beer-hall dishes such as *Eisbein* (boiled pork knuckle) are imaginatively reinterpreted and beautifully plated. A perennial favourite is the Königsberger Klopse (veal dumplings with capers, beetroot and mashed potatoes).

🅭 DRINKING & NIGHTLIFE
🅞 Mitte

Clärchens Ballhaus   Club
(Map p500; ✆030-282 9295; www.ballhaus.de; Auguststrasse 24; ⏰11am-late; 🚇M1, ⑤Oranienburger Strasse) Yesteryear is right now at this late, great 19th-century dance hall where groovers and grannies hoof it across the parquet without even a touch of irony. There are different sounds nightly – salsa to swing, tango to disco – and a live band on Saturday. Dancing kicks off from 9pm or 9.30pm. Easy door but often packed, so book a table.

Strandbar Mitte   Bar
(Map p500; ✆030-2838 5588; www.strandbar-mitte.de; Monbijoustrasse 3; dancing €4; ⏰10am-late May-Sep; 🚇M1, ⑤Oranienburger Strasse) With a full-on view of the Bode-Museum, palm trees and a relaxed ambience, Germany's first beach bar (since 2002) is great for balancing a surfeit of sightseeing stimulus with a reviving drink and thin-crust pizza. At night, there's dancing under the stars with tango, cha-cha, swing and salsa, often preceded by dance lessons.

Kaffee Burger   Club
(Map p500; www.kaffeeburger.de; Torstrasse 60; ⏰from 9pm Mon-Thu, from 10pm Fri-Sun; Ⓤ Rosa-Luxemburg-Platz) Nothing to do with either coffee or meat patties, this sweaty cult club with lovingly faded Communist-era decor is a fun-for-all concert and party pen. The sound policy swings from indie and electro to klezmer punk without missing a beat. Also has readings and poetry slams.

🅞 Potsdamer Platz & Tiergarten

Fragrances   Cocktail Bar
(Map p507; ✆030-337 777; www.ritzcarlton.com; Ritz-Carlton, Potsdamer Platz 3; ⏰from 7pm Wed-Sat; 📶; 🚌200, ⑤Potsdamer Platz, Ⓤ Potsdamer Platz) Berlin cocktail maven Arnd

 East Berlin's Stasi Museum

The **Stasimuseum** (✆030-553 6854; www.stasimuseum.de; Haus 1, Ruschestrasse 103; adult/concession €6/4.50; ⏰10am-6pm Mon-Fri, 11am-6pm Sat & Sun; Ⓤ Magdalenenstrasse) provides an overview of the structure, methods and impact of the Ministry of State Security (Stasi), the secret police of former East Germany, inside the feared institution's fortress-like headquarters. At its peak, more than 8000 people worked in this compound alone; the scale model in the entrance foyer will help you grasp its vast dimensions. Other rooms introduce the ideology, rituals and institutions of East German society. You can marvel at cunningly low-tech surveillance devices (hidden in watering cans, rocks, even neckties), a prisoner transport van with tiny, lightless cells, and the stuffy offices of Stasi chief Erich Mielke. There's also background on the SED party and on the role of the youth organisation Junge Pioneere (Young Pioneers). Panelling is partly in English, and there are free English tours at 3pm Saturday and Sunday.

The museum is in the eastern district of Lichtenberg, just north of U-Bahn station Magdalenenstrasse.

Conference room in the Stasi headquarters

Heissen's newest baby is the world's first 'perfume bar', a libation station where he mixes potable potions mimicking famous scents. The black-mirrored space in the Ritz-Carlton is like a 3D menu where adventurous drinkers sniff out their favourite

 ### Sachsenhausen Concentration Camp

About 35km north of Berlin, **Sachsen-hausen** (Memorial & Museum Sachsen-hausen; ☏03301-200 200; www.stiftung-bg. de; Strasse der Nationen 22, Oranienburg; ⊙8.30am-6pm mid-Mar–mid-Oct, to 4.30pm mid-Oct–mid-Mar, museums closed Mon mid-Oct–mid-Mar; **P**; **S**Oranienburg) **FREE** was built by prisoners and opened in 1936 as a prototype for other concentration camps. By 1945, some 200,000 people had passed through its sinister gates, most of them political opponents, Jews, Roma people and, after 1939, POWs. Tens of thousands died here from hunger, exhaustion, illness, exposure, medical experiments and executions. Thousands more succumbed during the death march of April 1945, when the Nazis evacuated the camp in advance of the Red Army.

A tour of the memorial site with its remaining buildings and exhibits will leave no one untouched.

The S1 makes the trip thrice hourly from central Berlin (eg Friedrichstrasse station) to Oranienburg (€3.30, 45 minutes). Hourly regional RE5 and RB12 trains leaving from Hauptbahnhof are faster (€3.30, 25 minutes). The camp is about 2km from the Oranienburg train station.

from among a row of perfume bottles, then settle back into flocked couches to enjoy exotic blends served in unusual vessels, including a birdhouse.

Café am Neuen See   Beer Garden

(Map p508; ☏030-254 4930; www.cafeamneuen see.de; Lichtensteinallee 2; ⊙restaurant 9am-11pm, beer garden 11am-late Mon-Fri, 10am-late Sat & Sun; ♿; ☐200, **U**Zoologischer Garten, **S**Zoologischer Garten, Tiergarten) Next to an idyllic pond in Tiergarten, this restaurant gets jammed year-round for its sumptuous breakfast and seasonal fare, but it really comes into its own during beer garden season. Enjoy a microvacation over a cold one and a pretzel or pizza, then take your sweetie for a spin in a rowing boat.

Prenzlauer Berg

Prater Biergarten   Beer Garden

(☏030-448 5688; www.pratergarten.de; Kastanienallee 7-9; snacks €2.50-6; ⊙noon-late Apr-Sep, weather permitting; **U**Eberswalder Strasse) Berlin's oldest beer garden has seen beer-soaked nights since 1837 and is still a charismatic spot for guzzling a custom-brewed Prater Pilsner beneath the ancient chestnut trees (self-service). Kids can romp around the small play area.

Weinerei Forum   Wine Bar

(☏030-440 6983; www.weinerei.com; Fehrbel-liner Strasse 57; ⊙10am-midnight; ☎; ☐M1, **U**Rosenthaler Platz) After 8pm, this living-room-style cafe turns into a wine bar that works on the honour principle: you 'rent' a wine glass for €2, then help yourself to as much vino as you like and in the end decide what you want to pay. Please be fair to keep this fantastic concept going.

Zum Starken August   Pub

(☏030-2520 9020; www.zumstarkenaugust.de; Schönhauser Allee 56; ⊙11am-1am Sun & Mon, to 2am Tue, to 3am Wed, to 4am Thu, to 5am Fri & Sat; ☐M1, M10, **U**Eberswalder Strasse) Part cir-cus, part burlesque bar, this vibrant venue dressed in Victorian-era exuberance is a fun and friendly addition to the Prenzlauer Berg pub culture. Join the unpretentious, international crowd over cocktails and craft beers while being entertained with drag-hosted bingo, burlesque divas, wicked cabaret or the hilarious 'porno karaoke'.

⦿ Kreuzberg
Schwarze Traube   Cocktail Bar
(☎030-2313 5569; www.schwarzetraube.de; Wrangelstrasse 24; ☺7pm-2am Sun-Thu, to 5am Fri & Sat; Ⓤ Görlitzer Bahnhof) Mixologist Atalay Aktas was Germany's Best Bartender of 2013 and this pint-sized drinking parlour is where he and his staff create their magic potions. Since there's no menu, each drink is calibrated to the taste and mood of each patron using premium spirits, expertise and a dash of psychology.

⦿ Friedrichshain
Berghain/Panorama Bar   Club
(www.berghain.de; Am Wriezener Bahnhof; ☺midnight Fri-Mon morning; Ⓢ Ostbahnhof) Only world-class spinmasters heat up this hedonistic bass-junkie hellhole inside a labyrinthine ex–power plant. Hard-edged minimal techno dominates the ex–turbine hall (Berghain) while house dominates at Panorama Bar, one floor up. Strict door; no cameras. Check the website for midweek concerts and record-release parties at the main venue and the adjacent **Kantine am**

Berghain (☎030-2936 0210; admission varies; ☺hours vary).

Briefmarken Weine   Wine Bar
(☎030-4202 5292; www.briefmarkenweine.de; Karl-Marx-Allee 99; ☺7pm-midnight; Ⓤ Weberwiese) For *dolce vita* right on socialist Karl-Marx-Allee, head to this charmingly nostalgic Italian wine bar ensconced in a former stamp shop. The original wooden cabinets cradle a hand-picked selection of Italian bottles that complement a snack menu of yummy cheeses, prosciutto and salami, plus a pasta dish of the day.

Hops & Barley   Pub
(☎030-2936 7534; www.hopsandbarley-berlin.de; Wühlischstrasse 22/23; ☺from 5pm Mon-Fri, from 3pm Sat & Sun; ⓂM13, Ⓤ Warschauer Strasse, Ⓢ Warschauer Strasse) Conversation flows as freely as the unfiltered Pilsner, malty *Dunkel* (dark) and fruity *Weizen* (wheat) produced right here at one of Berlin's oldest craft breweries. The pub is inside a former butcher's shop and still has the tiled walls to prove it. Two projectors show football (soccer) games.

Cocktail bar in Kreuzberg

😊 Charlottenburg
Bar am Steinplatz   Bar
(Map p508; ☎030-554 4440; www.hotelam
steinplatz.com; Steinplatz 4; ⏰4pm-late; 🚌M45,
245, Ⓤ Ernst-Reuter-Platz) Christian Gen-
temann's liquid playground may reside at
art deco Hotel am Steinplatz, but it hardly
whispers 'stuffy hotel bar'. The classic and
creative drinks (how about a Red Beet Old
Fashioned?) often showcase regionally produced spirits and ingredients, and even the
draught beer hails from the Berlin-based
Rollberg brewery. Inventive bar bites complement the drinks.

Diener Tattersall   Pub
(Map p508; ☎030-881 5329; www.diener-berlin.
de; Grolmanstrasse 47; ⏰6pm-2am; Ⓢ Savigny-
platz) In business for over a century, this
Old Berlin haunt was taken over by German
heavyweight champion Franz Diener in
the 1950s and has since been one of West

Berlin's pre-eminent artist pubs. From Billy
Wilder to Harry Belafonte, they all came for
beer and *Bulette* (meat patties), and left
behind signed black-and-white photographs that grace Diener's walls to this day.

Monkey Bar   Bar
(Map p508; ☎030-120 221 210; www.25hours-
hotel.com; Budapester Strasse 40; ⏰noon-1am
Sun-Thu, to 2am Fri & Sat; 🛜; 🚌100, 200,
Ⓢ Zoologischer Garten, Ⓤ Zoologischer Garten)
On the 10th floor of the 25hours Hotel Bikini
Berlin, this 'urban jungle' hot spot delivers
fabulous views of the city and the Berlin Zoo.
On balmy days, the sweeping terrace is a
handy perch for sunset drinks selected from
a menu that gives prominent nods to tiki
concoctions (including the original Trader
Vic's Mai Tai) and gin-based cocktail sorcery.

⭐ ENTERTAINMENT
Berliner
Philharmonie   Classical Music
(☎tickets 030-254 888 999; www.berliner-
philharmoniker.de; Herbert-von-Karajan-Strasse 1;
tickets €30-100; 🚌M29, M48, M85, 200, Ⓢ Pots-

> *supreme acoustics and not a bad seat in the house*

Berliner Philharmonie

MATO/SHUTTERSTOCK ©

damer Platz, Potsdamer Platz) This world-famous concert hall has supreme acoustics and, thanks to Hans Scharoun's terraced vineyard configuration, not a bad seat in the house. It's the home turf of the Berliner Philharmoniker, who will be led by Sir Simon Rattle until 2018. One year later, Russia-born Kirill Petrenko will pick up the baton as music director.

Chamäleon Varieté — Cabaret

(☎030-400 0590; www.chamaeleonberlin. com; Rosenthaler Strasse 40/41; tickets €29-69; ▣M1, ⓢHackescher Markt) A marriage of art nouveau charms and high-tech theatre trappings, this intimate 1920s-style venue in an old ballroom hosts classy variety shows – comedy, juggling acts and singing – often in sassy, sexy and unconventional fashion.

INFORMATION

Visit Berlin (☎030-2500 25; www.visitberlin. de), the Berlin tourist board, operates five walk-in offices, info desks at the airports, and a **call centre** (☎030-2500 2333, ⊙9am-7pm Mon-Fri, 10am-6pm Sat, 10am-2pm Sun) whose multilingual staff field general questions and make hotel and ticket bookings.

Brandenburger Tor (South Wing, Pariser Platz; ⊙9.30am-7pm Apr-Oct, to 6pm Nov-Mar; ⓢBrandenburger Tor, ⓤBrandenburger Tor)

Hauptbahnhof (Europaplatz entrance, ground fl; ⊙8am-10pm; ⓢHauptbahnhof, ▣Hauptbahnhof)

Europa-Center (Tauentzienstrasse 9, ground fl; ⊙10am-8pm Mon-Sat; ▣100, 200, ⓤKurfürstendamm)

Rankestrasse (cnr Rankestrasse & Kurfürstendamm; ⊙10am-6pm Apr-Oct, to 4pm Nov-Mar; ▣100, 200, ⓤKurfürstendamm)

TV Tower (Panoramastrasse 1a, ground fl; ⊙10am-6pm Apr-Oct, to 4pm Nov-Mar; ▣100, 200, TXL, ⓤAlexanderplatz, ⓢAlexanderplatz)

GETTING THERE & AWAY

AIR

Most visitors arrive in Berlin by air. Berlin's new central airport, about 24km southeast of the

⚲ LGBT Berlin

Berlin's legendary liberalism has spawned one of the world's biggest, most divine and diverse GLBT playgrounds. Anything goes in 'Homopolis' (and we do mean anything!), from the highbrow to the hands-on, the bourgeois to the bizarre, the mainstream to the flamboyant. Except for the most hardcore places, gay spots get their share of opposite-sex and straight patrons.

Generally speaking, Berlin's gayscape runs the entire spectrum from mellow cafes, campy bars and cinemas to saunas, cruising areas, clubs with darkrooms and all-out sex venues. In fact, sex and sexuality are entirely everyday matters to the unshockable city folks and there are very few, if any, itches that can't be quite openly and legally scratched. As elsewhere, gay men have more options for having fun, but grrrrls of all stripes won't feel left out either.

SERGEY KOHL/SHUTTERSTOCK ©

city centre, is under construction. Check www. berlin-airport.de for the latest. In the meantime, flights continue to land at the city's **Tegel** (TXL; ☎030-6091 1150; www.berlin-airport.de; ▣Tegel Flughafen) and **Schönefeld** (SXF; ☎030-6091 1150; www.berlin-airport.de; ▣Airport-Express, RE7 & RB14) airports.

BUS

Most long-haul buses arrive at the **Zentraler Omnibusbahnhof** (ZOB; ☎030-3010 0175; www.iob-berlin.de; Masurenallee 4-6; ⓢMesse/

ICC Nord, U Kaiserdamm) near the trade fair-grounds on the western city edge. Some stop at Alexanderplatz or other points in town. The closest U-Bahn station to ZOB is Kaiserdamm, about 400m north and served by the U2 line, which travels to Zoologischer Garten in about eight minutes and to Alexanderplatz in 28 minutes.

TRAIN

Berlin's **Hauptbahnhof** (Main Train Station; www.berliner-hbf.de; Europaplatz, Washingtonplatz; S Hauptbahnhof, U Hauptbahnhof) is in the heart of the city, just north of the Government Quarter and within walking distance of major sights and hotels. From here, the U-Bahn, the S-Bahn, trams and buses provide links to all parts of town. Taxi ranks are located outside the north exit (Europaplatz) and the south exit (Washingtonplatz).

GETTING AROUND

Berlin's extensive and efficient public transport system is operated by BVG (www.bvg.de) and consists of the U-Bahn (underground, or subway), the S-Bahn (light rail), buses and trams.

For trip planning and general information, call the 24-hour hotline (☎030-194 49) or check the website.

U-Bahn Most efficient way to travel; operates 4am to 12.30am and all night Friday, Saturday and public holidays. From Sunday to Thursday, half-hourly night buses take over in the interim.

S-Bahn Less frequent than U-Bahn trains, but with fewer stops, and thus useful for longer distances. Same operating hours as the U-Bahn.

Bus Slow but useful for sightseeing on the cheap. Run frequently 4.30am to 12.30am; half-hourly night buses in the interim. Metro-Buses (designated eg M1, M19) operate 24/7.

Tram Only in the eastern districts; MetroTrams (designated eg M1, M2) run 24/7.

Cycling Bike lanes and rental stations abound; bikes allowed in specially marked U-Bahn and S-Bahn carriages.

Taxi Can be hailed; fairly inexpensive; avoid during daytime rush hour.

Uber The only Uber option is uberTaxi. Prices are identical to regular taxis, including a surcharge of €1.50 for cash-free payments.

Where to Stay

Berlin offers the full gamut of places to unpack your suitcase – you can even sleep in a former bank, boat or factory, in the home of a silent-movie diva or in a 'flying bed'.

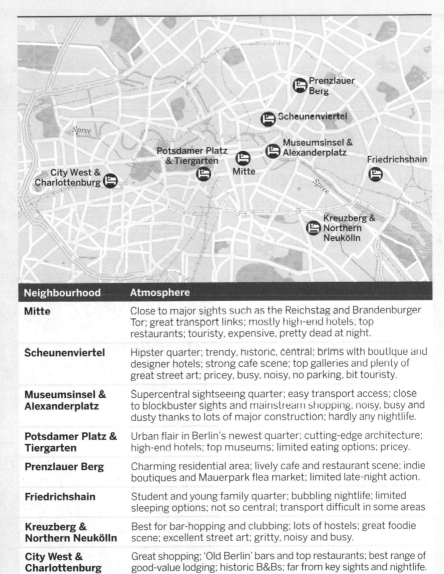

Neighbourhood	Atmosphere
Mitte	Close to major sights such as the Reichstag and Brandenburger Tor; great transport links; mostly high-end hotels; top restaurants; touristy, expensive, pretty dead at night.
Scheunenviertel	Hipster quarter; trendy, historic, central; brims with boutique and designer hotels; strong cafe scene; top galleries and plenty of great street art; pricey, busy, noisy, no parking, bit touristy.
Museumsinsel & Alexanderplatz	Supercentral sightseeing quarter; easy transport access; close to blockbuster sights and mainstream shopping; noisy, busy and dusty thanks to lots of major construction; hardly any nightlife.
Potsdamer Platz & Tiergarten	Urban flair in Berlin's newest quarter; cutting-edge architecture; high-end hotels; top museums; limited eating options; pricey.
Prenzlauer Berg	Charming residential area; lively cafe and restaurant scene; indie boutiques and Mauerpark flea market; limited late-night action.
Friedrichshain	Student and young family quarter; bubbling nightlife; limited sleeping options; not so central; transport difficult in some areas
Kreuzberg & Northern Neukölln	Best for bar-hopping and clubbing; lots of hostels; great foodie scene; excellent street art; gritty, noisy and busy.
City West & Charlottenburg	Great shopping; 'Old Berlin' bars and top restaurants; best range of good-value lodging; historic B&Bs; far from key sights and nightlife.

Schloss Neuschwanstein

Appearing through the mountain-ous forest like a mirage, Schloss Neuschwanstein was the model for Disney's Sleeping Beauty *castle.*

Great For...

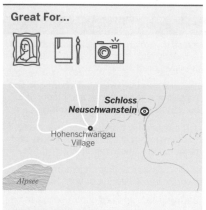

❶ Need to Know

✆tickets 08362-930 830; www.neuschwan stein.de; Neuschwansteinstrasse 20; adult/ concession €12/11, incl Hohenschwangau €23/21; ⊙9am-6pm Apr–mid-Oct, 10am-4pm mid-Oct–Mar

★ **Top Tip**
Arrive as early as 8am to make sure
you bag a ticket for that day.

Ludwig II, the Fairy-Tale King

King Ludwig II drew the blueprints for this fairy-tale pile himself. He envisioned it as a giant stage on which to re-create the world of Germanic mythology, inspired by the operatic works of Wagner. His obsession with French culture and the Sun King, Louis XIV, further inspired the fantastical design.

Ludwig was an enthusiastic leader initially, but Bavaria's days as a sovereign state were numbered, and he became a puppet king after the creation of the German Reich in 1871. Ludwig withdrew completely to drink, draw up castle plans and view concerts and operas in private.

In January 1886, several ministers and relatives arranged a hasty psychiatric test that diagnosed Ludwig as mentally unfit to rule. That June, he was removed to Schloss Berg on Lake Starnberg. A few days later the dejected bachelor and his doctor took a Sunday-evening lakeside walk and were found several hours later, drowned in just a few feet of water. No one knows with certainty what happened that night, and conspiracy theories abound. That summer the authorities opened Neuschwanstein to the public to help pay off Ludwig's huge debts. King Ludwig II was dead, but the myth was just being born.

Construction

Built as a romantic medieval castle, the grey-white granite pile was begun in 1869 but was an anachronism from the start: at the time of Ludwig's death in 1886, the first high-rises had pierced New York's skyline. However, despite his love for the old-fashioned look, the palace had plenty of high-tech features, including a hot-air

Schloss Hohenschwangau

heating system and running water. Like so many of the king's grand schemes, Neuschwanstein was never finished. For all the coffer-depleting sums spent on it, the king spent just over 170 days in residence.

The Interior

The most impressive room is the **Sängersaal** (Minstrels' Hall), whose frescoes depict scenes from Wagner's opera *Tannhäuser*. Other completed sections include Ludwig's *Tristan and Isolde*–themed

> ☑ **Don't Miss**
>
> The excellent **Museum der Bayerischen Könige** (www.museumderbay erischenkoenige.de; Alpseestrasse 27; adult/concession €9.50/8; ⊙10am-6pm) is a short walk from the castle ticket office.

bedroom, dominated by a huge Gothic-style bed crowned with intricately carved cathedral-like spires; a gaudy artificial grotto (another allusion to the *Tannhäuser*); and the Byzantine-style **Thronsaal** (Throne Room) with an incredible mosaic floor containing over two million stones. The painting opposite the (throneless) throne platform depicts another castle dreamed up by Ludwig that was never built.

Schloss Hohenschwangau

King Ludwig II grew up at the sun-yellow **Schloss Hohenschwangau** (☑08362-930 830; www.hohenschwangau.de; Alpseestrasse 30; adult/concession €12/11, incl Neuschwanstein €23/21; ⊙8am-5pm Apr–mid-Oct, 9am-3.30pm mid-Oct–Mar) and later enjoyed summers here until his death in 1886. His father, Maximilian II, built this palace in a neo-Gothic style atop 12th-century ruins left by Schwangau knights. Far less showy than Neuschwanstein, Hohenschwangau has a distinctly lived-in feel where every piece of furniture is a used original. After his father died, Ludwig's main alteration was having stars, illuminated with hidden oil lamps, painted on the ceiling of his bedroom.

Castle Tickets & Tours

Schloss Neuschwanstein and Hohenschwangau can only be visited on guided tours (in German or English), which last about 35 minutes each (Hohenschwangau is first). Strictly timed tickets are available from the **Ticket Centre** (☑08362-930 830; www.hohenschwangau.de; Alpenseestrasse 12; ⊙8am-5pm Apr–mid-Oct, 9am-3.30pm mid Oct Mar) at the foot of the castles.

Enough time is left between tours for the steep 30- to 40-minute walk between the castles. All Munich's tour companies run day excursions out to the castles.

> ★ **Classic Image**
>
> For the postcard view of Neuschwanstein, walk 10 minutes up to Marienbrücke (Mary's Bridge).

Prague, Czech Republic

Everyone who visits the Czech Republic starts with Prague, the cradle of Czech culture and one of Europe's most fascinating cities. Prague offers a near-intact medieval core of Gothic architecture that can transport you back 500 years – the 14th-century Charles Bridge, connecting two historic neighbourhoods across the Vltava River, with the castle ramparts and the spires of St Vitus Cathedral rising above, is one of the classic sights of world travel. But the city is not just about history, it's also a vital urban centre with a rich array of cultural offerings and a newly emerging foodie scene.

Two Days in Prague

Start the day wandering through the courtyards of **Prague Castle** (p527) before the main sights open, then spend the afternoon visiting the baroque beauty of **St Nicholas Church** (p532). End the day with dinner at **Augustine** (p541). Spend the morning of day two in the **Old Town Square** (p532), before visiting the half-dozen monuments that comprise the **Prague Jewish Museum** (p532).

Four Days in Prague

Explore the passages and arcades around **Wenceslas Square** (p535) on day three, then take in the historical and artistic treasures of the **Prague City Museum** (p535). On the final day take a metro ride out to Vyšehrad and explore Prague's other castle, the **Vyšehrad Citadel** (p538), with its gorgeous views along the Vltava. In the evening catch a performance at the **National Theatre** (p543) or the **Palác Akropolis** (p543).

After Prague travel to Budapest (p546) or Vienna (p564).

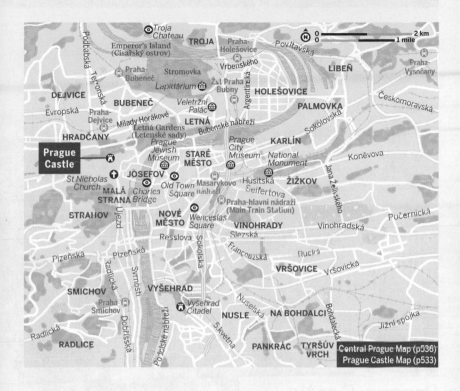

Arriving in Prague

Václav Havel Airport Buses to metro stops Nádraží Veleslavín (service No 119) and Zličín (No 100) depart every 10 minutes from 4am to midnight, from stops just outside the arrivals terminal (32Kč). A taxi to the centre costs 500Kč.

Praha hlavní nádraží Prague's main train station is in the city centre and is accessible by metro line C (red); all international rail connections arrive here.

Florenc bus station International buses arrive here, just east of Prague centre, with metro and tram links to the rest of the city.

Where to Stay

Gone are the days when Prague was a cheap destination. The Czech capital now ranks alongside most Western European cities when it comes to the quality, range and price of hotels. Accommodation ranges from cosy, romantic hotels set in historic townhouses to the new generation of funky design hotels and hostels. Book as far in advance as possible (especially during festival season in May, and at Easter and Christmas/New Year).

St Vitus Cathedral (p528) surrounded by Prague Castle

Prague Castle

Prague Castle – Pražský hrad, or just hrad to Czechs – is Prague's most popular attraction. Looming above the Vltava's left bank, its serried ranks of spires, towers and palaces dominate the city centre like a fairy-tale fortress.

Within the castle walls lies a varied and fascinating collection of historic buildings, museums and galleries that are home to some of the Czech Republic's greatest artistic and cultural treasures.

First Courtyard

The First Courtyard lies within the castle's main gate on Hradčany Square (Hradčan-ské náměstí), flanked by huge, baroque statues of battling **Titans** (1767–70) that dwarf the castle guards standing beneath them. After the fall of communism in 1989, then-president Václav Havel hired his old pal Theodor Pistek, the costume designer on the film *Amadeus* (1984), to replace the guards' communist-era khaki uniforms with the stylish pale-blue kit they now wear, which harks back to the army of the first Czechoslovak Republic of 1918 to 1938.

Great For...

☑ Don't Miss

The tiny, colourful 16th-century cottages on Golden Lane, or the Princely Collections at Lobkowicz Palace.

Titans battle on the main gate

❶ Need to Know

Pražský hrad; Map p533; ☑224 372 423; www.hrad.cz; Hradčanské náměstí 1; grounds free, sights adult/concession Tour A & C 350/175Kč, Tour B 250/125Kč; ☺grounds 6am-11pm year-round, gardens 10am-6pm Apr-Oct, closed Nov-Mar, historic buildings 9am-5pm Apr-Oct, to 4pm Nov-Mar; Ⓜ Malostranská, ☎22

✕ Take a Break

Stop by **Lobkowicz Palace Café** (Map p533; ☑233 312 925; Jiřská 3; mains 200-300Kč; ☺10am-6pm; ☎✿; ☎22) for great goulash and superb city views.

The **changing of the guard** takes place every hour on the hour, but the longest and most impressive display is at noon, when banners are exchanged while a brass band plays a fanfare from the windows of the Plečnik Hall, which overlooks the First Courtyard.

Second Courtyard

Beyond the Matthias Gate lies the Second Courtyard, centred on a baroque fountain and a 17th-century well with lovely Renaissance latticework.

On the right, the Chapel of the Holy Cross (1763) houses the **St Vitus Treasury** (Svatovitský poklad; Map p533; ☑224 373 442; adult/child 300/150Kč, admission incl with Prague Castle Tour C ticket; ☺10am-6pm Apr-Oct, to 5pm Nov-Mar), a spectacular collection of ecclesiastical bling that was founded by

Charles IV in the 14th century. The oldest items include a reliquary arm of St Vitus dating from the early 10th century, while the most impressive treasures include a gold coronation cross of Charles IV (1370) and a diamond-studded baroque monstrance from 1708.

The **Prague Castle Picture Gallery** (Map p533; adult/child 100/50Kč, admission incl with Prague Castle Tour C ticket; ☺9am-5pm Apr-Oct, to 4pm Nov-Mar), in the castle's beautiful Renaissance stables, houses an exhibition of 16th- to 18th-century European art, based on the Habsburg collection that was begun in 1650 to replace stolen paintings; it includes works by Cranach, Holbein, Rubens, Tintoretto and Titian

Third Courtyard

As you pass through the passage on the eastern side of the Second Courtyard, the huge western facade of St Vitus Cathedral soars directly above you; to its south (to the right as you enter) lies the Third Courtyard. At its entrance you'll see a 16m-tall **granite monolith** dedicated to the victims of WWI, designed by Jože Plečnik in 1928, and a copy of a 14th-century bronze figure of **St George** slaying the dragon; the original is on display in the **Story of Prague Castle** (adult/child 140/70Kč, admission incl with Prague Castle Tour A ticket; ⊙9am-5pm Apr-Oct, to 4pm Nov-Mar) exhibition.

The **Old Royal Palace** (Starý královský palác; Map p533; admission incl with Prague Castle tour A & B tickets; ⊙9am-5pm Apr-Oct, to 4pm Nov-Mar) at the courtyard's eastern end is one of the oldest parts of the castle, dating from 1135. It was originally used only by Czech princesses, but from the 13th to the 16th centuries it was the king's own palace.

The courtyard is dominated by the southern facade of **St Vitus Cathedral** (Katedrála sv Víta; Map p533; ☏257 531 622; www.katedralasvatehovita.cz; admission incl with Prague Castle Tour A & B tickets; ⊙9am-5pm Mon-Sat, noon-5pm Sun Apr-Oct, to 4pm Nov-Mar), one of the most richly endowed cathedrals in central Europe, and pivotal to the religious and cultural life of the Czech Republic. It houses treasures that range from the 14th-century mosaic of the Last Judgement and the tombs of St Wenceslas and Charles IV, to the baroque silver tomb of St John of Nepomuck, the ornate Chapel of St Wenceslas, and art nouveau stained glass by Alfons Mucha.

Golden Lane

St George Square

St George Sq (Jiřské náměstí), the plaza to the east of St Vitus Cathedral, lies at the heart of the castle complex.

The striking, brick-red, early-baroque facade that dominates the square conceals the **Basilica of St George** (Bazilika sv Jiří; Jiřské náměstí; Map p533; admission incl with Prague Castle tour A & B tickets; ⊙9am-5pm Apr-Oct, to 4pm Nov-Mar), the Czech Republic's best-preserved Romanesque basilica, established in the 10th century by Vratislav I (the father of St Wenceslas). What you see

★ **A World Record**

According to the *Guinness World Records*, Prague Castle is the largest ancient castle in the world – 570m long, an average of 128m wide and occupying 7.28 hectares.

today is mostly the result of restorations made between 1887 and 1908.

George Street

George Street (Jiřská) runs from the Basilica of St George to the castle's eastern gate.

The picturesque alley known as **Golden Lane** (Zlatá ulička; Map p533; admission incl with Prague Castle tour A & B tickets; ⊙9am-5pm Apr-Oct, to 4pm Nov-Mar) runs along the northern wall of the castle. Its tiny, colourful cottages were built in the 16th century for the sharpshooters of the castle guard, but were later used by goldsmiths. In the 19th and early 20th centuries they were occupied by artists, including the writer Franz Kafka (who frequently visited his sister's house at No 22 from 1916 to 1917).

Sixteenth-century **Lobkowicz Palace** (Lobkovický palác; Map p533; ☏233 312 925; www.lobkowicz.com; Jiřská 3; adult/concession/family 275/200/690Kč; ⊙10am-6pm) houses a private museum known as the **Princely Collections**, which includes priceless paintings, furniture and musical memorabilia. Your tour includes an audio guide dictated by owner William Lobkowicz and his family – this personal connection really brings the displays to life, and makes the palace one of the castle's most interesting attractions.

DESPERADO/GETTY IMAGES ©

★ **South Gardens**

At the castle's eastern gate, you can take a sharp right and wander back to Hradčany Square through the **South Gardens** (Zahrada na valech; Map p533; ⊙10am-6pm Apr-Oct, closed Nov-Mar) FREE. The terrace garden offers superb views across the rooftops of Malá Strana.

Prague River Stroll

The Vltava River runs through the heart of Prague and served as muse for composer Bedřich Smetana in writing his moving 'Vltava' (Moldau) symphony. But you don't need to be a musician to enjoy the river's breath-taking bridges and backdrops on this extended walk along the waterway.
Start Convent of St Agnes
Distance 8km
Duration Three hours

2 Amble around **Letná Gardens** (p542) and take in the view of the Old Town and Malá Strana below.

Royal Garden (Královská zahrada)

Brusnice

Old Castle Steps (Staré Zámecké schody)

Malostranská Ⓜ

Valdštejnská

MALÁ STRANA

❸

Hradu

Thunovská

Wallenstein Garden (Valdštejnská zahrada)

Nerudova

Vojan Gardens (Vojanovy sady)

Josefská

Malá Strana Square (Malostranské náměstí)

Tržiště

Mostecká

Na Kampě

Karmelitská

Čertovka

Janáčkovo nábřeží

Classic Photo: Photogenic Prague Castle from any angle.

3 Enjoy views over the Vltava and the red roofs of Malá Strana from the ramparts of **Prague Castle** (p527) or from the beautifully manicured royal gardens.

6 The whimsical yet elegant **Dancing House**, by architects Vlado Milunić and Frank Gehry, surprisingly fits in with its ageing neighbours.

nice

ova

SMÍCHOV

Ⓝ 0 _____ 500 m
0 _____ 0.25 miles

Letná
Terása

2

nábřeží Edvarda Beneše

Klárov

Cechuv
most

Dvořákovo nábřeží

Na Františku

Dušní

JOSEFOV **START**

1

Dvořákovo nábřeží

17.listopadu

Pařížská

Bílkova

Kozí

Haštalská

Revoluční

Máchas Bridge
(Mánesuv most)

Vezeňská

Kozí

Dlouhá

1 The **Convent of St Agnes**
(p532) is the oldest Gothic building in Bohemia – building began in
1231 – and is supposedly haunted.

M Staroměstská

Kaprova

Platnérská

Charles Bridge
(Karluv most)

4

Křížovnické
náměstí

Linhartská

Karlova

Anenská

Liliová

Náprstkova

Betlémská

Vltava River

Smetanovo nábřeží

Divadelní

Konviktská

Bartolomejská

Národní třída

Legion Bridge
(Legii most)

Marksmen's Island
(Strelecký ostrov)

Ostrovní

5

Slav Island
(Slovanský
ostrov)

Masarykovo nábřeží

Opatovická

Children's
Island
(Detský
ostrov)

Myslíkova

Jirásek
Square
(Jiráskovo
náměstí)

Karlovo
Náměstí

M

Jiráskuv Bridge
(Jiráskuv most)

6

FINISH

Resslova

Rašínovo
nábřeží

Dittrichova

M IP Pavlova

Nábřežní

Lidická

Na Moráni

4 Always gorgeous **Charles Bridge**
(p535) is a great spot to admire
your surroundings – the towering
medieval gates, the castle, the lazy
river.

🍴🍽️

Take a Break... Old-fashioned
Kavárna Slavia (Národní třída 1;
8am-midnight Mon-Fri, ⏱9am-
midnight Sat & Sun) is the place
to stop for coffee and cake.

5 Slav Island is a delightfully quiet
place to enjoy a picnic or take a
nap in the shade.

3 LMSPENCER/SHUTTERSTOCK © 4 NAUGHTYNUT/SH_TTERSTOCK © 6 VLADIMIR SAZONOV/SHUTTERSTOCK ©

◎ SIGHTS

◎ Hradčany

Loreta   Church

(☑220 516 740; www.loreta.cz; Loretánské náměstí 7; adult/child/family 150/80/310Kč, photography permit 100Kč; ☺9am-5pm Apr-Oct, 9.30am-4pm Nov-Mar; 🚊22) The Loreta is a baroque place of pilgrimage founded by Benigna Kateřina Lobkowicz in 1626, designed as a replica of the supposed Santa Casa (Sacred House; the home of the Virgin Mary) in the Holy Land. Legend says that the original Santa Casa was carried by angels to the Italian town of Loreto as the Turks were advancing on Nazareth.

Strahov Library   Historic Building

(Strahovská knihovna; ☑233 107 718; www.strahovskyklaster.cz; Strahovské nádvoří 1; adult/child 100/50Kč; ☺9am-noon & 1-5pm; 🚊22) Strahov Library is the largest monastic library in the country, with two magnificent baroque halls dating from the 17th and 18th centuries. You can peek through the doors but, sadly, you can't go into the halls themselves – it was found that fluctuations in humidity caused by visitors' breath was endangering the frescoes. There's also a display of historical curiosities.

◎ Malá Strana

St Nicholas Church   Church

(Kostel sv Mikuláše; Map p533; ☑257 534 215; www.stnicholas.cz; Malostranské náměstí 38; adult/child 70/50Kč; ☺9am-5pm Mar-Oct, to 4pm Nov-Feb; 🚊12, 15, 20, 22) Malá Strana is dominated by the huge green cupola of St Nicholas Church, one of Central Europe's finest baroque buildings. (Don't confuse it with the other Church of St Nicholas on the Old Town Square.) On the ceiling, Johann Kracker's 1770 *Apotheosis of St Nicholas* is Europe's largest fresco (clever *trompe l'œil* technique has made the painting merge almost seamlessly with the architecture).

Petřín   Hill

(🚡Nebozízek, Petřín) This 318m-high hill is one of Prague's largest green spaces. It's great for quiet, tree-shaded walks and fine views over the 'City of a Hundred Spires'. Most of the attractions atop the hill, including a lookout tower and mirror maze, were built in the late 19th to early 20th century, lending the place an old-fashioned, fun-fair atmosphere.

◎ Staré Město

Convent of St Agnes   Gallery

(Klášter sv Anežky; Map p536; ☑224 810 628; www.ngprague.cz; U Milosrdných 17; incl admission to all National Gallery venues adult/child 300/150Kč; ☺10am-6pm Tue-Sun; 🚊6, 8, 15, 26) In the northeastern corner of Staré Město is the former Convent of St Agnes, Prague's oldest surviving Gothic building. The 1st-floor rooms hold the National Gallery's permanent collection of medieval and early Renaissance art (1200–1550) from Bohemia and Central Europe, a treasure house of glowing Gothic altar paintings and polychrome religious sculptures.

Old Town Square   Square

(Staroměstské náměstí; Map p536; Ⓜ Staroměstská) One of Europe's biggest and most beautiful urban spaces, the Old Town Square (Staroměstské náměstí, or Staromák for short) has been Prague's principal public square since the 10th century, and was its main marketplace until the beginning of the 20th century.

Prague Jewish Museum   Museum

(Židovské muzeum Praha; Map p536; ☑222 749 211; www.jewishmuseum.cz; Reservation Centre, Maiselova 15; ordinary ticket adult/child 300/200Kč, combined ticket incl entry to Old-New Synagogue 480/320Kč; ☺9am-6pm Sun-Fri Apr-Oct, to 4.30pm Nov-Mar; Ⓜ Staroměstská) This museum consists of six Jewish monuments clustered together in Josefov: the **Maisel Synagogue** (Maiselova synagóga; Map p536; Maiselova 10); the **Pinkas Synagogue** (Pinkasova synagóga; Map p536; Široká 3); the **Spanish Synagogue** (Španělská synagóga; Map p536; Vězeňská 1); the **Klaus Synagogue** (Klauzová synagóga; Map p536; U starého hřbitova 1; 🚊17); the **Ceremonial Hall** (Obřadní síň; Map p536; Old Jewish Cemetery; 🚊17); and the **Old Jewish Cemetery** (Starý židovský hřbitov; Map p536; Pinkas Synagogue,

Prague Castle

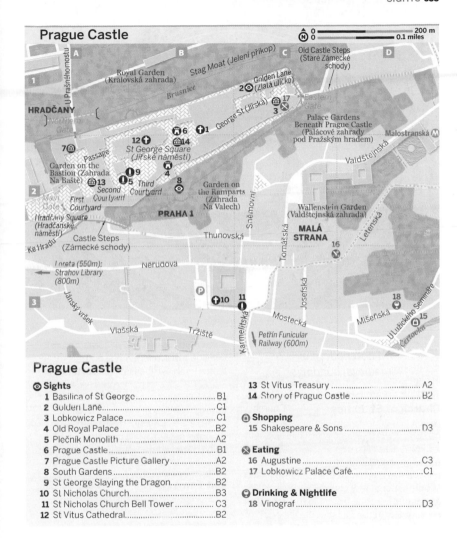

Prague Castle

Široká 3), Europe's oldest surviving Jewish graveyard. There is also the **Old-New Synagogue** (Staronová synagóga; Map p536; Červená 2; adult/child 200/140Kč; ⊠17), which is still used for religious services, and requires a separate ticket or additional fee.

Church of Our Lady Before Týn
Church

(Kostel Panny Marie před Týnem; Map p536; ☎222 318 186; www.tyn.cz; Staroměstské náměstí; suggested donation 25Kč; ⊙10am-1pm & 3-5pm Tue-Sat, 10am-noon Sun Mar-Dec; Ⓜ Staroměstská) Its distinctive twin Gothic spires make the Týn Church an unmistakable Old Town landmark. Like something out of a 15th-century – and probably slightly cruel – fairy tale, they loom over the Old Town Square, decorated with a golden image of the Virgin Mary made in the 1620s from the melted-down Hussite chalice that previously adorned the church.

Astronomical Clock

NIK PHOT/500PX ©

> *a hotchpotch of medieval buildings*

Church of St James   Church

(Kostel sv Jakuba; Map p536; http://praha.
minorite.cz; Malá Štupartská 6; ⊘9.30am-noon &
2-4pm Tue-Sat, 2-4pm Sun; Ⓜ Náměstí Republiky)
FREE The great Gothic mass of the Church
of St James began in the 14th century as a
Minorite monastery church, and was given
a beautiful baroque facelift in the early 18th
century. But in the midst of the gilt and
stucco is a grisly memento: on the inside of
the western wall (look up to the right as you
enter) hangs a shrivelled human arm.

Municipal House   Historic Building

(Obecní dům; Map p536; ⍅222 002 101; www.
obecnidum.cz; náměstí Republiky 5; guided tours
adult/concession/child under 10yr 290/240Kč/
free; ⊘public areas 7.30am-11pm, information
centre 10am-8pm; Ⓜ Náměstí Republiky, 🚋6, 8,
15, 26) Restored in the 1990s after decades
of neglect, Prague's most exuberantly art
nouveau building is a labour of love, every

detail of its design and decoration carefully
considered, every painting and sculpture
loaded with symbolism. The **restaurant**
(⍅222 002 770; www.francouzskarestaurace.cz;
mains 695Kč; ⊘noon-11pm) and **cafe** (⍅222
002 763; www.kavarnaod.cz; ⊘7.30am-11pm;
🛜) here are like walk-in museums of art
nouveau design, while upstairs there are
half a dozen sumptuously decorated halls
that you can visit by guided tour.

Old Town Hall   Historic Building

(Staroměstská radnice; Map p536; ⍅236
002 629; www.staromestskaradnicepraha.cz;
Staroměstské náměstí 1; guided tours adult/child
100/70Kč, incl tower 180Kč; ⊘11am-6pm Mon,
9am-6pm Tue-Sun; Ⓜ Staroměstská) Prague's
Old Town Hall, founded in 1338, is a
hotchpotch of medieval buildings acquired
piecemeal over the centuries, presided
over by a tall Gothic tower with a splendid
Astronomical Clock (Map p536; ⊘chimes
on the hour 9am-9pm). As well as housing
the Old Town's main tourist information
office, the town hall has several historic
attractions, and hosts art exhibitions on the
ground floor and 2nd floor.

The town hall's best feature is the view across the Old Town Square from its 60m-tall **clock tower** (Věž radnice; Map p536; adult/child 130/80Kč, incl Old Town Hall tour 180Kč; ⊗11am-10pm Mon, 9am-10pm Tue-Sun). It's well worth the climb up the modern, beautifully designed steel spiral staircase; there's also a lift.

◎ Nové Město

Wenceslas Square   Square
(Václavské náměstí; Map p536; MMůstek, Muzeum) More a broad boulevard than a typical city square, Wenceslas Square has witnessed a great deal of Czech history – a giant Mass was held here during the revolutionary upheavals of 1848; in 1918 the creation of the new Czechoslovak Republic was celebrated here; and it was here in 1989 that the fall of communism was announced. Originally a medieval horse market, the square was named after Bohemia's patron saint during the nationalist revival of the mid-19th century.

Mucha Museum   Gallery
(Muchovo muzeum; Map p536; ☑221 451 333; www.mucha.cz; Panská 7; adult/child 240/160Kč; ⊗10am-6pm; ☐3, 5, 6, 9, 14, 24) This fascinating (and busy) museum features the sensuous art nouveau posters, paintings and decorative panels of Alfons Mucha (1860–1939), as well as many sketches, photographs and other memorabilia. The exhibits include countless artworks showing Mucha's trademark Slavic maidens with flowing hair and piercing blue eyes, bearing symbolic garlands and linden boughs.

National Memorial to the Heroes of the Heydrich Terror   Museum
(Národní památník hrdinů Heydrichiády; ☑224 916 100; www.pamatnik-heydrichiady.cz; Resslova 9; ⊗9am-5pm Tue-Sun Mar-Oct, 9am-5pm Tue-Sat Nov-Feb; MKarlovo Náměstí) **FREE** The Church of Sts Cyril & Methodius houses a moving memorial to the seven Czech paratroopers who were involved in the assassination of Reichsprotektor Reinhard Heydrich in 1942, with an exhibit and video about Nazi persecution of the Czechs. The

🏛 Charles Bridge

Strolling across **Charles Bridge** (Karlův most; Map p536; ⊗24hr; ☐2, 17, 18 to Karlovy lázně, 12, 15, 20, 22 to Malostranské náměstí) – browsing the stalls of hawkers and caricaturists and listening to buskers beneath the impassive gaze of the baroque statues that line the parapets – is everybody's favourite Prague activity. Don't forget to look at the bridge itself (the bridge towers have great views) and at the grand vistas up and down the river.

EMPERORCOSAR/SHUTTERSTOCK ©

church appeared in the 2016 movie based on the assassination, *Anthropoid*.

Prague City Museum   Museum
(Muzeum hlavního města Prahy; Map p536; ☑224 816 773; www.muzeumprahy.cz; Na Poříčí 52; adult/child 120/50Kč; ⊗9am-6pm Tue-Sun; MFlorenc) This excellent museum, opened in 1898, is devoted to the history of Prague from prehistoric times to the 20th century (labels are in English as well as Czech). Among the many intriguing exhibits are an astonishing scale model of Prague, and the Astronomical Clock's original 1866 calendar wheel with Josef Mánes' beautiful painted panels representing the months – that's January at the top, toasting his toes by the fire, and August near the bottom, sickle in hand, harvesting the corn.

◎ Holešovice

Veletržní Palác   Museum
(Trade Fair Palace; ☑224 301 111; www.ngprague.cz; Dukelských hrdinů 47; incl admission to all

Central Prague

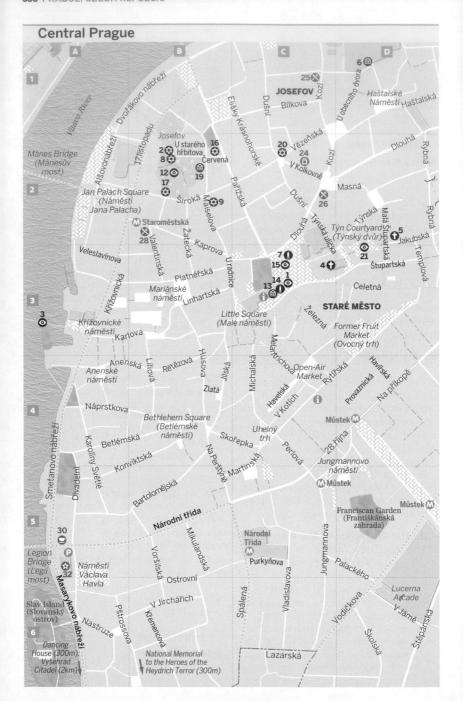

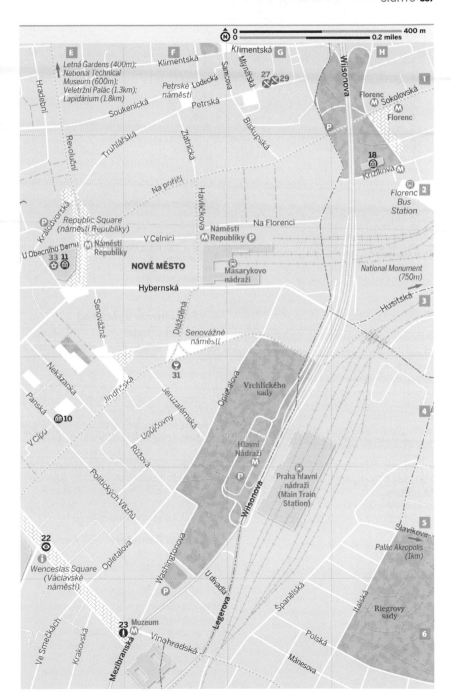

Central Prague

National Gallery venues; adult/child 300/150Kč; ⊙10am-6pm Tue-Sun; Ⓜ Vltavská, 🚃1, 6, 8, 12, 17, 25, 26) The National Gallery's collection of 'Art of the 19th, 20th and 21st Centuries' is spread out over four floors and is a strong contender for Prague's best museum. It has an unexpectedly rich collection of world masters, including works from Van Gogh, Picasso, Schiele, Klimt and on and on, but the holdings of Czech interwar abstract, surrealist and cubist art are worth the trip alone.

National Technical
Museum   Museum
(Národní Technické Muzeum; ☎220 399 111; www.ntm.cz; Kostelní 42; adult/concession 190/90Kč; ⊙9am-5.30pm Tue-Fri, 10am-6pm Sat & Sun; 🚼; 🚃1, 8, 12, 25, 26 to Letenské náměstí) Prague's most family-friendly museum got a high-tech renovation in 2012 and is a dazzling presentation of the country's industrial heritage. If that sounds dull, it's anything but. Start in the main hall, filled to the rafters with historic planes, trains and automobiles. There are separate halls devoted to exhibits on astronomy, photography, printing and architecture.

◎ Smíchov & Vyšehrad

Vyšehrad Citadel   Fortress
(☎261 225 304; www.praha-vysehrad.cz; information centre at V pevnosti 159/5b; admission to grounds free; ⊙grounds 24hr; Ⓜ Vyšehrad) **FREE** The Vyšehrad Citadel refers to the complex of buildings and structures atop Vyšehrad Hill that have played an important role in Czech history for over 1000 years as a royal residence, religious centre and military fortress. While most of the surviving structures date from the 18th century, the citadel is still viewed as the city's spiritual home. The sights are spread out over a wide area, with commanding views out over the Vltava and surrounding city.

Vyšehrad Cemetery   Cemetery
(Vyšehradský hřbitov; ☎274 774 835; www.praha-vysehrad.cz; K Rotundě 10, Vyšehrad; ⊙8am-7pm May-Sep, shorter hours Oct-Apr; Ⓜ Vyšehrad) **FREE** Vyšehrad Cemetery is a main attraction for many visitors, being the final resting place for dozens of Czech luminaries, including Antonín Dvořák, Bedřich Smetana and Alfons Mucha. Many tombs and headstones are works of art – Dvořák's is a sculpture by Ladislav Šaloun, the art

nouveau sculptor who created the Jan Hus monument in the Old Town Square.

◎ Žižkov & Karlín
National Monument   Museum
(Národní Památník na Vítkově; ☑224 497 600; www.nm.cz; U Památníku 1900, Žižkov; adult/child exhibition only 80/60Kč, roof terrace 80/50Kč, combined ticket 120/80Kč; ◎10am-6pm Wed-Sun Apr-Oct, Thu-Sun Nov-Mar; ☐133, 175, 207) While this monument's massive functionalist structure has all the elegance of a nuclear power station, the interior is a spectacular extravaganza of polished art-deco marble, gilt and mosaics, and is home to a fascinating museum of 20th-century Czechoslovak history.

⊙ TOURS
Taste of Prague   Food & Drink
(☑775 577 275; www.tasteofprague.com; per person 2700Kč) Locals Jan and Zuzi are passionate about Prague's restaurant scene. They lead four-hour foodie tours of the city, tasting trad and modern Czech dishes and drinks in a variety of venues, with intriguing asides on Czech history and culture along the way. Private one- or two-day tasting tours of Moravian vineyards can also be arranged.

AlenaGuide   Tours
(☑724 129 201; www.alenaguide.com; tours from 2300Kč) Alena Vopalkova is a graduate of La Salle University in Philadelphia, USA, who has returned to Prague to lead private, customised tours of her home city. Subjects range from general sightseeing to more specialised tours covering the Jewish Museum, food or shopping, and from three-hour walking tours to day trips exploring off-the-beaten-track spots such as the scenic Český raj (Bohemian Paradise).

Biko Adventures Prague   Cycling
(☑733 750 990; www.bikoadventures.com; Vratislavova 3, Vyšehrad; standard rental per day 450Kč, group tours per person from 1250Kč; ◎9am-6pm Apr-Oct; ☐2, 3, 7, 17, 21) Italian owner Fillippo Mari loves to cycle, ski and

hike and has created this small outfit dedicated to outdoor pursuits of all kinds. From April to October Biko rents bikes and offers day-long guided cycling trips for riders of all levels, as well as hiking and skiing tours. Rental bikes include standard mountain bikes and high-end hardtails from Giant.

🛍 SHOPPING
Shakespeare & Sons   Books
(Map p533; ☑257 531 894; www.shakes.cz; U Lužického semináře 10; ◎11am-9pm; ☐12, 15, 20, 22) Though its shelves groan with a formidable range of literature in English, French and German, this is more than just a bookshop (with Prague's best range of titles on Eastern European history) – it's a congenial literary hang-out with knowledgeable staff, occasional author events, and a cool downstairs space for sitting and reading.

Wine Food Market   Food
(☑733 338 650; www.winemarket.cz; Strakonická 1, Smíchov; ◎7am-11pm Mon-Sat, 8am-11pm Sun; ☎; MSmíchovské Nádraží) This rather unpromising, industrial corner in a forgotten Smíchov neighbourhood holds arguably the city's best Italian market, with all manner of breads, cheeses, meats, and Italian goodies such as marinated mushrooms and peppers. It's the perfect spot to assemble a picnic lunch. There's a dining room in the back where you can treat yourself to the spoils. A real treasure.

TEG1   Fashion & Accessories
(Map p536; ☑222 327 358; www.timoure.cz; V Kolkovně 6; ◎10am-7pm Mon-Fri, 11am-5pm Sat; MStaroměstská) TEG (Timoure et Group) is the design team created by Alexandra Pavalová and Ivana Šafránková, two of Prague's most respected fashion designers. This boutique showcases their quarterly collections, which feature a sharp, imaginative look that adds zest and sophistication to everyday, wearable clothes.

Obchod s Uměním   Art, Antiques
(☑224 252 779; Korunní 34, Vinohrady; ◎11am-5pm Mon-Fri; MNáměstí Míru, ☐10, 16)

Náplavka Farmers Market

Stretching along the embankment from Trojická to Výton, the weekly **Náplavka Farmers Market** (www.farmarsketrziste. cz; Rašínovo nábřeží; ⊙8am-2pm Sat; 🚇2, 3, 7, 17, 21) 🍴 makes the most of its riverside setting with live music and outdoor tables scattered among stalls selling freshly baked bread, organic locally grown vegetables, homemade cakes and pastries, wild mushrooms (in season), herbs, flowers, wild honey, hot food, Czech cider, coffee and a range of arts and crafts.

The 'Shop with Art' specialises in original paintings, prints and sculpture from 1900 to 1940, when Czech artists were at the forefront in movements such as constructivism, surrealism and cubism. Naturally, these artworks now fetch astronomical prices, but it's still fun to drop by and browse.

EATING

Restaurace U Veverky   Czech €
(📞603 781 997; www.uveverky.com; Eliášova 14, Dejvice; mains 140-240Kč; ⊙11am-11pm; MHradčanská) This highly rated traditional pub has some of the best-tasting and best-value lunches in the city and is worth a detour. The set-up is classic, with a drinking room out the front and two big dining rooms in the back. The restaurant is filled with the welcoming smell of grilled onions and beer. Reserve in advance.

Mistral Café   Bistro €
(Map p536; 📞222 317 737; www.mistralcafe. cz; Valentinská 11; mains 130-250Kč; ⊙10am-11pm; 🌐📶; MStaroměstská) Is this the coolest bistro in the Old Town? Pale stone, bleached birchwood and potted shrubs make for a clean, crisp, modern look, and the clientele of local students and office workers clearly appreciate the competi-

tively priced, well-prepared food. Fish and chips in crumpled brown paper with lemon and black-pepper mayo – yum!

Můj Šálek Kávy   Cafe €
(📞725 556 944; www.mujsalekkavy.cz; Křižíkova 105, Karlín; mains 80-160Kč; ⊙9am-10pm Mon-Sat, 10am-6pm Sun; 🌐📶; MKřižíkova) A symbol of Karlín's up-and-coming, neighbourhood-to-watch status, 'My Cup of Coffee' uses Direct Trade beans prepared by expert baristas, and serves what is probably the city's best caffeine hit. Add on a friendly, laid-back atmosphere and superb breakfast and lunch dishes, and you can see why it's often full – reservations are recommended at weekends.

Café Savoy   European €€
(📞257 311 562; http://cafesavoy.ambi.cz; Vítězná 5; mains 200-400Kč; ⊙8am-10.30pm Mon-Fri, 9am-10.30pm Sat & Sun; 🌐; 🚇9, 12, 15, 20, 22) The Savoy is a beautifully restored belle époque cafe, with smart, suited waiting staff and a Viennese-style menu of hearty soups, salads, roast meats and schnitzels. There's also a 'gourmet menu' (mains 400Kč to 700Kč) where the star of the show is Parisian steak tartare mixed at your table, and a superb wine list (ask the staff for recommendations).

Sansho   Asian, Fusion €€
(Map p536; 📞222 317 425; www.sansho.cz; Petrská 25; lunch mains 190-245Kč, 6-course dinner 900-1200Kč; ⊙11.30am-2pm Tue-Fri, 6-11pm Tue-Sat, last orders 10pm; 🍴; 🚇3, 8, 14, 24) 🍴 'Friendly and informal' best describes the atmosphere at this ground-breaking restaurant where British chef Paul Day champions Czech farmers by sourcing all his meat and vegetables locally. There's no menu as such – the waitstaff will explain what dishes are available, depending on market produce. Typical dishes include curried rabbit, pork belly with watermelon and hoisin, and 12-hour beef rendang. Reservations recommended.

Nejen Bistro   Bistro €€
(📞222 960 515; www.nejenbistro.cz; Křižíkova 24, Karlín; mains 200-380Kč; ⊙10am-11pm;

3, 8, 24) 🖉 Nejen (Not Only) is emblematic of the new breed of restaurant that is transforming Karlín into one of Prague's hottest neighbourhoods, its quirky interior nominated for a slew of design awards. But just as much attention is lavished on the food, which makes the most of the kitchen's fancy Josper grill, turning out superb steaks, beef ribs and Nejen's signature Black Angus burger.

Augustine   Czech, European €€€

(Map p533; 266 112 280; www.augustine-restaurant.cz; Letenská 12, Augustine Hotel; mains 350-590Kč, 4 course tasting menu 1350Kč; 7am-11pm; ; 12, 15, 20, 22) Hidden away in the historic Augustine Hotel (check out the ceiling fresco in the bar), this sophisticated yet relaxed restaurant is well worth seeking out. The menu ranges from down-to-earth but delicious dishes such as pork cheeks braised in the hotel's own St Thomas beer, to inventive dishes built around fresh Czech produce. The two-course business lunch costs 380Kč

Field   Czech €€€

(Map p536; 222 316 999; www.fieldrestau rant.cz; U Milosrdných 12; mains 590-620Kč, 6-course tasting menu 2800Kč; 11am-2.30pm & 6-10.30pm Mon-Fri, noon-3pm & 6-10.30pm Sat, noon-3pm & 6-10pm Sun; 17) 🖉 Prague's third Michelin-starred restaurant is its least formal and most fun. The decor is an amusing art-meets-agriculture blend of farmyard implements and minimalist chic, while the chef creates painterly presentations from the finest of local produce along with freshly foraged herbs and edible flowers. You'll have to book at least a couple of weeks in advance to have a chance of a table.

Kalina   French €€€

(Map p536; 222 317 715; www kalinarestau rant.cz; Dlouhá 12; mains 500-900Kč; noon-3pm & 6-11.30pm; ; 6, 8, 15, 26) Setting a trend for taking the best of fresh Czech produce and giving it the French gourmet treatment, this smart but unfailingly friendly little restaurant offers dishes such as Prague snails with beef marrow and parsley purée, and roast sweetbreads with glazed

Drinks beside a Bedřich Smetana statue and the Vltava River

salsify and black truffles. Weekday lunch specials are good value at 150Kč to 300Kč.

🍺 DRINKING & NIGHTLIFE

Beer Geek
Pub

(https://beergeek.cz; Vinohradská 62, Vinohrady; ⊙3pm-2am; 🛜; Ⓜ Jiřího z Poděbrad) One of the most successful of a new generation of multi-tap pubs in Prague to offer the best beers from local Czech producers as well as brewers from around the world. They have 32 taps in all, and regularly rotate in obscure and hard-to-find labels. The 'geek' part of the name extends to the cool, lab-like presentation of the pub.

Cross Club
Club

(🗋736 535 010; www.crossclub.cz; Plynární 23; admission free-200Kč; ⊙cafe noon-2am, club 6pm-4am; 🛜; Ⓜ Nádraží Holešovice) An industrial club in every sense of the word: the setting in an industrial zone; the thumping music (both DJs and live acts); and the interior, an absolute must-see jumble of gadgets, shafts, cranks and pipes, many of which move and pulsate with light to the music. The program includes occasional live music, theatre performances and art happenings.

Letná Beer Garden
Beer Garden

(🗋233 378 208; www.letenskyzamecek.cz; Letenské sady 341; ⊙11am-11pm May-Sep; 🚋1, 8, 12, 25, 26) No accounting of watering holes in the neighbourhood would be complete without a nod toward the city's best beer garden, with an amazing panorama, situated at the eastern end of the **Letná Gardens** (Letenské sady; ⊙24hr; 👪). Buy a takeaway beer from a small kiosk and grab a picnic table, or sit on a small terrace where you can order beer by the glass and decent pizza.

Vinograf
Wine Bar

(Map p536; 🗋214 214 681; www.vinograf.cz; Senovážné náměstí 23; ⊙11.30am-midnight Mon-Sat, 5pm-midnight Sun; 🛜; 🚋3, 5, 6, 9, 14, 24) With knowledgeable staff, a relaxed atmosphere and an off-the-beaten-track feel, this appealingly modern wine bar is a great place to discover Moravian wines. There's good finger food to accompany

Cross Club

RADIOKAFKA/SHUTTERSTOCK ©

your wine, mostly cheese and charcuterie, with food and wine menus (in Czech and English) on big blackboards behind the bar. Very busy at weekends, when it's worth booking a table.

There's another branch in **Malá Strana** (Map p533; ☑604 705 730; Míšeňská 8; ⊙4pm-midnight Mon-Sat, 2-10pm Sun; ☎; ☒12, 15, 20, 22).

Pivovarský Klub   Pub

(☑222 315 777; www.pivovarskyklub.com; Křižíkova 17, Karlín; ⊙11.30am-11.30pm; Ⓜ Florenc) This bar is to beer what the Bodleian Library is to books – wall-to-wall shelves lined with more than 200 varieties of bottled beer from all over the world, and six guest beers on tap. Perch on a bar stool or head downstairs to the snug cellar and order some of the pub's excellent grub, such as authentic *guláš* (goulash) with bacon dumplings, to soak up the beer.

U Slovanské Lípy   Pub

(☑734 743 094; www.uslovanskelipy.cz; Tachovské náměstí 6, Žižkov; ⊙11am-midnight; ☎; ☒133, 175, 207) A classic Žižkov pub, plain and unassuming in and out, 'At the Linden Trees' (the linden is a Czech and Slovak national emblem) is something of a place of pilgrimage for beer lovers. The reason is its range of artisan brews (from 28Kč for 0.5L), such as those from the Kocour brewery, including its superb Sumeček 11° (Catfish pale ale).

⊕ ENTERTAINMENT

Palác Akropolis   Live Music

(☑296 330 913; www.palacakropolis.cz; Kubelíkova 27, Žižkov; tickets free-250Kč; ⊙club 6.30pm-5am; ☎; ☒5, 9, 15, 26) The Akropolis is a Prague institution, a smoky, labyrinthine, sticky-floored shrine to alternative music and drama. Its various performance spaces host a smorgasbord of musical and cultural events, from DJs to string quartets to Macedonian Roma bands to local rock gods to visiting talent – Marianne Faithfull, the Flaming Lips and the Strokes have all played here.

 Czech Beer

There are two main varieties of beer: *světlé* (light) and *tmavy* or *černé* (dark). The *světlé* is a pale amber or golden lager-style beer with a crisp, refreshing, hoppy flavour. Dark beers are sweeter and more full-bodied, with a rich, malty or fruity flavour.

Czechs like their beer served at cellar temperature (around 6°C to 10°C) with a tall, creamy head (known as *pěna*, meaning 'foam'). Americans and Australians may find it a bit warm, but this improves the flavour. Most draught beer is sold in *půl-litr* (0.5L) glasses; if you prefer a small beer, ask for a *malé pivo* (0.3L). Some bars confuse the issue by using 0.4L glasses, while others offer a German-style 1L mug known as a *tuplák*.

Prague pubs traditionally offered just three beers on tap, all from one large brewery such as Pilsner Urquell; some pioneering bar owners added a *čtvrtá pípa* ('fourth pipe') to allow them to offer a rotating range of guest beers from various independent regional breweries. Many now have five, six or even more pipes.

MATT MUNRO/LONELY PLANET ©

National Theatre   Opera, Ballet

(Národní divadlo; Map p536; ☑224 901 448; www.narodni-divadlo.cz; Národní třída 2; tickets 100-1290Kč; ⊙box offices 10am-6pm; ☒2, 9, 18, 22) The much-loved National Theatre provides a stage for traditional opera, drama and ballet by the likes of Smetana, Shakespeare and Tchaikovsky, sharing the

Troja Chateau

Troja Chateau (Zámek Troja; ☑283 851 614; www.ghmp.cz; U Trojského Zámku 1, Troja; adult/concession 120/60Kč; ☺10am-6pm Tue-Sun, from 1pm Fri Apr-Oct, closed Nov-Mar; ☐112, M Nádraží Holešovice) is a 17th-century baroque palace that was built for the Šternberk family, inspired by Roman country villas seen by the architect on a visit to Italy. A visit to the chateau can easily be combined with a trip to **Prague Zoo** (Zoo Praha; ☑296 112 230; www.zoopraha.cz; U Trojského zámku 120, Troja; adult/concession/family 200/150/600Kč; ☺9am-7pm Jun-Aug, to 6pm Apr, May, Sep & Oct, to 5pm Mar, to 4pm Nov-Feb; ⛲; ☐112, M Nádraží Holešovice), as the two are side by side. It's a pleasant 20-minute walk from Stromovka park, including crossing a dramatic footbridge over the Vltava.

The sumptuously decorated palace now houses collections of the Prague City Gallery and exhibits explaining the sculptures and frescoes that adorn the palace itself. There's free admission to the grounds, where you can wander in the beautiful French gardens.

Troja Chateau
MILONK/SHUTTERSTOCK ©

program alongside more modern works by composers and playwrights such as Philip Glass and John Osborne. The box offices are in the Nový síň building next door, in the Kolowrat Palace (opposite the Estates Theatre) and at the State Opera.

La Fabrika Theatre, Performing Arts (☑box office 774 417 644; www.lafabrika.cz; Komunardů 30; admission 200-400Kč; ☺box office 2-7.30pm Mon-Fri; ☐1, 6, 12, 14, 25) The name refers to a 'factory', but this is actually a former paint warehouse that's been converted into an experimental performance space. Depending on the night, come here to catch live music (jazz or cabaret), theatre, dance or film. Consult the website for the latest program. Try to reserve in advance as shows typically sell out.

❶ INFORMATION

Prague City Tourism (☑221 714 714; www.prague.eu) branches are scattered around town at the **Old Town Hall** (Staroměstské náměstí 5; ☺9am-7pm; M Staroměstská), in **Staré Město** (Rytířská 12; ☺9am-7pm; M Můstek) and at **Wenceslas Square** (Václavské náměstí 42; ☺10am-6pm; M Můstek, Muzeum), and at both airport arrivals terminals at **Václav Havel Airport Prague** (Terminals 1 & 2; ☺8am-8pm; ☐100, 119). Offices are good sources of maps and general information; they also sell Prague Card discount cards and can book guides and tours.

❶ GETTING THERE & AWAY

AIR

Václav Havel Airport Prague (Prague Ruzyně International Airport; ☑220 111 888; www.prg.aero; K letišti 6, Ruzyně; ☎; ☐100, 119), 17km west of the city centre, is the main international gateway to the Czech Republic and the hub for the national carrier Czech Airlines, which operates direct flights to Prague from many European cities. There are also direct flights from North America (from April to October) as well as to select cities in the Middle East and Asia.

BUS

Several bus companies offer long-distance coach service connecting Prague to cities around Europe. Nearly all international buses (and most domestic services) use the renovated and user-friendly **Florenc bus station** (ÚAN

Praha Florenc; ☑900 144 444; www.florenc.cz;
Křižíkova 2110/2b, Karlín; ☺5am-midnight; ☎;
Ⓜ Florenc).

CAR

Prague lies at the nexus of several European
four-lane highways and is a relatively easy drive
from many major regional cities, including Berlin
(four hours), Vienna (four hours) and Budapest
(five hours).

TRAIN

Prague is well integrated into European rail
networks. **České dráhy** (ČD, Czech Rail; ☑221
111 122, www.cd.cz), the Czech state rail operator,
sells tickets for international destinations. Train
travel makes the most sense if coming from
Berlin or from Vienna and Budapest in the east
and south.

Most domestic and international trains arrive
at **Praha hlavní nádraží** (Prague Main Train
Station; ☑840 112 113; www.cd.cz; Wilsonova
8, Nové Město; ☺3.30am-12.30am; Ⓜ Hlavní
nádraží). Some international trains, particularly
those travelling to or coming from Berlin, also
stop at a smaller station, **Praha-Holešovice**
(Nádraží Holešovice; ☑840 112 113; www.cd.cz;
Vrbenského, Holešovice; Ⓜ Nádraží Holešovice),
north of the centre. Both stations have stops on
metro line C (red)

ⓘ GETTING AROUND

Central Prague is easily managed on foot
(though be sure to wear comfortable shoes).
For longer trips, the city has a reliable public-
transport system of metros, trams and buses
operated by the **Prague Public Transport**

Authority (DPP; ☑296 191 817; www.dpp.cz;
☺7am-9pm). The system is integrated, meaning
that the same tickets are valid on all types of
transport, and for transfers between them.

METRO

Prague's excellent metro operates daily from
5am to midnight. The metro has three lines:

Line A (shown on transport maps in green) Links
the airport bus to Malá Strana, Old Town Square,
Wenceslas Square and Vinohrady.

Line B (Yellow) Cross-river route from Smíchov
in southwest to central Náměstí Republiky and
Florenc bus station.

Line C (Red) Links main train station to Florenc
bus station, Wenceslas Square and Vyšehrad.

BUS & TRAM

To supplement the metro, there is a comprehensive system of trams (streetcars) and buses that
reach virtually every nook and cranny in the city.
The DPP website has a handy 'Journey Planner'
tab in English to allow you to plan your route.

○ Trams are convenient for crossing the river
and moving between neighbourhoods.

○ Buses are less useful for visitors and normally
connect far-flung residential neighbourhoods to
nearby metro stations or the centre.

○ Always validate an unstamped ticket on
entering the tram or bus.

○ Trams and buses run from around 5am to
midnight daily. After the system shuts down, a
smaller fleet of night trams (51 to 59) and night
buses rumble across the city about every 40
minutes (only full-price 32Kč tickets are valid on
these services).

Budapest, Hungary

Budapest is paradise for explorers. Architecturally, the city is a treasure trove, with enough baroque, neoclassical and art nouveau buildings to satisfy everyone. Amid these splendid edifices, history waits around every corner, with bullet holes and shrapnel pockmarks poignant reminders of past conflicts. And to buoy the traveller on their explorations, the city generously supplies delicious Magyar cuisine (among an array of other top eats), excellent wines, rip-roaring nightlife and an abundance of hot springs to soak the day's aches away.

Two Days in Budapest

Spend most of the first day on **Castle Hill** (p557), taking in the views and visiting the **Royal Palace** (p549) and a museum or two. In the afternoon, ride the **Sikló** (p557) down to Clark Ádám tér and make your way to the **Gellért Baths** (p551). In the evening, head to Erzsébetváros and the Jewish Quarter. On the second day take a walk up Andrássy út, stopping off at the **House of Terror** (p552). In the afternoon, take the waters at the **Széchenyi Baths** (p551).

Four Days in Budapest

The next day, concentrate on the two icons of Hungarian nationhood and the places that house them: the Crown of St Stephen in **Parliament** (p553) and the saint-king's mortal remains in the **Basilica of St Stephen** (p553). In the evening, go for drinks at a **ruin pub** (p561). On day four visit the **Great Synagogue** (p552) and in the afternoon cross over to idyllic **Margaret Island** (p553). Spend the rest of the afternoon at **Veli Bej Bath** (p551).

Next waltz on to Vienna (p564), 2½ hours by train or 5½ to 6½ hours by boat.

Map labels:
Aquincum • Vác (30 km) • 0 2 km / 0 1 mile • ISTVÁNTELEK • Óbuda Island (Óbudai-sziget) • ÓBUDA • REMETEHEGY • Danube River • Váci út • Béke u • ANGYALFÖLD • HŰVÖSVÖLGYI ÚT • MÁTYÁSHEGY • ÚJLAK • Margaret Island (Margit-sziget) • FELHÉVÍZ • Budakeszi út • RÓZSADOMB • Museum of Fine Arts • Nyugati Train Station • Dózsa György út • HERMINAMEZŐ • RÉZMÁL • City Park (Városliget) • ORBÁNHEGY • Bem rkp • Keleti Train Station • Kerepsei út • Déli Train Station • Attila u • Royal Palace • József krt • Fiumei út • Piety Museum • FARKASRÉT • TABÁN • Kerepesi Cemetery • Farkasréti temető • Jubilee Park • JÓZSEFVÁROS • SASHEGY • Budaörsi út • Üllői út • Népliget • SASAD • Egyetemisták parkja • FERENCVÁROS • Soroksári út • KELENFÖLD • LÁGYMÁNYOS • Budapest Map (p554)

Arriving in Budapest

Ferenc Liszt International Airport

Minibuses, buses and trains to central Budapest run from 4am to midnight. A taxi will cost from 6500Ft.

Keleti, Nyugati & Déli Train Stations

All three are connected to metro lines of the same name and night buses call when the metro is closed.

Stadion & Népliget Bus Stations Both

are on metro lines and are served by trams.

Where to Stay

Accommodation in Budapest runs the gamut from hostels in converted flats and private rooms in far-flung housing estates to luxury guesthouses in the Buda Hills and five-star properties charging upwards of €350 a night.

Because of the changing value of the forint, many midrange and top-end hotels quote their rates in euros.

Royal Palace

The enormous Royal Palace (Királyi Palota) has been razed and rebuilt six times over the past seven centuries. Today it contains two museums, the national library and an abundance of statues and monuments. It is the focal point of Buda's Castle Hill and the city's most visited sight.

Great For...

☑ Don't Miss

Late Gothic altarpieces, Gothic statues and heads, and the Renaissance door frame.

Hungarian National Gallery

The **Hungarian National Gallery** (Nemzeti Galéria; ☎1-201 9082; www.mng.hu; Bldgs A-D; adult/concession 1800/900Ft, audio guide 1000Ft; ☉10am-6pm Tue-Sun) boasts an overwhelming collection that traces Hungarian art from the 11th century to the present day. The largest collections include medieval and Renaissance stonework, Gothic wooden sculptures and panel paintings, late Gothic winged altars and late Renaissance and baroque art. The museum also has an important collection of Hungarian paintings and sculpture from the 19th and 20th centuries. Much of the gallery was closed for renovations at the time of writing, and by 2019 the collection is due to move to a purpose-built gallery in City Park.

Royal Palace

❶ Need to Know

Királyi Palota; I Szent György tér; 🚌16, 16A, 116

✕ Take a Break

If you need something hot and/or sweet after your visit, head for **Ruszwurm Cukrászda** (☑1-375 5284; www.ruszwurm. hu; I Szentháromság utca 7; ☉10am-7pm Mon-Fri, to 6pm Sat & Sun; 🚌16, 16A, 116).

★ Top Tip

Exiting through the museum's back courtyard door will take you straight down to I Szarvas tér in the Tabán.

Castle Museum

Part of the multibranched Budapest History Museum, the **Castle Museum** (Vármúzeum; ☑1-487 8800; www.btm.hu; Bldg E; adult/concession 2000/1000Ft; ☉10am-6pm Tue-Sun Mar-Oct, to 4pm Nov-Feb) explores the city's 2000-year history over three floors. Restored palace rooms dating from the 15th century can be entered from the basement, where there are three vaulted halls. One of the halls features a magnificent Renaissance door frame in red marble, leading to the Gothic and Renaissance Halls, the Royal Cellar and the vaulted Tower Chapel (1320) dedicated to St Stephen.

On the ground floor, exhibits showcase Budapest during the Middle Ages, with dozens of important Gothic statues, heads and fragments of courtiers, squires and saints, discovered during excavations in 1974.

A wonderful exhibit on the 1st floor called '1000 Years of a Capital' traces the history of Budapest from the arrival of the Magyars and the Turkish occupation to modern times, taking an interesting look at housing, ethnic diversity, religion and other such issues over the centuries. The excellent audioguide is 1200Ft.

National Széchenyi Library

The **National Széchenyi Library** (Országos Széchenyi Könyvtár; ☑1-224 3700; www.oszk. hu; Bldg F; ☉9am-8pm, stacks to 7pm Tue-Sat) contains codices and manuscripts, a large collection of foreign newspapers and a copy of everything published in Hungary or the Hungarian language. It was founded in 1802 by Count Ferenc Széchenyi, father of the heroic István, who endowed it with 15,000 books and 2000 manuscripts.

Széchenyi Baths

Thermal Baths & Spas

Budapest sits on a crazy quilt of almost 125 thermal springs, and 'taking the waters' is very much a part of everyday life here. Some baths date from Turkish times, others are art nouveau marvels and still others are chic modern spas boasting all the mod cons.

Great For...

☑ Don't Miss

The sight of locals playing chess on floating boards (regardless of the weather) at Széchenyi Baths.

History of a Spa City

The remains of two sets of baths found at Aquincum – for the public and the garrisons – indicate that the Romans took advantage of Budapest's thermal waters almost two millennia ago. But it wasn't until the Turkish occupation of the 16th and 17th centuries that bathing became an integral part of everyday Budapest life. In the late 18th century, Habsburg Empress Maria Theresa ordered that Budapest's mineral waters be analysed/recorded in a list at the Treasury's expense. By the 1930s Budapest had become a fashionable spa resort.

Healing Waters

Of course, not everyone goes to the baths for fun and relaxation. The warm, mineral-rich waters are also believed to relieve a number of specific complaints, ranging from

Gellért Baths

MARTCHAN/SHUTTERSTOCK ©

arthritis and muscle pain to poor blood circulation and post-traumatic stress. They are also a miracle cure for that most unpleasant of afflictions: the dreaded hangover.

Choosing a Bath

The choice of bathhouses today is legion, and which one you choose is a matter of taste and what exactly you're looking for – be it fun, a hangover cure, or relief for something more serious.

Rudas Baths (Rudas Gyógyfürdő; ☏1-356 1322; www.rudasfurdo.hu; I Döbrentei tér 9; with cabin Mon-Fri/Sat & Sun 3200/3500Ft, morning/night ticket 2500/4600Ft; ⊙men 6am-8pm Mon & Wed-Fri, women 6am-8pm Tue, mixed 10pm-4am Fri, 6am-8pm & 10pm-4am Sat, 6am-8pm Sun; ◻7, 86, ◻18, 19) These renovated baths are the most Turkish of all in Budapest, built in 1566, with an octagonal pool, domed

cupola and eight massive pillars. They're mostly men-only during the week, but turn into a real zoo on mixed weekend nights.

Gellért Baths (Gellért gyógyfürdő; ☏1-466 6166; www.gellertbath.hu; XI Kelenhegyi út 4, Danubius Hotel Gellért; with locker/cabin Mon-Fri 5100/5500Ft, Sat & Sun 5300/5700Ft; ⊙6am-8pm; ◻7, 86, ⓂM4 Szent Gellért tér, ◻18, 19, 47, 49) Soaking in these art nouveau baths, now open to both men and women at all times, has been likened to taking a bath in a cathedral.

Széchenyi Baths (Széchenyi Gyógyfürdő; ☏1-363 3210; www.szechenyibath.hu; XIV Állatkerti körút 9-11; tickets incl locker/cabin Mon-Fri 4700/5200Ft, Sat & Sun 4900/5400Ft; ⊙6am-10pm; ⓂM1 Széchenyi fürdő) The gigantic 'wedding-cake' building in City Park houses these baths, which are unusual for three reasons: their immensity (a dozen thermal baths and three outdoor swimming pools); the bright, clean atmosphere; and the high temperature of the water (up to 40°C).

Veli Bej Baths (Veli Bej Fürdője; ☏1-438 8500; www.irgalmas.hu/veli-bej-furdo; II Árpád fejedelem útja 7 & Frankel Leó út 54; 6am-noon 2240Ft, 3-7pm 2800Ft, after 7pm 2000Ft; ⊙6am-noon & 3-9pm; ◻9, 109, ◻4, 6, 17, 19) This venerable (1575) Turkish bath in Buda has got a new lease of life after having been forgotten for centuries.

◎ SIGHTS

Budapest's most important museums are found on Castle Hill, in City Park, along Andrássy út in Erzsébetváros, and in Southern Pest. The area surrounding the splendid Parliament building is also home to Budapest's most iconic church; both Parliament and Belváros feature some of the city's best art nouveau architecture. Margaret Island and City Park are the city's most appealing green spaces, while the Buda Hills is a veritable playground for hikers, cavers and bikers. Óbuda is home to extensive Roman ruins and quirky museums, and Gellért Hill gives you some of the best views of the city.

Great Synagogue   Synagogue
(Nagy Zsinagóga; ☑1-462 0477; www.dohany-zsi nagoga.hu; VII Dohány utca 2; adult/concession incl museum 3000/2000Ft; ⊗10am-6pm Sun-Thu, to 4pm Fri Mar-Oct, 10am-4pm Sun-Thu, to 2pm Fri Nov-Feb; ⋈M2 Astoria, ➋47, 49) Budapest's stunning Great Synagogue is the largest Jewish house of worship in the world outside New York City. Built in 1859, the synagogue has both Romantic and Moorish ar-

chitectural elements. Inside, the **Hungarian Jewish Museum & Archives** (Magyar Zsidó Múzeum és Levéltár; ☑1-343 6756; www.milev.hu) contains objects relating to both religious and everyday life. On the synagogue's north side, the **Holocaust Tree of Life Memorial** (Raoul Wallenberg Memorial Park, opp VII Wesselényi utca 6) presides over the mass graves of those murdered by the Nazis.

House of Terror   Museum
(Terror Háza; ☑1-374 2600; www.terrorhaza. hu; VI Andrássy út 60; adult/concession 2000/1000Ft, audioguide 1500Ft; ⊗10am-6pm Tue-Sun; ⋈M1 Oktogon) The headquarters of the dreaded secret police is now the startling House of Terror, focusing on the crimes and atrocities of Hungary's fascist and Stalinist regimes in a permanent exhibition called Double Occupation. But the years after WWII leading up to the 1956 Uprising get the lion's share of the exhibition space (almost three-dozen spaces on three levels). The reconstructed prison cells in the basement and the Perpetrators' Gallery, featuring photographs of the turncoats, spies and torturers, are chilling.

Holocaust Tree of Life Memorial

Liberty Monument — Monument

(Szabadság-szobor; 🚌27) The Liberty Monument, the lovely lady with the palm frond proclaiming freedom throughout the city, is to the east of the Citadella. Some 14m high, she was raised in 1947 in tribute to the Soviet soldiers who died liberating Budapest in 1945. The victims' names in Cyrillic letters on the plinth and the soldiers' statues were removed in 1992 and sent to Memento Park. The inscription reads: 'To those who gave up their lives for Hungary's independence, freedom and prosperity'.

Memento Park — Historic Site

(🗹1-424 7500; www.mementopark.hu; XXII Balatoni út & Szabadkai utca; adult/student 1500/1000Ft; ⏰10am-dusk; 🚌101, 150) Home to more than 40 statues, busts and plaques of Lenin, Marx, Béla Kun and others whose likenesses have ended up on rubbish heaps elsewhere, Memento Park, 10km southwest of the city centre, is truly a mind-blowing place to visit. Ogle the socialist realism and try to imagine that some of these relics were erected as recently as the late 1980s.

Basilica of St Stephen — Cathedral

(Szent István Bazilika; 🗹06 30 703 6599, 1-311 0839; www.basilica.hu; V Szent István tér; requested donation 200Ft; ⏰9am-7pm Mon-Sat, 7.45am-7pm Sun; MM3 Arany János utca) Budapest's neoclassical cathedral was built over half a century and completed in 1905. Much of the interruption during construction had to do with a fiasco in 1868 when the dome collapsed during a storm, and the structure had to be demolished and then rebuilt from the ground up. The basilica is rather dark and gloomy inside, but take a trip to the top of the dome for incredible views.

Hungarian State Opera House — Notable Building

(Magyar Állami Operaház; 🗹1-332 8197; www.operavisit.hu; VI Andrássy út 22; adult/concession 2990/1990Ft; ⏰tours in English 2pm, 3pm & 4pm; MM1 Opera) The neo-Renaissance Hungarian State Opera House was designed by Miklós Ybl in 1884 and is among the most beautiful buildings in Budapest. Its facade is decorated with statues of muses and

Margaret Island

Situated in the middle of the Danube, leafy Margaret Island is neither Buda nor Pest, but its shaded walkways, large swimming complexes, thermal spa and gardens offer refuge to the denizens of both sides of the river. The island was always the domain of one religious order or another until the Turks turned it into a harem, and it remains studded with picturesque ruins.

The island is bigger than you think, so rent a bicycle or other wheeled equipment from **Bringóhintó** (🗹1-329 2073; www.bringohinto.hu; per 30/60min mountain bikes 690/990Ft, pedal coaches for 4 people 2280/3680Ft; ⏰8am-dusk; 🚌26) at the refreshment stand near the Japanese Garden in the northern part of the island, then work your way south. The island is at its best during the day, though you can also check out the on-site club, **Holdudvar** (🗹1-236 0155; www.facebook.com/holdudvaroldal; XIII Margitsziget; ⏰11am-2am Sun-Wed, to 4am Thu, to 5am Fri & Sat; 🚌4, 6), in the evening.

Church ruins
GASCHWALD/SHUTTERSTOCK ©

opera greats such as Puccini, Mozart, Liszt and Verdi, while its interior dazzles with marble columns, gilded vaulted ceilings, chandeliers and near-perfect acoustics. If you cannot attend a performance, join one of the three daily tours. Tickets are available from the souvenir shop inside the lobby.

Parliament — Historic Building

(Országház; 🗹1-441 4904; www.hungarianparliament.com; V Kossuth Lajos tér 1-3; adult/

Budapest

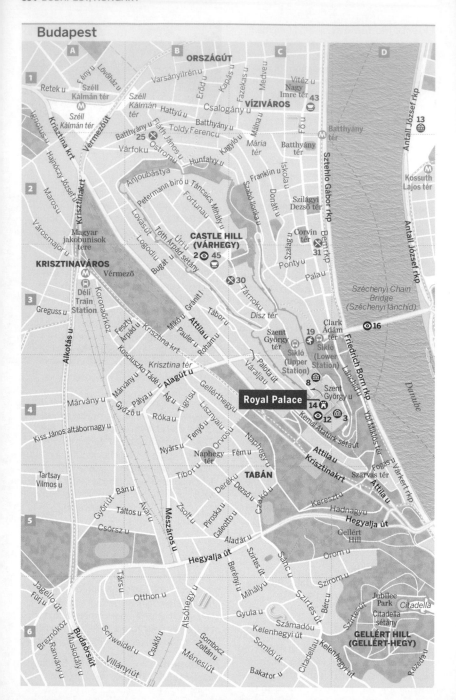

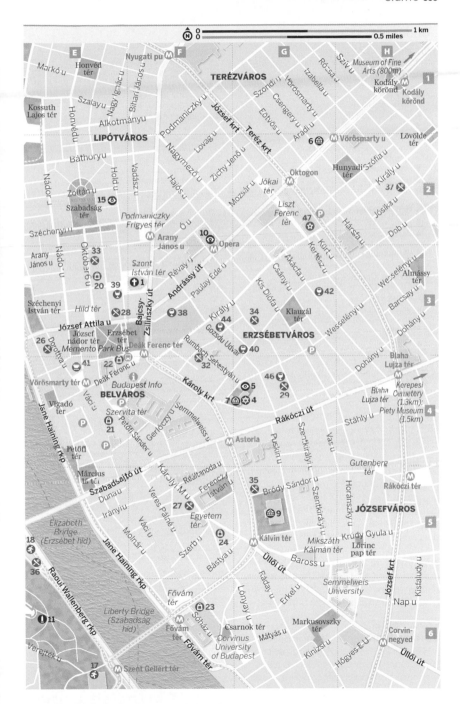

Ⓝ 0 ——————————— 1 km
0 ——————————— 0.5 miles

TERÉZVÁROS

Nyugati pu Ⓜ

Museum of Fine
Arts (800m)

Markó u

Honvéd
tér

Kodály Ⓜ
körönd

Kodály
körönd

Kossuth
Lajos tér

Szalay u

Bihari János u

Nagy Ignác u

József krt

Teréz krt

Szondi u

Vörösmarty u

Izabella u

Róza u

Szív u

Eötvös u

Aradi u

Csengery u

6 🏛

Ⓜ Vörösmarty u

Lövölde
tér

Alkotmány u

Honvéd u

LIPÓTVÁROS

Podmaniczky u

Lovag u

Nagymező u

Zichy Jenő u

Mozsár u

Jókai
tér

Oktogon Ⓜ

Hunyadi
tér

Szófia u

Király u

Báthory u

Vadász u

Hold u

Hajós u

Nádor u

Zoltán u

15 ☉

Szabadság
tér

31 ✕

Josika u

Liszt
Ferenc
tér

47 🅿
✪

Kürt u

Kertész u

Hárs u

Dob u

Széchenyi u

Podmaniczky
Frigyes tér

Ó u

Ⓜ Arany
János u

10

🅿 Opera

Akácfa u

Csányi u

Wesselényi u

Almássy
tér

Nádor u

Arany
János u

Október 6 u

33
✕

Szent
István tér

20   39

Andrássy út

Révay u

Paulay Ede u

Kis Diófa u

42

Barcsay u

Dohány u

Széchenyi
István tér

Hild tér

28

Bajcsy-
Zsilinszky út

38

Király u

44

34

Klauzál
tér

Wesselényi u

József Attila u

József
nádor tér

Erzsébet
tér

Gozsdu Udvar

ERZSÉBETVÁROS

26 ✕

Dorottya u

Memento Park Bus

Deák Ferenc tér

Rumbach Sebestyén u

🅿

Dohány u

Blaha
Lujza tér

41

22

Deák Ferenc u

32

40

Vörösmarty tér Ⓜ

Ⓜ Deák Ferenc tér

Budapest Info

BELVÁROS

Károly krt

46
29

Blaha
Lujza tér

Kerepesi
Cemetery
(1.3km);
Piety Museum
(1.5km)

Vigadó
tér

Váci u

Szervita tér

21

Petőfi Sándor u

Gerlóczy u

Semmelweis u

7

5

4

Rákóczi út

Sztáhly u

Vas u

Petőfi
tér

Jane Haining rkp

Astoria Ⓜ

Puskin u

Szentkirályi u

Gutenberg
tér

Rákóczi tér Ⓜ

Március
15 tér

Szabadsajtó út

Károly u

Reáltanoda u

Ferenc
István u

35
✕

Bródy Sándor u

Szentkirályi u

Horánszky u

JÓZSEFVÁROS

Dunau

Irányi u

Veres Pálné u

Váci u

27

Egyetem
tér

9 🏛

Kálvin tér Ⓜ

Mikszáth
Kálmán tér

Krúdy Gyula u

Lőrinc
pap tér

Elizabeth
Bridge
(Erzsébet híd)

18
✪

Molnár u

Szerb u

24

Bástya u

Üllői út

Baross u

Semmelweis
University

Nap u

József krt

Kisfaludy u

36

Raoul Wallenberg rkp

Fővám
tér

Lónyay u

Ráday u

Erkel u

Markusovszky
tér

Corvin-
negyed

Üllői út

11 ❗

Liberty Bridge
(Szabadság
híd)

23

Sóház u

Csarnok tér

Mátyás u

Hőgyes E. u

Kinizsi u

Vereiték u

17

Ⓜ Szent Gellért tér

Fővám
tér

Corvinus
University
of Budapest

Fővám tér

Budapest

student EU citizen 2200/1200Ft, non-EU citizen 5400/2800Ft; ⊗8am-6pm Mon-Fri, to 4pm Sat, to 2pm Sun; Ⓜ M2 Kossuth Lajos tér, ☒2) The Eclectic-style Parliament, designed by Imre Steindl and completed in 1902, has 691 sumptuously decorated rooms, but you'll only get to see several of these and other features on a guided tour of the North Wing: the Golden Staircase; the Domed Hall, where the **Crown of St Stephen**, the nation's most important national icon, is on display; the Grand Staircase and its wonderful landing; Loge Hall; and Congress Hall, where the House of Lords of the one-time bicameral assembly sat until 1944.

Royal Postal Savings Bank
Notable Building
(V Hold utca 4; ☒15) East of Szabadság tér, the former Royal Postal Savings Bank is a Secessionist extravaganza of colourful tiles and folk motifs, built by Ödön Lechner in 1901. One of the most beautiful buildings in Pest, it is now part of the National Bank of Hungary.

Hungarian National Museum
Museum
(Magyar Nemzeti Múzeum; ☎1-338 2122; www. hnm.hu; VIII Múzeum körút 14-16; adult/concession 1600/800Ft; ⊗10am-6pm Tue-Sun; ☒47, 49, Ⓜ M3/4 Kálvin tér) The Hungarian National Museum houses the nation's most important collection of historical relics in an impressive neoclassical building, purpose built in 1847. Exhibits trace the history of the Carpathian Basin from earliest times to the end of the Avar period, and the ongoing story of the Magyar people from the conquest of the basin to the end of communism. Don't miss King Stephen's crimson silk coronation mantle and the Broadwood piano, used by both Beethoven and Liszt.

Kerepesi Cemetery   Cemetery

(Kerepesi temető; ☑06 30 331 8822; www.
nemzetisirkert.hu; VIII Fiumei út 16; ⊘7am-8pm
May-Jul, to 7pm Apr & Aug, to 6pm Sep, to 5pm
Mar & Oct, 7.30am-5pm Nov-Feb; Ⓜ M2/4 Keleti
train station, 🚋24) FREE Budapest's equivalent of London's Highgate or Père Lachaise
in Paris, this 56-hectare necropolis was
established in 1847 and holds some 3000
gravestones and mausoleums, including
those of statesmen and national heroes
Lajos Kossuth, Ferenc Deák and Lajos
Batthyány. Maps indicating the location of
noteworthy graves are available free at the
entrance. Plot 21 contains the graves of
many who died in the 1956 Uprising.

Castle Hill   Hill

(Várhegy; 🚋16, 16A, 116, Ⓜ M2 Batthyány tér,
Széll Kálmán tér, 🚋19, 41;) Castle Hill is a
kilometre-long limestone plateau towering
170m above the Danube. It contains some
of Budapest's most important medieval
monuments and museums, and is a Unesco
World Heritage Site. Below it is a 28km-long
network of caves formed by thermal springs.

The walled area consists of two distinct
parts: the Old Town, where commoners
once lived, and the Royal Palace, the original site of the castle built by Béla IV in the
13th century and reserved for the nobility.

The easiest way to reach Castle Hill from
Pest is to take bus 16 from Deák Ferenc tér
to Dísz tér, more or less the central point
between the Old Town and the Royal Palace.
Much more fun, though, is to stroll across
Széchenyi Chain Bridge and board the **Sikló**
(www.bkv.hu; I Szent György tér; one way/return
adult 1200/1800Ft, 3-14yr 700/1100Ft; ⊘7.30am-
10pm, closed 1st & 3rd Mon of month; 🚋16, 16A,
🚋19, 41), a funicular railway built in 1870 that
ascends steeply from Clark Ádám tér to
Szent György tér near the Royal Palace.

Alternatively, you can walk up the Király
lépcső (Royal Steps) leading northwest off
Clark Ádám tér.

Another option is to take metro M2 to
Széll Kálmán tér, go up the stairs in the
southeastern part of the square and walk
up Várfok utca to Vienna Gate. This medieval entrance to the Old Town was rebuilt in

Budapest's Flea Markets

Jostling with locals shopping for bargains
at **Ecseri Piac** (Ecseri Market; www.piacon
line.hu; XIX Nagykőrösi út 156; ⊘8am-4pm
Mon-Fri, 5am-3pm Sat, 8am-1pm Sun; 🚋54,
84E, 89E 94F), one of Central Europe's
largest flea markets, is a fabulous way to
spend a Saturday morning. Lose yourself
amid a cornucopia of gramophones,
rocking horses, uniforms, violins and
even suits of armour. If you can't make
it here, the smaller **PECSA Bolhapiac**
(www.bolhapiac.com; XIV Zichy Mihály utca
14; admission 150Ft; ⊘7am-2pm Sat & Sun;
🚋trolleybus 72, 74, 🚋1) offers a less impressive jumble of vintage knick-knacks.

Old radios and TVs for sale at Ecseri Piac
WESTEND61 PREMIUM/SHUTTERSTOCK ©

1936 to mark the 250th anniversary of the
castle being taken back from the Turks. Bus
16A follows the same route from the start
of Várfok utca.

Museum of Fine Arts   Museum

(Szépmüvészeti Múzeum; ☑1-469 7100; www.
mfab.hu; XIV Dózsa György út 41; Ⓜ M1 Hősök
tere) Housed in a grand neoclassical
building, the Museum of Fine Arts is home
to the city's most outstanding collection of
foreign works of art, ranging from articles
from ancient Egypt and ancient Mediterranean cultures to stellar collections of
Spanish, Flemish, Italian and German art.
The private collection of Count Miklós
Esterházy, purchased by the state in 1870,
forms the nucleus of this collection. At
research time, the museum was closed for
renovation until March 2018.

The Danube and Its Bridges

Budapest's dustless highway is ever present, neatly dividing the city and still serving as an important means of transport. The Danube bridges (all eight of them, not counting train bridges), at once landmarks and vantage points over the river, are the stitches that have bound Buda and Pest together since well before the two were linked politically in 1873. The four bridges in the centre stand head and shoulders above the rest: Margaret Bridge, wonderful **Széchenyi Chain Bridge** (Széchenyi lánchíd; 🚌16, 🚋19, 41), Elizabeth Bridge and Liberty Bridge.

Széchenyi Chain Bridge
PAOLO PARADISO/SHUTTERSTOCK ©

Aquincum   Archaeological Site
(🖉1-250 1650; www.aquincum.hu; III Szentendrei út 133-135; adult/concession museum & park 1600/800Ft, park only 1000/500Ft; ☺museum 10am-6pm Tue-Sun Apr-Oct, to 4pm Nov-Mar, park 9am-6pm Tue-Sun Apr-Oct; 🚌34, 106, 🚉HÉV to Aquincum) The most complete Roman civilian town in Hungary was built around AD 100 and became the seat of the Roman province of Pannonia Inferior in AD 106. Visitors can explore its houses, baths, courtyards, fountains and sophisticated underfloor heating systems, as well as a recreation of a Roman painter's dwelling. Alight at the Aquincum stop.

The purpose-built Aquincum Museum, just inside the entrance, puts the ruins in perspective, with a vast collection of Roman daily life objects and wall paintings.

🛍 SHOPPING

Nagycsarnok   Market
(Great Market Hall; 🖉1-366 3300; www.piacon line.hu; IX Vámház körút 1-3; ☺6am-5pm Mon, to 6pm Tue-Fri, to 3pm Sat; 🚇M4 Fővám tér) This is Budapest's biggest market, though it has become a tourist magnet since its renovation for the millecentenary celebrations in 1996. Still, plenty of locals come here for fruit, vegetables, deli items, fish and meat. Head up to the 1st floor for Hungarian folk costumes, dolls, painted eggs, embroidered tablecloths, carved hunting knives and other souvenirs.

Bestsellers   Books
(🖉1-312 1295; www.bestsellers.hu; V Október 6 utca 11; ☺9am-6.30pm Mon-Fri, 11am-6pm Sat, noon-6pm Sun; 🚇M1/2/3 Deák Ferenc tér) Our favourite English-language bookshop in town, with fiction, travel guides and lots of Hungarica, as well as a large selection of newspapers and magazines overseen by master bookseller Tony Láng. Helpful staff are at hand to advise and recommend.

Le Parfum Croisette   Perfume
(🖉06 30 405 0668; www.leparfum.hu; V Deák Ferenc utca 18; ☺10am-7pm Mon-Fri, to 5pm Sat & Sun; 🚇M1/2/3 Deák Ferenc tér, 🚌47, 48, 49) 🖋 Hungary's only *parfumier*, Zsolt Zólyomi, creates scents at his atelier-shop, as well as selling cutting-edge, animal-friendly perfumes from around the globe, such as Romano Ricci's Juliette Has a Gun range of cognac scents, whose recipes go back 750 years. Zólyomi, who foresees a renaissance in the once-great Hungarian perfume industry, holds perfume-making workshops here too.

Rózsavölgyi Csokoládé   Chocolate
(🖉06 30 814 8929; www.rozsavolgyi.com; V Királyi Pál utca 6; ☺10.30am-1pm & 1.30-6.30pm Mon-Fri, noon-6pm Sat; 🚇M3/4 Kálvin tér) A tiny, low-lit boutique selling delicious and artfully packaged, award-winning bean-to-bar chocolate. The range of handmade chocolates includes such interesting flavours as coffee and balsamic vinegar, and star anise with red peppercorn.

Bomo Art — Arts & Crafts

(📞1-318 7280; www.bomoart.hu; V Régi Posta utca 14; ☺10am-6.30pm Mon-Fri, to 6pm Sat; Ⓜ M3 Ferenciek tere) This tiny shop just off Váci utca sells some of the finest paper and paper goods in Budapest, including leather-bound notebooks, photo albums and address books.

EATING

Budavári Rétesvár — Hungarian €

(Strudel Castle; 📞06 70 408 8696; www. budavariretesvar.hu; I Balta köz 4; strudel 310Ft; ☺8am-7pm; 🚌16, 16A, 116) Strudel in all its permutations – from poppyseed with sour cherry to dill with cheese and cabbage – is available at this hole-in-the wall dispensary in a narrow alley of the Castle District.

Bors Gasztro Bár — Sandwiches €

(www.facebook.com/BorsGasztroBar; VII Kazinczy utca 10; soups 600Ft, baguettes 670-890Ft; ☺11.30am-midnight; ✈; Ⓜ M2 Astoria) We love this thimble-sized place, not just for its hearty, imaginative soups (how about sweet potato with coconut or tiramisu?) but also for its equally good grilled baguettes: try 'Bors Dog' (spicy sausage and cheese) or 'Brain Dead' (pig's brains are the main ingredient). It's not a sit-down kind of place, most chow down on the pavement outside.

Zeller Bistro — Hungarian €€

(📞06 30 651 0880, 1-321 7879; VII Izabella utca 38; mains 2900-5400Ft; ☺noon-3pm & 6-11pm Tue-Sat; Ⓜ M1 Vörösmarty utca, 🚋4, 6) You'll receive a very warm welcome at this lovely candlelit cellar where the attentive staff serve food sourced largely from the owner's family and friends in the Lake Balaton area. The Hungarian home cooking includes some first-rate dishes such as grey beef, duck leg, oxtail and lamb's knuckle. Superb desserts, too. Popular with both locals and expats; reservations are essential.

Borkonyha — Hungarian €€

(Wine Kitchen; 📞1-266 0835; www.borkonyha. hu; V Sas utca 3; mains 3150-7950Ft; ☺noon-4pm & 6pm-midnight Mon-Sat; 🚌15, 115, Ⓜ M1 Bajcsy-Zsilinszky út) Chef Ákos Sárközi's approach to Hungarian cuisine at this

Outdoor dining

Gerbeaud

Michelin-starred restaurant is contemporary, and the menu changes every week or two. Go for the signature foie gras appetiser wrapped in strudel pastry and a glass of sweet Tokaj wine. If *mangalica* (a special type of Hungarian pork) is on the menu, try it with a glass of dry *furmint*.

Kőleves   Jewish €€

(☎06 20 213 5999; www.kolevesvendeglo.hu; VII Kazinczy utca 37-41; mains 2120-4920Ft; ⊕8am-1am Mon-Fri, 9am-1am Sat & Sun; 🐕🍴; Ⓜ M1/2/3 Deák Ferenc tér) Always buzzy and lots of fun, the 'Stone Soup' attracts a young crowd with its Jewish-inspired (but not kosher) menu, lively decor, great service and reasonable prices. Good vegetarian choices. Breakfast (890Ft to 1250Ft) is served from 8am to 11.30am. The daily lunch is just 1250Ft, or 1100Ft for the vegetarian version.

Gerbeaud   Cafe €€

(☎1-429 9001; www.gerbeaud.hu; V Vörösmarty tér 7-8; ⊕noon-10pm; Ⓜ M1 Vörösmarty tér) Founded on the northern side of Pest's busiest square in 1858, Gerbeaud has been the most fashionable meeting place for the city's elite since 1870. Along with exquisitely prepared cakes and pastries, it serves continental/full breakfast and a smattering of nicely presented Hungarian dishes with international touches. A visit is mandatory.

Baraka   Fusion €€€

(☎1-200 0817; www.barakarestaurant.hu; V Dorottya utca 6; mains 7200-17,500Ft, 3-course lunches 6900Ft, 7-course tasting menus 27,000Ft; ⊕11am-3pm & 6-11.30pm Mon-Sat; 🐕; Ⓜ M1 Vörösmarty tér) If you only eat in one fine-dining establishment while in Budapest, make it Baraka. You're ushered into the monochrome dining room, where chef Norbert Bíró works his magic in the half-open kitchen. Seafood features heavily, with French, Asian and Hungarian elements in the beautifully presented dishes. The bar, with its vast array of Japanese whiskies and pan-Asian tapas, is a treat.

Múzeum   Hungarian €€€

(☎1-267 0375; www.muzeumkavehaz.hu; VIII Múzeum körút 12; mains 3600-7200Ft; ⊕6pm-midnight Mon-Sat, noon-3pm Sun;

 M3/4 Kálvin tér) This cafe-restaurant is the place to come if you like to dine in old-world style with a piano softly tinkling in the background. It's still going strong after 130 years at the same location. The goose-liver parfait (3400Ft) is to die for, the goose leg and cabbage (3900Ft) iconic. There's also a good selection of Hungarian wines.

🥤 DRINKING & NIGHTLIFE

In recent years Budapest has justifiably gained a reputation as one of Europe's top nightlife destinations. Alongside its age-old cafe culture, it offers a magical blend of unique drinking holes, fantastic wine, home-grown firewaters and emerging craft beers, all served up with a warm Hungarian welcome and a wonderful sense of fun. The website www.wheretraveler.com/budapest is useful for nightlife listings.

Doblo   Wine Bar
(www.budapestwine.com; VII Dob utca 20; ⊙1pm-2am Sun-Wed, to 4am Thu-Sat; M1/2/3 Deák Ferenc tér) Brick lined and candlelit, Doblo is where you go to taste Hungarian wines, with scores available by the 1.5cL (15mL) glass for 900Ft to 2150Ft. There's food too, such as meat and cheese platters.

Léhűtő   Bar
(📞06 30 731 0430; www.facebook.com/lehuto.kezmuvessorozo; VII Holló utca 12-14; ⊙4pm-midnight Mon, to 2am Tue-Thu, to 4am Fri & Sat; 🛜; M1/2/3 Deák Ferenc tér) Drop into this very friendly basement bar if you fancy a craft beer, of which it has a large Hungarian and international range, with staff willing to advise and let you try before you buy. Coffee-based craft beer? Yep. There's also above-ground seating amid an often-buzzing crowd that gathers at this crossroads on warm nights.

DiVino Borbár   Wine Bar
(📞06 70 935 3980; www.divinoborbar.hu; V Szent István tér 3; ⊙4pm-midnight Sun-Wed, to 2am Thu-Sat; M1 Bajcsy-Zsilinszky út) Central and always heaving, DiVino is Budapest's most popular wine bar, as the crowds

 Ruin Pubs

Romkocsmák (ruin pubs) began to appear in the city from the early 2000s, when entrepreneurial free thinkers took over abandoned buildings and turned them into pop-up bars. At first a very word-of-mouth scene, the ruin bars' popularity grew exponentially and many have transformed from ramshackle, temporary sites full of flea-market furniture to more slick, year-round fixtures with covered areas to protect patrons from the winter elements. Budapest's first romkocsmá, **Szimpla Kert** (📞06 20 261 8669; www.szimpla.hu; VII Kazinczy utca 14; ⊙noon-4am Mon-Thu & Sat, 10am-4am Fri, 9am-5am Sun; M2 Astoria) is firmly on the drinking-tourists' trail, but remains a landmark place for a beverage.

Szimpla Kert
LUMOKRAJLINIOJ/SHUTTERSTOCK ©

spilling out onto the square in front of the Basilica of St Stephen in the warm weather attest. Choose from more than 140 wines produced by 36 winemakers under the age of 35, but be careful: those 0.15dL (15mL) glasses (650Ft to 3500Ft) go down quickly.

The glass deposit is 500Ft.

Instant   Club
(📞06 30 830 8747, 1-311 0704; www.instant.co.hu; VII Akácfa utca 51; ⊙4pm-6am; M1 Opera) We still love this 'ruin pub' on one of Pest's most vibrant nightlife strips and so do all our friends. It has 26 rooms, seven bars, seven stages and two gardens with underground DJs and dance parties. It's always heaving.

Where to Stay

In general, accommodation is more limited in the Buda neighbourhoods than on the other side of the Danube River in Pest. The districts of Erzsébetváros and Terézváros have the lion's share of Budapest's accommodation, though the area can be very noisy at night. Options on Castle Hill tend to be somewhat limited and in the upper price bracket. Belváros is close to just about everything, especially drinking and entertainment options, while Parliament is a great area to lay your hat as it's central but still just that little bit away from the noise. Accommodation in Óbuda and Buda Hills is thin on the ground.

Szatyor Bár és Galéria   Bar
(Carrier Bag Bar & Gallery; ☑1-279 0290; www.szatyorbar.com; XIII Bartók Béla út 36-38; ⊗noon-1am; ⓂM4 Móricz Zsigmond körtér, 🚋18, 19, 47, 49) Sharing the same building as the cafe **Hadik Kávéház** (☑1-279 0291; www.hadikkavehaz.com; XIII Bartók Béla út 36; ⊗noon-1am) and separated by just a door, the Szatyor is the funkier of the twins, with cocktails, street art on the walls and a Lada driven by the poet Endre Ady. Cool or what? There's food here, too (mains 1900Ft to 2400Ft).

Double Shot   Coffee
(☑06 70 674 4893; www.facebook.com/doubleshotspecialtycoffee; XIII Pozsonyi út 16; ⊗7am-8pm Mon-Thu, to 9pm Fri, 8am-9pm Sat, 8am-7pm Sun; 🚋4, 6) With an unfinished, grungy look, and break-your-neck stairs to the small seating area upstairs, this thimble-sized coffee shop is the brainchild of two expats. The artisan coffee from around the globe is excellent.

Kávé Műhely   Coffee
(☑06 30 852 8517; www.facebook.com/kavemuhely; II Fő utca 49; ⊗7.30am-6.30pm Mon-Fri, 9am-5pm Sat & Sun; ⓂM2 Batthyány tér, 🚋19, 41) This tiny coffee shop is one of the best

in the city. These guys roast their own beans, and their cakes and sandwiches are fantastic. Too hot for coffee? They've got craft beers and homemade lemonades, too. The attached gallery stages vibrant contemporary art exhibitions.

⭐ ENTERTAINMENT

Hungarian State Opera House   Opera
(Magyar Állami Operaház; ☑1-814 7100, box office 1-353 0170; www.opera.hu; VI Andrássy út 22; ⊗box office 10am-8pm; ⓂM1 Opera) The gorgeous neo-Renaissance opera house is worth a visit as much to admire the incredibly rich decoration inside as to view a performance and hear the perfect acoustics.

Liszt Music Academy   Classical Music
(Liszt Zeneakadémia; ☑1-462 4600, box office 1-321 0690; www.zeneakademia.hu; VI Liszt Ferenc tér 8; ⊗box office 10am-6pm; ⓂM1 Oktogon, 🚋4, 6) Performances at Budapest's most important concert hall are usually booked up at least a week in advance, but more expensive (though still affordable) last-minute tickets can sometimes be available. It's always worth checking.

Palace of Arts   Concert Venue
(Művészetek Palotája; ☑1-555 3300; www.mupa.hu; IX Komor Marcell utca 1; ⊗box office 10am-6pm; 🚋; 🚋2, 24, 🚈HÉV 7 Közvágóhíd) The two concert halls at this palatial arts centre by the Danube are the 1700-seat **Béla Bartók National Concert Hall** (Bartók Béla Nemzeti Hangversenyterem) and the smaller **Festival Theatre** (Fesztivál Színház), accommodating up to 450 people. Both are purported to have near-perfect acoustics. Students can pay 500Ft one hour before all performances for a standing-only ticket.

ℹ️ INFORMATION

Budapest Info (☑1-438 8080; www.budapestinfo.hu; V Sütő utca 2; ⊗8am-8pm; ⓂM1/2/3

Hungarian State Opera House

Deák Ferenc tér) is the main tourist office; there is another **branch** (Olof Palme sétány 5, City Ice Rink; ⊙9am-7pm; ⓂM1 Hősök tere) in City Park and info desks in the arrivals sections of Ferenc Liszt International Airport's Terminals 2A and 2B.

GETTING THERE & AWAY

AIR

Budapest's **Ferenc Liszt International Airport** (BUD; ☑1-296 7000; www.bud.hu) has two modern terminals side by side 24km southeast of the city centre.

TRAIN

Keleti Train Station (Keleti pályaudvar; VIII Kerepesi út 2-6; ⓂM2/M4 Keleti pályaudvar) Most international trains (and domestic traffic to/from the north and northeast) arrive here. **MÁV** (Magyar Államvasutak, Hungarian State Railways; ☑1-349 4949; www.mavcsoport.hu) links up with the European rail network in all directions.

Nyugati Train Station (Western Train Station; VI Nyugati tér) Trains from some international

destinations (eg Romania) and from the Danube Bend and Great Plain.

Déli Train Station (Déli pályaudvar; I Krisztina körút 37; ⓂM2 Déli pályaudvar) Trains from some destinations in the south, eg Osijek in Croatia and Sarajevo in Bosnia, as well as some trains from Vienna.

ⓘ GETTING AROUND

Travel passes valid for one day to one month are valid on all trams, buses, trolleybuses, HÉV suburban trains (within city limits) and metro lines.

Metro The quickest but least scenic way to get around. Runs from 4am to about 11.15pm.

Bus Extensive network of regular buses runs from around 4.15am to between 9pm and 11.30pm; from 11.30pm to just after 4am a network of 41 night buses (three digits beginning with '9') kicks in.

Tram Faster and more pleasant for sightseeing than buses; a network of 30 lines. Tram 6 runs overnight.

Trolleybus Mostly useful for getting to and around City Park in Pest.

Vienna, Austria

Few cities in the world waltz so effortlessly between the present and the past like Vienna. Its splendid historical face is easily recognised: grand imperial palaces and bombastic baroque interiors, revered opera houses and magnificent squares. But Vienna is also one of Europe's most dynamic urban spaces. A stone's throw from the Hofburg (Imperial Palace), the MuseumsQuartier houses provocative and high-profile contemporary art behind a striking basalt facade. In the Innere Stadt (Inner City), up-to-the-minute design stores sidle up to old-world confectioners, and Austro-Asian fusion restaurants stand alongside traditional Beisl (small taverns).

Two Days in Vienna

Start your day at Vienna's heart, the **Stephansdom** (p575), being awed by the cathedral's cavernous interior. Soak up the grandeur of the **Hofburg** (p570), a Habsburg architectural masterpiece, before ending the day with a craft beer at **Brickmakers Pub & Kitchen** (p583). Spend the morning of the second day in the **Kunsthistorisches Museum** (p569) and the afternoon in at least one of the museums in the **MuseumsQuartier** (p574).

Four Days in Vienna

Divide your morning between **Schloss Belvedere** (p576) and its magnificently landscaped French-style formal **gardens** (p577). Make your way to the **Prater** (p571), Vienna's playground of woods, meadows and sideshow attractions. Dedicate your final day to **Schloss Schönbrunn** (p567). If there's any time left check out **Karlskirche** (p576) or **Secession** (p576).

Looking for more castles? Take a train to Schloss Neuschwanstein (p520) or fly to Dubrovnik (p470).

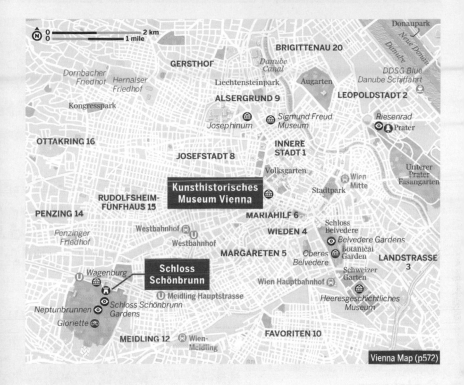

Arriving in Vienna

Vienna International Airport The frequent City Airport Train (CAT; €11, 15 minutes) runs from 6am to 11.30pm. There's also a cheaper but slower S7 suburban train (€4.40, 25 minutes) from the airport to Wien Mitte. A taxi costs €25 to €50.

Wien Hauptbahnhof Situated 3km south of Stephansdom, Vienna's main train station handles all international trains. It's linked to the centre by U-Bahn line 1, trams D and O, and buses 13A and 69A. A taxi to the centre costs about €10.

Where to Stay

Vienna's lodgings cover it all, from inexpensive youth hostels to luxury establishments where chandeliers, antique furniture and original 19th-century oil paintings abound. In between are homey, often family-run *Pensionen* (guesthouses), many traditional, and less ostentatious hotels, plus a smart range of apartments. It's wise to book ahead at all times; for the best value, especially in the centre, at least a few weeks in advance is advisable.

Schloss Schönbrunn

The Habsburg Empire is revealed in all its frescoed, gilded, chandelier-lit glory in the wondrously ornate apartments of Schloss Schönbrunn, which are among Europe's best-preserved baroque interiors.

Great For...

☑ **Don't Miss**

The Great Gallery, Neptunbrunnen, Gloriette and Wagenburg.

State Apartments

The frescoed **Blue Staircase** makes a regal ascent to the palace's upper level. First up are the 19th-century apartments of Emperor Franz Josef I and his beloved wife Elisabeth. The tour whisks you through lavishly stuccoed, chandelier-lit apartments such as the **Billiard Room**, where army officials would pot a few balls while waiting to attend an audience, and Franz Josef's **study**, where the emperor worked tirelessly from 5am.

In the exquisite white-and-gold **Mirror Room**, a six-year-old Mozart performed for a rapturous Maria Theresia in 1762. Fairest of all, however, is the 40m-long **Great Gallery**, where the Habsburgs threw balls and banquets, a frothy vision of stucco and chandeliers, topped with a fresco by Italian artist Gregorio Guglielmi showing the glorification of Maria Theresia's reign. Decor

Schönbrunn Palace Main Courtyard with fountain

SCHLOSS SCHÖNBRUNN KULTUR- UND BETRIEBSGESMBH PHOTOGRAPHER: ALEXANDER E. KOLLER ©

ⓘ Need to Know

www.schoenbrunn.at; 13, Schönbrunner Schlossstrasse 47; adult/child Imperial Tour €13.30/9.80, Grand Tour €16.40/10.80, Grand Tour with guide €19.40/12.30; ⊘8.30am-6.30pm Jul & Aug, to 5.30pm Sep, Oct & Apr-Jun, to 5pm Nov-Mar; ⓊHietzing

✕ Take a Break

Head to **Waldemar** (www.waldemar-tages bar.at; 13, Altgasse 6; lunch mains €4.30-6.90; ⊘7.30am-8pm Mon-Fri, 9am-8pm Sat & Sun) for bolstering coffee and cake or a superhealthy lunch.

★ Top Tip

If you plan to see several sights at Schönbrunn, it's worth buying one of the combined tickets, which can be purchased in advance online.

aside, this was where the historic meeting between John F Kennedy and Soviet leader Nikita Khrushchev took place in 1961.

If you have a Grand Tour ticket, you can continue through to the palace's **east wing** Franz Stephan's apartments begin in the sublime **Blue Chinese Salon**, where the intricate floral wall paintings are done on Chinese rice paper. The negotiations that led to the collapse of the Austro-Hungarian Empire in 1918 were held here.

Schloss Schönbrunn Gardens

The beautifully tended formal **gardens** (⊘6.30am-dusk) FREE of the palace, arranged in the French style, are appealing whatever the season: a symphony of colour in the summer and a wash of greys and browns in winter. The grounds, which were opened to the public by Joseph II in 1779,

hide a number of attractions in the tree-lined avenues (arranged according to a grid and star-shaped system between 1750 and 1755), including the 1781 **Neptunbrunnen** (Neptune Fountain, adult/child €3.60/2.80), a riotous ensemble from Greek mythology, and the crowning glory, the 1775 **Gloriette** (adult/child €3.60/2.80, ⊘9am-6pm, closed early Nov–mid-Mar).

Wagenburg

The **Wagenburg** (Imperial Coach Collection; www.kaiserliche-wagenburg.at; adult/child €8/ free; ⊘9am-5pm mid-Mar–Nov, 10am-4pm Dec–mid-Mar) is *Pimp My Ride* imperial style. On display is a vast array of carriages, including Emperor Franz Stephan's coronation carriage, with its ornate gold plating, Venetian glass panes and painted cherubs. The whole thing weighs an astonishing 4000kg.

 ANDREI RYBACHUK/GETTY IMAGES ©

Kunsthistorisches Museum Vienna

Occupying a neoclassical building as sumptuous as the art it contains, this museum takes you on a time-travel treasure hunt – from classical Rome to Egypt and the Renaissance.

Great For...

☑ Don't Miss

Dutch Golden Age paintings, the Kunstkammer and the Offering Chapel of Ka-ni-nisut.

Picture Gallery

The vast Picture Gallery is by far and away the most impressive of the museum's collections. First up is the German Renaissance, where the key focus is the prized Dürer collection, followed by the Flemish baroque, epitomised by Rubens, Van Dyck and Pieter Bruegel the Elder.

In the 16th- and 17th-century Dutch Golden Age paintings, the desire to faithfully represent reality is captured in works by Rembrandt, Ruisdael and Vermeer.

High on your artistic agenda in the 16th-century Venetian rooms should be Titian's *Nymph and Shepherd* (1570), Veronese's dramatic *Lucretia* (1583) and Tintoretto's *Susanna at her Bath* (1556).

Devotion is central to Raphael's *Madonna of the Meadow* (1506), one of the true masterpieces of the High Renaissance, just as it is to the *Madonna of the Rosary* (1601),

Museum interior

Kunsthistorisches Museum Vienna

❶ Need to Know

KHM, Museum of Art History; www.khm.at; 01, Maria-Theresien-Platz; adult/child incl Neue Burg museums €15/free; ⊙10am 6pm Fri-Wed, to 9pm Thu Jun-Aug, closed Mon Sep-May; Ⓤ Museumsquartier, Volkstheater

✕ Take a Break

Head to hip **Said the Butcher to the Cow** (www.butcher-cow.at; 01, Opernring 11; mains €10.80-31.90; ⊙kitchen 5-11pm Tue-Sat, bar 5pm-1am Tue & Wed, 5pm-2am Thu-Sat; ⍟D, 1, 2, 71 Kärntner Ring/Oper, Ⓤ Karlsplatz) for a post-museum burger.

★ Top Tip

If your time's limited, skip straight to the Old Master paintings in the Picture Gallery.

a stirring Counter-Reformation altarpiece by Italian baroque artist Caravaggio.

Of the artists represented in the final rooms dedicated to Spanish, French and English painting, the undoubted star is Spanish court painter Velázquez.

Kunstkammer

The Habsburgs filled their Kunstkammer (cabinet of art and curiosities) with an encyclopaedic collection of the rare and the precious: from narwhal-tusk cups to table holders encrusted with fossilised shark teeth. Its 20 themed rooms containing 2200 artworks open a fascinating window on the obsession with collecting curios in royal circles in Renaissance and baroque times.

Egyptian & Near Eastern Art

Decipher the mysteries of Egyptian civil-isations with a chronological romp through this miniature Giza of a collection. Here the **Offering Chapel of Ka-ni-nisut** spells out the life of the high-ranking 5th-dynasty official in reliefs and hieroglyphs.

In the Near Eastern collection, the representation of a prowling lion from Babylon's triumphal Ishtar Gate (604–562 BC) is the big attraction.

Greek & Roman Antiquities

This rich Greek and Roman repository reveals the imperial scope for collecting classical antiquities, with 2500 objects traversing three millennia from the Cypriot Bronze Age to early medieval times.

Among the Greek art is a fragment from the Parthenon's northern frieze, while the sizeable Roman stash includes the 4th-century AD *Theseus Mosaic* from Salzburg and the captivating 3rd-century AD *Lion Hunt* relief.

◎ SIGHTS

◎ The Hofburg & Around

Hofburg   Palace
(Imperial Palace; www.hofburg-wien.at; 01,
Michaelerkuppel; 🚌1A, 2A Michaelerplatz, 🚋D,
1, 2, 46, 49, 71 Burgring, Ⓤ Herrengasse) FREE
Nothing symbolises Austria's resplendent
cultural heritage more than its Hofburg,
home base of the Habsburgs from 1273 to
1918. The oldest section is the 13th-century
Schweizerhof (Swiss Courtyard), named
after the Swiss guards who used to protect
its precincts. The Renaissance **Swiss gate**
dates from 1553. The courtyard adjoins
a larger courtyard, **In der Burg**, with a
monument to Emperor Franz II adorning its
centre. The palace now houses the Austrian
president's offices and a raft of museums.

Kaiserappartements   Palace
(Imperial Apartments; 📞01-533 75 70; www.
hofburg-wien.at; 01, Michaelerplatz; adult/
child €12.90/7.70, incl guided tour €15.90/9.20;
🕘9am-6pm Jul & Aug, to 5.30pm Sep-Jun; Ⓤ Herrengasse) The Kaiserappartements, once
the official living quarters of Franz Josef I

and Empress Elisabeth, are dazzling in their
chandelier-lit opulence. The highlight is the
Sisi Museum, devoted to Austria's most
beloved empress, which has a strong focus
on the clothing and jewellery of Austria's
monarch. Multilingual audio guides are included in the admission price. Guided tours
take in the Kaiserappartements, the Sisi
Museum and the **Silberkammer** (Silver
Depot), whose largest silver service caters
to 140 dinner guests.

Kaiserliche
Schatzkammer   Museum
(Imperial Treasury; www.kaiserliche-schatz
kammer.at; 01, Schweizerhof; adult/child €12/free;
🕘9am-5.30pm Wed-Mon; Ⓤ Herrengasse) The
Kaiserliche Schatzkammer contains secular
and ecclesiastical treasures, including
devotional images and altars, particularly
from the baroque era, of priceless value and
splendour – the sheer wealth of this collection of crown jewels is staggering. As you
walk through the rooms you see magnificent
treasures such as a golden rose, diamond-
studded Turkish sabres, a 2680-carat

Sisi Museum, Imperial Apartments and Silver Collection, Hofburg

Colombian emerald and, the highlight of the treasury, the imperial crown.

Spanish Riding School
Performing Arts

(Spanische Hofreitschule; ☑01-533 90 31; www.srs.at; 01, Michaelerplatz 1; performances €25-217; ☺hours vary; ☐1A, 2A Michaelerplatz, ⓤHerrengasse) The world-famous Spanish Riding School is a Viennese institution truly reminiscent of the imperial Habsburg era. This unequalled equestrian show is performed by Lipizzaner stallions formerly kept at an imperial stud established at Lipizza (hence the name). These graceful stallions perform an equine ballet to a program of classical music while the audience watches from pillared balconies – or from a cheaper standing-room area – and the chandeliers shimmer above.

Albertina
Gallery

(www.albertina.at; 01, Albertinaplatz 3; adult/child €12.90/free; ☺10am-6pm Thu-Tue, to 9pm Wed; ☐D, 1, 2, 71 Kärntner Ring/Oper, ⓤKarlsplatz, Stephansplatz) Once used as the Habsburgs' imperial apartments for guests, the Albertina is now a repository for what's regularly touted as the greatest collection of graphic art in the world. The permanent Batliner Collection – with over 100 paintings covering the period from Monet to Picasso – and the high quality of changing exhibitions really make the Albertina worthwhile.

Multilingual audio guides (€4) cover all exhibition sections and tell the story behind the apartments and the works on display.

Neue Burg Museums
Museum

(☑01-525 240; www.khm.at; 01, Heldenplatz; adult/child €15/free; ☺10am-6pm Wed-Sun; ☐D, 1, 2, 71 Burgring, ⓤHerrengasse, Museumsquartier) The Neue Burg is home to the three Neue Burg Museums. The **Sammlung Alter Musik Instrumente** (Collection of Ancient Musical Instruments) contains a wonderfully diverse array of instruments. The **Ephesos Museum** features artefacts unearthed during Austrian archaeologists' excavations at Ephesus in Turkey

 Prater & the Riesenrad

Spread across 60 sq km, central Vienna's largest **park** (www.wiener-prater.at; ♿; ⓤPraterstern) comprises woodlands of poplar and chestnut, meadows, and tree-lined boulevards, as well as children's playgrounds, a swimming pool, a golf course and a race track. Fringed by statuesque chestnut trees that are ablaze with russet and gold in autumn and frilly with white blossom in spring, the central Hauptallee avenue is the main vein. It runs straight as an arrow from the Praterstern to the **Lusthaus** (☑01-728 95 65; 02, Freudenau 254; mains €11-19; ☺noon-10pm Mon-Fri, to 6pm Sat & Sun, shorter hours winter; ☎; ☐77A), a former 16th-century Habsburg hunting lodge that today shelters a chandelier-lit cafe and restaurant serving classic Viennese fare.

Twirling above the **Würstelprater** amusement park is one of the city's most visible icons, the **Riesenrad** (www.wienerriesenrad.com; 02, Prater 90; adult/child €9.50/4; ☺9am-11.45pm, shorter hours winter; ♿; ⓤPraterstern). It's top of every Prater wish-list; at least for anyone of an age to recall Orson Welles' cuckoo clock speech in British film noir *The Third Man* (1949), set in a shadowy postwar Vienna. Built in 1897 by Englishman Walter B Basset, the Ferris wheel rises to 65m and takes about 20 minutes to rotate its 430-tonne weight one complete circle – giving you ample time to snap some fantastic shots of the city spread out below.

Riesenrad Ferris wheel and the Prater
MRGB/SHUTTERSTOCK ©

Vienna

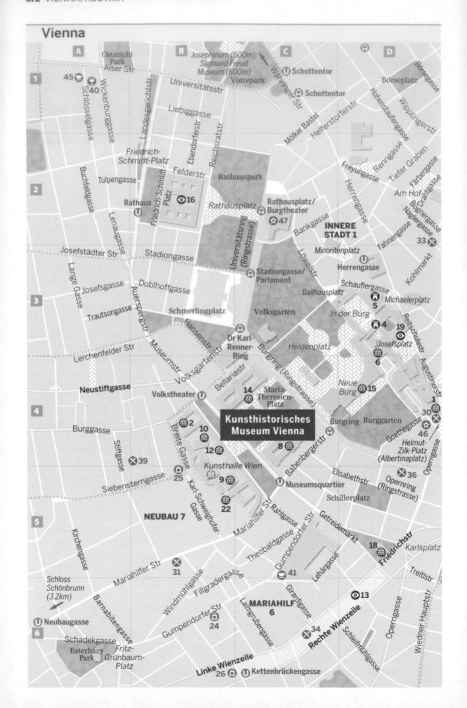

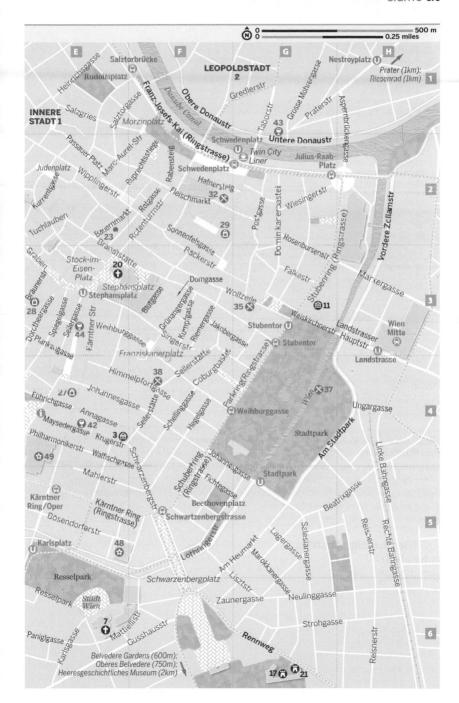

Vienna

between 1895 and 1906. The **Hofjägd und Rüstkammer** (Arms and Armour) museum contains ancient armour dating mainly from the 15th and 16th centuries. Admission includes the Kunsthistorisches Museum (p568) and all three Neue Burg museums. An audio guide costs €4.

◉ The Museum District & Neubau

MuseumsQuartier Museum
(Museum Quarter; MQ; www.mqw.at; 07, Museumsplatz; ⊙information & ticket centre 10am-7pm; ⓊMuseumsquartier, Volkstheater) The MuseumsQuartier is a remarkable ensemble of museums, cafes, restaurants and bars inside former imperial stables designed by Fischer von Erlach. This breeding ground of Viennese cultural life

is the perfect place to hang out and watch or meet people on warm evenings. With over 60,000 sq metres of exhibition space – including the Leopold Museum (p575), MUMOK (p575), **Kunsthalle** (Arts Hall; ☏01-521 890; www.kunsthallewien.at; both halls adult/child €12/free; ⊙11am-7pm Fri-Wed, to 9pm Thu), **Architekturzentrum** (Vienna Architecture Centre; ☏01-522 31 15; www.azw.at; exhibition prices vary, library admission free; ⊙architecture centre 10am-7pm, library 10am-5.30pm Mon, Wed & Fri, to 7pm Sat & Sun, closed Thu; ◻49 Volkstheater, ⓊVolkstheater, Museumsquartier) and **Zoom** (☏01-524 79 08; www.kindermuseum.at; exhibition adult/child €4/free, activities child €4-6, accompanying adult free; ⊙12.45-5pm Tue-Sun Jul & Aug, 8.30am-4pm Tue-Fri, 9.45am-4pm Sat & Sun Sep-Jun, activity times vary) – the complex is one of the world's most ambitious cultural hubs.

Leopold Museum   Museum

(www.leopoldmuseum.org; 07, Museumsplatz 1;
adult/child €13/8; ⊙10am-6pm Fri-Wed, to 9pm
Thu Jun-Aug, 10am-6pm Wed & Fri-Mon, to 9pm
Thu Sep-May; ⓊVolkstheater, Museumsquartier)
Part of the MuseumsQuartier, the Leopold
Museum is named after ophthalmologist
Rudolf Leopold, who, after buying his first
Egon Schiele for a song as a young student
in 1950, amassed a huge private collection
of mainly 19th-century and modernist
Austrian artworks. In 1994 he sold the
lot – 5266 paintings – to the Austrian
government for €160 million (individually,
the paintings would have made him €574
million), and the Leopold Museum was
born. **Café Leopold** (www.cafe-leopold.at;
⊙10am midnight Sun Wed, to 4am Thu, to 6am
Fri & Sat; 🛜) is located on the top floor.

MUMOK   Gallery

(Museum Moderner Kunst; Museum of Modern
Art; www.mumok.at; 07, Museumsplatz 1; adult/
child €11/free; ⊙2-7pm Mon, 10am-7pm Tue, Wed
& Fri-Sun, 10am-9pm Thu; 🚌49 Volkstheater,
ⓊVolkstheater, Museumsquartier) The dark
basalt edifice and sharp corners of the
Museum Moderner Kunst are a complete
contrast to the MuseumsQuartier's historical sleeve. Inside, MUMOK contains Vienna's finest collection of 20th-century art,
centred on fluxus, nouveau realism, pop art
and photo-realism. The best of expressionism, cubism, minimal art and Viennese
Actionism is represented in a collection of
9000 works that are rotated and exhibited
by theme – but note that sometimes all this
Actionism is packed away to make room for
temporary exhibitions.

Naturhistorisches
Museum   Museum

(Museum of Natural History; www.nhm-wien.ac.at;
01, Maria-Theresien-Platz; adult/child €10/free,
rooftop tours €8; ⊙9am-6.30pm Thu-Mon, to
9pm Wed, rooftop tours in English 3pm Fri, Sat &
Sun; ⓊMuseumsquartier, Volkstheater) Vienna's
astounding Naturhistorisches Museum
covers four billion years of natural history in
a blink. With its exquisitely stuccoed, frescoed halls and eye-catching cupola, this late
19th-century building is the identical twin of
the Kunsthistorisches Museum which sits
opposite. Among its minerals, fossils and
dinosaur bones are one-of-a-kind finds like
the minuscule 25,000-year-old Venus von
Willendorf and a peerless 1100-piece me-
teorite collection. Panoramic rooftop tours
take you onto the building's roof to view
the ornate architecture up-close; children
under 12 aren't allowed.

Rathaus   Landmark

(City Hall; www.wien.gv.at; 01, Rathausplatz 1;
⊙tours 1pm Mon, Wed & Fri Sep-Jun, 1pm Mon-Fri
Jul & Aug; 🚊D, 1, 2 Rathaus, ⓊRathaus) **FREE**
The crowning glory of the Ringstrasse
boulevard's 19th-century architectural
ensemble, Vienna's neo-Gothic City Hall
was completed in 1883 by Friedrich von
Schmidt of Cologne Cathedral fame and
modelled on Flemish city halls. From the
fountain-filled **Rathauspark**, where Josef
Lanner and Johann Strauss I, fathers of the
Viennese waltz, are immortalised in bronze,
you get the full effect of its facade of lacy
stonework, pointed arch windows and spin-
dly turrets. One-hour guided tours are in
German; multilingual audio guides are free.

◉ Stephansdom &
the Historic Centre

Stephansdom   Cathedral

(St Stephen's Cathedral; 📞tours 01-515 323 054;
www.stephanskirche.at; 01, Stephansplatz; main
nave adult & one child €6, additional child €1.50;
⊙public visits 9-11.30am & 1-4.30pm Mon-Sat,
1-4.30pm Sun; ⓊStephansplatz) Vienna's
Gothic masterpiece, Stephansdom – or
Steffl (Little Stephan), as it's ironically nicknamed – is Vienna's pride and joy. A church
has stood here since the 12th century, and
reminders of this are the Romanesque
Riesentor (Giant Gate) and **Heidentürme**.
From the exterior, the first thing that will
strike you is the glorious tiled **roof**, with
its dazzling row of chevrons and Austrian
eagles. Inside, the magnificent Gothic
stone **pulpit** presides over the main nave,
fashioned in 1515 by Anton Pilgrim.

Haus der Musik — Museum

(www.hausdermusik.com; 01, Seilerstätte 30; adult/child €13/6, with Mozarthaus Vienna €18/8; ☺10am-10pm; ⌂D, 1, 2, 71 to Kärntner Ring/Oper, ⓊKarlsplatz) The Haus der Musik explains the world of sound and music to adults and children alike in an amusing and interactive way (in English and German). Exhibits are spread over four floors and cover everything from how sound is created, from Vienna's Philharmonic Orchestra to street noises. The staircase between floors acts as a piano, and the glassed-in ground-floor courtyard hosts musical events. Admission is discounted after 8pm.

◉ Alsergrund & the University District

Sigmund Freud Museum — Museum, House

(www.freud-museum.at; 09, Berggasse 19; adult/child €10/4; ☺10am-6pm; ⌂D, ⓊSchottentor, Schottenring) Sigmund Freud is a bit like the telephone – once he happened, there was no going back. This is where Freud spent his most prolific years and developed the most significant of his ground-breaking theories; he moved here with his family in 1891 and stayed until forced into exile by the Nazis in 1938.

Josephinum — Museum

(www.josephinum.meduniwien.ac.at; 09, Währinger Strasse 25; adult/child €8/free, guided tours €4; ☺4-8pm Wed, 10am-6pm Fri-Sat, guided tours 11am Fri; ♿; ⓊWähringer Strasse/Volksoper) Architecture fans sometimes visit this Enlightenment-era complex for its superb 1785 neo-classical structures alone, although Joseph II's purpose-built medical academy for army surgeons does, in fact, house the city's most unusual museum. The highlight is its large collection of 200-year-old anatomical and obstetric models made of wax: while designed as visual aids for teaching, they were also intended for public viewing and to this day are exhibited in their original display cases, made of rosewood and Venetian glass.

◉ Karlsplatz & Around Naschmarkt

Secession — Museum

(www.secession.at; 01, Friedrichstrasse 12; adult/child €9/5.50; ☺10am-6pm Tue-Sun; ⓊKarlsplatz) In 1897, 19 progressive artists swam away from the mainstream Künstlerhaus artistic establishment to form the *Wiener Secession* (Vienna Secession). Among their number were Klimt, Josef Hoffman, Kolo Moser and Joseph M Olbrich. Olbrich designed the new exhibition centre of the Secessionists, which combined sparse functionality with stylistic motifs. Its biggest draw is Klimt's exquisitely gilded *Beethoven Frieze*. Guided tours in English (€3) lasting one hour take place at 11am Saturday. An audio guide costs €3.

Karlskirche — Church

(St Charles Church; www.karlskirche.at; 04, Karlsplatz; adult/child €8/free; ☺9am-6pm Mon-Sat, noon-7pm Sun; ⓊKarlsplatz) Built between 1716 and 1739, after a vow by Karl VI at the end of the 1713 plague, Vienna's finest baroque church rises at the southeast corner of Resselpark. It was designed and commenced by Johann Bernhard Fischer von Erlach and completed by his son Joseph. The huge elliptical copper **dome** reaches 72m; the highlight is the lift (elevator) to the cupola (included in admission) for a close-up view of the intricate frescoes by Johann Michael Rottmayr. Audio guides cost €2.

◉ Schloss Belvedere to the Canal

Schloss Belvedere — Palace

(www.belvedere.at; adult/child Oberes Belvedere €14/free, Unteres Belvedere €12/free, combined ticket €20/free; ☺10am-6pm; ⌂D, 71 Schwarzenbergplatz, ⓊTaubstummengasse, Südtiroler Platz) A masterpiece of total art, Schloss Belvedere is one of the world's finest baroque palaces. Designed by Johann Lukas von Hildebrandt (1668–1745), it was built for the brilliant military strategist Prince Eugene of Savoy, conqueror of the Turks in 1718. What giddy romance is evoked in its

Karlskirche

sumptuously frescoed halls, replete with artworks by Klimt, Schiele and Kokoschka; what stories are conjured in its landscaped **gardens** (03, Rennweg/Prinz-Eugen-Strasse; ☺6.30am-8pm, shorter hours in winter; 🚊D), which drop like the fall of a theatre curtain to reveal Vienna's skyline.

The first of the palace's two buildings is the **Oberes Belvedere** (Upper Belvedere; 03, Prinz-Eugen-Strasse 27; adult/child €14/free; ☺10am-6pm), showcasing Gustav Klimt's *The Kiss* (1908), the perfect embodiment of Viennese art nouveau, alongside other late 19th- to early 20th-century Austrian works. The lavish **Unteres Belvedere** (Lower Belvedere; 03, Rennweg 6; adult/child €12/free; ☺10am-6pm Thu-Tue, to 9pm Wed; 🚊D), with its richly frescoed Marmorsaal (Marble Hall), sits at the end of sculpture-dotted gardens.

Heeresgeschichtliches Museum   Museum

(Museum of Military History; www.hgm.or.at; 03, Arsenal; adult/under 19yr €6/free, 1st Sun of month free; ☺9am-5pm; ⓤSüdtiroler Platz) The superb Heeresgeschichtliches Museum is housed in the Arsenal, a large neo-Byzantine barracks and munitions depot. Spread over two floors, the museum works its way from the Thirty Years' War (1618–48) to WWII, taking in the Hungarian Uprising and the Austro-Prussian War (ending in 1866), the Napoleonic and Turkish Wars, and WWI. Highlights on the 1st floor include the Great Seal of Mustafa Pasha, which fell to Prince Eugene of Savoy in the Battle of Zenta in 1697.

Museum für Angewandte Kunst   Museum

(MAK, Museum of Applied Arts; www.mak.at; 01, Stubenring 5; adult/under 19yr €9.90/free, 6-10pm Tue free, tours €2; ☺10am-6pm Wed-Sun, to 10pm Tue, English tours noon Sun; 🚊2 Stubentor, ⓤStubentor) MAK is devoted to craftsmanship and art forms in everyday life. Each exhibition room showcases a different style, which includes Renaissance, baroque, orientalism, historicism, empire, art deco and the distinctive metalwork of the Wiener Werkstätte. Contemporary artists were invited to present the rooms in ways they felt were appropriate, resulting in eye-catching and unique displays. The

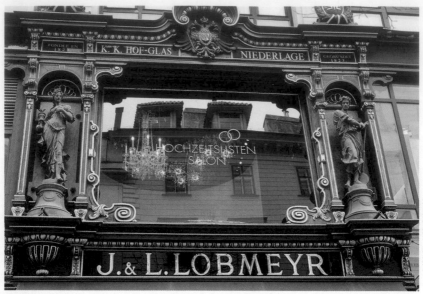

J&L Lobmeyr Vienna

20th-century design and architecture room is one of the most fascinating, and Frank Gehry's cardboard chair is a gem.

🏃 ACTIVITIES

Wrenkh Cookery School   Cooking
(📞01-533 15 26; www.wrenkh-wien.at; 01, Bauernmarkt 10; 🕐per person from €48; Ⓤ Stephansplatz) This cookery school based in its eponymous **restaurant** (mains €8-25; 🕐11am-11pm Mon-Sat; 🖊) has classes in English and German covering Austrian classics such as schnitzels, *Tafelspitz* (boiled beef), fresh-water fish, and apple strudel, along with international cuisines (Indian, Thai etc) and vegetarian and vegan cuisine. Look out for foraging expeditions, too. Courses start from €48 for 2½ hours to €130 for 6 hours. Check programs online.

Donauinsel   Island
(Danube Island; Ⓤ Donauinsel) The svelte Danube Island stretches some 21.5km from opposite Klosterneuburg in the north to the Nationalpark Donau-Auen in the south and splits the Danube in two, creating a separate arm known as the Neue Donau (New Danube). Created in 1970, it is Vienna's aquatic playground, with sections of beach (don't expect much sand) for swimming, boating and a little waterskiing.

🛍 SHOPPING

Beer Lovers   Drinks
(www.beerlovers.at; 06, Gumpendorfer Strasse 35; 🕐11am-8pm Mon-Fri, 10am-5pm Sat; Ⓤ Kettenbrückengasse) A wonderland of craft beers, this emporium stocks over 1000 labels from over 125 different breweries in over 70 styles, with more being sourced every day. Tastings are offered regularly, and cold beers are available in the walk-in glass fridge and in refillable growlers. It also stocks craft ciders, small-batch liqueurs and boutique nonalcoholic drinks such as ginger beers.

Meinl am Graben   Food & Drinks
(www.meinlamgraben.at; 01, Graben 19; 🕐8am-7.30pm Mon-Fri, 9am-6pm Sat; Ⓤ Stephansplatz) Vienna's most prestigious providore brims with quality European foodstuffs.

Chocolate and confectionery dominate the ground floor, and impressive cheese and cold meats are tantalisingly displayed upstairs. The basement stocks European and Austrian wine and fruit liqueurs and has a classy on-site wine bar; there's also an exceptional on-site restaurant (p583).

Wiener Rosenmanufaktur   Food, Cosmetics
(www.wienerrosenmanufaktur.at; 01, Schönlaterngasse 7; ⊙3-7pm Mon-Fri, 11am-5pm Sat Jul & Aug, 1-6.30pm Mon-Fri, 11am-6.30pm Sat, 2-5pm Sun Sep-Jun; Ⓤ Schwedenplatz) Roses grown by Ingrid Maria Heldstab in her garden in Vienna's 23rd district are used in an incredible array of products, from jams (including spicy versions with ginger), jellies and liqueurs – which you can taste in store – to soaps, aromatic oils and other cosmetics. The tiny shop occupies one of Vienna's oldest buildings, the Basiliskenhaus, which dates from 1212.

J&L Lobmeyr Vienna   Homewares
(www.lobmeyr.at; 01, Kärntner Strasse 26; ⊙10am-7pm Mon-Fri, to 6pm Sat; Ⓤ Stephansplatz) Reached by a beautifully ornate wrought-iron staircase, this is one of Vienna's most lavish retail experiences. The collection of Biedermeier pieces, Loos-designed sets, fine/arty glassware and porcelain on display here glitters from the lights of the chandelier-festooned atrium. Lobmeyr has been in business since 1823, when it exclusively supplied the imperial court.

Steiff   Toys
(www.steiff-galerie-wien.at; 01, Bräunerstrasse 3; ⊙10am-12.30pm & 1.30-6pm Mon-Fri, 10am-12.30pm & 1.30-5pm Sat; Ⓤ Stephansplatz) Founded in Germany in the late 19th century, Steiff is widely regarded as the original creator of the teddy bear, which it presented at the Leipzig Toy Fair in 1903: an American businessman bought 3000 and sold them under the name 'teddy bear' after US president Theodore ('Teddy') Roosevelt. Today its flagship Austrian shop is

 ### Naschmarkt & Flohmarkt

Vienna's famous **market** (www.wiener naschmarkt.eu; 06, Linke & Rechte Wienzeile; ⊙6am-7.30pm Mon-Fri, to 6pm Sat; Ⓤ Kettenbrückengasse) and **eating strip** (www.naschmarkt-deli.at; 04, Naschmarkt stand 421-436; dishes €6.50-16.50; ⊙7am-midnight Mon-Sat; Ⓤ Kettenbrückengasse) began life as a farmers market in the 18th century, when the fruit market on Freyung was moved here.

The fruits of the Orient poured in, the predecessors of the modern-day sausage stand were erected, and sections were set aside for coal, wood and farming tools and machines. Officially, it became known as Naschmarkt ('munch market') in 1905, a few years after Otto Wagner bedded the Wien River down in its open-topped stone and concrete sarcophagus. This Otto Wagnerian horror was a blessing for Naschmarkt, because it created space to expand. Today the Naschmarkt is not only the place to shop for food, but also has the weekly Flohmarkt antique market.

One of the best flea markets in Europe, and a Vienna institution, **Flohmarkt** (Flea Market; 05, Linke Wienzeile; ⊙6.30am-6pm Sat; Ⓤ Kettenbrückengasse) brims with antiques and *Altwaren* (old wares). Stalls hawking books, clothes, records, ancient electrical goods, old postcards, ornaments and carpets stretch for several blocks. Arrive early, as it gets increasingly crammed as the morning wears on, and be prepared to haggle.

Naschmarkt

🍽 Viennese Specialities

Vienna has a strong repertoire of traditional dishes. One or two are variations on dishes from other regions. Classics include the following:

Schnitzel *Wiener Schnitzel* should always be crumbed veal, but pork is gaining ground in some places.

Goulash *Rindsgulasch* (beef goulash) is everywhere in Vienna. Originating in Hungary, the Austrian version is often served with *Semmelknoedel* (bread dumplings).

Tafelspitz Traditionally this boiled prime beef swims in the juices of locally produced *Suppengrün* (fresh soup vegetables), before being served with *Kren* (horseradish) sauce.

Beuschel Offal, usually sliced lung and heart, with a slightly creamy sauce.

Backhendl Fried, breaded chicken, often called *steirischer Backhendl* (Styrian fried chicken).

Zwiebelrostbraten Slices of roast beef smothered in gravy and fried onions.

Schinkenfleckerln Oven-baked ham and noodle casserole.

Bauernschmaus Platter of cold meats.

The undeniable monarchs of all desserts are *Kaiserschmarrn* (sweet pancake with raisins) and *Apfelstrudel* (apple strudel), but also look out for *Marillenknödel* (apricot dumplings) in summer.

Wiener Schnitzel
CARLY HULLS/LONELY PLANET ©

filled with adorable bears, along with other premium quality cuddly toys.

Die Werkbank Design
(www.werkbank.cc; 07, Breite Gasse 1; ⊙noon-6.30pm Tue-Fri, 11am-5pm Sat; UVolkstheater) Furniture, lamps, rugs, vases, jewellery, watches, graphic art, bags, even bicycles are among the creations you might find on display at 'The Workbench', an all-white space that operates as a design collective, where some of Vienna's most innovative designers showcase their works.

Dirndlherz Clothing
(www.dirndlherz.at; 07, Lerchenfelder Strasse 50; ⊙11am-6pm Thu & Fri, to 4pm Sat; UVolkstheater) Putting her own spin on alpine fashion, Austrian designer Gabriela Urabl creates one-of-a-kind, high-fashion *Dirndls* (women's traditional dress), from sassy purple-velvet bosom-lifters to 1950s-style gingham numbers and *Dirndls* emblazoned with quirky motifs like pop-art and punk-like conical metal studs. T-shirts with taglines like *'Mei Dirndl is in da Wäsch'* ('My Dirndl is in the wash') are also available.

🍴 EATING

Mamamon Thai €
(☑01-942 31 55; www.mamamonthaikitchen.com; 08, Albertgasse 15; mains €7-9.50; ⊙11.30am-9.30pm Mon-Fri, noon-9.30pm Sat; UJosefstädter Strasse, Rathaus) Owner Piano, who named her restaurant for her mum Mon, has spiced up Vienna's burgeoning Southeast Asian food scene with a menu of southern Thai flavours, street-style decor and an indie soundtrack. On mild nights, a young, happy crowd spills out into the courtyard, while single diners pull up a stool at the large communal table or window seats within.

Bitzinger Würstelstand am Albertinaplatz Street Food €
(www.bitzinger-wien.at; 01, Albertinaplatz; sausages €3.40-4.40; ⊙8am-4am; 🚋Kärntner Ring/Oper, UKarlsplatz, Stephansplatz) Behind

the Staatsoper, Vienna's best sausage stand has cult status. Bitzinger offers the contrasting spectacle of ladies and gents dressed to the nines, sipping beer, wine (from €2.30) or Joseph Perrier Champagne (€19.90 for 0.2L) while tucking into sausages at outdoor tables or the heated counter after performances. Mustard (€0.40) comes in *süss* (sweet; ie mild) or *scharf* (fiercely hot).

Eis Greissler   Ice Cream €

(www.eis-greissler.at; 06, Mariahilfer Strasse 33; 1/2/3/4/5 scoops €1.50/2.80/3.80/4.80/5.30; ⏰11am-10pm; Ⓤ Museumsquartier) 🍽 The inevitable queue makes Eis Greissler easy to spot. Locals flock here whatever the weather for ice cream made from organic milk, yoghurt and cream from its own farm in Lower Austria, and vegans are well catered for with soy and oat milk varieties. All-natural flavours vary seasonally but might include cinnamon, pear, strawberry, raspberry, chocolate, hazelnut or butter caramel.

Lingenhel   Modern European €€

(📞01-710 15 66; www.lingenhel.com; 03, Landstrasser Hauptstrasse 74; mains €19-24; ⏰shop 8am-8pm, restaurant 8am-10pm Mon-Sat; Ⓤ Rochusgasse) One of Vienna's most exciting gastro newcomers, Lingenhel is an ultra-slick deli-shop-bar-restaurant, lodged in a 200-year-old house. Salamis, wines and own-dairy cheeses tempt in the shop, while much-lauded chef Daniel Hoffmeister helms the kitchen in the pared-back, whitewashed restaurant. The season-inflected food – simple as char with kohlrabi and pork belly with aubergines – tastes profoundly of what it ought to.

Punks   Modern European €€

(📞0664 275 70 72; www.punks.wien; 08, Florianigasse 50; small plates €4.50) The name might be a giveaway, but this guerilla-style restaurant *is* indeed shaking up an otherwise genteel neighbourhood. Patrick Müller, Anna Schwab and René Steindachner have 'occupied' a former wine bar and eschewed the usual refit or any form of interior decoration; the focus is, quite literally, on

Griechenbeisl (p582)

the kitchen, with a menu of inventive small dishes prepared behind the bar.

Griechenbeisl   Bistro €€

(📞01-533 19 77; www.griechenbeisl.at; 01, Fleischmarkt 11; mains €15-28; ⏱11.30am-11.30pm; 🖼; 🚋1, 2, Ⓤ Schwedenplatz) Dating from 1447 and frequented by Beethoven, Brahms, Schubert and Strauss among other luminaries, Vienna's oldest restaurant has vaulted rooms, wood panelling and a figure of Augustin trapped at the bottom of a well inside the front door. Every classic Viennese dish is on the menu, along with three daily vegetarian options. In summer, head to the plant-fringed front garden.

Tian Bistro   Vegetarian €€

(📞01-890 466 532; www.tian-bistro.com; 07, Schrankgasse 4; mains €10-18; ⏱11.30am-10pm Mon-Fri, 9am-10pm Sat & Sun; 🖼; 🚋49 Siebensterngasse/Stiftgasse, Ⓤ Volkstheater) Colourful tables set up on the cobbled laneway outside Tian Bistro in summer, while indoors, a glass roof floods the atrium-style, greenery-filled dining room in light. It's the cheaper, more relaxed offspring of Michelin-starred vegetarian restaurant Tian (📞01-890 46 65-2; www.taste-tian.com; 01, Himmelpfortgasse 23; 2-/3-course lunch menus €29/34, 4-/6-course dinner menus €93/108; ⏱noon-2pm & 5.45-9pm Tue-Sat; 🖼; 🚋2, Ⓤ Stephansplatz) 🌿, and serves sublime vegetarian and vegan dishes such as black truffle risotto with Piedmont hazelnuts, as well as breakfast until 2pm on weekends.

Steirereck im Stadtpark   Gastronomy €€€

(📞01-713 31 68; www.steirereck.at; 03, Am Heumarkt 2a; mains €48-52, 6-/7-course menus €142/152; ⏱11.30am-2.30pm & 6.30pm-midnight Mon-Fri; Ⓤ Stadtpark) Heinz Reitbauer is at the culinary helm of this two-starred Michelin restaurant, beautifully lodged in a 20th-century former dairy building in the leafy Stadtpark. His tasting menus are an exuberant feast, fizzing with natural, integral flavours that speak of a chef with exacting standards. Wine pairing is an additional €79/89 (six/seven courses).

Café Sperl

HELEN CATHCART/LONELY PLANET/GETTY IMAGES ©

Meinl's
Restaurant International €€€

(📞01-532 33 34 6000; www.meinlamgraben.
at; 01, Graben 19; mains €16-39, 4-/5-course
menus €67/85; 🕐noon-midnight Mon-Sat;
📶🍴; ⓤStephansplatz) Meinl's combines
cuisine of superlative quality with an
unrivalled wine list and views of Graben.
Creations at its high-end restaurant span
calamari and white-truffle risotto, and
apple-schnapps-marinated pork fillet with
green beans and chanterelles. Its on-site
providore (p578) has a cafe and sushi bar,
and its cellar **wine bar** (🕐11am-midnight Mon-
Sat) serves great-value lunch menus.

Plachutta Austrian €€€

(📞01-512 15 77; www.plachutta.at; 01, Wollzeile
38; mains €16.50-27.20; 🕐11.30am-11.15pm;
ⓤStubentor) If you're keen to taste
Tafelspitz, you can't beat this specialist
wood-panelled, white-tableclothed restaurant. It serves no fewer than 13 varieties
from different cuts of Austrian-reared beef,
such as *Mageres Meisel* (lean, juicy shoulder meat), *Beinfleisch* (larded rib meat)
and *Lueger Topf* (shoulder meat with beef
tongue and calf's head). Save room for the
Austrian cheese plate.

🍷 DRINKING & NIGHTLIFE
Le Loft Bar

(02, Praterstrasse 1; 🕐10am-2am; 🚃2 Gredler-
strasse, ⓤSchwedenplatz) Wow, what a view!
Take the lift to Le Loft on the Sofitel's 18th
floor to reduce Vienna to toy-town scale in
an instant. From this slinky, glass-walled
lounge, you can pick out landmarks such
as the Stephansdom and the Hofburg over
a pomegranate martini or mojito. By night,
the backlit ceiling swirls with an impressionist painter's palette of colours.

Brickmakers
Pub & Kitchen Craft Beer

(📞01-997 44 14; www.brickmakers.at; 07, Ziegler-
gasse 42; 🕐4pm-2am Mon-Fri, 10am-2am Sat,
10am-1am Sun; ⓤZieglergasse) British
racing-green metro tiles, a mosaic floor and
a soundtrack of disco, hip-hop, funk and
soul set the scene for brilliant craft beers
and ciders: there are 30 on tap at any one
time and over 150 by the bottle. Pop-ups
take over the kitchen, and at lunch and
dinner guest chefs cook anything from
gourmet fish and chips to BBQ-smoked
beef brisket.

Loos American Bar Cocktail Bar

(www.loosbar.at; 01, Kärntner Durchgang
10; 🕐noon-5am Thu-Sat, to 4am Sun-Wed;
ⓤStephansplatz) Loos is *the* spot in the Innere Stadt for a classic cocktail such as its
signature dry martini, expertly whipped up
by talented mixologists. Designed by Adolf
Loos in 1908, this tiny 27-sq-metre box
(seating just 20-or-so patrons) is bedecked
from head to toe in onyx and polished
brass, with mirrored walls that make it
appear far larger.

POC Cafe Coffee

(www.poccafe.com; 08, Schlösselgasse 21;
🕐8am-5pm Mon-Fri; 🚃5, 43, 44 to Lange Gasse,
ⓤSchottentor) Friendly Robert Gruber is
one of Vienna's coffee legends and his
infectious passion ripples through this
beautifully rambling, lab-like space. POC
stands for 'People on Caffeine'; while filter,
espresso-style or a summertime iced cold-
brew are definitely this place's raison d'être,
it's also known for moreish sweets like killer
poppy-seed cake, cheesecake or seasonal
fruit tarts.

Café Sperl Coffee

(www.cafesperl.at; 06, Gumpendorfer Strasse
11; 🕐7am-11pm Mon-Sat, 11am-8pm Sun; 📶;
ⓤMuseumsquartier, Kettenbrückengasse)
With its gorgeous *Jugendstil* (art nouveau)
fittings, grand dimensions, cosy booths and
unhurried air, 1880-opened Sperl is one
of the finest coffee houses in Vienna. The
must-try is *Sperl Torte,* an almond-and-
chocolate-cream dream. Grab a slice and a
newspaper (over 10 daily in English, French
and German), order a coffee (from 34
types), and join the rest of the people-
watching patrons.

Opera & Classical Music

The glorious **Staatsoper** (☎01-514 44 7880; www.wiener-staatsoper.at; 01, Opernring 2; tickets €10-208, standing room €3-4; ⬛D, 1, 2, 71 to Kärntner Ring/Oper, ⓊKarlsplatz) is Vienna's premiere opera and classical-music venue. Productions are lavish, formal affairs, where people dress up accordingly. In the interval, wander the foyer and refreshment rooms to fully appreciate the gold-and-crystal interior. Opera is not performed here in July and August (tours still take place). Tickets can be purchased from the **state ticket office** (☎01-514 44 7810; www.bundestheater.at; 01, Operngasse 2; ⊙8am-6pm Mon-Fri, 9am-noon Sat & Sun; ⓊStephansplatz) up to two months in advance.

Tickets to the annual **Opernball** (www.wiener-staatsoper.at; ⊙Jan/Feb) range from €490 to an eye-watering €21,000 and sell out years in advance.

Staatsoper
IZIM M. GULCUK/SHUTTERSTOCK ©

Kruger's American Bar   Bar

(www.krugers.at; 01, Krugerstrasse 5; ⊙6pm-4am Mon-Sat, 7pm-4am Sun; ⬛D, 1, 2, 71 to Kärntner Ring/Oper, ⓊStephansplatz) Retaining some of its original decor from the 1920s and '30s, this dimly lit, wood-panelled American-style bar is a legend in Vienna, furnished with leather Chesterfield sofas and playing a soundtrack of Frank Sinatra, Dean Martin and the like. The drinks list runs to 71 pages; there's a separate cigar and smoker's lounge.

Achtundzwanzig   Wine Bar

(www.achtundzwanzig.at; 08, Schlösslegasse 28; ⊙4pm-1am Mon-Thu, to 2am Fri, 7pm-2am Sat; ⬛5, 43, 44, ⓊSchottentor) Austrian wine fans with a rock-and-roll sensibility will feel like they've found heaven at this black-daubed *vinothek* (wine bar) that vibes casual but takes its wines super seriously. Wines by the glass are all sourced from small producers – many of them are organic or minimal-intervention and friends of the owners – and are well priced at under €4 a glass.

★ ENTERTAINMENT

Burgtheater   Theatre

(National Theatre; ☎01-514 44 4440; www.burgtheater.at; 01, Universitätsring 2; seats €7.50-61, standing room €3.50, students €9; ⊙box office 9am-5pm Mon-Fri; ⬛D, 1, 2 to Rathaus, ⓊRathaus) The Burgtheater hasn't lost its touch over the years – this is one of the foremost theatres in the German-speaking world, staging some 800 performances a year, which reach from Shakespeare to Woody Allen plays. The theatre also runs the 500-seater Akademietheater, which was built between 1911 and 1913.

Musikverein   Concert Venue

(☎01-505 81 90; www.musikverein.at; 01, Musikvereinsplatz 1; tickets €24-95, standing room €4-6; ⊙box office 9am-8pm Mon-Fri, to 1pm Sat Sep-Jun, 9am-noon Mon-Fri Jul & Aug; ⓊKarlsplatz) The opulent Musikverein holds the proud title of the best acoustics of any concert hall in Austria, which the Vienna Philharmonic Orchestra embraces. The lavish interior can be visited by 45-minute guided tour (in English and German; adult/child €6.50/4) at 10am, 11am and noon Monday to Saturday. Smaller-scale performances are held in the Brahms Saal. There are no student tickets.

MuTh   Concert Venue

(☎01-347 80 80; www.muth.at; 02, Obere Augartenstrasse 1e; Vienna Boys' Choir Fri performance €39-89; ⊙4-6pm Mon-Fri & 1 hour before performances; ⓊTaborstrasse) Opened to much acclaim in December 2012, this striking baroque meets contemporary concert hall is the new home of the Wiener Sängerknaben (Vienna Boys' Choir), who previously only performed at the Hofburg. Besides Friday afternoon choral sessions with the angelic-voiced lads, the venue also stages a top-drawer roster of dance, drama, opera, classical, rock and jazz performances.

INFORMATION

Tourist Info Wien (☎01-245 55; www.wien.info; 01, Albertinaplatz; �9am-7pm; ☎; ☐D, 1, 2, 71 to Kärntner Ring/Oper, ⓤStephansplatz) Vienna's main tourist office, with a ticket agency, hotel booking service, free maps and every brochure under the sun.

GETTING THERE & AWAY

Vienna sits at the crossroads of Western and Eastern Europe, and has excellent air, road and rail connections to both regions, as well as services further afield.

AIR

Located 19km southwest of the city centre, **Vienna International Airport** (VIE, ☎01-700 722 233; www.viennaairport.com; ☎) operates services worldwide. Facilities include restaurants and bars, banks and ATMs, money-exchange counters, supermarkets, a post office, car-hire agencies and two left-luggage counters open 5.30am to 11pm (€4 to €8 per 24 hours; maximum six-month storage). Bike boxes (€35) and baggage wrapping (€12 per item) are available.

BOAT

The Danube is a traffic-free access route for arrivals and departures from Vienna. Eastern Europe is the main destination; **Twin City Liner** (☎01-904 88 80; www.twincityliner.com; 01, Schwedenplatz; one-way adult €20-35; ☐1, 2, ⓤSchwedenplatz) connects Vienna with Bratislava in 1½ hours, while its sister company **DDSG Blue Danube Schiffahrt** (☎01-588 80; www.ddsg-blue-danube.at; 02, Handelskai 265, Reichsbrücke; one-way €99-109, return €125; ☉9am-5pm Mon-Fri, 10am-4pm Sat & Sun, closed

Sat & Sun Nov-Feb) links Budapest with Vienna from mid-May to September, departing Vienna Wednesday, Friday and Sunday, departing Budapest Tuesday, Thursday and Saturday. DDSG tickets may also be obtained or picked up at Twin City Liner.

CAR & MOTORCYCLE

Bordering eight countries, Austria is easily reached by road. If you're bringing your own vehicle, you'll need a Motorway Vingette (toll sticker). For 10 days/two months it costs €8.80/25.70 per car; €5.50/12.90 per motorcycle. Buy it at petrol stations in neighbouring countries before entering Austria. More information is available at www.austria.info.

TRAIN

Vienna's main train station, the Wien Hauptbahnhof, 3km south of Stephansdom, handles all international trains as well as trains from all of Austria's provincial capitals, and many local and regional trains.

GETTING AROUND

Tickets and passes for **Wiener Linien** (☎01-7909-100; www.wienerlinien.at) services can be purchased at U-Bahn stations, on trams and buses, or in a *Tabakladen* (*Trafik;* tobacco kiosk), as well as from a few staffed ticket offices. Tickets should be validated prior to boarding (U-Bahn) or on boarding (tram and bus).

U-Bahn Fast, comfortable and safe. Trains run from 5am to midnight Monday to Thursday and continuously from 5am Friday through to midnight Sunday.

Tram Slower but more enjoyable. Depending on route, trams run from around 5.15am to about 11.45pm. Tickets bought from the driver are more expensive.

Bus Reliable and punctual, with several very useful routes for visitors. Most run from 5am to midnight; services can be sporadic or nonexistent on weekends.

Night Bus Especially useful for outer areas; runs every 30 minutes from 12.30am to 5am. Main stops are located at Schwedenplatz, Schottentor and Kärntner Ring/Oper.

Swiss Alps, Switzerland

You can sense the anticipation on the train from Täsch: couples gaze wistfully out of the window, kids fidget, folk rummage for their cameras. And then, as they arrive in Zermatt, all give little whoops of joy at the pop-up-book effect of the Matterhorn, the hypnotically beautiful, one-of-a-kind peak that rises like a shark's fin above town.

Since the mid-19th century, Zermatt has starred among Switzerland's glitziest resorts. Today skiers cruise along well-kept pistes, spellbound by the scenery, while style-conscious darlings flash designer threads in the town's swish lounge bars. But all are smitten with the Matterhorn, an unfathomable monolith you can't quite stop looking at.

Two Days in the Swiss Alps

Get up high with Europe's highest-altitude **cable car** (p589) or **cog-wheel railway** (p589) and walk or ski down – never taking your eyes off the pyramid-perfect, bewitching Matterhorn. Dedicate day two to exploring **Zermatt** (p592) and gorging yourself on delicious **raclette** or **fondue** (p596).

Four Days in the Swiss Alps

Spend the morning hiking the Matterhorn **Glacier Trail** (p594) for more stunning views before taking to the **slopes** (p593) for the rest of the day. On the fourth day, hop aboard the **Glacier Express** (p591) in Zermatt, sit back and enjoy a spectacular train journey to St Moritz.

At the end of your trip, take a train to Florence (p418) or Provence (p252).

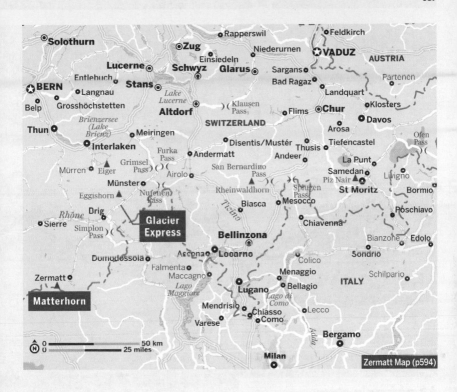

Zermatt Map (p594)

Arriving in the Swiss Alps

Train Direct trains to Zermatt depart hourly from Brig (Sfr38, 1½ hours), stopping at Visp en route. Zermatt is also the start/end point of the **Glacier Express** (p591) to/from St Moritz.

Car Zermatt is car-free. Motorists have to park in the Matterhorn Terminal Täsch (www.matterhornterminal.ch; Sfr15.50 per 24 hours) in Täsch and ride the Zermatt Shuttle train (return adult/child Sfr16.80/8.40, 12 minutes) the last 5km up to Zermatt.

Where to Stay

Book well ahead in winter, and bear in mind that nearly everywhere closes from May to mid- or late June and mid-October to November or early December. With advance warning, many places will pick you and your bags up at the station in an electro-shuttle. Check when you book.

Sleeping choices in Zermatt run from hostel beds to ultra-chic designer digs, with plenty of chalet-style midrange options in between.

JAKL LUBOS/SHUTTERSTOCK ©

Matterhorn

No mountain has so much pulling power and natural magnetism or – is so easy to become obsessed with – as this charismatic peak.

Beautiful Matterhorn demands to be admired, ogled and repeatedly photographed at sunrise and sunset, in different seasons, and from every last infuriating angle.

Climbing Matterhorn

Some 3000 alpinists summit Europe's most photographed, 4478m-high peak each year. You don't need to be superhuman to do it, but you do need to be a skilled climber (with crampons), be in tip-top physical shape (12-hours-endurance performance) and have a week in hand to acclimatise beforehand to make the iconic ascent up sheer rock and ice.

No one attempts the Matterhorn without local know-how: mountain guides at the Snow & Alpine Center (p593) charge Sfr1790 per person for the eight-hour return climb, including cable car from

Great For...

☑ **Don't Miss**

Visiting the Matterhorn Museum (p592) to learn about the first successful ascent of the peak.

Matterhorn Glacier Paradise cable car

ℹ Need to Know

Mid-July to mid-September is the best time of year to attempt the ascent.

✕ Take a Break

There are restaurants at Riffelalp (2211m) and Riffelberg (2582m) along the Gornergratbahn path.

★ Top Tip

For outstanding views of the Matterhorn, jump aboard the *Sunnegga Express* funicular (p592) to the top of Sunnegga.

and an ice slide to swoosh down bum first. End with some exhilarating **snow tubing** outside in the snowy surrounds.

Zermatt to Schwarzee and half-board accommodation in a mountain hut. Client:guide ratios are 1:1. You'll probably be required to do training climbs first, just to prove you really are 100% up to it. The Matterhorn claims more than a few lives each year.

Matterhorn Glacier Paradise

Views from Zermatt's cable cars are all remarkable, but the **Matterhorn Glacier Paradise** (www.matterhornparadise.ch; adult/child return Sfr100/50; ⏲8.30am-4.20pm) is the icing on the cake. Ride Europe's highest-altitude cable car to 3883m and gawp at 14 glaciers and 38 mountain peaks over 4000m from the **Panoramic Platform** (only open in good weather). Don't miss the **Glacier Palace**, an ice palace complete with glittering ice sculptures

Gornergratbahn

Europe's highest **cogwheel railway** (www.gornergrat.ch; Bahnhofplatz 7; adult/child return trip Sfr94/47; ⏲7am-7.15pm) has climbed through picture-postcard scenery to **Gornergrat** (3089m) – a 30-minute journey – since 1898. On the way up, sit on the right-hand side of the little red train to goggle at the Matterhorn. Tickets allow you to get on and off en route at stops including Riffelalp (2211m) and Riffelberg (2582m). In summer an extra train runs once a week at sunrise and sunset – the most spectacular trips of all.

Glacier Express

The Glacier Express is one of Europe's mythical train journeys. It starts and ends in two of Switzerland's oldest, glitziest mountain resorts – Zermatt and St Moritz – and the Alpine scenery is magnificent in parts.

Hop aboard the red train with floor-to-ceiling windows in St Moritz or Zermatt, and savour shot after cinematic shot of green peaks, glistening Alpine lakes, glacial ravines and other hallucinatory natural landscapes. Pulled by steam engine when it first puffed out of the station in 1930, the Glacier Express traverses 191 tunnels and 291 bridges on its famous 290km journey.

Highlights include the one-hour ride from Disentis to Andermatt, across the Oberalp Pass (2033m) – the highest point of the journey in every way; and the celebrity six-arch, 65m-high Landwasser Viaduct, pictured on almost every feature advertising the Glacier Express, that dazzles passengers during the 50km leg between Chur and Filisur.

Great For...

☑ Don't Miss

The ride from Disentis to Andermatt and the Landwasser Viaduct.

❶ Need to Know

www.glacierexpress.ch; adult/child one way
St Moritz–Zermatt Sfr153/76.50, obligatory
seat reservation summer/winter Sfr33/13, on-
board 3-course lunch Sfr45; ⊙3 trains daily
May Oct, 1 train daily mid-Dec–Feb

✗ Take a Break

Have lunch in the vintage restaurant car
or bring your own Champagne picnic.

★ Top Tip

**Check the weather forecast before
committing: a blue sky is essential
for the eight-hour train ride to be
worthwhile.**

A ticket is not cheap, and to avoid dis-
appointment it pays to know the nuts and
bolts of this long mountain train ride.

◦ Don't asume it is hard-core mountain
porn for the duration of the journey: the
views in the tunnels the train passes
through are not particularly wonderful, for
starters.

◦ The complete trip takes almost eight
hours. If you're travelling with children or
can't bear the thought of sitting all day
watching mountain scenery that risks becoming monotonous, opt for just a section
of the journey: the best bit is the one-hour
ride from Disentis to Andermatt.

◦ Windows in the stylish panoramic
carriages are sealed and can't be opened,
making it tricky to take good photographs

or film. If photography/video is the reason
you're aboard, ditch the direct glamour
train for regional express SBB trains along
the same route – cheaper, no reservations
required, with windows that open and the
chance to stretch your legs when changing
trains.

◦ The southern side of the train is said to
have the best views.

◦ Children aged under six travel free (buy
an extra seat reservation if you don't fancy
a young child on your lap for eight hours),
and children aged six to 16 years pay half-
price plus a seat reservation fee.

Zermatt

SIGHTS

Meander main-strip **Bahnhofstrasse** with its flashy boutiques and stream of horse-drawn sleds or carriages and electric taxis, then head downhill towards the noisy Vispa river along **Hinterdorfstrasse**. This old-world street is crammed with 16th-century pig stalls and archetypal Valaisian timber granaries propped up on stone discs and stilts to keep out pesky rats; look for the **fountain** commemorating Ulrich Inderbinen (1900–2004), a Zermatt-born mountaineer who climbed the Matter-horn 370 times, the last time at age 90. Nicknamed the King of the Alps, he was the oldest active mountain guide in the world when he retired at the ripe old age of 95.

Matterhorn Museum   Museum
(027 967 41 00; www.zermatt.ch/museum; Kirchplatz; adult/child Sfr10/5; ⏰11am-6pm Jul-Sep, 3-6pm Oct–mid-Dec, 3-7pm mid-Dec–Mar, 2-6pm Apr-Jun) This crystalline, state-of-the-art museum provides fascinating insight into Valaisian village life, mountaineering, the dawn of tourism in Zermatt and the lives the Matterhorn has claimed. Short films portray the first successful ascent of the Matterhorn on 13 July 1865 led by Edward Whymper, a feat marred by tragedy on the descent when four team members crashed to their deaths in a 1200m fall. The infamous rope that broke is exhibited.

Gornerschlucht   Gorge
(027 967 20 96; www.gornergorge.ch; adult/child Sfr5/2.50; ⏰9.15am-5.45pm Jun–mid-Oct) It is a 20-minute walk from town along the river to this dramatic gorge, carved out of green serpentinite rock and accessed by a series of wooden staircases and walkways. Good fun for families.

Sunnegga   Funicular
(www.matterhornparadise.ch; adult/child one way Sfr12/6, return Sfr24/12) Take the *Sunnegga Express* 'tunnel funicular' up to Sunnegga (2288m) for amazing views of the Matter-horn. This is a top spot for families – take the Leisee Shuttle (free) down to the lake for beginner ski slopes at Wolli's Park in winter, and a children's playground plus splashing around in the lake in summer. A

From left: Zermatt and the Matterhorn; Mountaineers' Cemetery; Skiing in the Swiss Alps

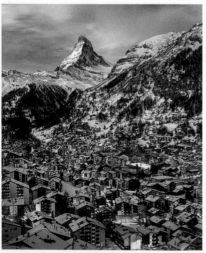

marmot-watching station is a few minutes' walk from Sunnegga. It's a relatively easy downhill walk back to Zermatt via Findeln in about 1½ hours.

Ricola Herb Garden
Gardens

(www.ricola.com; Blatten; ⊗Jun-Sep) FREE The Ricola Herb Garden in the pretty mountain hamlet of Blatten bristles with aromatic herbs that end up in Ricola sweets; and there's a family-fun 'touch and smell' quiz.

Mountaineers' Cemetery
Cemetery

(Kirchstrasse) A walk in Zermatt's twinset of cemeteries – the Mountaineers' Cemetery in the garden of Zermatt's **St Mauritius Church** (Kirchplatz) and the main cemetery across the road – is a sobering experience. Numerous gravestones tell of untimely deaths on Monte Rosa, the Matterhorn and Breithorn.

🕚 ACTIVITIES

An essential stop in activity planning is the **Snow & Alpine Center** (☏027 966 24 00, www.alpincenter.zermatt.ch; Bahnhofstrasse 58; ⊗9am-noon & 3-7pm Mon-Fri, 4-7pm Sat & Sun Dec-Apr, 9am-noon & 3-7pm Jul-Sep), home to Zermatt's ski school and mountain guides. In winter buy lift passes here (Sfr79/430 for a one-day/one-week pass excluding Cervinia; Sfr92/494 including Cervinia).

🕚 Skiing

Zermatt is cruising heaven, with mostly long, scenic red runs, plus a smattering of blues for ski virgins and knuckle-whitening blacks for experts. The main skiing areas in winter are **Rothorn**, **Stockhorn** and **Klein Matterhorn** – 360km of ski runs in all with a link from Klein Matterhorn to the Italian resort of **Cervinia** and a freestyle park with half-pipe for snowboarders.

Summer skiing (20km of runs) and boarding (gravity park at Plateau Rosa on the Theodul glacier) is Europe's most extensive. Count on Sfr84/125 for a one-/two-day summer ski pass.

🕚 Hiking

Zermatt is a hiker's paradise, with 400km of summer trails through some of the most incredible scenery in the Alps – the

OLIVER FOERSTNER/SHUTTERSTOCK ©

Zermatt

N | 0 ————— 200 m
0 ————— 0.1 miles

Zermatt

◎ Sights
1 Glacier Express	B1
2 Gornergratbahn	C1
3 Matterhorn Museum	B3
Mountaineers' Cemetery	(see 4)
4 St Mauritius Church	B3
5 Sunnegga	C2

☻ Activities, Courses & Tours
6 Snow & Alpine Center	B2

☒ Eating
7 Bayard Metzgerei	B2
8 Brown Cow Pub	B2
9 Le Gitan – Zermatterstübli	B2
10 Snowboat Bar & Yacht Club	C2
11 Whymper Stube	B3

◎ Drinking & Nightlife
12 Elsie Bar	B3
13 Papperla Pub	B3
14 Vernissage Bar Club	B2

tourist office has trail maps. For Matterhorn close-ups, nothing beats the highly dramatic **Matterhorn Glacier Trail** (two hours, 6.5km) from Trockener Steg to Schwarzsee; 23 information panels en route tell you everything you could possibly need to know about glaciers and glacial life.

For those doing lots of walking, local excursion passes offer a convenient way to get into the high country. A **Peak Pass** – offering unlimited use of the Schwarzsee, Rothorn and Matterhorn Glacier Paradise (p589) cable cars plus the Gornergrat-

bahn (p589) cog railway – costs Sfr220 for three days or Sfr315 for a week. To find your perfect walk, search by duration, distance and difficulty on the hiking page of the excellent tourist office website.

☒ EATING

You won't go hungry in Zermatt. The entire town centre is packed with restaurants, with the greatest concentration along busy Bahnhofstrasse.

Snowboat Bar & Yacht Club International €

(☎027 967 43 33; www.zermattsnowboat.com; Vispastrasse 20; mains Sfr22-39; ☺noon-midnight) This hybrid eating-drinking, riverside address, with deckchairs sprawled across its rooftop sun terrace, is a blessing. When fondue tires, head here for barbecue-sizzled burgers (not just beef, but crab and veggie burgers too), creative salads (the Omega 3 buster is a favourite) and great cocktails. The vibe? 100% friendly, fun and funky.

Klein Matterhorn Pizza €

(☎027 967 01 42; www.kleinmatterhorn-zermatt. com; Schluhmattstrasse 50; pizza Sfr17-22; ☺8am-midnight, kitchen 11.30am-10pm) For first-rate Italian pizza in the sun with a Matterhorn view, this simple pizzeria and cafe-bar opposite the Matterhorn Glacier Express cable car station is the address.

Bayard Metzgerei Swiss €

(☎027 967 22 66; www.metzgerei-bayard. ch; Bahnhofstrasse 9; sausage Sfr6; ☺noon-6.30pm Jul-Sep, 4-6.30pm Dec-Mar) Join the line for a street-grilled sausage (pork, veal or beef) and chunk of bread to down with a beer on the hop — or at a bar stool with the sparrows in the alley by this first-class butcher's shop.

Chez Vrony Swiss €€

(☎027 967 25 52; www.chezvrony.ch; Findeln; breakfast Sfr15-28, mains Sfr25-45; ☺9.15am-5pm Dec-Apr & mid-Jun–mid-Oct) Ride the Sunnegga Express funicular (p592) to 2288m, then ski down or summer-hike 15 minutes to Zermatt's tastiest slope-side address in the Findeln hamlet. Delicious dried meats, homemade cheese and sausage come from Vrony's own cows that graze away the summer on the high alpine pastures (2100m) surrounding it, and the Vrony burger (Sfr31) is legendary. Advance reservations essential in winter.

Le Gitan – Zermatterstübli Swiss €€

(☎027 968 19 40; www.legitan.ch; Bahnhof-strasse 64; mains Sfr23-39; ☺noon-3pm &

Hiking with Kids

Try out these short-walk favourites for families with younger children.

○ Take the Sunnegga Express up to Sunnegga then the Leisee Shuttle (or walk the 10 minutes) downhill to **Leisee**, a lake made for bracing summer dips with bijou pebble beach and old-fashioned wooden raft for children to tug themselves across the water pirate-style.

○ In town, embark on the 20-minute walk along the river to the Gorner-schlucht (p592), a dramatic gorge carved out of green serpentinite rock and accessed by a series of wooden staircases and walkways.

○ The easy circular walk around the Ricola Herb Garden (p593), in the pretty mountain hamlet of Blatten (signposted from Gornergratschlucht).

○ The 1¼-hour circular walk (2.9km) in **Füri** takes in the Gletschergarten Dos-sen (Dossen Glacier Garden) with its bizarre glacial rock formations, a picnic area with stone-built barbecues to cook up lunch, and the dizzying 90m-high, 100m-long steel suspension bridge above the Gornerschlucht Gorge.

7-10pm) Le Gitan stands out for its elegant chalet-style interior and extra-tasty cuisine. Plump for a feisty pork or veal sausage with onion sauce and rösti, or dip into a cheese fondue – with Champagne (yes!), or, if you're feeling outrageously indulgent, Champagne and fresh truffles. End with coffee ice cream doused in kirsch, or apricot sorbet with abricotine (local Valais apricot liqueur).

Whymper Stube Swiss €€

(☎027 967 22 96; www.whymper-stube.ch; Bahnhofstrasse 80; raclette Sfr9, fondue Sfr25-48; ☺11am-11pm Nov-Apr & Jun–mid-Oct) This cosy bistro, attached to the Monte Rosa

🍽 A Feast of a Meal: Fondue & Raclette

It is hard to leave Switzerland without dipping into a fondue. A pot of gooey melted cheese is placed in the centre of the table and kept on a slow burn while diners dip in cubes of crusty bread using slender two-pronged fondue forks. Traditionally a winter dish, the Swiss tend to eat it mostly if there's snow around or they're at a suitable altitude – unlike tourists who tuck in year-round and wherever they find it.

The classic fondue mix in Switzerland is equal amounts of emmental and gruyère cheese, grated and melted with white wine and a shot of kirsch (cherry-flavoured liquor), then thickened slightly with potato or corn flour. It is served with a basket of bread slices (which are soon torn into small morsels) and most people order a side platter of cold meats and tiny gherkins to accompany it.

Switzerland's other signature alpine cheese dish is raclette. Unlike fondue, raclette – both the name of the dish and the cheese at its gooey heart – is eaten year-round. A half-crescent slab of the cheese is screwed onto a specially designed 'rack oven' that melts the top flat side. As it melts, cheese is scraped onto plates for immediate consumption with boiled potatoes, cold meats and pickled onions or gherkins.

Fondue
SILKENPHOTOGRAPHY/GETTY IMAGES ©

Hotel that Whymper left from to climb the Matterhorn in 1865, is legendary for its excellent raclette and fondues. The icing on the cake is a segmented pot bubbling with three different cheese fondues. Service is relaxed and friendly, tables are packed tightly together, and the place – all inside – buzzes come dusk.

Brown Cow Pub   Pub Food

(☏027 967 19 31; www.hotelpost.ch; Bahnhofstrasse 41; ⊙9am-2am, kitchen 9am-10.30pm) Dozens of dining joints line Bahnhofstrasse, including this busier-than-busy pub, one of several eating spots inside the legendary Hotel Post. The Brown Cow serves pub grub (hot dogs from Sfr9, burgers from Sfr16) all day.

🍷 DRINKING & NIGHTLIFE

Still fizzing with energy after hurtling down the slopes? Zermatt pulses in party-mad après-ski huts, suave lounge bars and Brit-style pubs. Most close (and some melt) in low season.

Elsie Bar   Wine Bar

(☏027 967 24 31; www.elsiebar.ch; Kirchplatz 16; ⊙4pm-1am) In a building originally erected in 1879, this elegant, old-world wine bar with wood-panelled walls, across from the church, has been known as Elsie's since 1961. Oysters, caviar and snails are on the winter menu, along with a top selection of wine and whisky.

Hennu Stall   Bar

(☏027 966 35 10; www.facebook.com/HennustallZermatt; Klein Matterhorn; ⊙2-10pm Dec-Apr) Last one down to this snowbound 'chicken run' is a rotten egg. Hennu is the wildest après-ski shack on Klein Matterhorn. Order a caramel vodka and take your ski boots grooving to live music on the terrace. A metre-long 'ski' of shots will make you cluck all the way down to Zermatt. Below Furi on the way to Zermatt.

Vernissage Bar Club   Bar

(☏027 966 69 70; www.backstagehotel.ch; Hofmattstrasse 4; ⊙5pm-midnight Sun-Wed, to 2am Thu-Sat) The ultimate après-ski antithesis, Vernissage at the Backstage Hotel exudes

Al fresco restaurant with Matterhorn views

grown-up sophistication. Local artist Heinz Julen has created a theatrical space with flowing velvet drapes, film-reel chandeliers and candlelit booths. Catch an exhibition, watch a movie, or pose in the lounge bar.

Papperla Pub   Pub
(www.julen.ch; Steinmattstrasse 34; ☺2pm-2am; ☜) Rammed with sloshed skiers in winter and happy hikers in summer, this buzzing pub with red director chairs on its pavement terrace blends pulsating music with lethal Jägermeister bombs, good vibes and pub grub (from 5pm). Its downstairs **Schneewittli club** rocks until dawn in season.

ⓘ INFORMATION

Make the Swiss tourist board, **Switzerland Tourism** (www.myswitzerland.com), your first port of call. For detailed information, contact the local **tourist office** (☏027 966 81 00; www. zermatt.ch; Bahnhofplatz 5; ☺8.30am-6pm; ☜). Information and maps are free and somebody invariably speaks English. In German-speaking Switzerland tourist offices are called *Verkehrsbüro*, or *Kurverein* in some resorts.

ⓘ GETTING AROUND

Dinky electro-taxis zip around town transporting goods and the weary (and taking pedestrians perilously by surprise – watch out!). Pick one up at the main rank in front of the train station on Bahnhofstrasse.

Parliament building (p553), Budapest

In Focus

German train station

ROMAN BABAKIN/SHUTTERSTOCK ©

Europe Today

These are challenging times for Europe. Economically, many countries are still struggling, while politically, pro- and anti- European Union (EU) forces are engaged in a titanic struggle. The UK public narrowly voted for 'Brexit' – leaving the EU – and that process is now underway. Across the Channel, voters in France and the Netherlands have backed candidates and parties that favour a stronger, united Europe.

State of the Union

Where Europe should be headed as a political entity remains a burning question for EU nations, especially those hostile to relinquishing further powers to the EU parliament. In 2016 a referendum in the UK over the issue saw voters opt by a slim majority for 'Brexit'. The Conservative government went on to trigger Article 50 of the Treaty of Lisbon at the end of March 2017 setting the UK on course to leave the EU by 2019.

EU membership also raises questions about democratic representation: in exchange for their financial bailouts, financially strapped countries have been forced to follow the political will of Brussels, often in direct contradiction to the wishes of their own constituents and, in some cases, the platforms on which their governments were elected. Despite the unease over this, the French presidential election in 2017 saw a decisive victory for

belief systems
(% of population)

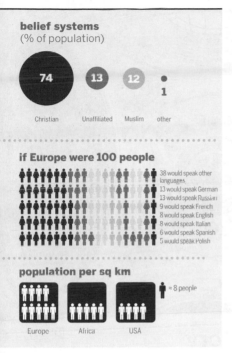

| 74 | 13 | 12 | 1 |
| Christian | Unaffiliated | Muslim | other |

if Europe were 100 people

38 would speak other languages
13 would speak German
13 would speak Russian
9 would speak French
8 would speak English
8 would speak Italian
6 would speak Spanish
5 would speak Polish

population per sq km

≈ 8 people

Europe   Africa   USA

the pro-EU centrist candidate Emmanuel Macron, over the far right Front National leader Marine Le Pen.

Refugee Crisis

It was a similar story in the Netherlands. In the March 2017 general election the centre-right VVD party prevailed over the right-wing Partij voor de Vrijheid (PVV) led by Geert Wilders, an anti-EU politician advocating a ban on immigration from Muslim countries and closing down mosques.

Such hostility to Muslims has been on the rise in the wake of the worst refugee crisis to hit Europe since the end of WWII. Since 2015 over one million refugees and migrants have arrived in the EU, the majority of them fleeing from war and terror in Syria and other troubled countries. The response has ranged from some countries in the EU's Schengen Area closing previously open borders to Germany's open arms policy of accepting refugees.

Greener Europe

On a brighter note, many European countries are stepping up efforts to combat climate change. Increasingly, high-speed rail services provide an ecofriendly alternative to short-haul flights, green spaces flourish in urban areas, share-bicycle schemes are becoming prevalent in cities and towns, and vehicle emissions are being reduced with more electric and hybrid engines and biofuels. London mayor Sadiq Khan has added a £10 charge for motorists driving older, more polluting vehicles on top of the congestion charge that already exists for central London. The mayors of Paris, Madrid and Athens also plan to to take diesel cars and vans off their roads by 2025.

The Eurovision Issue

On a lighter note, every May Europe plops down on the sofa to enjoy the Eurovision Song Contest. This one-of-a-kind musical marathon has been screened every year since 1956, making it the longest-running television show of its kind.

Created to symbolise Euro harmony, the contest has also developed into a reflection of Euro discord. Is the voting system rigged? Should acts sing in English or in their own language? Is that kitschy pop song some kind of coded political statement?

Each country enters one song, and then votes for their favourites among the competitors. Inevitably this leads to accusations of 'block voting' (neighbouring countries tending to vote for each other, for example). Confusingly, too, several non-European countries are allowed to enter. The host city, with a few exceptions, is in the winner country of the previous year, with cities competing domestically for the honour and associated tourism boost.

Ceiling at Széchenyi Baths (p551), Budapest

History

Understanding Europe's long and often troubled history is a crucial part of figuring out what makes this continent tick. Fragments of that history can be encountered in the tumbledown remains of Roman ampitheatres and bathhouses, in the fabulously ostentatious architecture of French chateaux and German castles, and in the winding streets, broad boulevards and governing institutions of its many stately cities.

4500–2500 BC
Neolithic tribes build burial tombs, barrows, stone circles and alignments across Europe.

1st century BC–AD 4
The Romans conquer much of Europe. The Roman Empire flourishes under Augustus and his successors.

410
The sacking of Rome by the Goths brings an end to Roman dominance.

Roman Forum (p372), Rome

Prehistory

The first settlers arrived in Europe around two million years ago, but it wasn't until the end of the last major ice age between 12,000 BC and 8000 BC that humans really took hold. As the glaciers and ice sheets retreated, hunter-gatherer tribes extended their reach northwards in search of new land. Some of Europe's earliest human settlements were left behind by Neolithic tribes.

Greeks & Romans

The civilisation of ancient Greece emerged around 2000 BC and made huge leaps forward in science, technology, architecture, philosophy and democratic principles. Many of the writers, thinkers and mathematicians of ancient Greece, from Pythagoras to Plato, exert a profound influence to this day. Then came the Romans, who set about conquering most of Europe and devised the world's first republic. At its height, Roman power extended all the

1066	**1340s–1350s**	**15th century**
William the Conqueror defeats the English King Harold at the Battle of Hastings.	The Black Death reaches its peak in Europe, killing between 30% and 60% of Europe's population.	The Italian Renaissance brings about a revolution in art, architecture and science.

Trinity College entrance, Dublin

way from Celtic Britain to ancient Persia (Iran). The Romans' myriad achievements are almost too numerous to mention: they founded cities, raised aqueducts, constructed roads, laid sewers and built baths all over the continent, and produced a string of brilliant writers, orators, politicians, philosophers and military leaders.

Dark Ages to Middle Ages

Rome's empire-building ambitions eventually proved too much, and a series of political troubles and military disasters resulted in the sacking of Rome (in 410) by the Goths. Although Roman emperors clung onto their eastern Byzantine empire for another thousand years, founding a new capital at Constantinople (modern day Istanbul), Rome's dominance over Western Europe was over. A new era, the Dark Ages, had begun.

The next few centuries were marked by a series of conflicts in which the various kingdoms of the European mainland sought to gain political and strategic control. In AD 711, the Moors – Arabs and Berbers who had converted to the Islamic religion prevailing throughout northern Africa – crossed the Straits of Gibraltar, defeating the Visigothic army. They went on to rule the Iberian Peninsula for almost 800 years, until the fall of Granada in 1492, leaving behind a flourishing architectural, scientific and academic legacy.

Meanwhile, in the late 8th century Charlemagne, King of the Franks, brought together much of Western Europe under what would become known as the Holy Roman Empire. This alliance of Christian nations sent troops to reclaim the Holy Land from Islamic control in a series of campaigns known as the Crusades.

The Renaissance

Europe's troubles rumbled on into the 14th and 15th centuries. In the wake of further conflicts and political upheavals, as well as the devastating outbreak of the Black Death (estimated to have wiped out somewhere between 30% to 60% of Europe's population), control over the Holy Roman Empire passed into the hands of the Austrian Habsburgs, a

1517
Martin Luther nails his demands to the church door in Wittenburg, sparking the Reformation.

1789
France becomes a republic following the French Revolution. Numerous aristocrats are executed by guillotine.

1815
France's defeat at the Battle of Waterloo ends First French Empire and military career of Napoleon Bonaparte.

political dynasty that became one of the continent's dominant powers.

The Italian city-states of Genoa, Venice, Pisa and Amalfi consolidated their control over the Mediterranean, establishing trading links with much of the rest of Europe and the Far East, and embarking on some of the first journeys in search of the New World.

In the mid-15th century, a new age of artistic and philosophical development broke out across the continent. The Renaissance encouraged writers, artists and thinkers to challenge the accepted doctrines of theology, philosophy, architecture and art. The centre of this artistic tsunami was Florence, Italy, where such inspirational figures as Michelangelo and Leonardo da Vinci made great strides in art and architecture. Another epoch-changing development was under way in Germany, thanks to the invention of the printing press by Johannes Gutenburg in around 1440. The advent of 'movable type' made printed books available to the masses for the first time.

The Reformation

While the Renaissance challenged artistic ideas, the Reformation dealt with questions of religion. Challenging Catholic 'corruption' and the divine authority of the Pope, the German theologian Martin Luther established his own breakaway branch of the Church, to which he gave the name 'Protestantism', in 1517. Luther's stance was soon echoed by the English monarch Henry VIII, who cut ties with Rome in 1534 and went on to found his own (Protestant) Church of England, sowing the seeds for centuries of conflict between Catholics and Protestants.

The New World

The schisms of the Church weren't the only source of tension. The discovery of the 'New World' in the mid-16th century led to a colonial arms race between the major European nations, in which each country battled to lay claim to the newly discovered lands – often enslaving or killing the local populace in the process.

More trouble followed during the Thirty Years' War (1618–48), which began as a conflict between Catholics and Protestants and eventually sucked in most of Europe's principal powers. The war was ended by the Peace of Westphalia in 1648, and Europe entered a period of comparative stability.

The Enlightenment

The Enlightenment (sometimes known as 'The Age of Reason') is the name given to a philosophical movement that spread throughout European society during the mid- to late-17th century. It emphasised the importance of logic, reason and science over the doctrines of religion. Key figures included the philosophers Baruch Spinoza, John Locke, Immanuel Kant and Voltaire, as well as scientists such as Isaac Newton.

19th century	1914	1939–45
The Industrial Revolution transforms European society; with railways and factories bringing in the modern age.	The assassination of Archduke Franz Ferdinand leads to the outbreak of WWI (1914–18).	WWII rages across Europe, devastating many cities. After peace is declared, much of Eastern Europe falls under communist rule.

The Enlightenment also questioned the political status quo. Since the Middle Ages, the majority of Europe's wealth and power had been concentrated in the hands of an all-powerful elite, largely made up of monarchs and aristocrats. This stood in direct contradiction to one of the core values of the Enlightenment – equality. Many thinkers believed it was an impasse that could only be solved by revolution.

Revolution

Things came to a head in 1789 when armed mobs stormed the Bastille prison in Paris, thus kick-starting the French Revolution. The Revolution began with high ideals, inspired by its iconic slogan of *liberté, egalité, fraternité* (liberty, equality, brotherhood). Before long things turned sour and heads began to roll. Hard-line republicans seized control and demanded retribution for centuries of oppression. Scores of aristocrats met their end under the guillotine's blade, including the French monarch Louis XVI, who was publicly executed in January 1793 in Paris' Place de la Concorde, and his queen, Marie-Antoinette, killed in October that year.

The Reign of Terror between September 1793 and July 1794 saw religious freedoms revoked, churches closed, cathedrals turned into 'Temples of Reason' and thousands beheaded. In the chaos, a dashing young Corsican general named Napoleon Bonaparte (1769– 1821) seized his chance.

Napoleon assumed power in 1799 and in 1804 was crowned Emperor. He fought a series of campaigns across Europe and conquered vast swathes of territory for the French empire but, following a disastrous campaign to conquer Russia in 1812, his grip on power faltered and he was defeated by a coalition of British and Prussian forces at the Battle of Waterloo in 1815.

Industry, Empire & WWI

Having vanquished Napoleon, Britain emerged as Europe's predominant power. With such innovations as the steam engine, the railway and the factory, Britain unleashed the Industrial Revolution and, like many of Europe's major powers (including France, Spain, Belgium and the Austro-Hungarian empire), set about developing its colonies across much of Africa, Australasia and the Middle and Far East.

Before long these competing empires clashed again, with predictably catastrophic consequences. The assassination of the heir to the Austro-Hungarian Empire Franz Ferdinand in 1914 led to the outbreak of the Great War, or WWI, as it came to be known. By the end of hostilities in 1918, huge tracts of northern France and Belgium had been razed and over 16 million people across Europe had been killed.

In the Treaty of Versailles, the defeated powers of Austro-Hungary and Germany lost large areas of territory and found themselves saddled with a massive bill for reparations,

1957	**1989**	**1993**
The European Economic Community (EEC) is formed by a collection of Western European countries.	The fall of the Berlin Wall heralds the downfall of oppressive regimes across much of Eastern Europe.	The Maastricht Treaty leads to the formation of the European Union (EU).

sowing seeds of discontent that would be exploited a decade later by a fanatical Austrian painter by the name of Adolf Hitler.

Rise of Fascism

Hitler's rise to power was astonishingly swift. By 1933 he had become Chancellor and, as the head of the Nazi Party, assumed total control of Germany. Having spent much of the 1930s building up a formidable war machine, assisting General Franco's nationalist forces during the Spanish Civil War, Hitler annexed former German territories in Austria and parts of Czechoslovakia, before extending his reach onwards into Poland in 1939.

The occupation of Poland proved the final straw. Britain, France and its Commonwealth allies declared war on Germany, which had formed its own alliance of convenience with the Axis powers of Italy (led by the fascist dictator Mussolini) and Japan.

WWII

Having done a secret deal with Stalin over the Soviet Union's spheres of influence to the east, Hitler unleashed his blitzkrieg on an unsuspecting western Europe, and within a few short months had conquered huge areas of territory, forcing the French into submission and driving the British forces to a humiliating retreat at Dunkirk. Europe was to remain under Nazi occupation for the next six years.

The Axis retained the upper hand until the Japanese attack on Pearl Harbor forced a reluctant USA into the war in 1941. Hitler's subsequent decision to invade the Soviet Union in 1941 proved to be a catastrophic error, resulting in devastating German losses that opened the door for the Allied invasion of Normandy in June 1944.

After several months of bitter fighting, Hitler's remaining forces were pushed back towards Berlin. Hitler committed suicide on 30 April 1945 and the Russians took the city, crushing the last pockets of German resistance. By 8 May Germany and Italy had unconditionally surrendered to the Allied powers, bringing the war in Europe to an end.

The Iron Curtain

Differences of opinion between the Western powers and the communist Soviet Union soon led to a stand-off. The USSR closed off its assigned sectors, including East Berlin, East Germany and much of Eastern Europe, which heralded the descent of the Iron Curtain and the beginning of the Cold War. This period of political tension and social division in Europe lasted for 40 years and saw popular uprisings in Prague and Budapest put down by Communist forces.

By the late 1980s the Soviet Union's grip on Eastern Europe was weakening as the former superpower's economic feet of clay crumbled. The Cold War era came to an end in 1989 with the fall of the Berlin Wall. Germany was reunified in 1990; a year later the

2002	**2009**	**2014**
Twelve member states of the EU ditch their national currencies in favour of the euro.	Europe is rocked by a series of financial crises, leading to costly bailouts for Ireland, Greece, Portugal and Spain.	Scotland votes on and rejects becoming a fully independent nation and so remains part of the United Kingdom.

USSR was dissolved. Shortly afterwards Romania, Bulgaria, Poland, Hungary and Albania had implemented multiparty democracy. In Czechoslovakia (now the Czech Republic and Slovakia), the so-called Velvet Revolution brought about the downfall of the communist government through mass demonstrations and other nonviolent means.

Europe United

The process of political and economic integration across Europe continued apace after the end of WWII. The formation of the European Economic Community (EEC) in 1957 began as a loose trade alliance between six nations. By 1992 this alliance had evolved into the European Union (EU) and when the Treaty of Maastricht came into effect in 1993 its core membership had expanded to 28 countries. Even though the UK is in the process of leaving the EU, five other candidates – Turkey, Macedonia, Montenego, Albania and Serbia – are on the books for future membership. All except Albania and Macedonia have started negotiations for entry.

Another key development was the implementation of the Schengen Agreement in 1995, which abolished border checks across much of mainland Europe and allowed EU citizens to travel freely throughout member states (with the notable exceptions of the UK and Ireland).

Even more momentous was the adoption of the single currency of the euro on 1 January 1999 as a cashless accounting currency; euro banknotes and coins have been used since 1 January 2002. To date, 19 countries have joined the Eurozone, while the UK, Denmark and Sweden have chosen to retain their national currencies. In future any new states joining the EU will be required to adopt the euro as a condition of entry. It's a hot topic, especially since the financial crash in countries including Greece and Spain, which has required richer nations (principally France and Germany) being called on to bail out several of their more indebted European neighbours.

Economic Challenges

Since the 2009 European debt crisis, growth throughout the EU has been sluggish, with many countries dipping in and out of recession. Unemployment figures across many European nations remain high, especially in Spain and Greece.

Although the euro stabilised after a series of multi billion-euro rescue packages for Greece, Ireland, Portugal and Spain, the currency is still subject to uncertainty. In 2015 an extension of Greece's bailout was granted in the hope of keeping the country within the Eurozone, to avoid a Greek exit (aka 'Grexit'), and to avoid other debt-saddled countries following suit. And the European Central Bank launched massive quantitative easing measures involving money printing and bond buying, pumping over €1 trillion into the economy in an effort to resuscitate it.

2015
Greece defaults on loan payments. Bailout proposals with tough conditions trigger riots and Greek banks close.

2016
Some EU borders are shut as millions of refugees and other unofficial migrants attempt to reach save European havens.

2017
Following a referendum in favour of quitting the EU, the UK triggers Article 50 setting in motion 'Brexit'.

La Pedrera (p294), Barcelona

Arts & Architecture

For millennia great art and architecture has sprung forth from Europe. The continent's museums and galleries are repositories of all kinds of creative treasures. Caesars, royal families and wealthy elites served as patrons to artists of the stature of Michelangelo, Rembrandt and Monet. Modernist and contemporary architects such as Antonio Gaudí and Richard Rogers have designed buildings that are mammoth works of art in their own right.

Arts

Ancient Art

Art was a crucial part of everyday life for ancient civilisations: decorative objects were a sign of status and prestige, while statues were used to venerate and honour the dead, and monuments and temples lavishly decorated in an attempt to appease the gods.

You'll find sculptures and artefacts from early civilisations in all Europe's top art museums, including the British Museum, the Louvre in Paris and the Pergamonmuseum in Berlin. Perhaps the most famous ancient artwork is the *Venus de Milo* at the Louvre, thought to have been created between 130 BC and 100 BC by the master sculptor Alexandros of Antioch.

Tate Modern, London

★ **Best Modern Art Galleries**
Tate Modern (p77), London
Museu Picasso (p292), Barcelona
Centre Pompidou (p228), Paris
Museo Guggenheim (p311), Bilbao
Designmuseum Danmark (p141),
Copenhagen

Medieval Art

During the Middle Ages, the power of the Church and its importance as an artistic patron meant that the majority of medieval art dealt with religious subjects. The Old Testament, the crucifixion, the apostles and the Last Judgment were common topics. Some of the finest medieval artworks are actually woven into the fabric of Europe's churches in the form of frescoes painted onto panels or walls.

Flemish and German painting produced several important figures during the period, including Jan van Eyck (c 1390–1441) and Hans Memling (c 1430–94), known for their lifelike oils, and Hieronymus Bosch (1450–1516), known for his use of fantastic imagery and allegorical concepts.

The Renaissance

The Renaissance marked Europe's golden age of art. Artists such as Leonardo da Vinci (1452–1519), Michelangelo (1475–1564), Raphael (1483–1520), Titian (c 1488/90–1576) and Botticelli (1445–1510) introduced new techniques, colours and forms into the artistic lexicon, drawing inspiration from the sculptors and artists of the classical world.

Landscape and the human form gained increasing importance during the Renaissance. Michelangelo's masterpiece, *David*, is often cited as the perfect representation of the human figure (despite the fact that the artist deliberately distorted its proportions to make it more pleasing to the eye). The sculpture is now displayed at the Galleria dell'Accademia in Florence. Florence's Galleria degli Uffizi contains the greatest collection of Italian Renaissance art.

In the wake of the Renaissance came the great names of the baroque period, epitomised by the Italian artist Caravaggio (1571–1610) and the Dutch artists Rembrandt (1606–69), Rubens (1577–1640) and Johannes Vermeer (1632–75). The baroque artists employed light and shadow (*chiaroscuro*) to heighten the drama of a scene and give their work a photographic intensity.

Romanticism & Impressionism

During the 18th century, Romantic artists such as Caspar David Friedrich (1774–1840) and JMW Turner (1775–1851) explored the drama of the natural landscape – cloudcapped mountains, lonely hilltops, peaceful meadows and moody sunsets. Other artists, such as Théodore Géricault (1791–1824) and Eugène Delacroix (1798–1863), drew inspiration from French history and prominent people of the day. One of Spain's most important artists, Francisco Goya (1746–1828), covered everything from royal portraits to war scenes, bull-fight etchings and tapestry designs.

During the late 19th century, artists such as Claude Monet (1840–1926), Edgar Degas (1834–1917), Camille Pissarro (1830–1903), Edouard Manet (1832–83) and Pierre-

Auguste Renoir (1841–1919) aimed to capture the general 'impression' of a scene rather than its naturalistic representation (hence the name of their movement, 'Impressionism').

Their bold experiments with light, colour and form segued into that of their successors, the post-Impressionists such as Paul Cézanne (1839–1906), Vincent van Gogh (1853–90) and Paul Gauguin (1848–1903).

From Fauvism to Conceptual Art

The upheavals of the 20th century inspired many new artistic movements. The fauvists were fascinated by colour, typified by Henri Matisse (1869–1954), while the cubists, such as Georges Braque (1882–1963) and Pablo Picasso (1881–1973), broke their work down into abstract forms, taking inspiration from everything from primitive art to psychoanalysis.

The dadaists and surrealists took these ideas to their illogical extreme, exploring dreams and the subconscious: key figures include René Magritte (1898–1967) from Belgium, Max Ernst (1891–1976) from Germany, and Joan Miró (1893–1983) and Salvador Dalí (1904–89) from Spain.

European Cinema

Europe is the birthplace of cinema. It was in Paris that Antoine Lumière debuted his Cinematograph in 1885 and Georges Méliès set up the world's first movie studio two years later. Germany was also an early country to the cinematic party with classics such as Fritz Lang's *Metropolis* (1927).

France has gone on to produce some of cinema's greatest talents, including François Truffaut (1932-84) and Jean-Luc Godard (1930–). It also hosts the Cannes film festival, one of Europe's top-three annual movie jamborees along with Venice and Berlin.

The 1940s were the golden age of British cinema with classics including David Lean's *Brief Encounter*, Carol Reed's *The Third Man* and Powell and Pressburger's *The Red Shoes*. In the 1960s, Britain gave the world James Bond and, in recent times, the Harry Potter series.

Conceptual art, which stresses the importance of the idea behind a work rather than purely its aesthetic value, also got its start in the early 20th century with the works of Marcel Duchamp (1887-1968) having a seminal influence on the movement.

Modern & Contemporary Art

After 1945 abstract art became a mainstay of the European scene, with key figures such as Joseph Beuys (1921–86) and Anselm Kiefer (1945–) from Germany and the Dutch-American Willem de Kooning (1904–97).

The late 20th century and 21st century to date have introduced many more artistic movements: abstract expressionism, neoplasticism, minimalism, formalism and pop art, to name a few.

Britain has a particularly vibrant contemporary art scene: key names such as Tracey Emin (1963–), Dinos (1962–) and Jake (1966–) Chapman (known as the Chapman Brothers), Rachel Whiteread (1963–), Mark Wallinger (1959–) and Damien Hirst (1965–), famous for his pickled shark and diamond-encrusted skull, continue to provoke controversy.

Architecture

The Ancient World

Europe's oldest examples of architecture are the many hundreds of stone circles, henges, barrows, burial chambers and alignments built by Neolithic people between 4500 BC and 1500 BC. The most impressive examples of these ancient structures are at Carnac in Brittany and, of course, Stonehenge in the southwest of England.

No one is quite sure what the purpose of these structures was, although theories abound. Some say they could be celestial calendars, burial monuments or tribal meeting places, although it's generally agreed these days that they served some sort of religious function.

Greek & Roman Architecture

Several ancient cultures have left their mark around the shores of the Mediterranean, including the Etruscans (in present-day Tuscany) and the ancient Greeks and Romans. Athens is the best place to appreciate Greece's golden age: the dramatic monuments of the Acropolis illustrate the ancient Greeks' sophisticated understanding of geometry, shape and form, and set the blueprint for many of the architectural principles that have endured to the present day

The Romans were even more ambitious, and built a host of monumental structures designed to project the might and majesty of the Roman Empire. Roman architecture was driven by a combination of form and function – structures such as the Pont du Gard in southern France show how the Romans valued architecture that looked beautiful but also served a practical purpose. Rome has the greatest concentration of architectural treasures, including the famous Colosseum, but remains of Roman buildings are scattered all over the continent.

Romanesque & Gothic Architecture

The solidity and elegance of ancient Roman architecture echoed through the 10th and 11th centuries in buildings constructed during the Romanesque period. Many of Europe's earliest churches are classic examples of Romanesque construction, using rounded arches, vaulted roofs, and massive columns and walls.

Even more influential was the development of Gothic architecture, which gave rise to many of Europe's most spectacular cathedrals. Tell-tale characteristics include the use of pointed arches, ribbed vaulting, great showpiece windows and flying buttresses. Notre-Dame in Paris is an ideal place to see Gothic architecture in action.

Renaissance & Baroque Architecture

The Renaissance led to a huge range of architectural experiments. Pioneering Italian architects such as Brunelleschi, Michelangelo and Palladio shifted the emphasis away from Gothic austerity towards a more human approach. They combined elements of classical architecture with new building materials, and specially commissioned sculptures and decorative artworks. Florence and Venice are particularly rich in Renaissance buildings, but the movement's influence can be felt right across Europe.

Architectural showiness reached its zenith during the baroque period, when architects pulled out all the stops to show off the wealth and prestige of their clients. Baroque buildings are all about creating drama, and architects often employed swathes of craftsmen and used the most expensive materials available to create the desired effect. Paris' Hôtel des Invalides is a good example of the ostentation and expense that underpinned baroque architecture.

The Industrial Age

The 19th century was the great age of urban planning, when the chaotic streets and squalid slums of many of Europe's cities were swept away in favour of grand squares and ruler-straight boulevards. This was partly driven by an attempt to clean up the urban environment, but it also allowed architects to redesign the urban landscape to suit the industrial age, merging factories, public buildings, museums and residential suburbs into a seamless whole. One of the most obvious examples of urban remodelling was Baron Haussmann's reinvention of Paris during the late 19th century, which resulted in the construction of the city's great boulevards and many of its landmark buildings.

Nineteenth-century architects began to move away from the showiness of the baroque and rococo periods in favour of new materials such as brick, iron and glass. Neo-Gothic architecture was designed to emphasise permanence, solidity and power, reflecting the confidence of the industrial age. It was an era that gave rise to many of Europe's great public buildings, including many landmark museums, libraries, town halls and train stations.

Top Musical Destinations

Vienna The Staatsoper is the premier venue in a city synonymous with opera and classical music.

Berlin Everything from the world's most acclaimed techno venue to the Berlin Philharmonic can be seen in Germany's music-obsessed capital.

Dublin The Irish have music in their blood and it takes little to get them singing, particularly down the pub.

Lisbon Portuguese love the melancholic and nostalgic songs of fado; hear it in the city's Alfama district.

Reykjavík Iceland's capital has a vibrant live-music scene producing famous pop talents such as Björk and Sigur Rós.

The 20th Century

By the turn of the 20th century, the worlds of art and architecture had both begun to experiment with new approaches to shape and form. The flowing shapes and natural forms of art nouveau had a profound influence on the work of Charles Rennie Mackintosh in Glasgow, the Belgian architect Victor Horta and the Modernista buildings of Spanish visionary Antonio Gaudí. Meanwhile, other architects stripped their buildings back to the bare essentials, emphasising strict function over form: Le Corbusier, Ludwig Mies van der Rohe and Walter Gropius are among the most influential figures of the period.

Functional architecture continued to dominate much of mid-20th-century architecture, especially in the rush to reconstruct Europe's shattered cities in the wake of two world wars, although the 'concrete box' style of architecture has largely fallen out of fashion over recent decades. Europeans may have something of a love-hate relationship with modern architecture, but the best buildings eventually find their place – a good example is the inside-out Centre Pompidou in Paris (designed by the architectural team of Richard Rogers, Renzo Piano and Gianfranco Franchini), which initially drew howls of protest but is now considered one of the icons of 20th-century architecture.

Contemporary Architecture

Regardless of whether you approve of the more recent additions to Europe's architectural landscape, one thing's for sure – you won't find them boring.

The fashion for sky-high skyscrapers seems to have caught on in several European cities, especially London, where a rash of multistorey buildings have recently been completed, all with their own nickname (the Walkie Talkie, the Cheesegrater and so on). The official name for the Norman Foster–designed 'Gerkin' buildling is 30 St Mary Axe. Topping them all is the Shard, which became the EU's highest building at 309.6m when it was completed in 2013.

A quirky peacock among Rome's classical architecture is the Maxxi, a contemporary art museum designed by the late Zaha Hadid. Norman Foster's Reichstag is a icon of modern, unified Germany, while Frank Gehry's Museo Guggenheim is a silvery masterpiece that is perhaps Europe's most dazzling piece of modern architecture.

Macarons, France

Food & Drink

Europe is united by its passion for eating and drinking with gusto. Every country has its own flavours, incorporating olive oils and sun-ripened vegetables in the hot south, rich cream and butter in cooler areas, fresh-off-the-boat seafood along the coast, delicate river and lake fish, and meat from fertile mountains and pastures. Each country has its own tipples, too, spanning renowned wines, beers, stouts and ciders, and feistier firewater.

Great Britain & Ireland

Great Britain might not have a distinctive cuisine, but it does have a thriving food culture, with a host of celebrity chefs and big-name restaurants. Great Britain's colonial legacy has also left it with a taste for curry – a recent poll suggested the nation's favourite food was chicken tikka masala.

The Brits love a good roast, traditionally eaten on a Sunday and accompanied by roast potatoes, vegetables and gravy. The classic is roast beef with Yorkshire pudding (a crisp batter puff), but lamb, pork and chicken are equally popular. 'Bangers and mash' (sausages and mashed potato) and fish and chips (battered cod or haddock served with thick-cut fried potatoes) are also old favourites.

Specialities in Scotland include haggis served with 'tatties and neeps' (potato and turnip).

Ireland's traditional dishes reflect the country's rustic past: look out for colcannon (mashed potato with cabbage), coddle (sliced sausages with bacon, potato and onion) and boxty (potato pancake), plus classic Irish stew (usually made with lamb or mutton).

The traditional British brew is ale, served at room temperature and flat, in order to bring out the hoppy flavours. It's an acquired taste, especially if you're used to cold, fizzy lagers.

Ireland's trademark ale is stout – usually Guinness, but you can also sample those produced by Murphy's or Beamish.

Scotland and Ireland are both known for whisky-making, with many distilleries open for tours and tasting sessions. Note that in Scotland it's always spelt 'whisky'; only in Ireland do you add the 'e'.

The Netherlands

The Netherlands' colonial legacy has given the Dutch a taste for Indonesian and Surinamese-inspired meals like *rijsttafel* (rice table): an array of spicy dishes such as braised beef, pork satay and ribs, all served with white rice.

Other Dutch dishes to look out for are *erwertensoep* (pea soup with onions, carrots, sausage and bacon), *krokotten* (filled dough balls that are crumbed and deep-fried) and, of course, *friet* (fries). Here they're thin, crispy and eaten with mayonnaise rather than ketchup (tomato sauce).

Beer is the tipple of choice. Small Dutch brewers like Gulpen, Haarlem's Jopen, Bavaria, Drie Ringen and Leeuw are all excellent. Jenever (gin) is also a favourite in the Netherlands.

France

Each French region has its distinctive dishes. Broadly, the hot south favours dishes based on olive oil, garlic and tomatoes, while the cooler north tends towards root vegetables, earthy flavours and creamy or buttery sauces. The French are famously unfussy about which bits of the animal they eat – kidney, liver, cheek and tongue are as much of a delicacy as a fillet steak or a prime rib.

Bouillabaisse, a saffron-scented fish stew, is a signature southern dish. It is served with spicy rouille sauce, gruyère cheese and croutons.

The Alps are the place to try fondue: hunks of toasted bread dipped into cheese sauces. Brittany and Normandy are big on seafood, especially mussels and oysters.

Sweet Treats

From pralines to puddings, Europe specialises in foods that are sweet, sticky and sinful. Germans and Austrians have a particularly sweet tooth – treats include *Salzburger nockerl* (a fluffy soufflé) and *Schwarzwälder kirschtorte* (Black Forest cherry cake), plus many types of *apfeltasche* (apple pastry) and *strudel* (filled filo pastry).

The Brits are another big cake-eating nation – a slice of cake or a dunked biscuit is an essential teatime ritual. The Italians are famous for their *gelaterie* (ice-cream stalls; the best will be labelled *produzione propria*, indicating that it's handmade on the premises). In Lisbon don't miss out on the deliciously cream egg custard tarts known as *pastel de nata*.

But it's the French who have really turned dessert into a fine art. Stroll past the window of any *boulangerie* (bakery) or patisserie and you'll be assaulted by temptations, from creamy *éclairs* (filled choux buns) and crunchy *macarons* (meringue-based biscuits with a ganache filling) to fluffy *madeleines* (shell-shaped sponge cakes) and wicked *gâteaux* (cakes).

Go on – you know you want to.

Outdoor restaurant, Rome

ALEXANDER MAZURKEVICH /SHUTTERSTOCK ©

Central France prides itself on its hearty cuisine, including *foie gras* (goose liver), *boeuf bourguignon* (beef cooked in red wine), *confit de canard* (duck cooked in preserved fat) and black truffles.

France is Europe's biggest wine producer. The principal regions are Alsace, Bordeaux, Burgundy, Languedoc, the Loire and the Rhône, all of which produce reds, whites and rosés. Then, of course, there's Champagne – home to the world's favourite bubbly, aged in centuries-old cellars beneath Reims and Épernay.

Spain

Spain's cuisine is typical of the flavours of Mediterranean cooking, making extensive use of herbs, tomatoes, onions, garlic and lashings of olive oil.

The nation's signature dish is *paella*, consisting of rice and chicken, meat or seafood, simmered with saffron in a large pan. Valencia is considered the spiritual home of *paella*.

Spain also prides itself on its ham and spicy sausages (including *chorizo*, *lomo* and *salchichón*). These are often used in making the bite-size Spanish dishes known as tapas (or *pintxos* in the Basque region). Tapas is usually a snack, but it can also be a main meal – three or four dishes is generally enough for one person.

Spain boasts the largest area (1.2 million hectares) of wine cultivation in the world. La Rioja and Ribera del Duero are the principal wine-growing regions.

Portugal

The Portuguese take pride in simple but flavourful dishes honed to perfection over the centuries. Bread remains integral to every meal, and it even turns up in some main courses. Be on the lookout for *açorda* (bread stew, often served with shellfish), *migas* (bread pieces prepared as a side dish) and *ensopados* (stews with toasted or deep-fried bread).

Seafood stews are superb, particularly *caldeirada*, which is a mix of fish and shellfish in a rich broth, not unlike a *bouillabaisse*. *Bacalhau* (dried salt-cod) is bound up in myth, history and tradition, and is excellent in baked dishes. Classic meat dishes include *porco preto* (sweet 'black' pork), *cabrito assado* (roast kid) and *arroz de pato* (duck risotto).

Portuguese wines are also well worth sampling such as fortified port and reds from the Douro valley and *alvarinho* and *vinho verde* (crisp, semi-sparkling wine) from the Minho.

Italy

Italian cuisine is dominated by the twin staples of pizza and pasta, which have been eaten in Italy since Roman times. A full meal comprises an *antipasto* (starter), *primo* (pasta or rice dish), *secondo* (usually meat or fish), *contorno* (vegetable side dish or salad), *dolce*

(dessert) and coffee. When eating out it's
OK to mix and match any combination.

Italian pasta comes in numerous shapes,
from bow-shaped *farfalle* to twisty *fusilli*,
ribbed *rigatoni* and long *pappardelle*. Italian
pasta is made with durum flour, which gives
it a distinctive *al dente* bite; the type of pasta used is usually dictated by the type of
dish being served (ribbed or shaped pastas
hold sauce better, for example).

Italian pizza comes in two varieties: the
Roman pizza with a thin crispy base, and
the Neapolitan pizza, which has a higher,
doughier base. The best are always prepared in a *forno a legna* (wood-fired oven).
Flavours are generally kept simple – the
best pizza restaurants often serve only a
couple of toppings, such as *margherita*
(tomato and mozzarella) and *marinara*
(tomato, garlic and oregano).

Italy's wines run the gamut from big-
bodied reds such as Piedmont's Barolo, to
light white wines from Sardinia and sparkling *prosecco* from the Veneto.

Europe's Favourite Cheeses

Britain Cheddar is tops but also try
Wensleydale, Red Leicester and Stilton.

Netherlands Edam and Gouda,
sometimes served as bar snacks with
mustard.

France The big names are camembert,
Brie, Livarot, Pont l'Évêque and Époisses
(all soft cheeses); Roquefort and Bleu
d'Auvergne (blue cheeses); and Comté,
cantal and gruyère (hard cheeses).

Spain Manchego, a semi-hard sheep's
cheese with a buttery flavour, is often
used in tapas.

Italy Prestigious varieties include Parmesan, ricotta and mozzarella.

Switzerland Emmental and Gruyère are
the best-known Swiss cheeses.

Germany Sample hard cheeses, especially Allgäu Emmentaler and Bergkäse
(mountain cheese).

Germany, Austria & Switzerland

The Germanic nations are all about big flavours and big portions. *Wurst* (sausage) comes
in hundreds of forms, and is often served with *Sauerkraut* (fermented cabbage).

The most common types of *Wurst* include *Bratwurst* (roast sausage), *Weisswurst*
(veal sausage) and *Currywurst* (sliced sausage topped with ketchup and curry powder).
Austria's signature dish is *Wiener Schnitzel* (breaded veal cutlet) but schnitzel in general
(usually featuring pork) are also popular in Germany.

Other popular mains include *Rippenspeer* (spare ribs), *Rotwurst* (black pudding), *Rost-
brätl* (grilled meat) and *Putenbrust* (turkey breast). Potatoes are served as *Bratkartoffeln*
(fried), *Kartoffelpüree* (mashed), Swiss-style *Rösti* (grated then fried) or *Pommes Frites*
(French fries).

The Swiss are known for their love of fondue and the similar dish *Raclette* (melted
cheese with potatoes).

Beer is the national beverage. *Pils* is the crisp pilsner Germany is famous for, which is
often slightly bitter. *Weizenbier* is made with wheat instead of barley malt and served in a
tall, 500mL glass. *Helles Bier* means light beer, while *dunkles* means dark.

Germany is principally known for white wines – inexpensive, light and intensely fruity.
The Rhine and Moselle Valleys are the largest wine-growing regions.

Czech Republic

Like many nations in Eastern Europe, Czech cuisine revolves around meat, potatoes and
root vegetables, dished up in stews, goulashes and casseroles. *Pečená kachna* (roast duck)

Vegetarians & Vegans

Vegetarians will have a tough time in many areas of Europe – eating meat is still the norm, and fish is often seen as a vegetarian option. However, you'll usually find something meat-free on most menus, though don't expect much choice. Vegans will have an even tougher time – cheese, cream and milk are integral ingredients of most European cuisines.

Vegetable-based *antipasti* (starters), tapas, meze, pastas, side dishes and salads are good options for a meat-free meal. Shopping for yourself in markets is an ideal way of trying local flavours without having to compromise your principles.

is the quintessential Czech restaurant dish, while *klobása* (sausage) is a common beer snack. A common side dish is *knedliky*, boiled dumplings made from wheat or potato flour.

The Czechs have a big beer culture, with some of Europe's best *pivo* (beer), usually lager style. The Moravian region is the up-and-coming area for Czech wines.

Denmark & Iceland

In Copenhagen you can sample creations inspired by the New Nordic culinary movement that has got foodies the world over talking. Simpler but no less tasty are *smørrebrød*, slices of rye bread topped with anything from beef tartar to egg and prawns.

The caraway-spiced schnapps *akvavit* is Denmark's best loved spirit – drink it as a shot followed by a chaser of *øl* (beer). Speaking of which, Denmark is also the home of Carlsberg as well as a battalion of microbreweries including Mikkeller and Grauballe.

Traditional Icelandic dishes reflect a historical need to eat every scrap and make it last through winter. Fish, seafood, lamb, bread and simple vegetables still form the typical Icelandic diet. A popular snack is Harðfiskur – dried strips of haddock eaten with butter. More challenging dishes include *svið* (singed sheep's head, complete with eyes, sawn in two, boiled and eaten fresh or pickled) and the famous stomach churner *hákarl* – Greenland shark, an animal so inedible it has to rot away underground for six months before humans can even digest it.

Wash it all down with the traditional alcoholic brew *brennivin* (schnapps made from potatoes and caraway seeds), a drink fondly known as 'black death'. If that's not to your taste, there are plenty of craft beers.

GORILLAIMAGES/SHUTTERSTOCK ©

Survival Guide

Directory A–Z

Accommodation

Reservations

During peak holiday periods, particularly Easter, summer and Christmas – and any time of year in popular destinations such as London, Paris and Rome – it's wise to book ahead. Most places can be reserved online. Always try to book directly with the establishment; this means you're paying just for your room, with no surcharge going to a hostel- or hotel-booking website.

B&Bs & Guest Houses

Guesthouses (pension, gasthaus, chambre d'hôte etc) and B&Bs (bed and breakfasts) offer greater

---

Book Your Stay Online

For more accommodation reviews by Lonely Planet authors, check out http://hotels.lonelyplanet.com/europe. You'll find independent reviews, as well as recommendations on the best places to stay. Best of all, you can book online.

---

comfort than hostels for a marginally higher price. Most are simple affairs, normally with shared bathrooms.

In some destinations, particularly in Eastern Europe, locals wait in train stations touting rented rooms. Just be sure such accommodation isn't in a far-flung suburb that requires an expensive taxi ride to and from town. Confirm the price before agreeing to rent a room and remember that it's unwise to leave valuables in your room when you go out.

B&Bs in the UK and Ireland often aren't really budget accommodation – even the lowliest tend to have midrange prices and there is a new generation of 'designer' B&Bs that are positively top end.

Camping

Most camping grounds are some distance from city centres. National tourist offices provide lists of camping grounds and camping organisations. Also see www.coolcamping.co.uk for details on prime campsites across Europe.

Homestays & Farmstays

You needn't volunteer on a farm to sleep on it. In Switzerland and Germany, there's the opportunity to sleep in barns or 'hay hotels'. Farmers provide cotton undersheets (to avoid straw pricks) and woolly blankets for extra warmth, but guests

need their own sleeping bag and torch. For further details, visit Abenteuer im Stroh (www.schlaf-im-stroh.ch).

Italy has a similar and increasingly popular network of farmstays called *agriturismi*. Participating farms must grow at least one of their own crops. Otherwise, accommodation runs the gamut from small rustic hideaways to grand country estates. See www.agriturismo.it for more details.

Hostels

There's a vast variation in hostel standards across Europe.

HI Hostels (those affiliated to Hostelling International; www.hihostels.com), usually offer the cheapest (secure) roof over your head in Europe and you don't have to be particularly young to use them. That said, if you're over 26 you'll frequently pay a small surcharge (usually about €3) to stay in an official hostel.

Hostel rules vary per facility and country, but some ask that guests vacate the rooms for cleaning purposes or impose a curfew. Most offer a complimentary breakfast, although the quality varies. Hostels are also great places to meet other travellers and pick up all kinds of information on the region you are visiting. They often usurp tourist offices in this respect.

You need to be a YHA or HI member to use HI-affiliated hostels, but nonmembers can stay by paying a few extra euros,

Price Ranges

Rates in our reviews are for high season and often drop outside high season by as much as 50%. High season in ski resorts is usually between Christmas and New Year and around the February to March winter holidays. Price categories are broken down differently for individual countries – see each country for full details.

which will be set against future membership. After sufficient nights (usually six), you automatically become a member. To join, ask at any hostel or contact your national hostelling office, which you'll find on the HI website – where you can also make online bookings.

Europe has many private hostelling organisations and hundreds of unaffiliated backpacker hostels. These have fewer rules, more self-catering kitchens and fewer large, noisy school groups. Dorms in many private hostels can be mixed sex. If you aren't happy to share mixed dorms, be sure to ask when you book.

Hotels

Hotels are usually the most expensive accommodation option, though at their lower end there is little to differentiate them from guesthouses or even hostels.

Cheap hotels around bus and train stations can be convenient for late-night or early-morning arrivals and departures, but some are also unofficial brothels or just downright sleazy. Check the room beforehand and make sure you're clear on the price and what it covers.

Discounts for longer stays are usually possible and hotel owners in southern Europe *might* be open to a little bargaining if times are slack. In many countries it's common for business hotels (usually more than two stars) to slash their rates by up to 40% on Friday and Saturday nights.

Climate

London

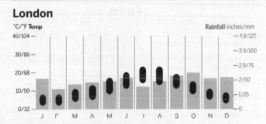

Paris

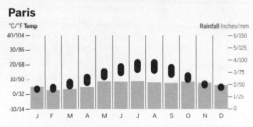

Rome

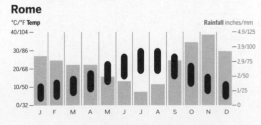

Customs Regulations

The European Union (EU) has a two-tier customs system: one for goods bought duty-free to import to or export from the EU, and one for goods bought in another EU country where taxes and duties have been paid.

○ Entering or leaving the EU, you are allowed to carry duty-free: 200 cigarettes, 50 cigars or 250g of tobacco; 2l of still wine plus 1L of spirits over 22% alcohol or another

4L of wine (sparkling or otherwise); 50g of perfume, 250cc of eau de toilette.

○ Travelling from one EU country to another, the duty-paid limits are: 800 cigarettes, 200 cigars, 1kg of tobacco, 10L of spirits, 20L of fortified wine, 90L of wine (of which not more than 60L is sparkling) and 110L of beer.

○ Non-EU countries often have different regulations and many countries forbid the export of antiquities and cultural treasures.

Electricity

Europe generally runs on 220V, 50Hz AC, but there are exceptions. The UK runs on 230/240V AC, and some old buildings in Italy and Spain have 125V (or even 110V in Spain). The continent is moving towards a

230V standard. If your home country has a vastly different voltage you will need a transformer for delicate and important appliances.

The UK and Ireland use three-pin square plugs (Type G). Most of Europe uses a 'europlug' with two round pins. Greece, Italy and Switzerland use a third round pin in a way that the two-pin plug usually (but not always in Italy and Switzerland) fits. Buy an adapter before leaving home; those on sale in Europe generally go the other way, but ones for visitors to Europe are also available.

Food

Rates in our reviews are based on the price of a main meal. Price categories are broken down differently for individual countries – see each country for full details.

Gay & Lesbian Travellers

Across Western Europe you'll find very liberal attitudes towards homosexuality. London, Paris, Berlin, Amsterdam and Lisbon have thriving gay communities and pride events.

Eastern Europe tends to be far less progressive. Outside the big cities, attitudes become more conservative and discretion is advised.

Health

Before You Go
Recommended Vaccinations

No jabs are necessary for Europe. However, the World Health Organization

Type C
220V/50Hz

Type F
230V/50Hz

Type G
230V/50Hz

(WHO) recommends that all travellers be covered for diphtheria, tetanus, measles, mumps, rubella and polio, regardless of their destination. Since most vaccines don't produce immunity until at least two weeks after they're given, visit a physician at least six weeks before departure.

Health Insurance

It is unwise to travel anywhere in the world without travel insurance. A good policy should include comprehensive health insurance including medical care and emergency evacuation. If you are engaging in hazardous sports, you may need to pay for extra cover.

If you're an EU citizen, the free EHIC (European Health Insurance Card) covers you for most medical care in the 28 EU member states, including maternity care and care for chronic illnesses such as diabetes (though not for emergency repatriation). However, you will normally have to pay for medicine bought from pharmacies, even if prescribed, and perhaps for some tests and procedures. The EHIC does not cover private medical consultations and treatment out of your home country; this includes nearly all dentists, and some of the better clinics and surgeries. In the UK, you can apply for an EHIC online, by telephone, or by filling out a form available at post offices.

Non-EU citizens should find out if there is a recip-rocal arrangement for free medical care between their country and the EU country they are visiting.

Websites

The **World Health Organization** (www.who.int/ith/en) publishes the annually revised, free online book *International Travel and Health*. **MD Travel Health** (www.mdtravelhealth.com) provides up-to-date travel-health recommendations for every country.

It's usually a good idea to consult your government's website before departure, if one is available:
Australia (www.smartraveller.gov.au)
Canada (www.phac-aspc.gc.ca)
UK (www.gov.uk/foreign-travel-advice)
USA (www.cdc.gov/travel)

In Europe

Good health care is readily available in Western Europe and, for minor illnesses, pharmacists can give valuable advice and sell over-the-counter medication. They can also advise if you need specialised help and point you in the right direction. The standard of dental care is usually good.

While the situation in Eastern Europe is improving since the EU accession of many countries, quality medical care is not always readily available outside major cities, but embassies, consulates and five-star hotels can usually recommend doctors or clinics.

Tap Water

Tap water is generally safe to drink in Western Europe. However, bottled water is recommended in most of Eastern Europe, and is a must in some countries where the giardia parasite can be a problem. Do not drink water from rivers or lakes as it may contain bacteria or viruses.

Condoms are widely available in Europe, however emergency contraception may not be, so take the necessary precautions.

Insurance

It's foolhardy to travel without insurance to cover theft, loss and medical problems. There are a wide variety of policies, so check the small print.

Some policies specifically exclude 'dangerous activities', which can include scuba diving, motorcycling, winter sports, adventure sports or even hiking.

Check that the policy covers ambulances or an emergency flight home.

Worldwide travel insurance is available online at www.lonelyplanet.com/travel-insurance. You can buy, extend and claim online anytime – even if you're already on the road.

Internet Access

Internet access varies enormously across Europe. In most places, you'll be able to find wireless (wi-fi, also called WLAN in some countries), although whether it's free varies greatly.

Where the wi-fi icon appears, it means that the establishment offers free wi-fi that you can access immediately, or by asking for the access code from staff.

Access is generally straightforward, although a few tips are in order. If you can't find the @ symbol on a keyboard, try Alt Gr + 2, or Alt Gr + Q. Watch out for German keyboards, which reverse the Z and the Y positions. Using a French keyboard is an art unto itself.

Where necessary in relevant countries, click on the language prompt in the bottom right-hand corner of the screen or hit Ctrl + Shift to switch between the Cyrillic and Latin alphabets.

Legal Matters

You can generally purchase alcohol (beer and wine) from between 16 and 18 years (usually 18 for spirits), but if in doubt, ask. Although you can drive at 17 or 18, you might not be able to hire a car until you're 25.

Drugs are often quite openly available in Europe, but that doesn't mean they're legal. The Netherlands is most famed for its liberal attitudes, with *coffeeshops* openly selling cannabis even though the drug is *not* technically legal. However, a blind eye is generally turned to the trade as the possession and purchase of small amounts (5g) of 'soft drugs' (ie marijuana and hashish) is allowed and users won't be prosecuted for smoking or carrying this amount. Don't take this relaxed attitude as an invitation to buy harder drugs; if you get caught, you'll be punished. Since 2008 magic mushrooms have been banned in the Netherlands.

Spain also has pretty liberal laws regarding marijuana although its use is usually reserved for private 'cannabis clubs'.

Switzerland, Portugal, Austria and the Czech Republic have decriminalised possession of marijuana; however, selling remains illegal.

Getting caught with drugs in some parts of Europe can lead to imprisonment. If in any doubt, err on the side of caution, and don't even think about taking drugs across international borders.

Maps

Tourist offices usually provide free but fairly basic maps.

Road atlases are essential if you're driving or cycling. Leading brands are Freytag & Berndt, Hallwag, Kümmerly + Frey and Michelin.

Maps published by European automobile associations, such as Britain's **AA** (www.theaa.co.uk) and Germany's **ADAC** (www.adac.de), are usually excellent and sometimes free if membership of your local association gives you reciprocal rights.

Money

ATMs

Across major European towns and cities international ATMs are common, but you should always have a back-up option, as there can be glitches. In some remote areas, ATMs might be scarce.

Much of Western Europe now uses a chip-and-pin system for added security. You will have problems if you don't have a four-digit PIN number and might have difficulties if your card doesn't have a metallic chip. Check with your bank.

Always cover the keypad when entering your PIN and make sure there are no unusual devices attached to the machine, which can copy your card's details or cause it to stick in the machine. If your card disappears and the screen goes blank before you've even entered your PIN, don't enter it –

especially if a 'helpful' by-stander tells you to do so. If you can't retrieve your card, call your bank's emergency number, if you can, before leaving the ATM.

Cash

It's a good idea to bring some local currency in cash, if only to cover yourself until you get to an exchange facility or find an ATM. The equivalent of €150 should usually be enough. Some extra cash in an easily exchanged currency is also a good idea, especially in Eastern Europe.

Credit Cards

Visa and MasterCard/Eurocard are more widely accepted in Europe than Amex and Diners Club; Visa (sometimes called Carte Bleue) is particularly strong in France and Spain.

There are, however, regional differences in the general acceptability of credit cards; in Germany, for example, it's rare for restaurants to take credit cards. Cards are not widely accepted once you're off the beaten track.

To reduce the risk of fraud, always keep your card in view when making transactions; for example, in restaurants that do accept cards, pay as you leave, following your card to the till. Keep transaction records and either check your statements when you return home, or check your account online while still on the road.

Letting your credit-card company know roughly where you're going lessens the chance of fraud – or of your bank cutting off the card when it sees (your) unusual spending.

Currency

Apart from Denmark, Switzerland and the UK (which have their own currencies), all the countries covered in this guide use the euro, which is made up of 100 cents. Notes come in denominations of €5, €10, €20, €50, €100, €200 and €500 euros, though any notes above €50 are rarely used on a daily basis. Coins come in 1c, 2c, 5c, 10c, 20c, 50c, €1 and €2.

Debit Cards

It's always worthwhile having a Maestro-compatible debit card, which differs from a credit card in deducting money straight from your bank account. Check with your bank or MasterCard (Maestro's parent) for compatibility.

Exchanging Money

Euros, US dollars and UK pounds are the easiest currencies to exchange. You may have trouble exchanging some lesser-known ones at small banks.

Importing or exporting some currencies is restricted or banned, so try to get rid of any local currency before you leave. Get rid of Scottish pounds before leaving the UK; nobody outside Britain will touch them.

Most airports, central train stations, big hotels and many border posts have banking facilities outside regular business hours, at times on a 24-hour basis. Post offices in Europe often perform banking tasks, tend to open longer hours and outnumber banks in remote places. While they always exchange cash, they might balk at handling travellers cheques not in the local currency.

The best exchange rates are usually at banks. *Bureaux de change* usually – but not always – offer worse rates or charge higher commissions. Hotels and airports are almost always the worst places to change money.

International Transfers

International bank transfers are good for secure one-off movements of large amounts of money, but they might take three to five days and there will be a fee (about £25 in the UK, for example). Be sure to specify the name of the bank, plus the sort code and address of the branch where you'd like to pick up your money.

In an emergency it's quicker but more costly to have money wired via an Amex office (www.american express.com), Western Union (www.westernunion. com) or MoneyGram (www. moneygram.com).

Taxes & Refunds

When non-EU residents spend more than a certain

amount (around €75, but amounts vary from country to country), they can usually reclaim any sales tax when leaving the country.

Making a tax-back claim is straightforward. First, make sure the shop offers duty-free sales (often a sign will be displayed reading 'Tax-Free Shopping'). When making your purchase, ask the shop attendant for a tax-refund voucher, filled in with the correct amount and the date. This can be used to claim a refund directly at international airports, or stamped at ferry ports or border crossings and mailed back for a refund.

Tipping

o 'Service charges' are increasingly added to bills. In theory this means you're not obliged to tip. In practice that money often doesn't go to the server. Don't pay twice. If the service charge is optional, remove it and pay a tip. If it's not optional, don't tip.

o Tipping isn't such a big deal in Europe as it is say in North America. If you tip, 5% to 10% will usually suffice.

Travellers Cheques

It's become more difficult to find places that cash travellers cheques. In parts of Eastern Europe only a few banks handle them, and the process can be quite bureaucratic and costly.

That said, having a few cheques is a good back-up. If they're stolen you can claim a refund, provided you

have a separate record of cheque numbers.

Amex and Thomas Cook are reliable brands of travellers cheques, while cheques in US dollars, euros or British pounds are the easiest to cash. When changing them ask about fees and commissions as well as the exchange rate.

Opening Hours

Opening times vary significantly between countries. The following is a general overview.

Shops & Businesses 9am–6pm Monday to Friday, to 1pm or 5pm Saturday. In smaller towns there may be a one- to two-hour closure for lunch. Some shops close on Sunday. Businesses also close on national holidays and local feast days.

Banks 9am to between 3pm and 5pm Monday to Friday. Occasionally shut for lunch.

Restaurants noon to midnight

Bars 6pm to midnight or later.

Museums close Monday or (less commonly) Tuesday.

Post

From major European centres, airmail typically takes about five days to North America and about a week to Australasian destinations.

Courier services such as DHL are best for essential deliveries.

Public Holidays

There are large variations in statutory holidays in Europe. The following are the most common across the board:

New Year's Day 1 January

Good Friday March/April

Easter Sunday March/April

May Day 1 May

Pentecost/Whitsun May/June

Christmas Day 25 December

Safe Travel

Travelling in Europe is usually very safe.

Discrimination

In some parts of Europe travellers of African, Arab or Asian descent might encounter unpleasant attitudes that are unrelated to them personally. In rural areas travellers whose skin colour marks them out as foreigners might experience unwanted attention.

Attitudes vary from country to country. People tend to be more accepting in cities than in the country.

Druggings

Although rare, some drugging of travellers does occur in Europe. Travellers are especially vulnerable on trains and buses where a new 'friend' may offer you food or a drink that will knock you out, giving them time to steal your belongings.

Gassings have also been reported on a handful of overnight international trains. The best protection is to lock the door of your compartment (use your own lock if there isn't one) and to lock your bags to luggage racks, preferably with a sturdy combination cable.

If you can help it, never sleep alone in a train compartment.

Pickpockets & Thieves

Theft is definitely a problem in parts of Europe and you have to be aware of unscrupulous fellow travellers. The key is to be sensible with your possessions.

● Don't store valuables in train-station lockers or luggage-storage counters and be careful about people who offer to help you operate a locker. Also be vigilant if someone offers to carry your luggage: they might carry it away altogether.

● Don't leave valuables in your car, on train seats or in your room. When going out, don't flaunt cameras,

Emergency Numbers

The phone number ☎112 can be dialled free for emergencies in all EU states. See individual countries for country-specific emergency numbers.

laptops and other expensive electronic goods.

● Carry a small day pack, as shoulder bags are an open invitation for snatch-thieves. Consider using small zipper locks on your packs.

● Pickpockets are most active in dense crowds, especially in busy train stations and on public transport during peak hours. Be careful in these situations.

● Spread valuables, cash and cards around your body or in different bags.

● A money belt with your essentials (passport, cash, credit cards, airline tickets) is usually a good idea. However, so you needn't delve into it in public, carry a wallet with a day's worth of cash.

● Having your passport stolen is less of a disaster if you've recorded the number and issue date or, even better, photocopied the relevant data pages. You can also scan them and email them to yourself. If you lose your passport, notify the police immediately to get a statement and contact your nearest consulate.

● Carry photocopies of your credit cards, airline tickets and other travel documents.

Unrest & Terrorism

Civil unrest and terrorist bombings are relatively rare in Europe, all things considered, but they do occur. Attacks by Muslim extremists in the UK, France and Germany have occurred in recent years. Keep an eye

on the news and avoid areas where any flare-up seems likely.

Telephone

Mobile Phones

If your mobile phone is European, it's often perfectly feasible to use it on roaming throughout the Continent.

If you're coming from outside Europe, it's usually worth buying a prepaid local SIM in one European country. Even if you're not staying there long, calls across Europe will still be cheaper if they're not routed via your home country and the prepaid card will enable you to keep a limit on your spending. In several countries you need your passport to buy a SIM card.

In order to use other SIM cards in your phone, you'll need to have your handset unlocked by your home provider. Even if your phone is locked, you can use apps such as 'whatsapp' to send free text messages internationally wherever you have wi-fi access, or Skype to make free international calls whenever you're online.

Europe uses the GSM 900 network, which also covers Australia and New Zealand, but is not compatible with the North American GSM 1900 or the totally different system in Japan and South Korea. If you have a GSM phone, check with your service provider about using it in Europe. You'll need international roaming, but this is usually free to enable.

You can call abroad from almost any phone box in Europe. Public telephones accepting phonecards (available from post offices, telephone centres, news stands or retail outlets) are virtually the norm now; coin-operated phones are rare if not impossible to find.

Without a phonecard, you can ring from a telephone booth inside a post office or telephone centre and settle your bill at the counter. Reverse-charge (collect) calls are often possible. From many countries the Country Direct system lets you phone home by billing the long-distance carrier you use at home. These numbers can often be dialled from public phones without even inserting a phonecard.

Time

Europe is divided into four time zones. The countries covered in this guide fall into the following zones:

UTC (Coordinated Universal Time; Britain, Ireland, Portugal) the same as GMT (GMT+1 in summer)

CET (Central European Time; the majority of European countries) GMT+1 (GMT+2 in summer)

At 9am in Britain it's 1am (GMT/UTC minus eight hours) on the US west coast, 4am (GMT/UTC minus five hours) on the US east coast, 10am in Paris and Prague, 11am in Athens, midday in Moscow and 7pm (GMT/UTC plus 10 hours) in Sydney.

Nearly all of Europe, with several exceptions (including Iceland), observes daylight saving time on synchronised dates in late March (clocks go forward an hour) and late October (clocks go back an hour).

Toilets

Many public toilets require a small fee either deposited in a box or given to the attendant. Sit-down toilets are the rule in the vast majority of places. Squat toilets can still be found in rural areas, although they are definitely a dying breed.

Public-toilet provision is changeable from city to city. If you can't find one, simply drop into a hotel or restaurant and ask to use theirs.

Tourist Information

Unless otherwise indicated, tourist offices are common and widespread, although their usefulness varies enormously.

Travellers with Disabilities

Cobbled medieval streets, 'classic' hotels, congested inner cities and underground subway systems make Europe a tricky destination for people with mobility impairments. However, the train facilities are good and some destinations boast new tram services or lifts to platforms. Download Lonely Planet's free Accessible Travel guide from http://lptravel.to/AccessibleTravel. The following websites can help with specific details:

Accessible Europe (www.accessibleurope.com) Specialist European tours with van transport.

Mobility International Schweiz (www.mis-ch.ch) Good site (only partly in English) listing 'barrier-free' destinations in Switzerland and abroad, plus wheelchair-accessible hotels in Switzerland.

Mobility International USA (www.miusa.org) Publishes guides and advises travellers with disabilities on mobility issues.

DisabledGo.com (www.disabledgo.com) Detailed access information on thousands of venues across the UK and Ireland.

Society for Accessible Travel & Hospitality (SATH; www.sath.org) Reams of information for travellers with disabilities.

The Schengen Area

Twenty six European countries are signatories to the Schengen Agreement, which has effectively dismantled internal border controls between them. They are Austria, Belgium, Czech Republic, Denmark, Estonia, Finland, France, Germany, Greece, Iceland, Italy, Hungary, Latvia, Liechtenstein, Lithuania, Luxembourg, Malta, the Netherlands, Norway, Poland, Portugal, Slovenia, Slovakia, Spain, Sweden and Switzerland.

The UK and Ireland, as well as much of Eastern Europe, are not part of the Schengen Agreement. Visitors from non-EU countries will have to apply for visas to these countries separately.

Citizens of the US, Australia, New Zealand, Canada and the UK only need a valid passport to enter Schengen countries (as well as the UK and Ireland). However, other nationals, including South Africans, can apply for a single visa – a Schengen visa when travelling throughout this region.

Non-EU visitors (with or without a Schengen visa) should expect to be questioned, however perfunctorily, when first entering the region. However, later travel within the zone is much like a domestic trip, with no border controls.

If you need a Schengen visa, you must apply at the consulate or embassy of the country that's your main destination, or your point of entry. You may then stay up to a maximum of 90 days in the entire Schengen area within a six-month period. Once your visa has expired, you must leave the zone and may only re-enter after three months abroad. Shop around when choosing your point of entry, as visa prices may differ from country to country.

If you're a citizen of the US, Australia, New Zealand or Canada, you may stay visa-free a total of 90 days, during six months, within the entire Schengen region.

For up-to-date details see www.schengenvisainfo.com.

Visas

◦ Citizens of the USA, Canada, Australia, New Zealand and the UK need only a valid passport to enter nearly all countries in Europe, including the entire EU.

◦ Transit visas are usually cheaper than tourist or business visas but they allow only a very short stay (one to five days) and can be difficult to extend.

◦ All visas have a 'use-by' date and you'll be refused entry afterwards. In some cases it's easier to get visas as you go along, rather than arranging them all beforehand. Carry spare passport photos (you may need from one to four every time you apply for a visa).

◦ Visas to neighbouring countries are usually issued immediately by consulates in Eastern Europe, although some may levy a hefty surcharge for 'express service'.

◦ Consulates are generally open weekday mornings (if there's both an embassy and a consulate, you want the consulate).

◦ Because regulations can change, double-check with the relevant embassy or consulate before travelling.

Women Travellers

◦ Women might attract unwanted attention in rural Spain and southern Italy where many men view whistling and catcalling as flattery. Conservative dress can help to deter lascivious gazes and wolf whistles; dark sunglasses help avoid unwanted eye contact.

◦ Marriage is highly respected in southern Europe, and a wedding ring can help, along with talk about 'my husband'.

◦ Hitchhiking alone is not recommended anywhere.

○ **Journeywoman** (www.
journeywoman.com) main-
tains an online newsletter
about solo female travels all
over the world.

Transport

Getting There & Away

Europe is one of the world's
major destinations; sporting
many of its busiest airports
with routes fanning out to the
far corners of the globe. More
adventurous travellers can
enter from Asia on some epic
long-distance train routes.
Numerous ferries jockey
across the Mediterranean
between Europe and Africa.

Flights, cars and tours
can be booked online at
lonelyplanet.com/bookings.

Air
Airports & Airlines

To save money, it's best
to travel off-season. This
means, if possible, avoid
mid-June to early Septem-
ber, Easter, Christmas and
school holidays.

Regardless of your
ultimate destination, it's
sometimes better to pick a
recognised transport 'hub'
as your initial port of entry,
where high traffic volumes
help keep prices down.
Long-haul airfares to Eastern
Europe are rarely a bargain;
you're usually better flying to
a Western European hub and
taking an onward budget-
airline flight or train. The
main hubs in Eastern Europe
are Budapest and Prague.

Gateway cities such as
London and Paris are also
well serviced by low-cost
carriers that fly to other
parts of Europe.

Land

It's possible to reach Europe
by various different train
routes from Asia. Most
common is the Trans-
Siberian Railway, connecting Moscow to Siberia, the
Russian Far East, Mongolia
and China. See www.seat61.
com for more information
about these adventurous
routes.

Border Crossings

Border formalities have
been relaxed in most of the
EU, but still exist in all their
original bureaucratic glory
in the more far-flung parts
of Eastern Europe.

In line with the Schengen
Agreement (p629), there
are officially no passport
controls at the borders between 26 European states.
Sometimes, however, there
are spot checks on trains
crossing borders, so always
have your passport. The UK
maintains border controls
over traffic from other EU
countries (except Ireland,
with which it shares an open
border), although there is
no customs control. For
up-to-date details see www.
schengenvisainfo.com.

Sea

There are numerous ferry
routes between Europe and
Africa, including links from
Spain to Morocco, Italy to
Tunisia, France to Morocco
and France to Tunisia. Check
out www.traghettiweb.it for
comprehensive information
on all Mediterranean ferries.
Ferries are often filled to capacity in summer, especially
to and from Tunisia, so book
well in advance if you're
taking a vehicle across.

Climate Change & Travel

Every form of transport that relies on carbon-based
fuel generates CO_2, the main cause of human-induced
climate change. Modern travel is dependent on aero-
planes, which might use less fuel per kilometre per person than most cars but travel much greater distances.
The altitude at which aircraft emit gases (including CO_2)
and particles also contributes to their climate change
impact. Many websites offer 'carbon calculators' that
allow people to estimate the carbon emissions generat-
ed by their journey and, for those who wish to do so, to
offset the impact of the greenhouse gases emitted with
contributions to portfolios of climate-friendly initiatives
throughout the world. Lonely Planet offsets the carbon
footprint of all staff and author travel.

Passenger freighters (typically carrying up to 12 passengers) aren't nearly as competitively priced as airlines. Journeys also take a long time. However, if you have your heart set on a transatlantic journey, **TravLtips Cruise and Freighter** (www.travltips. com) has information on freighter cruises.

Getting Around

Air

Airlines

Low-cost carriers have revolutionised European transport. Most airlines, budget or otherwise, have a similar pricing system – namely that ticket prices rise with the number of seats sold on each flight, so book as early as possible to get a decent fare.

Some low-cost carriers – Ryanair being the prime example – have made a habit of flying to smaller, less convenient airports on the outskirts of their destination city, or even to the airports of nearby cities, so check the exact location of the departure and arrival airports before you book. Many flights also leave at the crack of dawn or arrive inconveniently late at night.

Departure and other taxes (including booking fees, checked-baggage fees and other surcharges) soon add up and are included in the final price by the end of the

online booking process – usually a lot more than you were hoping to pay – but with careful choosing and advance booking you can get great deals.

For a comprehensive overview of which low-cost carriers fly to or from which European cities, check out the excellent www. flycheapo.com.

Air Passes

Various travel agencies and airlines offer air passes including the three main airline alliances: **Oneworld** (www.oneworld.com), **Star Alliance** (www.staralliance. com) and **SkyTeam** (www. skyteam.com). Check with your travel agent for current promotions.

Bicycle

Much of Europe is ideally suited to cycling. It's easy to hire bikes throughout most of Europe but, for major cycling trips, it's best to have a bike you're familiar with, so consider bringing your own rather than buying on arrival. If coming from outside Europe, ask about the airline's policy on transporting bikes before buying your ticket.

A primary consideration on a cycling trip is to travel light, but you should take a few tools and spare parts, including a puncture-repair kit and an extra inner tube. Panniers are essential to balance your possessions on either side of the bike frame. Wearing a helmet is not compulsory in most countries, but is certainly sensible.

Seasoned cyclists can average 80km a day, but it depends on what you're carrying and your level of fitness.

Cyclists' Touring Club (CTC; www.ctc.org.uk) The national cycling association of the UK runs organised trips to Continental Europe.

European Cyclists' Federation (www.ecf.com) Has details of 'EuroVelo', the European cycle network of 12 pan-European cycle routes, plus tips for other tours.

SwitzerlandMobility (www. veloland.ch/en/cycling-in-switzerland.html) Details of Swiss national routes and more.

Boat

Several different ferry companies compete on the main ferry routes, resulting in a comprehensive but complicated service. The same ferry company can have a host of different prices for the same route, depending on the time of day or year, validity of the ticket and length of your vehicle. Vehicle tickets usually include the driver and often up to five passengers free of charge.

It's worth booking ahead where possible as there may be special reductions on off-peak crossings and advance-purchase tickets. On English Channel routes, apart from one-day or short-term excursion returns, there is little price advantage in buying a return ticket versus two singles.

Rail-pass holders are entitled to discounts or free travel on some lines. Food on ferries is often expensive (and lousy), so it is worth bringing your own. Also be aware that if you take your vehicle on board, you are usually denied access to it during the voyage.

Lake and river ferry services operate in many countries, Austria and Switzerland being just two. Some of these are very scenic.

Bus

International Buses

Europe's biggest organisation of international buses operates under the name **Eurolines** (www.eurolines. com), comprised of various national companies. A **Eurolines Pass** (www.eurolines. com/en/eurolines-pass) is offered for extensive travel, allowing passengers to visit a choice of 53 cities across Europe over 15 or 30 days. In the high season (mid-June to mid-September) the pass costs €315/405 for those aged under 26, or €375/490 for those 26 and over. It's cheaper in other periods.

Busabout (www. busabout.com) offers a 'hop-on, hop-off' service around Europe, stopping at major cities. Buses are often oversubscribed, so book each sector to avoid being stranded. It departs every two days from May to the end of October.

National Buses

Domestic buses provide a viable alternative to trains in most countries. Again, they are usually slightly cheaper and somewhat slower.

Buses are generally best for short hops, such as getting around cities and reaching remote villages, and they are often the only option in mountainous regions.

Reservations are rarely necessary. On many city buses you usually buy your ticket in advance from a kiosk or machine and validate it on entering the bus.

Car & Motorcycle

Travelling with your own vehicle gives flexibility and is the best way to reach remote places. However, the independence does sometimes isolate you from local life. Also, cars can be a target for theft and are often impractical in city centres, where traffic jams, parking problems and getting thoroughly lost can make it well worth ditching your vehicle and using public transport. Various car-carrying trains can help you avoid long, tiring drives.

Campervan

One popular way to tour Europe is for a group of three or four people to band together and buy or rent a campervan. London is the usual embarkation point. Look at the ads in London's free magazine *TNT* (www. tntmagazine.com) if you wish to form or join a group. *TNT* is also a good source for purchasing a van, as is Loot (www.loot.com).

Some secondhand dealers offer a 'buy-back' scheme for when you return from the Continent, but check the small print

before signing anything and remember that if an offer is too good to be true, it probably is. Buying and reselling privately should be more advantageous if you have time. In the UK, DUInsure (www.duinsure.com) offers a campervan policy.

Motorcycle Touring

Europe is made for motorcycle touring, with quality winding roads, stunning scenery and an active motorcycling scene. Just make sure your wet-weather motorcycling gear is up to scratch.

❍ Rider and passenger crash helmets are compulsory everywhere in Europe.

❍ Austria, France, Germany, Portugal and Spain require that motorcyclists use headlights during the day; in other countries it is recommended.

❍ On ferries, motorcyclists rarely have to book ahead as they can generally be squeezed on board.

❍ Take note of the local custom about parking motorcycles on pavements (sidewalks). Though this is illegal in some countries, the police often turn a blind eye provided the vehicle doesn't obstruct pedestrians.

Fuel

❍ Fuel prices can vary enormously (though fuel is always more expensive than in North America or Australia).

❍ Unleaded petrol only is available throughout

Europe. Diesel is usually cheaper, though the difference is marginal in Britain, Ireland and Switzerland.

○ Ireland's Automobile Association maintains a webpage of European fuel prices at www.theaa.ie/aa/motoring-advice/petrol-prices.aspx.

Insurance

○ Third-party motor insurance is compulsory. Most UK policies automatically provide this for EU countries. Get your insurer to issue a Green Card (which may cost extra), an internationally recognised proof of insurance, and check that it lists every country you intend to visit. You'll need this in the event of an accident outside the country where the vehicle is insured.

○ Ask your insurer for a European Accident Statement form, which can simplify things if worst comes to worst. Never sign statements that you can't read or understand – insist on a translation and sign that only if it's acceptable.

○ For non-EU countries, check the requirements with your insurer. Travellers from the UK can obtain additional advice and information from the **Association of British Insurers** (www.abi.org.uk).

○ Take out a European motoring assistance policy. Non-Europeans might find it cheaper to arrange international coverage with their national motoring organisation before leaving

home. Ask your motoring organisation for details about the free services offered by affiliated organisations around Europe.

○ Residents of the UK should contact the **RAC** (www.rac.co.uk) or the **AA** (www.theaa.co.uk) for more information. Residents of the US, contact **AAA** (www.aaa.com).

Rental

○ Renting a car is ideal for people who will need cars for 16 days or less. Anything longer, it's better to lease.

○ Big international rental firms will give you reliable service and good vehicles. National or local firms can often undercut the big companies by up to 40%.

○ Usually you will have the option of returning the car to a different outlet at the end of the rental period, but there's normally a charge for this and it can be very steep if it's a long way from your point of origin.

○ Book early for the lowest rates and make sure you compare rates in different cities. Taxes range from 15% to 20% and surcharges apply if rented from an airport.

○ If you rent a car in the EU you might not be able to take it outside the EU, and if you rent the car outside the EU, you will only be able to drive within the EU for eight days. Ask at the rental agencies for other such regulations.

○ Make sure you understand what is included

in the price (unlimited or paid kilometres, tax, injury insurance, collision damage waiver etc) and what your liabilities are. We recommend taking the collision damage waiver, though you can probably skip the injury insurance if you and your passengers have decent travel insurance.

○ The minimum rental age is usually 21 years and sometimes 25. You'll need a credit card and to have held your licence for at least a year.

○ Motorcycle and moped rental is common in some countries, such as Italy, Spain, Greece and southern France.

Road Conditions & Road Rules

○ Conditions and types of roads vary across Europe. The fastest routes are generally four- or six-lane highways known locally as motorways, autoroutes, autostrade, autobahnen etc. These tend to skirt cities and plough through the countryside in straight lines, often avoiding the most scenic bits.

○ Some highways incur tolls, which are often quite hefty (especially in Italy, France and Spain), but there will always be an alternative route. Motorways and other primary routes are generally in good condition.

○ Road surfaces on minor routes are unreliable in some countries (eg parts of eastern Europe and Ireland), although normally they will be more than adequate.

○ Except in Britain and Ireland, you should drive on the right. Vehicles brought to the continent from any of these locales should have their headlights adjusted to avoid blinding oncoming traffic (a simple solution on older headlight lenses is to cover up a triangular section of the lens with tape). Priority is often given to traffic approaching from the right in countries that drive on the right-hand side.

○ Speed limits vary from country to country. You may be surprised at the apparent disregard for traffic regulations in some places (particularly in Italy and Greece), but as a visitor it is always best to be cautious. Many driving infringements are subject to an on-the-spot fine. Always ask for a receipt.

○ European drink-driving laws are particularly strict. The blood-alcohol concentration (BAC) limit when driving is usually between 0.05% and 0.08%, but in certain areas it can be zero.

○ Always carry proof of ownership of your vehicle (Vehicle Registration Document for British-registered cars). An EU driving licence is acceptable for those driving through Europe. If you have any other type of licence, you should obtain an International Driving Permit (IDP) from your motoring organisation. Check what type of licence is

required in your destination prior to departure.

○ Every vehicle that travels across an international border should display a sticker indicating its country of registration. A warning triangle, to be used in the event of breakdown, is compulsory almost everywhere.

○ Some recommended accessories include a first-aid kit (compulsory in Austria and Croatia), a spare bulb kit (compulsory in Spain), a reflective jacket for every person in the car (compulsory in France, Italy and Spain) and a fire extinguisher.

Local Transport

European towns and cities have excellent local-transport systems, often encompassing trams as well as buses and underground-rail networks.

Most travellers will find areas of interest in European cities can be easily traversed by foot or bicycle. A growing number of European cities have bike-sharing schemes where you can casually borrow a bike from a docking station for short hops around the city for a small cost.

In Italy travellers sometimes rent mopeds and motorcycles for scooting around a city or island.

Taxi

Taxis in Europe are metered and rates are usually high. There might also be supplements for things such

as luggage, time of day, location of pick-up and extra passengers.

Good bus, rail and underground-railway networks often render taxis unnecessary, but if you need one in a hurry, they can be found idling near train stations or outside big hotels. Lower fares make taxis more viable in some countries such as Spain and Portugal.

Train

Comfortable, frequent and reliable, trains are the way to get around Europe.

○ Many state railways have interactive websites publishing their timetables and fares, including www.bahn.de (Germany) and www.sbb.ch (Switzerland), which both have pages in English. **Eurail** (www.eurail.com) links to 28 European train companies.

○ **The Man in Seat 61** (www.seat61.com) is very comprehensive and a gem, while the US-based **Budget Europe Travel Service** (www.budgeteuropetravel.com) can also help with tips.

○ European trains sometimes split en route to service two destinations, so even if you're on the right train, make sure you're also in the correct carriage.

○ A train journey to almost every station in Europe can be booked via Voyages-sncf.com (http://uk.voyages-sncf.com/en), which also sells InterRail and other passes.

Language

Don't let the language barrier get in the way of your travel experience. This section offers basic phrases and pronunciation guides to help you negotiate your way around Europe. Note that in our pronunciation guides, the stressed syllables in words are indicated with italics.

To enhance your trip with a phrasebook (covering all of these languages in much greater detail), visit **lonelyplanet.com**.

Czech

Hello.	*Ahoj.*	uh·hoy
Goodbye.		
Na shledanou.		nuh·skhle·duh·noh
Yes./No.	*Ano./Ne.*	uh·no/ne
Please.	*Prosím.*	pro·seem
Thank you.	*Děkuji.*	dye·ku·yi
Excuse me.	*Promiňte.*	pro·min'·te
Help!	*Pomoc!*	po·mots

Do you speak English?
Mluvíte anglicky?   mlu·vee·te uhn·glits·ki
I don't understand.
Nerozumím.   ne·ro·zu·meem
How much is this?
Kolik to stojí?   ko·lik to sto·yee
I'd like ..., please.
Chtěl/Chtěla bych ...,   khtyel/khtye·luh bikh ...
prosím. (m/f)   pro·seem
Where's (the toilet)?
Kde je (záchod)?   gde ye (za·khod)
I'm lost.
Zabloudil/   zuh·bloh·dyil/
Zabloudila jsem. (m/f)   zuh·bloh·dyi·luh ysem

Dutch

Hello.	*Dag.*	dakh
Goodbye.	*Dag.*	dakh
Yes.	*Ja.*	yaa
No.	*Nee.*	ney
Please.	*Alstublieft.*	al·stew·bleeft
Thank you.	*Dank u.*	dangk ew

Excuse me.	*Excuseer mij.*	eks·kew·zeyr mey
Help!	*Help!*	help

Do you speak English?
Spreekt u Engels?   spreykt ew eng·uhls
I don't understand.
Ik begrijp het niet.   ik buh·khreyp huht neet
How much is this?
Hoeveel kost het?   hoo·veyl kost huht
I'd like ..., please.
Ik wil graag ...   ik wil khraakh ...
Where's (the toilet)?
Waar zijn   waar zeyn
(de toiletten)?   (duh twa·le·tuhn)
I'm lost.
Ik ben verdwaald.   ik ben vuhr·dwaalt

French

Hello.	*Bonjour.*	bon·zhoor
Goodbye.	*Au revoir.*	o·rer·vwa
Yes.	*Oui.*	wee
No.	*Non.*	noh
Please.	*S'il vous*	seel voo
	plaît.	play
Thank you.	*Merci.*	mair·see
Excuse me.	*Excusez-moi.*	
ek·skew·zay·mwa		
Help!	*Au secours!*	o skoor

Do you speak English?
Parlez-vous anglais?   par·lay·voo ong·glay
I don't understand.
Je ne comprends pas.   zher ner kom·pron pa
How much is this?
C'est combien?   say kom·byun
I'd like ..., please.
Je voudrais ...,   zher voo·dray ...
s'il vous plaît.   seel voo play
Where's (the toilet)?
Où sont   oo son
(les toilettes)?   (lay twa·let)
I'm lost.
Je suis perdu(e). (m/f)   zhe swee·pair·dew

German

Hello.	*Guten Tag.*	*goo·*ten taak
Goodbye.	*Auf*	owf
	Wiedersehen.	*vee·*der·zey·en
Yes.	*Ja.*	yaa
No.	*Nein.*	nain
Please.	*Bitte.*	*bi·*te
Thank you.	*Danke.*	*dang·*ke
Excuse me.	*Entschuldi-*	ent·*shul·*di·
	gung.	gung
Help!	*Hilfe!*	*hil·*fe

Do you speak English?
Sprechen Sie Englisch?   shpre·khen zee *eng·*lish
I don't understand.
Ich verstehe nicht.   ikh fer·*shtey·*e nikht
How much is this?
Was kostet das?   vas *kos·*tet das
I'd like ..., please.
Ich hätte gern ..., bitte.   ikh *he·*te gern ... *bi·*te
Where's (the toilet)?
Wo ist   vaw ist
(die Toilette)?   (dee to·a·*le·*te)
I'm lost.
Ich habe mich verirrt.   ikh *haa·*be mikh fer·*irt*

Icelandic

Hello.	*Halló.*	*ha·*loh
Goodbye.	*Bless.*	bles
Yes.	*Já.*	yow
No.	*Nei.*	nay
Thank you.	*Takk./*	tak/ tak *fi·*rir
	Takk fyrir.	
Excuse me.	*Afsakið.*	*af·*sa·kidh
Help!	*Hjálp!*	hyowlp

Do you speak English?
Talar þú ensku?   ta·lar thoo ens·ku
I don't understand.
Ég skil ekki.   yekh skil e·ki
How much is this?
Hvað kostar þetta?   kvadh *kos·*tar *the·*ta
I'd like a/the..., please.
Get ég fengið..., takk   get yekh *fen·*gidh..., tak
Where's (the toilet)?
Hvar er snyrtingin?   kvar er *snir·*tin·gin
I'm lost.
Ég er villtur/villt. (m/f)   yekh er *vil·*tur/vilt

Italian

Hello.	*Buongiorno.*	bwon·*jor·*no
Goodbye.	*Arrive-*	a·ree·ve·
	derci.	*der·*chee
Yes.	*Sì.*	see
No.	*No.*	no
Please.	*Per favore.*	per fa·*vo·*re
Thank you.	*Grazie.*	*gra·*tsye
Excuse me.	*Mi scusi.*	mee *skoo·*zee
Help!	*Aiuto!*	a·*yoo·*to

Do you speak English?
Parla inglese?   *par·*la een·*gle·*ze
I don't understand.
Non capisco.   non ka·*pee·*sko
How much is this?
Quanto costa?   *kwan·*to ko·sta
I'd like ..., please.
Vorrei ..., per favore.   vo·*ray* ... per fa·*vo·*re
Where's (the toilet)?
Dove sono   do·ve *so·*no
(i gabinetti)?   (ee ga·bee·*ne·*ti)
I'm lost.
Mi sono perso/a. (m/f)   mee *so·*no *per·*so/a

Spanish

Hello.	*Hola.*	*o·*la
Goodbye.	*Adiós.*	a·*dyos*
Yes.	*Sí.*	see
No.	*No.*	no
Please.	*Por favor.*	por fa·*vor*
Thank you.	*Gracias.*	*gra·*thyas
Excuse me.	*Disculpe.*	dees·*kool·*pe
Help!	*¡Socorro!*	so·*ko·*ro

Do you speak English?
¿Habla inglés?   a·bla een·*gles*
I don't understand.
No entiendo.   no en·*tyen·*do
How much is this?
¿Cuánto cuesta?   *kwan·*to *kwes·*ta
I'd like ..., please.
Quisiera ..., por favor.   kee·*sye·*ra ... por fa·*vor*
Where's (the toilet)?
¿Dónde están   don·de es·*tan*
(los servicios)?   (los ser·*vee·*thyos)
I'm lost.
Estoy perdido/a. (m/f)   es·*toy* per·*dee·*do/a

Behind the Scenes

Acknowledgements

Climate map data adapted from Peel MC, Finlayson BL & McMahon TA (2007) 'Updated World Map of the Köppen-Geiger Climate Classification', Hydrology and Earth System Sciences, 11, 1633–44.

Illustrations pp214–15, pp220–1, 224–5, pp276–7, pp376–7 and pp468–9 by Javier Zarracina.

This Book

This guidebook was researched and written by Alexis Averbuck, Mark Baker, Oliver Berry, Abigail Blasi, Cristian Bonetto, Kerry Christiani, Fionn Davenport, Sally Davies, Peter Dragicevich, Steve Fallon, Emilie Filou, Duncan Garwood, Bridget Gleeson, Paula Hardy, Damian Harper, Anna Kaminski, Catherine Le Nevez, Virginia Maxwell, Craig McLachlan, Josephine Quintero, Kevin Raub, Andrea Schulte-Peevers, Regis St Louis, Nicola Williams, Neil Wilson. This guidebook was produced by the following:

Curators Simon Richmond, Kate Chapman, Sasha Drew, Liz Heynes, Sandie Kestell, Anne Mason, Martine Power, Kathryn Rowan, Jessica Ryan, Tracy Whitmey

Destination Editors Daniel Fahey, Gemma Graham, James Smart, Tom Stainer, Anna Tyler, Brana Vladisavljevic

Product Editors Kathryn Rowan, Martine Power

Senior Cartographer Mark Griffiths

Book Designer Katherine Marsh

Assisting Editors Pete Cruttenden, Victoria Harrison, Kate Mathews, Gabrielle Stefanos, Saralinda Turner

Assisting Cartographers Julie Dodkins, Julie Sheridan

Assisting Book Designer Meri Blazevski

Cover Researcher Naomi Parker

Thanks to Carolyn Boicos, Hannah Cartmel, Kate Chapman, Clara Monitto, Jenna Myers, Catherine Naghten, Susan Paterson, Mazzy Prinsep, Kirsten Rawlings, Wibowo Rusli, Tony Wheeler

---

Send Us Your Feedback

A–Z
Index

000 Map pages

N

O

Symbols & Map Key

Look for these symbols to quickly identify listings:

- Sights
- Activities
- Courses
- Tours
- Festivals & Events
- Eating
- Drinking
- Entertainment
- Shopping
- Information & Transport

These symbols and abbreviations give vital information for each listing:

- Sustainable or green recommendation
- **FREE** No payment required

- Telephone number
- Opening hours
- Parking
- Nonsmoking
- Air-conditioning
- Internet access
- Wi-fi access
- Swimming pool
- Bus
- Ferry
- Tram
- Train
- English-language menu
- Vegetarian selection
- Family-friendly

Find your best experiences with these Great For... icons.

 Art & Culture
 Beaches
Budget
 Cafe/Coffee
 Cycling
Detour
 Drinking
Entertainment
Events
Family Travel
Food & Drink

History
Local Life
Nature & Wildlife
Photo Op
Scenery
Shopping
 Short Trip
Sport
Walking
Winter Travel

Sights

- Beach
- Bird Sanctuary
- Buddhist
- Castle/Palace
- Christian
- Confucian
- Hindu
- Islamic
- Jain
- Jewish
- Monument
- Museum/Gallery/ Historic Building
- Ruin
- Shinto
- Sikh
- Taoist
- Winery/Vineyard
- Zoo/Wildlife Sanctuary
- Other Sight

Points of Interest

- Bodysurfing
- Camping
- Cafe
- Canoeing/Kayaking
- Course/Tour
- Diving
- Drinking & Nightlife
- Eating
- Entertainment
- Sento Hot Baths/ Onsen
- Shopping
- Skiing
- Sleeping
- Snorkelling
- Surfing
- Swimming/Pool
- Walking
- Windsurfing
- Other Activity

Information

- Bank
- Embassy/Consulate
- Hospital/Medical
- Internet
- Police
- Post Office
- Telephone
- Toilet
- Tourist Information
- Other Information

Geographic

- Beach
- Gate
- Hut/Shelter
- Lighthouse
- Lookout
- Mountain/Volcano
- Oasis
- Park
- Pass
- Picnic Area
- Waterfall

Transport

- Airport
- BART station
- Border crossing
- Boston T station
- Bus
- Cable car/Funicular
- Cycling
- Ferry
- Metro/MRT station
- Monorail
- Parking
- Petrol station
- Subway/S-Bahn/ Skytrain station
- Taxi
- Train station/Railway
- Tram
- Tube Station
- Underground/ U-Bahn station
- Other Transport

Kevin Raub

Atlanta native Kevin Raub started his career as a music journalist in New York, working for *Men's Journal* and *Rolling Stone* magazines. He ditched the rock 'n' roll lifestyle for travel writing and has written nearly 50 Lonely Planet guides, focused mainly on Brazil, Chile, Colombia, USA, India, the Caribbean and Portugal. Raub also contributes to a variety of travel magazines in both the USA and UK. Along the way, the self-confessed hophead is in constant search of wildly high IBUs in local beers. Follow him on Twitter and Instagram (@RaubOnTheRoad).

Andrea Schulte-Peevers

Born and raised in Germany and educated in London and at UCLA, Andrea has travelled the distance to the moon and back in her visits to some 75 countries. She has earned her living as a professional travel writer for over two decades and authored or contributed to nearly 100 Lonely Planet titles as well as to newspapers, magazines and websites around the world. She also works as a travel consultant, translator and editor. Andrea's destination expertise is especially strong when it comes to Germany, Dubai and the UAE, Crete and the Caribbean Islands. She makes her home in Berlin.

Regis St Louis

Regis grew up in a small town in the American Midwest—the kind of place that fuels big dreams of travel—and he developed an early fascination with foreign dialects and world cultures. He spent his formative years learning Russian and a handful of Romance languages, which served him well on journeys across much of the globe. Regis has contributed to more than 50 Lonely Planet titles, covering destinations across six continents. His travels have taken him from the mountains of Kamchatka to remote island villages in Melanesia, and to many grand urban landscapes. When not on the road, he lives in New Orleans. Follow him on www.instagram.com/regisstlouis.

Nicola Williams

Border-hopping is way of life for British writer, runner, foodie, art aficionado and mum-of-three Nicola Williams who has lived in a French village on the southern side of Lake Geneva for more than a decade. Nicola has authored more than 50 guidebooks on Paris, Provence, Rome, Tuscany, France, Italy and Switzerland for Lonely Planet and covers France as a destination expert for the *Telegraph*. She also writes for the *Independent, Guardian*, lonelyplanet.com, Lonely Planet Magazine, French Magazine, Cool Camping France and others. Catch her on the road on Twitter and Instagram at @tripalong.

Neil Wilson

Neil was born in Scotland and has lived there most of his life. Based in Perthshire, he has been a full-time writer since 1988, working on more than 80 guidebooks for various publishers, including the Lonely Planet guides to Scotland, England, Ireland and Prague. An outdoors enthusiast since childhood, Neil is an active hill-walker, mountain-biker, sailor, snowboarder, fly-fisher and rock-climber, and has climbed and tramped in four continents, including ascents of Jebel Toubkal in Morocco, Mount Kinabalu in Borneo, the Old Man of Hoy in Scotland's Orkney Islands and the Northwest Face of Half Dome in California's Yosemite Valley.

Duncan Garwood

From facing fast bowlers in Barbados to sidestepping hungry pigs in Goa, Duncan's travels have thrown up many unique experiences. These days he largely dedicates himself to Italy, his adopted homeland where he's been living since 1997. From his base in the Castelli Romani hills outside Rome, he's clocked up endless kilometres exploring the country's well-known destinations and far-flung reaches, working on guides to *Rome, Sardinia, Sicily, Piedmont* and *Naples & the Amalfi Coast*. Other LP titles include *Italy's Best Trips*, the *Food Lover's Guide to the World* and *Pocket Bilbao & San Sebastian*. He also writes on Italy for newspapers, websites and magazines.

Bridget Gleeson

Bridget has written and taken photos for a variety of web and print publications including Lonely Planet, BBC Travel, BBC Culture, The Guardian, Budget Travel, Afar, Wine Enthusiast, Mr & Mrs Smith, Jetsetter, Tablet Hotels, The Independent, Delta Sky, Continental, LAN Airlines and Korean Air, and she's lived in Italy, the Czech Republic, Nicaragua and Argentina.

Paula Hardy

Paula Hardy is an independent travel writer and editorial consultant, whose work for Lonely Planet and other flagship publications has taken her from nomadic camps in the Danakil Depression to Seychellois beach huts and the jewel-like bar at the Gritti Palace on the Grand Canal. Over two decades, she has authored more than 30 Lonely Planet guidebooks and spent five years as commissioning editor of Lonely Planet's bestselling Italian list. These days you'll find her hunting down new hotels, hip bars and up-and-coming artisans primarily in Milan, Venice and Marrakech. Get in touch at www.paulahardy.com.

Damian Harper

Damian has been working largely full time as a travel writer (and translator) since 1997 and has also written for *National Geographic Traveler*, the *Guardian*, the *Daily Telegraph*, Abbeville Press (*Celestial Realm: The Yellow Mountains of China*), Lexean, Frequent Traveller, China Ethos and variousother magazines and newspapers.

Anna Kaminski

Soviet-born, Anna finds a lot to appreciate about Hungary, a country she first visited as a dental tourist in the early 2000s and has been drawn back to since – from the familiar relics of Communism to the world's best poppyseed strudel. The latest research stint took her from the art galleries and palaces along the Danube and Lake Balaton's shores to Budapest's graveyards; she trawled the latter for her great-uncle who died during the Siege of Budapest.

Catherine Le Nevez

Catherine's wanderlust kicked in when she roadtripped across Europe from her Parisian base aged four, and she's been hitting the road at every opportunity since, travelling to around 60 countries and completing her Doctorate of Creative Arts in Writing, Masters in Professional Writing, and postgrad qualifications in Editing and Publishing along the way. Over the past dozen-plus years she's written scores of Lonely Planet guides and articles covering Paris, France, Europe and far beyond. Her work has also appeared in numerous online and print publications. Topping Catherine's list of travel tips is to travel without any expectations.

Virginia Maxwell

Although based in Australia, Virginia spends at least half of her year updating Lonely Planet destination coverage in Europe and the Middle East. The Mediterranean is her favourite place to travel, and she has covered Spain, Italy, Turkey, Syria, Lebanon, Israel, Egypt and Morocco for LP guidebooks – there are only eight more countries to go! Virginia also writes about Armenia, Iran and Australia. Follow her @maxwellvirginia on Instagram and Twitter.

Craig McLachlan

Craig has covered destinations all over the globe for Lonely Planet for two decades. Based in Queenstown, New Zealand for half the year, he runs an outdoor activities company and a sake brewery, then moonlights overseas for the other half, leading tours and writing for Lonely Planet. Craig has completed a number of adventures in Japan and his books are available on Amazon. Describing himself as a 'freelance anything', Craig has an MBA from the University of Hawai'i and is also a Japanese interpreter, pilot, photographer, hiking guide, tour leader, karate instructor and budding novelist. Check out www.craigmclachlan.com

Josephine Quintero

Josephine first got her taste of not-so-serious travel when she slung a guitar on her back and travelled in Europe in the early '70s. She eventually reached Greece and caught a ferry to Israel where she embraced kibbutz life and the Mexican-American she was to subsequently wed. Josephine primarily covers Spain and Italy for Lonely Planet.

Oliver Berry

Oliver is a writer and photographer from Cornwall. He has worked for Lonely Planet for more than a decade, covering destinations from Cornwall to the Cook Islands, and has worked on more than 30 guidebooks. He is also a regular contributor to many newspapers and magazines, including *Lonely Planet Traveller*. His writing has won several awards, including The Guardian Young Travel Writer of the Year and the TNT Magazine People's Choice Award. His latest work is published at www.oliverberry.com.

Abigail Blasi

A freelance travel writer, Abigail has lived and worked in London, Rome, Hong Kong, and Copenhagen. Lonely Planet have sent her to India, Egypt, Tunisia, Mauritania, Mali, Italy, Portugal, Malta and around Britain. She writes regularly for newspapers and magazines, such as the *Independent*, the *Telegraph* and *Lonely Planet Traveller*. She has three children and they often come along for the ride. Twitter/Instagram: @abiwhere

Cristian Bonetto

Cristian has contributed to over 30 Lonely Planet guides to date, including *New York City, Italy, Venice & the Veneto, Naples & the Amalfi Coast, Denmark, Copenhagen, Sweden* and *Singapore*. Lonely Planet work aside, his musings on travel, food, culture and design appear in numerous publications around the world, including *The Telegraph* (UK) and *Corriere del Mezzogiorno* (Italy). When not on the road, you'll find the reformed playwright and TV scriptwriter slurping espresso in his beloved hometown, Melbourne. Instagram: rexcat75.

Kerry Christiani

Kerry is an award-winning travel writer, photographer and Lonely Planet author, specialising in Central and Southern Europe. Based in Wales, she has authored/co-authored more than a dozen Lonely Planet titles. An adventure addict, she loves mountains, cold places and true wilderness. She features her latest work at https://its-a-small-world.com and tweets @kerrychristiani.

Fionn Davenport

Irish by birth and conviction, Fionn has been writing about his native country for more than two decades. He's come and gone over the years, pushed to travel in order to escape Dublin's comfortable stasis and by the promise of adventure, but it has cemented his belief that Ireland remains his favourite place to visit, if not always live in. These days,

he has a weekly commute home to Dublin from Manchester, where he lives with his partner Laura and their car Trevor. In Dublin he presents Inside Culture on RTE Radio 1 and writes travel features for a host of publications, including *The Irish Times*.

Sally Davies

Sally landed in Seville in 1992 with a handful of pesetas and five words of Spanish, and, despite a complete inability to communicate, promptly snared a lucrative number handing out leaflets at Expo '92. In 2001 she settled in Barcelona, where she is still incredulous that her daily grind involves researching fine restaurants, wandering about museums and finding ways to convey the beauty of this spectacular city.

Peter Dragicevich

After a successful career in niche newspaper and magazine publishing, both in his native New Zealand and in Australia, Peter finally gave into Kiwi wanderlust, giving up staff jobs to chase his diverse roots around much of Europe. Over the last decade he's written literally dozens of guidebooks for Lonely Planet on an oddly disparate collection of countries, all of which he's come to love. He once again calls Auckland, New Zealand his home – although his current nomadic existence means he's often elsewhere.

Steve Fallon

After a full 15 years living in the centre of the known universe – East London – Steve cockney-rhymes in his sleep, eats jellied eel for brekkie, drinks lager by the bucketful and dances around the occasional handbag. As always, during research he did everything the hard/fun way: walking the walks, seeing the sights, taking (some) advice from friends, colleagues and the odd taxi driver and digesting everything in sight. Steve is a qualified London Blue Badge Tourist Guide (www.steveslondon.com).

Emilie Filou

Emilie Filou is a freelance journalist specialising in business and development issues, with a particular interest in Africa. Born in France, Emilie is now based in London, UK, from where she makes regular trips to Africa. Her work has appeared in publications such as *The Economist*, *The Guardian*, the BBC, the *Africa Report* and the *Christian Science Monitor*. She has contributed to some 20 Lonely Planet guides, including *France, Provence & the Côte d'Azur, London, West Africa, Madagascar* and *Tunisia*. You can find out more on www.emiliefilou.com.

Our Story

A beat-up old car, a few dollars in the pocket and a sense of adventure. In 1972 that's all Tony and Maureen Wheeler needed for the trip of a lifetime – across Europe and Asia overland to Australia. It took several months, and at the end – broke but inspired – they sat at their kitchen table writing and stapling together their first travel guide, *Across Asia on the Cheap*. Within a week they'd sold 1500 copies. Lonely Planet was born.

Today, Lonely Planet has offices in Franklin, London, Melbourne, Oakland, Dublin, Beijing and Delhi, with more than 600 staff and writers. We share Tony's belief that 'a great guidebook should do three things: inform, educate and amuse'.

Our Writers

Simon Richmond

Journalist and photographer Simon Richmond has specialised as a travel writer since the early 1990s and first worked for Lonely Planet in 1999 on their Central Asia guide. He's long since stopped counting the number of guidebooks he's researched and written for the company, but countries covered include Australia, China, India, Iran, Japan, Korea, Malaysia, Mongolia, Myanmar (Burma), Russia, Singapore, South Africa and Turkey. For Lonely Planet's website he's penned features on topics from the world's best swimming pools to the joys of Urban Sketching – follow him on Instagram to see some of his photos and sketches. Simon contributed to the Plan and Survival Guide chapters.

Alexis Averbuck

Alexis has travelled and lived all over the world, from Sri Lanka to Ecuador, Zanzibar and Antarctica. In recent years she's been living on the Greek island of Hydra and exploring her adopted homeland; sampling oysters in Brittany and careening through hill-top villages in Provence; and adventuring along Iceland's surreal lava fields, sparkling fjords and glacier tongues. A travel writer for over two decades, Alexis has lived in Antarctica for a year, crossed the Pacific by sailboat and written books on her journeys through Asia, Europe and the Americas.

Mark Baker

Mark is a freelance travel writer with a penchant for offbeat stories and forgotten places. He's originally from the United States, but now makes his home in the Czech capital, Prague. He writes mainly on Eastern and Central Europe for Lonely Planet as well as other leading travel publishers, but finds real satisfaction in digging up stories in places that are too remote or quirky for the guides. Prior to becoming an author, he worked as a journalist for The Economist, Bloomberg News and Radio Free Europe, among other organisations. Instagram: @markbakerprague Twitter: @markbakerprague

←――――――― More Writers ―――――――→

STAY IN TOUCH LONELYPLANET.COM/CONTACT

AUSTRALIA The Malt Store, Level 3, 551 Swanston St, Carlton, Victoria 3053 ☏03 8379 8000, fax 03 8379 8111

IRELAND Unit E, Digital Court. The Digital Hub, Rainsford St, Dublin 8, Ireland

USA 124 Linden Street, Oakland, CA 94607 ☏510 250 6400, toll free 800 275 8555, fax 510 893 8572

UK 240 Blackfriars Road, London SE1 8NW ☏020 3771 5100, fax 020 3771 5101

 twitter.com/ lonelyplanet

 facebook.com/ lonelyplanet

 instagram.com/ lonelyplanet

 youtube.com/ lonelyplanet

 lonelyplanet.com/ newsletter